Vital Statistics
on American Politics

SAGE was founded in 1965 by Sara Miller McCune to support the dissemination of usable knowledge by publishing innovative and high-quality research and teaching content. Today, we publish more than 850 journals, including those of more than 300 learned societies, more than 800 new books per year, and a growing range of library products including archives, data, case studies, reports, and video. SAGE remains majority-owned by our founder, and after Sara's lifetime will become owned by a charitable trust that secures our continued independence.

Los Angeles | London | New Delhi | Singapore | Washington DC

Vital Statistics on American Politics 2015–2016

Harold W. Stanley

Southern Methodist University

Richard G. Niemi

University of Rochester

Los Angeles | London | New Delhi
Singapore | Washington DC

Los Angeles | London | New Delhi
Singapore | Washington DC

FOR INFORMATION:

CQ Press

An Imprint of SAGE Publications, Inc.

2455 Teller Road

Thousand Oaks, California 91320

E-mail: order@sagepub.com

SAGE Publications Ltd.

1 Oliver's Yard

55 City Road

London EC1Y 1SP

United Kingdom

SAGE Publications India Pvt. Ltd.

B 1/I 1 Mohan Cooperative Industrial Area

Mathura Road, New Delhi 110 044

India

SAGE Publications Asia-Pacific Pte. Ltd.

3 Church Street

#10-04 Samsung Hub

Singapore 049483

Printed in the United States of America.

ISBN 978-1-4833-8031-5

This book is printed on acid-free paper.

Associate Editor: Laura Notton

Editorial Assistant: Jordan Enobakhare

Production Editor: Kelly DeRosa

Typesetter: C&M Digitals (P) Ltd.

Proofreader: Jennifer Grubba

Cover Designer: Michael Dubowe

Marketing Manager: Carmel Schrire

SFI Certified Sourcing
www.sfiprogram.org
SFI-00453

15 16 17 18 19 10 9 8 7 6 5 4 3 2 1

Contents

Tables and Figures

Acknowledgments

Preparing each new edition of this volume brings new challenges. One of the most vexing is when a source changes the frequency with which it updates information, making it impossible to update a table or figure to the extent we would like. To the reader, it may even seem as if we've been careless—not adding two years of information even though two years have passed since the last edition. Or, an agency may simply delay release of new data for a month or two, which may put it beyond the "close date" of the book. In one or two instances—thankfully very few—a source stops collecting the data altogether. We can, however, assure the reader that we have included information that is as up-to-date as possible at the time the volume was finalized in late spring even when, as seems to have happened increasingly in recent years, this has meant looking for advance information that has been collected but not generally released.

In preparing this edition, we again thank all the people who have helped us over the years. These individuals, and the organizations to which they belong, are thanked in previous acknowledgments. For this edition, Christine Carberry and Jennifer McLernon again did a fine job of updating and proofreading many of the tables and figures. We could not have completed the work without their assistance. Harold Stanley, juggling administrative responsibilities along with work on this edition, would like to especially acknowledge the masterful management of revisions by Christine.

In this edition, as in the last, we have made considerable use of material from the Pew Research Center. For more than two decades now, this organization, under its various initiatives, has been conducting quality research and reporting it in ways that are informative and easy to understand, while adhering to the kind of technical standards academics appreciate. We are happy to acknowledge our reliance on Pew's wide-ranging research capabilities (*www.pewtrusts.org*).

Help with specific tables or figures was provided by Lawrence Baum, Kimball Brace, Walter Dean Burnham, Rhodes Cook, Richard Curtin, Sean Evans, Sheldon Goldman, Judith Ingram, Simon Jackman, Scott Keeter, Martha Joynt Kumar, Michael Malbin, Michael McDonald, Barbara Palmer, Sara Schiavoni, Dennis Simon, Elliot Slotnick, and David Wasserman.

We are especially grateful to the many, often anonymous government officials who helped us out with this and all previous editions. They have almost always been courteous, helpful, and prompt in providing us with information, books, Web site assistance, and so on. They clearly belie negative stereotypes of government bureaucrats.

And we again wish to thank all of the colleagues who have given us useful suggestions—whether by pointing out errors or by suggesting improvements in the content and format of individual tables or groups of tables.

CQ Press/SAGE has been helpful to us as always. We owe a special thanks to Laura Notton for making the process run especially smoothly and for her careful checking of tables and figures. Kelly DeRosa handled the production process efficiently and in a way that eased the process for all concerned.

Introduction

- **Accuracy of Published Data**
- **Obtaining Additional Material**

In creating this volume of basic statistical information on American government and politics, our goal has always been to provide broad coverage that spans, whenever possible, a lengthy time perspective. The 2015–2016 edition, its tables, and its Guide to References for Political Statistics once again will serve as a fundamental reference book for those who wish to stay informed about numerous aspects of American politics.

This volume covers a wide range of topics as we seek to offer readers the numbers that count in American politics. In addition to standard subjects such as elections, Congress, the presidency, and the judiciary, this book provides information on the media; campaign finances; foreign, social, and economic policy; and a variety of issues related to state and local government. Coverage is not limited to "hard" data such as votes cast and offices won; rankings of public officials' reputations, content analyses of media coverage, and public opinion data on policy issues are also included. The information ranges from simple lists to compilations of outcomes based on implicit analytical concerns. A historical perspective is maintained throughout; depending on the available data, the longest possible periods are covered, even with public opinion data. The sources of material range from the findable to the fugitive: reference volumes, government publications, political science journals, monographs, the Internet, and press releases, among others. Indeed, the time span is sometimes so great, and the amount of information so large, that we report data for a limited number of years in the present volume, noting that additional data can be found in previous editions of *Vital Statistics on American Politics*.

The quantity and quality of statistical information have grown enormously in recent years, and this trend is unlikely to peak anytime soon. In fact, the Internet makes data overload just a click away. But statistics have a bad image. Even the numerically innocent can retort that "there're lies, damn lies, and statistics" and that "figures don't lie but liars can figure." However, anyone seeking to understand politics—past, present, or future—would be ill advised to take refuge in such skepticism. Increasingly, both public debates and political analyses contain points couched in or accompanied by statistics. Democracy turns in part on the ability of an informed public to follow such debates and analyses. Now more than ever, understanding politics requires an ability to comprehend numerical data and the assumptions behind them.

Although data are more essential and more readily available, the potential users of data are all too often lacking interpretive skills. Unless one knows how to read them, tables and figures can be less than useful; rather, they can be intimidating, incomprehensible, and boring. Yet properly understood, tables and figures can be a resource of considerable value and, surprisingly to many students, even intelligible and interesting.

This volume does not teach statistical methods, but it does foster a greater familiarity with the appropriate cautions about reading too much or too little into tables and figures. This introduction, the chapter introductions, and the Guide to References are all intended to enhance readers' understanding of how to make better use of data displayed in tables and figures. More specifically, they are designed to help readers extract the maximum amount of information from tables and figures, understand the level of accuracy and kinds of inaccuracies in displays of data as well as the various sources used, and find additional information, including the up-to-date information that must be found in serial publications rather than in books.

Some readers, particularly students who are accustomed to working with numbers as they appear in textbooks, are at times frustrated, perhaps even mystified, when confronted with whole tables of numbers—not to mention a whole book of tables and figures. An important point of departure for these readers is to realize that this book is based principally on simple numerical data, not on the results of complicated statistical manipulations. The fanciest statistics presented are averages or medians. Regression coefficients, chi-squares, and the like can be revealing and useful, and, in fact, increasingly political science has become so methodologically sophisticated that many journal articles are opaque to those without the ability to cope with advanced statistics. This book, however, fills a more fundamental need for a single volume encompassing a broad range of data about American politics, and, as such, it should be useful to the methodologically skilled and unskilled alike.

The figures and tables are easy to read. Many are merely lists, but useful lists. They are often lengthy because they cover as many as two hundred twenty-five years. Long historical stretches mean change, and that creates some complexities, such as when the names of the dominant parties change so that going back in time introduces unfamiliar labels (Figure 1-3). Notes to the tables and figures contain the necessary explanations as well as important qualifications and details; they must be read to understand the table or figure content. Following conventional practice, large numbers are sometimes expressed in units of thousands, millions, or billions to enhance readability. Although this practice, too, can lead to minor problems for readers unaccustomed to reading tabular material, with a bit of practice readers should be able to overcome any such difficulties. In general, a little care and caution in reading and interpreting numbers are all that is required.

Accuracy of Published Data

Errors in Data

The material selected for this volume is intended to be the most accurate, up-to-date information possible from the most reputable sources available. But anyone who has used statistical information realizes that it is almost never completely error-free. This is inevitably true here as well. Consider, for example, Tables 11-4 and 11-5. Both are taken from the same government publication, a hundred pages apart. The figures reported for total federal budget outlays, which appear in both tables, typically match. For example, the $2,472.0 billion total outlay for 2005 noted in Table 11-4 matches exactly the 2005 outlay shown in Table 11-5. Similarly, the total outlays for the other years match perfectly. Yet inexplicably the figures for national defense never quite match, differing by as little as $0.6 billion and as much as $4.6 billion.

Why do such discrepancies and other kinds of errors (or what appear to be errors) occur? The answer varies.

Rounding.   Sometimes what appears to be an error is simply a matter of rounding. For example, 20.2 plus 20.4 equals 41 if one adds and then rounds, but equals 40 if one rounds and then adds. This explains why the sum of the numbers in certain columns in Table 10-4 does not quite match the total. A similar sort of "error" occurs when percentages sum to 99.8 or 100.2 rather than to 100 plus or minus 0.1 percent.

Exact Date of Data Collection.   Accurate interpretation of data depends on knowing the precise date of collection and the period covered. Sometimes the period of collection and any implication for interpretation are obvious. For example, the unemployment rate "at the end of the year" may differ if the phrase means the average of the November and December figures rather than the December figure alone. The time factor can be more subtle—for example, if a U.S. senator-elect dies and someone from the other party is appointed to fill the seat, the number of Democrats and Republicans elected will differ slightly from the number of Democrats and Republicans that actually take office a few months later. Even seemingly similar time spans sometimes conceal important differences. For example, dollar amounts for given years are likely to differ if the researcher is using calendar years rather than fiscal years.

The date of data collection is important from another perspective as well. Data are often updated, and researchers need to know whether they are dealing with the "original" or the "revised" figures. Sometimes data providers make it clear that their initial figures are subject to change (such as when the government reports preliminary economic statistics), and that they will label revised statistics as such. But not always. We have found numerous instances in which data have been revised—and not only for the most recent period. It is always a good idea to check the latest publication of a time series to see if there have been changes to previously reported information.

Handling of "Minor" Categories.   "Minor" categories may be uncounted, ignored, or dropped for analytical reasons. Often, for example, votes are given only for the candidates of the two major parties. The small number of votes for the Socialist, Libertarian, and Prohibition candidates, not to mention the stray ballots cast for Mickey Mouse or "none of the above," are unreported or lumped together under "other." Thus, a vote may be correctly reported as 42.7 percent (of the total vote) and just as correctly reported as 42.9 percent (of the two-party vote). Occasionally, minor categories create more complicated problems. For example, in New York State the same candidate may be nominated by two parties, such as the Democratic Party and the Liberal Party. The percentage of Democratic votes then differs from the percentage of votes received by the Democratic candidate.

A similar problem occurs in the reporting of survey data. In any large survey, in response to almost every question a small number of respondents give "oddball" responses, refuse to answer, or say that they do not know. Depending on how these responses are handled—often, but not always, they are eliminated before any further percentaging is done—simple distributions of responses can vary up to a few percentage points or more. "Don't know" responses are especially problematic. It is sometimes important to know how many individuals are uncertain of their response, so we include them in many of our tables (such as Table 3-12 and Tables 3-14 through 3-18). Tabulations of the same items with these responses removed will differ by varying, unknown amounts.

Changes in Measurement Techniques.   Changes in the way measurements are made can produce different figures and can lead to time series that are not fully comparable. Although the two categories sometimes meld together, we might distinguish between (1) changes in operationalization and (2) changes in conceptualization.

A change in operationalization occurs when the underlying idea remains the same but there is a change in the precise way in which the measurement is carried out. A classic example occurs in survey research, in trying to measure concepts such as "political efficacy" and "political trust" or even concepts such as "support for gun control." Researchers at different times may define the concept in the same way but believe that they can "improve" on previous measures by changing the specific questions used to determine a person's efficacy, trust, or support. A consequence of doing so may be that we cannot measure change in public opinion because the new results are not truly comparable with those of earlier polls. Sometimes such changes are forced on reluctant researchers. For example, the "market basket" of items in the Consumer Price Index (Table 11-2) has changed over time. Fountain pens or carbon paper might have been reasonable items to include in the 1950s but not in the 2000s; in the same vein, because of technological progress some items could not have been included until recently.

A change in conceptualization occurs when researchers develop a new understanding of what is meant by some idea. A good example comes from the Current Population Survey (CPS), in which the U.S. Department of Labor tries to determine the status of "discouraged workers"—defined for many years as persons who are not employed and who want a job, but who are not looking for work because of perceived job market factors. Also for many years, the measure of discouraged workers was based on the relatively subjective notion of "desire for work," whereas a newer definition relies on more objective measures of recent efforts to search for a job. This altered conceptualization of what it means to be looking for work was one of many changes made in the CPS during the early 1990s. (These changes are described in the September 1993 issue of the *Monthly Labor Review*.)

Inability to Carry out Exact Measurements.   Sometimes problems arise not because the underlying concept is unclear, but simply because researchers are unable to complete the measurements called for. Consider, for example, the decennial census—the effort to measure the total population of the United States. The concept is clear enough—count every individual living in the United States at a specific time (now designated as April 1 of each census year). However, in fact it is impossible to carry out such a measurement with absolute precision for such a vast population. Homeless persons, for example, are exceedingly difficult to count, and then there are always those individuals who for one reason or another do not want to be identified and make an effort not to be counted.

A more vexing example is the effort to estimate voter turnout. Some of the problems are questions of conceptualization. For example, in calculating "presidential" turnout (Table 1-1), does one want to include individuals who go to the polls but do not in fact cast a ballot for president? There is also the question of how well researchers can obtain the count they seek. If they define the basis for the calculation (the "denominator") as all those eligible to vote, numerous problems arise, such as determining the number of felons or ex-felons in the voting-age population who are ineligible. For this reason, even simple-sounding numbers are estimated variously.[1]

Ad Hoc Problems.   All sorts of small discrepancies can occur, with ad hoc explanations for each one. One fairly well-known example is counting presidents. Barack Obama is usually said to be the forty-fourth president, but he is only the forty-third person to hold the office. Grover Cleveland is counted twice because his two terms were separated by four years. So, is the correct number forty-three or forty-four? It depends on precisely what one means. A less obvious problem occurs in counting Supreme Court nominations that failed. In 1987 Douglas Ginsburg was publicly announced as President Ronald Reagan's choice, but his name was withdrawn before it was formally submitted to the Senate. Technically, was he nominated? This kind of subtlety is exacerbated when dealing with events of the distant past. It would be easy, for example, to think that the multiple listings of certain nominees to the Supreme Court by President John Tyler are an egregious typographical error. In fact, these multiple nominations occurred (all unsuccessfully) in a fight between the president and Congress (Table 7-4).

Solutions to Errors in Data

Awareness that data may contain inaccuracies is no reason to ignore the data, nor is it an excuse to ignore the possible inaccuracies. Consideration of some "solutions" to data errors helps illustrate this point. The solutions, like the problems just described, are suggestive rather than exhaustive.

Sometimes errors are relatively obvious and can be easily corrected. One example is misprints. One might encounter references to the 535 members of the House of Representatives when obviously the whole Congress is meant. Checking with alternative or more authoritative sources when mistakes are suspected can help remedy such problems.

Outlandish or illogical numbers should also be checked. A classic example of finding and explaining nonsensical results is the case of two researchers who were not willing to believe data from the 1950 census showing "a surprising number of widowed fourteen-year-old boys and, equally surprising, a decrease in the number of widowed teenage males at older ages."[2] They wrote a "detective story" about how they traced the problem to systematic errors in the way certain data were entered into the census records.

Another method—one that should always be used—is to check footnotes and accompanying text for exceptions and special comments. Recognize that the problem may not really be error, but misreading. Consider the table on U.S. casualties in the Vietnam War (Table 9-5). For 1973 through 1993, the bottom row shows there were no U.S. military forces in Vietnam but 1,118 battle deaths—surely an anomaly. The note reveals, however, that there were troops in Vietnam for nearly a month at the beginning of this period—the zero indicates the force count as of December 31, 1973, and U.S. forces were withdrawn on January 27, 1973. In addition, forces dying of wounds incurred earlier or those who were missing and later classified as deceased are also considered battle deaths.

Another solution is what is formally called sensitivity analysis. When values are inexact or differ across sources, a researcher should ask how sensitive the conclusion is to the precise values used. If the true values differ by some specified amount from the reported values, would the conclusion change? If not, the researcher can be more confident about the conclusion. Similarly, if sources differ, consider the actual values from several sources. If the conclusion to be drawn does not vary with the different values, the discrepancies are only a minor problem. For example, almost any conclusion about national defense expenditures would be the same whether 2005 expenditures were $495.3 billion (Table 11-4) or $493.6 billion (Table 11-5), even though the difference represents what in other contexts would be an astonishing $1.7 billion.

For the researcher examining over-time data, one way to avoid possible errors is to be sure the data are truly comparable. For one thing, check for indications that the data were revised or updated. Preliminary reports are sometimes not directly comparable with initial reports. In addition, check that the data were collected uniformly or know what the differences are over time and their probable effects. Occasionally, guesses about probable error can be confirmed by formal tests. An excellent example is a study in which both old and new survey questions were asked. Differences that had previously been attributed to changes in the electorate over time were shown to be methodological artifacts.[3]

Sometimes when changes occur, one can develop new estimates, or incorporate ones that are supplied, for an entire existing time series. For example, in the mid-1990s the Bureau of Economic Analysis undertook a comprehensive revision of the National Income and Product Accounts (NIPA), and in doing so it published new estimates of the gross domestic product back to 1929, which, in turn, affected many other calculations. Along the same lines, in 2004 the General Social Survey, used as a basis for some tables about public opinion in Chapter 3, changed its sample design. This change required the use of sample weights for that and earlier years, resulting in slight changes in previously reported figures. While frustrating in that the older series might have to be replaced entirely by the new numbers, the new data provide a comparable time series for the entire period. Of course, in such situations researchers also must ask themselves which figures should be used. The original calculations are arguably better if a researcher is asking questions that depend on how people viewed the world at the time the original data were collected.

All data, perhaps especially data over time, should be examined for "outliers." If a series of values, say the percentages of votes for the Republican candidate in a given district, are 52, 56, 49, 85, and 50, the accuracy of the 85 percent must be checked. Is the 85 a transposition of 58? If 85 is the correct number, what is the reason for it? Was the candidate essentially unopposed that year? What conclusion should be drawn if the 85 were omitted?

Researchers should always think carefully about what information is really wanted. There are instances in which it is necessary to decide which of two or three sets of equally valid data are most appropriate to answer a given question. We noted, for example, that one might wish to employ only the two-party vote or the vote for all parties, include survey respondents who answer "don't know" or eliminate them, or use contemporary data rather than reestimates made years later.

Finally, after taking all reasonable steps to ensure the data are as good as can be obtained and that they address the question at hand, the researcher should indicate known errors. It is better to point out that there is some question about certain figures than to pretend that they are perfect. If a loftier reason does not come to mind, being straightforward about inaccuracies at least prevents readers from lobbing them back, implying the researcher was too ignorant to notice the problems.

Obtaining Additional Material

This book provides essential figures and tables, but the coverage is far from exhaustive. Many readers may want data with a slightly different twist or of another sort altogether. The Guide to References for Political Statistics in this volume should help to orient readers who seek information beyond that contained here. The sources given for the tables and figures in this book should also be considered in such searches. They will especially alert readers to the many electronic sources now available.

Data on current events can be found in newspapers, weekly news magazines, *CQ Weekly*, and the *National Journal*. The indexes of *CQ Weekly*, *National Journal*, and the major newspapers are a valuable guide. Online sources such as 50states.com provide useful links to newspapers on the Web, as does Newslink.org, which also covers magazines as well as radio and television stations. Subscription services such as LexisNexis, Newsbank, and ProQuest Historical Newspapers provide additional coverage, not only of current events but also of historical and legal materials. And Google's news archive allows one to search online sources by month and year. Many of these services are now available on the Web or as electronic databases available at research libraries.

Reference librarians should never be overlooked in the quest for information. Librarians for government document collections are also invaluable resources. Interlibrary loans can help to secure less readily available volumes, although principal reference works and current material seldom circulate in this fashion.

For some material, one may need to contact organizations that compile or disseminate the data. Various directories (most now online as well as in hard copy) are available—of party organizations, interest groups, associations, research institutions, and state agencies. At the federal level, CQ Press's *Washington Information Directory* is a valuable guide to potential sources. The Council of State Governments, with its *CSG State Directories* of administrative and elected officials, provides a similar service at the state level.

Data and texts are now often available in electronic form. Numerous commercial vendors offer online data services, and government agencies have moved many publications onto the Web, some of them exclusively so. Although such a change makes information widely available, it also means that consumers of information must be computer literate. Fortunately, producers are providing more user-friendly sites at the same time that consumers are becoming more sophisticated.

Archives of electronic data also constitute a valuable source of information and were the source of several tables and figures for this volume. The Inter-university Consortium for Political and Social Research (ICPSR) at the University of Michigan has the largest collection of digital social science data. A guide to its resources is available at *www.icpsr.umich.edu*, and some of its data are made available there for observation and analysis online. Most major research universities are members of the consortium. Anyone wishing to learn how to obtain data should contact the official university representatives of ICPSR. Other large data repositories exist in other countries (see *www.iassistdata.org*).

Because of the tremendous growth of sites on the Web, the appearance and disappearance of useful sites, and the availability of powerful search engines, it would be pointless (as well as impossible) to try to develop anything like a comprehensive list. Nevertheless, the Guide to References lists sites that may be of special interest in searching for political statistics. As noted, we also recommend using the sources we cite in the tables and figures as a starting point for gathering additional information.

These hints are merely suggestions for those who wish to go beyond this volume to track down particular pieces of information. We hope readers will find the extensive coverage in this obviously not exhaustive volume to be convenient and valuable.

Notes

1. On this matter, see the lengthy but informative discussions in the following, along with the work cited in the notes and sources for Table 1-1: Walter Dean Burnham, "Triumphs and Travails in the Study of American Voting Participation Rates, 1788–2006," *Journal of the Historical Society* 7 (2007): 505–519; Curtis Gans, *Voter Turnout in the United States, 1788–2009* (Washington, D.C.: CQ Press, 2011).
2. Ansley J. Coale and Frederick F. Stephan, "The Case of the Indians and the Teen-Age Widows," *Journal of the American Statistical Association* 57 (1962): 338.
3. John L. Sullivan, James E. Piereson, and George E. Marcus, "Ideological Constraint in the Mass Public: A Methodological Critique and Some New Findings," *American Journal of Political Science* 22 (1978): 233–249.

1

Elections and Political Parties

- **Turnout**
- **Political Parties**
- **Election Results (President, Congress, and State)**
- **Minority Elected Officials**
- **Presidential Nominations**
- **Districting**
- **Voting Rights**
- **Term Limits**
- **Voting Equipment**

Elections and campaigns provide an abundance of numbers. Indeed, if asked for examples of political statistics, most people would think first of election results. Not only are there a great many electoral statistics, but they extend back to the early years of the country. Here, for example, data are provided on voter turnout (Figures 1-1 and 1-2 and Tables 1-1 and 1-2) and on presidential (Table 1-7) and congressional (Table 1-10) election results going back to 1788. Results abound as well because of the federal system in the United States and because of the nature of the U.S. party system. Thus, this volume provides the most recent results for elections to the governorships and to the state legislatures (Table 1-6), as well as information on presidential primaries and caucuses (Tables 1-23 through 1-26).

In part because there are so many results, some form of summarization is needed. Typically, such summaries are in partisan terms, such as in the contrast between a party's share of the vote won and the share of House seats gained (Table 1-12). Wins by the major parties are presented in a variety of ways, but sometimes such results need to be broken down further. Reporting results by region (Table 1-4 and Figure 1-4) or by state (Tables 1-3, 1-5, and 1-9) is frequently informative. In addition, historians and political scientists often report election results by so-called party systems separated by periods of "realignment"—that is, fundamental shifts in support for parties and the coalitions supporting them. Scholars most often claim that such realignments occurred in the 1850s, 1890s, between 1928 and 1932, and probably in the 1960s.[1] This way of defining party systems is freely employed in the reporting for this analysis (Tables 1-4, 1-8, and 1-11).

There is particular interest in the current period. The available data document recent trends in campaigns and elections: the decline in presidential voter turnout between 1960 and 1996 and the recent upsurge (Table 1-1 and Figure 1-1), the electoral advantages of incumbency (Table 1-19), the frequently lengthened quests for the presidential nominations (Figure 1-5), the greater emphasis on primaries (Tables 1-23 and 1-24), and, in Chapter 2, the growing contributions from political action committees (Table 2-14) and the expense of political campaigns (Tables 2-3 through 2-5).

Besides the arsenal of statistics reporting and summarizing election results by party, other characteristics of the individuals elected to office are of interest. Information is included on the election of African Americans, Hispanics, and women (Tables 1-21 and 1-22) and on their districts (Table 1-20). Political scientists and others also find it useful to consider the frequency of "divided government" between the presidency and Congress (Table 1-13), to tabulate numbers of House districts in which the votes for president and Congress go to different parties (Table 1-14), to determine individual and partisan turnover rates for members of Congress (Tables 1-15, 1-16, 1-18, and 1-19), and to document the regular pattern of losses by the president's party at midterm elections—disrupted, incidentally, in 1998 and 2002 (Table 1-17).

Auxiliary information is often useful in interpreting these election results. One helpful item is a list of political parties that have competed in elections at various times in U.S. history (Figure 1-3). The location and size of presidential nominating conventions (Table 1-27) are also provided, as well as information on the types of delegates who have attended them (Table 1-28). Relevant to the election of minorities is information on legislative districts (Table 1-29) and application of the Voting Rights Act (Table 1-30). Of recent interest is information on which states have passed term limits, the length of the limits they have imposed, the representatives in Congress who have pledged to limit their terms voluntarily, and the numbers of state representatives who have been "termed out" of office (Tables 1-31 through 1-33). In light of the experience in Florida during the 2000 presidential election and in the state's Sarasota County during the 2006 congressional election, a previously utilitarian table on types of voting equipment used throughout the country has taken on new meaning (Table 1-34).

Despite the large quantity of data in this chapter, there are gaps that reflect the limits on what is known about campaigns, elections, and parties. The lack of survey data on realignments before the 1930s, for example, is troublesome because it robs researchers of helpful historical comparisons. Also, not as many data are readily available on state and local elections as on federal elections. Nevertheless, in the area of campaigns and elections, more than anywhere, there is almost an embarrassment of riches.

Note

1. John Aldrich and Richard G. Niemi, "The Sixth American Party System: Electoral Change, 1952–1992," in *Broken Contract? Changing Relationships between Americans and Their Government*, ed. Stephen Craig (Boulder, Colo.: Westview Press, 1996).

Table 1-1   Voter Turnout Rates: United States, South, and Non-South, 1789–2014 (percent)

	Presidential elections[a]				Nonpresidential elections[b]		
Year	United States	Non-South	South[c]	Year	United States	Non-South	South[c]
1789	11.6	11.1	14.3	1790	19.3	18.5	23.5
1792	6.2	6.0	14.4	1794	23.0	22.9	23.5
1796	19.9	19.5	24.9	1798	34.7	33.4	38.0
1800	32.2	40.5	28.7	1802	38.0	36.8	41.0
1804	23.7	27.9	13.1	1806	36.5	35.2	40.2
1808	34.9	42.8	19.1	1810	42.1	40.7	46.8
1812	38.2	43.9	18.9	1814	45.5	45.4	46.0
1816	16.8	20.7	8.1	1818	37.1	33.9	45.8
1820	10.5	12.6	5.2	1822	41.4	38.9	48.0
1824	26.7	26.6	27.2	1826	48.9	46.3	58.9
1828	57.7	62.1	42.5	1830	54.2	55.3	50.6
1832	56.5	64.0	30.1	1834	63.0	63.7	60.7
1836	56.5	58.5	49.2	1838	70.2	72.0	63.7
1840	80.3	81.6	75.4	1842	62.4	63.5	58.3
1844	79.2	80.5	74.2	1846	60.6	62.2	55.2
1848	72.7	74.0	68.0	1850	60.5	61.0	58.5
1852	69.8	72.5	59.3	1854	66.1	65.0	70.0
1856	80.0	81.9	72.2	1858	69.6	71.7	61.5
1860	82.8	84.3	76.7	1862	64.9	64.9	—
1864	77.0	77.0	—	1866	71.2	71.8	51.2[d]
1868	80.9	82.8	71.6	1870	67.0	67.1	66.7
1872	72.5	74.2	67.2	1874	65.0	65.5	63.2
1876	83.4	86.0	75.1	1878	65.1	70.5	48.4
1880	81.2	86.4	65.2	1882	64.2	68.1	58.5
1884	79.1	83.7	64.3	1886	63.9	70.6	42.0
1888	80.9	86.1	64.0	1890	64.6	70.4	44.7
1892	76.2	81.2	59.4	1894	67.5	73.5	47.2
1896	79.9	86.4	57.7	1898	60.1	68.0	33.6
1900	73.9	82.9	43.5	1902	55.7	65.2	23.8
1904	65.8	76.8	29.0	1906	51.4	61.1	18.6
1908	65.9	76.4	30.8	1910	51.8	61.0	20.6
1912	59.0	67.5	27.9	1914	50.1	58.5	18.6
1916	60.7	67.7	31.6	1918	39.9	45.8	14.8
1920	49.3	57.4	21.8	1922	35.8	42.7	11.8
1924	49.0	57.7	19.0	1926	33.0	40.0	8.5
1928	57.1	66.8	23.6	1930	36.9	44.0	12.2
1932	57.3	66.7	24.5	1934	44.8	53.9	13.1
1936	61.4	72.0	25.0	1938	47.0	57.4	11.3
1940	62.9	73.6	26.5	1942	34.1	42.0	7.2
1944	56.2	65.6	24.5	1946	38.8	47.2	10.4
1948	52.2	59.1	23.7	1950	43.6	51.9	13.6
1952	62.3	70.0	38.9	1954	43.5	51.2	17.2
1956	60.2	67.2	37.4	1958	45.0	53.6	16.1
1960	63.8	70.1	40.2	1962	47.7	54.1	24.0
1964	62.8	67.4	45.6	1966	48.7	52.9	33.1
1968	62.5	64.4	51.4	1970	47.3	50.9	34.7
1972	56.2	59.6	44.8	1974	39.1	43.1	26.1
1976	54.8	57.1	47.6	1978[e]	39.0	41.8	30.0

Table 1-1   *(Continued)*

	Presidential elections[a]				Nonpresidential elections[b]		
Year	United States	Non-South	South[c]	Year	United States	Non-South	South[c]
1980	54.2	56.4	47.6	1982[e]	42.1	44.7	31.0
1984	55.2	57.2	49.7	1986	38.1	39.3	34.7
1988	52.8	54.7	47.3	1990	38.4	39.5	35.2
1992	58.1	59.9	53.0	1994	41.1	42.8	36.5
1996	51.7	53.1	47.7	1998	38.1	40.1	32.8
2000	54.2	55.5	51.1	2002	39.5	40.2	37.9
2004	60.1	61.1	57.8	2006	40.4	42.4	35.5
2008	61.6	61.8	61.1	2010	41.0	42.1	37.9
2012[f]	58.2	60.0	58.0	2014	35.9	37.2	35.8

Note: "—" indicates not available. In presidential election years, these turnout figures represent, insofar as possible, the percentage of the eligible electorate that cast votes in presidential elections. In nonpresidential election years through 1946, the figures are the percentage voting in elections for the U.S. House of Representatives. Since 1948, they are the "vote for highest office"—that is, the largest number of votes for a statewide office (U.S. senator or governor) or, if lacking a statewide office, the sum of the votes for the U.S. House of Representatives. In recent years, the problem of estimating turnout for the House has been complicated by the fact that Arkansas, Florida, Louisiana, Oklahoma, and Texas do not tally votes when races are uncontested. The definition of *eligibility* has varied considerably over the years, depending on age, race, gender, felony convictions, and citizenship status. Some states during some periods allowed noncitizens to vote, but this practice has not been permitted nationwide since 1924. Estimating the eligible electorate is especially difficult for the nineteenth century. For details, see Walter Dean Burnham, *Voting in American Elections: The Shaping of the American Political Universe since 1788* (Palo Alto, Calif.: Academia Press, 2010). Also see Curtis Gans, *Vote Turnout in the United States, 1788–2009* (Washington, D.C.: CQ Press, 2011). From 1924 through 1946, the base is what is known as the citizen voting-age population. From 1948 through 2014, the base is the citizen-eligible population, which begins with the voting-age population but removes noncitizens and ineligible felons and adds in overseas eligible voters. Turnout based on the voter-eligible population is higher than that based on the voting-age population. For 2000–2008, the figures for voters living abroad are apportioned between the South and the non-South based on a 2008 estimate, state by state, of the number of citizens living abroad. For the methodology, see George Mason University (*www.electproject.org*), and Michael P. McDonald and Samuel L. Popkin, "The Myth of the Vanishing Voter," *American Political Science Review* 95 (2001): 963–974. Note that the number of people actually going to the polls is slightly higher than these percentages indicate; some voters do not vote for a given office such as president or U.S. representative, and a small number of ballots are spoiled.

[a] Before 1828, only a limited number of states held popular votes for president. Numbers shown reflect turnout in those states.
[b] Before 1880, one or more states held elections for the U.S. House of Representatives in the year following the presidential election year. Before the Civil War, this practice was quite common, especially in the South and New England. Thus, for example, "1840" should be read as "1840/41."
[c] The eleven states of the Confederacy.
[d] Tennessee only.
[e] Because of Louisiana's second ballot system, Louisiana is excluded from the numerator and denominator for 1978 and 1982.
[f] The percentage for the U.S. includes overseas citizens in the denominator. The percentages for the Non-South and South do not and are therefore slightly inflated.

Sources: 1789–1946: Walter Dean Burnham, *Voting in American Elections: The Shaping of the American Political Universe since 1788* (Palo Alto, Calif.: Academica Press, 2010); 1948–2014: Michael P. McDonald, George Mason University (*www.electproject.org*) and personal communication.

6

Figure 1-1 Voter Turnout Rates: Presidential and Midterm Elections, 1789–2014

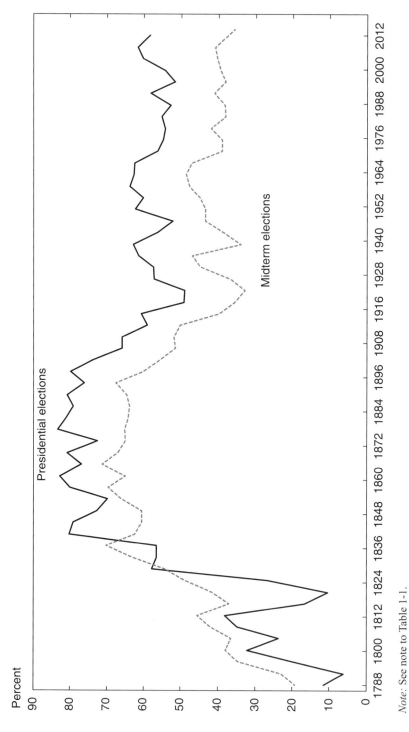

Percent

Figure 1-2 Voter Turnout Rates: Presidential Elections, South and Non-South, 1789–2012

Percent

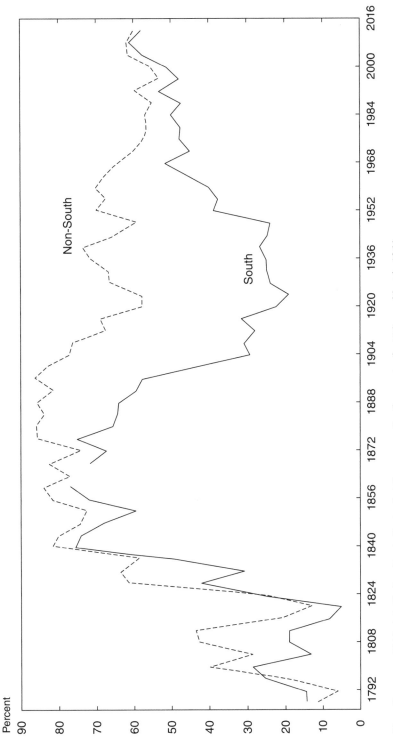

Note: See note to Table 1-1. Broken line indicates that there are no Southern votes for U.S. president in 1864.

Source: Table 1-1, this volume.

7

Table 1-2 Voting-Age Population Registered and Voting: Cross Sections, 1994–2012 (percent)

| | Percentage reporting they registered | | | | | | | | | | | | | | | Percentage reporting they voted | | | | | | | | | | | | | | |
| | Presidential election years | | | | | Congressional election years | | | | | Presidential election years | | | | | Congressional election years | | | | |
	1996	2000	2004	2008	2012	1994	1998	2002	2006	2010	1996	2000	2004	2008	2012	1994	1998	2002	2006	2010
Race/ethnicity																				
White[a]	68	66	68	67	67	65	64	63	64	62	56	56	60	60	58	47	43	44	46	43
Black[a]	64	64	64	66	69	58	60	59	57	59	51	54	56	61	62	37	40	40	39	41
Hispanic origin[b]	36	35	34	38	39	31	34	33	32	34	27	28	28	32	32	20	20	19	19	20
Hispanic citizen[b]	59	57	58	59	59	53	55	53	54	52	44	45	47	50	48	34	33	30	32	31
Sex																				
Men	64	62	64	63	63	61	61	59	60	58	53	53	56	56	54	45	41	41	42	41
Women	67	66	68	67	67	64	64	63	63	61	56	56	60	60	59	45	42	43	45	43
Region[c]																				
Northeast	65	64	65	64	65	61	61	61	60	60	54	55	59	57	57	45	41	41	43	42
Midwest	72	70	73	71	71	69	68	66	68	65	59	61	65	63	62	49	47	47	51	45
South	66	65	65	66	65	61	63	62	62	59	52	54	56	58	56	41	39	42	40	39
West	61	57	60	59	59	58	56	54	55	55	52	50	54	55	52	46	42	39	42	43
Age																				
18–20 years	46	41	51	49	44	37	32	33	37	34	31	28	41	41	35	17	14	15	17	16
21–24 years	51	49	52	56	53	46	45	42	45	47	33	35	42	47	40	22	19	19	22	22
25–34 years	57	55	56	57	57	52	52	50	50	50	43	44	47	48	46	32	28	27	28	27
35–44 years	67	64	64	61	62	63	62	60	59	57	55	55	57	55	53	46	41	40	40	38
45–64 years	74	71	73	70	70	71	71	69	70	66	64	64	67	65	63	56	54	53	54	51
65 years and older	77	76	77	75	77	76	75	76	75	73	67	68	69	68	70	61	60	61	60	59
Employment																				
Employed	67	65	67	66	67	63	63	62	63	62	55	56	60	60	59	45	41	42	44	43
Unemployed	53	46	56	57	57	46	48	48	48	52	37	35	46	49	46	28	28	27	28	32
Not in labor force	65	64	64	63	63	62	62	61	61	59	54	55	56	56	54	45	44	44	44	42

Education (years)																						
8 or less	41	36	33	30	29	40	40	32	30	27	30	27	24	23	24	23	22	23	24	19	17	16
1–3 of high school	48	46	45	43	43	45	43	42	39	38	34	34	34	34	34	34	32	27	25	23	22	21
4 of high school	62	60	60	59	59	59	59	57	55	53	49	49	50	51	50	49	49	40	37	37	36	35
1–3 of college	73	70	74	72	71	68	68	67	68	66	61	60	66	65	66	65	61	49	46	46	47	44
Total	66	64	66	65	65	62	62	61	62	60	54	55	58	58	58	57	57	45	42	42	44	42

Note: Figures for 2014 should be published in late 2015 and may be available at *www.census.gov.* Data for earlier years can be found in previous editions of *Vital Statistics on American Politics.*

[a] In 2002 and after, whites are individuals identifying with that race alone; blacks are individuals identifying with that race alone.
[b] Persons of Hispanic origin may be of any race.
[c] For composition of regions, see Table A-1, this volume.

Sources: Calculated by the editors from U.S. Census Bureau, "Current Population Reports, Voting and Registration in the Election of November 1994," series P-20, no. PPL-25RV; "November 1996," no. 504; "November 1998," no. 523; "November 2000," no. 542; "November 2002," no. 552; "November 2004," no. 556; "November 2006," no. 557; "November 2008," no. 562; "November 2010"; "November 2012" (*www.census.gov*).

Figure 1-3   American Political Parties since 1789

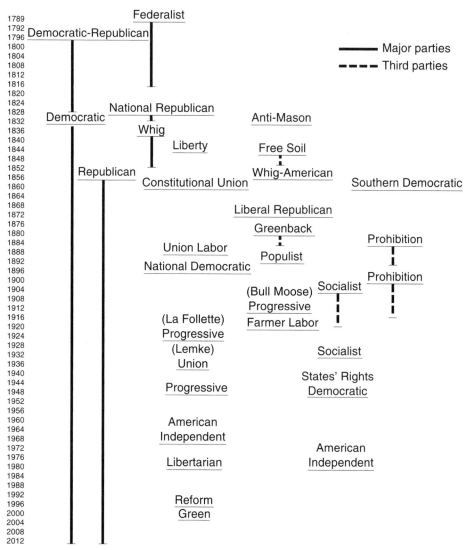

Note: In 1824 and later, the chart indicates the years in which the presidential candidate of a political party received 1.0 percent or more of the popular vote. Minor parties are not included if the minor-party candidate is also the candidate of one of the two major parties (as happened in 1896 when the Populists endorsed William Jennings Bryan, the Democratic candidate). Party candidates sometimes run under different designations in different states (in 1968 George C. Wallace ran for president under at least ten party labels). In such cases, the vote totals for the candidate were aggregated under a single party designation. Sometimes candidates run under no party label as H. Ross Perot did in 1992. (In 1996 Perot ran under the Reform Party label.)

Sources: 1789–1820: U.S. Bureau of the Census, *Historical Statistics of the United States, Colonial Times to 1970* (Washington, D.C.: Government Printing Office, 1975); 1824–2000: *Congressional Quarterly's Guide to U.S. Elections,* 4th ed. (Washington, D.C.: CQ Press, 2001), 225–232, 644–699; 2004–2012: Table 1-9, this volume, and previous editions of *Vital Statistics on American Politics.*

Table 1-3 Party Competition: Presidency, by State, 1992–2012

			Number of times Democratic presidential candidate carried the state		
0	1	2	3–4[a]	5	6
Alabama (9)	Arizona (11)	Arkansas (6)	Colorado (9)	Iowa (6)	California (55)
Alaska (3)	Georgia (16)	Kentucky (8)	Florida (29)	New Hampshire (4)	Connecticut (7)
Idaho (4)	Indiana (11)	Louisiana (8)	Nevada (6)	New Mexico (5)	Delaware (3)
Kansas (6)	Montana (3)	Missouri (10)	Ohio (18)		District of Columbia (3)
Mississippi (6)	North Carolina (15)	Tennessee (11)			Hawaii (4)
Nebraska (5)		Virginia (13)			Illinois (20)
North Dakota (3)		West Virginia (5)			Maine (4)
Oklahoma (7)					Maryland (10)
South Carolina (9)					Massachusetts (11)
South Dakota (3)					Michigan (16)
Texas (38)					Minnesota (10)
Utah (6)					New Jersey (14)
Wyoming (3)					New York (29)
					Oregon (7)
					Pennsylvania (20)
					Rhode Island (4)
					Vermont (3)
					Washington (12)
					Wisconsin (10)
Total electoral votes:					
102	56	61	62	15	242

Note: Numbers of electoral votes for 2012 are shown in parentheses. For similar data on other periods, see previous editions of *Vital Statistics on American Politics.*

[a] Colorado and Florida, three times each; Nevada and Ohio, four times each.

Sources: CQ Press Guide to U.S. Elections, 6th ed. (Washington, D.C.: CQ Press, 2010), 887–891; Table 1-9, this volume; and previous editions of *Vital Statistics on American Politics.*

Table 1-4   Party Competition, by Region, 1860–2014 (percent)

Region/office	1860–1895	1896–1931	1932–1965	1966–2014
New England				
President	85.2	85.5	53.7	37.5
Governor	74.3	85.5	63.1	47.5
U.S. representative	86.8	82.8	60.6	27.1
U.S. senator	a	83.3	65.1	41.5
Middle Atlantic				
President	38.9	88.9	47.2	35.4
Governor	34.9	66.7	51.4	45.1
U.S. representative	59.3	68.9	52.9	41.8
U.S. senator	a	76.9	57.7	40.3
Midwest				
President	77.8	84.4	44.4	55.0
Governor	78.8	78.9	46.9	69.2
U.S. representative	61.1	74.5	57.8	51.4
U.S. senator	a	83.3	50.8	35.7
Plains				
President	88.9	77.8	57.4	79.2
Governor	94.4	71.3	70.4	58.7
U.S. representative	88.6	84.2	76.4	60.2
U.S. senator	a	83.9	79.7	52.2
South				
President	18.4	6.1	15.8	76.5
Governor	21.2	4.2	0.0	57.6
U.S. representative	25.0	7.5	7.2	45.1
U.S. senator	a	0.0	1.5	65.0
Border South				
President	8.6	56.8	22.2	60.0
Governor	22.2	38.6	16.7	32.8
U.S. representative	19.4	36.5	18.7	39.5
U.S. senator	a	42.4	23.4	47.1
Rocky Mountain				
President	73.3	57.8	35.2	83.3
Governor	58.3	51.1	38.5	55.4
U.S. representative	70.0	67.6	30.3	61.9
U.S. senator	a	32.4	20.6	63.6
Pacific Coast				
President	75.0	75.0	37.5	48.3
Governor	47.4	70.8	59.4	37.5
U.S. representative	64.4	85.6	49.0	37.9
U.S. senator	a	73.7	44.4	38.8

Note: Table entries are the percentages of all elections won by Republicans. For composition of regions, see Table A-3, this volume.

[a] Direct election of U.S. senators began after passage of the Seventeenth Amendment in 1913.

Sources: Clerk of the House of Representatives (*http://clerk.house.gov*); *Congressional Quarterly's Guide to U.S. Elections*, 3rd ed. (Washington, D.C.: Congressional Quarterly, 1994), 1344; *Congressional Quarterly Weekly Report* (*CQ Weekly*) (1996), 3192, 3226, 3238, 3242; (1998), 3002, 3004, 3010–3011; (2000), 2671, 2704–2706; (2002), 3289–3297; (2004), 2653–2660; (2006), 3068–3078, 3132, 3186, 3238, 3381; (2008), 3019, 3043–3052, 3056, 3102, 3153, 3206, 3293, 3374; (2010), 2618–2627, 2716, 2766; (2012), 2284–2293, 2342, 2384, 2430; National Governors Association (*www.nga.org*); official election results from state websites; Table 1-9, this volume.

Table 1-5   Party Competition in the States, 1992–2014

Percentage of Democratic wins[a]				
0–20	21–40	41–60	61–80	81–100
Alaska	Indiana	Alabama	Arkansas	California
Arizona	Iowa	Colorado	Delaware	Connecticut
Florida	Michigan	Georgia	Illinois	Hawaii
Idaho	New Hampshire	Louisiana	Kentucky	Maryland
Kansas	Texas	Minnesota	Maine	Massachusetts
Montana	Virginia	Missouri	Mississippi	Rhode Island
Nebraska[b]	Wisconsin	Nevada	New Mexico	West Virginia
North Dakota		New Jersey	North Carolina	
Ohio		New York	Vermont	
Pennsylvania		Oklahoma	Washington	
South Carolina		Oregon		
South Dakota		Tennessee		
Utah				
Wyoming				

Note: For similar data on other periods, see previous editions of *Vital Statistics on American Politics.*

[a] The governorship, control of the lower chamber, and control of the upper chamber are figured separately—that is, if in a given state the Democrats won the governorship and control of one chamber, they had 66.7 percent of the wins in that election cycle.

[b] Results are for the governorship only because the legislature is nonpartisan.

Sources: Calculated by the editors. Council of State Governments, *The Book of the States, 1990–91* (Lexington, Ky.: Council of State Governments, 1990), 123; *1992–93* (1992), 141, 269–272; *1996–97* (1996), 68–69, 153–156; *2004* (2004), 269–270; *2006* (2006), 270–271; *2008* (2008), 305–306; *2010* (2010), 332–333; *2012* (2012), 332–333; *2014* (2014), 275–276; *Congressional Quarterly's Politics in America 1994* (Washington, D.C.: CQ Press, 1993); *Congressional Quarterly's Politics in America 1998* (Washington, D.C.: CQ Press, 1997); National Conference of State Legislatures (*www.ncsl.org*); National Governors Association (*www.nga.org*); and Richard Scammon and Rhodes Cook, eds., *America Votes 25, 2001–2002: A Handbook of Contemporary American Election Statistics* (Washington, D.C.: CQ Press, 2003).

Table 1-6 Partisan Division of Governors and State Legislatures, 2015

| | Governor | | | Legislature | | | | | |
| | | | | Upper house | | | Lower house | | |
State	Name	Party	Next up for election	Democrats	Republicans	Seats up in 2016	Democrats	Republicans	Seats up in 2016
Alabama	Robert Bentley	R	2018	8	26[a]	0[b]	33	72	0[b]
Alaska	Bill Walker	I[c]	2018	6	14	10	16	23[a]	40
Arizona	Doug Ducey	R	2018	13	17	30	22	38	60
Arkansas	Asa Hutchinson	R[c]	2018	11	24	17	36	64	100
California	Jerry Brown	D	2018	25[d]	14	20	52	28	80
Colorado	John Hickenlooper	D	2018	17	18[c]	17	33	32	65
Connecticut	Dan Malloy	D	2018	21	15	36	87	64	151
Delaware	Jack Markell	D	2016	12	9	11	25	16	41
Florida	Rick Scott	R	2018	14	26	20	37	82[d]	120
Georgia	Nathan Deal	R	2018	18	38	56	59	120[a]	180
Hawaii	David Ige	D	2018	24	1	13	43	8	51
Idaho	C. L. "Butch" Otter	R	2018	7	28	35	14	56	70
Illinois	Bruce Rauner	R[c]	2018	39	20	20	71	47	118
Indiana	Mike Pence	R	2016	10	40	25	30	70	100
Iowa	Terry Branstad	R	2018	26	24	25	43	57	100
Kansas	Sam Brownback	R	2018	8	32	40	27	98	125
Kentucky	Steven L. Beshear	D	2015	12	26	19	54	46	100
Louisiana	Bobby Jindal	R	2015	13	26	0[e]	44	59[f]	0[e]
Maine	Paul LePage	R	2018	15	20[c]	35	79[g]	68	151
Maryland	Larry Hogan	R[c]	2018	33	14	0[h]	90	51	0[h]
Massachusetts	Charlie Baker	R[c]	2018	34	6	40	125	35	160
Michigan	Rick Snyder	R	2018	11	27	0[i]	47	63	110
Minnesota	Mark Dayton	D	2018	39	28	0[j]	62	72[c]	134
Mississippi	Phil Bryant	R	2015	20	31[d]	0[k]	56	66	0[k]

State	Governor	Party	Year						
Missouri	Jay Nixon	D	2016	9	25	17	44	117[a,d]	163
Montana	Steve Bullock	D	2016	21[1]	29[1]	25[1]	41[1]	59[1]	100[1]
Nebraska	Pete Ricketts	R	2018						
Nevada	Brian Sandoval	R	2018	10	11[c]	10	15	27[c]	42
New Hampshire	Maggie Hassan	D	2016	10	14	24	160	239[a,c]	400
New Jersey	Chris Christie	R	2017	24	16	0[m]	48	32	0[m]
New Mexico	Susana Martinez	R	2018	25	17	42	33	37[c]	70
New York	Andrew Cuomo	D	2018	31	32[c]	63	106	44	150
North Carolina	Pat McCrory	R[c]	2016	16	34	50	46	74	150
North Dakota	Jack Dalrymple	R	2016	16	31	23	23	71	47
Ohio	John Kasich	R	2018	10	23	16	34	65	99
Oklahoma	Mary Fallin	R	2018	8	40	24	29	72	101
Oregon	Kate Brown[n]	D	2018	18	12	15	35	25	60
Pennsylvania	Tom Wolf	D[c]	2018	20	30	25	84	119	203
Rhode Island	Gina Raimondo	D[c]	2018	32[a]	5	38	63[a]	11	75
South Carolina	Nikki R. Haley	R	2018	18	28	46	46	78	124
South Dakota	Dennis Daugaard	R	2018	8	27	35	12	58	70
Tennessee	Bill Haslam	R	2018	6	27	16	26	73	99
Texas	Greg Abbott	R	2018	11	20	15	52	98	150
Utah	Gary R. Herbert	R	2016	4	23[o]	15	12	63	75
Vermont	Peter Shumlin	D	2016	20[a]	9	30	84[p]	54	150
Virginia	Terry McAuliffe	D[c]	2017	19	21	0[q]	32	67[d]	0[q]
Washington	Jay Inslee	D	2016	24	25[c]	25	51	47	98
West Virginia	Earl Ray Tomblin	D	2016	16	18[c]	17	36	64[c]	100
Wisconsin	Scott Walker	R	2018	14	19	16	36	63	99
Wyoming	Matthew Mead	R	2018	4	26	15	9	51	60
Total		D 18, I 1, R 31		830	1,086	1,071[r]	2,342	3,043	4,741[r]

Note: "D" indicates Democratic Party; "I" indicates independent; "R" indicates Republican Party. Governors and legislatures as of February 24, 2015. Legislative divisions reflect seated members; some vacancies exist. Data for earlier years can be found in previous editions of *Vital Statistics on American Politics.*

(Table continues)

Table 1-6 *(Continued)*

a Plus one independent.
b Thirty-five upper-house seats and 105 lower-house seats up for election in 2018.
c Change in party control from previous election.
d Plus one vacancy.
e Thirty-nine upper-house seats and 105 lower-house seats up for election in 2015.
f Plus two independents.
g Plus four independents.
h Forty-seven upper-house seats and 141 lower-house seats up for election in 2018.
i Thirty-eight upper-house seats up for election in 2018.
j Sixty-seven upper-house seats up for election in 2018.
k Fifty-two upper-house seats and 122 lower-house seats up for election in 2015.
l Nebraska's forty-nine-member state legislature is nonpartisan and unicameral; twenty-five seats are up for election in 2016.
m Eighty lower-house seats up for election in 2015; forty upper-house seats and eighty lower-house seats up for election in 2017.
n Kate Brown became governor on February 18, 2015, following the resignation of Gov. John Kitzhaber. There will be a special election in November 2016 to fill the last two years of Gov. Kitzhaber's term.
o Plus two vacancies.
p Plus twelve independents.
q Forty upper-house seats and one hundred lower-house seats up for election in 2015.
r Totals do not include the twenty-five seats in the unicameral, nonpartisan Nebraska legislature up for election in 2016.

Sources: Governors, name and party: National Governors Association (*www.nga.org*); state legislative partisan composition: National Conference of State Legislatures (*www.ncsl.org*); next up for election, governors and state legislatures: Council of State Governments, *The Book of the States, 2014* (Lexington, Ky.: Council of State Governments, 2014), 273–276; change in party control, governors and state legislatures: calculated by the editors from these sources and previous editions of *Vital Statistics on American Politics*.

Table 1-7 Popular and Electoral Votes for President, 1789–2012

Year	Number of states	Candidates	Electoral vote (number and percent)	Popular vote (number and percent)
1789[a]	10[b]	*(Federalist)* George Washington	*(Federalist)* 69 100%	
1792[a]	15	George Washington	132 98%	
1796[a]	16	*(Federalist)* John Adams	*(Federalist)* 71 51%	
		(Democratic-Republican) Thomas Jefferson	*(Democratic-Republican)* 68 49%	
1800[a]	16	Thomas Jefferson	73 53%	
		John Adams	65 47%	
1804	17	Thomas Jefferson	162 92%	
		Charles C. Pinckney	14 8%	
1808	17	James Madison	122 69%	
		Charles C. Pinckney	47 27%	
1812	18	James Madison	128 59%	
		George Clinton	89 41%	
1816	19	James Monroe	183 83%	
		Rufus King	34 15%	
		(Democratic-Republican) Daniel D. Tompkins	*(Democratic-Republican)*	
		(Independent Democratic-Republican) John Eager Howard	*(Independent Democratic-Republican)* 1 0%	
1820	24	James Monroe	231 98%	
		Daniel D. Tompkins Richard Stockton		

(Table continues)

Table 1-7 (Continued)

Year	Number of states	Candidates	Electoral vote (number and percent)	Popular vote (number and percent)
1824[c]	24	Andrew Jackson, Nathan Sanford *(Democratic-Republican)*	99 — 38% *(Democratic-Republican)*	
		John Q. Adams, John C. Calhoun *(National-Republican)*	84 — 32% *(National-Republican)*	
1828	24	Andrew Jackson, John C. Calhoun	178 — 68%	642,553 — 56.0% *(Democratic-Republican)*
		John Q. Adams, Richard Rush	83 — 32%	500,897 — 43.6% *(National-Republican)*
1832	24	Andrew Jackson, Martin Van Buren	219 — 76%	701,780 — 54.2%
		Henry Clay, John Sergeant	49 — 17%	484,205 — 37.4%
1836	26	Martin Van Buren, Richard M. Johnson *(Democratic)*	170 — 58% *(Democratic)*	764,176 — 50.8% *(Democratic)*
		William Henry Harrison, Francis Granger *(Whig)*	73[d] — 25% *(Whig)*	550,816 — 36.6% *(Whig)*
1840	26	Martin Van Buren, Richard M. Johnson	60 — 20%	1,128,854 — 46.8%
		William Henry Harrison, John Tyler	234 — 80%	1,275,390 — 52.9%
1844	26	James K. Polk, George M. Dallas	170 — 62%	1,339,494 — 49.5%
		Henry Clay, Theodore Frelinghuysen	105 — 38%	1,300,004 — 48.1%
1848	30	Lewis Cass, William O. Butler	127 — 44%	1,223,460 — 42.5%
		Zachary Taylor, Millard Fillmore	163 — 56%	1,361,393 — 47.3%
1852	31	Franklin Pierce, William R. King	254 — 86%	1,607,510 — 50.8%
		Winfield Scott, William A. Graham *(Democratic)*	42 — 14%	1,386,942 — 43.9%
1856	31	James Buchanan, John C. Breckinridge *(Democratic)*	174 — 59% *(Democratic)*	1,836,072 — 45.3% *(Democratic)*
		John C. Fremont, William L. Dayton *(Republican)*	114 — 39% *(Republican)*	1,342,345 — 33.1% *(Republican)*
1860	33	Stephen A. Douglas, Herschel V. Johnson	12 — 4%	1,380,202 — 29.5%
		Abraham Lincoln, Hannibal Hamlin	180 — 59%	1,865,908 — 39.8%
1864	36[e]	George B. McClellan, George H. Pendleton	21 — 9%	1,809,445 — 44.9%
		Abraham Lincoln, Andrew Johnson *(Democratic)*	212 — 91%	2,220,846 — 55.1%
1868	37[f]	Horatio Seymour, Francis P. Blair Jr.	80 — 27%	2,708,744 — 47.3%
		Ulysses S. Grant, Schuyler Colfax *(Republican)*	214 — 73%	3,013,650 — 52.7%

Year	№	Democratic candidate (Pres. / V.P.)	Republican candidate (Pres. / V.P.)	Electoral (D)	Electoral (R)	Popular (D)	Popular (R)
1872	37	Horace Greeley / Benjamin G. Brown	Ulysses S. Grant / Henry Wilson	g / g	286 / 78%	2,835,315 / 43.8%	3,598,468 / 55.6%
1876	38	Samuel J. Tilden / Thomas A. Hendricks	Rutherford B. Hayes / William A. Wheeler	184 / 50%	185 / 50%	4,288,191 / 51.0%	4,033,497 / 48.0%
1880	38	Winfield S. Hancock / William H. English	James A. Garfield / Chester A. Arthur	155 / 42%	214 / 58%	4,445,256 / 48.2%	4,453,611 / 48.3%
1884	38	Grover Cleveland / Thomas A. Hendricks	James G. Blaine / John A. Logan	219 / 55%	182 / 45%	4,915,586 / 48.9%	4,852,916 / 48.2%
1888	38	Grover Cleveland / Allen G. Thurman	Benjamin Harrison / Levi P. Morton	168 / 42%	233 / 58%	5,539,118 / 48.6%	5,449,825 / 47.8%
1892	44	Grover Cleveland / Adlai E. Stevenson	Benjamin Harrison / Whitelaw Reid	277 / 62%	145 / 33%	5,554,617 / 46.0%	5,186,793 / 43.0%
1896	45	William Jennings Bryan / Arthur Sewall	William McKinley / Garret A. Hobart	176 / 39%	271 / 61%	6,370,897 / 45.8%	7,105,144 / 51.1%
1900	45	William Jennings Bryan / Adlai E. Stevenson	William McKinley / Theodore Roosevelt	155 / 35%	292 / 65%	6,357,698 / 45.5%	7,219,193 / 51.7%
1904	45	Alton B. Parker / Henry G. Davis	Theodore Roosevelt / Charles W. Fairbanks	140 / 29%	336 / 71%	5,083,501 / 37.6%	7,625,599 / 56.4%
1908	46	William Jennings Bryan / John W. Kern	William Howard Taft / James S. Sherman	162 / 34%	321 / 66%	6,406,874 / 43.0%	7,676,598 / 51.6%
1912	48	Woodrow Wilson / Thomas R. Marshall	William Howard Taft / James S. Sherman[h]	435 / 82%	8 / 2%	6,294,326 / 41.8%	3,486,343 / 23.2%
1916	48	Woodrow Wilson / Thomas R. Marshall	Charles E. Hughes / Charles W. Fairbanks	277 / 52%	254 / 48%	9,126,063 / 49.2%	8,547,039 / 46.1%
1920	48	James M. Cox / Franklin D. Roosevelt	Warren G. Harding / Calvin Coolidge	127 / 24%	404 / 76%	9,134,074 / 34.2%	16,151,916 / 60.3%
1924	48	John W. Davis / Charles W. Bryan	Calvin Coolidge / Charles G. Dawes	136 / 26%	382 / 72%	8,386,532 / 28.8%	15,724,310 / 54.0%
1928	48	Alfred E. Smith / Joseph T. Robinson	Herbert C. Hoover / Charles Curtis	87 / 16%	444 / 84%	15,004,336 / 40.8%	21,432,823 / 58.2%

(Table continues)

Table 1-7 *(Continued)*

Year	Number of states	Candidates	Electoral vote (number and percent)	Popular vote (number and percent)
1932	48	Franklin D. Roosevelt	472 / 89%	22,818,740 / 57.4%
		John Nance Garner		
		Herbert C. Hoover	59 / 11%	15,760,425 / 39.6%
		Charles Curtis		
1936	48	Franklin D. Roosevelt	523 / 98%	27,750,866 / 60.8%
		John Nance Garner		
		Alfred M. Landon	8 / 2%	16,679,683 / 36.5%
		Frank Knox		
1940	48	Franklin D. Roosevelt	449 / 85%	27,343,218 / 54.7%
		Henry A. Wallace		
		Wendell L. Willkie	82 / 15%	22,334,940 / 44.8%
		Charles L. McNary		
1944	48	Franklin D. Roosevelt	432 / 81%	25,612,610 / 53.4%
		Harry S. Truman		
		Thomas E. Dewey	99 / 19%	22,021,053 / 45.9%
		John W. Bricker		
1948	48	Harry S. Truman	303 / 57%	24,105,810 / 49.5%
		Alben W. Barkley		
		Thomas E. Dewey	189 / 36%	21,970,064 / 45.1%
		Earl Warren		
1952	48	Dwight D. Eisenhower	442 / 83%	33,777,945 / 54.9%
		Richard Nixon		
		Adlai E. Stevenson II	89 / 17%	27,314,992 / 44.4%
		John J. Sparkman		
1956	48	Dwight D. Eisenhower	457 / 86%	35,590,472 / 57.4%
		Richard Nixon		
		Adlai E. Stevenson II	73 / 14%	26,022,752 / 42.0%
		Estes Kefauver		
1960	50	John F. Kennedy	303 / 56%	34,226,731 / 49.7%
		Lyndon B. Johnson		
		Richard Nixon	219 / 41%	34,108,157 / 49.5%
		Henry Cabot Lodge Jr.		
1964	50	Lyndon B. Johnson	486 / 90%	43,129,566 / 61.1%
		Hubert H. Humphrey		
		Barry M. Goldwater	52 / 10%	27,178,188 / 38.5%
		William E. Miller		
1968	50	Richard Nixon	301 / 56%	31,785,480 / 43.4%
		Spiro T. Agnew		
		Hubert H. Humphrey	191 / 36%	31,275,166 / 42.7%
		Edmund S. Muskie		
1972	50	Richard Nixon	520 / 97%	47,169,911 / 60.7%
		Spiro T. Agnew		
		George S. McGovern	17 / 3%	29,170,383 / 37.5%
		R. Sargent Shriver Jr.		
1976	50	Jimmy Carter	297 / 55%	40,830,763 / 50.1%
		Walter F. Mondale		
		Gerald R. Ford	240 / 45%	39,147,793 / 48.0%
		Robert J. Dole		
1980	50	Ronald Reagan	489 / 91%	43,904,153 / 50.7%
		George H. W. Bush		
		Jimmy Carter	49 / 9%	35,483,883 / 41.0%
		Walter F. Mondale		
1984	50	Ronald Reagan	525	54,455,075
		Walter F. Mondale	13	37,577,185

Year	States			Electoral votes		Popular votes	
		Geraldine Ferraro	George H. W. Bush	2%	98%	40.6%	58.8%
1988	50	Michael S. Dukakis	George H. W. Bush	111	426	41,809,074	48,886,097
		Lloyd M. Bentsen Jr.	Dan Quayle	21%	79%	45.6%	53.4%
1992	50	Bill Clinton	George H. W. Bush	370	168	44,909,326	39,103,882
		Al Gore	Dan Quayle	69%	31%	43.0%	37.4%
1996	50	Bill Clinton	Robert J. Dole	379	159	47,402,357	39,198,755
		Al Gore	Jack Kemp	70%	30%	49.2%	40.7%
2000	50	Al Gore	George W. Bush	266	271	50,992,335	50,455,156
		Joseph I. Lieberman	Dick Cheney	49%	50%	48.4%	47.9%
2004	50	John Kerry	George W. Bush	251	286	59,028,439	62,040,610
		John Edwards	Dick Cheney	47%	53%	48.3%	50.7%
2008	50	Barack Obama	John McCain	365	173	69,498,516	59,948,323
		Joseph R. Biden Jr.	Sarah Palin	68%	32%	52.9%	45.7%
2012	50	Barack Obama	Mitt Romney	332	206	65,587,106	60,848,302
		Joseph R. Biden Jr.	Paul Ryan	62%	38%	51.0%	47.3%

Note: For details of the electoral system as well as popular and electoral votes polled by minor candidates, see first source. Popular vote returns are shown beginning in 1828 because of availability and because by that time most electors were chosen by popular vote.

a The elections of 1789–1800 were held under different rules, which did not include separate voting for president and vice president. Scattered electoral votes are not shown.

b Eleven states could have voted, but a dispute between its two chambers prevented the New York state legislature from choosing electors. North Carolina and Rhode Island had not yet ratified the Constitution.

c All candidates in 1824 represented factions of the Democratic-Republican Party. Figures are for the two candidates with the highest number of electoral votes. The two other candidates were William H. Crawford and Henry Clay with forty-one and thirty-seven electoral votes, respectively.

d Three Whig candidates ran in 1836. Their electoral votes totaled 113.

e Eleven southern states had seceded from the Union and did not vote; twenty-five states voted.

f Mississippi, Texas, and Virginia were not yet readmitted to the Union and did not vote; thirty-four states voted.

g The Democratic presidential nominee, Horace Greeley, died between the popular vote and the meeting of presidential electors. Democratic electors split sixty-three votes among several candidates. Congress refused to count the three Georgians who insisted on casting their votes for Greeley, and an additional fourteen electoral votes were not cast. Congress also did not count the electoral votes from Arkansas and Louisiana because of "disruptive conditions during Reconstruction."

h James S. Sherman died on October 12, 1912. Nicholas Murray Butler was nominated as the substitute candidate.

Sources: 1789–2008: *CQ Press Guide to U.S. Elections*, 6th ed. (Washington, D.C.: CQ Press, 2010), 755–801, 836–891; 2012: Table 1-9, this volume.

Table 1-8 Party Winning Presidential Election, by State, 1789–2012

State	1789–1824			1828–1856			1860–1892			1896–1928			1932–1964			1968–2012		
	D	F	O	D	R	O	D	R	O	D	R	O	D	R	O	D	R	O
Alabama	2	0	0	8	0	0	6	2	0	9	0	0	7	1	1	1	10	1
Alaska	—	—	—	—	—	—	—	—	—	—	—	—	1	1	0	0	12	0
Arizona	—	—	—	—	—	—	—	—	—	2	3	0	5	4	0	1	11	0
Arkansas	—	—	—	6	0	0	6	1	0	9	0	0	9	0	0	3	8	1
California	—	—	—	2	0	0	2	7	0	1	7	1	6	3	0	6	6	0
Colorado	—	—	—	—	—	—	0	4	1	5	4	0	4	5	0	3	9	0
Connecticut	2	8	0	2	6	0	4	4	0	1	8	0	5	4	0	7	5	0
Delaware	2	8	0	2	6	0	7	1	0	1	8	0	5	4	0	7	5	0
District of Columbia[a]	—	—	—	—	—	—	—	—	—	—	—	—	1	0	0	12	0	0
Florida	—	—	—	2	1	0	4	3	1	8	1	0	6	3	0	4	8	0
Georgia	8	2	0	5	3	0	7	0	1	9	0	0	8	1	0	3	8	1
Hawaii	—	—	—	—	—	—	—	—	—	—	—	—	2	0	0	10	2	0
Idaho	—	—	—	—	—	—	—	—	1	4	5	0	6	3	0	0	12	0
Illinois	2	0	0	8	0	0	1	8	0	1	8	0	7	2	0	6	6	0
Indiana	3	0	0	6	2	0	3	6	0	1	8	0	3	6	0	1	11	0
Iowa	—	—	—	2	1	0	0	9	0	1	8	0	4	5	0	6	6	0
Kansas	—	—	—	—	—	—	0	7	1	3	6	0	3	6	0	0	12	0
Kentucky	8	1	0	2	6	0	8	0	1	6	3	0	7	2	0	3	9	0
Louisiana	4	0	0	6	2	0	5	1	1	9	0	0	6	2	1	3	8	1
Maine	2	0	0	5	3	0	0	9	0	1	8	0	1	8	0	7	5	0
Maryland	4	6	0	1	6	1	7	1	1	4	5	0	6	3	0	9	3	0
Massachusetts	3	7	0	0	8	0	0	9	0	2	7	0	7	2	0	10	2	0
Michigan	—	—	—	4	2	0	0	9	0	0	8	1	5	4	0	10	2	0
Minnesota	—	—	—	—	—	—	0	9	0	0	8	1	7	2	0	11	1	0
Mississippi	2	0	0	7	1	0	5	1	1	9	0	0	6	1	2	1	10	1
Missouri	—	—	—	8	0	0	7	2	0	4	5	0	8	1	0	3	9	0
Montana	—	—	—	—	—	—	0	1	0	4	5	0	6	3	0	1	11	0
Nebraska	—	—	—	—	—	—	0	7	0	4	5	0	3	6	0	0	12	0

State																		
Nevada	—	—	—	1	—	—	1	6	1	5	4	0	7	2	0	4	8	0
New Hampshire	4	6	0	6	2	0	0	9	0	2	7	0	4	5	0	5	7	0
New Jersey	5	5	0	3	5	0	7	2	0	1	8	0	6	3	0	6	6	0
New Mexico	—	—	—	—	—	—	—	—	—	2	3	0	7	2	0	5	3	0
New York	6	3	0	5	3	0	4	5	0	1	8	0	6	3	0	9	3	0
North Carolina	8	1	0	5	3	0	5	2	1	8	1	0	9	3	0	2	10	0
North Dakota	—	—	—	—	—	—	—	—	—	2	7	0	3	6	0	0	12	0
Ohio	6	0	0	4	4	0	0	9	0	2	7	0	5	4	0	5	7	0
Oklahoma	—	—	—	—	—	—	—	—	—	4	2	0	6	3	0	0	12	0
Oregon	—	—	—	—	—	—	1	8	0	1	8	1	5	4	0	7	5	0
Pennsylvania	8	2	0	6	2	0	0	9	0	0	8	0	5	4	0	8	4	0
Rhode Island	4	5	0	2	6	0	0	9	0	2	7	0	7	2	0	10	2	0
South Carolina	8	2	0	6	0	2	4	3	1	9	0	1	7	1	1	1	11	0
South Dakota	—	—	—	—	—	—	—	—	—	1	7	1	3	6	0	0	12	0
Tennessee	8	0	0	3	5	0	6	1	0	7	2	0	6	3	0	3	9	0
Texas	—	—	—	3	0	0	7	0	0	8	1	0	7	3	0	2	10	0
Utah	—	—	—	—	—	—	—	—	—	2	7	0	6	3	0	0	12	0
Vermont	6	3	0	7	1	0	0	9	0	0	9	0	1	8	0	6	6	0
Virginia	8	2	0	8	0	0	5	1	1	8	1	0	6	3	0	2	10	0
Washington	—	—	—	—	—	—	—	—	—	2	6	1	6	3	0	8	4	0
West Virginia	—	—	—	—	—	—	5	3	0	1	8	0	8	1	0	6	6	0
Wisconsin	—	—	—	2	1	0	1	8	0	1	7	1	5	4	0	8	4	0
Wyoming	—	—	—	—	—	—	—	—	—	3	6	0	5	4	0	0	12	0
Total[b]	113	61	0	136	79	3	118	189	15	170	244	7	274	158	5	225	382	5

Note: Table entries indicate number of times party indicated won the state. "D" indicates the Democratic-Republican Party from 1796 to 1820 and in 1828, the Jackson faction in 1824, and the Democratic Party in 1832 and later; "F" indicates the Federalists from 1792 to 1816, Independent Democratic-Republicans in 1820, and the Adams faction in 1824; "R" indicates the National Republicans in 1828 and 1832, Whigs from 1836 to 1852, and the Republican Party in 1856 and later. The "O" column refers to other (third) parties. Southern Democrats in 1860 are counted as Democratic. "—" indicates that the state was not yet admitted to the Union.

[a] Residents of the District of Columbia received the presidential vote in 1961.

[b] Fewer total votes for a given state within a party system indicate admission of the state during the party system or nonvoting in certain southern states in 1864, 1868, and 1872.

Sources: Compiled by the editors from *CQ Press Guide to U.S. Elections,* 6th ed. (Washington, D.C.: CQ Press, 2010), 836–891; Table 1-9, this volume; and previous editions of *Vital Statistics on American Politics.*

Table 1-9 Presidential General Election Returns, by State, 2012

| State | Popular vote | | | | | | | Plurality[a] | | Electoral vote | |
| | Obama (Democratic) | | Romney (Republican) | | Other | | Total vote | | | Dem. | Rep. |
	Vote	%	Vote	%	Vote	%		Vote	%		
Alabama	795,696	38.4	1,255,925	60.6	22,717	1.1	2,074,338	460,229	22.2		9
Alaska	122,640	40.8	164,676	54.8	13,179	4.4	300,495	42,036	14.0		3
Arizona	1,025,232	44.6	1,233,654	53.6	40,368	1.8	2,299,254	208,422	9.1		11
Arkansas	394,409	36.9	647,744	60.6	27,315	2.6	1,069,468	253,335	23.7		6
California	7,854,285	60.2	4,839,958	37.1	344,304	2.6	13,038,547	3,014,327	23.1	55	
Colorado	1,322,998	51.5	1,185,050	46.1	61,165	2.4	2,569,213	137,948	5.4	9	
Connecticut	905,083	58.1	634,892	40.8	17,311	1.1	1,557,286	270,191	17.4	7	
Delaware	242,584	58.6	165,484	40.0	5,822	1.4	413,890	77,100	18.6	3	
District of Columbia	267,070	90.9	21,381	7.3	5,313	1.8	293,764	245,689	83.6	3	
Florida	4,237,756	50.0	4,163,447	49.1	72,976	0.9	8,474,179	74,309	0.9	29	
Georgia	1,773,827	45.5	2,078,688	53.3	45,324	1.2	3,897,839	304,861	7.8		16
Hawaii	306,658	70.5	121,015	27.8	7,024	1.6	434,697	185,643	42.7	4	
Idaho	212,787	32.6	420,911	64.5	18,576	2.9	652,274	208,124	31.9		4
Illinois	3,019,512	57.6	2,135,216	40.7	87,286	1.7	5,242,014	884,296	16.9	20	
Indiana	1,152,887	43.9	1,420,543	54.1	51,104	2.0	2,624,534	267,656	10.2		11
Iowa	822,523	52.0	730,593	46.2	29,018	1.8	1,582,134	91,930	5.8	6	
Kansas	440,726	38.0	692,634	59.7	26,611	2.3	1,159,971	251,908	21.7		6
Kentucky	679,370	37.8	1,087,190	60.5	30,652	1.7	1,797,212	407,820	22.7		8
Louisiana	809,141	40.6	1,152,262	57.8	32,662	1.6	1,994,065	343,121	17.2		8
Maine	401,306	56.3	292,276	41.0	19,598	2.8	713,180	109,030	15.3	4	
Maryland	1,677,844	62.0	971,869	35.9	57,614	2.1	2,707,327	705,975	26.1	10	
Massachusetts	1,921,290	60.7	1,188,314	37.5	58,163	1.8	3,167,767	732,976	23.1	11	
Michigan	2,564,569	54.2	2,115,256	44.7	51,136	1.1	4,730,961	449,313	9.5	16	
Minnesota	1,546,167	52.6	1,320,225	45.0	70,169	2.4	2,936,561	225,942	7.7	10	
Mississippi	562,949	43.8	710,746	55.3	11,889	0.9	1,285,584	147,797	11.5		6

Missouri	1,223,796	44.4	1,482,440	53.8	51,087	1.9	2,757,323	258,644	9.4	10	
Montana	201,839	41.7	267,928	55.4	14,165	2.9	483,932	66,089	13.7	3	
Nebraska	302,081	38.0	475,064	59.8	17,234	2.2	794,379	172,983	21.8	5	
Nevada	531,373	52.4	463,567	45.7	19,978	2.0	1,014,918	67,806	6.7		6
New Hampshire	369,561	52.0	329,918	46.4	11,493	1.6	710,972	39,643	5.6		4
New Jersey	2,122,786	58.3	1,478,088	40.6	37,625	1.0	3,638,499	644,698	17.7		14
New Mexico	415,335	53.0	335,788	42.8	32,635	4.2	783,758	79,547	10.1		5
New York	4,159,441	62.5	2,401,799	36.1	99,202	1.5	6,660,442	1,757,642	26.4		29
North Carolina	2,178,391	48.4	2,270,395	50.4	56,586	1.3	4,505,372	92,004	2.0	15	
North Dakota	124,966	38.7	188,320	58.3	9,646	3.0	322,932	63,354	19.6	3	
Ohio	2,827,621	50.7	2,661,407	47.7	91,794	1.6	5,580,822	166,214	3.0		18
Oklahoma	443,547	33.2	891,325	66.8	—	—	1,334,872	447,778	33.5	7	
Oregon	970,488	54.2	754,175	42.1	64,607	3.6	1,789,270	216,313	12.1		7
Pennsylvania	2,990,274	52.1	2,680,434	46.7	71,332	1.2	5,742,040	309,840	5.4		20
Rhode Island	279,677	62.7	157,204	35.2	9,168	2.1	446,049	122,473	27.5		4
South Carolina	865,941	44.1	1,071,645	54.6	26,532	1.4	1,964,118	205,704	10.5	9	
South Dakota	145,039	39.9	210,610	57.9	8,166	2.2	363,815	65,571	18.0	3	
Tennessee	960,709	39.1	1,462,330	59.5	35,538	1.5	2,458,577	501,621	20.4	11	
Texas	3,308,124	41.4	4,569,843	57.2	115,884	1.5	7,993,851	1,261,719	15.8	38	
Utah	251,813	24.8	740,600	72.8	25,027	2.5	1,017,440	488,787	48.0	6	
Vermont	199,239	66.6	92,698	31.0	7,353	2.5	299,290	106,541	35.6		3
Virginia	1,971,820	51.2	1,822,522	47.3	60,147	1.6	3,854,489	149,298	3.9		13
Washington	1,755,396	56.2	1,290,670	41.3	79,450	2.5	3,125,516	464,726	14.9		12
West Virginia	238,269	35.5	417,655	62.3	14,514	2.2	670,438	179,386	26.8	5	
Wisconsin	1,620,985	52.8	1,410,966	45.9	39,483	1.3	3,071,434	210,019	6.8		10
Wyoming	69,286	27.8	170,962	68.6	8,813	3.5	249,061	101,676	40.8	3	
Total	65,587,106	51.0	60,848,302	47.3	2,214,755	1.7	128,650,163	4,738,804	3.7	206	332

Note: "—" indicates not available. Based on official returns as of mid-December 2012, subject to amendment. Percentage for "Plurality" calculated by the editors. Data for earlier years can be found in previous editions of *Vital Statistics on American Politics.*

[a] "Plurality" indicates the vote margin between the leader and the second-place finisher.

Source: "The Rhodes Cook Letter," December 2012, 12–13 (*www.rhodescook.com*).

Figure 1-4   Presidential General Election Map, 2012

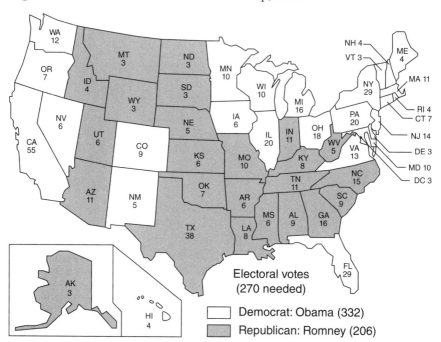

Note: Most states award electoral votes statewide on a winner-take-all basis. Maine and Nebraska award electoral votes by a district system, one for the candidate carrying each congressional district, two for the candidate carrying the state. In 2012 Nebraska awarded all five electoral votes to Romney. Maine awarded all four electoral votes to Obama.

Source: Table 1-9, this volume.

Table 1-10 House and Senate Election Results, by Congress, 1788–2014

Election year	Congress	House Dem.[a]	House Rep.[b]	House Other	House Gains/losses[c] Dem.	House Gains/losses[c] Rep.	Senate Dem.[a]	Senate Rep.[b]	Senate Other	Senate Gains/losses[c] Dem.	Senate Gains/losses[c] Rep.	President[d]
1788	1st	26	38		a	b	9	17		a	b	Washington (F)
1790	2nd	33	37		a	b	13	16		a	b	Washington (F)
1792	3rd	57	48		24	11	13	17		0	1	Washington (F)
1794	4th	52	54		−5	6	13	19		0	2	
1796	5th	48	58		−4	4	12	20		−1	1	J. Adams (F)
1798	6th	42	64		−6	6	13	19		1	−1	
1800	7th	69	36		27	−28	18	13		5	−6	Jefferson (DR)
1802	8th	102	39		33	3	25	9		7	−4	
1804	9th	116	25		14	−14	27	7		2	−2	Jefferson (DR)
1806	10th	118	24		2	−1	28	6		1	−1	
1808	11th	94	48		−24	24	28	6		0	0	Madison (DR)
1810	12th	108	36		14	−12	30	6		2	0	
1812	13th	112	68		4	32	27	9		−3	3	Madison (DR)
1814	14th	117	65		5	−3	25	11		−2	2	
1816	15th	141	42		24	−23	34	10		9	−1	Monroe (DR)
1818	16th	156	27		15	−15	35	7		1	−3	
1820	17th	158	25		2	−2	44	4		9	−3	Monroe (DR)
1822	18th	187	26		29	1	44	4		0	0	
1824	19th	105	97		a	b	26	20		a	b	J. Q. Adams (DR)
1826	20th	94	119		−11	22	20	28		−6	8	
1828	21st	139	74		a	b	26	22		a	b	Jackson (D)
1830	22nd	141	58	14	2	−16	25	21	2	−1	−1	
1832	23rd	147	53	60	6	−5	20	20	8	a	b	Jackson (D)
1834	24th	145	98		−2	45	27	25		a	b	

(Table continues)

Table 1-10 *(Continued)*

Election year	Congress	House Dem.[a]	House Rep.[b]	House Other	House Gains/losses[c] Dem.	House Gains/losses[c] Rep.	Senate Dem.[a]	Senate Rep.[b]	Senate Other	Senate Gains/losses[c] Dem.	Senate Gains/losses[c] Rep.	President[d]
1836	25th	108	107	24	-37	9	30	18	4	3	-7	Van Buren (D)
1838	26th	124	118		16	11	28	22		-2	4	
1840	27th	102	133	6	-22	15	28	22	2	0	0	Harrison (W)
1842	28th	142	79	1	40	-54	25	28	1	-3	6	Tyler (W)
1844	29th	143	77	6	1	-2	31	25		6	-3	Polk (D)
1846	30th	108	115	4	-35	38	36	21	1	5	-4	
1848	31st	112	109	9	4	-6	35	25	2	-1	4	Taylor (W)
1850	32nd	140	88	5	28	-21	35	24	3	0	-1	Fillmore (W)
1852	33rd	159	71	4	19	-17	38	22	2	3	-2	Pierce (D)
1854	34th	83	108	43	-76	37	40	15	5	[a]	[b]	
1856	35th	118	92	26	35	-16	36	20	8	-4	5	Buchanan (D)
1858	36th	92	114	31	-26	22	36	26	4	0	6	
1860	37th	42	106	28	-50	-8	11	31	7	-25	5	Lincoln (R)
1862	38th	80	103		38	-3	12	39		1	8	
1864	39th	46	145		-34	42	10	42		-2	3	Lincoln (R)
1866	40th	49	143		3	-2	11	42		1	0	A. Johnson (R)
1868	41st	73	170		24	27	11	61		0	19	Grant (R)
1870	42nd	104	139		31	-31	17	57		6	-4	
1872	43rd	88	203	3	-16	64	19	54		2	-3	Grant (R)
1874	44th	181	107		93	-96	29	46		10	-8	
1876	45th	156	137	14	-25	30	36	39	1	7	-7	Hayes (R)
1878	46th	150	128	11	-6	-9	43	33		7	-6	
1880	47th	130	152	6	-20	24	37	37	2	-6	4	Garfield (R)
1882	48th	200	119		70	-33	36	40		-1	3	Arthur (R)

Year	Congress											President
1884	49th	182	140	2	−18	21	34	41		−2	1	Cleveland (D)
1886	50th	170	151	4	−12	11	37	39		3	−2	
1888	51st	156	173	1	−14	22	37	47		0	8	Harrison (R)
1890	52nd	231	88	14	75	−85	39	47	2	2	0	
1892	53rd	220	126	8	−11	38	44	38	3	5	−9	Cleveland (D)
1894	54th	104	246	7	−116	120	30	44	5	−14	6	
1896	55th	134	206	16	30	−40	34	46	10	4	2	McKinley (R)
1898	56th	163	185	9	29	−21	26	53	11	−8	7	
1900	57th	153	198	5	−10	13	29	56	3	3	3	McKinley (R)
1902	58th	178	207		25	9	32	58		3	2	T. Roosevelt (R)
1904	59th	136	250		−42	43	32	58		0	0	T. Roosevelt (R)
1906	60th	164	222		28	−28	29	61		−3	3	
1908	61st	172	219	1	8	−3	32	59		3	−2	Taft (R)
1910	62nd	228	162	18	56	−57	42	49	1	10	−10	
1912	63rd	290	127	8	62	−35	51	44	1	9	−5	Wilson (D)
1914	64th	231	193	9	−59	66	56	39	1	5	−5	
1916	65th	210	216	7	−21	23	53	42		−3	3	Wilson (D)
1918	66th	191	237	1	−19	21	47	48		−6	6	
1920	67th	132	300	3	−59	63	37	59	2	−10	11	Harding (R)
1922	68th	207	225	5	75	−75	43	51	1	6	−8	
1924	69th	183	247	3	−24	22	40	54	1	−3	3	Coolidge (R)
1926	70th	195	237	1	12	−10	47	48	1	7	−6	
1928	71st	167	267	1	−28	30	39	56	1	−8	8	Hoover (R)
1930	72nd	220	214	5	53	−53	47	48	1	8	−8	
1932	73rd	313	117	10	93	−97	59	36	2	12	−12	F. Roosevelt (D)
1934	74th	322	103	13	9	−14	69	25	4	10	−11	
1936	75th	333	89	4	11	−14	75	17	4	6	−8	F. Roosevelt (D)
1938	76th	262	169	6	−71	80	69	23	2	−6	6	
1940	77th	267	162	4	5	−7	66	28	1	−3	5	F. Roosevelt (D)
1942	78th	222	209		−45	47	57	38		−9	10	

(Table continues)

Table 1-10 (Continued)

Election year	Congress	House Dem.[a]	House Rep.[b]	House Other	House Gains/losses[c] Dem.	House Gains/losses[c] Rep.	Senate Dem.[a]	Senate Rep.[b]	Senate Other	Senate Gains/losses[c] Dem.	Senate Gains/losses[c] Rep.	President[d]
1944	79th	243	190	2	21	−19	57	38	1	0	0	F. Roosevelt (D)
1946	80th	188	246	1	−55	56	45	51		−12	13	Truman (D)
1948	81st	263	171	1	75	−75	54	42		9	−9	Truman (D)
1950	82nd	234	199	2	−29	28	48	47	1	−6	5	
1952	83rd	213	221	1	−21	22	47	48	1	−1	1	Eisenhower (R)
1954	84th	232	203		19	−18	48	47	1	1	−1	
1956	85th	234	201		2	−2	49	47		1	0	Eisenhower (R)
1958	86th	283	154		49	−47	64	34		15	−13	
1960	87th	263	174		−20	20	64	36		0	2	Kennedy (D)
1962	88th	258	176	1	−5	2	67	33		3	−3	
1964	89th	295	140		37	−36	68	32		1	−1	L. Johnson (D)
1966	90th	248	187		−47	47	64	36		−4	4	
1968	91st	243	192		−5	5	58	42		−6	6	Nixon (R)
1970	92nd	255	180		12	−12	55	45		−3	3	
1972	93rd	243	192		−12	12	57	43		2	−2	Nixon (R)
1974	94th	291	144		48	−48	61	38		4	−5	Ford (R)
1976	95th	292	143		1	−1	62	38		1	0	Carter (D)
1978	96th	277	158		−15	15	59	41		−3	3	
1980	97th	243	192		−34	34	47	53		−12	12	Reagan (R)
1982	98th	269	166		26	−26	46	54		−1	1	
1984	99th	253	182		−16	16	47	53		−1	−1	Reagan (R)
1986	100th	258	177		5	−5	55	45		8	−8	
1988	101st	259	174		1	−3	55	45		0	0	G. H. W. Bush (R)
1990	102nd	267	167	1	8	−7	56	44		1	−1	
1992	103rd	258	176	1	−9	9	57	43		1	−1	Clinton (D)

Year	Congress	Democratic	Republican	Other	Dem. gain/loss	Rep. gain/loss	Democratic	Republican	Other	Dem. gain/loss	Rep. gain/loss	President
1994	104th	204	230	1	−54	54	47	53		−10	10	Clinton (D)
1996	105th	207	227	1	3	−3	45	55		−2	2	
1998	106th	211	223	1	4	−4	45	55		0	0	
2000	107th	212	221	2	1	−2	50	50		5	−5	G. W. Bush (R)
2002	108th	205	229	1	−7	8	48	51	1	−2	1	
2004	109th	201	232	1	−4	3	44	55	1	−4	4	G. W. Bush (R)
2006	110th	233	202		32	−30	49	49	2	5	−6	
2008	111th	257	178		24	−24	55	41	2	5	−8	Obama (D)
2010	112th	193	242		−63	64	51	47	2	−4	6	
2012	113th	200	233		7	−9	53	45	2	2	−2	Obama (D)
2014	114th	188	246		−12	13	44	54	2	−9	9	

Note: For parties, see Figure 1-3, this volume.

a "Democratic" column indicates Democratic partisans in 1828 and later, "Administration" in 1824 and 1826, "Democratic Republicans" from 1790 to 1822, and "Opposition" in 1788. Consequently, and because of changes within the "Republican" column noted in note b, gains/losses in the "Democratic" column are calculated only for 1792–1822, 1826, 1830, 1836–1852, and 1856 and later.

b The "Republican" column indicates Republican partisans in 1854 and later, "Whigs" from 1834 to 1852, "Anti-Masons" in 1832, "National Republicans" in 1828 and 1830, "Jacksonians" in 1824 and 1826, "Federalists" from 1790 to 1822, and "Administration" in 1788. Consequently, gains/losses in the "Republican" column are calculated only for 1792–1822, 1826, 1830, 1836–1852, and 1856 and later.

c The seat totals reflect the makeup of the House and Senate at the start of each Congress. Special elections that shifted party ratios between elections are not noted. Because of changes in the overall number of seats in the Senate and House, in the number of seats won by third parties, and in the number of vacancies, a Republican loss is not always matched precisely by a Democratic gain, or vice versa. Partisan seat shares at the start of each Congress need not match postelection seat shares: deaths, resignations, and special elections can cause further changes in party makeup. In the 1930 election, for example, Republicans won majority control, but when Congress organized, special elections held to fill fourteen vacancies resulted in a Democratic majority.

d President elected in the year indicated or, if a midterm election year, nonelected president in office at the time of the midterm election.

Sources: Seat gains and losses calculated by the editors. Other data: 1788–1858: U.S. Bureau of the Census, *Historical Statistics of the United States, Colonial Times to 1970* (Washington, D.C.: Government Printing Office, 1975), 1083–1084; 1860–2008: *CQ Press Guide to U.S. Elections*, 6th ed. (Washington, D.C.: CQ Press, 2010), 1748–1749; 2010–2012: *CQ Weekly* (2011), 119; (2013), 23; 2014: Clerk of the House of Representatives (*http://clerk.house.gov*).

Table 1-11 Party Victories in U.S. House Elections, by State, 1860–2014

State	Total 1860–1895 Dem.	Rep.	Other	Total 1896–1931 Dem.	Rep.	Other	Total 1932–1965 Dem.	Rep.	Other	Total 1966–2014 Dem.	Rep.	Other
Alabama	92	19	8	170	0	8	146	5	0	86	92	0
Alaska	—	—	—	—	—	—	4	0	0	2	23	0
Arizona	—	—	—	11	0	0	26	7	0	49	93	0
Arkansas	54	5	6	124	0	0	109	0	0	60	40	0
California[a]	29	46	8	30	133	15	234	212	0	716	469	0
Colorado	1	9	3	21	34	6	43	26	0	69	77	0
Connecticut	33	36	5	11	77	0	58	44	0	94	49	0
Delaware	15	3	2	5	14	0	9	8	0	8	17	0
Florida	18	8	1	57	4	0	111	8	0	238	262	0
Georgia	111	11	12	207	0	1	170	1	0	171	107	0
Hawaii	—	—	—	0	0	1	6	0	0	48	2	0
Idaho	0	4	0	5	42	2	20	14	0	7	43	0
Illinois	118	191	20	136	333	1	220	221	0	282	251	0
Indiana	104	105	17	97	139	0	85	108	0	123	128	0
Iowa	16	131	11	10	193	0	35	105	0	53	86	0
Kansas	0	62	12	30	114	0	16	90	0	26	87	0
Kentucky	133	20	38	151	54	0	122	25	0	75	88	0
Louisiana	69	20	2	136	0	2	139	0	0	104	82	0
Maine	3	76	7	4	71	0	8	41	0	31	19	0
Maryland	74	15	18	63	49	0	87	25	0	136	64	0
Massachusetts	31	165	17	60	211	2	103	136	0	235	34	0
Michigan	33	118	13	12	214	2	112	187	0	222	203	0
Minnesota	11	51	5	8	146	12	44	91	16	118	82	0
Mississippi	70	17	3	142	0	0	110	1	0	78	40	0
Missouri	143	43	38	202	88	0	157	49	0	143	88	0
Montana	1	3	0	13	14	1	23	12	0	17	21	0

Nebraska	3	28	5	36	63	9	21	50	0	6	69	0
Nevada	4	9	4	5	10	4	14	3	0	24	27	0
New Hampshire	11	33	3	3	33	0	3	31	0	14	36	0
New Jersey	53	58	5	66	137	0	84	158	0	197	147	0
New Mexico	—	—	—	7	5	0	29	0	1	29	38	0
New York	236	312	66	328	397	6	387	368	0	540	302	0
North Carolina	78	32	19	157	11	9	189	9	0	170	124	0
North Dakota	0	4	0	0	44	0	2	33	0	16	12	0
Ohio	146	186	39	123	264	0	163	238	0	200	309	0
Oklahoma	—	—	—	70	27	0	112	14	0	71	72	0
Oregon	7	13	2	2	44	0	22	41	0	86	31	0
Pennsylvania	158	300	38	83	522	17	255	291	0	283	274	0
Rhode Island	8	32	2	13	34	0	32	2	0	42	8	0
South Carolina	62	30	6	127	0	0	97	2	0	75	77	0
South Dakota	6	11	0	3	42	2	7	27	0	15	18	0
Tennessee	83	52	13	139	39	4	121	37	1	116	104	0
Texas	110	1	3	295	7	0	365	8	0	433	273	0
Utah	—	—	—	7	23	0	23	11	0	21	48	0
Vermont	0	42	5	0	36	0	1	16	0	5	12	0
Virginia	81	23	23	167	15	0	147	15	0	109	152	8
Washington	0	6	0	8	61	2	54	55	0	135	71	1
West Virginia	37	15	6	23	75	0	84	16	21	76	15	0
Wisconsin	40	94	9	18	176	4	46	105	0	113	108	0
Wyoming	1	2	0	1	17	0	3	14	0	4	21	0
Total	2,283	2,441	494	3,386	4,012	110	4,458	2,960	39	5,971	4,895	9

Note: Entries indicate the number of U.S. House seats won by the party in the state. "—" indicates that the state was not yet admitted to the Union. The period beginning in 1966 does not include special elections; candidates endorsed by both major and minor parties are counted as major-party candidates.

[a] When it could be determined, candidates who ran as both Republican and Democrat were classified by their usual party affiliation.

Sources: 1860–1964: *Congressional Quarterly's Guide to U.S. Elections*, 2nd ed. (Washington, D.C.: Congressional Quarterly, 1985), 1118–1119; 1966–2008: *CQ Press Guide to U.S. Elections*, 6th ed. (Washington, D.C.: CQ Press, 2010), 1286, 1287, 1306, 1379, 1383, 1750–1755; 2010–2012: Clerk of the House of Representatives (*http://clerk.house.gov*); *CQ Weekly* (2010), 2618–2627, 2716, 2766; (2012), 2284–2293, 2342, 2384, 2430; 2014: official election results from state websites.

Table 1-12   Popular Vote and Seats in House Elections, by Party, 1896–2014

| | Democratic candidates | | Republican candidates | | |
| | Percentage of all votes | Percentage of all seats | Percentage of all votes | Percentage of all seats | Difference between Democratic percentage of all seats and all votes[a] |
Year					
1896	43.3	37.6	46.7	57.9	−5.6
1898	46.7	45.7	45.7	51.8	−1.0
1900	44.7	43.0	51.2	55.6	−1.7
1902	46.7	46.2	49.3	53.8	−0.5
1904	41.7	35.2	53.8	64.8	−6.5
1906	44.2	42.5	50.7	57.5	−1.7
1908	46.1	44.0	49.7	56.0	−2.1
1910	47.4	58.3	46.5	41.4	10.9
1912	45.3	66.7	34.0	29.2	21.3
1914	43.1	53.5	42.6	44.7	10.3
1916	46.3	48.3	48.4	49.7	2.0
1918	43.1	43.9	52.5	54.5	0.8
1920	35.8	30.5	58.6	69.3	−5.4
1922	44.7	47.6	51.7	51.7	2.8
1924	40.4	42.1	55.5	56.8	1.7
1926	40.5	44.8	57.0	54.5	4.3
1928	42.4	37.8	56.5	61.9	−4.5
1930	44.6	49.7	52.6	50.1	5.1
1932	54.5	72.0	41.4	26.9	17.4
1934	53.9	74.0	42.0	23.7	20.1
1936	55.8	76.6	39.6	20.5	20.7
1938	48.6	60.2	47.0	38.9	11.6
1940	51.3	61.4	45.6	37.2	10.1
1942	46.1	51.0	50.6	48.0	5.0
1944	50.6	55.9	47.2	43.7	5.3
1946	44.2	43.2	53.5	56.6	−1.0
1948	51.9	60.5	45.5	39.3	8.6
1950	49.0	53.8	49.0	45.7	4.7
1952	49.7	49.0	49.3	50.8	0.8
1954	52.5	53.3	47.0	46.7	0.8
1956	51.1	53.8	48.7	46.2	2.7
1958	56.3	64.8	43.5	35.2	8.5
1960	54.2	60.2	45.4	39.8	6.0
1962	52.3	59.3	47.4	40.5	7.0
1964	57.4	67.8	42.1	32.2	10.4
1966	50.9	57.0	48.2	43.0	6.1
1968	50.2	55.9	48.5	44.1	5.7
1970	53.4	58.6	45.1	41.4	5.2
1972	51.7	55.9	46.4	44.1	4.2
1974	57.6	66.9	40.6	33.1	9.9
1976	56.2	67.1	42.1	32.9	10.9
1978	53.4	63.7	44.7	36.3	10.3
1980	50.4	55.9	48.0	44.1	5.5
1982	55.6	61.8	42.9	38.2	6.2

Table 1-12   *(Continued)*

Year	Democratic candidates		Republican candidates		Difference between Democratic percentage of all seats and all votes[a]
	Percentage of all votes	Percentage of all seats	Percentage of all votes	Percentage of all seats	
1984	52.1	58.2	47.0	41.8	6.0
1986	54.5	59.3	44.6	40.7	4.8
1988	53.3	59.8	45.5	40.2	6.5
1990	52.9	61.4	45.0	38.4	8.5
1992	50.8	59.3	45.6	40.5	8.5
1994	45.4	46.7	52.4	53.1	1.2
1996	48.5	47.6	48.9	52.2	−1.0
1998	47.8	48.5	48.9	51.3	0.7
2000	47.4	48.7	48.7	50.8	1.3
2002	45.2	47.1	51.6	52.6	1.9
2004	47.4	46.4	50.1	53.3	−1.0
2006	52.8	53.6	44.9	46.4	0.7
2008	53.9	59.1	42.9	40.9	5.2
2010	45.0	44.4	51.8	55.6	−0.7
2012	49.2	46.2	48.0	53.8	−2.9
2014	45.7	43.2	51.4	56.8	−2.5

Note: In recent years, there has been "built-in" inaccuracy in that some states have chosen not to put uncontested races on the ballot or to require the counting of votes in uncontested races.

[a] Calculated before rounding.

Sources: Votes, 1896–1970: U.S. Bureau of the Census, *Historical Statistics of the United States, Colonial Times to 1970* (Washington, D.C.: Government Printing Office, 1975), part 2, 1084; votes, 1972–1974: U.S. Bureau of the Census, *Statistical Abstract of the United States, 1976* (Washington, D.C.: Government Printing Office, 1976), 460; votes, 1976–1996: *Congressional Quarterly Weekly Report* (1977), 488; (1979), 571; (1981), 713; (1983), 387; (1985), 687; (1987), 484; (1989), 1063; (1991), 487; (1993), 965; (1995), 1079; (1997), 444; votes, 1998 and 2002: "The Rhodes Cook Letter," November 2002, 5; votes, 2000: calculated by the editors using unpublished data provided by Congressional Quarterly; votes, 2004–2010: "The Rhodes Cook Letter," January 2005, 14; December 2006, 16–17; February 2009, 3; December 2010, 5; February 2011, 14 (*www.rhodescook.com*); votes, 2012–2014: David Wasserman, "The Cook Political Report" (*www.cookpolitical.com*); seats: Clerk of the House of Representatives (*http://clerk.house.gov*); Table 1-10, this volume.

Table 1-13 Divided Government in the United States, by Congress, 1861–2017

Years	Congress	Unified/ divided	President (party)	Senate majority	House majority
1861–1863	37th	unified	Lincoln (R)	R	R
1863–1865	38th	unified	Lincoln (R)	R	R
1865–1867	39th	unified	Lincoln (R)	R	R
1867–1869	40th	unified	Grant (R)	R	R
1869–1871	41st	unified	Grant (R)	R	R
1871–1873	42nd	divided	Grant (R)	R	D
1873–1875	43rd	unified	Grant (R)	R	R
1875–1877	44th	divided	Grant (R)	R	D
1877–1879	45th	divided	Hayes (R)	R	D
1879–1881	46th	divided	Hayes (R)	D	D
1881–1883	47th	unified	Garfield (R)	even[a]	R
1883–1885	48th	divided	Arthur (R)	R	D
1885–1887	49th	divided	Cleveland (D)	R	D
1887–1889	50th	divided	Cleveland (D)	R	D
1889–1891	51st	unified	Harrison (R)	R	R
1891–1893	52nd	divided	Harrison (R)	R	D
1893–1895	53rd	unified	Cleveland (D)	D	D
1895–1897	54th	divided	Cleveland (D)	R	R
1897–1899	55th	unified	McKinley (R)	R	R
1899–1901	56th	unified	McKinley (R)	R	R
1901–1903	57th	unified	McKinley (R)	R	R
1903–1905	58th	unified	T. Roosevelt (R)	R	R
1905–1907	59th	unified	T. Roosevelt (R)	R	R
1907–1909	60th	unified	T. Roosevelt (R)	R	R
1909–1911	61st	unified	Taft (R)	R	R
1911–1913	62nd	divided	Taft (R)	R	D
1913–1915	63rd	unified	Wilson (D)	D	D
1915–1917	64th	unified	Wilson (D)	D	D
1917–1919	65th	divided	Wilson (D)	D	R
1919–1921	66th	divided	Wilson (D)	R	R
1921–1923	67th	unified	Harding (R)	R	R
1923–1925	68th	unified	Harding (R)	R	R
1925–1927	69th	unified	Coolidge (R)	R	R
1927–1929	70th	unified	Coolidge (R)	R	R
1929–1931	71st	unified	Hoover (R)	R	R
1931–1933	72nd	divided	Hoover (R)	R	D
1933–1935	73rd	unified	F. Roosevelt (D)	D	D
1935–1937	74th	unified	F. Roosevelt (D)	D	D
1937–1939	75th	unified	F. Roosevelt (D)	D	D
1939–1941	76th	unified	F. Roosevelt (D)	D	D
1941–1943	77th	unified	F. Roosevelt (D)	D	D
1943–1945	78th	unified	F. Roosevelt (D)	D	D
1945–1947	79th	unified	F. Roosevelt (D)	D	D
1947–1949	80th	divided	Truman (D)	R	R
1949–1951	81st	unified	Truman (D)	D	D
1951–1953	82nd	unified	Truman (D)	D	D
1953–1955	83rd	unified	Eisenhower (R)	R	R
1955–1957	84th	divided	Eisenhower (R)	D	D
1957–1959	85th	divided	Eisenhower (R)	D	D
1959–1961	86th	divided	Eisenhower (R)	D	D
1961–1963	87th	unified	Kennedy (D)	D	D
1963–1965	88th	unified	Kennedy (D)	D	D

Table 1-13   *(Continued)*

Years	Congress	Unified/ divided	President (party)	Senate majority	House majority
1965–1967	89th	unified	L. Johnson (D)	D	D
1967–1969	90th	unified	L. Johnson (D)	D	D
1969–1971	91st	divided	Nixon (R)	D	D
1971–1973	92nd	divided	Nixon (R)	D	D
1973–1975	93rd	divided	Nixon (R)	D	D
1975–1977	94th	divided	Ford (R)	D	D
1977–1979	95th	unified	Carter (D)	D	D
1979–1981	96th	unified	Carter (D)	D	D
1981–1983	97th	divided	Reagan (R)	R	D
1983–1985	98th	divided	Reagan (R)	R	D
1985–1987	99th	divided	Reagan (R)	R	D
1987–1989	100th	divided	Reagan (R)	D	D
1989–1991	101st	divided	G. H. W. Bush (R)	D	D
1991–1993	102nd	divided	G. H. W. Bush (R)	D	D
1993–1995	103rd	unified	Clinton (D)	D	D
1995–1997	104th	divided	Clinton (D)	R	R
1997–1999	105th	divided	Clinton (D)	R	R
1999–2001	106th	divided	Clinton (D)	R	R
2001–2003	107th	unified	G. W. Bush (R)	even[a]	R
2003–2005	108th	unified	G. W. Bush (R)	R	R
2005–2007	109th	unified	G. W. Bush (R)	R	R
2007–2009	110th	divided	G. W. Bush (R)	D	D
2009–2011	111th	unified	Obama (D)	D	D
2011–2013	112th	divided	Obama (D)	D	R
2013–2015	113th	divided	Obama (D)	D	R
2015–2017	114th	divided	Obama (D)	R	R

	Summary[b]	
	Unified	*Divided*
1861–1896	9 (50%)	9
1897–1932	14 (78%)	4
1933–1966	13 (76%)	4
1967–2016	8 (32%)	17

Note: "R" indicates Republican; "D" indicates Democrat.

[a] Divided or unified government is as of the start of each Congress. In the Forty-seventh Congress (1881), the Senate was initially composed of thirty-seven Republicans and thirty-seven Democrats, one independent (David Davis of Illinois, who voted with the Democrats), and one variously described as an independent or a Readjuster (William Mahone of Virginia, who voted with the Republicans). Vice President Chester A. Arthur's deciding vote resulted in the Republicans organizing the Senate. In the 107th Congress, the Senate was composed of fifty Republicans and fifty Democrats. On January 20, the Republicans organized the Senate. When James M. Jeffords of Vermont switched to independent effective June 6 and caucused with the Democrats, control shifted to the Democrats. This is the only instance for the years indicated in which party control shifted in one chamber after the start of a Congress and led to a change in the organization of that chamber. See the source on party changes in the Eighty-third Congress.

[b] 1861–1896 covers the elections of 1860–1894; 1897–1932 covers the elections of 1896–1930; 1933–1966 covers the elections of 1932–1964; 1967–2016 covers the elections of 1966–2014.

Sources: Table 1-10, this volume. Information on party switching and party control in evenly divided Congresses is from "Party Division in the Senate, 1789–Present" (*www.senate.gov*).

Table 1-14   Split Presidential and House Election Outcomes in Congressional Districts, 1900–2012

Year	Total number of districts[a]	Number of districts with split results[b]	Percentage of total
1900	295	10	3.4
1904	310	5	1.6
1908	314	21	6.7
1912	333	84	25.2
1916	333	35	10.5
1920	344	11	3.2
1924	356	42	11.8
1928	359	68	18.9
1932	355	50	14.1
1936	361	51	14.1
1940	362	53	14.6
1944	367	41	11.2
1948	422	90	21.3
1952	435	84	19.3
1956	435	130	29.9
1960	437	114	26.1
1964	435	145	33.3
1968	435	139	32.0
1972	435	192	44.1
1976	435	124	28.5
1980	435	143	32.8
1984	435	196	45.0
1988	435	148	34.0
1992	435	100	23.0
1996	435	111	25.5
2000	435	86	19.8
2004	435	59	13.6
2008	435	83	19.1
2012	435	26	6.0

[a] For years 1900–1948, data on every congressional district are not available.
[b] Congressional districts carried by a presidential candidate of one party and a House candidate of another party.

Sources: Norman J. Ornstein, Thomas E. Mann, and Michael J. Malbin, eds., *Vital Statistics on Congress, 1993–1994* (Washington, D.C.: Congressional Quarterly, 1994), 64; *Congressional Quarterly Weekly Report (CQ Weekly)* (1997), 862; (2000), 1062; (2005), 879; (2009), 659; David Wasserman, "The Cook Political Report" (*www.cookpolitical.com*).

Table 1-15   Mean Turnover in the House of Representatives from Various Causes, by Decade and Party System, 1789–2014

Period	Total turnover	Deaths	Retired[a]	Not renominated	General election defeat	Unknown[b]
1790s	0.379	0.017	0.164	0.002	0.027	0.170
1800s	0.361	0.018	0.154	0.001	0.032	0.157
1810s	0.488	0.025	0.181	0.008	0.065	0.209
1820s	0.401	0.018	0.142	0.002	0.079	0.159
1830s	0.483	0.029	0.175	0.006	0.117	0.156
1840s	0.594	0.030	0.253	0.009	0.098	0.205
1850s	0.580	0.018	0.252	0.015	0.140	0.154
1860s	0.492	0.025	0.237	0.026	0.119	0.086
1870s	0.482	0.020	0.220	0.035	0.147	0.060
1880s	0.442	0.023	0.189	0.045	0.130	0.056
1890s	0.394	0.026	0.170	0.043	0.126	0.028
1900s	0.276	0.028	0.114	0.033	0.086	0.015
1910s	0.290	0.029	0.112	0.028	0.114	0.006
1920s	0.223	0.035	0.076	0.026	0.085	0.000
1930s	0.283	0.039	0.084	0.047	0.114	0.000
1940s	0.245	0.025	0.084	0.032	0.104	0.000
1950s	0.168	0.025	0.073	0.014	0.056	0.000
1960s	0.166	0.016	0.073	0.021	0.057	0.000
1970s	0.190	0.010	0.112	0.014	0.053	0.000
1980s	0.120	0.010	0.069	0.007	0.033	0.000
1990s	0.167	0.007	0.106	0.013	0.042	0.000
2000s	0.148	0.006	0.083	0.009	0.051	0.000
2010s	0.180	0.002	0.112	0.020	0.045	0.000
Overall, 1789–2014	0.295	0.021	0.127	0.022	0.084	0.042
Grouped by party system						
First, 1789–1824	0.415	0.020	0.162	0.004	0.048	0.180
Second, 1825–1854	0.524	0.026	0.206	0.007	0.111	0.175
Third, 1855–1896	0.476	0.022	0.215	0.036	0.137	0.067
Fourth, 1897–1932	0.275	0.032	0.103	0.034	0.098	0.008
Fifth, 1933–1964	0.218	0.027	0.080	0.026	0.084	0.000
Sixth, 1965–2014	0.156	0.008	0.091	0.012	0.045	0.000

Note: Figures are proportions of the House membership for each Congress failing to return to the following Congress, averaged across all Congresses within a decade (or a party system). Decades are defined by the first year of a Congress (for example, the 1980s spans 1981–1982 through 1989–1990); each decade mean is based on five Congresses, except for the 1790s (six) and the 2010s (two). Results reflect the final disposition of challenged elections. Data are current through January 2015.

[a] Includes retirements from public office, retirements to seek or accept other elective office (including the Senate), retirements to accept federal executive branch appointments, resignations, and expulsions.

[b] "Unknown" are cases in which the member was not a candidate in the next general election, but it could not be determined whether he or she deliberately chose not to seek reelection or was denied renomination.

Sources: Revised from John W. Swain, Stephen A. Borrelli, Brian C. Reed, and Sean F. Evans, "A New Look at Turnover in the U.S. House of Representatives, 1789–1998," *American Politics Quarterly* 28 (2000): 435–457; other data supplied by the authors.

Table 1-16   House and Senate Seats That Changed Party, 1954–2014

Chamber/ year	Total changes	Incumbent defeated		Open seat	
		Democrat to Republican	Republican to Democrat	Democrat to Republican	Republican to Democrat
House					
1954	26	3	18	2	3
1956	20	7	7	2	4
1958	50	1	35	0	14
1960	37	23	2	6	6
1962	19	9	5	2	3
1964	57	5	39	5	8
1966	47	39	1	4	3
1968	11	5	0	2	4
1970	25	2	9	6	8
1972	23	6	3	9	5
1974	55	4	36	2	13
1976	22	7	5	3	7
1978	33	14	5	8	6
1980	41	27	3	10	1
1982	31	1	22	3	5
1984	22	13	3	5	1
1986	21	1	5	7	8
1988	9	2	4	1	2
1990	21	6	9	0	6
1992	43	16	8	11	8
1994	61	35	0	22	4
1996	35	3	18	10	4
1998	17	1	5	5	6
2000	18	2	4	6	6
2002	12	2	2	4	4
2004	10	3	2	2	3
2006	30	0	22	0	8
2008	31	5	14	0	12
2010	69	52	2	14	1
2012	29	6	16	5	2
2014	19	11	2	5	1
Senate					
1954	8	2	4	1	1
1956	8	1	3	3	1
1958	13	0	11	0	2
1960	2	1	0	1	0
1962	8	2	3	0	3
1964	4	1	3	0	0
1966	3	1	0	2	0
1968	9	4	0	3	2
1970	6	3	2	1	0
1972	10	1	4	3	2
1974	6	0	2	1	3

Table 1-16   *(Continued)*

Chamber/ year	Total changes	Incumbent defeated		Open seat	
		Democrat to Republican	Republican to Democrat	Democrat to Republican	Republican to Democrat
1976	14	5	4	2	3
1978	13	5	2	3	3
1980	12	9	0	3	0
1982	4	1	1	1	1
1984	4	1	2	0	1
1986	10	0	7	1	2
1988	7	1	3	2	1
1990	1	0	1	0	0
1992	4	2	2	0	0
1994	8	2	0	6	0
1996	4	0	1	3	0
1998	6	1	2	2	1
2000	8	1	5	1	1
2002	4	2	1	1	0
2004	8	1	0	5	2
2006	6	0	6	0	0
2008	8	0	5	0	3
2010	6	2	0	4	0
2012	3	0	1	1	1
2014	9	5	0	4	0

Note: This table reflects shifts in party control from before to after the November elections. It does not include shifts from the creation of districts or redistricting that result in incumbents from different districts running against each other in the same district.

Sources: 1954–1992: Norman J. Ornstein, Thomas E. Mann, and Michael J. Malbin, eds., *Vital Statistics on Congress, 1993–1994* (Washington, D.C.: Congressional Quarterly, 1994), 54, 56; 1994–2000: *Congressional Quarterly Weekly Report (CQ Weekly)* (1994), 3232–3233, 3240; (1996), 3228, 3238, 3402; (1998), 3004, 3010–3011; (2000), 2646–2647, 2652–2654; 2002: *2003 Congressional Staff Directory* (Washington, D.C.: CQ Press, 2003), 7, 215; 2004: *2005 Congressional Staff Directory* (Washington, D.C.: CQ Press, 2005), 7, 237; 2006: *CQ Weekly* (2006), 3066, 3068–3075, 3132, 3186, 3238, 3381; 2008: *CQ Weekly* (2008), 3043–3052, 3056, 3102, 3153, 3206, 3293, 3374; (2009), 216; 2010: Clerk of the House of Representatives (*http:// clerk.house.gov*); *CQ Weekly* (2010), 2618–2629, 2716, 2717, 2766; 2012: *CQ Weekly* (2012), 2284–2293, 2308–2309, 2342, 2384, 2430; 2014: Clerk of the House of Representatives (*http:// clerk.house.gov*); *CQ Weekly* (2014), 60–61; official election results from state websites.

Table 1-17   Losses by President's Party in Midterm Elections, 1862–2014

Year	Party holding presidency	President's party: gain/loss of seats in House	President's party: gain/loss of seats in Senate
1862	R	−3	8
1866	R	−2	0
1870	R	−31	−4
1874	R	−96	−8
1878	R	−9	−6
1882	R	−33	3
1886	D	−12	3
1890	R	−85	0
1894	D	−116	−14
1898	R	−21	7
1902	R	9[a]	2
1906	R	−28	3
1910	R	−57	−10
1914	D	−59	5
1918	D	−19	−6
1922	R	−75	−8
1926	R	−10	−6
1930	R	−53	−8
1934	D	9	10
1938	D	−71	−6
1942	D	−45	−9
1946	D	−55	−12
1950	D	−29	−6
1954	R	−18	−1
1958	R	−47	−13
1962	D	−5	3
1966	D	−47	−4
1970	R	−12	3
1974	R	−48	−5
1978	D	−15	−3
1982	R	−26	1
1986	R	−5	−8
1990	R	−7	−1
1994	D	−54	−10
1998	D	4	0
2002	R	8	1
2006	R	−30	−6
2010	D	−63	−4
2014	D	−12	−9

Note: Each entry is the difference between the number of seats held by the president's party at the start of Congress after the midterm election and the number of seats held by that party at the start of Congress after the preceding general election. Special elections that shifted partisan seat totals between elections are not noted. Because of changes in the overall number of seats in the Senate and House, in the number of seats won by third parties, and in the number of vacancies, a Republican loss is not always matched precisely by a Democratic gain, or vice versa.

[a] Although the Republicans gained nine seats in the 1902 elections, they actually lost ground to the Democrats, who gained twenty-five seats after the increase in the overall number of representatives after the 1900 census.

Source: Table 1-10, this volume.

Table 1-18 House and Senate Incumbents Retired, Defeated, or Reelected, 1946–2014

Chamber/ year	Retired[a]	Number seeking reelection	Defeated Primaries	Defeated General election	Reelected Total	Reelected Percentage of those seeking reelection
House						
1946	32	398	18	52	328	82.4
1948	29	400	15	68	317	79.3
1950	29	400	6	32	362	90.5
1952	42	389	9	26	354	91.0
1954	24	407	6	22	379	93.1
1956	21	411	6	16	389	94.6
1958	33	396	3	37	356	89.9
1960[b,c]	27	405	6	25	375	92.6
1962[d]	24	402	12	22	368	91.5
1964	33	397	8	45	344	86.6
1966	23	411	8	41	362	88.1
1968[e]	24	408	4	9	395	96.8
1970[c]	30	401	10	12	379	94.5
1972[c,f]	40	392	14	13	366	93.4
1974	43	391	8	40	343	87.7
1976	47	384	3	13	368	95.8
1978	49	382	5	19	358	93.7
1980[c]	34	398	6	31	361	90.7
1982	31	387	4	29	354	91.5
1984	22	411	3	16	392	95.4
1986	40	394	3	6	385	97.7
1988	23	409	1	6	402	98.3
1990	27	407	1	15	391	96.1
1992	65	368	19	24	325	88.3
1994[c]	48	387	4	34	349	90.2
1996	49	384	2	21	361	94.0
1998	33	402	1	6	395	98.3
2000	32	403	3	6	394	97.8
2002	35	398	8	8	382	96.0
2004	29	404	2	7	395	97.8
2006[g]	27	404	2	22	380	94.1
2008	32	403	4	19	380	94.3
2010	36	397	4	54	339	85.4
2012	39	391	13	27	351	89.8
2014	41	392	4	14	374	95.4
Senate						
1946	9	30	6	7	17	56.7
1948	8	25	2	8	15	60.0
1950	4	32	5	5	22	68.8
1952	4	31	2	9	20	64.5
1954	6	32	2	6	24	75.0

(Table continues)

Table 1-18   *(Continued)*

Chamber/ year	Retired[a]	Number seeking reelection	Defeated		Reelected	
			Primaries	General election	Total	Percentage of those seeking reelection
1956	6	29	0	4	25	86.2
1958	6	28	0	10	18	64.3
1960	4	29	0	1	28	96.6
1962	4	35	1	5	29	82.9
1964	2	33	1	4	28	84.8
1966	3	32	3	1	28	87.5
1968[c]	6	28	4	4	20	71.4
1970	4	31	1	6	24	77.4
1972	6	27	2	5	20	74.1
1974	7	27	2	2	23	85.2
1976	8	25	0	9	16	64.0
1978	10	25	3	7	15	60.0
1980[c]	5	29	4	9	16	55.2
1982	3	30	0	2	28	93.3
1984	4	29	0	3	26	89.7
1986	6	28	0	7	21	75.0
1988	6	27	0	4	23	85.2
1990	3	32	0	1	31	96.9
1992	7	28	1	4	23	82.1
1994	8	26	0	2	24	92.3
1996	13	21	1	1	19	90.5
1998	5	29	0	3	26	89.7
2000	5	29	0	6	23	79.3
2002	6	28	1	3	24	85.7
2004	8	26	0	1	25	96.2
2006[h]	4	29	1	6	23	79.3
2008	5	30	0	5	25	83.3
2010[i]	12	25	3	2	21	84.0
2012	10	23	1	1	21	91.3
2014	7	28	0	5	23	82.1

[a] Does not include persons who died or resigned from office before the election.

[b] Harold B. McSween, D-La., lost the Democratic primary in 1960 and is counted as an incumbent defeated in the primary. However, his victorious primary opponent, Earl K. Long, died after winning the primary, and McSween was appointed to replace Long in the general election by the Eighth District Democratic Committee. McSween won the general election and is counted as an incumbent winning the general election.

[c] In this year, an incumbent candidate lost the party primary and is counted as an incumbent defeated in the primary. The candidate then ran in the general election on a minor-party label or as a write-in candidate and lost again, but is not also counted (here or in Table 1-19) as an incumbent defeated in the general election. House: 1960, Ludwig Teller, D-N.Y.; 1970, Philip Philbin, D-Mass.; 1972, Emanuel Celler, D-N.Y.; 1980, John Buchanan, R-Ala.; 1994, David A. Levy, R-N.Y. Senate: 1968, Ernest Gruening, D-Alaska; 1980, Jacob K. Javits, R-N.Y.

[d] Clem Miller, D-Calif., was killed in a plane crash on October 7, 1962, but his name remained on the 1962 general election ballot. He won the election posthumously and is counted here as an incumbent winning the general election.

Table 1-18   *(Continued)*

---

[e] Adam Clayton Powell, D-N.Y., won a special election on April 11, 1967, but he was prevented from taking the oath of office and did not take his seat in Congress. Therefore, he is not counted here (or in Table 1-19) as an incumbent in the 1968 general election.

[f] Bella Abzug, D-N.Y., lost the Democratic primary in 1972 and is counted as an incumbent defeated in the primary. However, her victorious primary opponent, William F. Ryan, died after winning the primary, and Abzug was appointed to replace him in the general election by the local party committee. Abzug won the general election and is counted as an incumbent winning the general election.

[g] In 2006 three representatives withdrew from the general election after winning their primaries: Tom DeLay, R-Texas; Mark Foley, R-Fla.; and Bob Ney, R-Ohio. Because they did not run in the general election, they are not counted as incumbents seeking reelection (here or in Table 1-19).

[h] Joseph I. Lieberman, D-Conn., lost the Democratic primary in 2006 and is counted as an incumbent defeated in the primary. He ran as an independent in the general election and won. He is counted as an incumbent winning the general election.

[i] Lisa Murkowski, R-Alaska, lost the Republican primary in 2010 and is counted as an incumbent defeated in the primary. She ran as a write-in candidate in the general election and won. She is counted as an incumbent winning the general election.

Sources: Clerk of the House of Representatives (*http://clerk.house.gov*); Congressional Quarterly; official election results from state websites.

Table 1-19   Incumbent Reelection Rates: Representatives, Senators, and Governors, General Elections, 1960–2014

	Number of incumbents			Incumbents winning election[a]	Incumbents reelected with 60+ percent of the major-party vote[a]
Year/office	Ran	Won	Lost		
1960					
House[b,c]	400	375	25	93.5%	59.3%
Senate	29	28	1	96.6	44.8
Governor	14	8	6	57.1	14.3
1962					
House[d]	390	368	22	96.2	61.0[e]
Senate	34	29	5	85.3	32.4
Governor	26	15	11	57.7	7.7
1964					
House	389	344	45	88.4	58.1
Senate	32	28	4	87.5	46.9
Governor	14	12	2	85.7	50.0
1966					
House	403	362	41	90.0	67.0
Senate	29	28	1	96.6	44.8
Governor	22	15	7	68.2	22.7
1968					
House[f]	404	395	9	98.8	70.8
Senate[c]	24	20	4	83.3	45.8
Governor	14	10	4	71.4	21.4
1970					
House[c]	391	379	12	96.9	76.7
Senate	30	24	6	79.3	33.3
Governor	22	17	5	77.3	9.1
1972					
House[c,g]	379	366	13	96.6	76.3
Senate	25	20	5	80.0	48.0
Governor	9	7	2	77.8	44.4
1974					
House	383	343	40	89.6	66.6
Senate	25	23	2	92.0	44.0
Governor	21	16	5	76.2	42.9
1976					
House	381	368	13	96.6	72.7
Senate	25	16	9	64.0	44.0
Governor	7	5	2	71.4	28.6
1978					
House	377	358	19	95.0	75.3
Senate	22	15	7	68.2	31.8
Governor	20	15	5	75.0	30.0
1980					
House[c]	392	361	31	92.1	73.2
Senate[c]	25	16	9	64.0	38.5
Governor	10	7	3	70.0	40.0

Table 1-19   *(Continued)*

	Number of incumbents			Incumbents winning election[a]	Incumbents reelected with 60+ percent of the major-party vote[a]
Year/office	Ran	Won	Lost		
1982					
House	383	354	29	92.4	69.9
Senate	30	28	2	93.3	46.7
Governor	24	19	5	79.2	45.8
1984					
House	408	392	16	96.1	77.2
Senate	29	26	3	89.7	65.5
Governor	6	4	2	66.7	50.0
1986					
House	391	385	6	98.5	84.4
Senate	28	21	7	75.0	50.0
Governor	17	15	2	88.2	52.9
1988					
House	408	402	6	98.5	87.0
Senate	27	23	4	85.2	55.6
Governor	9	8	1	88.9	33.3
1990					
House	406	391	15	96.3	74.9
Senate	32	31	1	96.9	62.5
Governor	23	17	6	73.9	47.8
1992					
House	349	325	24	93.1	65.6
Senate	27	23	4	85.2	48.1
Governor	4	4	0	100.0	100.0
1994					
House[c]	383	349	34	91.9	67.2
Senate	26	24	2	92.3	38.5
Governor	21	17	4	81.0	38.1
1996					
House	382	361	21	94.5	67.8
Senate	20	19	1	95.0	30.0
Governor	7	7	0	100.0	71.4
1998					
House	401	395	6	98.5	77.3
Senate	29	26	3	89.6	65.5
Governor	26	24	2	92.3	50.0
2000					
House	400	394	6	98.5	78.0
Senate	29	23	6	79.3	58.6
Governor	6	5	1	83.3	0.0
2002					
House	390	382	8	97.9	86.4
Senate	27	24	3	88.9	65.4
Governor	16	12	4	75.0	25.0

(Table continues)

Table 1-19   *(Continued)*

Year/office	Number of incumbents			Incumbents winning election[a]	Incumbents reelected with 60+ percent of the major-party vote[a]
	Ran	Won	Lost		
2004					
House	402	395	7	98.3	85.3
Senate	26	25	1	96.2	69.2
Governor	6	4	2	66.7	33.3
2006					
House[h]	402	380	22	94.5	75.1
Senate[i]	29	23	6	79.3	58.6
Governor	26	25	1	96.1	46.2
2008					
House	399	380	19	95.2	76.4
Senate	30	25	5	83.3	56.7
Governor	8	8	0	100.0	87.5
2010					
House	393	339	54	86.3	63.9
Senate[j]	23	21	2	91.3	56.5
Governor	13	11	2	84.6	38.5
2012					
House	378	351	27	92.9	66.4
Senate	22	21	1	95.5	54.5
Governor	6	6	0	100.0	66.7
2014					
House	388	374	14	96.4	77.3
Senate	28	23	5	82.1	46.4
Governor	28	25	3	89.3	28.6

Note: Percentage gaining more than 60 percent of the vote (among incumbents who ran) is calculated on the basis of the vote for the two major parties. Incumbents running unopposed are considered to have won with over 60 percent of the major-party vote. "Off-off" year gubernatorial elections, held in Kentucky, Louisiana, Mississippi, New Jersey, and Virginia, are not included in the preceding totals. For these gubernatorial election outcomes, see *CQ Press Guide to U.S. Elections*, 6th ed. (Washington, D.C.: CQ Press, 2010).

[a] Percentage is calculated based on all incumbents running in the general election.
[b] Harold B. McSween, D-La., lost the Democratic primary in 1960 and is counted as an incumbent defeated in the primary in Table 1-18. However, his victorious primary opponent, Earl K. Long, died after winning the primary, and McSween was appointed to replace Long in the general election by the Eighth District Democratic Committee. McSween won the general election and is counted as an incumbent winning the general election.
[c] In this year, an incumbent candidate lost the party primary and is counted as an incumbent defeated in the primary in Table 1-18. The candidate then ran in the general election on a minor-party label or as a write-in candidate and lost again, but is not also counted (here or in Table 1-18) as an incumbent defeated in the general election. House: 1960, Ludwig Teller, D-N.Y.; 1970, Philip Philbin, D-Mass.; 1972, Emanuel Celler, D-N.Y.; 1980, John Buchanan, R-Ala.; 1994, David A. Levy, R-N.Y. Senate: 1968, Ernest Gruening, D-Alaska; 1980, Jacob K. Javits, R-N.Y.
[d] Clem Miller, D-Calif., was killed in a plane crash on October 7, 1962, but his name remained on the 1962 general election ballot. He won the election posthumously and is counted here as an incumbent winning the general election.

Table 1-19   *(Continued)*

---

[e] Data not available for Alabama. The percentage is calculated excluding the number of incumbents winning House seats in Alabama for this year.

[f] Adam Clayton Powell, D-N.Y., won a special election on April 11, 1967, but he was prevented from taking the oath of office and did not take his seat in Congress. Therefore, he is not counted here (or in Table 1-18) as an incumbent in the 1968 general election.

[g] Bella Abzug, D-N.Y., lost the Democratic primary in 1972 and is counted as an incumbent defeated in the primary in Table 1-18. However, her victorious primary opponent, William F. Ryan, died after winning the primary, and Abzug was appointed to replace him in the general election by the local party committee. Abzug won the general election and is counted as an incumbent winning the general election.

[h] In 2006 three representatives withdrew from the general election after winning their primaries: Tom DeLay, R-Texas; Mark Foley, R-Fla.; and Bob Ney, R-Ohio. Because they did not run in the general election, they are not counted as incumbents seeking reelection (here or in Table 1-18).

[i] Joseph I. Lieberman, D-Conn., lost the Democratic primary in 2006 and is counted as an incumbent defeated in the primary in Table 1-18. He ran as an independent in the general election and won. He is counted as an incumbent winning the general election.

[j] Lisa Murkowski, R-Alaska, lost the Republican primary in 2010 and is counted as an incumbent defeated in the primary in Table 1-18. She ran as a write-in candidate in the general election and won. She is counted as an incumbent winning the general election.

Sources: Clerk of the House of Representatives (*http://clerk.house.gov*); Congressional Quarterly; National Governors Association (*www.nga.gov*); official election results from state websites.

Table 1-20 Congressional Districts with a Racial or Ethnic Minority Representative or a "Majority-Minority" Population, 2015

| State | District number | Non-Hispanic (percent) | | | | Two or more races | Hispanic (percent) | Representative elected in 2014 | Party | Representative's race/ethnicity |
| | | Single race | | | | | | | | |
		White	Black	Asian	Other					
Racial or ethnic minority representatives in congressional districts without a majority-minority population										
California	7	55.1	7.3	14.3	1.4	4.7	17.2	Bera	D	Indian-American
California	33	66.3	2.7	13.9	0.6	3.5	12.9	Lieu	D	Asian
Idaho	1	84.8	0.4	1.3	1.2	1.9	10.2	Labrador	R	Hispanic
Illinois	8	54.1	4.7	11.4	0.3	1.5	28.0	Duckworth	D	Asian
Indiana	7	54.7	29.4	2.0	0.5	2.4	10.8	Carson	D	Black
Minnesota	5	63.8	15.1	6.2	1.3	4.1	9.5	Ellison	D	Black
Missouri	5	65.5	21.3	1.5	0.9	2.4	8.4	Cleaver	D	Black
Ohio	3	54.2	32.0	3.6	0.4	4.0	5.9	Beatty	D	Black
Oklahoma	2	65.3	3.5	0.5	16.3	9.7	4.7	Mullin	R	American Indian
Oklahoma	4	72.1	6.4	2.2	5.3	6.2	7.9	Cole	R	American Indian
Texas	17	56.3	12.6	4.0	0.3	2.0	24.7	Flores	R	Hispanic
Utah	4	75.2	1.6	3.0	2.1	1.7	16.5	Love	R	Black
Washington	3	82.0	1.5	3.2	1.3	3.6	8.4	Herrera Beutler	R	Hispanic
West Virginia	2	90.7	3.7	0.6	0.4	2.7	1.9	Mooney	R	Hispanic
Congressional districts with a majority-minority population										
Alabama	7	32.6	62.9	0.6	0.5	1.1	2.4	Sewell	D	Black
Arizona	3	28.1	4.3	1.6	3.3	1.4	61.3	Grijalva	D	Hispanic
Arizona	7	20.1	9.4	1.8	2.5	1.5	64.6	Gallego	D	Hispanic
California	3	48.9	6.3	10.2	1.5	4.3	28.8	Garamendi	D	White
California	6	38.4	11.9	15.7	1.8	5.2	27.1	Matsui	D	Asian
California	8	46.8	7.6	2.4	1.2	2.1	39.9	Cook	R	White
California	9	35.9	8.1	14.3	0.8	3.5	37.4	McNerney	D	White
California	10	44.4	3.0	6.6	1.0	3.2	41.8	Denham	R	White
California	11	47.0	8.8	12.4	1.1	4.3	26.4	DeSaulnier	D	White

California	12	42.9	5.5	31.5	1.2	3.4	15.5	Pelosi	D	White
California	13	33.8	18.1	20.7	1.2	4.7	21.4	Lee	D	Black
California	14	35.7	3.1	31.8	1.8	3.4	24.1	Speier	D	White
California	15	35.3	5.6	29.7	1.5	4.2	23.8	Swalwell	D	White
California	16	23.5	5.9	9.1	0.7	1.4	59.5	Costa	D	White
California	17	26.3	2.6	51.5	0.8	3.2	15.6	Honda	D	Asian
California	19	25.3	3.3	26.7	0.6	2.4	41.7	Lofgren	D	White
California	20	37.7	1.8	5.3	0.6	2.5	52.0	Farr	D	White
California	21	18.2	4.1	3.3	0.6	1.4	72.5	Valadao	R	White
California	22	40.9	2.9	7.9	0.7	1.8	45.8	Nunes	R	White
California	23	48.3	5.6	4.7	1.0	2.2	38.2	McCarthy	R	White
California	25	44.4	7.6	7.4	0.7	3.3	36.6	Knight	R	White
California	26	43.9	1.6	6.9	0.5	2.4	44.7	Brownley	D	White
California	27	27.4	4.6	38.4	0.4	2.1	27.2	Chu	D	Asian
California	29	17.8	3.8	8.0	0.4	1.3	68.7	Cardenas	D	Hispanic
California	30	49.6	3.8	12.2	0.5	3.3	30.6	Sherman	D	White
California	31	28.5	10.4	7.1	0.7	1.6	51.6	Aguilar	D	Hispanic
California	32	16.5	3.0	16.8	0.5	1.5	61.7	Napolitano	D	Hispanic
California	34	9.8	4.2	18.3	0.7	1.2	65.9	Becerra	D	Hispanic
California	35	15.5	7.0	7.0	0.8	2.2	67.5	Torres	D	Hispanic
California	36	43.1	3.9	2.5	1.0	2.0	47.6	Ruiz	D	Hispanic
California	37	26.3	22.1	9.3	0.9	2.7	38.8	Bass	D	Black
California	38	17.6	4.1	14.9	1.2	1.6	60.6	Sánchez	D	Hispanic
California	39	32.6	2.1	29.1	0.7	2.2	33.3	Royce	R	White
California	40	4.9	4.5	2.1	0.4	0.3	87.7	Roybal-Allard	D	Hispanic
California	41	24.6	8.6	4.8	0.7	1.9	59.3	Takano	D	Asian
California	42	44.3	5.3	9.7	0.8	3.3	36.6	Calvert	R	White
California	43	14.4	22.1	12.9	0.6	3.0	47.0	Waters	D	Black
California	44	6.2	16.4	5.8	0.9	1.4	69.4	Hahn	D	White
California	46	18.8	1.5	12.1	0.5	1.0	66.2	Sanchez	D	Hispanic
California	47	32.3	7.4	20.9	1.2	2.8	35.4	Lowenthal	D	White
California	51	13.1	6.7	7.7	0.9	1.6	69.9	Vargas	D	Hispanic
California	53	41.8	6.9	13.1	1.2	4.0	33.0	Davis	D	White

(Table continues)

Table 1-20 (Continued)

State	District number	Non-Hispanic (percent)					Hispanic (percent)	Representative elected in 2014	Party	Representative's race/ethnicity
		Single race				Two or more races				
		White	Black	Asian	Other					
Florida	5	30.0	51.6	2.7	0.8	2.3	12.5	Brown	D	Black
Florida	9	37.4	9.6	4.4	0.4	2.1	46.1	Grayson	D	White
Florida	14	41.6	24.5	3.0	0.8	2.0	28.2	Castor	D	White
Florida	20	24.2	52.1	1.6	0.4	1.4	20.3	Hastings	D	Black
Florida	23	46.9	9.8	3.3	1.1	1.7	37.3	Wasserman Schultz	D	White
Florida	24	11.5	52.0	2.1	0.6	0.6	33.2	Wilson	D	Black
Florida	25	18.5	7.0	1.8	0.4	0.2	72.1	Diaz-Balart	R	Hispanic
Florida	26	20.0	9.5	2.2	0.3	0.9	67.1	Curbelo	R	Hispanic
Florida	27	16.5	5.9	1.3	0.2	0.7	75.4	Ros-Lehtinen	R	Hispanic
Georgia	2	40.8	51.1	1.2	0.3	1.5	5.1	Bishop	D	Black
Georgia	4	25.3	58.0	5.3	0.7	1.9	8.7	Johnson	D	Black
Georgia	5	28.9	57.3	3.9	0.4	1.8	7.7	Lewis	D	Black
Georgia	7	48.3	17.8	12.2	0.7	1.8	19.2	Woodall	R	White
Georgia	13	29.7	55.4	2.7	0.4	1.8	9.9	Scott	D	Black
Hawaii	1	16.4	2.5	49.2	7.6	15.9	8.4	Takai	D	Asian
Hawaii	2	29.6	1.5	24.7	10.7	22.3	11.3	Gabbard	D	Pacific Islander
Illinois	1	35.5	51.0	2.3	0.4	1.5	9.4	Rush	D	Black
Illinois	2	30.4	55.0	0.7	0.1	1.5	12.3	Kelly	D	Black
Illinois	4	20.8	4.1	3.3	0.3	0.9	70.5	Gutierrez	D	Hispanic
Illinois	7	28.4	50.8	6.2	0.3	1.7	12.6	Davis	D	Black
Louisiana	2	27.8	62.0	2.8	0.3	1.2	5.8	Richmond	D	Black
Maryland	4	26.9	52.3	3.1	0.4	1.7	15.7	Edwards	D	Black
Maryland	5	47.8	37.7	4.1	0.8	2.2	7.4	Hoyer	D	White
Maryland	7	33.7	54.0	6.3	0.6	1.8	3.6	Cummings	D	Black
Massachusetts	7	43.1	22.9	9.2	1.7	2.9	20.2	Capuano	D	White
Michigan	13	33.5	55.9	1.0	0.6	1.9	7.1	Conyers	D	Black

State	District							Name	Party	Race
Michigan	14	31.4	57.3	3.7	0.3	2.6	4.7	Lawrence	D	Black
Mississippi	2	31.5	65.1	0.5	0.4	0.7	1.9	Thompson	D	Black
Missouri	1	42.1	48.7	2.7	0.4	3.1	3.0	Clay	D	Black
Nevada	1	34.0	10.5	7.8	0.8	2.9	44.0	Titus	D	White
Nevada	4	46.1	13.3	5.2	2.0	3.2	30.2	Hardy	R	White
New Jersey	6	49.6	9.3	17.5	0.4	1.6	21.7	Pallone	D	White
New Jersey	8	25.5	8.4	8.2	1.6	1.2	55.1	Sires	D	Hispanic
New Jersey	9	40.6	9.7	13.7	0.3	1.0	34.7	Pascrell	D	White
New Jersey	10	20.6	51.7	6.7	1.0	1.5	18.5	Payne	D	Black
New Jersey	12	48.8	17.3	16.5	1.1	1.6	14.8	Watson Coleman	D	Black
New Mexico	1	40.9	2.5	2.2	3.6	1.8	48.9	Lujan Grisham	D	Hispanic
New Mexico	2	38.4	1.6	0.6	4.8	1.6	53.1	Pearce	R	White
New Mexico	3	38.5	1.2	1.0	17.6	1.8	40.0	Luján	D	Hispanic
New York	5	11.5	47.8	13.2	5.3	3.1	19.1	Meeks	D	Black
New York	6	37.6	2.8	38.7	0.5	1.8	18.6	Meng	D	Asian
New York	7	28.2	7.3	18.9	1.0	1.5	43.1	Velázquez	D	Hispanic
New York	8	21.8	54.0	5.0	1.1	1.3	16.8	Jeffries	D	Black
New York	9	31.3	48.6	7.4	0.6	1.6	10.5	Clarke	D	Black
New York	13	14.3	24.8	4.0	1.1	1.2	54.6	Rangel	D	White
New York	14	22.8	9.7	16.0	0.4	1.2	49.8	Crowley	D	White
New York	15	2.9	28.6	2.2	0.9	0.8	64.7	Serrano	D	Hispanic
New York	16	39.4	30.3	4.3	0.8	1.7	23.4	Engel	D	White
North Carolina	1	34.0	54.1	1.5	0.8	2.2	7.4	Butterfield	D	Black
North Carolina	4	48.5	30.9	5.5	0.7	2.6	11.7	Price	D	White
North Carolina	12	27.7	50.6	4.6	0.5	1.8	14.8	Adams	D	Black
Ohio	11	37.6	53.5	2.1	0.4	2.5	3.8	Fudge	D	Black
Pennsylvania	1	38.7	34.6	7.2	0.5	2.0	17.1	Brady	D	White
Pennsylvania	2	29.8	57.6	4.6	0.3	1.9	5.8	Fattah	D	Black
South Carolina	6	35.3	57.3	0.9	0.4	1.6	4.4	Clyburn	D	Black
Tennessee	9	25.3	64.9	1.6	0.2	1.4	6.7	Cohen	D	White
Texas	7	44.0	13.7	11.2	0.8	2.0	28.3	Culberson	R	White
Texas	9	11.7	38.7	11.0	0.4	1.5	36.8	Green	D	Black
Texas	15	15.9	1.8	1.2	0.1	0.3	80.7	Hinojosa	D	Hispanic

(Table continues)

Table 1-20 (Continued)

| State | District number | Non-Hispanic (percent) Single race | | | | Two or more races | Hispanic (percent) | Representative elected in 2014 | Party | Representative's race/ethnicity |
		White	Black	Asian	Other					
Texas	16	14.9	3.5	1.2	0.5	1.0	79.0	O'Rourke	D	White
Texas	18	17.2	37.0	3.7	0.3	1.4	40.4	Jackson Lee	D	Black
Texas	20	21.6	5.3	3.2	0.3	1.3	68.3	Castro	D	Hispanic
Texas	22	43.2	13.9	16.7	0.3	1.6	24.3	Olson	R	White
Texas	23	24.5	2.7	1.3	0.7	1.0	69.9	Hurd	R	Black
Texas	27	41.6	5.1	1.6	0.2	0.9	50.6	Farenthold	R	White
Texas	28	16.8	3.3	0.6	0.4	1.1	77.8	Cuellar	D	Hispanic
Texas	29	10.0	10.4	1.1	0.2	0.3	78.0	Green	D	White
Texas	30	16.1	42.7	1.7	0.2	1.3	37.9	Johnson	D	Black
Texas	33	15.8	16.8	2.1	0.3	0.5	64.6	Veasey	D	Black
Texas	34	14.3	0.9	0.7	0.1	0.3	83.7	Vela	D	Hispanic
Texas	35	24.8	9.4	1.1	0.3	1.4	63.0	Doggett	D	White
Virginia	3	32.4	56.3	1.8	0.7	3.0	5.8	Scott	D	Black
Virginia	11	47.4	12.6	17.9	0.4	3.2	18.5	Connolly	D	White
Washington	9	48.5	10.4	21.9	1.6	5.6	12.0	Smith	D	White
Wisconsin	4	43.8	33.4	3.5	0.6	2.8	15.9	Moore	D	Black

Note: "D" indicates Democratic; "R" indicates Republican. Majority-minority districts are those in which the non-Hispanic white population does not constitute a majority of the total population. Population values are based on the 2013 American Community Survey one-year estimates from the U.S. Census Bureau. The six population categories sum to 100 percent. Non-Hispanic white, non-Hispanic black, and non-Hispanic other are single-race counts, indicating persons who considered themselves only one race, not two or more races. The percentage for all non-Hispanics who considered themselves to be of two or more races is indicated separately. Data for earlier years can be found in previous editions of *Vital Statistics on American Politics*.

Sources: Derived by the editors from CQ Roll-Call, *Guide to the New Congress*, November 6, 2014, 58; Office of the Clerk, U.S. House of Representatives, *Statistics of the Congressional Election from Official Sources for the Election of November 4, 2014* (*http://clerk.house.gov*); U.S. Census Bureau, 2013 American Community Survey 1-Year Estimates (*www.census.gov*).

Table 1-21 Latino Elected Officials in the United States, 1996–2014

	1996	2000	2005	2007	2010	2011	2012	2014
Members of Congress	17	19	25	26	24	26	26	31
State officials	6	8	9	6	7	9	8	9
State legislators	156	190	232	238	245	251	258	294
County officials	358	398	498	512	563	551	555	547
Municipal officials	1,295	1,469	1,651	1,640	1,707	1,731	1,738	1,766
Judicial and law enforcement	546	465	678	685	874	864	881	878
School board members	1,240	1,392	1,760	1,847	2,071	2,173	2,225	2,322
Special district officials	125	119	188	175	248	245	237	237
Total	3,743	4,060	5,041	5,129	5,739	5,850	5,928	6,084

Note: After the 2014 election, there were 32 Latino members of Congress and 292 state legislators.

Sources: 1996–2005: National Association of Latino Elected Officials, "NALEO At-A-Glance" (September 4, 2006) (*www.naleo.org*); 2007: National Association of Latino Elected Officials, *2007 National Directory of Latino Elected Officials*; 2010: *2010*; 2011: *2011*; 2012: *2012*; 2014: *2014*; Note: National Association of Latino Elected Officials, "2015 Class of Latino State Legislators to Make History" (November 6, 2014) (*www.naleo.org*).

Table 1-22 Blacks, Hispanics, and Women as a Percentage of State Legislators and State Voting-Age Population

State	Total number of legislators	Blacks				Hispanics				Women			
		Legislators	Percentage	Percentage VAP	Ratio[a]	Legislators	Percentage	Percentage VAP	Ratio[a]	Legislators	Percentage	Percentage VAP	Ratio[a]
Alabama	140	32	22.9	24.8	0.923	0	0.0	3.0	0.000	20	14.3	52.6	0.272
Alaska	60	0	0.0	4.1	0.000	0	0.0	4.5	0.000	17	28.3	49.4	0.573
Arizona	90	1	1.1	4.3	0.256	18	20.0	28.7	0.697	32	35.6	51.4	0.693
Arkansas	135	15	11.1	14.2	0.782	0	0.0	6.5	0.000	27	20.0	52.5	0.381
California	120	11	9.2	6.4	1.438	27	22.5	35.0	0.643	31	25.8	51.0	0.506
Colorado	100	5	5.0	3.7	1.351	12	12.0	17.8	0.674	42	42.0	50.7	0.828
Connecticut	187	14	7.5	10.2	0.735	13	7.0	10.7	0.654	54	28.9	52.4	0.552
Delaware	62	4	6.5	20.5	0.317	2	3.2	8.1	0.395	15	24.2	52.4	0.462
Florida	160	26	16.3	14.9	1.094	18	11.3	22.3	0.507	39	24.4	52.2	0.467
Georgia	236	58	24.6	30.0	0.820	2	0.8	6.8	0.118	54	22.9	52.3	0.438
Hawaii	76	1	1.3	1.8	0.722	2	2.6	8.0	0.325	22	28.9	51.3	0.563
Idaho	105	1	1.0	0.6	1.667	0	0.0	10.5	0.000	28	26.7	51.1	0.523
Illinois	177	32	18.1	13.7	1.321	14	7.9	12.4	0.637	55	31.1	51.9	0.599
Indiana	150	12	8.0	7.9	1.013	3	2.0	3.8	0.526	30	20.0	52.1	0.384
Iowa	150	5	3.3	2.3	1.435	0	0.0	5.2	0.000	34	22.7	51.1	0.444
Kansas	165	9	5.5	5.0	1.100	6	3.6	9.3	0.387	41	24.8	51.5	0.482
Kentucky	138	8	5.8	6.8	0.853	0	0.0	2.5	0.000	23	16.7	52.0	0.321
Louisiana	144	30	20.8	30.0	0.693	1	0.7	3.8	0.184	18	12.5	53.2	0.235
Maine	186	1	0.5	0.8	0.625	1	0.5	1.0	0.500	54	29.0	51.2	0.566
Maryland	188	46	24.5	28.7	0.854	3	1.6	7.7	0.208	59	31.4	52.8	0.595
Massachusetts	200	7	3.5	7.4	0.473	5	2.5	8.8	0.284	50	25.0	52.6	0.475
Michigan	148	15	10.1	13.7	0.737	3	2.0	3.8	0.526	31	20.9	52.0	0.402
Minnesota	201	3	1.5	4.4	0.341	3	1.5	3.4	0.441	67	33.3	50.9	0.654
Mississippi	174	49	28.2	34.5	0.817	0	0.0	1.6	0.000	30	17.2	53.0	0.325
Missouri	197	20	10.2	10.7	0.953	2	1.0	3.1	0.323	48	24.4	52.0	0.469
Montana	150	0	0.0	0.3	0.000	0	0.0	2.0	0.000	47	31.3	50.7	0.617
Nebraska	49	2	4.1	3.7	1.108	0	0.0	8.0	0.000	9	18.4	50.6	0.364

State												
Nevada	63	6	9.5	8.3	1.145	7	11.1	22.8	0.487	20	31.7	50.2	0.631
New Hampshire	424	3	0.7	1.2	0.583	3	0.7	2.8	0.250	122	28.8	51.1	0.564
New Jersey	120	16	13.3	13.5	0.985	10	8.3	17.4	0.477	35	29.2	52.2	0.559
New Mexico	112	2	1.8	2.8	0.643	49	43.8	40.2	1.090	29	25.9	51.4	0.504
New York	213	33	15.5	16.5	0.939	21	9.9	15.7	0.631	51	23.9	52.5	0.455
North Carolina	170	35	20.6	21.0	0.981	1	0.6	8.3	0.072	39	22.9	52.7	0.435
North Dakota	141	0	0.0	1.1	0.000	0	0.0	3.0	0.000	27	19.1	50.2	0.380
Ohio	132	15	11.4	11.7	0.974	2	1.5	2.9	0.517	33	25.0	52.3	0.478
Oklahoma	149	5	3.4	6.8	0.500	1	0.7	6.2	0.113	19	12.8	51.6	0.248
Oregon	90	2	2.2	1.9	1.158	3	3.3	7.5	0.440	28	31.1	50.6	0.615
Pennsylvania	253	21	8.3	10.2	0.814	3	0.8	5.1	0.157	45	17.8	52.0	0.342
Rhode Island	113	6	5.3	6.1	0.869	4	3.5	11.6	0.302	30	26.5	53.1	0.499
South Carolina	170	39	22.9	26.1	0.877	0	0.0	3.2	0.000	23	13.5	52.8	0.256
South Dakota	105	0	0.0	1.0	0.000	0	0.0	2.6	0.000	22	21.0	50.6	0.415
Tennessee	132	17	12.9	15.8	0.816	1	0.8	5.0	0.160	23	17.4	52.5	0.331
Texas	181	19	10.5	11.9	0.882	41	22.7	36.6	0.620	36	19.9	51.5	0.386
Utah	104	1	1.0	1.2	0.833	4	3.8	12.2	0.311	16	15.4	51.0	0.302
Vermont	180	2	1.1	1.0	1.100	1	0.6	1.2	0.500	74	41.1	51.4	0.800
Virginia	140	19	13.6	18.6	0.731	1	0.7	6.3	0.111	24	17.1	52.6	0.325
Washington	147	1	0.7	3.1	0.226	4	2.7	8.8	0.307	48	32.7	51.3	0.637
West Virginia	134	2	1.5	2.8	0.536	0	0.0	1.0	0.000	20	14.9	51.4	0.290
Wisconsin	132	6	4.5	5.6	0.804	2	1.5	4.9	0.306	33	25.0	51.4	0.486
Wyoming	90	2	2.2	0.7	3.143	2	2.2	7.5	0.293	12	13.3	49.9	0.267
United States	7,383	659	8.9	12.2	0.730	294	4.0	15.0	0.267	1,786	24.2	51.9	0.466

Note: Hispanics may be of any race. The black voting-age population (VAP) figures are for the black-alone racial category. The counts of black legislators are as of February 2015, of Hispanic legislators as of June 2014, of female legislators as of January 2015.

[a] The ratio between the group's indicated percentage of state legislators and the group's percentage of the state voting-age population. Calculated before rounding.

Sources: Total number of legislators and women legislators: Center for American Women and Politics, "Women in State Legislatures 2015" (*www.cawp.rutgers.edu*); black legislators: unpublished data from the National Black Caucus of State Legislators (*www.nbcsl.org*); Hispanic legislators: National Association of Latino Elected and Appointed Officials (NALEO) Educational Fund, *2014 National Directory of Latino Elected Officials* (*www.naleo.org*); voting-age population percentages calculated by the editors from U.S. Census Bureau, "Current Population Reports, Voting and Registration in the Election of November 2012" (*www.census.gov*).

Table 1-23 Presidential Primaries, 1912–2012

	Democratic Party			Republican Party		
Year	Number of primaries	Votes cast	Percentage of delegates selected through primaries	Number of primaries	Votes cast	Percentage of delegates selected through primaries
1912	12	974,775	32.9	13	2,261,240	41.7
1916	20	1,187,691	53.5	20	1,923,374	58.9
1920	16	571,671	44.6	20	3,186,248	57.8
1924	14	763,858	35.5	17	3,525,185	45.3
1928	16	1,264,220	42.2	15	4,110,288	44.9
1932	16	2,952,933	40.0	14	2,346,996	37.7
1936	14	5,181,808	36.5	12	3,319,810	37.5
1940	13	4,468,631	35.8	13	3,227,875	38.8
1944	14	1,867,609	36.7	13	2,271,605	38.7
1948	14	2,151,865	36.3	12	2,653,255	36.0
1952	16	4,928,006	38.7	13	7,801,413	39.0
1956	19	5,832,592	42.7	19	5,828,272	44.8
1960	16	5,687,742	38.3	15	5,537,967	38.6
1964	16	6,247,435	45.7	16	5,935,339	45.6
1968	15	7,535,069	40.2	15	4,473,551	38.1
1972	21	15,993,965	65.3	20	6,188,281	56.8
1976	27	16,052,652	76.0	26	10,374,125	71.0
1980	34	18,747,825	71.8	34	12,690,451	76.0
1984	29	18,009,217	52.4	25	6,575,651	71.0
1988	36	22,961,936	66.6	36	12,165,115	76.9
1992	39	20,239,385	66.9	38	12,696,547	83.9
1996	35	10,996,395	65.3	42	14,233,939	84.6
2000	40	14,045,745	64.6	43	17,156,117	83.8
2004	37	16,182,439	67.5	27	7,940,331	55.5
2008	38	36,995,069[a]	68.9	39	20,840,681	79.8
2012	26	9,187,665	47.2	36	18,767,217	71.3

Note: The number of primaries held include those in which delegates were elected and pledged to specific candidates. A few states also held "beauty contest" primaries that were nonbinding; in those states pledged delegates were selected in caucuses.

[a] Includes 149,181 votes cast in a New Mexico contest in February. That contest was technically a caucus but had many characteristics of a regular primary.

Sources: 1912–2008: *CQ Press Guide to U.S. Elections*, 6th ed. (Washington, D.C.: CQ Press, 2010), 363; 2012: Rhodes Cook, personal communication.

Table 1-24 State Methods for Choosing National Convention Delegates, 1968–2012

State	1968	1972	1976	1980	1984	1988	1992	1996	2000	2004	2008	2012
Alabama	DP	↓	OP	↓	↓	↓	↓	↓	↓	↓	↓	↓
Alaska	CL	↓	↓	↓	↓	↓	↓	↓	↓	↓	↓	↓
Arizona	(D)CS (R)CL	CL	↓	↓	↓	↓	↓	(D)CL (R)P	P	(D)P (R)CL	P	↓
Arkansas	CS	CL	OP	(D)OP (R)CL	CL	OP	↓	↓	↓	↓	↓	↓
California	P	↓	↓	↓	↓	↓	↓	↓	↓	(D)PI (R)P	P	P
Colorado	CL	↓	↓	↓	↓	↓	OP	↓	↓	↓	↓	↓
Connecticut	CL	↓	↓	P	(D)P (R)CL	P	↓	↓	↓	CL	↓	↓
Delaware	CL	↓	↓	↓	↓	↓	↓	(D)CL (R)P	(D)X (R)CL	(D)P (R)CL	P	↓
District of Columbia	P	↓	↓	↓	↓	↓	↓	↓	↓	(D)X (R)CL	P	↓
Florida	P	↓	↓	↓	↓	↓	↓	↓	↓	↓	↓	↓
Georgia	(D)CS (R)CL	CL	OP	↓	↓	↓	↓	↓	↓	↓	↓	↓
Hawaii	CL	↓	↓	↓	↓	↓	↓	↓	↓	↓	↓	↓
Idaho	CL	↓	OP	(D)CL (R)OP	(D)PI (R)OP	(D)X (R)OP	↓	↓	(D)X (R)OP,CS	(D)CL (R)OP	OP	CL
Illinois	DP,CL	P	OP	↓	DP	↓	↓	↓	(D)OP (R)DP,CS	(D)OP (R)DP	(D)OP (R)DP	↓
Indiana	OP	↓	↓	↓	↓	↓	↓	↓	(D)OP (R)OP,CS	OP	OP	↓
Iowa	CL	↓	↓	↓	↓	↓	↓	↓	↓	↓	↓	↓
Kansas	CL	↓	↓	PI	CL	↓	PI	↓	↓	CL	↓	↓

(Table continues)

Table 1-24 *(Continued)*

State	1968	1972	1976	1980	1984	1988	1992	1996	2000	2004	2008	2012
Kentucky	CL	↓	P	↓	CL	P	↓	↓	↓	↓	↓	↓
Louisiana	CS	CL	↓	P	↓	↓	↓	(D)P (R)CL PI	P	↓	↓	↓
Maine	CL	↓	↓	↓	↓	↓	↓	CL	↓	CL	↓	↓
Maryland	(D)CS (R)CL	P	↓	↓	DP	P	↓	↓	(D)P (R)PI	(D)P (R)PI	P	↓
Massachusetts	PI	↓	↓	↓	↓	↓	↓	↓	↓	↓	↓	↓
Michigan	CL	OP	↓	(D)CL (R)OP	CL	(D)CL (R)X	P	(D)CL (R)OP	↓	(D)PI (R)CL	P	↓
Minnesota	CL	↓	↓	↓	↓	↓	↓	↓	↓	↓	↓	↓
Mississippi	CL	↓	↓	(D)CL (R)DP	CL	OP	↓	↓	↓	↓	↓	↓
Missouri	(D)CL,CS (R)CL	CL	↓	↓	↓	OP	CL	↓	OP	↓	↓	CL
Montana	CL	↓	OP	↓	DP	(D)OP (R)X	↓	↓	↓	↓	↓	CL
Nebraska	OP	↓	↓	↓	P	↓	↓	PI	(D)P (R)DP	(D)P (R)X	(D)CL (R)X	X
Nevada	CL	↓	P	↓	CL	↓	↓	(D)CL (R)P	CL	↓	↓	↓
New Hampshire	PI	↓	↓	↓	↓	↓	↓	↓	↓	↓	↓	↓
New Jersey	PI	↓	↓	↓	DP	↓	↓	(D)PI (R)DP	↓	↓	PI	↓
New Mexico	CL	P	CL	P	↓	↓	↓	↓	↓	(D)CL (R)P	↓	P
New York	DP,CS	↓	DP	(D)P (R)DP,CS	(D)DP (R)DP,CS	↓	(D)P (R)OP	↓	(D)P (R)DP,CS	P	↓	↓
North Carolina	CL	P	↓	↓	↓	↓	↓	(D)P (R)PI	PI	CL	PI	↓

North Dakota	CL	↓	↓	↓	↓	DP	(D)X (R)OP	↓	CS	CL	↓
Ohio	OP	↓	↓	↓	PI	↓	P	↓	OP	↓	PI
Oklahoma	CL	↓	↓	↓	↓	↓	↓	↓	↓	↓	↓
Oregon	P	OP	↓	↓	DP	P	↓	↓	↓	↓	↓
Pennsylvania	P,CS	P	↓	↓	(D)P (R)DP,CS	DP	↓	↓	(D)P (R)DP,CS	↓	P
Rhode Island	(D)CS (R)CL	PI	↓	↓	↓	↓	↓	↓	↓	↓	↓
South Carolina	CL	↓	(D)CL (R)OP	↓	OP	↓	OP	↓	(D)OP (R)CL	OP	↓
South Dakota	P	↓	↓	↓	↓	↓	↓	↓	↓	↓	↓
Tennessee	CL	OP	↓	↓	P	↓	(D)CL (R)OP	↓	↓	↓	↓
Texas	CL	↓	OP	P	OP	(D)CL (R)OP	(D)OP,CS (R)OP	OP	(D)OP,CS (R)OP	↓	↓
Utah	CL	↓	↓	↓	↓	↓	↓	↓	PI	↓	PI
Vermont	CL	↓	X	CL	↓	↓	OP	↓	↓	↓	↓
Virginia	CL	↓	↓	↓	↓	↓	(D)OP (R)X	CL	(D)OP (R)CL	OP	↓
Washington	(D)CL,CS (R)CL	(D)CL (R)P	↓	↓	CL	CL	↓	P	(D)X (R)P;CL	CL	(D)CL (R)OP
West Virginia	P	↓	↓	↓	↓	(D)P (R)PI	↓	(D)P (R)DP	(D)P (R)DP	↓	PI
Wisconsin	OP	↓	↓	↓	↓	↓	(D)PI (R)OP	OP	PI	↓	↓
Wyoming	CL (D)CL	↓ CL	↓	↓	OP	(D)PI (R)CL	(D)X (R)OP	↓	(D)CL (R)OP	↓	↓ OP
(Puerto Rico)							PI				

(Table continues)

Table 1-24 *(Continued)*

Note: "←" indicates method(s) same as in previous presidential election; "CL" indicates delegates chosen by state and local caucuses and conventions; "CS" indicates delegates chosen by state party committee; "(D)" indicates Democrats; "DP" indicates delegates chosen directly by voters in primaries with nonbinding presidential preference poll; "OP" indicates delegates chosen or bound by presidential preference primaries open to all registered voters with no regard for party preregistration (or voters can switch party affiliation at the polls on primary day); "P" indicates delegates chosen or bound by presidential preference primaries open only to voters pre-registered as members of the particular parties; "PI" indicates delegates chosen or bound by presidential preference primaries open only to voters preregistered as members of the particular parties or as independents; "(R)" indicates Republicans; "X" indicates having nonbinding presidential preference primaries, but delegates are chosen by party caucus and conventions. States with primaries but without voter registration by party are coded "OP."

Sources: 1968–1984: Austin Ranney, ed., *The American Elections of 1984* (Durham, N.C.: Duke University Press, 1985), 330–332; 1988: derived by the editors from Kevin Coleman, "A Summary of National and State Party Rules and State Laws Concerning the Election of Delegates to the 1988 Democratic and Republican National Conventions," Report no. 88-102 GOV, Congressional Research Service, Washington, D.C., 1988; 1992: derived by the editors from Congressional Quarterly, *The First Hurrah: A 1992 Guide to the Nomination of the President* (Washington, D.C.: Congressional Quarterly, 1991); *Congressional Quarterly Weekly Report* (1991), 3478; and Thomas M. Durbin and L. Paige Whitaker, *Nomination and Election of the President and Vice President of the United States, 1992: Including the Manner of Selecting Delegates to National Party Conventions* (Washington, D.C.: Government Printing Office, 1992); 1996: derived by the editors from *Congressional Quarterly Weekly Report* (1995), 2485–2599; 2000–2008: derived by the editors from Rhodes Cook, *Race for the Presidency* (Washington, D.C.: CQ Press, 2000, 2004, and 2008); 2012: derived by the editors from "Presidential Primaries 2012: Democratic Delegate Selection and Voter Eligibility" and "Presidential Primaries 2012: Republican Delegate Selection and Voter Eligibility" (*www.thegreenpapers.com*). Because several of the sources of these methods are published prior to the nomination season and because last-minute changes are made in some states' methods, occasionally later publications have led to revisions of a classification for an earlier year.

Figure 1-5   Democratic and Republican Presidential Nominations, Campaign
Lengths, 1968–2012

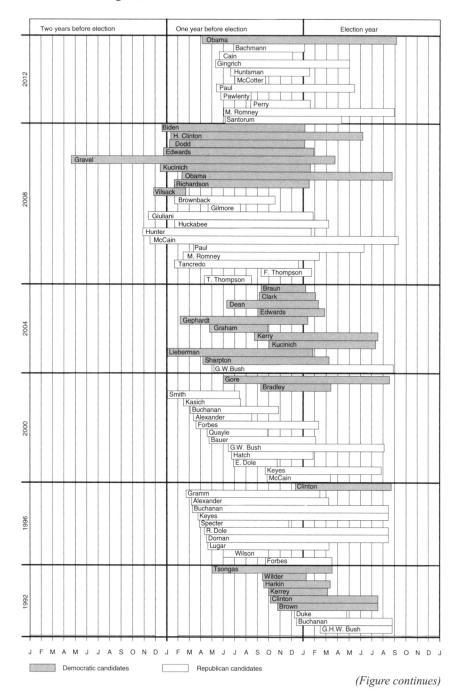

(Figure continues)

Figure 1-5   *(Continued)*

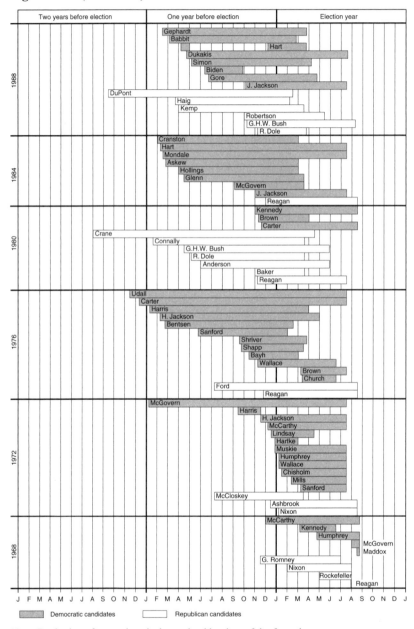

Note: Beginning of campaigns is determined by date of the formal announcement.

Sources: 1968–1984: Congressional Quarterly, *Elections '80* (Washington, D.C.: Congressional Quarterly, 1980), and *Congressional Quarterly's Guide to U.S. Elections,* 2nd ed. (Washington, D.C.: Congressional Quarterly, 1985), 387; 1988–1996: *Congressional Quarterly Weekly Report* (1987), 2732; (1988), 1894, 1896, 1899; (1991), 3735; (1992), 66, 361, 556, 633, 1086; (1995), 2, 13, 15, 3025, 3606; (1996), 641, 716; 2000–2012: compiled by the editors from news reports, various sources.

Table 1-25 Republican Presidential Primary Returns, 2012

	Date	Turnout	Gingrich	Paul	Romney	Santorum	Others
New Hampshire	Jan. 10	248,475	9%	23%	39%	9%	19%
South Carolina	Jan. 21	603,770	40	13	28	17	2
Florida	Jan. 31	1,672,634	32	7	46	13	1
Missouri[a]	Feb. 7	252,185	—	12	25	55	7
Arizona	Feb. 28	510,258	16	9	47	27	1
Michigan	Feb. 28	996,499	7	12	41	38	3
Georgia	March 6	901,470	47	7	26	20	1
Massachusetts	March 6	369,617	5	10	72	12	2
Ohio	March 6	1,213,879	15	9	38	37	1
Oklahoma	March 6	286,523	27	10	28	34	1
Tennessee	March 6	554,573	24	9	28	37	2
Vermont	March 6	60,850	8	25	39	24	4
Virginia	March 6	265,570	—	40	60	—	
Alabama	March 13	622,514	29	5	29	35	2
Mississippi	March 13	294,112	31	4	31	33	1
Illinois	March 20	933,454	8	9	47	35	1
Louisiana	March 24	186,410	16	6	27	49	2
District of Columbia	April 3	5,104	11	12	70	—	7
Maryland	April 3	248,468	11	10	49	29	2
Wisconsin	April 3	787,847	6	11	44	37	2
Connecticut	April 24	59,578	10	13	67	7	2
Delaware	April 24	28,592	27	11	56	6	—
New York	April 24	189,599	13	15	63	10	—
Pennsylvania	April 24	808,115	10	13	58	18	—
Rhode Island	April 24	14,564	6	24	63	6	1
Indiana	May 8	635,589	6	15	65	13	—
North Carolina	May 8	973,206	8	11	66	10	5

(Table continues)

Table 1-25 *(Continued)*

	Date	Turnout	Gingrich	Paul	Romney	Santorum	Others
West Virginia	May 8	112,416	6	11	70	12	1
Nebraska	May 15	185,402	5	10	71	14	—
Oregon	May 15	287,955	5	13	71	9	2
Arkansas	May 22	152,360	5	13	68	13	—
Kentucky	May 22	176,160	6	13	67	9	6
Texas	May 29	1,443,781	5	12	69	8	6
California	June 5	1,894,233	4	10	80	5	1
Montana	June 5	140,457	4	14	68	9	4
New Jersey	June 5	227,108	3	10	81	5	—
New Mexico	June 5	90,113	6	10	73	11	—
South Dakota	June 5	51,145	4	13	66	11	5
Utah	June 26	220,960	0	5	93	2	—

Note: "—" indicates that the candidate was not listed on the ballot; in the "Others" column, it can also mean that the aggregate vote for the other candidates rounded to less than 1% of the primary vote. Percentages are rounded and thus do not always sum to 100. Primary results are based on official state returns for all states that voted through May 22. Results after that date are based on nearly complete, but unofficial, returns. Data for earlier years can be found in previous editions of *Vital Statistics on American Politics*.

[a] Nonbinding primary.

Source: "The Rhodes Cook Letter," June 2012, 8, 10 (*www.rhodescook.com*).

Table 1-26 Republican Presidential Caucus Results, 2012

	Date	Turnout	Gingrich	Paul	Romney	Santorum
Iowa	Jan. 3	121,503	13%	21%	25%	25%
Nevada	Feb. 4	32,894	21	19	50	10
Colorado	Feb. 7	66,027	13	12	35	40
Minnesota	Feb. 7	48,795	11	27	17	45
Maine	Feb. 4–11	6,281	6	36	38	18
Wyoming	Feb. 9–29	2,108	8	21	39	32
Washington	March 3	50,764	10	25	38	24
Alaska	March 6	13,219	14	24	32	29
Idaho	March 6	44,672	2	18	62	18
North Dakota	March 6	11,349	8	28	24	40
Kansas	March 10	29,857	14	13	21	51
Hawaii	March 13	10,228	11	19	44	25

Note: Percentages are rounded and thus do not always sum to 100. Caucus results are primarily from the websites of the state Republican parties. Data for earlier years can be found in previous editions of *Vital Statistics on American Politics*. Missouri had already scheduled a February presidential primary, but state Republican leaders sought to comply with national Republican party rules penalizing states for scheduling delegate contests too early and instituted a March caucus, leaving the primary as nonbinding. The multistep caucus results, however, were not made known until June, after Romney had clinched the Republican nomination.

Source: "The Rhodes Cook Letter," April 2012, 10 (*www.rhodescook.com*).

Table 1-27   Location and Size of National Party Conventions, 1932–2016

	Democrats		Republicans	
Year	Location	Delegate votes	Location	Delegate votes
1932	Chicago	1,154	Chicago	1,154
1936	Philadelphia	1,100	Cleveland	1,003
1940	Chicago	1,100	Philadelphia	1,000
1944	Chicago	1,176	Chicago	1,056
1948	Philadelphia	1,234	Philadelphia	1,094
1952	Chicago	1,230	Chicago	1,206
1956	Chicago	1,372	San Francisco	1,323
1960	Los Angeles	1,521	Chicago	1,331
1964	Atlantic City	2,316	San Francisco	1,308
1968	Chicago	2,622	Miami Beach	1,333
1972	Miami Beach	3,016	Miami Beach	1,348
1976	New York	3,008	Kansas City	2,259
1980	New York	3,331	Detroit	1,994
1984	San Francisco	3,933	Dallas	2,235
1988	Atlanta	4,161	New Orleans	2,277
1992	New York	4,288	Houston	2,210
1996	Chicago	4,289	San Diego	1,990
2000	Los Angeles	4,339	Philadelphia	2,066
2004	Boston	4,353	New York	2,509
2008	Denver	4,440	St. Paul	2,380
2012	Charlotte	5,552	Tampa	2,286
2016	Philadelphia	—	Cleveland	—

Note: "—" indicates not available. The number of delegates (persons attending) may be larger because of fractional votes.

Sources: 1932–2008: *CQ Press Guide to U.S. Elections*, 6th ed. (Washington, D.C.: CQ Press, 2010), 489–490, 492; 2012: "The Rhodes Cook Letter," August 2012, 7, 11 (*www.rhodescook. com*), and Rhodes Cook, personal communication; 2016: news reports.

Table 1-28 Profile of National Convention Delegates, 1968–2008 (percent)

	1968		1972		1976		1980		1984		1988		1992		1996		2000		2004		2008	
	D	R	D	R	D	R	D	R	D	R	D	R	D	R	D	R	D	R	D	R	D	R
Female	13	16	40	29	33	31	49	29	49	44	48	33	48	43	50	36	48	35	50	43	49	32
Black	5	2	15	4	11	3	15	3	18	4	23	4	16	5	19	3	19	4	18	6	23	2
Hispanic	—	—	—	—	—	—	5	1	6	4	6	3	7	4	9	3	12	6	12	7	11	5
Lawyer	28	22	12	—	16	15	13	15	17	14	16	17	14	—	10	11	9	9	13	—	17	16
Teacher	8	2	11	—	12	4	15	4	16	6	14	5	9	—	9	2	7	2	13	—	8	—
Union member	—	—	16	—	21	3	27	4	25	4	25	3	26	—	35	4	31	4	25	3	24	5
Attending first convention	67	66	83	78	80	78	87	69	78	69	65	68	62	—	61	65	49	54	57	55	57	58
Protestant	—	—	42	—	47	73	47	72	49	71	50	69	47	—	47	62	47	63	43	65	43	57
Catholic	—	—	26	—	34	18	37	22	29	22	30	22	30	—	30	25	30	27	32	26	26	30
Jewish	—	—	9	—	9	3	8	3	8	2	7	2	10	—	6	3	8	2	8	2	9	3
Liberal	—	—	—	—	40	3	46	2	48	1	43	0	48	1	43	0	36	1	41	1	43	0
Moderate	—	—	—	—	47	45	42	36	42	35	43	35	44	32	48	27	56	34	52	33	50	26
Conservative	—	—	—	—	8	48	6	58	4	60	5	58	5	63	5	70	5	63	3	63	3	72
Under age 30	3	4	22	6	15	7	11	5	8	4	4	3	4	—	6	2	4	3	7	4	7	3
Median age (years)	49	49	42	—	43	48	44	49	43	51	46	51	46	—	49	52	51	53	—	54	54	54

Note: "D" indicates Democrat; "R" indicates Republican; "—" indicates not available. Data for additional years can be found in previous editions of *Vital Statistics on American Politics*. Similar surveys were not conducted in 2012.

Sources: 1992 (Democrat, median age, teacher, attending first convention): "New York *Newsday* Democratic Delegate Survey"; Democrats (all other), 1968–2008: CBS News/*New York Times* Poll, "Overview of the Democratic Delegates, 1968–2008," August 24, 2008 (*www.cbsnews.com*); Republicans, 1968–2008: CBS News/ *New York Times* Poll, "Overview of the Republican Delegates, 1968–2008," August 31, 2008 (*www.cbsnews.com*).

Table 1-29 Legislative Districting: Deviations from Equality in Congressional and State Legislative Districts (percent)

| | Congressional districts | | | | State legislative districts | | | | | | | |
| | | | | | Senate | | | | House | | | |
State	1980s	1990s	2000s	2010s	1980s	1990s	2000s	2010s	1980s	1990s	2000s	2010s
Alabama	2.45	[a]	0	0	8.50	9.22	9.73	1.98	9.80	10.20	9.93	1.98
Alaska	AL	AL	AL	AL	9.77	11.70	9.32	8.45	9.99	15.50	9.96	9.04
Arizona	0.08	[a]	0	0	8.40	9.85	3.79	8.78	8.40	9.85	3.79	8.78
Arkansas	0.73	0.73	0.04	0.06	9.15	9.27	9.81	8.20	9.15	9.52	9.87	8.36
California	0.08	0.49	0	[a]	4.60	1.60	0	0.63	3.60	1.80	0	0.45
Colorado	[a]	[a]	0	0	3.98	4.90	4.95	4.99	4.94	4.96	4.88	4.98
Connecticut	0.46	0.05	0	0	3.92	7.98	8.03	9.79	8.35	8.78	9.20	5.99
Delaware	AL	AL	AL	AL	9.78	10.18	9.96	10.73	25.10	9.58	9.98	9.93
Florida	0.13	[a]	0.01	0	1.05	0.86	0.03	1.99	0.46	4.99	2.79	3.98
Georgia	[a]	0.93	0.32	0.10	9.99	9.95	1.94	1.84	9.94	9.95	1.96	1.98
Hawaii	[a]	[a]	0.60	0.09	18.60	9.86	38.90	44.23	8.60	9.78	20.10	21.57
Idaho	0.04	[a]	0	0	5.35	9.88	9.70	9.70	5.35	9.88	9.70	9.70
Illinois	0.03	[a]	0.02	0	1.75	[a]	0	0	2.80	[a]	0	0
Indiana	2.96	[a]	0.02	0.01	4.04	2.19	3.80	2.88	4.45	3.36	1.92	1.74
Iowa	0.05	0.05	0	0	0.71	1.45	1.46	1.65	1.78	1.97	1.89	1.93
Kansas	0.34	0.01	0	0	6.50	6.89	9.27	2.03	9.90	9.72	9.95	2.87
Kentucky	1.39		0.04	0	7.52	6.13	9.53	9.84	13.47	9.91	10.00	10.00
Louisiana	0.42	0.04	0	0.03	8.40	9.78	9.95	9.86	9.69	9.97	9.88	9.89
Maine	[a]	[a]	0	0	10.18	4.16	3.57	[d]	10.94	43.74[b]	9.33	[d]
Maryland	0.35	[a]	0.39	[a]	9.80	9.84	9.91	8.87	15.70	10.67	9.89	8.87
Massachusetts	1.09	[a]	0	0	—	4.75	9.33	9.77	—	9.92	9.68	9.74
Michigan	[a]	[a]	0	0	16.24	15.83	9.92	9.79	16.34	16.13	9.92	9.96
Minnesota	0.01		0	0	4.61	3.42	1.35	1.60	3.93	5.90	1.56	1.42
Mississippi	—	0.02	0	0.20	4.61	8.96	9.30	9.77	4.90	9.97	9.98	9.95
Missouri	0.18	0.20	0	0	6.10	8.42	6.81	8.50	9.30	8.96	6.08	7.80
Montana	—	AL	AL	AL	—	9.51	9.82	5.26	—	9.97	9.85	5.44
Nebraska	0.23	0.20	0	0	9.43	3.81	9.21	7.39	[c]	[c]	[c]	[c]

State											
Nevada	0.60	[a]	0	8.20	2.28	9.91	0.80	9.70	4.55	1.97	1.33
New Hampshire	0.24	0.07	0.10	7.60	12.36	9.50	8.83	13.74	14.53	9.26	9.90
New Jersey	0.69	[a]	0	7.70	4.60	1.83	5.20	7.70	4.60	1.83	5.20
New Mexico	0.87	0.16	0.03	9.83	9.58	9.60	8.70	9.87	9.89	9.70	6.68
New York	1.64	[a]	0	5.29	4.29	9.78	8.80	8.17	9.43	9.43	7.94
North Carolina	1.76	[a]	0	9.46	9.94	9.96	9.74	9.66	9.97	9.98	9.90
North Dakota	AL	AL	AL	9.93	8.71	10.00	8.86	9.93	8.71	10.00	8.86
Ohio	0.68	[a]	0	8.88	13.60	8.81	9.20	9.67	13.60	12.46	16.44
Oklahoma	0.58	[a]	0	5.60	3.93	4.71	2.03	10.98	6.13	2.05	1.81
Oregon	0.15	[a]	0	3.73	1.69	1.77	2.99	5.34	1.89	1.90	3.10
Pennsylvania	0.24	0.01	0	1.93	1.86	3.98	7.96	2.82	4.94	5.54	7.88
Rhode Island	0.02	0.02	0	—	13.00	9.91	5.01	10.47	14.70	9.88	4.98
South Carolina	0.28	[a]	0	1.00	1.00	9.87	9.55	9.88	5.20	4.99	4.99
South Dakota	AL	AL	AL	12.90	9.47	9.69	9.47	12.40	9.47	9.69	9.47
Tennessee	2.40	[a]	0	10.22	13.92	9.98	9.74	1.66	9.96	9.99	9.17
Texas	0.28	[a]	0	1.82	9.98	9.71	8.04	9.95	9.99	9.74	9.92
Utah	0.43	0.02	0	7.80	7.60	7.02	0.39	5.41	7.94	8.00	1.55
Vermont	AL	AL	AL	16.18	16.36	14.28	18.20	19.33	17.62	18.99	18.90
Virginia	1.81	[a]	0	10.65	8.53	4.00	4.00	5.11	9.67	3.90	2.00
Washington	0.06	[a]	0	5.40	[a]	0.30	0.07	5.70	[a]	0.30	0.07
West Virginia	0.50	0.09	0.22	8.96	9.98	10.92	10.00	9.94	9.96	9.98	9.99
Wisconsin	0.14	[a]	0	1.23	0.52	0.98	0.62	1.74	0.92	1.60	0.76
Wyoming	AL	AL	AL	63.70	9.60	9.51	9.37	89.40	9.97	9.81	9.84

Note: "AL" indicates at-large district (only one congressional representative); "—" indicates not available. Figures represent the absolute sum of the maximum percentage deviations (positive and negative) from the average district population. 1980s data are as of April 1983; 1990s data are as of August 1994. The 1980 state house plans for Delaware and Rhode Island contained errors that increased total deviation, but had not been corrected. 2000s data are as of March 2005; 2010s data are from February 2013. Data for the 1960s can be found in previous editions of *Vital Statistics on American Politics*.

a Less than 0.01 percent.

b Apart from two districts, the deviation is 8.15.

c Nebraska's state legislature is unicameral.

d Maine will redraw its state legislative districts in 2013.

Sources: 1980s: Election Data Services, Inc.; 1990s: Supreme Judicial Court of Maine, *In re Apportionment of 1993* (Docket #JC–93–229), and unpublished data from the National Conference of State Legislators, Illinois State Board of Elections, Michigan Information Center (Department of Management and Budget), and Tennessee Office of Local Government; 2000s and 2010s: National Conference of State Legislatures (*www.ncsl.org*).

Table 1-30   Jurisdictions Subject to Federal Preclearance of Election Law Changes and to Minority Language Provisions of the Voting Rights Act

Coverage under preclearance provisions[a]	*Coverage under minority language provisions*[b]	
Alabama	Alaska (9)[c]	New Jersey (8)
Alaska	Arizona (10)	New Mexico (21)
Arizona	California	New York (6)
California (4)	Colorado (3)	Pennsylvania (3)
Florida (5)	Connecticut (9)[c]	Rhode Island (3)[c]
Georgia	Florida	Texas
Louisiana	Hawaii (2)	Utah (1)
Michigan (2)[c]	Illinois (4)	Virginia (1)
Mississippi	Kansas (4)	Washington (4)
New York (5)	Maryland (1)	Wisconsin (1)[c]
North Carolina (40)	Massachusetts (12)[c]	
South Carolina	Michigan (3)[c]	
South Dakota (2)	Mississippi (10)	
Texas	Nebraska (3)	
Virginia	Nevada (1)	

Note: "Preclearance" means that changes in election laws must be approved by the U.S. Justice Department. "Language provisions" require covered jurisdictions to provide bilingual voting materials to members of specified minority language groups. Numbers in parentheses indicate the number of counties in the state affected by the provisions. If there are no parentheses, coverage is statewide. The Supreme Court decision in *Shelby County v. Holder*, 133 S. Ct. 2612 (2013) held that Section 4 of the Voting Rights Act, which set out the formula that is used to determine which state and local governments must comply with Section 5's preclearance requirement, is unconstitutional and can no longer be used. Section 5 will have no actual effect unless a jurisdiction is covered by a separate court order entered under Section 3(c) of the VRA or Congress enacts a new statute to determine which jurisdictions should be covered by Section 5. The above table listing jurisdictions subject to federal preclearance indicates the situation immediately before *Shelby County v. Holder*.

[a] Approximately 250 governmental units and jurisdictions once subject to the preclearance provisions of Section 5 were no longer subject to such coverage because they availed themselves of the bailout process set forth in Section 4 of the Voting Rights Act.
[b] Covered jurisdictions under the minority language provisions are determined by the U.S. Census Bureau after each census, based on a formula set out in the Voting Rights Act. The most recent determinations were made on October 13, 2011.
[c] Number of towns, townships, cities, boroughs, or areas.

Sources: U.S. Department of Justice, Voting Section, "Section 4 of the Voting Rights Act," "Section 5 Covered Jurisdictions," and "About Language Minority Voting Rights" (*www.usdoj.gov*).

Table 1-31 Term Limits on State Legislators

State[a]	Lower house (years)[b]	Upper house (years)[b]	Year adopted	Percent support	Year of first impact		Mechanism[c]	Break in service[d]
					Lower house	Upper house		
Arizona	8	8	1992	74	2000	2000	S	2 years
Arkansas	6	8	1992	60	1998	2000	S	lifetime
California	12 years total in legislature[e]		1990	52	1996	1998	S	lifetime
Colorado	8	8	1990	71	1998	1998	S	4 years
Florida	8	8	1992	77	2000	2000	B	2 years
Louisiana	12	12	1995	76	2007	2007	S	4 years
Maine	8	8	1993	68	1996	1996	S	2 years
Michigan	6	8	1992	59	1998	2002	S	lifetime
Missouri[f]	8	8	1992	75	2002	2002	S	lifetime
Montana	8/16	8/16	1992	67	2000	2000	B	contingent
Nebraska	g	8g	2000	56	g	2006	S	2 years
Nevada[h]	12	12	1996	70	2010	2010	S	lifetime
Ohio	8	8	1992	68	2000	2000	S	4 years
Oklahoma	12 years total in legislature		1990	67	2004	2004	S	lifetime
South Dakota	8	8	1992	64	2000	2000	S	2 years

Note: States have varying provisions for counting partial terms stemming from appointment or special election. In many states, limits are defined in terms of times elected rather than years served or contain a clause such as "or, but for resignation, would have served."

[a] In addition to the states listed here, Washington, Oregon, and Wyoming passed state legislative term limits in 1992 and Massachusetts, Idaho, and Utah in 1994, but they were overturned by the courts in the first four states (in 1998, 2002, 2004, and 1997, respectively) and by the legislatures in Idaho (in 2002) and Utah (in 2003). In Oregon, some legislators were "termed out" in 1998 and 2000.

[b] Number of years an individual may serve before term limits are applied. In Arkansas and Florida, all senate seats are up for election in the first election of the decade (i.e., after redistricting), so some senators may in fact serve for 10 years. In Montana, an individual may not serve more than eight out of sixteen years, whether or not those years are consecutive.

(Table continues)

Table 1-31 *(Continued)*

c Strict term limits (S) prohibit service in the legislature. Ballot access restrictions (B) prevent a candidate's name from being placed on the ballot, but do not prevent a candidate from being elected on write-in votes.

d Length of time an individual must "sit out" before serving (or having ballot access) again in the same house. The time is "contingent" when the term limit law specifies that an individual may serve no more than a certain number of years over a longer period.

e Prior to 2012, California's limits were identical to those in Arkansas. The prior rules govern those who were in the legislature as of June 5, 2012.

f Because of special elections, term limits were effective in 2000 for eight members of the House and in 1998 for one senator.

g Nebraska's legislature is unicameral.

h The Nevada Legislative Council and attorney general ruled that Nevada's term limits could not be applied to those legislators elected in the same year term limits were passed (1996). They first applied to persons elected in 1998.

Sources: National Conference of State Legislatures (*www.ncsl.org*) and texts of state measures.

Table 1-32   Members of Congress under Self-Imposed Term Limits,
1998–2024

Year[a]	Member	State	District/chamber	Party	Kept pledge
1998					
	Coats	Indiana	Senate	R	yes[b]
	Furse	Oregon	1	D	yes
	Inglis	South Carolina	4	R	yes
				2R, 1D	
2000					
	Burns	Montana	Senate	R	no/reelected
	Canady	Florida	12	R	yes
	Chenoweth	Idaho	1	R	yes
	Coburn	Oklahoma	2	R	yes/elected to Senate
	Fowler	Florida	4	R	yes
	McInnis	Colorado	3	R	no/reelected
	Meehan	Massachusetts	5	D	no/reelected
	Metcalf	Washington	2	R	yes
	Nethercutt	Washington	5	R	no/reelected
	Salmon	Arizona	1	R	yes
	Sanford	South Carolina	1	R	yes
				10R, 1D	
2002					
	Baldacci	Maine	2	D	yes
	Cooksey	Louisiana	5	R	yes
	Lewis	Kentucky	2	R	no/reelected
	Miller	Florida	13	R	yes
	Riley	Florida	3	R	yes
	Schaffer	Colorado	4	R	yes
	Thune	South Dakota	AL	R	yes/elected to Senate
	Weldon	Florida	15	R	no/reelected
	Wellstone	Minnesota	Senate	D	no[c]
				7R, 2D	
2004					
	Bond	Missouri	Senate	R	no/reelected
	Boswell	Iowa	3	D	no/reelected
	Calvert	California	43	R	no/reelected
	Campbell	Colorado	Senate	R	yes
	Capps	California	22	D	no/reelected
	Deal	Georgia	9	R	no/reelected
	DeMint	South Carolina	4	R	yes/elected to Senate
	Ganske	Iowa	4	R	yes
	Goodlatte	Virginia	6	R	no/reelected
	Goss	Florida	14	R	[d]
	Green	Wisconsin	8	R	no/reelected
	Hoekstra	Michigan	2	R	no/reelected
	Knollenberg	Michigan	11	R	no/reelected
	LaTourette	Ohio	19	R	no/reelected

(Table continues)

Table 1-32   *(Continued)*

Year[a]	Member	State	District/ chamber	Party	Kept pledge
	Lucas	Kentucky	4	D	yes
	Maloney	Connecticut	5	D	yes
	Napolitano	California	34	D	no/reelected
	Ose	California	3	R	yes
	Radanovich	California	19	R	no/reelected
	Smith	Michigan	7	R	yes
	Tancredo	Colorado	6	R	no/reelected
	Toomey	Pennsylvania	15	R	yes
				17R, 5D	
2006					
	Bryant	Tennessee	7	R	[e]
	Cubin	Wyoming	AL	R	no/reelected
	English	Pennsylvania	3	R	no/reelected
	Flake	Arizona	6	R	no/reelected
	Frist	Tennessee	Senate	R	yes
	Graham	South Carolina	Senate	R	yes[f]
	Gutknecht	Minnesota	1	R	no[g]
	Hilleary	Tennessee	4	R	yes
	Hutchison	Texas	Senate	R	no/reelected
	Johnson	Illinois	15	R	no/reelected
	Keller	Florida	8	R	no/reelected
	Largent	Oklahoma	1	R	yes
	LoBiondo	New Jersey	2	R	no/reelected
	Souder	Indiana	3	R	no/reelected
	Wamp	Tennessee	3	R	no/reelected
				15R	
2008					
	Allard	Colorado	Senate	R	yes
	Collins	Maine	Senate	R	no/reelected
	Hutchinson	Arkansas	Senate	R	no[h]
	Thompson	Tennessee	Senate	R	yes[i]
				4R	
2010[j]					
	Brownback	Kansas	Senate	R	yes[k]
	Bunning	Kentucky	Senate	R	yes
	Fitzgerald	Illinois	Senate	R	yes[l]
	Voinovich	Ohio	Senate	R	yes
				4R	
2016					
	Coburn	Oklahoma	Senate	R	yes[m]
	Fitzpatrick	Pennsylvania	8	R	
	Walsh	Illinois	8	R	[n]
				3R	
2018					
	Runyan	New Jersey	3	R	yes[o]
	Scott	South Carolina	1	R	yes[p]
	West	Florida	22	R	[q]
				3R	

Table 1-32   *(Continued)*

Year[a]	Member	State	District/ chamber	Party	Kept pledge
2022					
	Ayotte	New Hampshire	Senate	R	
	Griffin	Arkansas	2	R	yes[r]
	Schweikert	Arizona	6	R	
				3R	
2024					
	Grothman	Wisconsin	6	R	
	Palmer	Alabama	6	R	
				2R	
2026					
	Brat	Virginia	7	R	
	Perdue	Georgia	Senate	R	
				2R	
	Total		62 House 19 Senate	72R, 9D	

Note: "R" indicates Republican; "D" indicates Democratic; "AL" indicates "at large." Members who kept their pledge did not run for reelection to the chamber they were in when they made the pledge. They may have resigned or run for another office at the time their pledge ended or before.

[a] The year that the member's time in Congress ended or will end if he or she is not defeated earlier and the self-imposed term limit is observed.
[b] Sen. Dan Coats, after being out of office for twelve years, was reelected to the Senate in 2010.
[c] Sen. Paul Wellstone died while campaigning for reelection.
[d] Rep. Porter Goss announced that he would break his term limits pledge, but he was appointed head of the Central Intelligence Agency by President George W. Bush.
[e] Rep. Ed Bryant ran for reelection in 2002 and was defeated.
[f] Sen. Lindsay Graham was elected to the U.S. House in 1994 and pledged to serve no more than six terms. In 2002 he ran for the U.S. Senate and won.
[g] Rep. Gil Gutknecht ran for reelection in 2006 and was defeated.
[h] Sen. Tim Hutchinson ran for reelection in 2002 and was defeated.
[i] Sen. Fred Thompson retired in 2006.
[j] In 2010, according to the pro–term limits organization U.S. Term Limits, some fifty-six candidates for the U.S. House and Senate signed a pledge to support an amendment to the U.S. Constitution that, if passed, would limit U.S. House members to three consecutive terms in office and U.S. senators to two consecutive six-year terms. The electoral tally was the following: Democrats: zero winners, eight losers; Republicans: twelve winners, thirty-five losers; Libertarian: one loser. Of the Republicans, one winner (Coburn, Okla.) and one loser (Raese, W.V.) were in the Senate.
[k] Sen. Sam Brownback ran for and won the governorship of Kansas in 2010.
[l] Sen. Peter G. Fitzgerald retired in 2004.
[m] Sen. Tom Coburn, M.D. retired in January, 2015.
[n] Rep. William Walsh ran for reelection in 2012 and was defeated.
[o] Rep. Jon Runyan did not seek reelection in 2014.
[p] Rep. Timothy Scott was appointed U.S. Senator from South Carolina on December 17, 2012.
[q] Rep. Allen West ran for reelection in 2012 and was defeated.
[r] Sen. Tim Griffin ran for and won the lieutenant governorship of Arkansas in 2014.

Sources: U.S. Term Limits (*www.ustl.org*); updated by the editors using candidate and other websites.

Table 1-33 Members "Termed Out" of State Legislatures, 1996–2014

State	Chamber	Membership	1996	1998	2000	2002	2004	2006	2008	2010	2012	2014
							Members termed out in					
Arizona	House	60	—	—	15	9	5	3	7	13	3	3
	Senate	30	—	—	7	6	2	3	2	10	3	1
Arkansas	House	100	—	48	25	14	36	29	28	34	24	25
	Senate	35	—	—	13	11	0	1	4	13	11	0
California	Assembly	80	22	16	19	20	18	26	24	19	22	16
	Senate	40	13	11	8	7	8	12	10	8	6	6
Colorado	House	65	—	18	10	7	7	11	8	8	8	9
	Senate	35	—	9	11	5	5	4	7	4	9	5
Florida	House	120	—	—	55	14	7	19	28	24	11	15
	Senate	40	—	—	11	12	0	5	5	7	11	0
Louisiana	House	105	—	—	—	—	—	—	a	a	a	a
	Senate	39	—	—	—	—	—	—	a	a	a	a
Maine	House	151	26	11	17	28	21	19	15	21	26	22
	Senate	35	4	1	7	8	7	1	6	4	9	1
Michigan	House	110	—	64	21	23	37 b	23	44 b	34	14	29
	Senate	38	—	—	—	27	—	6	—	29	0	7
Missouri	House	163	—	—	8 c	73	15	10	21	52	25	10
	Senate	34	—	1 c	—	12	10	3	4	10	9	4
Montana	House	100	—	—	33	7	10	16	17	15	17	7
	Senate	50	—	—	14	15	6	5	10	15	8	8
Nebraska	Senate	49	—	—	—	—	—	20	13	1	9	17
Nevada	House	42	—	—	—	—	—	—	—	10	1	2
	Senate	21	—	—	—	—	—	—	—	7	4	1
Ohio	House	99	—	—	45	9	7	14	21	13	7	15
	Senate	33	—	—	6	4	5	7	4	7	2	3
Oklahoma	House	101	—	—	—	—	28	15	7	4	6	7

	Senate	48	—	—	—	—	13	7	5	6	2	4
Oregon[d]	House	60	—	22	17	—	3	7	13	8	6	6
	Senate	30	—	2	5	—	7	2	6	4	3	2
South Dakota	House	70	—	—	20	7	3	7	13	8	6	6
	Senate	35	—	—	13	4	7	2	6	4	3	2
Total		1,811	65	203	380	322[e]	257[f]	268	309	380	256	225

Note: "—" indicates term limits were not yet applicable.

[a] Louisiana holds its legislative elections in odd-numbered years. In 2007, forty-four House and sixteen Senate members were termed out; in 2011, the numbers were eleven House members and six Senators, respectively.

[b] No election in this year.

[c] Because of special elections, term limits were effective in 2000 for eight members of the House and in 1998 for one senator.

[d] Term limits were overturned by Oregon's state supreme court in 2002.

[e] Does not include eight "termed-out" legislators in three states who resigned midterm.

[f] Does not include four "termed-out" legislators in Colorado and Ohio who resigned midterm.

Source: National Conference of State Legislatures (*www.ncsl.org*).

Table 1-34 Types of Voting Equipment Used in U.S. Elections, November 2012

Type of voting equipment used	Number of counties	Percent	Number of precincts	Percent	Voting-age population	Percent	Number of registered voters	Percent
Punch card[a]	4	0.1	101	0.1	87,000	<0.1	65,424	<0.1
Paper ballots	48	1.5	639	0.4	294,353	0.1	238,851	0.1
Optical scan[b]	1,958	62.8	122,080	66.6	145,920,706	66.1	118,293,560	65.0
Electronic[c]	1,023	32.8	55,633	30.3	65,308,948	29.6	54,931,897	30.2
Mixed	85	2.7	4,903	2.7	9,277,880	4.2	8,173,764	4.5
Total	3,118	99.9	183,356	100.1	220,888,887	100.1	181,703,496	99.9

Note: Data for earlier years can be found in previous editions of *Vital Statistics on American Politics.*

[a] Voters mark their ballots by punching holes in paper cards.
[b] Voters fill in circles, ovals, or squares that are printed on the ballot or complete a broken arrow. Ballots are then read with optical scanning equipment. Also called mark-sense ballots.
[c] Voters cast ballots by pressing buttons or images on a computer screen. Often called Direct Recording Electronic (DRE) machines.

Source: Election Data Services Inc., Washington, D.C. (*www.electiondataservices.com*).

2

Campaign Finance and Political Action Committees

- **Contribution Limits**
- **Presidential Campaign Financing**
- **Party Expenditures**
- **Political Action Committees (PACs)**

One of the most important aspects of election campaigns and political activities more generally is money: who gives it, who spends it, who regulates it, and what effect it has. Surprisingly, a huge quantity of information is available on the subject. This abundance stems chiefly from the large number of elections in the United States and the effort over the last four decades to collect data about them and make those data available to the public. The Bipartisan Campaign Reform Act (BCRA) of 2002, a recent attempt to regulate the role of money in campaigns, enacted new contribution limits (Table 2-1), changed the law on "soft" money (Table 2-8), and otherwise reworked campaign finance law. Likewise, a Supreme Court decision, *Citizens United v. Federal Election Commission* in January 2010, allowed the emergence of "super" political action committees. These Super PACs could raise unlimited money from corporations, labor unions, and individuals, spending that money supporting and opposing presidential or congressional candidates so long as they did not directly coordinate with the campaigns (Table 2-10). In *American Tradition Partnership, Inc. v. Bullock,* a Montana case, the U.S. Supreme Court held that *Citizens United* applied to state elections.

This chapter presents information on the amounts of money collected and spent by individual presidential candidates (Tables 2-3 and 2-4), along with more aggregated information about expenditures by the political parties (Tables 2-6 through 2-8). The most recent campaign expenditures for all 435 representatives and 100 senators can be found in Chapter 5 on Congress (Tables 5-11 and 5-12).

One could, in fact, easily be inundated by numbers on campaign finance. The publications of the Federal Election Commission (FEC) alone run to multiple volumes every two years, with detailed accountings of the receipts and expenditures of candidates in federal elections. Additional volumes are produced, though inconsistently and much less systematically, by various state agencies. Because such information is so voluminous, it is often summarized as it is here: how much was spent by various types of political action committees (Table 2-11), which PACs are the biggest contributors (Table 2-13), and so on.

This wealth of information has been collected since the mid-1970s, when the FEC was established. Although studies of campaign costs were conducted before then, the present time series are often limited to this span of about forty years. Laws regulating campaign contributions, expenditures, and interest group activities change so frequently that longer time series are often unobtainable and would be misleading if they could be compiled. For example, the growth of PACs dates from 1974 because changes in the laws at that time allowed their establishment (Table 2-9). Similarly, data on public funding of presidential campaigns date from 1976 (Table 2-5).

Concern about money is not limited strictly to candidate spending. Indeed, researchers and watchdog groups are probably more concerned about interest group spending and about where candidates' funds come from and what, if anything, that money buys. Fortunately, more and more data are now available on interest group finances and on candidates' fund-raising as well as on expenditures. Many of the data are related to PACs, the dominant organizations through which interest groups raise and spend money (Table 2-10). The information presented here is related primarily to the general categories of PACs (Tables 2-9, 2-11, 2-12, and 2-14); the list of the largest PAC contributors illustrates the variety of organizations that fall into these categories (Table 2-13).

Because money is at the heart of interest group activities, matters of campaign finance law are directly relevant to this chapter. At the federal level, these regulations consist mainly of fairly straightforward contribution limits—limits that were recently changed by the BCRA (Table 2-1) and *Citizens United* (Table 2-10). At the state level, there is a myriad of contribution and expenditure limits (Table 2-2).

Of course, not all questions about efforts to influence the electoral or the political process involve money (directly anyway). Other aspects of interest group activity that can be quantified are depicted in Chapters 5 and 11, such as the growth and decline of labor unions (Table 11-8) and interest groups' ratings of members of Congress on how favorable their votes were to the groups' interests (Tables 5-11 and 5-12).

For obvious reasons, no one is able to collect systematically what would surely be the most captivating data on organized interests: that on any bribes, threats, and blackmail that may insinuate themselves into campaign finance. Although political analysts now have access to a larger body of material on campaign finances and related matters than ever before, much of this information is buried in hard-to-digest volumes or in bland lists of what interests are represented in various politicians' support groups. Yet such data provide unprecedented knowledge and research potential about the scope and possible influence of organized interests.

Table 2-1 Contribution Limits under the Bipartisan Campaign Reform Act of 2002

Donors	Candidate committee per election	Recipients			
		National party committee per calendar year	State/district/local party committee per calendar year	PAC per calendar year[a]	Additional national party committee accounts per calendar year[b]
Individual	$2,700[c]	$33,400[c]	$10,000 (combined limit)	$5,000	$100,200[c] per account
National party committee	$5,000[d]	Unlimited transfers	Unlimited transfers	$5,000	
State/district/local party committee	$5,000	Unlimited transfers	Unlimited transfers	$5,000	
PAC multicandidate	$5,000	$15,000	$5,000 (combined limit)	$5,000	$45,000 per account
PAC not multicandidate	$2,700[c]	$33,400[c]	$10,000 (combined limit)	$5,000	$100,200[c] per account
Candidate committee	$2,000	Unlimited transfers	Unlimited transfers	$5,000	

[a] "PAC" here refers to a committee that makes contributions to other federal political committees. Independent expenditure-only political committees (sometimes called "Super PACs") may accept unlimited contributions, including from corporations and labor organizations.

[b] The limits in this column apply to a national party committee's accounts for: (a) the presidential nominating convention; (b) election recounts and contests and other legal proceedings; and (c) national party headquarters buildings. A party's national committee, Senate campaign committee, and House campaign committee are each considered separate party committees with separate limits. Only a national party committee, not the parties' national congressional campaign committees, may have an account for the presidential nominating convention.

[c] These limits will be indexed for inflation. Amounts shown are for the 2015–2016 election cycle.

[d] Additionally, a national party committee and its Senatorial campaign committee may contribute up to $46,800 combined per campaign to each Senate candidate.

Source: Federal Election Commission, "FEC Chart: 2015–2016 Campaign Cycle Contribution Limits," March 20, 2015 (*www.fec.gov*).

Table 2-2   Contribution Limits on Funding of State Election Campaigns

State	Individuals	Corporations	Labor unions	Political action committees	State parties
Alabama	no	no	no	no	no
Alaska	yes	prohibited	prohibited	yes	yes
Arizona	yes	prohibited	prohibited	yes	yes
Arkansas	yes	yes	yes	yes	yes
California	yes	yes	yes	yes	no
Colorado	yes	prohibited	prohibited	yes	yes
Connecticut	yes	prohibited	prohibited	yes	yes
Delaware	yes	yes	yes	yes	yes
Florida	yes	yes	yes	yes	yes
Georgia	yes	yes	yes	yes	yes
Hawaii	yes	yes	yes	yes	yes
Idaho	yes	yes	yes	yes	yes
Illinois	yes	yes	yes	yes	no[a]
Indiana	no	yes	yes	no	no
Iowa	no	prohibited	no	no	no
Kansas	yes	yes	yes	yes	no[a]
Kentucky	yes	prohibited	yes	yes	yes
Louisiana	yes	yes	yes	yes	no
Maine	yes	yes	yes	yes	yes
Maryland	yes	yes	yes	yes	yes
Massachusetts	yes	prohibited	yes	yes	yes
Michigan	yes	prohibited	prohibited	yes	yes
Minnesota	yes	prohibited	yes	yes	yes
Mississippi	no	yes	no	no	no
Missouri	no	no	no	no	no
Montana	yes	prohibited	yes	yes	yes
Nebraska	no	no	no	no	no
Nevada	yes	yes	yes	yes	yes
New Hampshire	yes	yes	prohibited	yes	yes
New Jersey	yes	yes	yes	yes	no
New Mexico	yes	yes	yes	yes	yes
New York	yes	yes	yes	yes	no[a]
North Carolina	yes	prohibited	prohibited	yes	no
North Dakota	no	prohibited	prohibited	no	no
Ohio	yes	prohibited	prohibited	yes	yes
Oklahoma	yes	prohibited	prohibited	yes	yes
Oregon	no	no	no	no	no
Pennsylvania	no	prohibited	prohibited	no	no
Rhode Island	yes	prohibited	prohibited	yes	yes
South Carolina	yes	yes	yes	yes	yes
South Dakota	yes	prohibited	prohibited	no	no
Tennessee	yes	yes	yes	yes	yes
Texas	no	prohibited	prohibited	no	no
Utah	no	no	no	no	no
Vermont	yes	yes	yes	yes	no

(Table continues)

Table 2-2   *(Continued)*

State	Individuals	Corporations	Labor unions	Political action committees	State parties
Virginia	no	no	no	no	no
Washington	yes	yes	yes	yes	yes
West Virginia	yes	prohibited	yes	yes	yes
Wisconsin	yes	prohibited	prohibited	yes	yes
Wyoming	yes	prohibited	prohibited	yes	no

Note: The definitions of "contributions" and "candidates," as well as the limits on sizes of contributions and other restrictions (for example, from government employees, regulated industries), vary widely across states. For details, see source.

[a] Unlimited, except for primary elections in Illinois (subject to limitations), contested primary elections in Kansas (subject to limitations), and primaries in New York (prohibited).

Source: National Conference of State Legislatures, "State Limits on Contributions to Candidates" (*www.ncsl.org*).

Table 2-3 Presidential Campaign Finance, 2012

Party/candidate	Federal funds	Contributions from individuals	Contributions from parties	Contributions from committees	Contributions/loans from the candidate	Other loans	Transfers and offsets[a]	Other receipts	Total
Republicans Romney, Mitt	$0	$303,822,811	$10,138	$1,126,220	$0	$20,000,000	$156,244,077	$2,249,087	$483,452,332
Democrats Obama, Barack	0	549,580,640	8,610	0	5,000	0	188,813,707	68,503	738,476,460
Others	923,204	2,986,822	0	0	52,000	0	2,402	0	3,964,428
Total general election candidates	923,204	856,390,274	18,748	1,126,220	57,000	20,000,000	345,060,185	2,317,590	1,225,893,220
Total primary-only candidates	351,961	140,569,934	16,451	616,653	6,127,557	0	5,068,241	1,205,312	153,956,109
Grand total	1,275,165	996,960,208	35,199	1,742,873	6,184,557	20,000,000	350,128,426	3,522,902	1,379,849,329

Party/candidate	Operating expenditures	Transfers to other committees	Fundraising disbursements	Total loan repayments	Total contribution refunds	Other disbursements[b]	Total disbursements	Latest cash on hand	Debts owed by campaign[c]
Republicans Romney, Mitt	$458,697,503	$444,687	$0	$20,000,000	$3,837,192	$90,299	$483,069,680	$383,275	$825,749
Democrats Obama, Barack	694,538,510	0	0	0	8,975,296	33,543,647	737,057,454	3,301,800	5,884,507

(Table continues)

Table 2-3 (Continued)

Party/ candidate	Operating expenditures	Transfers to other committees	Fundraising disbursements	Total loan repayments	Total contribution refunds	Other disbursements[b]	Total disbursements	Latest cash on hand	Debts owed by campaign[c]
Others	3,700,628	37,819	105,090	0	1,440	903	3,845,880	118,548	1,178,604
Total general election candidates	1,156,936,641	482,506	105,090	20,000,000	12,813,928	33,634,849	1,223,973,014	3,803,624	7,888,860
Total primary-only candidates	132,439,587	1,119	857,536	424,900	2,053,163	94,974	135,871,277	1,733,940	5,955,125
Grand total	1,289,376,228	483,625	962,626	20,424,900	14,867,091	33,729,823	1,359,844,292	5,537,563	13,843,985

Note: General election "Others" category and general election totals include two candidates, Gary Earl Johnson and Jill Stein, not shown separately. The total for primary-only candidates exclude general election candidates. The ten primary-only candidates were Michelle Bachmann, Herman Cain, Newt Gingrich, John Huntsman, Thaddeus McCotter, Ron Paul, Timothy Pawlenty, Rick Perry, Charles E. "Buddy" Roemer, and Rick Santorum.

a Although combined here, transfers and offsets are separate totals in the FEC source table.
b Includes legal and accounting disbursements, which is presented as a separate category in the FEC source table.
c There is also a total of $761 in debts owned to campaigns for primary-only candidates (not shown).

Sources: Federal Election Commission, "Table 1: Presidential Campaign Receipts Through December 31, 2012" and "Table 2: Presidential Campaign Disbursements Through December 31, 2012" (*www.fec.gov*).

Table 2-4 Presidential Campaign Finance, Aggregated Contributions from Individual Donors to Leading Presidential Candidates, 2008 and 2012

Candidate	Total number of itemized individual donors	Net individual contributions	Percentage of individual contributions from donors aggregating to		
			$200 or less	$201–999	$1,000 or more
2008					
Democrats					
Obama	403,341	$452,852,990	26	27	47
Clinton	170,777	210,901,574	16	21	63
Edwards	33,135	38,638,348	15	22	63
Republicans					
McCain	169,783	206,363,245	21	20	59
Romney	44,795	63,065,340	14	13	73
Giuliani	39,489	61,022,495	15	9	76
Paul	32,234	34,336,193	39	29	32
Thompson, F.	17,058	23,369,742	38	18	44
Huckabee	13,728	15,991,901	29	24	47
2012					
Democrats					
Obama	812,858	781,800,000	28	34	39
Republicans					
Romney	393,603	470,500,000	12	22	66
Paul	41,609	39,600,000	34	35	31
Gingrich	20,835	23,200,000	43	28	29
Santorum	20,441	22,200,000	44	28	27
Perry	11,072	19,400,000	5	6	89
Cain	12,632	15,900,000	52	24	24
Bachmann	6,010	7,300,000	59	26	15
Huntsman	2,862	3,600,000	13	14	73
Roemer	3	400,000	100	0	0

Note: Amounts are through August 31, 2008, and November 26, 2012. Similar data for earlier years can be found in previous editions of *Vital Statistics on American Politics*.

Sources: 2008: Michael J. Malbin, "Small Donors, Large Donors and the Internet: The Case for Public Financing after Obama," Campaign Finance Institute, April 2009, 16; 2012: "Money vs. Money-Plus: Post-Election Reports Reveal Two Different Campaign Strategies," Campaign Finance Institute, January 2013, Table 3 (www.*CampaignFinanceInstitute.org*); derived by Campaign Finance Institute from data from the Federal Election Commission.

Table 2-5 Public Funding of Presidential Elections, 1976–2012 (millions)

Year	Spending limits Primary[a]	Spending limits Primary plus 20%[a]	Maximum entitlement, primary matching funds[b]	Public funds for each major-party convention[c]	Public funds for each major-party nominee for general election[d]	Coordinated party spending limit[e]
1976	$10.9	$13.1	$5.5	$2.2	$21.8	$3.2
1980	14.7	17.7	7.4	4.4	29.4	4.6
1984	20.2	24.2	10.1	8.1	40.4	6.9
1988	23.1	27.7	11.5	9.2	46.1	8.3
1992	27.6	33.1	13.8	11.0	55.2	10.3
1996	30.9	37.1	15.5	12.4	61.8	12.0
2000	33.8	40.5	16.9	13.5	67.6	13.7
2004	37.3	44.8	18.7	14.9	74.6	16.2
2008	42.1	50.5	21.0	16.8	84.1	19.1
2012	45.6	54.7	22.8	18.2	91.1	21.7

Note: Amounts are in current dollars. The following third party candidates received public funds for general elections: John B. Anderson (independent), $4.2 million in 1980; H. Ross Perot (Reform Party), $29.1 million in 1996; and Pat Buchanan (Reform Party), $12.6 million in 2000. Perot declined public funds in 1992.

[a] $10 million + COLA. (COLA is the cost-of-living adjustment over the base year of 1974.) Campaigns are also allowed to exempt fund-raising costs up to 20 percent of the overall limit, which, in effect, raises their total spending limit by 20 percent. Legal and accounting costs, up to 15 percent of the overall limit, if incurred to comply with the law, are also exempt from the limit.

[b] Eligible candidates in the presidential primaries may receive public funds to match the individual contributions they raise. Contributions from political action committees (PACs) and party committees are not matchable. Although an individual has been able to give up to $1,000 to a primary candidate (before the Bipartisan Campaign Reform Act of 2002 raised that limit to $2,000), only the first $250 of that contribution is matchable. Presidential candidates become eligible for matching funds by raising more than $5,000 in matchable contributions in each of twenty different states. Candidates must agree to use these public funds only for campaign expenses.

[c] $4 million + COLA. Originally, the limit was $2 million + COLA. The base was raised to $3 million for the 1980 convention, then to $4 million for the 1984 convention. The Reform Party received $2.523 million for its presidential nominating convention in 2000.

[d] $20 million + COLA. Legal and accounting costs incurred to comply with the law are exempt from the limit and may be defrayed from private monies raised in separate compliance funds (subject to contribution limitations and prohibitions). The Republican and Democratic candidates who win their party's nominations for president are each eligible to receive a grant to cover all the expenses of their general election campaigns. Nominees who accept the funds must agree not to raise private contributions (from individuals, PACs, or party committees) and to limit their campaign expenditures to the amount of public funds they receive. They may use the funds only for campaign expenses. A third-party presidential candidate may qualify for some public funds after the general election if he or she receives at least 5 percent of the popular vote.

[e] $.02 × voting-age population of U.S. + COLA. This is the amount the national party may spend on behalf of its nominee. The party may work in conjunction with the campaign, but the money is raised, spent, and reported by the national party committee.

Source: Federal Election Commission Press Office.

Table 2-6 Financial Activity of the National Political Parties, 1997–2014 (millions)

Party	1997–1998	1999–2000	2001–2002	2003–2004	2005–2006	2007–2008	2009–2010	2011–2012	2013–2014
Democratic									
Raised	$160.0	$275.2	$217.2	$688.8	$483.1	$763.3	$618.1	$800.1	$657.2
Spent	155.3	265.8	208.7	665.6	472.4	746.5	603.5	784.1	634.6
Contributions	1.2	1.4	2.3	1.8	4.1	2.5	2.0	2.3	1.8
Coordinated expenditures[a]	18.6	21.0	7.1	33.1	20.7	38.0	24.9	39.5	13.1
Independent expenditures[b]	1.5	2.3	1.7	176.5	108.1	156.2	107.4	113.8	123.6
Republican									
Raised	285.0	465.8	424.1	782.4	599.0	792.9	542.1	803.5	565.7
Spent	275.9	427.0	427.0	752.6	608.2	766.1	546.4	786.9	552.9
Contributions	2.6	2.3	4.7	2.6	1.9	8.6	2.4	2.6	2.6
Coordinated expenditures[a]	15.7	29.6	16.0	29.1	14.2	32.0	27.1	36.3	14.5
Independent expenditures[b]	0.3	1.6	1.9	88.0	115.6	124.7	76.1	140.3	105.3

Note: Amounts in current dollars. This table includes only federal activity. Total receipts and disbursements do not include monies transferred among committees. Building funds and state and local election spending are not reported to the Federal Election Commission. Data for earlier years can be found in previous editions of *Vital Statistics on American Politics.* Comparisons with earlier years must be made cautiously since subsequent data revisions can differ appreciably from previously published data.

[a] Party committees are also allowed to spend money on behalf of federal candidates, in addition to the money party committees may contribute directly. This spending may be coordinated with a candidate.
[b] The 1996 election cycle was the first in which party committees were permitted to make independent expenditures.

Sources: Federal Election Commission, "Party Table 2: Democratic Party Committees' Federal Financial Activity through December 31 of the Election Year," "Party Table 3: Republican Party Committees' Federal Financial Activity through December 31 of the Election Year" (*www.fec.gov*).

Table 2-7 Financial Activity of National, State, and Local Party Committees, 2013–2014 (millions)

Committee	Raised			Spent				Cash on hand	Debts by
	From individuals	From other committees	Total	Contributions made	Coordinated expenditures	Independent expenditures	Total		
Democratic National Committee	$155.5	$3.3	$163.3	$0.0	$1.1	$0.0	$160.7	$6.9	$5.9
Democratic Senatorial Campaign Committee	117.1	22.0	168.3	0.4	3.6	54.6	169.2	0.9	21.4
Democratic Congressional Campaign Committee	148.0	26.2	206.8	0.6	2.9	68.8	206.1	2.1	10.0
Democratic state and local committees	62.0	25.1	202.8	0.8	5.4	0.2	182.6	9.3	2.5
Total Democratic	482.6	76.7	657.2	1.8	13.1	123.6	634.6	19.2	39.8
Republican National Committee	176.7	1.6	194.9	0.0	0.2	0.0	194.6	5.0	3.5
National Republican Senatorial Committee	89.8	16.0	128.3	0.8	7.6	39.6	129.0	2.7	10.0
National Republican Congressional Committee	59.2	56.1	153.5	0.4	3.7	65.3	153.5	1.5	7.8
Republican state and local committees	68.8	9.9	149.2	1.4	3.0	0.5	136.0	8.6	2.7
Total Republican	394.5	83.6	565.7	2.6	14.5	105.3	552.9	17.8	24.0

Note: See notes to Table 2-6, this volume.

Sources: Federal Election Commission, "Party Table 2: Democratic Party Committees' Federal Financial Activity through December 31 of the Election Year," "Party Table 3: Republican Party Committees' Federal Financial Activity through December 31 of the Election Year" (*www.fec.gov*).

Table 2-8 National Party Campaign Finance: "Soft" and "Hard" Money, 1999–2014 (millions)

Type of money/party	1999–2000	2001–2002	2003–2004	2005–2006	2007–2008	2009–2010	2011–2012	2013–2014
Nonfederal, "soft" money[a]								
Democratic								
Raised	$245.2	$246.1	b	b	b	b	b	b
Spent	244.8	250.7	b	b	b	b	b	b
Republican								
Raised	249.9	250.0	b	b	b	b	b	b
Spent	252.8	258.9	b	b	b	b	b	b
Federal, "hard" money								
Democratic								
Raised	275.2	217.2	$688.8	$483.1	$763.3	$618.1	$800.1	$657.2
Spent	265.8	208.7	665.6	472.4	746.5	603.5	784.1	634.6
Republican								
Raised	465.8	424.1	782.4	599.0	792.9	542.1	803.5	565.7
Spent	427.0	427.0	752.6	608.2	766.1	546.4	786.9	552.9
Total, "soft" and "hard" money								
Democratic								
Raised	520.4	463.3	688.8	483.1	763.3	618.1	800.1	657.2
Spent	510.6	459.4	665.6	472.4	746.5	603.5	784.1	634.6
Republican								
Raised	715.7	674.1	782.4	599.0	792.9	542.1	803.5	565.7
Spent	679.8	685.9	752.6	608.2	766.1	546.4	786.9	552.9

Note: Amounts in current dollars. Totals do not include transfers among national party committees. Data for earlier years may be found in previous editions of *Vital Statistics on American Politics.* Comparisons with earlier years must be made cautiously since subsequent data revisions can differ appreciably from previously published data.

[a] Before 2003–2004, party committees could, without affecting their other contribution and expenditure limits, spend unlimited amounts ("soft" money) on grassroots activities specified in campaign finance law (for example, voter drives by volunteers in support of the parties' presidential nominees and campaign materials for volunteer distribution). Soft money could also be used to pay for issue advocacy and generic party advertising, to support the construction and maintenance of party headquarters, to pay a portion of the overhead expenses of party organizations, and to meet other shared expenses that benefited candidates in both federal and nonfederal elections. A portion could be transferred as well from national committees to state and local party committees, and some could be contributed directly to candidates in nonfederal races.
[b] The Bipartisan Campaign Reform Act (BCRA) of 2002 and court rulings prohibited political parties from raising soft money, starting with the 2003–2004 election cycle.

Sources: "Soft" money: Federal Election Commission, "Party Committees Raise More than $1 Billion in 2001–2002," press release, March 20, 2003; "hard" money: Federal Election Commission, "Party Table 2: Democratic Party Committees' Federal Financial Activity through December 31 of the Election Year," "Party Table 3: Republican Party Committees' Federal Financial Activity through December 31 of the Election Year" (*www.fec.gov*).

Table 2-9 Number of Political Action Committees (PACs), by Type, 1974–2015

Year	Corporate	Labor	Trade/ membership/ health[a]	Cooperative	Corporation without stock	Independent expenditure-only committees[b]	Political committees with non-contribution accounts[c]	Other nonconnected	Total
1974	89	201	318	—	—	—	—	—	608
1976	433	224	489	—	—	—	—	—	1,146
1978	785	217	453	12	24	—	—	162	1,653
1980	1,206	297	576	42	56	—	—	374	2,551
1982	1,469	380	649	47	103	—	—	723	3,371
1984	1,682	394	698	52	130	—	—	1,053	4,009
1986	1,744	384	745	56	151	—	—	1,077	4,157
1988	1,816	354	786	59	138	—	—	1,115	4,268
1990	1,795	346	774	59	136	—	—	1,062	4,172
1992	1,735	347	770	56	142	—	—	1,145	4,195
1994	1,660	333	792	53	136	—	—	980	3,954
1996	1,642	332	838	41	123	—	—	1,103	4,079
1998	1,567	321	821	39	115	—	—	935	3,798
2000	1,548	318	844	38	115	—	—	972	3,835
2002	1,508	316	891	41	116	—	—	1,019	3,891
2004	1,538	310	884	35	102	—	—	999	3,868
2006	1,622	290	925	37	103	—	—	1,233	4,210
2008	1,601	273	925	38	97	—	—	1,300	4,234
2009	1,598	272	995	49	103	—	—	1,594	4,611
2010	1,628	280	968	40	95	—	—	1,567	4,578
2011	1,683	283	1,004	39	103	—	—	1,747	4,859
2012	1,652	280	985	35	104	—	—	1,601	4,657
2013	1,664	290	960	40	107	1,015	62	2,193	6,331
2014	1,666	287	965	40	106	731	62	1,823	5,680
2015	1,680	280	938	38	96	917	84	1,730	5,763

Note: "___" indicates not available. Counts are as of December 31 for 1974–1998 and as of January 1 for 2000–2015. Counts for other years can be found in earlier editions of *Vital Statistics on American Politics*. The counts reflect federally registered PACs. Registration does not necessarily imply financial activity. The trade/membership/health category for 1974–1976 includes all PACs except corporate and labor; no further breakdown available.

[a] As of July 2011, health organizations are no longer an organization type but are included in either the trade or membership category.
[b] Independent expenditure-only committees may receive unlimited contributions from individuals, corporations, and labor unions for the purpose of financing independent expenditures and other independent political activity.
[c] Committees with non-contribution accounts, permitted to make contributions to federal candidates, solicit and accept unlimited contributions from individuals, corporations, labor organizations, and other political committees. These contributions are in a segregated bank account for the purpose of financing independent expenditures, other ads that refer to a federal candidate, and generic voter drives in federal elections, while maintaining a separate bank account, subject to all of the statutory amount limitations and source prohibitions.

Sources: Federal Election Commission, "PAC Count—1974 to the Present" (*www.fec.gov*); unpublished data.

Table 2-10   PACs: Receipts, Expenditures, and Contributions, 1975–2014

Election cycle[a]	Receipts[b] (millions)	Expenditures[b] (millions)	Contributions to congressional candidates[c] (millions)	Percentage of receipts contributed to congressional candidates
1975–1976	$54.0	$52.9	$22.6	42
1977–1978	80.0	77.4	34.1	43
1979–1980	137.7	131.2	60.2	44
1981–1982	199.5	190.2	87.6	44
1983–1984	288.7	266.8	113.0	39
1985–1986	353.4	340.0	139.8	40
1987–1988	384.6	364.2	159.2	41
1989–1990	372.1	357.6	159.1	43
1991–1992	385.5	394.8	188.9	49
1993–1994	391.8	388.1	189.6	48
1995–1996	437.4	429.9	217.8	50
1997–1998	502.6	470.8	219.9	44
1999–2000	604.9	579.4	259.8	43
2001–2002	685.3	656.5	282.0	41
2003–2004	915.7	842.9	310.5	34
2005–2006	1,085.5	1,055.3	372.1	34
2007–2008	1,212.4	1,180.0	412.8	34
2009–2010	1,197.8	1,174.1	431.5	36
2011–2012	2,259.1	2,198.4	444.5	20
2013–2014	2,368.6	2,304.8	435.9	18

Note: Amounts in current dollars. The 2012 presidential election was the first after a Supreme Court decision, *Citizens United v. Federal Election Commission* in January 2010, allowed the emergence of "super" political action committees (PACs). Super PACs can raise unlimited money from corporations, labor unions, and individuals, spending that money supporting and opposing presidential or congressional candidates, but cannot directly coordinate with the campaigns.

[a] Data cover January 1 of the odd-numbered year to December 31 of the even-numbered year.
[b] Receipts and expenditures for 1975–1984 exclude funds transferred between affiliated committees.
[c] Primarily contributions to candidates for election in the even-numbered year, made during the two-year election cycle. Some contributions went to candidates running for office in future years, or to debt retirement for candidates in past cycles.

Sources: 1975–1976: Joseph E. Cantor, "Political Action Committees: Their Evolution and Growth and Their Implications for the Political System," Report no. 83, Congressional Research Service, Washington, D.C., 1982, 87–88; 1977–1978: Federal Election Commission, "FEC Releases First PAC Figures for 1985–86," press release, May 21, 1987, 1; 1979–1988: "PAC Activity Falls in 1990 Elections," press release, March 31, 1991, 10; 1989–2010: "Table 4: Summary of PAC Activity, 1990–2010"; 2011–2014: "PAC Table 1: Summary of PAC Activity," "PAC Table 2: PAC Contributions to Candidates" (*www.fec.gov*).

Table 2-11 Spending, by Type of PAC, 1997–2014 (millions)

Election cycle[a]	Separate Segregated Funds (SSFs)					Nonconnected committees			Total
	Corporate	Labor	Trade/ membership[b]	Cooperative	Corporations without stock	Independent expenditure-only committees[c]	Committees with non-contribution accounts[c]	Other PACs[d]	
1997–1998	$141.4	$103.0	$141.5	$4.3	$8.6	—	—	$94.8	$493.7
1999–2000	162.8	129.4	178.6	3.3	12.2	—	—	125.2	611.5
2001–2002	184.3	159.3	175.9	3.7	9.6	—	—	153.8	686.5
2003–2004	225.3	184.4	219.8	3.9	9.3	—	—	495.9	1,138.50
2005–2006	272.9	198.5	251.9	4.6	11.1	—	—	328.7	1,067.70
2007–2008	299.7	252.3	294.9	9.9	12.7	—	—	310.7	1,180.30
2009–2010	302.8	256.9	268.8	6.3	15.9	90.9	—	333.1	1,274.60
2011–2012	343.0	279.4	264.5	6.7	16.2	796.9	175.3	316.3	2,198.40
2013–2014	370.7	289.2	290.5	7.0	19.4	687.2	312.6	328.0	2,304.80

Note: "—" indicates not available. Amounts in current dollars. Detail may not add to totals because of rounding. Data for earlier years may be found in previous editions of *Vital Statistics on American Politics*.

a Data cover January 1 of the odd-numbered year to December 31 of the even-numbered year.
b This category combines the Federal Election Commission categories of trade and membership.
c For details, see notes for Table 2-9, this volume.
d This category includes the Federal Election Commission category of leadership PACs (initiated in 2011–2012).

Sources: 1997–2012: Federal Election Commission, "PAC Table 1: Summary of PAC Activity through December 31 of the Election Year"; 2013–2014: "PAC Table 1: Summary of PAC Activity, January 1, 2013 through December 31, 2014" (*www.fec.gov*).

Table 2-12 Contributions and Independent Expenditures, by Type of PAC, 2003–2014

Election cycle/PAC type	Number[a]	Receipts[b]	Contributions to federal candidates[c]		Independent expenditures[d]	
			Amount	Percentage of receipts	Amount	Percentage of receipts
2003–2004						
Corporate	1,402	$238,984,115	$115,641,547	48%	$223,729	0.1%
Labor	206	191,651,043	52,103,572	27	20,737,373	10.8
Trade/membership/health	722	181,837,429	83,221,870	46	18,138,069	10.0
Cooperative	34	4,187,378	2,872,363	69	4,993	0.1
Corporations without stock	75	9,639,838	4,182,321	43	111,095	1.2
Nonconnected	819	289,423,580	52,467,328	18	18,159,133	6.3
Total	3,258	915,723,383	310,489,001	34	57,374,392	6.3
2005–2006						
Corporate	1,464	278,345,927	135,925,970	49	250,345	0.1
Labor	204	218,185,504	55,815,069	26	10,056,447	4.6
Trade/membership/health	745	218,448,147	101,803,507	47	19,050,740	8.7
Cooperative	35	6,166,566	3,454,915	56	3,865	0.1
Corporations without stock	89	11,441,713	4,885,718	43	377,849	3.3
Nonconnected	887	352,947,674	70,217,568	20	8,083,013	2.3
Total	3,424	1,085,535,531	372,102,747	34	37,822,259	3.5
2007–2008						
Corporate	1,470	313,350,975	158,323,496	51	221,207	0.1
Labor	203	262,055,837	62,675,294	24	58,630,780	22.4
Trade/membership/health	794	240,983,640	112,897,919	47	44,911,854	18.6
Cooperative	39	10,283,949	6,861,823	67	0	0.0
Corporations without stock	84	13,025,360	5,461,525	42	582,735	4.5
Nonconnected	1,023	372,720,837	66,627,495	18	30,834,925	8.3
Total	3,613	1,212,420,598	412,847,552	34	135,181,501	11.1
2009–2010						
Corporate	1,470	316,954,250	165,455,021	52	360,039	0.1
Labor	203	259,066,268	64,162,708	25	25,881,237	10.0
Trade/membership/health	794	227,397,841	115,335,850	51	31,734,037	14.0

	Number	Receipts	Contributions	%	Independent Expenditures	%
Cooperative	39	10,060,381	4,959,203	49	0	0.0
Corporations without stock	84	14,253,911	7,488,570	53	712,598	5.0
Nonconnected	1,023	451,730,393	74,089,193	16	10,308,213	2.3
Total	3,613	1,279,469,044	431,490,545	34	68,996,124	5.4
2011–2012						
Corporate	1,851	361,088,386	181,141,433	50	—	—
Labor	300	282,589,623	57,476,379	20	—	—
Trade/membership[e]	993	270,443,042	121,324,660	45	—	—
Cooperative	41	7,318,621	5,345,052	73	—	—
Corporations without stock	118	17,343,198	7,529,555	43	—	—
Nonconnected[f]	4,008	1,320,350,343	73,532,041	6	78,044,150	3.5
Total	7,311	2,259,133,213	446,349,121	20	—	—
2013–2014						
Corporate	1,804	384,831,590	178,086,417	46	—	—
Labor	288	305,740,812	50,647,727	17	—	—
Trade/membership[e]	967	302,705,703	119,232,896	39	—	—
Cooperative	41	7,699,678	4,928,775	64	—	—
Corporations without stock	114	19,705,058	7,025,307	36	—	—
Nonconnected[f]	4,334	1,347,934,933	76,025,813	6	—	—
Total	7,548	2,368,617,774	435,946,935	18	47,449,852	2.0

Note: "—" indicates not available. Amounts in current dollars. Data for earlier years can be found in previous editions of *Vital Statistics on American Politics.*

[a] For 2003–2010, the numbers shown are those PACs that actually made contributions.

[b] Not adjusted for money transferred between affiliated committees. Receipts are for all PACs whether or not they made contributions to candidates in the election cycle.

[c] Figures include contributions to all federal candidates, including those who did not run for office during the years indicated.

[d] Independent expenditures include money spent for candidates and against candidates.

[e] As of July 2011, health organizations are no longer an organization type but are included in either the trade or the membership category.

[f] This category includes independent expenditure-only committees (1,251 in 2011–2012, 1,618 in 2013–2014), which are prohibited from making contributions to candidates.

Sources: Federal Election Commission, "PAC Activity Increases for 2004 Elections," press release, April 13, 2005; "PAC Activity Continues Climb in 2006," press release, October 5, 2007; "Growth in PAC Financial Activity Slows," press release, April 24, 2009; "Table 1: PAC Financial Activity, 2009–2010," "Table 3: 2009–2010 Summary of Independent Expenditures," "Independent Expenditure Table 1: Independent Expenditures Made for or against Candidates through December 31 of the Election Year (2012 and 2010)," "PAC Table 1: Summary of PAC Activity through December 1 of the Election Year," "PAC Table 2: PAC Contributions to Candidates, January 1, 2011–December 31, 2012," "PAC Table 1: Summary of PAC Activity, January 1, 2013 through December 31, 2014," "PAC Table 2: PAC Contributions to Candidates, January 1, 2013–December 31, 2014," "Independent Expenditure Table 2: Independent Expenditures Made For or Against Congressional Candidates, January 1, 2013 through December 31, 2014" (*www.fec.gov*).

Table 2-13   Top Twenty PACs in Overall Spending and in Contributions to Federal Candidates, 2013–2014

Rank	PAC	Overall spending
1	Emily's List	$44,878,362
2	SEIU COPE (Service Employees International Union Committee on Political Education)	36,346,872
3	National Rifle Association of America Political Victory Fund	20,785,386
4	American Federation of State, County, and Municipal Employees—P E O P L E	19,792,136
5	Senate Conservatives Fund	17,255,137
6	DRIVE (Democrat, Republican, Independent Voter Education) The PAC of the International Brotherhood of Teamsters	15,043,785
7	1199 Service Employees International Union Federal Political Action Fund	14,039,397
8	Our Country Deserves Better PAC—TeaPartyExpress.org	12,606,795
9	American Federation of Teachers, AFL-CIO Committee on Political Education	12,026,184
10	United Food and Commercial Workers International Union Active Ballot Club	11,145,605
11	International Brotherhood of Electrical Workers Political Action Committee	10,361,663
12	Moveon.org PAC	10,199,097
13	UAW-V-CAP (UAW Voluntary Community Action Program)	8,870,820
14	Voice of Teachers for Education/Committee on Political Education of NY State United Teachers (VOTE/COPE) of NYSUT	8,013,686
15	Honeywell International Political Action Committee	7,879,570
16	Democracy for America	7,629,671
17	American Legacy Political Action Committee	7,182,060
18	American Association for Justice Political Action Committee (AAJ PAC)	7,181,618
19	Engineers Political Education Committee (EPEC)/International Union of Operating Engineers	7,074,160
20	United Association Political Education Committee (United Association of Journeymen and Apprentices of the Plumbing & Pipefitting Industry of the United States and Canada)	7,042,716

Rank	PAC	Contributions to federal candidates and other committees[a]
1	American Federation of Teachers, AFL-CIO Committee on Political Education	$5,655,000
2	Honeywell International Political Action Committee	5,134,461
3	Engineers Political Education Committee (EPEC)/International Union of Operating Engineers	4,969,291

Table 2-13   *(Continued)*

Rank	PAC	*Contributions to federal candidates and other committees*[a]
4	National Association of Realtors Political Action Committee	4,968,436
5	Senate Conservatives Fund	4,935,265
6	United Food and Commercial Workers International Union Active Ballot Club	4,562,475
7	NEA Fund for Children and Public Education	4,363,997
8	Committee on Letter Carriers Political Education (Letter Carriers Political Action Fund)	4,275,800
9	National Air Traffic Controllers Association PAC	4,239,200
10	International Brotherhood of Electrical Workers Political Action Committee	4,199,757
11	American Federation of State, County, and Municipal Employees—P E O P L E	4,126,400
12	National Beer Wholesalers Association Political Action Committee	4,086,000
13	Lockheed Martin Corporation Employees' Political Action Committee	3,723,500
14	Employees of Northrop Grumman Corporation PAC	3,720,750
15	DRIVE (Democrat, Republican, Independent Voter Education) The PAC of the International Brotherhood of Teamsters	3,690,950
16	AT&T Inc. Federal Political Action Committee (AT&T Federal PAC)	3,598,000
17	Laborers' International Union of North America (LIUNA) PAC	3,495,750
18	Comcast Corporation & NBCUniversal Political Action Committee–Federal	3,366,000
19	SEIU COPE (Service Employees International Union Committee on Political Education)	3,355,171
20	Dealers Election Action Committee of the National Automotive Dealers Association	3,310,100

Note: Amounts in current dollars. Information for earlier years can be found in previous editions of *Vital Statistics on American Politics.*

[a] Includes contributions to candidate committees, other PACs, and party committees.

Source: Federal Election Commission, "PAC Table 4b: Top 50 PACs by Disbursements, January 1, 2013–December 31, 2014" and "PAC Table 4c: Top 50 PACs by Contributions to Candidates and Other Committees, January 1, 2013–December 31, 2014" (*www.fec.gov*).

Table 2-14 PAC Congressional Campaign Contributions, by Type of PAC and Incumbency Status of Candidate, 1999–2014 (millions)

	House						Senate					
	Candidate party		Type of contest				Candidate party		Type of contest			
Election cycle/ PAC type	Dem.	Rep.	Incum-bent	Chal-lenger	Open seat[a]	Total	Dem.	Rep.	Incum-bent	Chal-lenger	Open seat[a]	Total
1999–2000												
Corporate	$22.0	$40.0	$54.5	$2.3	$5.3	$62.1	$5.1	$16.9	$16.0	$1.5	$4.6	$22.1
Trade/membership/ health	22.3	32.6	45.7	3.4	5.7	55.0	3.8	9.4	9.3	1.2	2.8	13.3
Labor	39.9	3.5	30.1	8.0	5.3	43.5	6.2	0.4	2.3	2.8	1.5	6.6
Nonconnected	11.4	15.6	15.0	5.7	6.2	27.1	3.0	5.5	4.9	1.5	2.2	8.6
Total[b]	98.2	94.7	150.1	19.8	23.0	193.4	18.7	33.2	33.5	7.1	11.3	51.9
2001–2002												
Corporate	23.6	44.6	59.7	1.6	6.9	68.2	7.0	16.4	15.8	4.3	3.4	23.4
Trade/membership/ health	23.0	34.2	47.1	2.1	8.0	57.2	4.9	9.3	9.5	3.1	1.7	14.3
Labor	39.9	4.3	31.4	5.2	7.7	44.4	7.0	0.5	4.1	2.4	1.1	7.5
Nonconnected	14.0	18.1	18.5	4.8	8.9	32.2	5.8	6.6	6.6	4.1	1.8	12.5
Total[b]	102.6	104.2	160.9	13.8	32.0	206.9	25.4	33.8	37.0	14.2	8.1	59.2
2003–2004												
Corporate	24.8	54.3	72.6	1.9	4.6	79.1	8.9	16.3	17.2	1.2	6.7	25.2
Trade/membership/ health	23.0	40.1	55.4	2.3	5.4	63.2	5.7	9.3	9.9	1.1	4.0	15.0
Labor	37.3	5.4	32.9	5.2	4.6	42.8	6.8	0.8	4.3	0.9	2.3	7.6
Nonconnected	11.4	23.8	21.6	6.0	7.6	35.2	6.3	8.3	6.9	2.2	5.4	14.6
Total[b]	98.6	126.6	187.1	15.6	22.5	225.4	28.4	35.3	39.3	5.6	18.8	63.7
2005–2006												
Corporate	31.7	64.2	90.0	1.7	4.2	95.9	9.1	17.1	21.9	1.7	2.6	26.2
Trade/membership/ health	30.3	49.0	70.2	3.4	5.7	79.3	6.0	9.8	12.1	1.8	2.0	15.8

Labor	42.1	5.5	32.2	10.3	5.1	47.6	5.8	0.5	3.3	2.1	0.9	6.3
Nonconnected	18.2	32.0	31.5	10.5	8.2	50.2	7.1	9.4	9.5	4.3	2.7	16.5
Total[b]	124.9	154.2	229.3	26.2	23.5	279.2	28.6	37.5	47.7	10.0	8.3	66.1
2007–2008												
Corporate	57.3	54.4	103.2	5.0	3.6	111.7	11.4	21.8	27.4	2.7	3.1	33.3
Trade/membership/health	48.0	40.0	76.0	7.2	4.8	88.0	7.3	12.5	15.2	2.6	2.0	19.8
Labor	49.9	3.9	37.9	11.3	4.6	53.8	6.6	0.5	2.8	3.0	1.2	7.1
Nonconnected	25.3	19.6	27.9	11.6	5.4	44.9	7.8	10.0	10.9	4.4	2.5	17.8
Total[b]	185.6	122.4	253.5	35.7	18.8	308.1	33.9	45.9	57.7	13.0	9.1	79.8
2009–2010												
Corporate	58.0	55.7	102.1	6.4	5.3	113.7	13.6	23.2	22.6	3.2	11.0	36.8
Trade/membership/health	45.6	40.8	74.2	6.7	5.5	86.4	8.3	13.1	12.6	2.2	6.6	21.4
Labor	50.8	3.5	46.6	3.7	3.9	54.2	7.1	0.6	2.9	1.4	3.4	7.7
Nonconnected	25.1	24.7	31.8	12.4	5.6	49.8	9.9	10.9	9.6	3.4	7.8	20.8
Total[b]	184.4	129.2	262.8	30.0	20.7	313.6	39.9	49.0	48.9	10.4	29.5	88.8
2011–2012												
Corporate	45.1	88.9	125.4	5.0	4.1	134.5	20.9	24.7	34.9	4.4	6.5	45.8
Trade/membership[c]	34.2	62.4	84.8	7.2	4.9	96.9	11.5	12.5	16.8	2.7	4.6	24.2
Labor	44.1	5.2	32.2	11.8	5.4	49.4	7.3	0.5	4.8	1.2	2.1	8.1
Nonconnected	21.0	29.4	34.1	11.5	4.9	50.6	12.4	9.8	12.3	4.2	5.8	22.3
Total[b]	148.1	192.1	285.4	36.1	19.8	341.3	53.5	48.9	70.7	12.8	19.7	103.2
2013–2014												
Corporate	49.2	89.7	130.7	2.2	6.0	138.9	14.9	24.3	28.5	5.3	5.4	39.1
Trade/membership[c]	36.8	60.7	88.1	2.9	6.5	97.6	8.2	13.5	14.8	3.3	3.6	21.7
Labor	39.3	5.2	35.3	4.3	4.8	44.5	5.8	0.3	4.3	0.5	1.3	6.2
Nonconnected	19.6	30.8	35.3	7.9	7.3	50.4	12.1	13.5	14.9	5.5	5.3	25.6
Total[b]	149.3	192.3	298.9	17.6	25.1	341.6	41.8	52.5	63.6	14.8	15.9	94.3

(Table continues)

Table 2-14   *(Continued)*

Note: Amounts are current dollar amounts contributed during the two-year election cycle indicated to all candidates in primary, general, runoff, and special elections. Figures are for all House and Senate candidates, not just those up for election in the two-year cycle. Data for earlier years can be found in previous editions of *Vital Statistics on American Politics*.

[a] "Open seat" refers to candidates in elections in which an incumbent did not seek reelection.
[b] Includes PACs classified by the Federal Election Commission as cooperatives and corporations without stock.
[c] As of July 2011, health organizations are no longer an organization type but are included in either the trade or membership category.

Sources: Federal Election Commission, "PAC Contributions to Candidates 1996 through 2010 Election Cycles," "PAC Table 2: PAC Contributions to Candidates, January 1, 2011–December 31, 2012," "PAC Table 2: PAC Contributions to Candidates, January 1, 2013 through December 31, 2014" (*www.fec.gov*).

3
Public Opinion and Voting

- **Partisanship**
- **Ideology**
- **Voting by Groups**
- **Presidential and Congressional Approval**
- **Confidence in Government and the Economy**
- **Most Important Problem**
- **Specific Issues**

Public opinion data are everywhere. For example, preelection polls give the pundits and the voters an idea of who is ahead and who is behind. Other polls give candidates and officeholders a glimpse into what the public thinks and how it would react to changes in public policies. Survey data are also used, in a more partisan way, by politicians, commentators, and interest groups to support their positions. And, in a slightly different form, they are used even more widely by advertisers and manufacturers to gauge consumer reactions to new products and services. Reflecting this frequent and varied use of surveys, this chapter presents public opinion on issues ranging from the very broad, such as the government and the economy, to the specific, such as gun control and the death penalty.

This chapter also includes tables and figures on how specific groups of voters cast their ballots in elections. Chapter 1 presented overall election results, indicating which party or individual won an election, whereas this chapter shows votes by region, gender, race, religion, and so on, as well as for groups of ideologues, such as liberals and conservatives, partisan groups, and sometimes special groups such as first-time voters. Because these data are analogous to public opinion data in that they come from sample surveys and indicate group opinions rather than overall election outcomes, they are included in this chapter.

Figures 3-1 through 3-4 and Tables 3-1 through 3-3 cover two of the most frequently cited components of public opinion—partisanship and political ideology. These characteristics merit emphasis because of their practical political significance. They are of interest not only to analysts who wish to understand scientifically why people behave as they do, but also to those who assess long-term political and social trends, as well as those who track day-to-day politics.

From another perspective, these results are important because they illustrate the reliability and validity of public opinion polling, as well as the hazards of gauging personal opinion. Figures 3-1 and 3-2, showing self-proclaimed party identification, are reasonably similar for the period they jointly cover. If public opinion data were totally unreliable, as some contend, such similarity would be unlikely. Moreover, these figures illustrate two aspects of reliability and validity. First, polling as few as fifteen hundred people is a window to the opinion of the entire population; the two separate polling organizations represented in Figures 3-1 and 3-2 would not obtain such similarity over decades of interviewing if their results represented only those actually interviewed. (Of course, one must choose the fifteen hundred respondents according to scientific sampling procedures, as do all the major polling organizations.) Second, poll results are not completely dependent on exact question wording. The Pew question (Figure 3-2) focuses on the immediate situation ("In politics today . . . "), while the American National Election Studies question (Table 3-1) is broader ("Generally speaking . . . "), suggesting that the Pew question might pick up more short-term fluctuations in partisanship. Yet the results are quite similar.

Both the American National Election Studies and Pew surveys probe those who claim to be independents to determine whether they lean toward one party or the other. The responses to this probe as well as other evidence (Table 3-7) raise the question of whether independents are really closet partisans. How that question is answered, as the contrast between the two plots in Figures 3-1 and 3-2 shows, has major implications for conclusions about the relative strengths of the parties. As emphasized in earlier introductions, even simple data descriptions involve interpretation.

Because surveys are not exact counts of the whole population, "sampling error" is often reported to convey the range within which the true population result lies. For example, results are said to be accurate to within plus or minus 3 percent. Yet even with greater precision (achieved by increasing the size of the sample), survey results still require interpretation. Suppose one could ask every American adult simultaneously whether he or she is a Democrat, an independent, or a Republican. There would then be no sampling error; because everyone was asked, the information would describe the entire U.S. population at that particular time. But that leads back to an equally vexing question: What does it mean to be an independent?

The "don't know" responses to the ideology question about liberal or conservative self-identification in Table 3-3—and in the other public opinion tables—illustrate a similar point. Whether pollsters ask about a general position or a specific issue, some proportion of the sample—often as much as 15 percent and sometimes much more—responds "don't know." It is not immediately apparent how to interpret such responses. Some people have information about the subject matter but no opinion; some have no information and no opinion; and a few have no information but have an opinion anyway. The pollster's decision about how to treat such responses can make a large difference. For example, in a preelection poll should a pollster assume that those respondents who have not yet chosen candidates to support will eventually (1) split votes between candidates in similar proportions as those who have already decided, (2) not vote, (3) divide evenly between the candidates, or (4) overwhelmingly support particular candidates?

For public officials seeking guidance on public sentiment, no simple reading suffices because they must assess intensity as well as direction. Those pursuing a theoretical understanding of politics face the same problem. Take the matter of gun control. A majority of Americans—at times approaching two-thirds—thought it was more important to "control gun ownership" than to "protect the right to own guns," according to polls between 1993 and 2008 (Table 3-14). If that is true, why is it more stringent gun control laws were not enacted? The answer has to do, in part, with the strength of feeling—and organization—of the anti–gun control lobby. Those supporting Second Amendment rights (as they would probably prefer to be known) have historically been much better organized and have outspent those who would restrict gun ownership, presumably because gun advocates feel more strongly about the issue. Understanding the importance of public opinion in politics requires more than a simple nose count. The salience of an opinion to the person holding it also counts.

Another factor in polling is that a particular survey result usually says little in isolation. The soundest interpretations depend on several surveys stretching over time, often over a period of years. Consider the decline and partial recovery in public confidence in government (Figure 3-8). The confidence level at a particular time is a mere point, difficult or impossible to interpret. Yet that point, when viewed with comparable points from similar surveys over the years, indicates a trend—decline, upsurge, constancy, whatever. Consequently, reports of public opinion increasingly emphasize extended time series, as is done here (Figures 3-11, 3-12, 3-15, 3-16, and 3-17, and Tables 3-11 through 3-17). Such time series data can be usefully supplemented by cross sections (Table 3-2). Such within-survey contrasts convey whether and how groups differ in attitudes. Where long time series are impossible because of the nature of the event—such as the U.S. military actions in Iraq (Figure 3-20) and the war on terrorism (Table 3-18)—comparison of multiple time series can aid interpretation.

The issues most salient in the public's mind vary across time. This fact itself has been measured by asking people what they regard as the nation's most important problem (Figures 3-11 and 3-12). Yet many issues are of perennial interest, and over-time assessments (which sometimes require the use of earlier editions of this volume) often date back to the 1940s (Tables 3-11 and 3-16). From the point of view of elections, the significance of public opinion lies chiefly in how the public translates its feelings into summary judgments of the president (Figure 3-6), Congress (Figure 3-7), and government and society as a whole (Figures 3-8 and 3-9). Yet another set consists of favorable versus unfavorable opinions of the two parties (Figure 3-13). Finally, public satisfaction with the status quo and evaluations of the economy, both personal and national and present and future, are perennial concerns in politics (Figures 3-9 and 3-10).

Of course, the most direct and important judgments about political leaders, candidates, and parties occur in elections, but election results tell us only the overall results (and outcomes in different geographical areas). Surveys are the prime means of looking into the behavior of individuals and groups. This chapter reveals how various kinds of individuals voted for president, both in the general election (Table 3-4) and in presidential primaries (Tables 3-5 and 3-6), and for Congress (Table 3-8). These data also answer questions of great theoretical and practical interest, such as the extent to which individuals vote in accordance with their general party preference and in straight or split tickets (Tables 3-7, 3-9, and 3-10).

A final note: Even a firm understanding of public opinion can be contradicted by events because one cannot blindly equate opinion with behavior. The growth of racial tolerance in the South is a telling counterpoint to a political atmosphere formerly committed to white supremacy. As one respondent, a segregationist, told a pollster in the mid-1960s: "You asked me what I favored, not what I will accept graciously, not what I thought was right."[1]

Note

1. Donald R. Matthews and James W. Prothro, *Negroes and the New Southern Politics* (New York: Harcourt, Brace and World, 1966), 363. See also Robert Weissberg's thoughtful discussion of different types of tolerance, especially his distinction between "hearts and minds" tolerance and various forms of behavioral tolerance. Weissberg, *Political Tolerance: Balancing Community and Diversity* (Thousand Oaks, Calif.: Sage, 1998).

Table 3-1 Partisan Identification, American National Election Studies, 1952–2012 (percent)

Year	Democrat			Independent	Republican			Total	Number of interviews
	Strong	Weak	Independent		Independent	Weak	Strong		
1952	23	26	10	5	8	14	14	100	1,689
1954	23	26	9	8	6	15	13	100	1,088
1956	22	24	7	9	9	15	16	102	1,690
1958	28	23	7	8	5	17	12	100	1,737
1960	21	26	6	10	7	14	16	100	1,864
1962	24	24	8	8	6	17	13	100	1,237
1964	27	25	9	8	6	14	11	100	1,536
1966	18	28	9	12	7	15	10	99	1,263
1968	20	26	10	11	9	15	10	101	1,531
1970	20	24	10	13	8	15	9	99	1,490
1972	15	25	11	15	10	13	10	99	2,695
1974	18	21	13	18	9	14	8	101	2,492
1976	15	25	12	16	10	14	9	101	2,833
1978	15	24	14	16	10	13	8	100	2,269
1980	18	23	11	15	10	14	9	100	1,612
1982	20	24	11	13	8	14	10	100	1,403
1984	17	20	11	13	12	15	12	100	2,228
1986	18	22	10	14	11	15	11	101	2,157
1988	18	18	12	12	13	14	14	101	2,026
1990	20	19	12	12	12	15	10	100	1,965
1992	18	17	14	13	12	14	11	99	2,473
1994	15	18	13	11	12	15	15	99	1,780
1996	18	19	14	10	12	15	12	100	1,706
1998	19	18	14	12	11	16	10	100	1,267
2000	19	15	15	13	13	12	12	99	1,790
2002	17	17	16	7	13	16	15	101	1,466
2004	17	16	17	10	12	12	16	100	1,194
2008	19	15	17	11	12	13	13	100	2,293
2012	20	15	12	14	12	12	15	100	5,892

Note: Question: "Generally speaking, do you consider yourself a Republican, a Democrat, an Independent, or what?" If Republican or Democrat: "Would you call yourself a strong (R/D) or a not very strong (R/D)?" If Independent or other: "Do you think of yourself as closer to the Republican or Democratic party?" Regarding the data: "The percentages above for the 7-category party identification variable reflect the following: 1) the apolitical category is eliminated, 2) respondents who fail or refuse to say whether they are a 'strong' partisan are not imputed to be a 'weak' partisan, ... 3) respondents who identify as members of other parties are coded as missing from the Democrat-independent-Republican scale." For further consideration, see "Clarification of 'apolitical' codes in the party identification summary variable on ANES datasets," December 8, 2009 (*www.electionstudies.org*). There was no update of the American National Election Studies series in 2006, 2010, and 2014.

Source: Calculated by the editors from American National Election Studies data, University of Michigan, Ann Arbor, MI, and Stanford University, Palo Alto, CA (*www.electionstudies.org*).

110

Figure 3-1 Partisan Identification, American National Election Studies, 1952–2012

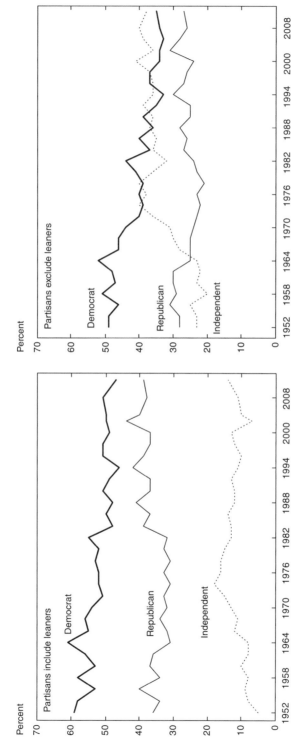

Note: See Table 3-1, this volume, for question. "Leaners" are independents who consider themselves closer to one party. There was no update of the American National Election Studies series in 2006, 2010, and 2014.

Source: Calculated by the editors from American National Election Studies data, University of Michigan, Ann Arbor, MI, and Stanford University, Palo Alto, CA (*www.electionstudies.org*).

Figure 3-2 Partisan Identification, Pew Surveys, 1987–2015

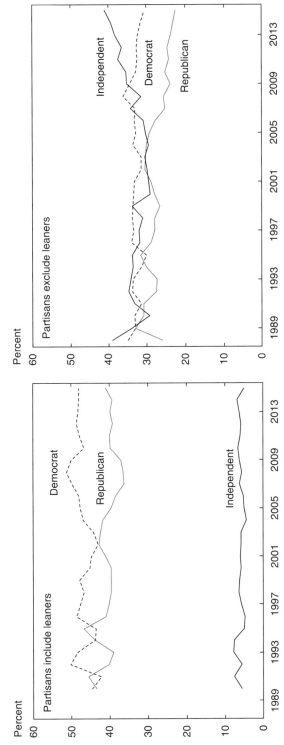

Note: Data for 2015 are through February. Question: "In politics today, do you consider yourself a Republican, Democrat, or Independent?" If answered other than Republican or Democrat: "As of today do you lean more to the Republican Party or more to the Democratic Party?" Related data for additional years can be found in previous editions of *Vital Statistics on American Politics.*

Source: Pew Research Center for the People and the Press, "Democrats Have More Positive Image, But GOP Runs Even or Ahead on Key Issues," February 26, 2015, 26 (*http://people-press.org*).

Table 3-2 Partisan Identification, by Groups, 2004–2012 (percent)

	2004				2008						2012					
	Dem.	Ind.	Rep.	Democratic advantage	Dem.	Ind.	Rep.	Democratic advantage	Democratic gain, 2004–2008	Sample size, 2008	Dem.	Ind.	Rep.	Democratic advantage	Democratic gain, 2008–2012	Sample size, 2012
Sex																
Men	43	9	48	−5	47	11	42	5	4	8,308	43	9	48	−5	−4	6,212
Women	51	9	40	11	55	11	34	21	4	9,235	52	8	39	13	−3	7,217
Age																
18–29 years	50	9	40	10	58	10	33	25	8	1,710	55	9	36	19	−3	1,408
30–49 years	45	8	47	−2	50	10	39	11	5	5,416	47	8	45	2	−3	3,358
50–64 years	48	8	44	4	51	11	38	13	3	5,647	48	8	43	5	−3	4,453
65 years and over	50	9	42	8	49	11	40	9	−1	4,408	45	7	48	−3	−4	3,942
Race and ethnicity																
White	42	8	50	−8	46	10	44	2	4	14,391	40	8	52	−12	−6	10,374
All others	70	12	18	52	73	12	15	58	3	3,152	73	8	20	53	0	2,810
Black	83	8	9	74	86	8	7	79	3	1,776	87	5	8	79	1	1,371
Hispanic	56	10	34	22	62	11	27	35	6	926	61	10	29	32	−1	800
Region[a]																
Northeast	52	9	40	12	55	11	34	21	3	3,194	54	9	37	17	−1	2,316
Midwest	46	10	45	1	50	12	38	12	4	4,513	47	9	43	4	−3	3,370
South	45	8	46	−1	49	10	41	8	4	6,405	45	8	47	−2	−4	4,892
West	48	8	43	5	53	10	37	16	5	3,431	49	9	43	6	−4	2,851
Education																
Less than high school	57	11	32	25	60	13	27	33	3	930	—					—
High school graduate	48	10	43	5	52	11	38	14	4	4,786	—					—
Some college	44	9	48	−4	50	11	39	11	6	4,541	46	8	46	0	−4	3,848
College graduate	44	7	50	−6	47	10	43	4	3	4,179	48	7	45	3	1	3,143
Postgraduate	51	7	42	9	53	9	38	15	2	3,020	54	7	39	15	1	2,624

Income																
<$20,000	60	10	30	30	63	12	24	39	3	1,973	57	11	32	25	-6	1,716
$20,000–29,999	56	9	35	21	58	10	32	26	2	1,460	54	9	37	17	-4	1,258
$30,000–49,999	47	8	45	2	54	9	36	18	7	3,076	49	7	44	5	-5	2,396
$50,000–74,999	43	6	51	-8	51	8	41	10	8	2,854	46	7	46	0	-5	1,978
$75,000–99,999	40	6	54	-14	48	8	45	3	8	2,212	46	7	46	0	-2	1,713
$100,000+	42	7	52	-10	45	8	47	-2	3	3,335	45	5	49	-4	0	2,614
Community type																
Urban	56	9	35	21	58	11	32	26	2	4,751	57	8	35	22	-1	3,789
Suburban	44	9	48	-4	49	11	40	9	5	7,301	46	8	46	0	-3	6,553
Rural	43	9	47	-4	45	12	43	2	2	3,069	40	9	51	-11	-5	2,616
Religious preference																
Total, white Protestant	36	7	57	-21	37	10	53	-16	1	7,843	—	—	—	—	—	—
White, evangelical Protestant	28	6	66	-38	30	8	62	-32	2	3,947	22	7	71	-49	-8	2,965
White, mainline Protestant	43	8	49	-6	45	11	44	1	2	3,896	40	8	52	-12	-5	2,572
White, non-Hispanic Catholic	45	8	47	-2	49	10	40	9	4	3,146	41	8	50	-9	-8	2,235
Union household																
Yes	56	8	36	20	58	12	30	28	2	581	62	8	30	32	4	202
No	46	9	46	0	50	11	39	11	4	3,217	46	6	48	-2	-4	1,354

(Table continues)

Table 3-2 *(Continued)*

	2004				2008						2012					
	Dem.	Ind.	Rep.	Democratic advantage	Dem.	Ind.	Rep.	Democratic advantage	Democratic gain, 2004–2008	Sample size, 2008	Dem.	Ind.	Rep.	Democratic advantage	Democratic gain, 2008–2012	Sample size, 2012
Homeowner																
Yes	44	8	47	-3	47	10	43	4	3	5,579	40	9	51	-11	-7	912
No	59	9	32	27	62	12	26	36	3	1,491	55	12	33	22	-7	243
Marital status																
Married	40	8	51	-11	45	10	45	0	5	9,643	42	8	50	-8	-3	4,899
Divorced/ separated	54	9	36	18	60	11	29	31	6	2,296	54	11	35	19	-6	1,153
Widowed	55	9	36	19	55	13	32	23	0	1,363	48	9	44	4	-7	744
Never married	59	9	32	27	61	11	28	33	2	2,002	58	9	33	25	-3	1,248
Living with partner	—	—	—	—	61	10	29	32	—	858	62	9	29	33	1	589
Parent or guardian																
Yes	44	8	48	-4	47	12	41	6	3	1,579	46	9	45	1	-1	1,502
No	49	9	42	7	53	13	35	18	4	3,855	48	9	43	5	-5	4,804
Total	47	9	44	3	51	11	38	13	4	17,543	48	9	43	5	-3	13,429

Note: "—" indicates not available. Percentages are from pooled surveys of 17,543 registered voters for 2004 and 2008 interviewed by the Pew Research Center from January through August of 2004 and 2008; for 2012, the percentages are from 13,429 registered voters interviewed from January through July of 2012. Not all characteristics were available in each of the pooled surveys, making sample sizes vary. A Democratic gain is not always matched precisely by a Republican loss, or vice versa. Related data for additional years can be found in previous editions of *Vital Statistics on American Politics*. For partisan identification question, see Figure 3-2, this volume. Percentages in the table count leaners as partisans.

[a] For composition of regions, see Table A-1, this volume.

Sources: 2004–2008: Pew Research Center for the People and the Press, "Convention Backgrounder: A Closer Look at the Parties in 2008," August 22, 2008, 5–6; 2012: "A Closer Look at the Parties in 2012," August 23, 2012, 6–7 (*http://peoplepress.org*).

Table 3-3 Liberal or Conservative Self-Identification, 1973–2014 (percent)

Year	Extremely liberal	Liberal	Slightly liberal	Moderate	Slightly conservative	Conservative	Extremely conservative	Don't know	Number of interviews
1973	4	14	13	36	13	13	3	6	1,484
1975	3	12	13	38	16	11	2	5	1,478
1978	2	9	16	37	18	13	2	4	1,509
1980	3	8	14	40	19	12	3	1	1,451
1983	2	8	12	40	18	13	2	3	802
1985	2	11	11	37	18	14	3	4	1,526
1986	2	9	11	39	17	15	3	4	1,468
1987	2	12	13	37	16	12	2	4	1,436
1988	2	12	12	35	17	16	2	4	1,472
1989	3	12	12	37	16	13	2	5	1,532
1990	3	10	13	34	18	14	4	4	1,369
1991	2	10	14	39	14	14	3	3	1,512
1993	2	12	13	35	17	16	3	3	1,598
1994	2	11	13	35	16	16	3	3	2,981
1996	2	10	12	36	16	16	3	5	2,898
1998	2	12	12	36	15	15	3	5	2,824
2000	4	11	10	38	14	15	3	5	2,797
2002	3	11	12	38	15	16	3	3	1,362
2004	3	9	12	37	16	17	4	2	1,325
2006	3	11	11	37	14	15	4	3	1,323
2008	3	12	11	37	14	16	4	4	2,010
2010	4	13	12	37	13	16	4	3	3,752
2012	4	12	11	36	14	15	3	4	1,961
2014	4	12	10	39	13	14	4	3	2,514

Note: General Social Survey interviews are conducted in the spring of the year indicated, usually March–June. Question: "We hear a lot of talk these days about liberals and conservatives. I'm going to show you a seven-point scale on which the political views that people might hold are arranged from extremely liberal—point 1—to extremely conservative—point 7. Where would you place yourself on this scale?" Data for additional years can be found in previous editions of *Vital Statistics on American Politics.*

Source: General Social Survey, National Opinion Research Center, University of Chicago.

116

Figure 3-3 Liberal, Moderate, and Conservative Self-Identification, 1973–2014

Percent

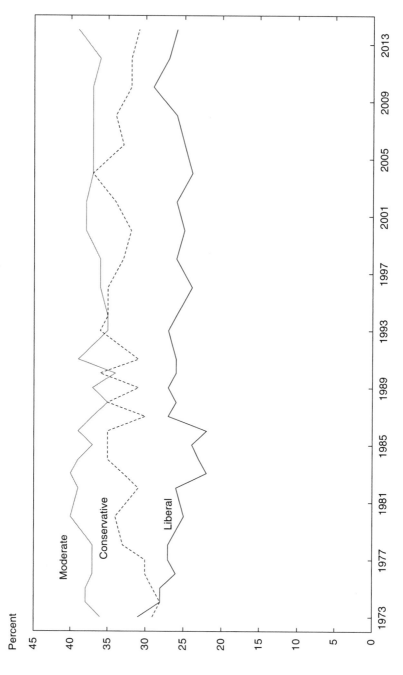

Note: See Table 3-3, this volume.

Source: Table 3-3, this volume.

Figure 3-4 Ideological Self-Identification of College Freshmen, 1970–2014

Percent

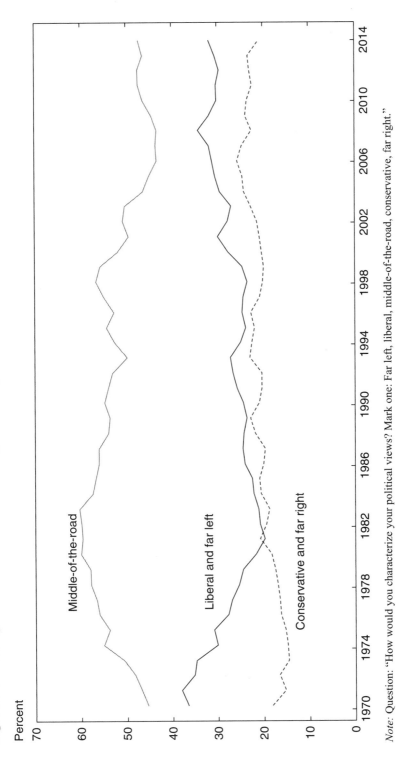

Note: Question: "How would you characterize your political views? Mark one: Far left, liberal, middle-of-the-road, conservative, far right."

Sources: Alexander Astin et al., *The American Freshman: Thirty Year Trends* (Los Angeles: Higher Education Research Institute, University of California, Los Angeles, 1997); *The American Freshman: National Norms for Fall 1997–* (Los Angeles: Higher Education Research Institute, University of California, Los Angeles, annual).

Table 3-4 Presidential Vote in General Elections, by Groups, Network Exit Polls, 1996–2012 (percent)

	Percentage of voters					1996			2000			2004		2008		2012	
	1996	2000	2004	2008	2012	D	R	I	D	R	I	D	R	D	R	D	R
Sex																	
Men	48	48	46	47	47	43	44	10	42	53	3	44	55	49	48	45	52
Women	52	52	54	53	53	54	38	7	54	43	2	51	48	56	43	55	44
Race/ethnicity																	
White	83	82	77	74	72	43	46	9	42	54	3	41	58	43	55	39	59
Black	10	10	11	13	13	84	12		90	8	1	88	11	95	4	93	6
Hispanic/Latino	5	4	8	9	10	72	21	6	67	31	2	53	44	67	31	71	27
Age																	
Younger than 30 years	17	17	17	18	19	53	34	10	48	46	5	54	45	66	32	60	37
30–44 years	33	33	29	29	27	48	41	9	48	49	2	46	53	52	46	52	45
45–59 years	26	28	30	37[a]	38[a]	48	41	9	48	49	2	48	51	50[a]	49[a]	47[a]	51[a]
60 years and older	24	22	24	16[b]	16[b]	48	44	7	51	47	2	46	54	45[b]	53[b]	44[b]	56[b]
Education																	
Not high school graduate	6	5	4	4	3	59	28	11	59	39	1	50	49	63	35	64	35
High school graduate	24	21	22	20	21	51	35	13	48	49	1	47	52	52	46	51	48
College incomplete	27	32	32	31	29	48	40	10	45	51	3	46	54	51	47	49	48
College graduate	43	24	42	45	47	47	44	7	48	48	3	49	49	53	45	50	48
Religion																	
White Protestant	34	47	41	42	39	38	53	8	34	63	2	32	67	34	65	30	69
White fundamentalist	24	14	23	26	26	26	65	8	18	80	2	21	78	24	74	21	78
Catholic	29	26	27	27	25	53	37	9	49	47	2	47	52	54	45	50	48
Jewish	3	4	3	2	2	78	16	3	79	19	1	74	25	78	21	69	30

Region																	
East	23	23	22	21[c]	—	55	34	9	56	39	3	56	43	59[c]	40[c]	—	—
Midwest	26	26	26	24	—	48	41	10	48	49	2	48	51	54	44	—	—
South	30	31	32	32	—	46	46	7	43	55	1	42	58	45	54	—	—
West	20	21	20	23	—	48	40	8	48	46	4	50	49	57	40	—	—
Union household	23	26	24	21	18	59	30	9	59	37	3	59	40	59	39	58	40
Family income																	
Under $15,000	11	7	8	6	—	59	28	11	57	37	4	63	36	73	25	—	—
$15,000–29,999	23	16	15	12	20[d]	53	36	9	54	41	3	57	42	60	37	63[d]	35[d]
$30,000–49,999	27	24	22	19	21	48	40	10	49	48	2	50	49	55	43	57	42
$50,000–74,999	21	25	23	21	31[e]	47	45	7	46	51	2	43	56	48	49	46[e]	52[e]
Over $75,000	18	28	32	41	28[f]	41	51	7	44	53	2	43	57	50	49	44[f]	54[f]
Party																	
Democratic	39	39	37	39	38	84	10	5	86	11	2	89	11	89	10	92	7
Independent	26	27	26	29	29	43	35	17	45	47	6	49	48	52	44	45	50
Republican	35	35	37	32	32	13	80	6	8	91	1	6	93	9	90	6	93
Ideology																	
Liberal	20	20	21	22	25	78	11	7	80	13	6	85	13	89	10	86	11
Moderate	47	50	45	44	41	57	33	9	52	44	2	54	45	60	39	56	41
Conservative	33	29	34	34	35	20	71	8	17	81	1	15	84	20	78	17	82
Previous presidential vote																	
Democratic	47	46	37	37	—	85	9	4	82	15	2	90	10	89	9	—	—
Independent/third party	14	6	3	4	—	22	44	33	27	64	7	71	21	66	24	—	—
Republican	38	31	43	46	—	13	82	4	7	91	1	9	91	17	82	—	—
Congressional vote																	
Democratic	49	49	49	54	50	84	8	7	85	11	3	88	11	88	10	93	6
Republican	49	49	50	44	48	15	76	8	12	86	1	9	91	9	89	7	92
First-time voter	9	9	11	11	—	54	34	11	52	43	4	53	46	69	30	—	—
Total	100	100	100	100	100	49	41	8	48	48	2	48	51	53	45	50	48

(Table continues)

Table 3-4 *(Continued)*

Note: "D" indicates Democrat; "R" indicates Republican; "I" indicates H. Ross Perot's candidacy in 1996 and Ralph Nader's in 2000; "—" indicates not available. Data based on questionnaires completed by voters leaving polling places around the nation on election day. Differing questions and question formats make comparability across elections of some of these groups problematic. For example, in some years the "white fundamentalist" category is "evangelicals," "born-again Christians," or members of the "religious right." See sources for details. The number of respondents in 1996 was 16,637; in 2000, 13,279; in 2004, 13,660; in 2008, 17,836; and in 2012, 26,565. Data for earlier years can be found in previous editions of *Vital Statistics on American Politics*.

[a] Age category is 45–64 years for 2008 and 2012.
[b] Age category is 65 years and older for 2008 and 2012.
[c] Region is "Northeast" for 2008.
[d] Income category is under $30,000 for 2012.
[e] Income category is $50,000–$99,999 for 2012.
[f] Income category is over $100,000 for 2012.

Sources: Percentages calculated by the editors from Voter News Service, General Election Exit Polls, National Files, 1996 and 2000; National Election Pool General Election Exit Polls, 2004, National Data; CNN Presidential Election National Exit Poll, 2008 (*www.cnn.com*); National Election Pool, National Exit Poll, 2012, as reported by Fox News (*www.foxnews.com*); some data obtained through the Inter-university Consortium for Political and Social Research (*www.icpsr.umich.edu*). Neither the collectors of the original data nor the consortium bear any responsibility for the results presented here.

Figure 3-5 Presidential Preferences during 2012

Percent

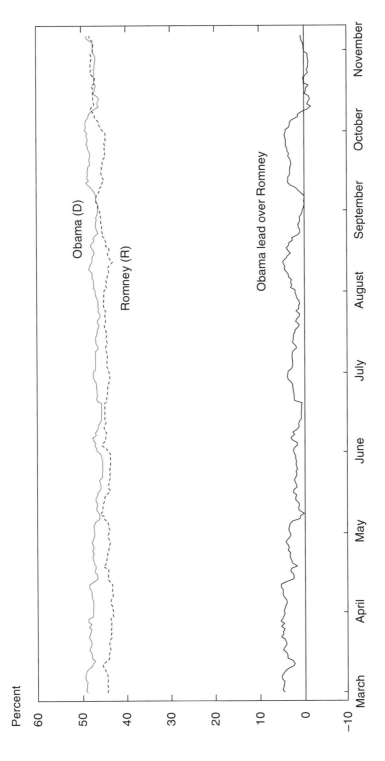

Note: Figure shows five-day moving average from national polls gauging support for Pres. Barack Obama and Gov. Mitt Romney for president.

Source: Real Clear Politics (*www.realclearpolitics.com*).

Table 3-5 Vote in Democratic Presidential Primaries, by Groups, 1988–2008 (percent)

Group	Percentage of primary voters 1988	1992	2000	2004	2008	1988 Dukakis	Jackson	Others	1992 Clinton	Brown	Tsongas	2000 Bradley	Gore	2004 Edwards	Kerry	Others	2008 Clinton	Obama
Sex																		
Men	47	47	43	46	43	41	29	30	50	21	20	27	71	25	54	21	43	50
Women	53	53	57	54	57	43	30	26	51	20	21	22	76	26	55	20	52	43
Race/ethnicity																		
White	75	80	69	73	65	54	12	35	47	23	25	29	69	28	53	19	55	39
Black	21	14	17	16	19	4	92	4	70	15	8	12	86	19	56	25	15	82
Hispanic	3	4	10	8	12	48	30	20	51	30	15	11	89	13	70	17	61	35
Age																		
Younger than 30 years	14	12	9	10	14	35	38	27	47	24	19	26	72	25	48	27	38	58
30–44 years	31	33	26	23	—	37	36	26	45	26	22	24	74	25	52	23	—	—
45–59 years	25	25	31	34	—	42	30	28	51	19	20	27	71	27	56	18	—	—
60 years and older	30	30	33	33	18[a]	53	19	29	59	15	18	21	77	25	63	12	59[a]	34[a]
Religion																		
Catholic	30	50	29	29	—	60	18	22	55	14	21	26	72	23	61	16	—	—
White Protestant	36	30	49	—	—	43	10	47	44	24	24	26	71	—	—	—	—	—
Jewish	7	6	8	5	—	75	8	17	75	15	33	31	68	17	70	13	—	—
Party																		
Democratic	72	67	84	73	76	43	33	24	57	19	17	21	77	23	60	17	51	45
Independent	20	29	14	22	19	44	20	34	36	25	27	42	55	31	42	28	40	52
Ideology																		
Liberal	27	35	47	46	47	41	41	19	47	26	20	21	72	22	58	20	47	48
Moderate	47	45	41	39	40	47	25	28	54	18	19	22	77	28	54	18	50	45

Conservative	22	20	12	15	13	38	23	38	48	17	23	27	68	30	43	26	47	44
Union household	—	—	28	32	—	—	—	—	—	—	—	22	75	23	58	19	—	—
Total	100	100	100	100	—	43	29	28	50	21	20	24	74	25	54	21	—	—

Note: "—" indicates not available. Entries are derived from exit poll data in thirty-three contested delegate selection primaries in 1988, twenty-nine in 1992, twenty in 2000, and eighteen in 2004; for 2008, exit poll data include thirty-six contested delegate selection primaries and three caucuses (Iowa, Nevada, and New Mexico). No exit poll in Montana, Oregon, and District of Columbia in 1988; in Arizona, Michigan, Utah, and Washington State in 2000; in Michigan, New Mexico, and Utah in 2004; and in Idaho, Nebraska, Puerto Rico, District of Columbia, and Washington State in 2008. In 2012 President Obama was uncontested for renomination.

[a] Age 65 years and older for 2008.

Sources: Percentages calculated by the editors from CBS News/*New York Times* Primary Election Day Exit Polls, 1988; Voter Research and Surveys, Presidential Primary Exit Polls, 1992; Voter News Service, Presidential Primary Exit Polls, 2000; Edison Media Research, Mitofsky International, National Election Pool Democratic Presidential Preference Primary Exit Polls, 2004; and ABC News Presidential Primary Exit Polls (*http://abcnews.go.com*), 2008; obtained through the Inter-university Consortium for Political and Social Research (*www.icpsr.org*). Neither the collectors of the original data nor the consortium bear any responsibility for the results presented here.

Table 3-6 Vote in Republican Presidential Primaries, by Groups, 2000, 2008, and 2012 (percent)

Group	Percentage of voters 2000	2008	2012	2000 G. W. Bush	McCain	2008 Huckabee	McCain	Romney	2012 Gingrich	Paul	Romney	Santorum
Sex												
Men	51	54	52	55	38	21	43	25	22	12	38	26
Women	49	46	48	60	35	24	41	25	20	8	41	29
Race/ethnicity												
White	—	89	93	—	—	22	42	25	21	10	40	28
Black	—	2	1	—	—	27	42	17	—	—	—	—
Hispanic	—	6	—a	—	—	19	46	19	25	5	46	10
Age												
Younger than 30 years	10	11	9	56	34	29	34	21	13	27	30	28
30–44 years	26	—	18	59	33	—	—	—	18	15	34	31
45–64 years	31b	—	46	55b	39b	—	—	—	21	8	40	29
65 years and older	34b	23	27	60b	37b	16	48	26	25	5	46	22
Party												
Democrat	6	3	5	18	77	22	48	16	6	17	22	46
Independent	25	21	26	38	55	19	42	20	16	20	36	25
Republican	70	76	70	67	27	23	42	26	23	6	42	28
Ideology												
Liberal	11	9	—	40	54	15	55	16	—	—	22	46
Moderate	33	27	33c	46	50	14	55	18	15c	16c	44c	21c
Conservative	55	63	67	68	25	27	35	29	23	7	38	30
Evangelical or member of religious right												
No	72	56	48	52	43	10	49	28	15	13	49	20
Yes	23	44	52	74	17	39	33	20	26	8	31	34
Time of vote decision												
In last three days	18	25	—d	48	42	24	39	27	—d	—d	—d	—d

Within last week	17	—	—[d]	49	44	—	—	—	—[d]	—[d]	—[d]	—[d]
Earlier this year	48	—	—[d]	50	46	—	—	—	—[d]	—[d]	—[d]	—[d]
Last year	18	—	—[d]	69	26	—	—	—	—[d]	—[d]	—[d]	—[d]
Military veteran												
Yes	—	22	—	—	—	19	47	25	—	—	—	25
No	—	78	—	—	—	23	41	25	—	—	—	25
Percentage of total vote	100	100	100	58	36	22	42	25	21	10	40	27

Note: "—" indicates not available. The small percentage of votes going to other candidates is not shown. For 2000, based on combined vote totals and results from exit polls conducted by Voter News Service in twenty-five primary states between February 1 and March 14. Some questions were not asked in each state. There was no exit poll in Washington State. There were no exit polls for the 2004 primaries when President Bush was uncontested for renomination. For 2008, based on combined vote totals and results from exit polls conducted by Edison Media Research/Mitofsky International in twenty-seven primaries and two caucuses (Iowa and Nevada) between January 8 and March 11. There were no exit polls for primaries held in Rhode Island, the District of Columbia, and Washington State. For 2012, based on combined vote totals and results from exit polls conducted by Edison Research for the National Election Pool in eighteen primaries and two caucuses (Iowa and Nevada) held between January 3 and April 3. There were no exit polls for primaries held in Missouri and the District of Columbia.

[a] Exit polls surveyed Hispanic participation and preferences in twelve states in 2008 but in only four states—Arizona, Florida, Michigan, and Nevada—in 2012.
[b] The two oldest age categories in 2000 are 45 to 59 and 60 years and older.
[c] In 2012 moderate and liberal responses are combined.
[d] Time of vote decision was asked, but variation in responses precluded summarizing across eighteen primaries and two caucuses.

Sources: Calculated by the editors from data in previous editions of *Vital Statistics on American Politics* and exit poll data as reported by CNN (*www.cnn.com*), ABC News (*http://abcnews.go.com*), and MSNBC (*www.nbcnews.com*).

Table 3-7 Strength of Party Identification and the Presidential Vote, 1952–2012 (percent)

Year/candidate	Strong Democrat	Weak Democrat	Independent Democrat	Independent	Independent Republican	Weak Republican	Strong Republican	Total
1952								
Stevenson (D)	84	62	61	20	7	6	2	42
Eisenhower (R)	16	38	39	80	93	94	98	58
1956								
Stevenson (D)	85	63	67	17	6	7	0	40
Eisenhower (R)	15	37	33	83	94	93	100	60
1960								
Kennedy (D)	91	72	90	46	12	13	2	49
Nixon (R)	9	28	10	54	88	87	98	51
1964								
L. Johnson (D)	95	82	90	77	25	43	10	68
Goldwater (R)	5	18	10	23	75	57	90	32
1968								
Humphrey (D)	92	68	64	30	5	11	3	46
Nixon (R)	8	32	36	70	95	89	97	54
1972								
McGovern (D)	73	48	61	30	13	9	3	36
Nixon (R)	27	52	39	70	87	91	97	64
1976								
Carter (D)	92	75	76	44	14	22	3	51
Ford (R)	8	25	24	56	86	78	97	49
1980								
Carter (D)	89	65	60	26	13	5	5	44
Reagan (R)	11	35	40	74	87	95	95	56
1984								
Mondale (D)	89	68	79	28	7	6	3	42
Reagan (R)	11	32	21	72	93	94	97	58

1988								
Dukakis (D)	94	72	88	35	15	17	2	47
G. H. W. Bush (R)	6	28	12	65	85	83	98	53
1992								
Clinton (D)	97	84	92	65	15	20	2	58
G. H. W. Bush (R)	3	16	8	35	85	80	98	42
1996								
Clinton (D)	98	91	93	49	23	23	5	58
Dole (R)	2	9	7	51	77	77	95	42
2000								
Gore (D)	97	85	78	45	14	16	2	52
G. W. Bush (R)	3	15	22	55	86	84	98	48
2004								
Kerry (D)	98	85	88	58	15	11	3	50
G. W. Bush (R)	2	15	12	42	85	89	97	50
2008								
Obama (D)	95	86	91	57	18	12	4	55
McCain (R)	5	14	9	43	82	88	96	45
2012								
Obama (D)	99	85	91	54	9	12	3	54
Romney (R)	1	15	9	46	91	88	97	46

Note: "D" indicates Democrat; "R" indicates Republican. Results are from surveys in which voters are asked with which party they identify and for whom they voted. For the party identification questions, see Table 3-1, this volume. Votes for candidates other than Democratic or Republican were excluded.

Source: Calculated by the editors from American National Election Studies data, University of Michigan, Ann Arbor, MI, and Stanford University, Palo Alto, CA (*www.electionstudies.org*).

Table 3-8 Congressional Vote in General Elections, by Groups, 2004–2014 (percent)

	Percentage of voters						2004		2006		2008		2010		2012		2014	
Group	2004	2006	2008	2010	2012	2014	D	R	D	R	D	R	D	R	D	R	D	R
Sex																		
Men	46	49	47	48	47	49	45	53	50	47	52	46	41	55	45	53	42	56
Women	54	51	53	52	53	51	52	46	55	43	56	42	48	49	55	44	52	47
Race/ethnicity																		
White	77	79	74	77	72	75	42	57	47	51	45	53	37	60	39	59	38	60
Black	12	10	13	11	13	12	89	10	89	10	93	5	89	9	91	8	89	10
Hispanic/Latino	8	8	8	8	10	8	55	44	69	30	68	29	60	38	68	30	63	35
Asian	2	2	2	2	3	3	56	41	62	37	63	31	58	40	73	25	50	49
Age																		
Younger than 30 years	16	12	18	12	19	13	55	44	60	38	63	34	55	42	60	38	54	43
30–44 years	29	24	29	24	26	22	47	51	53	45	53	44	46	50	51	46	50	48
45–64 years	30[a]	34[a]	38	43	38	43	49[a]	49[a]	53[a]	46[a]	51	46	45	53	47	51	45	53
65 years and older	25[b]	29[b]	15	21	17	22	46[b]	53[b]	50[b]	48[b]	49	48	38	59	44	55	42	57
Education																		
Not a high school graduate	4	3	4	3	3	2	49	48	64	35	67	30	57	36	62	35	54	44
High school graduate	22	21	21	17	21	18	49	50	55	44	55	43	46	52	52	46	46	53
College incomplete	32	31	31	28	29	29	47	51	51	47	53	45	43	53	48	50	45	53
College graduate	43	45	45	51	47	50	49	49	53	46	52	45	45	53	49	49	48	50
Region																		
East	22	22	23[c]	21[c]	—	21	57	40	63	35	61[c]	38[c]	54[c]	44[c]	—	—	55	43
Midwest	26	27	25	25	—	24	49	50	52	47	53	45	44	53	—	—	45	53
South	32	30	34	31	—	33	43	56	45	53	48	50	37	61	—	—	39	58
West	20	21	18	23	—	22	48	50	54	43	58	39	49	48	—	—	51	47

Religion																		
White Protestant	41	44	42	44	39	39	34	65	37	61	35	63	28	69	29	70	27	71
White fundamentalist	23	24	26	25	26	26	25	74	28	70	28	70	19	77	20	78	21	78
Catholic	27	26	26	23	25	24	49	50	55	44	55	42	44	54	50	49	45	53
Jewish	3	2	2	2	2	3	76	22	87	12	81	19	—	—	69	29	65	33
Union household	24	23	21	17	18	17	61	37	64	34	64	34	61	37	56	43	59	38
Family income																		
Less than $15,000	8	7	6	—	—	—	64	34	67	30	74	25	57[d]	40[d]	63[d]	35[d]	59[d]	39[d]
$15,000–29,999	15	12	12	17[d]	20[d]	16[d]	58	39	61	36	63	35	51	46	56	42	51	47
$30,000–49,999	22	21	19	19	21	20	51	47	56	43	57	40	45	40	46	52	44	54
$50,000–74,999	23	22	21	21	31[e]	34[e]	44	54	50	48	51	46	45	51	52[e]	56	44	54[e]
More than $75,000	33	39	41	42	28[f]	30[f]	43	56	49	50	49	49	41	58	42[f]	56[f]	42[f]	57[f]
Party																		
Democratic	38	38	40	35	39	36	90	9	93	7	92	7	94	7	94	6	92	7
Independent	25	26	28	29	28	28	49	46	57	39	51	43	37	56	44	51	42	54
Republican	38	36	33	35	33	36	7	93	8	91	9	89	5	94	5	94	5	94
Ideology																		
Liberal	21	20	22	20	25	23	83	14	87	11	87	11	90	8	86	12	87	11
Moderate	45	47	44	38	40	40	56	43	60	38	61	37	55	42	57	41	53	44
Conservative	34	32	34	42	35	37	17	81	20	78	23	75	13	84	16	82	13	85
Previous presidential vote																		
Democratic	37	43	45	45	—	—	86	12	92	7	88	8	84	14	86	12	92	—
Independent/third party	3	4	4	4	—	—	70	19	66	23	63	28	33	58	57	51	42	—
Republican	43	49	46	45	—	—	13	86	15	83	19	80	7	91	12	87	—	—
First-time voter	11	—	3	3	—	—	53	46	—	—	63	35	45	43	41	53	—	51
Total	100	100	100	100	100	100	49	50	53	45	54	44	52	45	52	50	48	51

(Table continues)

Table 3-8 *(Continued)*

Note: "D" indicates Democrat; "R" indicates Republican; "__" indicates not available. Percentages based on Democratic, Republican, and other (not shown) votes. Data based on questionnaires completed by voters leaving polling places around the nation on election day. Differing questions and question formats make comparability across elections of some of these groups problematic. For example, in some years the "white fundamentalist" category is "evangelicals," "born-again Christians," or members of the "religious right." See sources for details. The number of respondents in 2004 was 12,649; in 2006, 13,251; in 2008, 16,521; in 2010, 17,504; in 2012, 25,058; and in 2014, 19,436. Data for earlier years can be found in previous editions of *Vital Statistics on American Politics*.

[a] Age category is 45–59 years for 2004 and 2006.
[b] Age category is 60 years and older for 2004 and 2006.
[c] Region is "Northeast" for 2008 and 2010.
[d] Income category is less than $30,000 for 2010–2014.
[e] Income category is $50,000–$99,999 for 2012 and 2014.
[f] Income category is more than $100,000 for 2012 and 2014.

Sources: Percentages calculated by the editors from Voter News Service, General Election Exit Polls, National Files, 2004 and 2006, obtained through the Inter-university Consortium for Political and Social Research (*www.icpsr.umich.edu*); CNN U.S. House National Exit Poll, 2008 and 2010 (*www.cnn.com*); National Election Pool, House National Exit Poll, 2012 and 2014, as reported by Fox News (*www.foxnews.com*). Neither the collectors of the original data nor the consortium bears any responsibility for the results presented here.

Table 3-9 Party-Line Voting in Presidential and Congressional Elections, 1952–2012 (percent)

Year	Presidential elections			U.S. Senate elections			U.S. House elections		
	Party-line voters[a]	Defectors[b]	Independents	Party-line voters[a]	Defectors[b]	Independents	Party-line voters[a]	Defectors[b]	Independents
1952	77	18	5	79	16	5	80	15	5
1956	76	15	9	80	12	8	82	9	9
1960	79	13	8	79	12	9	80	11	8
1964	79	15	5	78	16	6	79	15	5
1968	69	24	7	73	20	7	74	19	7
1972	67	25	8	69	22	9	74	17	8
1976	73	16	11	69	19	12	72	19	9
1980	68	24	8	71	21	8	69	23	8
1984	79	13	8	72	20	9	70	23	7
1988	81	12	7	72	20	7	74	19	7
1992	68	24	9	74	20	7	71	21	7
1996	78	16	5	77	16	7	77	17	5
2000	79	12	8	79	13	7	76	17	7
2004	85	10	5	81	14	5	79	15	6
2008	84	9	7	81	12	7	80	13	6
2012	83	8	9	82	9	9	82	8	8

Note: "—" indicates not available. In presidential elections, the base for percentages is all voters. In Senate and House elections, the base for percentages is all voters supporting Democratic or Republican candidates. Data for additional years may be found in previous editions of *Vital Statistics on American Politics*.

[a] Democratic or Republican identifiers who vote for the candidate of their party. Party identification is based on surveys in which voters are asked with which party they identify. See Table 3-1, this volume, for question. "Independent partisans," or "leaners," are included here as party-line voters or defectors.

[b] Democratic or Republican identifiers who do not vote for the candidate of their party.

Source: Calculated by the editors from American National Election Studies data, University of Michigan, Ann Arbor, MI, and Stanford University, Palo Alto, CA (*www.electionstudies.org*).

131

Table 3-10   Split-Ticket Voting, 1952–2012 (percent)

Year	President–House	Senate–House	State–local
1952	13	9	26
1956	16	10	29
1958		10	31
1960	14	9	27
1962		—	42
1964	14	18	41
1966		21	50
1968	17	21	47
1970		20	51
1972	30	22	58
1974		24	61
1976	25	23	—
1978		35	—
1980	28	31	59
1982		24	55
1984	25	20	52
1986		28	—
1988	25	27	—
1990		25	—
1992	22	25	—
1994		24	—
1996	18	19	—
1998		23	—
2000	19	18	—
2002		21	—
2004	17	16	—
2008	17	16	—
2012	14	14	—

Note: "—" indicates not available. Entries are the percentages of voters who "split" their ticket by supporting candidates of different parties for the offices indicated. Those who cast ballots for other than Democratic and Republican candidates are excluded in presidential and congressional calculations. The state–local figure is based on a general question: "Did you vote for other state and local offices? Did you vote a straight ticket or did you vote for candidates from different parties?" There was no update of the American National Election Studies series in 2006, 2010, and 2014.

Source: Calculated by the editors from American National Election Studies data, University of Michigan, Ann Arbor, MI, and Stanford University, Palo Alto, CA (*www.electionstudies.org*).

Figure 3-6 Presidential Approval, 1993–2015

Percent

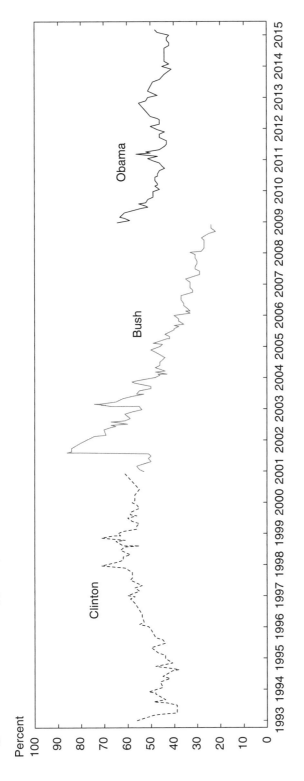

Note: Data for 2015 are through February. Question: "Do you approve or disapprove of the way _____ (Bill Clinton/George W. Bush/Barack Obama) is handling his job as president?" Related data for additional years can be found in previous editions of *Vital Statistics on American Politics.*

Sources: Clinton: Pew Research Center for the People and the Press, "It's the Economy Again!: Clinton Nostalgia Sets in, Bush Reaction Mixed," January 11, 2001, 27–28; Bush: "Reviewing the Bush Years and the Public's Final Verdict: Bush and Public Opinion," December 18, 2008, 24–25; Obama: "Democrats Have More Positive Image, but GOP Runs Even or Ahead on Key Issues," February 26, 2015, 15 *(http://people-press.org).*

Figure 3-7   Rating of Congress, 1985–2014

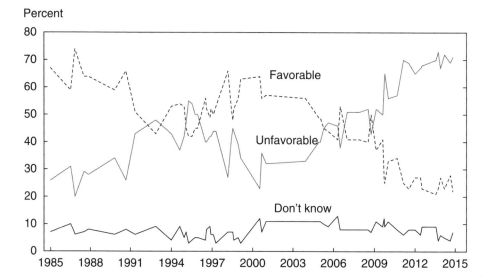

Note: Data for 2014 are through December. Question: "Is your overall opinion of Congress very favorable, mostly favorable, mostly unfavorable, or very unfavorable?" Related data for additional years can be found in previous editions of *Vital Statistics on American Politics.*

Source: Pew Research Center for the People and the Press, "Few See Quick Cure for Nation's Political Divisions," December 11, 2014, 24, 26–27 *(http://people-press.org).*

Figure 3-8   Individual Confidence in Government, 1952–2012

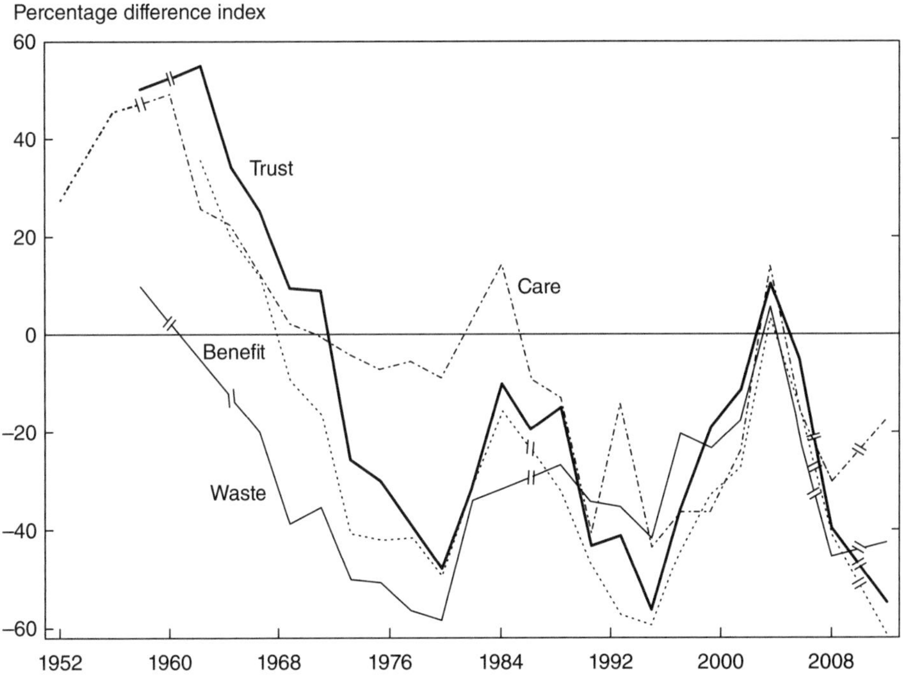

Note: Broken line indicates question not asked that year in the biennial American National Election Studies. Questions: (Care) "I don't think public officials care much about what people like me think." (Trust) "How much of the time do you think you can trust the government in Washington to do what is right—just about always, most of the time, or only some of the time?" (Benefit) "Would you say the government is pretty much run by a few big interests looking out for themselves or that it is run for the benefit of all people?" (Waste) "Do you think that people in the government waste a lot of money we pay in taxes, waste some of it, or don't waste very much of it?" The percentage difference index is calculated by subtracting the percentage giving a nontrusting response from the percentage giving a trusting response. There was no update of the American National Election Studies series in 2006, 2010, and 2014.

Source: American National Election Studies, University of Michigan, Ann Arbor, MI, and Stanford University, Palo Alto, CA (*www.electionstudies.org*).

136

Figure 3-9 Satisfaction with "The Way Things Are Going," 1988–2015

Percent

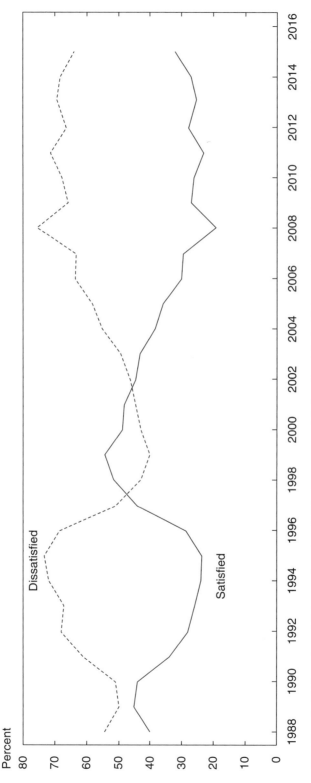

Note: Data for 2015 are through February. Question: "All in all, are you satisfied or dissatisfied with the way things are going in this country today?" Related data for additional years can be found in previous editions of *Vital Statistics on American Politics.*

Sources: Pew Research Center for the People and the Press, "Independents Take Center Stage in Obama Era," May 21, 2009, 118; "Democrats Have More Positive Image, But GOP Runs Even or Ahead on Key Issues," February 26, 2015, 16–17 (*http://people-press.org*).

Figure 3-10 Consumer Confidence, 1960–2014

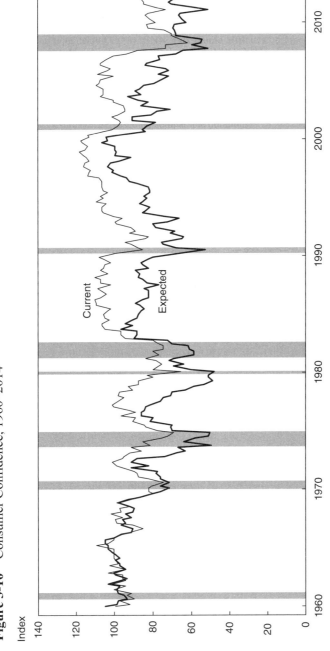

(Figure continues)

138

Figure 3-10 *(Continued)*

Note: Shaded areas indicate periods of economic recession, as determined by the National Bureau of Economic Research (*www.nber.org*). The curves reflect data from surveys conducted quarterly from 1960 through 1977, and monthly since 1978 (though aggregated by quarter). "Current" indicates the Index of Current Economic Conditions (ICC) and "Expected" the Index of Consumer Expectations (ICE).

The current index includes the following survey questions: (X1) "We are interested in how people are getting along financially these days. Would you say that you (and your family living there) are better off or worse off financially than you were a year ago?" (X5) "About the big things people buy for their homes—such as furniture, a refrigerator, stove, television, and things like that. Generally speaking, do you think now is a good or a bad time for people to buy major household items?"

The expected index includes the following survey questions: (X2) "Now looking ahead—do you think that a year from now you (and your family living there) will be better off financially, or worse off, or just about the same as now?" (X3) "Now turning to business conditions in the country as a whole—do you think that during the next twelve months we'll have good times financially, or bad times, or what?" (X4) "Looking ahead, which would you say is more likely—that in the country as a whole we'll have continuous good times during the next five years or so, or that we will have periods of widespread unemployment or depression?"

As a first step in calculating each index, a relative score is calculated from the percent giving favorable replies minus the percent giving unfavorable replies, plus 100 percent, for each question used. Each relative score is rounded to the nearest whole number. Using the following equation for each index, the relative scores of the appropriate survey questions are summed, divided by the 1966 base period constant for the index, and 2 is added (a constant to correct for sample design changes from the 1950s).

$$ICC = ((X1 + X5) / 2.6424) + 2.0$$

$$ICE = ((X2 + X3 + X4) / 4.1134) + 2.0$$

The Index of Consumer Sentiment is a weighted average of the current and expected indexes.

Sources: "Surveys of Consumers," Reuters/University of Michigan (*www.sca.isr.umich.edu*); recession periods determined by the National Bureau of Economic Research (*www.nber.org*). Reprinted with permission.

Figure 3-11   The Most Important Problem: Foreign Affairs, 1987–2014

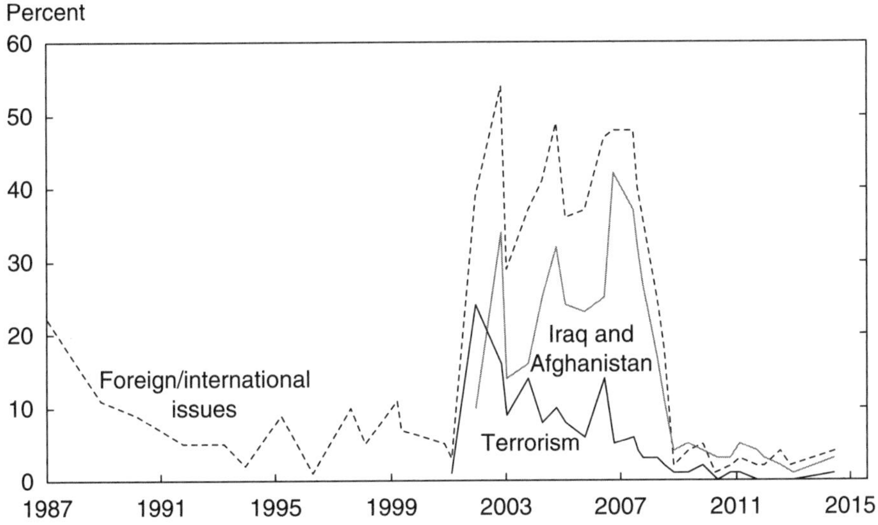

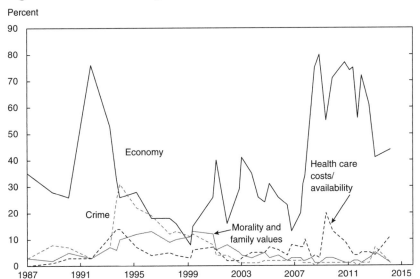

Note: Question: "What do you think is the most important problem facing the country today?" Verbatim responses recorded. Multiple responses allowed. Iraq/Afghanistan mentions are also included in foreign/international issues.

Source: Pew Research Center for the People and the Press *(http://people-press.org).*

Figure 3-12   The Most Important Problem: Domestic Issues, 1987–2014

Note: See Figure 3-11, this volume, for question.

Source: Pew Research Center for the People and the Press *(http://people-press.org).*

Figure 3-13 Favorable Opinions of the Democratic and Republican Parties, 1992–2015

Percent

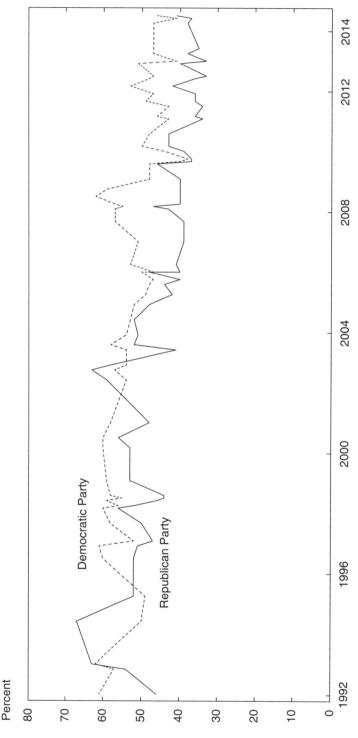

Note: Shown is the percentage "very" or "mostly" favorable to the question "I'd like to get your opinion of some groups and organizations in the news. Is your overall opinion of the [Democratic] [Republican] Party very favorable, mostly favorable, mostly unfavorable, or very unfavorable?" Typically, 5 to 10 percent of the respondents volunteer that they cannot rate the parties.

Source: Pew Research Center for the People and the Press (*http://people-press.org*).

Figure 3-14   Condition of Nation's Economy and Citizens' Personal Financial
Situations over the Last Year, 1980–2012 (percent)

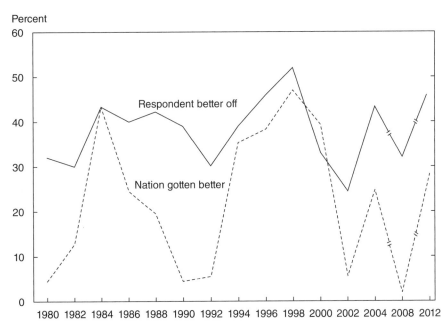

Note: Broken line indicates question not asked that year in the biennial American National Election Studies. Questions: Nation's economy: "How about (1996–later: Now thinking about) the economy (1990, 1994–later: in the country as a whole)?" All years except 2000: "Would you say that over the past year the nation's economy has gotten better, stayed (all years except 1984: about) the same, or gotten worse?" (2000:) "Would you say that over the past year the nation's economy has gotten worse, stayed about the same, or gotten better?"; personal financial situation: 1962–1998, 2004–2008: "We are interested in how people are getting along financially these days. Would you say that (1962, 1966–1974: you [and your family]; 1976 and later: you [and your family living here]) are better off or worse off financially than you were a year ago?"; 2000–2002: "We are interested in how people are getting along financially these days. Would you say that you (and your family [2000 face-to-face only: living here]) are better off, worse off, or just about the same financially as you were a year ago?": There was no update of the American National Election Studies series in 2006, 2010, and 2014.

Source: Calculated by the editors from American National Election Studies data, University of Michigan, Ann Arbor, MI, and Stanford University, Palo Alto, CA (*www.electionstudies.org*).

Table 3-11   Public Opinion on Civil Liberties, 1940–2014 (percent)

Issue/year		Allow[a]	Don't forbid[b]
Public speeches against democracy			
1940		25	46
1974		56	72
1976		55	80
1976		52	79

Issue/year	Allow to speak	Allow to teach college	Keep book in library
Atheist[c]			
1954	37	12	35
1964[d]	—	—	61
1972	66	41	61
1973[a]	66	42	62
1973[b]	62	39	57
1974	62	42	60
1976	65	42	60
1977	63	40	59
1978	63	—	60
1980	66	46	62
1982	65	46	61
1985	65	46	61
1987	70	47	67
1988	70	46	64
1989	72	52	68
1990	73	51	67
1991	73	51	68
1993	71	53	68
1994	73	53	70
1996	74	56	68
1998	75	58	70
2000	75	57	68
2002	77	60	72
2004	76	64	72
2006	77	60	71
2008	76	61	71
2010	76	60	73
2012	77	63	75
2014	79	66	77
Admitted communist[c]			
1954	27	6	27
1972	53	33	53
1973[a]	61	40	59
1973[b]	53	30	54
1974	58	42	59
1976	55	42	57
1977	56	39	56
1978	60	—	61
1982	56	43	57

Table 3-11   *(Continued)*

Issue/year	Allow to speak	Allow to teach college	Keep book in library
1985	58	46	58
1987	60	46	62
1988	61	48	60
1989	65	51	63
1990	65	53	64
1991	68	54	67
1993	70	57	68
1994	67	55	67
1996	64	58	65
1998	67	57	67
2000	66	57	66
2002	69	59	69
2004	69	63	70
2006	67	60	68
2008	65	58	67
2010	64	61	69
2012	66	62	73
2014	68	63	71
Racist[c]			
1943[e]	17	—	—
1976	61	41	60
1977	59	41	62
1978	62	—	64
1980	62	42	64
1982	59	43	60
1985	56	42	60
1987	60	43	64
1988	61	41	61
1989	62	46	65
1990	64	45	65
1991	62	41	65
1993	61	45	65
1994	62	43	66
1996	61	46	64
1998	62	47	63
2000	60	46	63
2002	62	52	65
2004	62	46	65
2006	61	46	64
2008	59	45	63
2010	56	47	65
2012	59	47	64
2014	60	47	63
Admitted homosexual[c]			
1973	61	48	54
1974	63	51	56

(Table continues)

Table 3-11   *(Continued)*

Issue/year	Allow to speak	Allow to teach college	Keep book in library
1976	63	53	56
1977	62	50	55
1980	66	55	58
1982	65	55	56
1985	67	58	56
1987	68	57	58
1988	70	57	61
1989	77	64	66
1990	75	65	65
1991	77	63	69
1993	79	69	67
1994	80	71	69
1996	81	75	69
1998	81	75	70
2000	81	76	71
2002	83	78	75
2004	83	79	73
2006	82	78	74
2008	82	79	76
2010	86	84	78
2012	86	83	77
2014	89	87	80

Note: "—" indicates not available.

[a] Question: "Do you think the United States should allow public speeches against democracy?"
[b] Question: "Do you think the United States should forbid public speeches against democracy?"
[c] Question: "There are always some people whose ideas are considered bad or dangerous by other people. For instance, somebody who (is against all churches and religion/admits he is a communist/believes that blacks are genetically inferior/admits that he is a homosexual). If such a person wanted to make a speech in your (city/town/community), should he be allowed to speak or not? Should such a person be allowed to teach in a college or university or not? If some people in your community suggested that a book he wrote (against churches and religion/promoting communism/which said blacks are inferior/in favor of homosexuality) should be taken out of your public library, would you favor removing this book or not?" (Slight variations in wording across groups.) A "don't know" response is considered a "no."
[d] In 1964 the question was as follows: "Suppose a man admitted in public that he did not believe in God. Do you think a book he wrote should be removed from a public library?"
[e] In 1943 the question was as follows: "In peacetime, do you think anyone in the United States should be allowed to make speeches against certain races in this country?"

Sources: Public speeches against democracy: Howard Schuman and Stanley Presser, *Questions and Answers in Attitude Surveys* (New York: Academic Press, 1981), 277; Atheist: 1943, 1964, and 1973a: National Opinion Research Center surveys; 1954: Samuel A. Stouffer, *Communism, Conformity, and Civil Liberties* (Garden City, N.Y.: Doubleday, 1955), 32–34, 40–43; 1973b: Clyde Z. Nunn et al., *Tolerance for Nonconformity* (San Francisco: Jossey-Bass, 1978), 40–43; data for all other years from General Social Survey, National Opinion Research Center, University of Chicago.

Table 3-12   Public Opinion on the Death Penalty, 1972–2014 (percent)

Year	Favor	Oppose	Don't know
1972	53	39	8
1973	60	35	5
1974	63	32	5
1975	60	33	7
1976	66	29	5
1977	68	26	6
1978	67	28	5
1980	68	27	5
1982	74	21	5
1983	74	21	5
1984	72	23	5
1985	75	20	5
1986	72	23	5
1987	69	25	6
1988	71	22	7
1989	74	21	5
1990	75	20	6
1991	72	22	6
1993	72	21	7
1994	75	19	6
1996	72	21	7
1998	68	25	7
2000	64	28	8
2002	67	29	4
2004	65	30	5
2006	64	30	5
2008	64	31	5
2010	65	30	5
2012	61	33	7
2014	61	34	6

Note: General Social Survey interviews are conducted in the spring of the year indicated, usually March–June. Question: "Do you favor or oppose the death penalty for persons [or: "people"] convicted of murder?" Data for additional years can be found in previous editions of *Vital Statistics on American Politics.*

Source: General Social Survey, National Opinion Research Center, University of Chicago.

Table 3-13   Public Opinion on Abortion, 1965–2014 (percent)

Year	Mother's health	Rape	Birth defect	Low income	Single mother	As form of birth control	Any reason
	Abortion should be legal under these circumstances						
1965	70	56	55	21	17	15	—
1972	84	75	75	46	41	38	—
1973	90	81	82	52	47	47	—
1974	91	83	82	52	48	45	—
1975	88	80	80	50	46	43	—
1976	89	81	82	51	48	45	—
1977	89	81	83	51	47	44	36
1978	88	80	80	45	39	38	32
1980	88	80	81	50	46	45	39
1982	90	84	82	49	45	46	38
1983	87	78	76	41	36	37	32
1984	88	76	78	45	42	41	37
1985	88	78	77	42	40	39	36
1987	86	77	76	43	40	40	37
1988	86	77	76	40	38	39	35
1989	88	80	79	46	43	43	39
1990	90	81	78	45	43	43	42
1991	88	83	80	46	43	42	41
1993	86	79	77	47	45	44	42
1994	88	81	79	48	46	46	45
1996	88	80	78	44	43	44	42
1998	84	76	74	41	39	39	38
2000	85	76	75	39	36	38	37
2002	89	76	75	42	39	41	40
2004	83	73	69	39	40	39	38
2006	84	73	70	40	37	40	38
2008	85	72	70	41	40	43	40
2010	84	77	72	44	41	47	41
2012	84	73	72	43	41	45	43
2014	86	75	73	44	42	46	44

Note: "—" indicates not available. Question: "Please tell me whether or not you think it should be possible for a pregnant woman to obtain a legal abortion [in the order asked in the survey] if there is a strong chance of serious defect in the baby? If she is married and does not want any more children? If the woman's own health is seriously endangered by the pregnancy? If the family has a very low income and cannot afford any more children? If she became pregnant as a result of rape? If she is not married and does not want to marry the man? The woman wants it for any reason?" A "don't know" response is considered a "no." Data for additional years can be found in previous editions of *Vital Statistics on American Politics.*

Sources: 1965: National Opinion Research Center surveys; 1972–2014: General Social Survey, National Opinion Research Center, University of Chicago.

Figure 3-15   Public Opinion on Interracial Dating, 1987–2013

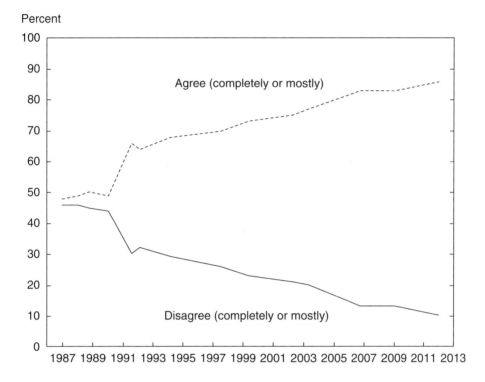

Percent

Note: Question: "It's all right for blacks and whites to date each other."

Source: Pew Research Center for the People and the Press (*http://people-press.org*).

Figure 3-16   Public Opinion on Same-Sex Marriage, 1996–2015

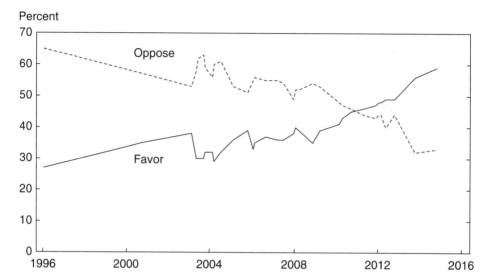

Note: Question: 1996–2013: "Do you strongly favor, favor, oppose, or strongly oppose allowing gay and lesbian couples to marry legally?" In some surveys, the question asked about "allowing gays and lesbians to marry legally." 2014: "Do you agree or disagree with the following statement: Homosexuals should have the right to marry one another." 2015: "Do you favor or oppose allowing gay and lesbian couples to enter into same-sex marriages?" Typically, 8 to 12 percent of the respondents volunteer that they don't know.

Sources: 1996–2013: Pew Research Center for the People and the Press *(http://people-press.org)*; 2013: General Social Survey; 2015: *www.wsj.com/public/resources/documents/NBC_WSJ_MARCH_POLL.pdf.*

Figure 3-17 Public Opinion on Legalization of Marijuana, 1973–2014

Percent

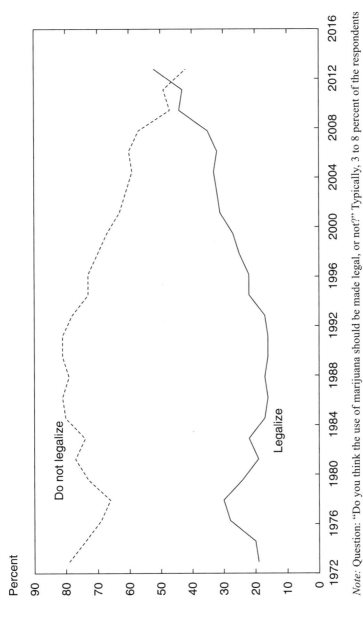

Note: Question: "Do you think the use of marijuana should be made legal, or not?" Typically, 3 to 8 percent of the respondents volunteer that they don't know.

Source: General Social Survey, National Opinion Research Center, University of Chicago.

Figure 3-18   Religious Affiliation of the U.S. Population and Political Ideology, by Religious Affiliation, 2007

Religious affiliation

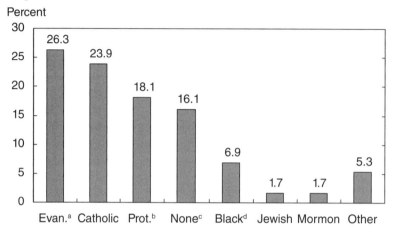

Conservative

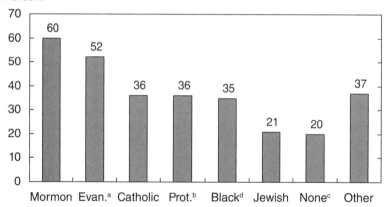

Note: Other affiliations (each less than 1 percent of the population) are Buddhist, Jehovah's Witness, Hindu, Orthodox, Muslim, and "others." The bottom figure shows the percentages responding "very conservative" or "conservative" in response to the question "In general, would you describe your political views as very conservative, conservative, moderate, liberal, or very liberal?"

[a] Evangelical Protestant.
[b] Mainline Protestant.
[c] Unaffiliated.
[d] Historically black churches.

Source: Pew Forum on Religion and Public Life, "U.S. Religious Landscape Survey" (*http://pew forum.org*).

Figure 3-19   Recent Trends in the Religiously Unaffiliated, by Generation, 2007–2014

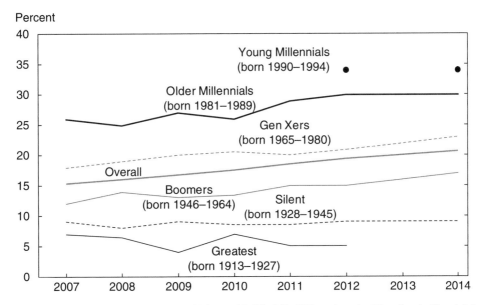

Sources: 2007–2012: Pew Forum on Religion and Public Life, "'Nones' on the Rise: One-in-Five Adults Have No Religious Affiliation," October 9, 2012, 13, 16 *(http://pewforum.org)*; 2014: General Social Survey.

Table 3-14   Public Opinion on Gun Control, 1993–2014 (percent)

Date	Protect right to own guns	Control gun ownership	Don't know, refused
December 1993	34	57	9
May 1999	30	65	5
June 1999	33	62	5
March 2000	29	66	5
April 2000	37	55	8
May 2000	38	57	5
June 2003	42	54	4
February 2004	37	58	5
April 2007	32	60	8
November 2007	42	55	3
April 2008	37	58	5
April 2009	45	49	6
March 2010	46	46	7
September 2010	46	50	4
January 2011	49	46	6
February 2011	48	47	6
September 2011	47	49	5
April 2012	49	45	6
July 2012	46	47	6
December 2012	42	49	9
January 2013	45	51	5
February 2013	46	50	4
May 2013	48	50	2
February 2014	49	48	3
December 2014	52	46	3

Note: Question: "What do you think is more important – to protect the right of Americans to own guns, or to control gun ownership?"

Source: Pew Center for the People and the Press (*http://people-press.org*).

Table 3-15   Public Opinion on the Courts, 1972–2014 (percent)

Year	Too harsh	About right	Not harsh enough	Don't know
1972	8	16	66	11
1973	5	13	73	9
1974[a]	5	6	60	29
1974	6	10	78	6
1975	4	10	79	7
1976	3	10	82	6
1977	3	8	83	5
1978	3	7	85	5
1980	3	7	84	5
1981 (Jan.)	3	13	77	7
1982[a]	4	5	76	14
1982	3	6	86	4
1983	4	6	85	4
1984	3	11	82	4
1985	3	10	84	3
1986	3	8	85	4
1987	3	12	80	5
1988	4	10	82	4
1989	3	9	84	5
1990	4	10	82	4
1991	4	11	80	5
1993	4	9	82	5
1994	3	8	85	4
1996	5	10	78	7
1998	6	13	75	6
2000	7	15	69	8
2002	9	17	67	6
2004	9	20	65	6
2006	9	21	64	5
2008	12	19	63	6
2010	14	18	61	8
2012	14	19	58	9
2014	15	19	57	8

Note: General Social Survey interviews are conducted in the spring of the year indicated, usually March–June. Question: "In general, do you think the courts in this area deal too harshly or not harshly enough with criminals?" Data for additional years can be found in previous editions of *Vital Statistics on American Politics.*

[a] In 1974 and 1982, half of the General Social Survey sample was asked the question as noted above and half the sample was asked the same question but with the phrase "or don't you have enough information about the courts to say" added at the end. The "don't know" column for these rows includes those saying "not enough information."

Sources: 1981: *Los Angeles Times* survey; others: General Social Survey, National Opinion Research Center, University of Chicago.

Table 3-16   Public Opinion on U.S. Involvement in World Affairs,
1987–2014 (percent)

	Agree		Disagree		
Date	Completely	Mostly	Mostly	Completely	*Don't know*
May 1987	32	55	7	1	5
May 1988	47	43	6	1	3
February 1989	51	42	3	1	3
May 1990	39	50	6	1	4
November 1991	54	38	4	2	2
June 1992	47	44	5	2	2
May 1993	33	54	9	1	3
July 1994	51	39	7	2	1
November 1997	48	43	6	2	1
September 1999	45	43	8	2	2
August 2002	49	41	5	3	2
August 2003	50	40	6	2	2
January 2007	42	44	7	3	4
April 2009	51	39	5	2	3
April 2012	42	41	9	4	3

Note: Question: "Now I am going to read you another series of statements on some different topics. For each statement, please tell me if you completely agree with it, mostly agree with it, mostly disagree with it, or completely disagree with it. It's best for the future of our country to be active in world affairs." A slightly different question was posed at other times. When asked in 2014 (January 23–March 16) "Which statement comes closer to your own views," 35% of respondents sided with, "It's best for the future of our country to be active in world affairs," while 60% sided with, "We should pay less attention to problems overseas and concentrate on problems here at home." This compares with 33% and 58%, respectively, for February 22–March 1, 2011, and with 44% and 49%, respectively, for December 2004. Related data for additional years can be found in previous editions of *Vital Statistics on American Politics*.

Sources: Pew Research Center for the People and the Press, "Partisan Polarization Surges in Bush, Obama Years: Trends in American Values: 1987–2012," June 4, 2012, 152–153; "Beyond Red vs. Blue: The Political Typology," June 26, 2014, 152, 155 (*http://people-press.org*).

Table 3-17 Public Opinion on Peace through Military Strength, 1987–2012 (percent)

	Agree		Disagree		
Date	Completely	Mostly	Mostly	Completely	Don't know
May 1987	14	40	30	10	6
May 1988	22	37	25	12	4
February 1989	22	39	26	10	3
May 1990	17	35	31	13	4
November 1991	21	31	29	16	3
June 1992	21	33	30	13	3
May 1993	16	38	33	10	3
July 1994	20	35	27	17	1
November 1997	23	34	29	11	3
September 1999	23	32	30	12	3
August 2002	26	36	24	10	4
August 2003	23	30	29	15	3
January 2007	18	31	30	17	4
April 2009	22	31	27	15	5
April 2012	22	31	27	15	4
September 2012	23	37	24	13	3

Note: Question: "Now I am going to read you another series of statements on some different topics. For each statement, please tell me if you completely agree with it, mostly agree with it, mostly disagree with it, or completely disagree with it. The best way to ensure peace is through military strength." Related data for additional years can be found in previous editions of *Vital Statistics on American Politics.*

Sources: Pew Research Center for the People and the Press, "Partisan Polarization Surges in Bush, Obama Years: Trends in American Values: 1987–2012," June 4, 2012, 151–152; "Obama Ahead with Stronger Support, Better Image and Lead on Most Issues," September 12, 2012, 78 (*http://people-press.org*).

Figure 3-20   Public Opinion on U.S. Military Involvement in Iraq, 2003–2014

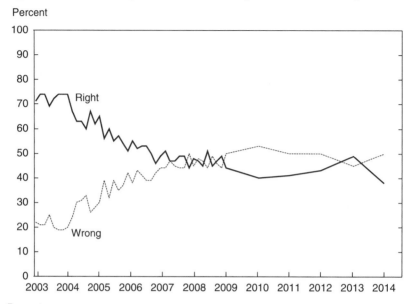

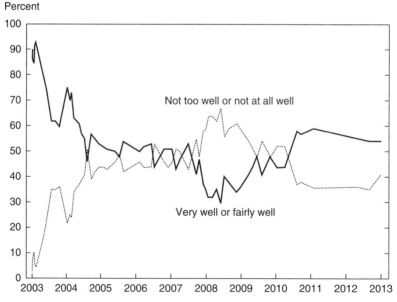

Note: Questions: "Do you think the U.S. made the right decision or the wrong decision in using military force in Iraq?" (In earlier years, the question wording was, ". . . in using military force against Iraq?") "How well is the U.S. military effort in Iraq going—very well, fairly well, not too well, or not at all well?" Related data for additional years can be found in previous editions of *Vital Statistics on American Politics.*

Sources: Pew Research Center for the People and the Press, "Obama's Ratings Little Affected by Recent Turmoil," June 24, 2010, 35–36; "More Now See Failure than Success in Iraq, Afghanistan," January 30, 2014, 9–10 (*http://people-press.org*).

Table 3-18   Public Opinion on Terrorism, 2001–2015 (percent)

Ability to launch another major attack on the United States

Date	Greater	The same	Less	Don't know, refused
August 2002	22	39	34	5
July 2004	24	39	34	3
July 2005	28	40	29	3
January 2006	17	39	39	5
August 2006	25	37	33	5
December 2006	23	41	31	5
February 2008	16	41	39	4
February 2009	17	44	35	4
October–November 2009	29	38	29	4
January 2010	33	35	29	3
August 2011	23	39	35	3
October–November 2013	34	36	29	2
July 2014	34	34	30	2

U.S. government reducing the threat of terrorism

Date	Very well	Fairly well	Not too well	Not at all well	Don't know, refused
October 10–14, 2001	48	40	6	2	4
October 15–21, 2001	38	46	9	4	3
June 2002	16	60	16	4	4
August 2003	19	56	16	7	2
July 2004	18	53	17	8	4
July 2005	17	53	19	8	3
February 2006	16	52	20	10	2
August 2006	22	52	16	8	2
December 2006	17	48	21	11	3
January 2007	17	37	27	17	2
February 2008	21	45	19	12	3
February 2009	22	49	16	6	7
March–April 2009	19	56	15	5	5
January 2010	15	50	21	12	2
August 2011	27	49	16	6	2
July 2013	20	47	21	9	3
October–November 2013	26	47	18	8	2
September 2014	17	39	22	19	2
January 2015	22	50	17	9	2

Note: Questions: "Overall, do you think the ability of terrorists to launch another major attack on the U.S. is greater, the same, or less than it was at the time of the September 11th terrorist attacks?" "In general, how well do you think the U.S. government is doing in reducing the threat of terrorism?" Related data for additional years can be found in previous editions of *Vital Statistics on American Politics.*

Sources: Pew Research Center for the People and the Press, "Most Think the U.S. Has No Responsibility to Act in Iraq," July 18, 2014, 9–10; "Terrorism Worries Little Changed; Most Give Government Good Marks for Reducing Threat," January 12, 2015, 14–15 (*http://people-press.org*).

4

The Media

- **National Reach**
- **Presence in Washington**
- **Public Use**
- **Coverage and Viewership of Presidential Campaigns, Conventions, and Debates**
- **Newspaper Endorsements**

The mass media thrive on numbers. Nearly every American adult has heard of the audience ratings games—serious games with millions of dollars and many individual careers at stake—played by television, newspapers, radio, and magazines. Will the top-ranked television show remain first in the ratings, and how much will it help the show that follows it? Will a new e-zine be profitable? Will a radio station increase its audience ratings—and what kind of audience will it attract—by playing more hard rock? How many extra copies and how much more advertising will a weekly news magazine sell with excerpts of a soon-to-be-published political memoir—and how much can the publisher afford to pay for those excerpts? So much money is at stake that media organizations spend millions of dollars each year to find the answers to such questions.

Politics, as it relates to the media, also involves numbers. What is the reach or penetration of different media (Tables 4-1 and 4-2)? Some questions simply involve market share and audience, much like the questions just noted: To what extent do people now get their news from cable networks and the Internet, and to what extent from other sources (Tables 4-4 through 4-9, and 4-11)? What is the availability of information about specific parts of government, and how has it changed over time (Figure 4-1 and Table 4-3)? How much attention do people pay to political campaign coverage, political party conventions, campaign debates, and so on (Tables 4-12, 4-16, and 4-17)? The broadcast networks have reduced coverage of the national nominating conventions (Table 4-16). Somewhat more complicated is the question of how much confidence people have in what the media report (Table 4-13). Of course, all of these matters, while important, are relatively straightforward. More complex and controversial are other matters that involve numbers. Some critics charge, for example, that the media have a political bias and that people pick the news channel that fits their political leanings (Tables 4-9, 4-10, and 4-14).

Although data specifically about politics and the media are not as plentiful as one might think (for example, some information, such as candidates' private surveys, is proprietary), more is available now than in the past. Television coverage extends more than sixty years (with extended coverage since the 1960s), and congressional proceedings have been televised for multiple decades (since 1979 in the House and 1986 in the Senate). Thus, researchers should now be in a position to do more extensive studies of the media and politics than they were before. Predictably, there has been a spurt in such studies. Perhaps as a consequence of the closer attention, there is an increasingly stronger sense of media influence on individual voters and on the political system generally.

As for media coverage of presidential campaigns, the greater amounts of data now available include the political tone of the campaign in the news (Table 4-14) and the coverage given candidates for the nomination and the general election (Figure 4-2 and Table 4-15). Some information is now available for multiple election cycles, including the public's use of media to follow the campaigns (Table 4-12), and the electorate's viewing of the nominating conventions (Table 4-16) and presidential and vice presidential debates (Table 4-17). Longstanding tabulations are also available of newspaper endorsements of the presidential candidates (Table 4-18 and Figure 4-3).

The media themselves are increasingly well preserved and documented in ways that make them highly accessible. Magazines are saved and are well indexed. Major newspapers are widely available and also well indexed, and small newspapers—increasingly available online—combine to give widespread coverage of politics as practiced and perceived throughout the country. CBS News has published transcripts and indexes of its news programs since 1975 to facilitate research. LexisNexis, an online subscription service, contains transcripts of various news programs. Google's news archive allows one to search for online sources by month and year. And network television news programs since 1968 have been stored at Vanderbilt University; the archives are indexed and available to researchers. These efforts at preservation mean that studies can be undertaken of both past and contemporary events. Indeed, some of the most interesting studies of politics and the media are yet to come, because they will be able to cover long expanses of time.

As in all areas of research, data about the media are rarely self-interpreting. One specific problem here is that the media both shape the news and reflect it. The shift in emphasis from parties to candidates (see, for example, Tables 1-14 and 3-10 on split-ticket voting) is a case in point. To some degree, this shift simply reflects, on one hand, the weakening hold of political parties over American voters, a process that began as long ago as the beginning of the twentieth century, well before the advent of television. On the other hand, the power of television to bring individual candidates directly into one's living room has accelerated the declining influence of party organizations in particular and of party affiliation more generally. An added interpretive difficulty is that the ties between parties and voters have restrengthened in recent years (see the recent decline in split-ticket voting in Table 3-10).

Problems of interpretation—especially whether the media cause or simply reflect events—thus make inferences about media influence difficult. The usual response to such problems of inference is to bring additional data to bear on the subject. With more data now available, researchers can safely anticipate better answers to questions about media audiences, coverage, emphasis, and influence as they relate to the political process.

Table 4-1   Reach and Use of Selected Media, 1950–2014

Year	Percentage of households with		Percentage of adults who use Internet[b]	Percentage of TV households with		Average hours viewing per TV home per day
	Telephone service[a]	Television sets		Cable television	Satellite television[c]	
1950	62.0	9.0	—	—	—	4.6
1960	78.5	87.1	—	—	—	5.1
1970	87.0	95.3	—	6.7	—	5.9
1975	—	97.1	—	12.6	—	6.1
1980	93.0	97.9	—	19.9	—	6.6
1985	91.8	98.1	—	42.8	—	7.2
1990	93.3	98.2	—	56.4	—	6.9
1991	93.6	98.2	—	58.9	—	7.0
1992	93.9	98.3	—	60.2	—	7.1
1993	94.2	98.3	—	61.4	—	7.2
1994	93.9	98.3	—	62.4	—	7.3
1995	93.9	98.3	14	63.4	—	7.3
1996	93.8	98.3	23	69.5	6.0	7.2
1997	93.9	98.4	36	69.4	7.6	7.2
1998	94.1	98.3	36	69.8	9.0	7.2
1999	94.0	98.2	—	70.7	9.1	7.4
2000	94.1	98.2	50	70.2	11.4	7.6
2001	94.9	98.2	59	70.5	13.9	7.7
2002	95.3	98.2	61	69.1	16.5	7.7
2003	94.7	98.2	61	67.4	18.2	8.0
2004	93.5	98.2	63	66.4	19.2	8.0
2005	92.9	98.2	72	64.8	20.8	8.2
2006	93.4	98.2	70	62.1	24.5	8.2
2007	94.9	98.2	75	61.3	28.0	8.2
2008	95.0	98.2	75	61.3	28.7	8.3
2009	95.7	98.9	79	61.7	29.3	8.3
2010	95.9	98.9	79	60.7	30.5	—
2011	95.6	98.9	79	60.4	31.1	—
2012	95.8	—	85	—	—	—
2013	—	98.0	85	83.0		—
2014	—	—	87	—	—	—

Note: "—" indicates not available. Data for additional years can be found in previous editions of *Vital Statistics on American Politics.*

[a] Includes cell phone service. It is estimated that 85 percent of U.S. adults had a cell phone in 2010. As early as 2003, less than 2 percent were estimated to have no phone service at all.
[b] Questions have varied over the years, but usually a variant of "Do you use the Internet or email, at least occasionally?" In years with multiple surveys, the highest value is shown.
[c] Includes a small number of other delivery systems. Entry for 2013–2014 is for either cable or satellite television.

Sources: Telephone service: *ProQuest Statistical Abstract of the United States, 2015* (Bernan Press, *www.bernan.com*, 2014), "Utilization and Number of Selected Media" (table), and earlier editions of *Statistical Abstract*; television sets, cable and satellite television, viewing, 1950–2011: Television Bureau of Advertising (*www.tvb.org*), various years; 2013–2014: Consumer Electronics Association, "Mobile Devices Lead Electronics Purchases," "Only Seven Percent of TV Households Rely on Over-the-Air Signals," *www.ce.org*; Internet: Pew Research Center's Internet & American Life Project (*www.pewinternet.org*).

Table 4-2   Newspaper Circulation, Daily Papers, 1850–2013

Year	Number	Circulation (thousands)	Circulation as a percentage of population
1850	254	758	3.3
1860	387	1,478	4.7
1870	574	2,602	6.5
1880	971	3,566	7.1
1890	1,610	8,387	13.3
1900	2,226	15,102	19.8
1904	2,452	19,633	23.4
1909	2,600	24,212	26.2
1914	2,580	28,777	28.6
1919	2,441	33,029	31.0
1921	2,334	33,742	31.7
1923	2,271	35,471	30.6
1925	2,116	37,407	32.3
1927	2,091	41,368	35.7
1929	2,086	42,015	34.1
1931	2,044	41,294	33.6
1933	1,903	37,630	29.6
1935	2,037	40,871	32.1
1937	2,065	43,345	34.1
1939	2,040	42,966	32.4
1947	1,854	53,287	37.0
1950	1,772	53,800	35.3
1954	1,820	56,410	34.6
1958	1,778	58,713	33.6
1960	1,763	58,900	32.6
1963	1,766	63,831	33.7
1965	1,751	60,400	31.1
1967	—	66,527	33.5
1970	1,748	62,100	30.3
1975	1,756	60,700	28.1
1978	1,756	62,000	27.9
1979	1,763	62,200	27.6
1980	1,745	62,200	27.3
1981	1,730	61,400	26.7
1982	1,711	62,500	26.9
1983	1,701	62,600	26.7
1984	1,688	63,300	26.8
1985	1,676	62,800	26.3
1986	1,657	62,500	26.0
1987	1,645	62,826	25.9
1988	1,642	62,695	25.6
1989	1,626	62,649	25.3
1990	1,611	62,328	24.9
1991	1,586	60,687	24.4
1992	1,570	60,164	23.1

(Table continues)

Table 4-2 *(Continued)*

Year	Number	Circulation (thousands)	Circulation as a percentage of population
1993	1,556	59,812	22.6
1994	1,548	59,305	22.2
1995	1,533	58,193	21.9
1996	1,520	56,983	21.1
1997	1,509	56,728	20.7
1998	1,489	56,182	20.3
1999	1,483	55,979	20.2
2000	1,480	55,773	19.8
2001	1,468	55,578	19.2
2002	1,457	55,186	18.9
2003	1,456	55,185	18.6
2004	1,457	54,626	18.6
2005	1,452	53,345	18.0
2006	1,437	52,329	17.5
2007	1,422	50,742	16.8
2008	1,408	48,598	15.9
2009	1,397	46,278	15.1
2010	—	—	—
2011	—	—	—
2012	1,427	43,433	13.8
2013	1,395	40,712	12.9

Note: "—" indicates not available. Data are for English language newspapers only. In 1900 and earlier, figures include a small number of periodicals. In 1970 and later, the number of newspapers is for February of the following year, and circulation figures are as of September 30 of the year indicated.

Sources: Daily papers, 1850–1967: U.S. Bureau of the Census (Washington, D.C.: Government Printing Office, 1975), 810; 1970–2009: *Editor & Publisher International Yearbook* (New York: Editor & Publisher, annual); 2012–2013: *Editor & Publisher Newspaper Data Book*; population, 1850–1990, 1998–1999, 2004–2009: U.S. Bureau of the Census, *Statistical Abstract of the United States* (Washington, D.C.: Government Printing Office, annual); 1991–1997, 2000–2003: estimated by Editor & Publisher; population, 2012–2013: Proquest LLC., *Proquest Statistical Abstract of the United States, 2015* (Bethesda, MD: Bernan, 2014).

Figure 4-1   Growth of Congressional Press Corps, 1864–2014

Number

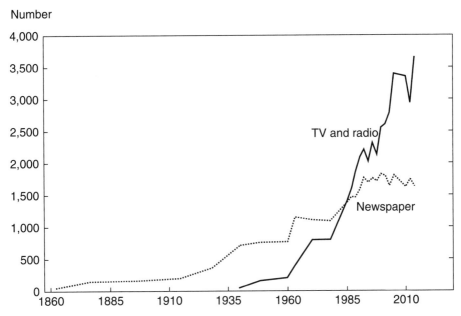

Note: Press corps members are those correspondents entitled to admission to the Senate and House press galleries and radio and television galleries. Before 1986, the number of press corps members was recorded about every ten years. Since 2000, the numbers are from the revised, online edition of the *Official Congressional Directory* (see source) for the year indicated.

Sources: Samuel Kernell, *Going Public: New Strategies of Presidential Leadership* (Washington, D.C.: CQ Press, 1986), 57; updated by the editors from successive volumes of U.S. Congress Joint Committee on Printing, *Official Congressional Directory* (Washington, D.C.: Government Printing Office); as of 2000 from the online version *(www.gpo.gov).*

Table 4-3   Presidential News Conferences, 1913–2015

President	Total number of solo press conferences	Total number of press conferences	Average number of press conferences per month
Wilson (1913–1921)	159	159	1.7
Harding (1921–1923)	—	—	—
Coolidge (1923–1929)	521	521	7.8
Hoover (1929–1933)	267	268	5.6
F. Roosevelt (1933–1945)	984	1,020	7.0
Truman (1945–1953)	311	324	3.4
Eisenhower (1953–1961)	192	193	2.0
Kennedy (1961–1963)	65	65	1.9
L. Johnson (1963–1969)	118	135	2.2
Nixon (1969–1974)	39	39	0.6
Ford (1974–1977)	39	40	1.3
Carter (1977–1981)	59	59	1.2
Reagan (1981–1989)	46	46	0.5
G. H. W. Bush (1989–1993)	85	143	3.0
Clinton (1993–2001)	62	193	2.0
G. W. Bush (2001–2009)	50	208	2.2
Obama (2009–)	50	122	1.7

Note: "—" indicates not available. Obama count is through January 20, 2015. Counting news conferences—even distinguishing between solo and joint conferences—requires judgment because of the variety of contacts presidents have with the press. In almost all cases, the solo counts exclude those news conferences in which the president appears jointly with foreign leaders or other U.S. officials. For details, see Martha Joynt Kumar, "'Does This Constitute a Press Conference?' Defining and Tabulating Modern Presidential Press Conferences," *Presidential Studies Quarterly* (March 2003). In addition to the more formal press conferences counted in the table, presidents submit to interviews with individual and groups of reporters, such as those with individual television anchors. The number of such interviews that recent presidents have conducted vary substantially. After one term in office, Barack Obama had 674; George W. Bush, 217; Bill Clinton, 191; George H. W. Bush, 382; and Ronald Reagan, 277. Some interview transcripts are found in the *Public Papers of the Presidents of the United States*, but many are not—the news organization conducting the interview controls the transcript and chooses whether to release it. A third type of presidential session with reporters is a short question-and-answer session that takes place mostly in the Oval Office, Roosevelt Room, Cabinet Room, or Diplomatic Room, where space is at a premium and a pool of reporters represents the whole of the press corps. After one term in office, Obama had 107 of these sessions; George W. Bush had 354; Clinton, 620; George H.W. Bush, 335; and Reagan, 161. Counts of interviews and question-and-answer sessions from Martha Joynt Kumar, "W.H. Press Conferences Turn 100," in *Politico*, March 28, 2013. For details on the distinctions among categories and for the total numbers for the Clinton and George W. Bush administrations, see Martha Joynt Kumar, *Managing the President's Message: The White House Communications Operation* (Baltimore: Johns Hopkins University Press, 2007).

Sources: Martha Joynt Kumar, "Source Material: Presidential Press Conferences: The Evolution of an Enduring Forum," *Presidential Studies Quarterly* (March 2005); data supplied by Kumar, February 2015.

Table 4-4   Use of Television for News, 1990–2013 (percent)

Date	Local TV news[a]	Network TV news[b]	Cable news channels[c]	Cable News Network (CNN)[d]	Fox News Cable Channel[e]	MSNBC[f]	CNBC[g]
			Regularly or sometimes watch				
January 1990	—	—	—	51	—	—	—
June 1990	—	—	—	57	—	—	—
February 1993	92	81	—	—	—	—	—
May 1993	93	88	—	69	—	—	—
March 1995	90	76	—	58	—	—	—
April 1996	88	71	—	59	—	—	—
February 1997	88	72	—	58	—	—	—
April 1998	86	67	—	57	47	31	39
August 1999	—	73	—	—	—	—	—
April 2000	80	58	—	55	45	38	42
April 2002	81	61	68	56	48	45	43
April 2004	82	62	71	55	54	42	41
April 2006	77	54	65	54	51	40	37
May 2008	77	54	67	57	50	46	38
June 2010	76	55	70	50	49	39	35
May–June 2012	73	53	64	50	48	39	—
Aug–Sept 2013[h]	72	59	52	—	—	—	—

Note: "—" indicates not available. Data for other months can be found in previous editions of *Vital Statistics on American Politics.*

[a] Question: "How often do you watch the local news about your viewing area which usually comes on before or after the national news in the evening and again later at night—regularly, sometimes, hardly ever, or never?" (Prior to 2002, the question was, "How often do you watch the local news about your viewing area? This usually comes on before the national news and then later at night at 10 or 11.") In 2013, the question was, "How often do you watch local television news—often, sometimes, hardly ever, or never?"

[b] Question: "How often do you watch the national nightly network news on CBS, ABC, or NBC? This is different from local news shows about the area where you live—regularly, sometimes, hardly ever, or never?" In 2013, the question was, "How often do you watch national evening network television news (such as ABC World News, CBS Evening News, or NBC Nightly News)—often, sometimes, hardly ever, or never?"

[c] Question: "How often do you watch cable news channels such as CNN, MSNBC, or the Fox News Cable Channel—regularly, sometimes, hardly ever, or never?" In 2013, the question was, "How often do you watch cable television news (such as CNN, The Fox News Cable channel, or MSNBC)—often, sometimes, hardly ever, or never?"

[d] Question: "How often do you watch CNN—regularly, sometimes, hardly ever, or never?" (Prior to 2008, the question was, "How often do you watch Cable News Network (CNN)—regularly, sometimes, hardly ever, or never?")

[e] Question: "How often do you watch the Fox News Cable Channel—regularly, sometimes, hardly ever, or never?"

[f] Question: "How often do you watch MSNBC—regularly, sometimes, hardly ever, or never?"

[g] Question: "How often do you watch CNBC—regularly, sometimes, hardly ever, or never?"

[h] Responses are for "often or sometimes watch."

Sources: Pew Research Center for the People and the Press, "Americans Spending More Time Following the News," September 12, 2010, 107–109; "In Changing News Landscape, Even Television Is Vulnerable," September 27, 2012, 59–61; "The Role of News on Facebook," October 24, 2013, 2 (*http://people-press.org*).

Table 4-5 Use of Internet and Newspapers for News, 1990–2012 (percent)

Date	Ever go online?[a]		Frequency of going online to get news[b]						Read newspaper regularly?[c]	
	Yes	No	Every day	3–5 days/week	1–2 days/week	Every few weeks	Less often	No/never (volunteered)	Yes	No
November 1990	—	—	—	—	—	—	—	—	74	26
July 1991	—	—	—	—	—	—	—	—	73	27
June 1992	—	—	—	—	—	—	—	—	75	25
October 1994	—	—	—	—	—	—	—	—	73	27
March 1995	—	—	—	—	—	—	—	—	71	29
June 1995	14	86	6	9	15	13	28	29	69	34
April 1996	21	79	—	—	—	—	28	71	28	—
April 1998	36	64	18	17	20	15	21	9	68	32
September 1998	42	58	23	16	21	14	19	7	—	—
November 1998	—	—	—	—	—	—	—	—	70	30
August 1999	52	48	22	15	19	15	20	9	—	—
April 2000	54	46	27	15	19	12	18	9	63	37
April 2002	62	38	25	16	16	13	21	9	63	37
April 2004	66	34	27	18	15	12	17	11	60	40
April 2006	67	33	27	20	17	12	16	8	59	41
May 2008	67	33	37	18	16	8	13	8	54	46
June 2010	82	18	39	17	13	8	15	7	49	51
May–June 2012	86	14	37	16	13	7	19	7	49	50

Note: "—" indicates not available. Data for other months can be found in previous editions of *Vital Statistics on American Politics.*

[a] Questions: "Do you use the Internet, at least occasionally?"; "Do you send or receive e-mail, at least occasionally?"; "Do you access the Internet on a cell phone, tablet or other mobile handheld device, at least occasionally?" A "yes" response to any question is considered a "yes" to "Ever go online?" (Prior to 2012, the question was, "Do you ever go online to access the Internet or to send and receive e-mail?" Prior to 2006, the question was, "Do you ever go online to access the Internet or World Wide Web or to send and receive e-mail?")

[b] Question: (Asked only of those who "ever" go online) "How frequently do you get news online or on a mobile device... Would you say every day, 3 to 5 days per week, 1 or 2 days per week, once every few weeks, or less often?" (For June 2010 and earlier, the question did not include the phrase, "or on a mobile device." For May 2008 and earlier, the question wording was, "How frequently do you go online to get news . . . ?")

[c] Question: "Do you happen to read any daily newspaper or newspapers regularly, or not?"

Source: Pew Research Center for the People and the Press (*http://people-press.org*).

Table 4-6   Use of Newspaper, Radio, and Television for News, 1993–2013 (percent)

Year	Read/listened yesterday		Regularly watch			
	Newspaper[a]	Radio news[b]	Cable TV news[c]	Local TV news[d]	Nightly network news[e]	Morning network news[f]
1993	58[g]	47[g]	—	77	60	—
1996	50	44	—	65	42	—
1998	48	49	—	64	38	23
2000	47	43	—	56	30	20
2002	41	41	33	57	32	22
2004	42	40	38	59	34	22
2006	40	36	34	54	28	23
2008	34	35	39	52	29	22
2010	31	34	39	50	28	20
2012	29	33	34	48	27	19
2013[h]	27	26	24	46	31	—

Note: "—" indicates not available.

[a] Question: "Did you get a chance to read a daily newspaper yesterday, or not?" In 2013, the question was, "How often do you read any newspapers in print—often, sometimes, hardly ever, or never?"

[b] Question: "About how much time, if any, did you spend listening to a radio news program or any news on the radio yesterday, or didn't you happen to listen to any radio news yesterday?" In 2010 and earlier, the final phrase of the question was "or didn't you happen to listen to the news on the radio yesterday?" In 2008 and earlier, the question wording did not include "a radio news program." In 2013, the question was, "How often do you listen to news on the radio—often, sometimes, hardly ever, or never?"

[c] Question: "Tell me if you watch cable news channels such as CNN, MSNBC, or the Fox News Cable Channel—regularly, sometimes, hardly ever, or never." In 2013, the question was, "How often do you watch cable television news (such as CNN, The Fox News Cable channel, or MSNBC)—often, sometimes, hardly ever, or never?"

[d] Question: "Tell me if you watch the local news about your viewing area which usually comes on before or after the national news in the evening and again later at night—regularly, sometimes, hardly ever, or never." In 2013, the question was, "How often do you watch local television news—often, sometimes, hardly ever, or never?"

[e] Question: "Tell me if you watch the national nightly network news on CBS, ABC, or NBC— regularly, sometimes, hardly ever, or never." In 2013, the question was, "How often do you watch national evening network television news (such as ABC World News, CBS Evening News, or NBC Nightly News)—often, sometimes, hardly ever, or never?"

[f] Question: "Now I'd like to know how often you watch or listen to certain TV and radio programs. For each that I read, tell me if you watch or listen to it regularly, sometimes, hardly ever or never . . . The Today Show, Good Morning America, or CBS This Morning." From 2000 through 2010, this item referred to "The Today Show, Good Morning America, or The Early Show."

[g] Data from 1994.

[h] Responses are for "often listened/read" or "often watch."

Sources: Pew Research Center for the People and the Press, "In Changing News Landscape, Even Television Is Vulnerable," September 27, 2012, 50, 52, 59, 61–62; "The Role of News on Facebook," October 24, 2013, 2 (*http://people-press.org*).

Table 4-7   Media Use, by Groups, 2012 (percent)

	Newspaper[a]	Nightly network news[b]	Cable news channels[c]	Local news[d]	Morning news programs[e]
Total	38	27	35	48	19
Sex					
Men	37	26	38	46	15
Women	39	28	32	49	23
Age					
18–29 years	21	11	23	29	10
30–49 years	35	26	34	46	17
50–64 years	43	35	35	57	26
65 years and older	60	41	52	64	24
Sex/age					
Men younger than 30 years	18	10	22	28	9
Women younger than 30 years	24	11	24	29	12
Men 30–49 years	35	28	39	46	12
Women 30–49 years	35	23	27	45	22
Men 50 years and older	52	34	44	58	21
Women 50 years and older	47	39	39	61	29
Education					
High school graduate or less	30	26	33	48	21
Some college	39	28	34	52	18
College graduate	48	29	38	44	18
Family income					
Less than $30,000	32	28	34	48	19
$30,000–49,999	39	29	32	51	22
$50,000–74,999	43	26	33	55	23
$75,000–99,999	39	30	39	49	16
$100,000 or more	47	25	40	41	18
Party identification					
Democrat	41	31	33	51	23
Independent	37	27	34	44	16
Republican	41	26	43	54	20
Ideology/partisanship					
Liberal Democrat	43	24	31	45	20
Conservative/moderate Democrat	41	36	34	56	26
Moderate/liberal Republican	40	28	38	51	23
Conservative Republican	30	25	46	56	18
Online use					
Internet user	38	27	34	46	19
Not an Internet user	37	28	40	58	22

Note: Percentages are those responding "regularly."

[a] Question: "Now I'd like to know how often you read certain types of publications in print or online. How often do you read a daily newspaper—regularly, sometimes, hardly ever, or never?"

Table 4-7   *(Continued)*

---

[b] Question: "Now I'd like to know how often you watch or listen to certain TV and radio programs. For each that I read, tell me if you watch or listen to it regularly, sometimes, hardly ever, or never. Watch the national nightly network news on CBS, ABC, or NBC? This is different from local news shows about the area where you live."

[c] Question: "Watch cable news channels such as CNN, MSNBC, or the Fox News CABLE Channel?"

[d] Question: "Watch the local news about your viewing area, which usually comes on before or after the national news in the evening and again later at night?"

[e] Question: "Watch the *Today Show, Good Morning America* or the *Early Show*?"

Source: Calculated by the editors from Pew Research Center for the People and the Press, "Biennial Media Consumption Survey 2012," May 9–June 3, 2012 (*http://people-press.org*).

Table 4-8   Network and Cable Television Audiences Compared, 2012 (percent)

| | Regularly watch | | |
	Nightly network news	Cable news channels	Share of population sampled
Sex			
Men	48	53	49
Women	52	47	51
Age			
18–29 years	9	15	23
30–49 years	31	32	33
50–64 years	35	27	27
65 years and older	25	25	17
Education			
High school graduate or less	33	40	43
Some college	30	29	28
College graduate	37	32	29
Party[a]			
Democrat	36	31	33
Independent	35	37	37
Republican	27	30	25

Note: For questions, see Table 4-4, notes b and c, this volume. Table entries indicate the percentage the group composes of regular watchers of nightly network or cable news programs.

[a] "Other" and "no preference" respondents, not shown here, make up a few percent of the sample.

Source: Calculated by the editors from Pew Research Center for the People and the Press, "Biennial Media Consumption Survey 2012," May 9–June 3, 2012 (*http://people-press.org*).

Table 4-9   Partisan Profile of TV News Audiences, 2006–2012

	Percentage of those who regularly watch who are			
	Democrats	Independents	Republicans	Don't know
CNN				
2006	45	26	22	7
2008	51	23	18	8
2010	47	31	17	5
2012	50	31	16	3
Fox News Channel				
2006	31	22	38	9
2008	33	22	39	6
2010	21	28	44	7
2012	22	33	40	5
MSNBC				
2006	48	26	19	7
2008	45	27	18	10
2010	53	30	14	3
2012	58	24	16	2
NewsHour				
2006	47	22	21	10
2008	46	23	21	10
2010	—	—	—	—
2012	—	—	—	—
Nightly network news				
2006	40	24	28	8
2008	45	26	22	7
2010	35	34	24	7
2012	36	37	23	4
General public				
2006	32	30	28	10
2008	36	29	25	10
2010	33	34	25	8
2012	32	36	24	8

Note: "—" indicates not available. Table entries are the shares of each audience who identify themselves as Republicans, Democrats, and independents. Questions: "How often do you watch *The NewsHour with Jim Lehrer*—regularly, sometimes, hardly ever, or never?" See Figure 3-2, this volume, for partisan identification question. See Table 4-4, this volume, for the other questions.

Sources: Pew Research Center for the People and the Press, "Audience Segments in a Changing News Environment," August 17, 2008, 15; "Americans Spending More Time Following the News," September 12, 2010, 56; "In Changing News Landscape, Even Television Is Vulnerable," September 27, 2012, 39 (*http://people-press.org*).

Table 4-10   Preference for News with a Point of View, 2004–2013 (percent)

| | Prefer news from | | |
	My point of view	No point of view	Don't know
2004	25	67	8
2006	23	68	9
2008	23	66	11
2010	25	62	13
2012	26	64	10
2013	27	71	—
Partisanship			
Democrat	30	—	—
Independent	19	—	—
Republican	33	—	—

Note: "—" indicates not available. Question: "Thinking about the different kinds of political news available to you, what do you prefer . . . getting news from sources that share your political point of view or getting news from sources that don't have a particular political point of view?" In 2013, the question was, "Thinking about the different kinds of news you get, do you mostly . . . get news from sources that share [your] point of view or get news from sources that don't have a particular point of view?"

Sources: Pew Research Center for the People and the Press, "Americans Spending More Time Following the News," September 12, 2010, 47; "In Changing News Landscape, Even Television Is Vulnerable," September 27, 2012, 32; "The Role of News on Facebook," October 24, 2013, 20; Topline, 3 (*http://people-press.org*).

Table 4-11   Sources of Campaign News, 1992–2012 (percent)

	1992	1996	2000	2004	2008	2012
Main source of campaign news[a]						
Television	82	72	70	76	68	67
Newspapers	57	60	39	46	33	27
Radio	12	19	15	22	16	20
Magazines	9	11	4	6	3	3
Campaign news from the Internet[b]						
Yes	—	10	30	41	56	67
No	—	90	70	59	44	33

Note: "—" indicates not available. Results are based on adults who voted. Data for additional years can be found in earlier editions of *Vital Statistics on American Politics*.

[a] Question: "How did you get most of your news about the presidential election campaign?" Sum may exceed 100 percent due to multiple responses: respondents were allowed to give two responses.
[b] Question in 2012: "Did you happen to get any news or information about the 2012 elections online on a computer, tablet, cell phone or other device, or not?" In 2008 and earlier, question was, "Did you happen to get any news or information about the [year] elections from the Internet, or not?"

Source: Pew Research Center for the People and the Press, "Low Marks for the 2012 Election: Voters Pessimistic about Partisan Cooperation," November 15, 2012, 38–39 (*http://people-press.org*).

Table 4-12 Public's Use of Media to Follow Presidential Campaigns, 1956–2012 (percent)

Media	1956	1960	1964	1968	1972	1976	1980	1984	1988	1992	1996	2000	2004	2008	2012
Read newspaper articles about the election															
Regularly	—	44	40	37	26	28	—	—	—	—	—	—	—	—	—
Often[a]	69	12	14	12	14	17	27	24	—	—	—	—	—	—	14
From time to time[b]	—	16	18	19	16	24	29	34	—	—	—	—	—	—	20
Once in a great while[c]	—	7	6	7	4	10	17	19	—	—	—	—	—	—	15
None	31	21	22	25	40	22	27	23	—	—	—	—	—	—	51
Paid attention to newspaper articles about the presidential campaign															
Great deal	—	—	—	—	—	—	—	8	6	9	5	6	8	9	—
Quite a bit	—	—	—	—	—	—	—	14	12	15	11	10	14	18	—
Some	—	—	—	—	—	—	—	28	22	20	19	19	21	31	—
Very little	—	—	—	—	—	—	—	20	9	6	7	6	6	9	—
None	—	—	—	—	—	—	—	31	52	50	58	60	51	33	—
Listened to speeches or discussions on radio															
Good many[d]	—	15	12	12	8	12	14	10	5	7	7	8	15	13	10
Several[e]	45	17	23	16	21	20	22	20	10	11	14	14	18	19	14
One or two[f]	—	10	12	12	13	16	15	16	17	18	18	15	18	15	13
None	55	58	52	59	59	52	50	55	69	64	61	62	49	53	64
Watched programs about the campaign on television															
Good many[d]	—	47	41	42	33	37	28	25	—	31	15	24	27	29	20
Several[e]	74	29	34	34	41	38	37	37	—	39	32	35	37	37	28
One or two[f]	—	11	13	13	16	15	22	24	—	19	28	23	22	20	28
None	26	13	11	11	9	10	13	14	—	11	25	18	14	14	24

Paid attention to television news about the presidential campaign

Great deal	—	—	—	—	—	—	17	15	20	—	27
Quite a bit	—	—	—	—	—	—	24	26	29	—	31
Some	—	—	—	—	—	—	28	29	28	—	23
Very little	—	—	—	—	—	—	11	13	11	—	8
None	—	—	—	—	—	—	20	17	13	—	11

Read about the campaign in magazines

Good many[d]	31	12	10	9	7	12	7	7	—	—	—
Several[e]	—	15	16	12	15	24	19	16	—	—	—
One or two[f]	—	13	13	15	14	15	12	11	—	—	—
None	69	59	61	64	64	49	62	66	—	—	—

Paid attention to magazine articles about the presidential campaign

Great deal	—	—	—	—	—	3	3	4	3	4	3
Quite a bit	—	—	—	—	—	4	6	7	7	7	8
Some	—	—	—	—	—	7	11	10	15	12	17
Very little	—	—	—	—	—	2	3	3	7	6	7
None	—	—	—	—	—	84	76	77	68	72	65

Note: "—" indicates question not asked or response category not offered. Data for earlier years can be found in previous editions of *Vital Statistics on American Politics.*

[a] "Quite a lot, pretty much" in 1952; "yes" in 1956; "good many" in 1980–1984 and 2012.
[b] "Not very much" in 1952; "several" in 1980–1984 and 2012.
[c] "One or two" in 1980–1984 and 2012.
[d] "Quite a lot, pretty much" in 1952; "yes" in 1956; "good many" in 1980–1984.
[e] "Yes" in 1956.
[f] "Not very much" in 1952.

Source: Calculated by the editors from American National Election Studies data, University of Michigan, Ann Arbor, MI, and Stanford University, Palo Alto, CA (www.electionstudies.org).

Table 4-13　Credibility of Television and Print Media, 1998–2012 (percent)

	1998	2000	2002	2004	2006	2008	2010	2012	Not rated, 2012[a]
TV news outlets									
60 Minutes (CBS)	34	34	34	32	27	30	33	30	10
ABC News	30	30	24	24	22	24	21	22	7
CBS News	28	29	26	24	22	22	21	20	6
CNN	43	39	37	32	28	31	29	25	6
C-SPAN	32	34	30	27	25	25	22	—	—
Fox News Channel	—	25	24	24	25	24	27	22	8
Local TV news	34	32	28	24	23	28	29	28	5
MSNBC	—	28	27	21	20	24	22	19	10
NBC News	30	29	25	23	23	24	19	20	5
NewsHour (PBS)	29	24	26	23	23	23	—	—	—
National Public Radio	18	25	23	22	22	27	28	24	21
Print news outlets									
Associated Press	18	21	17	18	17	16	—	—	—
National Enquirer	3	4	3	5	6	5	—	—	—
New York Times	—	—	—	21	20	18	21	17	19
Newsweek	24	24	20	19	18	16	—	—	—
People	10	10	9	7	8	8	—	—	—
Time	27	29	23	22	21	21	—	—	—
U.S. News	—	—	26	24	21	20	—	—	—
USA Today	23	23	20	19	19	16	17	14	17
Wall Street Journal	41	41	33	24	26	25	25	21	19
Your daily newspaper	29	25	22	18	19	23	21	20	8

Note: "—" indicates not available. The 1998–2012 percentages are, of respondents who could rate each organization, those who believe all or most of what the organization says. Question: "As I name some organizations, please rate how much you think you can believe each that I name on a scale of 4 to 1. On this four-point scale, '4' means you can believe all or most of what the organization says, and '1' means you believe almost nothing of what they say. First, how would you rate the believability of _____ on this scale of 4 to 1?"

[a] "Not rated" combines "never heard of " and "can't rate" responses.

Sources: Pew Research Center for the People and the Press, "Audience Segments in a Changing News Environment," August 17, 2008, 122–126; "Americans Spending More Time Following the News," September 12, 2010, 138–141; "Further Decline in Credibility Ratings for Most News Organizations," August 16, 2012, 11–14 (*http://people-press.org*).

Table 4-14 Tone of News Coverage of Presidential and Vice Presidential Candidates in 2012 General Election

		Percent of stories with tone						Totals for convention and general election campaign	
Candidate	Tone	Republican Convention Aug. 27–Sept. 2	Democratic Convention Sept. 3–9	Post conventions Sept. 10–Oct. 3	Post first presidential debate Oct. 4–16	Post second presidential debate Oct. 17–21	Final weeks Oct. 22–Nov. 5	Percent of stories with tone Aug. 27–Nov. 5	Number of stories Aug. 27–Nov. 5
Obama	Positive	3.2%	34.6%	19.9%	12.0%	17.2%	22.2%	19.7%	442
	Neutral	38.6	44.8	55.8	51.2	49.0	52.9	51.3	1148
	Negative	58.3	20.7	24.3	36.8	33.8	24.9	29.0	649
Biden	Positive	0.0	35.3	0.0	16.4	0.0	8.3	15.9	29
	Neutral	100.0	64.7	91.7	64.2	100.0	91.7	63.2	126
	Negative	0.0	0.0	8.3	19.4	0.0	0.0	14.8	27
Romney	Positive	35.9	8.7	3.9	22.9	13.7	17.1	15.1	295
	Neutral	48.9	44.9	44.6	53.7	41.0	50.1	48.0	936
	Negative	15.2	46.5	51.5	23.4	45.3	32.8	36.9	721
Ryan	Positive	37.7	7.1	2.1	10.6	0.0	8.3	13.6	38
	Neutral	47.2	67.9	52.1	60.6	85.7	83.3	58.9	165
	Negative	15.1	25.0	45.8	28.8	14.3	8.3	27.5	77

Note: In addition to the stories identified earlier, an additional number of stories were not rated because the candidate was not in at least 25 percent of the story and therefore were not given a tone. The number of these stories is 878 for Obama, 2,935 for Biden, 1,165 for Romney, and 2,837 for Ryan.

Sources: Pew Research Center's Project for Excellence in Journalism, "The Final Days of the Media Campaign 2012," Topline, 2 (*http://journalism.org*).

Figure 4-2　Media Exposure of Gingrich, Santorum, Romney, and Paul in
the 2012 Presidential Nominations

Percent

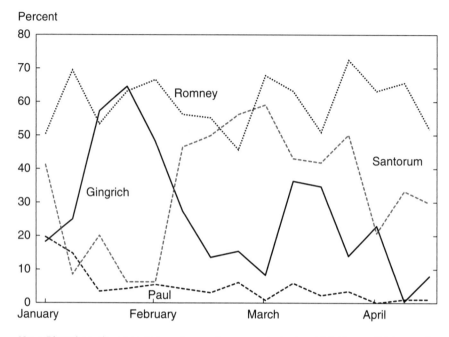

Note: Plotted are the percentages of campaign news stories in which the candidate was the
subject of 25 percent or more of the story. Related data for additional years can be found in
previous editions *of Vital Statistics on American Politics.*

Source: Pew Research Center's Project for Excellence in Journalism, "How the Media Covered
the 2012 Primary Campaign," April 23, 2012, 25 *(http://journalism.org).*

Table 4-15 Media Exposure of Presidential Candidates in 2008 and 2012 General Elections

Percentage of campaign stories where each candidate is a significant presence

2008 Election	Overall	Democratic Convention	Republican Convention	Post conventions	Post first presidential debate	Post second presidential debate	Final weeks
	Aug. 24–Nov. 2	Aug. 24–30	Aug. 31–Sept. 6	Sept. 7–27	Sept. 28–Oct. 11	Oct. 12–25	Oct. 26–Nov. 2
McCain	55.1%	56.0%	24.5%	56.7%	54.4%	72.1%	51.1%
Obama	59.9	77.7	56.9	47.7	49.7	75.0	65.7

2012 Election	Overall	Republican Convention	Democratic Convention	Post conventions	Post first presidential debate	Post second presidential debate	Final weeks
	Aug. 27–Nov. 5	Aug. 27–Sept. 2	Sept. 3–9	Sept. 10–Oct. 3	Oct. 4–16	Oct. 17–21	Oct. 22–Nov. 5
Obama	71.7	39.6	78.2	72.4	68.1	82.6	83.0
Romney	62.6	57.3	33.5	65.6	65.5	84.7	68.4

Note: A candidate is considered a significant presence if 25 percent or more of the story is about him.

Sources: Pew Research Center's Project for Excellence in Journalism, "Campaign Coverage Index," "The Final Days of the Media Campaign 2012," Topline, 1 (*http://journalism.org*).

Table 4-16   National Nominating Conventions: Television Coverage and Viewership, 1952–2012

Year/party	Audience rating[a] (percent)	Average hours viewed by household	Network hours telecast[b]
1952			
Republican	—	10.5	57.5
Democratic	—	13.1	61.1
1956			
Republican	—	6.4	22.8
Democratic	—	8.4	37.6
1960			
Republican	28.0	6.2	25.5
Democratic	29.2	8.3	29.3
1964			
Republican	21.8	7.0	36.5
Democratic	28.8	6.4	23.5
1968			
Republican	26.4	6.5	34.0
Democratic	28.5	8.5	39.1
1972			
Republican	23.4	3.5	19.8
Democratic	18.3	5.8	36.7
1976			
Republican	31.5	6.3	29.5
Democratic	25.2	5.2	30.4
1980			
Republican	21.6	3.8	22.7
Democratic	27.0	4.4	24.1
1984			
Republican	19.2	1.9	11.9
Democratic	23.4	2.5	12.9
1988			
Republican	18.3	—	—
Democratic	19.8	—	—
1992			
Republican	20.5	—	7.3
Democratic	22.0	—	8.0
1996			
Republican	16.5	—	5.0
Democratic	17.2	—	5.0
2000			
Republican	13.9	—	5.2
Democratic	15.3	—	5.3
2004			
Republican	15.3	—	3.0
Democratic	14.3	—	3.0
2008			
Republican	21.9	1.4	3.0[c]
Democratic	19.9	1.4	4.0
2012			
Republican	—[d]	—	3.0
Democratic	—[e]	—	3.0

Table 4-16   *(Continued)*

Note: "—" indicates not available.

[a] Sum of the percentage of television households viewing the convention during an average minute of common coverage periods. Through 1988, based on viewing of ABC, CBS, and NBC; for 1992 and 1996, based on viewing the three networks plus PBS and CNN (the 1996 Republican convention was also televised on the Family Channel, but that is not included in the rating); for 2000, includes the three networks, CNN, Fox News Channel, and MSNBC; for 2004, includes the three networks, CNN, Fox News Channel, and MSNBC; for 2008, includes the three networks, CNN, Fox News Channel, MSNBC, BET (Democratic convention only), TV One (Democratic convention only), Univision (day four only), and Telemundo (day four only). C-SPAN viewing not included.

[b] Number of hours during which one or more of ABC, CBS, or NBC was broadcasting the convention. CNN, Fox News Channel, and MSNBC provided extensive coverage, often entailing regular news programming anchored from the convention site.

[c] Four hours of network coverage of the Republican convention was originally planned. However, because of Hurricane Gustav the convention's first night was scaled back and networks aired storm coverage instead.

[d] An average audience rating for the convention is not available. There was no common coverage, and thus no rating calculated, for the first day of the convention due to Hurricane Isaac. For day two of the convention, the audience rating for all households was 14.7; for day three, 14.7; and for day four, 19.3.

[e] An average audience rating for the convention is not available. For day one of the convention, the audience rating for all households was 17.3; for day two, 16.7; and for day three, 22.7.

Sources: Audience rating, 1960–2004: The Nielsen Company, "Historical TV Ratings: Democratic Conventions" and "Historical TV Ratings: Republican Conventions," August 27, 2008; audience rating, 2008: The Nielsen Company, "Audience Estimates for the 2008 Republican Convention," September 5, 2008 (*http://blog.nielsen.com*); hours viewed, hours telecast, 1952–1980: Christopher Sterling, *Electronic Media: A Guide to Trends in Broadcasting and Newer Technologies, 1920–1983* (Praeger, 1984), 169; hours viewed, hours telecast, 1984: *Network Television Audiences to Primaries, Conventions, and Elections: 1987 Update Edition* (Northbrook, Ill.: A. C. Nielsen, 1987), 13, 17; hours telecast, 1992: A. C. Nielsen Co., *Nielsen Tunes in to Politics: Tracking the Presidential Election Years (1960–1992)* (New York: Nielsen Media Research, 1993), 2–3; hours telecast, 1996: John Carmody, "Convention Low-Show," *Washington Post*, August 19, 1996, B1; hours telecast, 2000: Robin Toner, "The Conventions Are Over, the Party's Just Starting," *New York Times*, August 20, 2000, iv; hours telecast, 2004: Michael Janofsky, "Each Convention to Get 3 Hours of Prime Time on TV Networks," *New York Times*, July 13, 2004, A16; hours telecast, 2008: "Networks Rethink Conventions," *Baltimore Sun*, August 25, 2008, 11A, and "TV Cameras Turn from G.O.P. to Storm," *New York Times*, September 1, 2008; hours viewed, 2008: The Nielsen Company, "Nielsen Examines TV Viewers to the Political Convention," September 2008, 3; hours telecast, 2012: "CBS, NBC and ABC Announce Just Three Hours of Primetime Coverage," *Tampa Bay Times,* August 20, 2012 (*www.tampabay.com*); note "d": The Nielsen Company, "Final Night of Republican National Convention Draws 30.3 Million Viewers," August 31, 2012 (*http://blog.nielsen.com*); note "e": The Nielsen Company, "Closing Night of Democratic National Convention Draws 35.7 Million Viewers," September 7, 2012 (*http://blog.nielsen.com*). Copyrighted information of The Nielsen Company, licensed for use herein.

Table 4-17　Television Viewership of Presidential and Vice Presidential Debates, 1960–2012

Year	Candidates	Date	Audience rating[a] (percentage)	Viewers (millions)
1960	Kennedy–Nixon	Sept. 26	59.5	—
		Oct. 7	59.1	—
		Oct. 13	61.0	—
		Oct. 21	57.8	—
1976	Carter–Ford	Sept. 23	53.5	69.7
		Oct. 6	52.4	63.9
		Oct. 22	47.8	62.7
	Mondale–Dole	Oct. 15	35.5	43.2
1980	Carter–Reagan	Oct. 28	58.9	80.6
1984	Mondale–Reagan	Oct. 7	45.3	65.1
		Oct. 21	46.0	67.3
	Ferraro–G. H. W. Bush	Oct. 11	43.6	56.7
1988	Dukakis–G. H. W. Bush	Sept. 25	36.8	65.1
		Oct. 13	35.9	67.3
	Bentsen–Quayle	Oct. 5	33.6	46.9
1992	Clinton–G. H. W. Bush–Perot	Oct. 11	38.3	62.4
		Oct. 15	46.3	69.9
		Oct. 19	45.2	66.9
	Gore–Quayle–Stockdale	Oct. 13	35.9	51.2
1996	Clinton–Dole	Oct. 6	31.6	36.1
		Oct. 16	26.1	36.3
	Gore–Kemp	Oct. 9	19.7	26.6
2000	Gore–G. W. Bush	Oct. 3	31.7	46.6
		Oct. 11	26.8	37.6
		Oct. 17	25.9	37.7
	Lieberman–Cheney	Oct. 5	21.0	29.0
2004	Kerry–G. W. Bush	Sept. 30	39.4	62.5
		Oct. 8	29.6	46.7
		Oct. 13	32.6	51.2
	Edwards–Cheney	Oct. 5	28.1	43.6
2008	Obama–McCain	Sept. 26	31.6	52.4
		Oct. 7	38.8	63.2
		Oct. 15	35.0	56.5
	Biden–Palin	Oct. 2	41.7	70.0
2012	Obama–Romney	Oct. 3	40.4	67.2
		Oct. 16	40.0	65.6
		Oct. 22	35.9	59.2
	Biden–Ryan	Oct. 11	31.9	51.4

Table 4-17 *(Continued)*

Note: "—" indicates not available. Vice presidential candidates are in italics. 1976–1988 debates include ABC, CBS, and NBC only; 1992 includes ABC, CBS (not Oct. 11), NBC, and CNN; 1996 includes ABC, CBS, NBC, CNN, and Fox (only Oct. 6); 2000 includes ABC, CBS, NBC (some affiliates on tape delay Oct. 3), CNN, Fox (some affiliates on tape delay Oct. 3, not included Oct. 5 or Oct. 11), Fox News Channel, and MSNBC; 2004 includes ABC, CBS, NBC, CNN, Fox (not Oct. 5 or Oct. 13), Fox News Channel, and MSNBC; 2008 includes ABC, CBS, Fox (not Oct. 15), NBC, Telefutura (not Oct. 7 or Oct. 15), Telemundo, Univision (not Sept. 26 or Oct. 2), BBC-America, CNBC, CNN, Fox News Channel, MSNBC, and MUN2 (only Oct. 15); 2012 includes ABC, CBS, Fox (not Oct. 22), NBC, Telemundo, Univision, PBS, CNN, Fox News Channel, MSNBC, CurrentTV, and CNBC. PBS (before 2012) and C-SPAN data not included. Combined audience estimates are based on comparable durations.

[a] Percentage of television households viewing the debates during an average minute.

Sources: Presidential debates, 1960–2004: Nielsen Media Research, "Political Debates: Presidential Debates;" 2008: "Media Advisory: 56.5 Million Watch the Final 2008 Presidential Debate;" 2012: "Final Presidential Debate Draws 59.2 Million Viewers;" vice presidential debates, 1976–2004: "Political Debates: Vice Presidential Debates;" 2008: "Media Advisory: 69.6 Million Watch the 2008 Vice Presidential Debate;" 2012: "51.4 Million Viewers Tune into Biden and Ryan's VP Debate" (*http://blog.nielsen.com*). Copyrighted information of The Nielsen Company, licensed for use herein.

Table 4-18   Newspaper Endorsements of Presidential Candidates, 1948–2012

Year/candidate endorsed	Papers		Circulation	
	Number	Percentage	Number	Percentage
1948				
Dewey (R)	771	65	35,152,807	79
Truman (D)	182	15	4,489,851	10
Thurmond	45	4	537,730	1
Wallace	3	0	60,233	0
Uncommitted	182	15	4,454,557	10
1952				
Eisenhower (R)	933	67	40,129,237	80
Stevenson (D)	202	15	5,466,781	11
Uncommitted	250	18	4,417,102	9
1956				
Eisenhower (R)	740	62	34,538,755	72
Stevenson (D)	189	15	6,122,491	13
Uncommitted	270	23	7,079,846	15
1960				
Nixon (R)	731	58	38,006,203	71
Kennedy (D)	208	16	8,448,677	16
Uncommitted	328	26	7,135,954	13
1964				
Goldwater (R)	359	35	8,977,214	21
L. Johnson (D)	440	42	26,997,400	62
Uncommitted	237	23	7,638,727	18
1968				
Nixon (R)	634	61	34,559,385	70
Humphrey (D)	146	14	9,572,948	19
1972				
Nixon (R)	753	71	30,560,535	77
McGovern (D)	56	5	3,044,534	8
Uncommitted	245	23	5,864,548	15
1976				
Ford (R)	411	62	20,951,798	62
Carter (D)	80	12	7,607,739	23
Uncommitted	168	26	5,074,069	15
1980				
Reagan (R)	443	42	17,561,333	49
Carter (D)	126	12	7,782,078	22
Anderson	40	4	1,614,740	4
Uncommitted	439	42	9,131,940	25
1984				
Reagan (R)	381	58	18,357,512	52
Mondale (D)	62	9	7,568,639	21
Uncommitted	216	33	9,611,058	27
1988				
G. H. W. Bush (R)	241	31	18,186,225	40

Table 4-18   *(Continued)*

Year/candidate endorsed	Papers Number	Papers Percentage	Circulation Number	Circulation Percentage
Dukakis (D)	103	13	11,644,600	25
Uncommitted	428	55	16,224,807	35
1992[a]				
G. H. W. Bush (R)	121	15	7,134,599	18
Clinton (D)	149	18	10,961,415	27
Uncommitted	542	67	22,225,342	55
1996[b]				
Dole (R)	111	19	4,741,645	13
Clinton (D)	65	11	4,581,337	13
Uncommitted	415	70	26,173,692	74
2000				
G. W. Bush (R)	93	48	—	—
Gore (D)	44	23	—	—
Uncommitted	56	29	—	—
2004				
G. W. Bush (R)	205	48	15,743,799	41
Kerry (D)	213	50	20,882,889	55
Uncommitted	12[c]	3	1,650,819[c]	4
2008				
McCain (R)	159	34	9,301,511	29
Obama (D)	287	61	23,086,607	71
Uncommitted	26	6	—	—
2012[d]				
Romney (R)	212	45	17,660,553[e]	46
Obama (D)	191	41	12,897,157[e]	34
Uncommitted	66	14	7,718,757[e]	20

Note: "D" indicates Democrat; "R" indicates Republican; "—" indicates not available. In 2000 *Editor & Publisher* changed the method used to conduct its poll of newspaper endorsements, which resulted in a much smaller number of responses, with an unknown but probably larger bias; also, circulation numbers were not indicated. Circulation numbers were not provided for all papers in 2012. Data for additional years can be found in previous editions of *Vital Statistics on American Politics*.

[a] One newspaper—circulation 9,075—endorsed H. Ross Perot, independent.
[b] One newspaper—circulation 3,300—endorsed Harry Browne, Libertarian.
[c] Based on the 2008 listing, which indicated those uncommitted in 2004.
[d] Two newspapers endorsed Gary Johnson, Libertarian (combined circulation 103,186).
[e] Usually Sunday circulation (except for weekly paper).

Sources: Editor & Publisher, October 30, 1948, 11; November 1, 1952, 9; November 3, 1956, 11; November 5, 1960, 10; October 31, 1964, 10; November 2, 1968, 9; November 7, 1972, 9; October 30, 1976, 5; November 1, 1980, 10; November 3, 1984, 9; November 5, 1988, 9; October 24, 1992, 9; October 26, 1996, 8; November 6, 2000, 9; November 5, 2004; November 7, 2008; November 2012 (*www.editorandpublisher.com*).

188

Figure 4-3 Newspaper Endorsements of Presidential Candidates: Democratic, Republican, and Uncommitted, 1932–2012

Percent

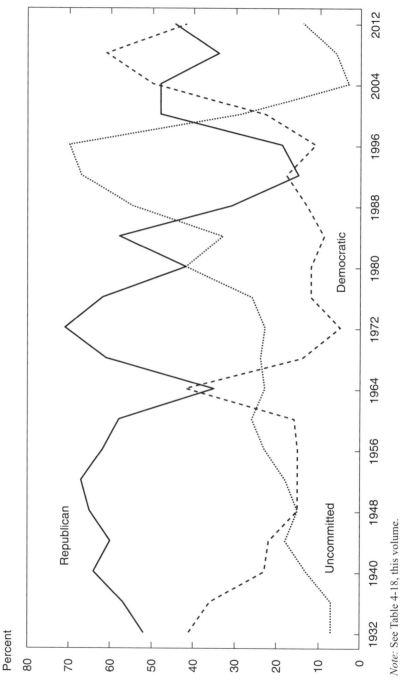

Note: See Table 4-18, this volume.

Source: Table 4-18, this volume.

5

Congress

- **Apportionment**
- **Membership Characteristics**
- **Committees**
- **Bills and Laws**
- **Voting Patterns**
- **Current Members**

Statistics about Congress abound. Capsule descriptions of senators and representatives and their districts run to more than a thousand pages for each Congress (see, for example, *Politics in America*, published by CQ Press, and the *Almanac of American Politics*, published by the National Journal Group). Elections are held every two years, generating mounds of electoral and financial data. Moreover, the annual number of record votes totals nearly six hundred in the House and more than three hundred in the Senate. It is thus hardly surprising that votes for Congress, votes in Congress, members of Congress themselves, and all those who surround them or contribute to their activities have been subjected to extensive statistical scrutiny.

Election-related material is one of the largest collections of data about Congress, and various aspects of these data are provided in several chapters of this book. Election results, including material associated specifically with congressional elections such as losses by the president's party at midterm, are provided in Chapter 1; information on the funding of congressional campaigns is provided in Chapter 2. Chapter 3 covers individual voting behavior in congressional elections, as well as public judgments of the institution—so-called congressional approval (see Figure 3-7).

Congress also generates many other kinds of statistics. Simply apportioning members among the states (Table 5-1 and Figure 5-1) has led to a surprising amount of controversy and statistical calculation, which has resulted in a fascinating book-length treatment.[1] As the composition of Congress changes to include more women and minorities, these and other characteristics have also been tabulated and analyzed (Tables 5-2 through 5-5).

Likewise, as Congress has become a larger and more complex operation, analysts have become more interested in its structure and workload. These aspects of Congress are represented here with information about the numbers of committees and their leadership (Table 5-6), numbers of measures considered and passed (Figure 5-2 and Table 5-7), and numbers of votes (Table 5-8). Although these items might at first be considered insignificant or analytically useless tabulations, analyses of the relationships among congressional voting, voter behavior, and legislative output suggest otherwise.

Voting by the members of Congress is of obvious interest. Indeed, cohesion within and contrasts between the political parties were the topics of some of the first statistical treatments of political subjects.[2] Increased numbers of roll calls and other record votes (Table 5-8) have done nothing to dampen this tradition. Party unity and presidential support by individual representatives and senators (Tables 5-11 and 5-12) and for groups (Tables 5-9, 5-10, and Figure 5-3) have become a standard part of congressional analyses.

For the statistically minded, the study of Congress has long been an inviting prospect. The traditional topics are still interesting because the turnover in personnel, the ongoing change in congressional leadership and of the president, the changes in regional strength, and so on make Congress anything but static. In addition, the reforms of congressional procedures and of campaign finance since the Watergate scandal in the 1970s, the technological changes that have resulted in electronic voting and the televising of proceedings in both chambers, and the changes in the size and scope of the government bureaucracy that Congress must deal with are reason enough to scrutinize anew the data underlying one's understanding of Congress.

Notes

1. Michel Balinski and H. P. Young, *Fair Representation* (New Haven, Conn.: Yale University Press, 1982).
2. Stuart Rice, *Quantitative Methods in Politics* (New York: Knopf, 1928).

Table 5-1 Apportionment of Membership of the House of Representatives, 1789–2010

| | | | | | | 1789–1890 | | | | | | |
State	1789[a]	1790	1800	1810	1820	1830	1840	1850	1860	1870	1880	1890
Alabama	—	—	—	—	3	5	7	7	6	8	8	9
Alaska	—	—	—	—	—	—	—	—	—	—	—	—
Arizona	—	—	—	—	—	—	—	—	—	—	—	—
Arkansas	—	—	—	—	—	—	1	2	3	4	5	6
California	—	—	—	—	—	—	—	2	3	4	6	7
Colorado	—	—	—	—	—	—	—	—	—	—	1	2
Connecticut	5	7	7	7	6	6	4	4	4	4	4	4
Delaware	1	1	1	2	1	1	1	1	1	1	1	1
Florida	—	—	—	—	—	—	—	1	1	2	2	2
Georgia	3	2	4	6	7	9	8	8	7	9	10	11
Hawaii	—	—	—	—	—	—	—	—	—	—	—	—
Idaho	—	—	—	—	—	—	—	—	—	—	—	1
Illinois	—	—	—	—	1	3	7	9	14	19	20	22
Indiana	—	—	—	—	3	7	10	11	11	13	13	13
Iowa	—	—	—	—	—	—	—	2	6	9	11	11
Kansas	—	—	—	—	—	—	—	—	1	3	7	8
Kentucky	—	2	6	10	12	13	10	10	9	10	11	11
Louisiana	—	—	—	—	3	3	4	4	5	6	6	6
Maine	—	—	—	—	7	8	7	6	5	5	4	4
Maryland	6	8	9	9	9	8	6	6	5	6	6	6
Massachusetts	8	14	17	20	13	12	10	11	10	11	12	13
Michigan	—	—	—	—	—	—	3	4	6	9	11	12
Minnesota	—	—	—	—	—	—	—	—	2	3	5	7
Mississippi	—	—	—	—	1	2	4	5	5	6	7	7
Missouri	—	—	—	—	1	2	5	7	9	13	14	15
Montana	—	—	—	—	—	—	—	—	—	—	—	1
Nebraska	—	—	—	—	—	—	—	—	—	1	3	6
Nevada	—	—	—	—	—	—	—	—	—	1	1	1
New Hampshire	3	4	5	6	6	5	4	3	3	3	2	2

(Table continues)

Table 5-1 *(Continued)*

1789–1890

State	1789[a]	1790	1800	1810	1820	1830	1840	1850	1860	1870	1880	1890
New Jersey	4	5	6	6	6	6	5	5	5	7	7	8
New Mexico	—	—	—	—	—	—	—	—	—	—	—	—
New York	6	10	17	27	34	40	34	33	31	33	34	34
North Carolina	5	10	12	13	13	13	9	8	7	8	9	9
North Dakota	—	—	—	—	—	—	—	—	—	—	—	1
Ohio	—	—	—	6	14	19	21	21	19	20	21	21
Oklahoma	—	—	—	—	—	—	—	—	—	—	—	—
Oregon	—	—	—	—	—	—	—	—	1	1	1	2
Pennsylvania	8	13	18	23	26	28	24	25	24	27	28	30
Rhode Island	1	2	2	2	2	2	2	2	2	2	2	2
South Carolina	5	6	8	9	9	9	7	6	4	5	7	7
South Dakota	—	—	—	—	—	—	—	—	—	—	—	2
Tennessee	—	—	3	6	9	13	11	10	8	10	10	10
Texas	—	—	—	—	—	—	—	2	4	6	11	13
Utah	—	—	—	—	—	—	—	—	—	—	—	—
Vermont	—	2	4	6	5	5	4	3	3	3	2	2
Virginia	10	19	22	23	22	21	15	13	11	9	10	10
Washington	—	—	—	—	—	—	—	—	—	—	—	2
West Virginia	—	—	—	—	—	—	—	—	—	3	4	4
Wisconsin	—	—	—	—	—	—	—	3	6	8	9	10
Wyoming	—	—	—	—	—	—	—	—	—	—	—	1
Representatives apportioned by census count	65	105	141	181	213	240	223	234	241	292	325	356
Apportionment population[c]	[d]	3,615,823	4,879,820	6,584,231	8,972,396	11,930,987	15,908,376	21,766,691	29,550,038	38,115,641	49,371,340	61,908,906
Apportionment ratio[e]	30,000[f]	34,436	34,609	36,377	42,124	49,712	71,338	93,020	122,614	130,533	151,912	173,901

1900–2010

State	1900	1910	1930[b]	1940	1950	1960	1970	1980	1990	2000	2010
Alabama	9	10	9	9	9	8	7	7	7	7	7
Alaska	—	—	—	—	—	1	1	1	1	1	1
Arizona	—	1	1	2	2	3	4	5	6	8	9
Arkansas	7	7	7	7	6	4	4	4	4	4	4
California	8	11	20	23	30	38	43	45	52	53	53
Colorado	3	4	4	4	4	4	5	6	6	7	7
Connecticut	5	5	6	6	6	6	6	6	6	5	5
Delaware	1	1	1	1	1	1	1	1	1	1	1
Florida	3	4	5	6	8	12	15	19	23	25	27
Georgia	11	12	10	10	10	10	10	10	11	13	14
Hawaii	—	—	—	—	—	2	2	2	2	2	2
Idaho	1	2	2	2	2	2	2	2	2	2	2
Illinois	25	27	27	26	25	24	24	22	20	19	18
Indiana	13	13	12	11	11	11	11	10	10	9	9
Iowa	11	11	9	8	8	7	6	6	5	5	4
Kansas	8	8	7	6	6	5	5	5	4	4	4
Kentucky	11	11	9	9	8	7	7	7	6	6	6
Louisiana	7	8	8	8	8	8	8	8	7	7	6
Maine	4	4	3	3	3	2	2	2	2	2	2
Maryland	6	6	6	6	7	8	8	8	8	8	8
Massachusetts	14	16	15	14	14	12	12	11	10	10	9
Michigan	12	13	17	17	18	19	19	18	16	15	14
Minnesota	9	10	9	9	9	8	8	8	8	8	8
Mississippi	8	8	7	7	6	5	5	5	5	4	4
Missouri	16	16	13	13	11	10	10	9	9	9	8
Montana	1	2	2	2	2	2	2	2	1	1	1
Nebraska	6	6	5	4	4	3	3	3	3	3	3
Nevada	1	1	1	1	1	1	1	2	2	3	4
New Hampshire	2	2	2	2	2	2	2	2	2	2	2
New Jersey	10	12	14	14	14	15	15	14	13	13	12

(Table continues)

Table 5-1 *(Continued)*

State	1900	1910	1930[b]	1940	1950	1960	1970	1980	1990	2000	2010
New Mexico	—	1	1	2	2	2	2	3	3	3	3
New York	37	43	45	45	43	41	39	34	31	29	27
North Carolina	10	10	11	12	12	11	11	11	12	13	13
North Dakota	2	3	2	2	2	2	1	1	1	1	1
Ohio	21	22	24	23	23	24	23	21	19	18	16
Oklahoma	—	8	9	8	6	6	6	6	6	5	5
Oregon	2	3	3	4	4	4	4	5	5	5	5
Pennsylvania	32	36	34	33	30	27	25	23	21	19	18
Rhode Island	2	3	2	2	2	2	2	2	2	2	2
South Carolina	7	7	6	6	6	6	6	6	6	6	7
South Dakota	2	3	2	2	2	2	2	1	1	1	1
Tennessee	10	10	9	10	9	9	8	9	9	9	9
Texas	16	18	21	21	22	23	24	27	30	32	36
Utah	1	2	2	2	1	2	2	3	3	3	4
Vermont	2	2	1	1	1	1	1	1	1	1	1
Virginia	10	10	9	9	10	10	10	10	11	11	11
Washington	3	5	6	6	7	7	7	8	9	9	10
West Virginia	5	6	6	6	6	5	4	4	3	3	3
Wisconsin	11	11	10	10	10	10	9	9	9	8	8
Wyoming	1	1	1	1	1	1	1	1	1	1	1
Representatives apportioned by census count	386	435	435	435	435	435	435	435	435	435	435
Apportionment population[c]	74,562,608	91,603,772	122,093,455	131,006,184	149,895,183	178,559,217	204,053,025	225,867,174	249,022,783	281,424,177	309,183,463
Apportionment ratio[e]	193,167	210,583	280,675	301,164	344,587	410,481	469,088	519,235	572,466	646,952	710,767

1900–2010

Note: "—" indicates state not yet admitted to Union. States mentioned in the decennial apportionment law or report are listed for that year. Several territories were counted in the census and admitted after the census year, but before the apportionment decade. The remaining states were admitted during the decade after an apportionment law or report. All new states were admitted with one seat unless noted. These states were, after the 1790 apportionment, Tennessee; after 1800, Ohio; after 1810, Alabama, Illinois, Indiana, Louisiana, and Mississippi; after 1830, Arkansas and Michigan; after 1840, California, Florida, Iowa, and Wisconsin; after 1870, Colorado; after 1880, Idaho, Montana, North Dakota, South Dakota, Washington, and Wyoming; after 1890, Utah; after 1900, Oklahoma; after 1950, Alaska and Hawaii. Twenty members were assigned to Massachusetts in the 1810 apportionment; seven of these were credited to Maine when that area became a state. Virginia had eleven representatives in 1860; three of these were credited to West Virginia when that area became a state. The only exception to the census apportionment or new state admittance manner of securing a representative was when California was given one additional representative for the Thirty-seventh Congress (1861–1863).

[a] Original apportionment made in Constitution, pending first census.

[b] No apportionment was made in 1920.

[c] Excludes the population of District of Columbia; the population of the territories; prior to 1940, the number of American Indians not taxed; and, prior to 1870, two-fifths of the slave population. In 1970 and 1990 includes selected segments of Americans abroad.

[d] No census prior to 1790.

[e] The ratio of apportionment population to the number of representatives apportioned by census.

[f] The minimum ratio of population to representative, as stated in Article I, section 2, of the U.S. Constitution.

Sources: Apportionment of membership, 1788–1990: Kenneth C. Martis and Greg A. Elmes, *The Historical Atlas of State Power in Congress, 1790–1990* (Washington, D.C.: Congressional Quarterly, 1993); apportionment population, 1790–1990: U.S. Census Bureau, "Population Base for Apportionment and the Number of Representatives Apportioned: 1790 to 1990" (*www.census.gov*); 2000: U.S. Census Bureau, "Apportionment Population and Number of Representatives, by State: Census 2000" (www.census.gov); 2010: U.S. Census Bureau, "Apportionment Population and Number of Representatives, by State: 2010 Census" (*www.census.gov*). Apportionment ratios calculated by the editors.

196

Figure 5-1 Apportionment of Membership of the House of Representatives, by Region, 1910 and 2010

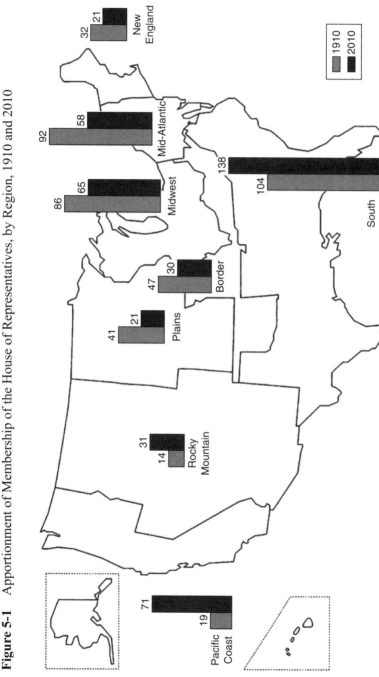

Note: For composition of regions, see Table A-3, this volume.

Source: Table 5-1, this volume.

Table 5-2 Members of Congress: Female, Black, Hispanic, Marital Status, and Age, 1971–2015

Congress		Female	Black	Hispanic	Not married[a]	Age					
						Under 40	40–49	50–59	60–69	70–79	80 and older
Representatives											
92nd	(1971)	12	12	5	26	40	133	152	86	19	3
93rd	(1973)	14	15	5	34	45	132	154	80	20	2
94th	(1975)	18	16	5	54	69	138	137	75	14	2
95th	(1977)	18	16	5	56	81	121	147	71	15	0
96th	(1979)	16	16	6	69	86	125	145	63	14	0
97th	(1981)	19	16	6	86	94	142	132	54	12	1
98th	(1983)	21	20	10	68	86	145	132	57	13	1
99th	(1985)	22	19	11	69	71	154	131	59	17	2
100th	(1987)	23	22	11	64	63	153	137	56	24	2
101st	(1989)	25	23	11	—	41	163	133	74	20	2
102nd	(1991)	28	25	10	—	39	153	133	86	20	4
103rd	(1993)	47	38	17	—	47	152	129	91	13	3
104th	(1995)	47	39	18	—	53	153	136	80	12	1
105th	(1997)	51	37	18	—	47	145	147	82	10	2
106th	(1999)	56	39	19	—	32	131	171	80	20	0
107th	(2001)	59	36	19	—	36	118	175	78	26	0
108th	(2003)	59	37	23	—	26	111	175	102	21	0
109th	(2005)	65	40	23	—	25	97	176	111	23	3
110th	(2007)	71	40	23	—	20	93	171	117	30	4
111th	(2009)	78	41	25	—	23	84	156	128	40	3
112th	(2011)	72	42	24	—	22	89	138	132	42	12
113th	(2013)	78	40	28	—	26	74	138	143	42	10
114th	(2015)	84	44	29	—	26	69	141	147	44	7
Senators											
92nd	(1971)	1	1	1	3	4	24	32	23	16	1
93rd	(1973)	0	1	1	4	3	25	37	23	11	1
94th	(1975)[b]	0	1	1	6	5	21	35	24	15	0

(Table continues)

Table 5-2 (Continued)

Congress		Female	Black	Hispanic	Not married[a]	Age					
						Under 40	40–49	50–59	60–69	70–79	80 and older
95th	(1977)	0	1	0	9	6	26	35	21	10	2
96th	(1979)	1	0	0	5	10	31	33	17	8	1
97th	(1981)	2	0	0	7	9	35	36	14	6	0
98th	(1983)	2	0	0	10	7	28	39	20	3	3
99th	(1985)	2	0	0	8	4	27	38	25	4	2
100th	(1987)	2	0	0	11	5	30	36	22	5	2
101st	(1989)	2	0	0	—	0	30	40	22	6	2
102nd	(1991)	2	1	0	—	0	22	47	24	5	2
103rd	(1993)	6	1	0	—	1	16	49	22	11	1
104th	(1995)	8	1	0	—	1	14	41	27	16	1
105th	(1997)	9	1	0	—	1	21	39	26	12	2
106th	(1999)	9	0	0	—	2	16	42	27	11	2
107th	(2001)	13	0	0	—	0	17	43	31	7	2
108th	(2003)	14	0	0	—	2	16	33	36	11	2
109th	(2005)	14	1	2	—	0	17	29	33	16	5
111th	(2009)	17	0	3	—	0	7	32	37	18	4
112th	(2011)	17	0	2	—	0	9	29	38	21	3
113th	(2013)	20	1	3	—	0	9	30	35	23	3
114th	(2015)	20	2	3	—	1	13	24	39	18	5

Note: "—" indicates not available. As of beginning of first session of each Congress. Figures for representatives exclude vacancies. The counts exclude nonvoting delegates and commissioners from American Samoa, Guam, Puerto Rico, the Virgin Islands, and Washington, D.C.

[a] Single, widowed, or divorced.
[b] Includes Sen. John Durkin, D-N.H., seated September 1975.

Sources: Hispanic (1971–1985): Congressional Quarterly, *American Leaders, 1789–1987* (Washington, D.C.: Congressional Quarterly, 1987), 55; female and black (1971–2009) and Hispanic (1987–2009), *Congressional Quarterly Weekly Report (CQ Weekly)* (1970), 2756; (1972), 2991; (1974), 3104; (1976), 3155; (1978), 3252; (1980), 3318; (1982), 2805; (1984), 2921; (1986), 2863; (1988), 3294; (1990), 3835–3836; (January 16, 1993, Supplement), 10; (November 12, 1994, Supplement), 10; (1997), 28; (1999), 62; (2001), 178; (2003), 192; (2005), 243; (2006), 3008, 3064; (2008), 2998, 3374; female, black, and Hispanic (2011–2015): CQ-Roll Call, *Guide to the New Congress,* November 4, 2010, 15; November 12, 2012, 17; November 6, 2014, 59, updated by the editors; not married and age (1971–1989): U.S. Bureau of the Census, *Statistical Abstract of the United States, 1988* (Washington, D.C.: Government Printing Office, 1987), 244; *1990,* 257; age (1991–2015): calculated by the editors from *Congressional Quarterly Weekly Report (CQ Weekly)* (1991), 118–127; (January 16, 1993, Supplement), 12, 160–168; (1995), 541–549; (1997), 497–505; Congressional Biographical Directory *(http://bioguide.congress.gov)*; Congressional Quarterly, unpublished data.

Table 5-3   Black Members of Congress, 1869–2017

Congress		Black members of U.S. House of Representatives	Black members of U.S. Senate	Total black members
41st	(1869–1871)	2	1	3
42nd	(1871–1873)	5	0	5
43rd	(1873–1875)	7	0	7
44th	(1875–1877)	7	1	8
45th	(1877–1879)	3	1	4
46th	(1879–1881)	0	1	1
47th	(1881–1883)	2	0	2
48th	(1883–1885)	2	0	2
49th	(1885–1887)	2	0	2
50th	(1887–1889)	0	0	0
51st	(1889–1891)	3	0	3
52nd	(1891–1893)	1	0	1
53rd	(1893–1895)	1	0	1
54th	(1895–1897)	1	0	1
55th	(1897–1899)	1	0	1
56th	(1899–1901)	1	0	1
57th	(1901–1903)	0	0	0
58th	(1903–1905)	0	0	0
59th	(1905–1907)	0	0	0
60th	(1907–1909)	0	0	0
61st	(1909–1911)	0	0	0
62nd	(1911–1913)	0	0	0
63rd	(1913–1915)	0	0	0
64th	(1915–1917)	0	0	0
65th	(1917–1919)	0	0	0
66th	(1919–1921)	0	0	0
67th	(1921–1923)	0	0	0
68th	(1923–1925)	0	0	0
69th	(1925–1927)	0	0	0
70th	(1927–1929)	0	0	0
71st	(1929–1931)	1	0	1
72nd	(1931–1933)	1	0	1
73rd	(1933–1935)	1	0	1
74th	(1935–1937)	1	0	1
75th	(1937–1939)	1	0	1
76th	(1939–1941)	1	0	1
77th	(1941–1943)	1	0	1
78th	(1943–1945)	1	0	1
79th	(1945–1947)	2	0	2
80th	(1947–1949)	2	0	2
81st	(1949–1951)	2	0	2
82nd	(1951–1953)	2	0	2
83rd	(1953–1955)	2	0	2
84th	(1955–1957)	3	0	3
85th	(1957–1959)	4	0	4
86th	(1959–1961)	4	0	4
87th	(1961–1963)	4	0	4
88th	(1963–1965)	5	0	5
89th	(1965–1967)	6	0	6

(Table continues)

Table 5-3   *(Continued)*

Congress		Black members of U.S. House of Representatives	Black members of U.S. Senate	Total black members
90th	(1967–1969)	5	1	6
91st	(1969–1971)	10	1	11
92nd	(1971–1973)	13	1	14
93rd	(1973–1975)	16	1	17
94th	(1975–1977)	17	1	18
95th	(1977–1979)	17	1	18
96th	(1979–1981)	17	0	17
97th	(1981–1983)	19	0	19
98th	(1983–1985)	21	0	21
99th	(1985–1987)	21	0	21
100th	(1987–1989)	23	0	23
101st	(1989–1991)	24	0	24
102nd	(1991–1993)	27	0	27
103rd	(1993–1995)	39	1	40
104th	(1995–1997)	40	1	41
105th	(1997–1999)	39	1	40
106th	(1999–2001)	39	0	39
107th	(2001–2003)	39	0	39
108th	(2003–2005)	39	0	39
109th	(2005–2007)	42	1	43
110th	(2007–2009)	42	1	43
111th	(2009–2011)	41	1	42
112th	(2011–2013)	42	0	42
113th	(2013–2015)	41	2	43
114th	(2015–2017)	44	2	46

Note: The numbers reflect the highest number of black members to serve in the House of Representatives or Senate at any one time during a Congress. For example, a record forty-six black members were elected to the 110th Congress, but only forty-three served at any one time during the Congress.

Sources: 41st–110th Congresses: Mildred L. Amer, "African American Members of the United States Congress: 1870–2008," RL30378, Congressional Research Service, Washington, D.C., July 23, 2008; 111th Congress: *CQ Weekly* (2008), 2998; (2009), 132; 112th Congress: CQ-Roll Call, *Guide to the New Congress*, November 4, 2010, 15; 113th Congress: CQ-Roll Call, *Guide to the New Congress*, November 8, 2012, 17; 114th Congress: *CQ Weekly* (2014), 59, updated by the editors.

Table 5-4 Women Nominated, by Party, 1956–2014, and Women Elected to U.S. House of Representatives, by Party, 1916–2014

Election year	Congress	Major-party nominees			Elected			Success rate			Serving		
		Democratic	Republican	Total	Democratic	Republican	Total	Democratic	Republican	Total	Democratic	Republican	Total
1916	65th	—	—	—	0	1	1	—	—	—	0	1	1
1918	66th	—	—	—	0	0	0	—	—	—	0	0	0
1920	67th	—	—	—	0	1	1	—	—	—	0	3	3
1922	68th	—	—	—	0	1	1	—	—	—	0	1	1
1924	69th	—	—	—	1	0	1	—	—	—	1	2	3
1926	70th	—	—	—	1	3	4	—	—	—	2	3	5
1928	71st	—	—	—	4	4	8	—	—	—	5	4	9
1930	72nd	—	—	—	3	3	6	—	—	—	4	3	7
1932	73rd	—	—	—	3	2	5	—	—	—	4	3	7
1934	74th	—	—	—	4	2	6	—	—	—	4	2	6
1936	75th	—	—	—	4	1	5	—	—	—	5	1	6
1938	76th	—	—	—	2	2	4	—	—	—	4	4	8
1940	77th	—	—	—	3	4	7	—	—	—	5	4	9
1942	78th	—	—	—	1	6	7	—	—	—	2	6	8
1944	79th	—	—	—	4	5	9	—	—	—	6	5	11
1946	80th	—	—	—	3	4	7	—	—	—	3	4	7
1948	81st	—	—	—	4	4	8	—	—	—	5	4	9
1950	82nd	—	—	—	2	6	8	—	—	—	4	6	10
1952	83rd	—	—	—	5	6	11	—	—	—	5	6	11
1954	84th	—	—	—	9	6	15	—	—	—	10	6	16
1956	85th	15	14	29	9	6	15	60.0%	42.9%	51.7%	9	6	15
1958	86th	13	14	27	8	8	16	61.5	57.1	59.3	9	8	17
1960	87th	15	8	23	9	6	15	60.0	75.0	65.2	11	7	18
1962	88th	12	11	23	6	5	11	50.0	45.5	47.8	6	6	12
1964	89th	11	7	18	6	4	10	54.5	57.1	55.6	7	4	11
1966	90th	10	13	23	6	5	11	60.0	38.5	47.8	6	5	11
1968	91st	13	6	19	6	4	10	46.2	66.7	52.6	6	4	10

(Table continues)

201

Table 5-4 *(Continued)*

Election year	Congress	Major-party nominees			Elected			Success rate			Serving		
		Democratic	Republican	Total	Democratic	Republican	Total	Democratic	Republican	Total	Democratic	Republican	Total
1970	92nd	14	10	24	9	3	12	64.3	30.0	50.0	10	3	13
1972	93rd	23	10	33	12	2	14	52.2	20.0	42.4	14	2	16
1974	94th	27	16	43	14	4	18	51.9	25.0	41.9	14	5	19
1976	95th	34	20	54	13	5	18	38.2	25.0	33.3	13	5	18
1978	96th	26	18	44	10	5	15	38.5	27.8	34.1	11	5	16
1980	97th	27	26	53	10	9	19	37.0	34.6	35.8	11	10	21
1982	98th	27	27	54	12	9	21	44.4	33.3	38.9	13	9	22
1984	99th	28	36	64	11	11	22	39.3	30.6	34.4	12	11	23
1986	100th	30	34	64	12	11	23	40.0	32.4	35.9	13	11	24
1988	101st	33	25	58	14	11	25	42.4	44.0	43.1	16	13	29
1990	102nd	38	29	67	19	9	28	50.0	31.0	41.8	20	9	29
1992	103rd	69	35	104	35	12	47	50.7	34.3	45.2	35	12	47
1994	104th	72	42	114	31	16	47	43.1	38.1	41.2	32	17	49
1996	105th	78	42	120	35	16	51	44.9	38.1	42.5	37	18	55
1998	106th	73	45	118	39	17	56	53.4	37.8	47.5	39	17	56
2000	107th	81	43	124	41	18	59	50.6	41.9	47.6	42	18	60
2002	108th	77	44	121	38	21	59	49.4	47.7	48.8	39	21	60
2004	109th	85	52	137	42	23	65	49.4	44.2	47.4	43	25	68
2006	110th	94	42	136	50	21	71	53.2	50.0	52.2	55	21	76
2008	111th	95	38	133	58	17	75	61.1	44.7	56.4	58	17	75
2010	112th	91	47	138	48	24	72	52.7	51.1	52.2	51	24	75
2012	113th	118	48	166	58	20	78	49.1	41.7	47.0	61	20	81
2014	114th	109	50	159	62	22	84	56.9	44.0	52.8	62	22	84

Note: "—" indicates not available. "Major-party nominees," "elected," and "success rate" refer to women candidates in regularly scheduled elections for the election year indicated. "Serving" includes women elected in regularly scheduled elections in the election year indicated as well as those elected in special elections over the course of the congressional session. One woman was elected as an independent: Jo Ann Emerson was elected simultaneously as a Republican to the 104th Congress and as an independent to the 105th Congress by special election to fill the vacancy caused by the death of her husband, U.S. Representative Bill Emerson. She changed from an independent to a Republican on January 8, 1997, and was elected as a Republican to the 106th and subsequent Congresses. In the counts, Emerson is considered a Republican.

Source: Unpublished data, Barbara Palmer, Baldwin Wallace University, and Dennis Simon, Southern Methodist University, published with permission.

Table 5-5 Members of Congress: Seniority and Occupation, 2005–2015

	Representatives								Senators							
	109th (2005)	110th (2007)	111th (2009)	112th (2011)	113th (2013)	114th (2015) Dem.	114th (2015) Rep.	114th (2015) Total	109th (2005)	110th (2007)	111th (2009)	112th (2011)	113th (2013)	114th (2015) Dem.	114th (2015) Rep.	114th (2015) Total
Seniority[a]																
Under 2 years	44	59	66	103	88	19	49	68	9	11[b]	15	20	15	3	12	15
2–9 years	185	159	165	146	172	81	125	206	41	32	31[b]	35[b]	45	29[b,c]	22	51
10–19 years	147[d]	161	142	125	104	47	49	96	28[e]	30	28	24	23	8	13	21
20–29 years	45	37	42	40	51	35	18	53	15	18	16[f]	13	11	3	3	6
30 years or more	13	17	18	21	18	6	5	11	7	9	9[g]	8	6	3	4	7
Total	434[g]	433[g]	433[g]	435	433[g]	188	246	434[g]	100	100	99[g]	100	100	46	54	100
Occupation																
Agriculture	29	23	26	24	26	—	—	25	5	6	5	5	5	—	—	5
Business	205	166	175	181	187	—	—	231	30	27	26	28	27	—	—	42
Education	91	88	78	68	77	—	—	80	13	14	16	13	15	—	—	25
Journalism	11	7	7	9	12	—	—	11	7	8	5	6	4	—	—	5
Law	178	162	152	148	156	—	—	174	64	59	54	52	55	—	—	60
Public service/ politics	209	174	182	172	184	—	—	271	45	32	32	36	42	—	—	60

Note: "—" indicates not available. Members of Congress may state more than one occupation; therefore, sum may be greater than total. Not all occupations reported are listed. Data for earlier years can be found in previous editions of *Vital Statistics on American Politics.*

[a] Represents consecutive years of service.
[b] Includes Sen. Bernard Sanders, I-Vt.
[c] Includes Sen. Angus King, I-Maine.
[d] Includes Rep. Bernard Sanders, I-Vt.
[e] Includes Sen. James M. Jeffords, I-Vt.
[f] Includes Sen. Joseph I. Lieberman, I-Conn.
[g] Includes one or more vacancies.

Sources: Seniority: *2005 Congressional Staff Directory* (Washington, D.C.: CQ Press, 2005), 5, 230–233; *2007* 5, 240–243; *2009* 5, 242–245 (revised by the editors); Congressional Quarterly, unpublished data; "Senators of the United States, 1789–present" (www.senate.gov); "Seniority List of the United States House of Representatives, 113th Congress" (www.house.gov); "U.S. House of Representatives, Seniority, 114th Congress" (http://pressgallery.house.gov); Occupation: *Congressional Quarterly Weekly Report (CQ Weekly)* (2005), 241; (2007), 605; *CQ Today,* November 26, 2008, 72; CQ-Roll Call, *Guide to the New Congress,* November 4, 2010, 14; November 8, 2012, 16; November 6, 2014, 58.

Table 5-6 Congressional Committees and Majority Party Chairmanships, 1981–2017

Congress		Number of committees[a]	Party in majority	Number of majority party members	Number of majority party members chairing standing committees and subcommittees	Percentage of majority party members chairing standing committees and subcommittees	Number of majority party members chairing all committees and subcommittees	Percentage of majority party members chairing all committees and subcommittees
House								
98th	(1983–1985)	172	D	267	124	46.4	127	47.6
99th	(1985–1987)	191	D	253	129	51.0	131	51.8
100th	(1987–1989)	192	D	258	128	49.6	132	51.2
101st	(1989–1991)	189	D	260	134	51.5	137	52.7
102nd	(1991–1993)	185	D	267	130	48.7	135	50.6
103rd	(1993–1995)	146	D	258	113	43.8	116	45.0
104th	(1995–1997)	110	R	230	86	37.4	86	37.4
105th	(1997–1999)	112	R	225	100	44.4	100	44.4
106th	(1999–2001)	108	R	222	100	45.0	100	45.0
107th	(2001–2003)	116	R	221	109	49.3	109	49.3
108th	(2003–2005)	122	R	228	89	39.0	97	42.5
109th	(2005–2007)	121	R	230	107	46.5	112	48.7
110th	(2007–2009)	131	D	232	114	49.1	119	51.3
111th	(2009–2011)	131	D	254	109	42.9	117	46.1
112th	(2011–2013)	130	R	241	121	50.2	122	50.6
113th	(2013–2015)	123	R	232	106	45.7	107[b]	46.1
114th	(2015–2017)	124	R	245	112	45.7	115[b]	46.9
Senate								
98th	(1983–1985)	137	R	54	52	96.3	52	96.3
99th	(1985–1987)	120	R	53	49	92.5	49	92.5
100th	(1987–1989)	118	D	54	47	87.0	47	87.0
101st	(1989–1991)	118	D	55	46	83.6	46	83.6
102nd	(1991–1993)	119	D	56	50	89.3	50	89.3

103rd	(1993–1995)	111	D	57	46	80.7	46	80.7
104th	(1995–1997)	92	R	54	44	81.5	44	81.5
105th	(1997–1999)	92	R	54	49	90.7	49	90.7
106th	(1999–2001)	94	R	55	52	94.5	52	94.5
107th	(2001–2003)	92	R[c]	50	49	98.0	49	98.0
108th	(2003–2005)	92	R	51	50	98.0	50	98.0
109th	(2005–2007)	96	R	55	52	94.5	53	96.4
110th	(2007–2009)	96	D	50[d]	40	80.0	40	80.0
111th	(2009–2011)	89	D	58[d]	46	79.3	46	79.3
112th	(2011–2013)	98	D	53[d]	49	92.5	49	92.5
113th	(2013–2015)	96	D	55[e]	49	89.1	49[b]	89.1
114th	(2015–2017)	97	R	54[e]	50	92.6	51[b]	94.4

Note: "D" indicates Democratic; "R" indicates Republican. Data for additional years can be found in previous editions of *Vital Statistics on American Politics.*

[a] Includes standing committees, subcommittees of standing committees, select and special committees, subcommittees of select and special committees, joint committees, and subcommittees of joint committees.

[b] Excludes joint committees formed for which chairs were not announced as of March 25, 2013 or as of March 2, 2015.

[c] Split 50–50 at the start of the session, the Senate was controlled by Republicans by virtue of Vice President Dick Cheney's vote. On May 24, 2001, Sen. James M. Jeffords, Vt., announced that he would switch from Republican to independent and that he would caucus with the Democrats. This change shifted control of the Senate to the Democratic Party.

[d] Includes Joseph I. Lieberman, Conn., elected in 2006 under the label "Connecticut for Lieberman," and Bernard Sanders, Vt., elected as an independent, both of whom caucused with the Democrats.

[e] Includes Angus S. King Jr., Md., and Bernard Sanders, Vt., elected as independents, both of whom caucus with the Democrats.

Sources: 98th–103rd: Norman J. Ornstein, Thomas E. Mann, and Michael J. Malbin, eds., *Vital Statistics on Congress, 1993–1994* (Washington, D.C.: Congressional Quarterly, 1994), 113, 117–118; 104th–111th: calculated by the editors from *Congressional Quarterly Weekly Report* (*CQ Weekly*), supplement to volumes 53 (March 25, 1995); (March 22, 1997); 57 (March 13, 1999); 59 (April 28, 2001); 61 (April 12, 2003); 63 (April 11, 2005); 65 (April 16, 2007); 67 (April 13, 2009); 1 (March 25, 2013); 112th–114th: calculated by *www.contactingthecongress.org*, supplemented by House committee list (*www.house.gov*) and Senate committee list (*www.senate.gov*).

Table 5-7   Congressional Measures Introduced and Enacted, 1947–2015

Congress		Bills	Joint resolutions	Total	Public	Private	Total
		Measures introduced			*Measures enacted*		
80th	(1947–1949)	10,108	689	10,797	906	457	1,363
81st	(1949–1951)	14,219	769	14,988	921	1,103	2,024
82nd	(1951–1953)	12,062	668	12,730	594	1,023	1,617
83rd	(1953–1955)	14,181	771	14,952	781	1,002	1,783
84th	(1955–1957)	16,782	905	17,687	1,028	893	1,921
85th	(1957–1959)	18,205	907	19,112	936	784	1,720
86th	(1959–1961)	17,230	1,031	18,261	800	492	1,292
87th	(1961–1963)	17,230	1,146	18,376	885	684	1,569
88th	(1963–1965)	16,079	1,401	17,480	666	360	1,026
89th	(1965–1967)	22,483	1,520	24,003	810	473	1,283
90th	(1967–1969)	24,786	1,674	26,460	640	362	1,002
91st	(1969–1971)	24,631	1,672	26,303	695	246	941
92nd	(1971–1973)	21,363	1,606	22,969	607	161	768
93rd	(1973–1975)	21,950	1,446	23,396	651	123	774
94th	(1975–1977)	19,762	1,334	21,096	588	141	729
95th	(1977–1979)	18,045	1,342	19,387	633	170	803
96th	(1979–1981)	11,722	861	12,583	613	123	736
97th	(1981–1983)	10,582	908	11,490	473	56	529
98th	(1983–1985)	10,134	1,022	11,156	623	54	677
99th	(1985–1987)	8,697	1,188	9,885	664	24	688
100th	(1987–1989)	8,515	1,073	9,588	713	48	761
101st	(1989–1991)	9,257	1,095	10,352	404	7	411
102nd	(1991–1993)	9,601	909	10,510	589	14	603
103rd	(1993–1995)	7,883	661	8,544	465	8	473
104th	(1995–1997)	6,545	263	6,808	234	2	236
105th	(1997–1999)	7,532	200	7,732	394	10	404
106th	(1999–2001)	8,968	190	9,158	580	24	604
107th	(2001–2003)	8,956	178	9,134	377	6	383
108th	(2003–2005)	8,468	157	8,625	498	6	504
109th	(2005–2007)	10,560	143	10,703	395	1	396
110th	(2007–2009)	11,081	147	11,228	416	0	416
111th	(2009–2011)	10,621	149	10,770	336	2	338
112th	(2011–2013)	10,439	173	10,612	238	1	239
113th	(2013–2015)	8,915	178	9,093	296	0	296

Note: Measures exclude simple and concurrent resolutions.

Sources: 80th–99th: United States Congress, *Calendars of the U.S. House of Representatives and History of Legislation*, 99th Cong., final ed., 19–57 through 19–68; 100th–106th: successive issues of *Congressional Quarterly Almanac* (Washington, D.C.: CQ Press); 107th–113th: "Résumé of Congressional Activity," *Congressional Record—Daily Digest*, various issues, 2005–2014.

Figure 5-2   Measures Introduced in Congress That Were Passed, 1789–2015 (percent)

Percent

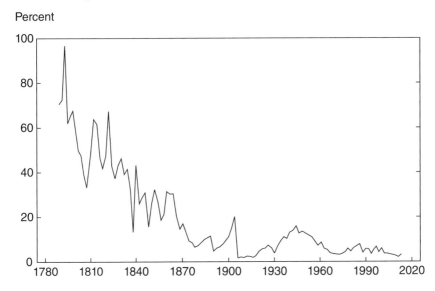

Note: Measures include bills and joint resolutions. Before 1824, only bills are included. Figures are for each Congress.

Sources: 1789–1968: U.S. Bureau of the Census, *Historical Statistics of the United States*, Series Y189-198 (Washington, D.C.: Government Printing Office, 1975), 1081–1082; 1969–2015: Table 5-7, this volume.

Table 5-8   Record Votes in the House and the Senate, 1947–2014

Year	House	Senate	Year	House	Senate
1947	84	138	1981	353	497
1948	79	110	1982	459	469
1949	121	226	1983	498	381
1950	154	229	1984	408	292
1951	109	202	1985	439	381
1952	72	129	1986	451	359
1953	71	89	1987	488	420
1954	76	181	1988	451	379
1955	73	88	1989	368	312
1956	74	136	1990	510	326
1957	100	111	1991	428	280
1958	93	202	1992	473	270
1959	87	215	1993	597	395
1960	93	207	1994	497	329
1961	116	207	1995	867	613
1962	124	227	1996	454	306
1963	119	229	1997	633	298
1964	113	312	1998	533	314
1965	201	259	1999	609	374
1966	193	238	2000	600	298
1967	245	315	2001	507	380
1968	233	280[a]	2002	483	253
1969	177	245	2003	675	459
1970	266	422	2004	543	216
1971	320	423	2005	669	366
1972	329	532	2006	539	279
1973	541	594	2007	1177	442
1974	537	544	2008	688	215
1975	612	611	2009	987	397
1976	661	700	2010	660	299
1977	706	636	2011	946[b]	235
1978	834	520	2012	657	251
1979	672	509	2013	640	291
1980	604	546	2014	563	366

Note: In the House, record votes are defined as yea-and-nay (roll call) votes plus so-called recorded votes, which refers to votes cast electronically using the system introduced in the House after the Legislative Reorganization Act of 1970. In the Senate, there is no electronic system, so record votes are simply yea-and-nay (roll call) votes. Quorum votes are excluded for both the House and the Senate.

[a] The Senate record vote total does not include one yea-and-nay vote that was ruled invalid for lack of a quorum.
[b] The House record vote total includes one roll call vote that was vacated by unanimous consent.

Source: "Résumé of Congressional Activity," *Congressional Record—Daily Digest*, various issues, Eightieth Congress (1947) through 113th Congress (2014).

Figure 5-3   Party Votes in the House, 1878–2014

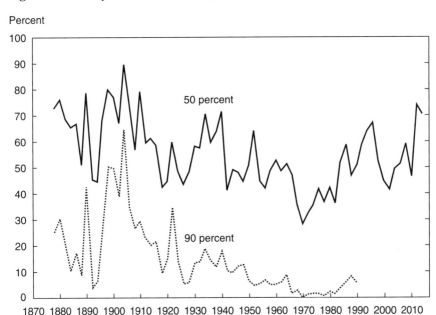

Percent

Note: Figures shown by Congress. A party vote occurs when the specified percentage (or more) of one party votes against the specified percentage (or more) of the other party.

Sources: 1878–1886 and 90 percent vote for 1972–1990: Brinck Kerr, "Structural Determinants of Party Voting in the U.S. Congress, 1877–1990," PhD diss., Texas A&M University, 1993; 1887–1969: Joseph Cooper, David William Brady, and Patricia A. Hurley, "The Electoral Basis of Party Voting: Patterns and Trends in the U.S. House of Representatives, 1887–1969," in *The Impact of the Electoral Process*, Louis Maisel and Joseph Cooper (Beverly Hills, Calif.: Sage Publications, 1977), 139; 1970–1990: *Congressional Quarterly Almanac* (Washington, D.C.: Congressional Quarterly, annual); 1991–2014: *Congressional Quarterly Weekly Report (CQ Weekly)* (1992), 3906; (1993), 3480; (1994), 3658; (1996), 199, 3432; (1998), 18; (1999), 79; (2000), 2975; (2001), 56; (2002), 114, 3240; (2004), 11, 2907; (2006), 93; (2007), 33; (2008), 144, 3333; (2010), 123; (2011), 30; (2012), 111; (2013), 132–136; (2014), 183; (2015), 37.

Table 5-9 Party Unity and Polarization in Congressional Voting,
1953–2014 (percent)

Year	House	Senate	Year	House	Senate
1953	52	52	1984	47	40
1954	38	48	1985	61	50
1955	41	30	1986	57	52
1956	44	53	1987	64	41
1957	59	36	1988	47	43
1958	40	44	1989	56	35
1959	55	48	1990	49	54
1960	53	37	1991	55	49
1961	50	62	1992	65	53
1962	46	41	1993	66	67
1963	49	47	1994	62	52
1964	55	36	1995	73	69
1965	52	42	1996	56	62
1966	42	50	1997	50	50
1967	36	35	1998	56	56
1968	35	32	1999	47	63
1969	31	36	2000	43	49
1970	27	35	2001	40	55
1971	38	42	2002	43	46
1972	27	37	2003	52	67
1973	42	40	2004	47	52
1974	29	44	2005	49	63
1975	48	48	2006	55	57
1976	36	37	2007	62	60
1977	42	42	2008	53	52
1978	33	45	2009	51	72
1979	47	47	2010	40	79
1980	38	46	2011	76	51
1981	37	48	2012	73	60
1982	36	43	2013	69	70
1983	56	44	2014	73	67

Note: Data indicate the percentage of all record votes on which a majority of voting Democrats opposed a majority of voting Republicans.

Source: 1953: *CQ Weekly* (2011), 37; 1954–1955: (2013), 138; 1956–2014: (2015), 42.

Table 5-10   Party Unity in Congressional Voting, 1954–2014 (percent)

	House			Senate		
Year	All Democrats	Southern Democrats	Republicans	All Democrats	Southern Democrats	Republicans
1954	80	—	84	77	—	89
1955	84	68	78	82	78	82
1956	80	79	78	80	75	80
1957	79	71	75	79	81	81
1958	77	67	73	82	76	74
1959	85	77	85	76	63	80
1960	75	62	77	73	60	74
1961	—	—	—	—	—	—
1962	81	—	80	80	—	81
1963	85	—	84	79	—	79
1964	82	—	81	73	—	75
1965	80	55	81	75	55	78
1966	78	55	82	73	52	78
1967	77	53	82	75	59	73
1968	73	48	76	71	57	74
1969	71	47	71	74	53	72
1970	71	52	72	71	49	71
1971	72	48	76	74	56	75
1972	70	44	76	72	43	73
1973	75	55	74	79	52	74
1974	72	51	71	72	41	68
1975	75	53	78	76	48	71
1976	75	52	75	74	46	72
1977	74	55	77	72	48	75
1978	71	53	77	75	54	66
1979	75	60	79	76	62	73
1980	78	64	79	76	64	74
1981	75	57	80	77	64	85
1982	77	62	76	76	62	80
1983	82	67	80	76	70	79
1984	81	68	77	75	61	83
1985	86	76	80	79	68	81
1986	86	76	76	74	59	80
1987	88	78	79	85	80	78
1988	88	81	80	85	78	74
1989	86	77	76	79	69	79
1990	86	78	78	82	75	77
1991	86	78	81	83	73	83
1992	86	79	84	82	70	83
1993	89	83	87	87	78	86
1994	88	83	87	86	77	81
1995	84	75	93	84	76	91
1996	84	76	90	86	75	91
1997	85	78	91	86	75	88
1998	86	79	89	90	85	88
1999	86	77	88	91	86	90
2000	86	80	90	90	80	91

(Table continues)

Table 5-10   *(Continued)*

Year	House			Senate		
	All Democrats	Southern Democrats	Republicans	All Democrats	Southern Democrats	Republicans
2001	86	77	94	90	79	90
2002	90	82	93	85	69	88
2003	91	85	95	90	76	95
2004	91	83	93	88	76	93
2005	91	84	93	90	81	90
2006	90	82	92	89	77	87
2007	95	85	90	92	93	84
2008	97	—	92	92	—	87
2009	94	—	90	94	—	87
2010	93	—	94	94	—	93
2011	91	—	94	94	—	89
2012	92	—	93	93	—	83
2013	92	—	95	96	—	89
2014	95	—	95	99	—	89

Note: "—" indicates not available. Data show percentage of members voting with a majority of their party on party unity votes. Party unity votes are those roll calls on which a majority of Democrats vote against a majority of Republicans. Percentages are calculated to eliminate the impact of absences as follows: unity = (unity)/(unity + opposition).

Sources: 1954–1992: Norman J. Ornstein, Thomas E. Mann, and Michael J. Malbin, eds., *Vital Statistics on Congress, 1993–1994* (Washington, D.C.: Congressional Quarterly, 1994), 201–202; 1993–2014: *Congressional Quarterly Weekly Report (CQ Weekly)* (1993), 3479; (1994), 3659; (1996), 245, 3461; (1998), 33; (1999), 92, 2993; (2001), 67; (2002), 142, 3281; (2004), 48, 2952; (2006), 97; (2007), 38; (2008), 147, 3337; (2011), 36; (2013), 137; (2015), 41.

Table 5-11 The 114th Congress: House of Representatives

State/district/representative	Party	Year born	Year first elected	% vote in 2014		Campaign expenditures (2013–2014)	Voting ratings[a]						
				Primary	General		VP	PS	PU	AFL-CIO	ADA	CCUS	ACU
Alabama													
1 Byrne	R	1955	2013	U	68	$1,655,999	94	11	99	—	—	—	—
2 Roby	R	1976	2010	U	67	793,565	99	14	91	14	0	77	64
3 Rogers	R	1958	2002	76	66	941,432	99	12	97	19	0	77	60
4 Aderholt	R	1965	1996	U	99	909,881	87	12	94	15	0	75	67
5 Brooks	R	1954	2010	80	74	299,838	99	8	95	14	0	62	84
6 Palmer	R	1954	2014	20	76	1,690,309	—	—	—	—	—	—	—
7 Sewell	D	1965	2010	84	98	1,468,013	98	88	92	95	65	62	13
Alaska													
AL Young	R	1933	1973	74	51	809,039	98	14	89	53	20	83	42
Arizona													
1 Kirkpatrick	D	1950	2008	100	53	3,340,585	93	76	88	100	55	62	23
2 McSally	R	1966	2014	69	50	4,466,678	—	—	—	—	—	—	—
3 Grijalva	D	1948	2002	100	56	561,116	94	88	98	100	100	23	17
4 Gosar	R	1958	2010	100	70	401,797	79	4	95	10	10	69	92
5 Salmon	R	1958	1994	100	70	578,157	98	2	97	10	5	69	100
6 Schweikert	R	1962	2010	100	65	1,119,894	99	6	96	10	5	85	100
7 Gallego	D	1979	2014	48	75	911,026	—	—	—	—	—	—	—
8 Franks	R	1957	2002	73	76	414,181	97	8	99	10	0	85	96
9 Sinema	D	1976	2012	100	55	3,464,333	99	57	75	90	50	77	24
Arkansas													
1 Crawford	R	1966	2010	U	63	665,075	90	11	92	25	0	75	72
2 Hill	R	1956	2014	55	52	2,149,744	—	—	—	—	—	—	—
3 Womack	R	1957	2010	U	79	574,944	100	14	93	14	0	92	72
4 Westerman	R	1967	2014	54	54	955,240	—	—	—	—	—	—	—

(Table continues)

Table 5-11 (Continued)

State/district/representative	Party	Year born	Year first elected	% vote in 2014 Primary	% vote in 2014 General	Campaign expenditures (2013–2014)	VP	PS	PU	AFL-CIO	ADA	CCUS	ACU
California													
1 LaMalfa	R	1960	2012	53	61	730,253	95	11	99	14	5	77	88
2 Huffman	D	1964	2012	68	75	887,468	97	94	99	95	100	31	8
3 Garamendi	D	1945	2009	53	53	1,320,607	97	69	92	95	75	46	12
4 McClintock	R	1956	2008	56	60	1,750,512	98	6	95	10	10	69	100
5 Thompson	D	1951	1998	80	76	1,712,298	99	95	98	90	85	38	13
6 Matsui	D	1944	2005	74	73	982,391	97	92	99	95	95	31	12
7 Bera	D	1965	2012	47	50	4,355,563	99	67	88	86	50	54	8
8 Cook	R	1943	2012	58	68	303,183	99	12	98	33	0	92	72
9 McNerney	D	1951	2006	49	52	1,109,115	98	82	95	95	65	38	8
10 Denham	R	1967	2010	59	56	1,753,321	98	17	91	29	0	77	60
11 DeSaulnier	D	1952	2014	59	67	541,228	—	—	—	—	—	—	—
12 Pelosi	D	1940	1987	74	83	2,395,066	89	95	99	90	85	31	8
13 Lee	D	1946	1998	83	88	1,100,730	95	90	99	95	100	38	20
14 Speier	D	1950	2008	77	77	841,039	94	89	98	89	80	42	14
15 Swalwell	D	1980	2012	49	70	1,669,314	99	88	97	100	85	46	8
16 Costa	D	1952	2004	44	51	1,116,677	96	62	69	79	45	69	8
17 Honda	D	1941	2000	48	52	3,447,979	94	89	99	100	95	33	5
18 Eshoo	D	1942	1992	68	68	1,540,093	98	91	99	95	90	31	8
19 Lofgren	D	1947	1994	76	67	682,507	99	89	98	90	95	31	12
20 Farr	D	1941	1993	74	75	747,789	98	92	97	95	100	31	4
21 Valadao	R	1977	2012	63	58	2,732,693	99	17	89	33	5	85	56
22 Nunes	R	1973	2002	68	72	1,536,605	99	14	95	26	0	85	64
23 McCarthy	R	1965	2006	99	75	5,935,084	99	14	97	19	0	85	72
24 Capps	D	1938	1998	44	52	2,493,170	99	88	97	95	80	42	12
25 Knight	R	1966	2014	28	53	410,835	—	—	—	—	—	—	—
26 Brownley	D	1952	2012	46	51	3,364,754	99	67	90	90	65	54	8

Voting ratings[a]

27 Chu	D	1953	2009	60	59	737,543	98	95	99	100	90	31	17
28 Schiff	D	1960	2000	74	76	870,295	99	94	99	95	85	31	16
29 Cardenas	D	1963	2012	63	75	953,305	96	88	97	95	70	42	16
30 Sherman	D	1954	1996	58	66	1,327,754	99	92	96	95	70	31	20
31 Aguilar	D	1979	2014	17	52	2,246,265	—	—	—	—	—	—	—
32 Napolitano	D	1936	1998	60	60	304,898	97	94	99	100	100	23	16
33 Lieu	D	1969	2014	19	59	2,249,521	—	—	—	—	—	—	—
34 Becerra	D	1958	1992	74	73	1,465,623	96	92	99	95	90	23	12
35 Torres	D	1965	2014	66	63	422,829	—	—	—	—	—	—	—
36 Ruiz	D	1972	2012	50	54	3,087,543	96	61	86	90	60	58	28
37 Bass	D	1953	2010	80	84	822,021	86	95	99	95	95	31	13
38 Sanchez	D	1969	2002	58	59	1,027,339	95	92	98	100	95	31	8
39 Royce	R	1951	1992	71	69	1,743,860	97	12	97	11	0	77	88
40 Roybal-Allard	D	1941	1992	66	61	498,231	98	92	99	95	100	25	8
41 Takano	D	1960	2012	45	57	1,312,896	100	89	99	95	90	38	12
42 Calvert	R	1953	1992	67	66	1,206,751	98	14	92	19	0	85	64
43 Waters	D	1938	1990	67	71	1,062,921	91	89	99	95	95	31	21
44 Hahn	D	1952	2011	100	87	723,718	99	91	98	95	95	38	12
45 Walters	R	1962	2014	45	65	1,323,770	—	—	—	—	—	—	—
46 Sanchez	D	1960	1996	51	60	1,284,392	94	77	94	95	75	38	13
47 Lowenthal	D	1941	2012	57	56	506,597	99	89	99	100	95	33	13
48 Rohrabacher	R	1947	1988	56	64	795,323	94	11	92	10	5	62	96
49 Issa	R	1953	2000	62	60	1,749,467	98	12	97	24	0	92	72
50 Hunter	R	1976	2008	70	71	841,310	98	11	96	14	0	77	78
51 Vargas	D	1961	2012	68	69	801,519	99	88	96	100	65	31	12
52 Peters	D	1958	2012	42	52	4,504,003	99	61	84	81	50	69	24
53 Davis	D	1944	2000	56	59	541,155	98	95	97	90	75	23	12
Colorado													
1 DeGette	D	1957	1996	100	66	1,068,909	96	94	99	95	80	33	8
2 Polis	D	1975	2008	100	57	1,207,969	90	88	93	85	65	46	25
3 Tipton	R	1956	2010	75	58	1,268,959	97	8	96	19	10	85	72
4 Buck	R	1959	2014	44	65	1,268,049	—	—	—	—	—	—	—

(Table continues)

Table 5-11 *(Continued)*

State/district/representative	Party	Year born	Year first elected	% vote in 2014 Primary	% vote in 2014 General	Campaign expenditures (2013–2014)	VP	PS	PU	AFL-CIO	ADA	CCUS	ACU
5 Lamborn	R	1954	2006	53	60	574,481	99	8	99	10	5	77	92
6 Coffman	R	1955	2008	100	52	4,711,132	99	12	93	19	5	92	84
7 Perlmutter	D	1953	2006	100	55	1,891,892	93	90	92	90	70	54	12
Connecticut													
1 Larson	D	1948	1998	U	62	1,659,154	97	86	97	95	75	31	13
2 Courtney	D	1953	2006	U	62	1,127,170	97	89	96	100	75	38	8
3 DeLauro	D	1943	1990	U	67	1,236,492	97	89	98	95	80	23	17
4 Himes	D	1966	2008	U	54	2,371,454	99	92	94	79	75	69	12
5 Esty	D	1959	2012	U	53	2,946,026	97	82	95	95	65	54	8
Delaware													
AL Carney	D	1956	2010	U	59	1,146,817	89	93	96	86	65	62	20
Florida													
1 Miller	R	1959	2001	75	70	543,974	94	10	98	10	0	85	92
2 Graham	D	1963	2014	U	50	3,663,383	—	—	—	—	—	—	—
3 Yoho	R	1955	2012	79	65	791,907	99	9	97	10	10	54	80
4 Crenshaw	R	1944	2000	71	78	1,642,951	99	14	92	21	0	85	52
5 Brown	D	1946	1992	U	65	607,418	96	91	96	100	75	38	21
6 DeSantis	R	1978	2012	U	63	430,188	99	5	98	10	5	77	100
7 Mica	R	1943	1992	72	64	727,556	100	12	98	10	5	77	92
8 Posey	R	1947	2008	U	66	1,042,652	99	5	93	14	10	54	88
9 Grayson	D	1958	2008	74	54	3,402,601	98	91	97	95	85	25	12
10 Webster	R	1949	2010	U	62	941,147	98	14	94	20	0	85	72
11 Nugent	R	1951	2010	U	67	317,246	99	8	96	5	5	73	76
12 Bilirakis	R	1963	2006	U	U	700,434	99	14	97	14	0	85	88
13 Jolly	R	1972	2014[b]	U	75	1,835,874	100	12	84	—	—	—	—
14 Castor	D	1966	2006	U	U	472,948	95	94	98	100	85	33	13

15 Ross	R	1959	2010	U	60	1,398,150	99	14	97	5	5	77	84
16 Buchanan	R	1951	2006	U	62	1,101,628	95	16	96	14	5	85	80
17 Rooney	R	1970	2008	U	63	669,304	98	11	94	10	0	77	76
18 Murphy	D	1983	2012	U	60	4,924,768	99	50	80	86	45	77	20
19 Clawson	R	1959	2014c	U	65	4,824,230	99	10	97	—	—	—	—
20 Hastings	D	1936	1992	79	82	811,995	91	90	98	100	90	42	4
21 Deutch	D	1966	2010	92	100	1,006,801	96	94	99	90	90	54	8
22 Frankel	D	1948	2012	U	58	1,354,369	97	89	98	95	75	31	16
23 Wasserman Schultz	D	1966	2004	U	63	2,753,276	94	97	96	95	65	36	9
24 Wilson	D	1942	2010	80	86	234,359	97	92	99	95	80	23	8
25 Diaz-Balart	R	1961	2002	U	U	605,137	98	17	88	32	0	83	52
26 Curbelo	R	1980	2014	47	51	2,357,633	—	18	—	37	—	—	—
27 Ros-Lehtinen	R	1952	1989	U	U	850,120	94	18	87	37	0	83	61
Georgia													
1 Carter	R	1957	2014	36	61	1,606,049	95	62	82	90	55	58	21
2 Bishop	D	1947	1992	100	59	1,091,589	95	10	97	19	0	83	76
3 Westmoreland	R	1950	2004	69	100	1,045,183	93	95	98	100	75	31	13
4 Johnson	D	1954	2006	55	100	640,573	85	90	99	95	85	33	4
5 Lewis	D	1940	1986	100	100	745,566	99	11	99	14	5	85	92
6 Price	R	1954	2004	100	66	1,724,935	98	15	97	10	5	85	80
7 Woodall	R	1970	2010	100	65	500,041	99	6	98	19	0	77	20
8 Scott	R	1969	2010	100	100	800,955	97	11	98	15	0	77	88
9 Collins	R	1966	2012	80	81	664,455	—	—	—	—	—	—	—
10 Hice	R	1960	2014	33	67	949,720	—	—	—	—	—	—	—
11 Loudermilk	R	1963	2014	37	100	1,034,392	—	—	—	—	—	—	—
12 Allen	R	1951	2014	54	55	3,083,060	—	—	—	—	—	—	—
13 Scott	D	1946	2002	82	100	1,157,434	95	88	92	95	80	54	12
14 Graves	R	1970	2010	74	100	736,722	98	12	98	14	5	85	92
Hawaii													
1 Takai	D	1967	2014	43	51	1,826,464	—	—	—	—	—	—	—
2 Gabbard	D	1981	2012	81	76	905,585	95	82	93	100	80	31	16

(Table continues)

Table 5-11 (*Continued*)

State/district/representative	Party	Year born	Year first elected	% vote in 2014 Primary	% vote in 2014 General	Campaign expenditures (2013–2014)	VP	PS	PU	AFL-CIO	ADA	CCUS	ACU
Idaho													
1 Labrador	R	1967	2010	79	65	425,011	97	14	94	10	10	69	100
2 Simpson	R	1950	1998	62	61	2,462,428	98	12	92	19	0	85	46
Illinois													
1 Rush	D	1946	1992	73	73	344,604	52	89	98	92	60	33	5
2 Kelly	D	1956	2013	71	78	1,421,097	98	91	99	100	70	55	16
3 Lipinski	D	1966	2004	50	65	618,212	97	71	85	90	40	62	33
4 Gutierrez	D	1953	1992	61	78	408,968	82	92	99	95	80	46	4
5 Quigley	D	1958	2009	99	63	779,868	98	92	98	89	75	54	8
6 Roskam	R	1961	2006	88	67	4,079,870	98	14	95	24	0	85	76
7 Davis	D	1941	1996	86	85	469,170	91	88	99	94	85	25	9
8 Duckworth	D	1968	2012	24	56	2,289,837	88	83	92	95	55	50	16
9 Schakowsky	D	1944	1998	52	66	1,327,081	98	95	99	95	95	31	16
10 Dold[d]	R	1969	2010	73	51	3,648,085	—	—	—	—	—	—	—
11 Foster	D	1955	2006	26	53	1,812,623	99	83	93	79	55	62	12
12 Bost	R	1960	2014	52	52	1,291,883	—	—	—	—	—	—	—
13 Davis	R	1970	2012	34	59	3,382,441	97	14	91	38	5	77	56
14 Hultgren	R	1966	2010	88	65	957,245	98	12	98	14	5	85	84
15 Shimkus	R	1958	1996	80	75	1,816,163	99	14	92	33	5	83	46
16 Kinzinger	R	1978	2010	67	71	1,377,467	99	14	91	19	0	85	52
17 Bustos	D	1961	2012	35	55	3,089,768	99	68	85	90	50	69	8
18 Schock[e]	R	1981	2008	87	75	1,534,176	97	14	91	20	0	92	52
Indiana													
1 Visclosky	D	1949	1984	100	61	892,913	98	85	96	95	70	38	12
2 Walorski	R	1963	2012	100	59	1,836,516	100	12	95	10	0	85	68
3 Stutzman	R	1976	2010	82	66	1,061,404	97	8	98	14	0	85	96
4 Rokita	R	1970	2010	71	67	1,157,769	99	12	98	10	0	85	82
5 Brooks	R	1960	2012	73	65	1,018,137	99	14	95	14	0	92	80

Voting ratings[a]

6 Messer	R	1969	2012	100	66	869,108	98	12	97	10	0	85	88
7 Carson	D	1974	2008	89	55	782,921	98	95	97	95	85	23	20
8 Bucshon	R	1962	2010	75	60	820,413	99	14	95	14	0	85	84
9 Young	R	1972	2010	79	62	1,405,165	99	12	94	19	0	92	84
Iowa													
1 Blum	R	1955	2014	51	51	1,035,952	—	—	—	—	—	—	—
2 Loebsack	D	1952	2006	86	52	1,721,736	99	71	90	95	70	31	8
3 Young	R	1968	2014	15	53	1,968,425	—	—	—	—	—	—	—
4 King	R	1949	2002	84	62	1,983,501	96	10	97	14	0	77	88
Kansas													
1 Huelskamp	R	1968	2010	55	68	878,253	98	3	95	10	10	62	96
2 Jenkins	R	1963	2008	69	57	3,122,372	99	12	98	19	5	92	80
3 Yoder	R	1976	2010	100	60	1,971,402	99	12	97	14	5	85	84
4 Pompeo	R	1963	2010	63	67	2,673,678	87	9	99	10	0	85	100
Kentucky													
1 Whitfield	R	1943	1994	U	73	1,447,566	95	15	91	30	0	85	60
2 Guthrie	R	1964	2008	U	69	1,292,843	98	14	96	14	0	92	72
3 Yarmuth	D	1947	2006	87	63	833,527	98	92	98	90	85	38	8
4 Massie	R	1971	2012	U	68	558,876	100	17	89	29	30	62	88
5 Rogers	R	1937	1980	U	78	1,125,832	98	14	92	20	0	85	65
6 Barr	R	1973	2012	U	60	2,295,731	99	14	96	10	0	85	76
Louisiana													
1 Scalise	R	1965	2008	78[f]	f	2,742,971	98	11	99	14	0	93	92
2 Richmond	D	1973	2010	69[f]	f	1,183,989	79	94	97	100	80	46	17
3 Boustany	R	1956	2004	79[f]	f	2,118,901	99	14	96	29	0	85	64
4 Fleming	R	1951	2008	73[f]	f	903,078	100	6	99	14	5	69	88
5 Abraham	R	1954	2014	23[f]	41[f]	884,868	—	—	—	—	—	—	—
6 Graves	R	1972	2014	27[f]	42[f]	1,527,595	—	—	—	—	—	—	—
Maine													
1 Pingree	D	1955	2008	89	58	381,502	97	83	98	95	100	23	17
2 Poliquin	R	1953	2014	53	45	1,720,116	—	—	—	—	—	—	—

(Table continues)

219

Table 5-11 (*Continued*)

220

State/district/representative	Party	Year born	Year first elected	% vote in 2014 Primary	% vote in 2014 General	Campaign expenditures (2013–2014)	VP	PS	PU	AFL-CIO	ADA	CCUS	ACU
Maryland													
1 Harris	R	1957	2010	78	70	1,169,106	97	6	98	14	5	77	92
2 Ruppersberger	D	1946	2002	78	61	893,339	92	81	93	95	65	54	17
3 Sarbanes	D	1962	2006	85	60	756,851	99	94	99	95	95	19	4
4 Edwards	D	1958	2008	87	70	567,094	97	94	99	95	95	23	13
5 Hoyer	D	1939	1981	100	64	3,843,176	98	95	96	90	75	42	12
6 Delaney	D	1963	2012	100	50	2,586,097	97	78	92	86	70	62	20
7 Cummings	D	1951	1996	91	70	787,933	99	91	99	100	90	23	12
8 Van Hollen	D	1959	2002	91	61	1,412,129	99	94	99	90	80	38	24
Massachusetts													
1 Neal	D	1949	1988	99	74	1,241,117	97	91	98	100	85	42	9
2 McGovern	D	1959	1996	99	72	855,087	98	91	99	95	100	33	8
3 Tsongas	D	1946	2007	99	60	958,140	97	88	98	95	90	42	12
4 Kennedy	D	1980	2012	99	72	1,629,037	99	91	98	95	90	33	8
5 Clark	D	1963	2013	81	71	1,943,089	95	89	99	—	—	—	—
6 Moulton	D	1978	2014	51	54	3,326,394	—	—	—	—	—	—	—
7 Capuano	D	1952	1998	99	81	653,147	91	90	98	100	95	25	12
8 Lynch	D	1955	2001	99	77	1,235,108	96	90	96	100	80	33	17
9 Keating	D	1952	2010	99	53	1,387,397	98	86	96	100	85	33	16
Michigan													
1 Benishek	R	1952	2010	70	52	2,176,822	94	14	93	19	0	85	68
2 Huizenga	R	1969	2010	100	64	1,105,248	99	12	99	10	5	69	80
3 Amash	R	1980	2010	57	58	1,554,134	99	20	89	24	25	58	92
4 Moolenaar	R	1961	2014	52	56	1,128,662	—	—	—	—	—	—	—
5 Kildee	D	1958	2012	100	67	938,757	100	97	99	100	85	31	8
6 Upton	R	1953	1986	71	56	3,941,684	96	14	91	24	0	92	72

District	Party	Born	Elected			Population							
7 Walberg	R	1951	2006	79	53	1,784,291	99	14	99	10	0	85	94
8 Bishop	R	1967	2014	60	55	1,018,365	—	—	—	—	—	—	—
9 Levin	D	1931	1982	100	60	1,491,687	100	94	99	100	80	77	12
10 Miller	R	1954	2002	100	69	795,742	100	14	96	14	0	77	76
11 Trott	R	1960	2014	66	56	4,958,200	—	—	—	—	—	—	—
12 Dingell	D	1961	2014	78	65	1,272,508	—	—	—	—	—	—	—
13 Conyers	D	1929	1964	74	79	833,999	97	95	99	95	100	23	13
14 Lawrence	D	1954	2014	36	78	660,743	—	—	—	—	—	—	—
Minnesota													
1 Walz	D	1964	2006	100	54	1,559,503	96	70	87	90	70	38	12
2 Kline	R	1947	2002	100	56	3,226,367	100	14	97	19	0	85	72
3 Paulsen	R	1965	2008	U	62	2,695,111	99	17	96	14	0	85	84
4 McCollum	D	1954	2000	U	61	740,086	95	91	98	95	90	31	12
5 Ellison	D	1963	2006	U	71	1,984,754	94	90	99	95	100	23	20
6 Emmer	R	1961	2014	73	56	2,030,950	—	—	—	—	—	—	—
7 Peterson	D	1944	1990	U	54	1,569,350	100	17	48	67	25	77	42
8 Nolan	D	1943	1974	U	49	2,113,281	99	68	93	100	80	40	8
Mississippi													
1 Nunnelee[g]	R	1958	2010	100	68	766,958	52	15	98	14	0	77	76
2 Thompson	D	1948	1993	96	68	1,138,674	94	86	97	100	90	38	17
3 Harper	R	1956	2008	92	69	804,136	97	14	96	29	0	85	52
4 Palazzo	R	1970	2010	51	70	1,180,696	91	13	99	24	0	77	80
Missouri													
1 Clay	D	1956	2000	100	73	384,887	92	92	98	100	95	46	8
2 Wagner	R	1962	2012	100	64	1,165,959	97	14	96	15	0	85	88
3 Luetkemeyer	R	1952	2008	79	68	801,186	99	14	96	15	0	77	80
4 Hartzler	R	1960	2010	75	68	707,937	91	14	98	14	0	77	72
5 Cleaver	D	1944	2004	82	52	1,015,923	87	91	98	100	85	38	18
6 Graves	R	1963	2000	77	67	1,124,266	94	15	97	19	5	85	72
7 Long	R	1955	2010	62	63	951,627	100	12	99	14	0	85	88
8 Smith	R	1980	2013	100	67	1,589,517	99	12	99	20	5	78	88

(Table continues)

Table 5-11 (Continued)

State/district/representative	Party	Year born	Year first elected	% vote in 2014		Campaign expenditures (2013–2014)	Voting ratings[a]						
				Primary	General		VP	PS	PU	AFL-CIO	ADA	CCUS	ACU
Montana													
AL Zinke	R	1961	2014	33	55	4,665,055	—	—	—	—	—	—	—
Nebraska													
1 Fortenberry	R	1960	2004	86	69	396,337	96	13	88	24	5	85	63
2 Ashford	D	1949	2014	81	49	1,231,468	—	—	—	—	—	—	—
3 Smith	R	1970	2006	68	75	877,940	99	12	99	19	0	85	84
Nevada													
1 Titus	D	1950	2008	86	57	1,012,672	99	82	97	100	70	54	13
2 Amodei	R	1958	2011	U	66	698,201	87	12	92	10	5	83	75
3 Heck	R	1961	2010	U	61	1,979,832	98	14	88	19	0	77	72
4 Hardy	R	1957	2014	43	49	383,494	—	—	—	—	—	—	—
New Hampshire													
1 Guinta[d]	R	1970	2010	49	52	1,261,539	—	—	—	—	—	—	—
2 Kuster	D	1956	2012	100	55	3,641,777	99	74	91	90	65	54	12
New Jersey													
1 Norcross	D	1958	2014[h]	53	57	2,076,614	98	80	92	—	—	—	—
2 LoBiondo	R	1946	1994	46	61	2,425,940	100	23	82	62	20	100	44
3 MacArthur	R	1960	2014	38	54	5,648,742	—	—	—	—	—	—	—
4 Smith	R	1953	1980	65	68	459,641	98	20	88	48	20	92	54
5 Garrett	R	1959	2002	60	55	2,245,456	99	6	96	19	5	77	100
6 Pallone	D	1951	1988	70	60	5,292,910	99	91	99	100	80	33	11
7 Lance	R	1952	2008	42	59	1,031,920	100	14	94	29	0	92	64
8 Sires	D	1951	2006	93	77	581,950	96	89	97	100	65	42	16
9 Pascrell	D	1937	1996	74	68	1,161,104	98	91	99	100	80	38	16
10 Payne	D	1958	2012	86	85	552,332	97	92	99	95	85	42	8

							99	14	91	29	5	92	54
11 Frelinghuysen	R	1946	1994	48	63	1,442,973	—	—	—	—	—	—	—
12 Watson Coleman	D	1945	2014	36	61	1,388,283	—	—	—	—	—	—	—
New Mexico													
1 Lujan Grisham	D	1959	2012	100	59	1,509,600	95	87	94	95	80	38	12
2 Pearce	R	1947	2002	100	64	2,282,213	99	12	95	20	5	69	76
3 Lujan	D	1972	2008	88	62	1,045,768	98	89	97	95	90	38	12
New York													
1 Zeldin	R	1980	2014	61	53	1,814,213	—	—	—	—	—	—	—
2 King	R	1944	1992	U	65	811,982	98	15	87	57	5	85	36
3 Israel	D	1958	2000	U	53	3,494,923	98	91	95	95	75	54	16
4 Rice	D	1965	2014	57	51	3,470,328	—	—	—	—	—	—	—
5 Meeks	D	1953	1998	80	80	882,334	93	94	98	90	70	46	12
6 Meng	D	1975	2012	U	72	613,820	94	87	98	95	70	46	17
7 Velazquez	D	1953	1992	81	83	715,659	93	90	100	95	95	33	16
8 Jeffries	D	1970	2012	U	81	650,169	99	91	99	95	85	46	13
9 Clarke	D	1964	2006	U	81	534,976	95	91	99	95	90	38	13
10 Nadler	D	1947	1992	U	79	1,276,210	98	92	99	95	100	31	4
11 Grimm[i]	R	1970	2010	U	53	2,034,807	94	17	88	67	25	92	27
12 Maloney	D	1948	1992	U	77	1,457,836	96	86	97	95	80	31	13
13 Rangel	D	1930	1970	48	74	1,515,861	72	91	99	95	85	31	13
14 Crowley	D	1962	1998	U	75	2,668,960	95	95	99	90	95	31	4
15 Serrano	D	1943	1990	91	90	165,919	97	89	97	95	100	31	12
16 Engel	D	1947	1988	U	72	1,015,032	97	92	98	95	70	33	21
17 Lowey	D	1937	1988	U	54	2,332,093	99	92	88	95	75	38	4
18 Maloney	D	1966	2012	U[j]	48	4,161,437	98	62	65	95	35	69	24
19 Gibson	R	1964	2010	U	63	2,981,041	99	36	98	62	30	77	36
20 Tonko	D	1949	2008	U	59	871,957	100	91	98	100	95	46	12
21 Stefanik	R	1984	2014	61	53	1,928,160	—	—	—	—	—	—	—
22 Hanna	R	1951	2010	54	74	1,272,661	90	19	84	42	15	92	48
23 Reed	R	1971	2010	U	59	3,471,224	97	15	90	30	5	83	52
24 Katko	R	1962	2014	U	58	1,017,698	—	—	—	—	—	—	—

(Table continues)

Table 5-11 (*Continued*)

State/district/representative	Party	Year born	Year first elected	% vote in 2014 Primary	% vote in 2014 General	Campaign expenditures (2013–2014)	VP	PS	PU	AFL-CIO	ADA	CCUS	ACU
25 Slaughter	D	1929	1986	U	49	796,859	90	90	98	100	95	25	10
26 Higgins	D	1959	2004	U	65	663,042	99	92	98	100	80	54	4
27 Collins	R	1950	2012	U	67	366,415	97	14	94	24	0	85	64
North Carolina													
1 Butterfield	D	1947	2004	81	73	703,902	97	92	96	95	75	42	16
2 Ellmers	R	1964	2010	59	59	1,820,394	99	14	93	14	0	77	76
3 Jones	R	1943	1994	51	68	677,381	89	34	71	38	30	33	84
4 Price	D	1940	1986	U	75	688,801	99	97	97	90	80	31	8
5 Foxx	R	1943	2004	75	61	693,139	100	11	98	10	0	85	92
6 Walker	R	1969	2014	25	59	824,586	—	—	—	—	—	—	—
7 Rouzer	R	1972	2014	53	59	1,492,826	—	—	—	—	—	—	—
8 Hudson	R	1971	2012	U	65	1,143,349	99	14	99	14	0	69	88
9 Pittenger	R	1948	2012	68	94	969,259	99	12	99	15	0	92	92
10 McHenry	R	1975	2004	78	61	1,031,565	97	14	98	16	5	92	80
11 Meadows	R	1959	2012	U	63	375,786	99	5	97	10	5	77	88
12 Adams	D	1946	2014[h]	44	75	743,807	96	80	100	—	—	—	—
13 Holding	R	1968	2012	U	57	1,449,387	99	11	99	10	0	83	92
North Dakota													
AL Cramer	R	1961	2012	100	56	1,505,728	94	14	95	29	5	77	64
Ohio													
1 Chabot	R	1953	1994	100	63	636,369	100	8	99	10	5	85	96
2 Wenstrup	R	1958	2012	100	66	917,602	99	12	97	10	0	85	96
3 Beatty	D	1950	2012	100	64	612,031	99	92	99	100	80	38	12
4 Jordan	R	1964	2006	100	68	1,016,223	99	2	97	10	5	85	100
5 Latta	R	1956	2007	100	66	777,771	100	14	99	14	0	85	76
6 Johnson	R	1954	2010	100	58	1,920,522	100	15	97	14	5	85	76

District	Party	Birth	Year			Population							
7 Gibbs	R	1954	2010	100	100	499,405	99	14	96	14	0	77	76
8 Boehner	R	1949	1990	71	67	18,032,172	1	100	80	—	—	—	—
9 Kaptur	D	1946	1982	100	68	652,304	97	90	98	100	75	33	8
10 Turner	R	1960	2002	80	65	931,476	99	14	91	38	0	77	48
11 Fudge	D	1952	2008	100	79	497,385	95	92	98	100	85	38	17
12 Tiberi	R	1962	2000	100	68	2,358,505	96	14	94	29	0	92	56
13 Ryan	D	1973	2002	85	68	787,870	89	88	98	95	80	31	20
14 Joyce	R	1957	2012	55	63	2,623,918	97	14	90	45	85	50	0
15 Stivers	R	1965	2010	90	66	2,020,213	96	15	93	24	0	92	56
16 Renacci	R	1958	2010	100	64	1,814,488	99	14	92	14	0	85	72
Oklahoma													
1 Bridenstine	R	1975	2012	U	U	365,520	99	6	98	19	15	62	88
2 Mullin	R	1977	2012	80	70	1,110,584	96	13	98	19	5	69	80
3 Lucas	R	1960	1994	83	79	1,254,509	99	14	94	24	0	77	64
4 Cole	R	1949	2002	84	71	1,147,517	97	14	92	33	0	83	56
5 Russell	R	1963	2014	27	60	845,411	—	—	—	—	—	—	—
Oregon													
1 Bonamici	D	1954	2012	99	57	947,513	100	95	99	95	90	31	12
2 Walden	R	1957	1998	76	70	3,463,666	98	14	92	14	0	77	64
3 Blumenauer	D	1948	1996	99	72	1,177,555	92	90	99	95	90	38	12
4 DeFazio	D	1947	1986	98	59	1,277,585	97	85	97	90	95	38	12
5 Schrader	D	1951	2008	83	54	1,365,699	97	70	81	86	70	69	21
Pennsylvania													
1 Brady	D	1945	1998	100	83	750,831	99	91	99	100	90	46	16
2 Fattah	D	1956	1994	100	88	524,914	96	94	97	95	90	38	8
3 Kelly	R	1948	2010	100	61	1,546,195	99	14	94	19	0	92	64
4 Perry	R	1962	2012	100	75	486,891	99	6	96	10	5	85	92
5 Thompson	R	1959	2008	100	64	1,114,806	97	17	90	24	5	92	56
6 Costello	R	1976	2014	100	56	1,674,283	—	—	—	—	—	—	—
7 Meehan	R	1955	2010	100	62	1,332,058	99	14	91	48	10	92	40
8 Fitzpatrick	R	1963	2004	100	62	2,093,800	97	20	82	43	10	92	36
9 Shuster	R	1961	2001	53	64	3,924,437	93	14	94	29	0	92	64

(Table continues)

Table 5-11 *(Continued)*

State/district/ representative	Party	Year born	Year first elected	% vote in 2014		Campaign expenditures (2013–2014)	Voting ratings[a]						
				Primary	General		VP	PS	PU	AFL-CIO	ADA	CCUS	ACU
10 Marino	R	1952	2010	100	63	977,726	98	14	94	24	0	85	60
11 Barletta	R	1956	2010	100	66	1,185,781	99	14	92	38	0	92	52
12 Rothfus	R	1962	2012	100	59	1,807,454	100	8	96	14	5	77	80
13 Boyle	D	1977	2014	41	67	956,281	—	—	—	—	—	—	—
14 Doyle	D	1953	1994	84	100	861,701	93	92	98	100	95	25	13
15 Dent	R	1960	2004	100	100	1,059,973	99	12	89	24	5	92	56
16 Pitts	R	1939	1996	100	58	1,314,732	99	12	97	10	0	85	92
17 Cartwright	D	1961	2012	100	57	878,616	99	89	98	95	85	31	12
18 Murphy	R	1952	2002	100	100	1,156,372	99	14	93	29	0	92	68
Rhode Island													
1 Cicilline	D	1961	2010	63	59	1,282,281	97	91	99	95	90	38	16
2 Langevin	D	1964	2000	100	62	811,117	99	86	98	95	75	46	13
South Carolina													
1 Sanford	R	1960	2013	U	93	1,317,937	99	17	90	9	10	78	100
2 Wilson	R	1947	2001	82	62	964,754	94	14	99	10	5	85	88
3 Duncan	R	1966	2010	U	71	582,705	99	3	97	10	5	69	100
4 Gowdy	R	1964	2010	U	85	588,778	99	6	98	10	5	85	100
5 Mulvaney	R	1967	2010	U	59	1,136,134	93	6	95	10	5	85	100
6 Clyburn	D	1940	1992	86	73	2,184,698	98	92	96	100	80	45	13
7 Rice	R	1957	2012	U	60	876,374	96	14	96	14	5	85	80
South Dakota													
AL Noem	R	1971	2010	U	67	1,684,069	93	14	96	14	0	77	64
Tennessee													
1 Roe	R	1945	2008	84	83	532,409	99	12	97	10	5	85	80
2 Duncan	R	1947	1988	60	72	992,997	99	12	90	14	20	69	96

3 Fleischmann	R	1962	2010	51	62	1,559,068	99	12	97	10	5	85	88
4 DesJarlais	R	1964	2010	45	58	643,369	75	4	97	14	5	77	76
5 Cooper	D	1954	1982	100	62	600,091	99	83	88	75	65	67	28
6 Black	R	1951	2010	77	71	587,243	98	14	99	10	5	85	88
7 Blackburn	R	1952	2002	84	70	1,444,429	99	9	99	10	5	83	84
8 Fincher	R	1973	2010	79	71	629,223	97	12	98	10	5	75	72
9 Cohen	D	1949	2006	66	75	915,467	98	94	98	95	95	31	16
Texas													
1 Gohmert	R	1953	2004	100	77	695,708	95	8	96	19	10	69	96
2 Poe	R	1948	2004	100	68	507,176	96	9	96	14	5	69	79
3 Johnson	R	1930	1991	81	82	1,261,812	92	8	98	15	0	77	92
4 Ratcliffe	R	1965	2014	29	100	1,388,481	—	—	—	—	—	—	—
5 Hensarling	R	1957	2002	100	85	3,408,252	98	11	98	10	0	85	96
6 Barton	R	1949	1984	73	61	1,659,725	91	7	97	20	5	85	87
7 Culberson	R	1956	2000	100	63	691,304	94	15	93	20	0	75	84
8 Brady	R	1955	1996	68	89	2,184,912	94	15	98	10	0	85	88
9 Green	D	1947	2004	100	91	483,696	90	89	97	95	75	54	12
10 McCaul	R	1962	2004	100	62	1,599,939	99	14	98	10	0	85	84
11 Conaway	R	1948	2004	74	90	1,560,657	98	14	98	14	0	77	76
12 Granger	R	1943	1996	100	71	1,317,818	96	15	96	20	0	75	74
13 Thornberry	R	1958	1994	68	84	1,693,677	99	14	99	14	0	77	80
14 Weber	R	1953	2012	100	62	595,588	99	6	98	10	5	69	84
15 Hinojosa	D	1940	1996	100	54	466,828	83	91	94	100	70	38	9
16 O'Rourke	D	1972	2012	100	67	409,513	99	86	98	95	80	46	20
17 Flores	R	1954	2010	100	65	1,437,623	98	12	98	10	0	85	88
18 Jackson Lee	D	1950	1994	100	72	384,140	92	89	97	100	80	23	13
19 Neugebauer	R	1949	2003	64	77	1,885,967	99	8	99	14	0	77	92
20 Castro	D	1974	2012	100	76	1,182,967	98	89	98	95	75	42	12
21 Smith	R	1947	1986	60	72	1,567,733	97	13	99	14	0	85	83
22 Olson	R	1962	2008	100	67	1,299,370	97	11	98	10	0	85	92
23 Hurd	R	1977	2014	41	50	1,437,694	—	—	—	—	—	—	—
24 Marchant	R	1951	2004	100	65	431,772	95	8	98	10	5	69	96
25 Williams	R	1949	2012	100	60	1,564,454	93	5	99	14	5	77	84

(Table continues)

Table 5-11 *(Continued)*

State/district/ representative	Party	Year born	Year first elected	% vote in 2014 Primary	% vote in 2014 General	Campaign expenditures (2013–2014)	Voting ratings[a] VP	PS	PU	AFL-CIO	ADA	CCUS	ACU
26 Burgess	R	1950	2002	83	83	1,068,923	99	6	94	14	5	85	92
27 Farenthold	R	1961	2010	100	64	1,081,932	99	14	96	19	5	77	76
28 Cuellar	D	1955	2004	100	82	937,078	99	45	73	76	35	77	20
29 Green	D	1947	1992	100	90	687,926	93	72	86	95	75	50	20
30 Johnson	D	1935	1992	70	88	546,099	97	88	97	100	80	38	24
31 Carter	R	1941	2002	100	64	862,690	96	13	96	19	0	77	71
32 Sessions	R	1955	1996	64	62	3,015,805	99	14	99	15	0	85	80
33 Veasey	D	1971	2012	73	87	1,224,552	99	83	96	100	75	46	12
34 Vela	D	1963	2012	100	59	867,735	96	66	86	81	55	62	12
35 Doggett	D	1946	1994	100	62	630,990	99	85	99	95	90	46	24
36 Babin	R	1948	2014	33	76	972,205	—	—	—	—	—	—	—
Utah													
1 Bishop	R	1951	2002	P	65	527,675	91	15	99	24	5	69	80
2 Stewart	R	1960	2012	P	61	665,016	96	15	95	14	5	85	80
3 Chaffetz	R	1967	2008	P	72	785,881	88	15	97	15	5	85	84
4 Love	R	1975	2014	P	51	5,159,840	—	—	—	—	55	88	42
Vermont													
AL Welch	D	1947	2006	100	64	700,783	99	91	97	90	95	31	12
Virginia													
1 Wittman	R	1959	2007	76	63	866,738	99	11	97	24	0	92	72
2 Rigell	R	1960	2010	U	59	1,605,821	99	14	94	19	0	85	84
3 Scott	D	1947	1992	U	94	473,415	99	91	97	90	85	31	8
4 Forbes	R	1952	2001	U	60	1,082,780	99	14	95	29	0	77	68
5 Hurt	R	1969	2010	U	61	1,227,681	96	9	98	10	0	85	88
6 Goodlatte	R	1952	1992	U	75	1,710,543	99	14	97	14	0	85	84
7 Brat	R	1964	2014[h]	56	61	1,408,693	98	0	92	—	—	—	—
8 Beyer	D	1950	2014	46	63	2,789,738	—	—	—	—	—	—	—
9 Griffith	R	1958	2010	U	72	889,987	99	14	92	14	20	69	72

District	Party	Born	Elected	P/U	%	Vote							
10 Comstock	R	1959	2014	P	56	3,403,550	—	—	—	—	—	—	—
11 Connolly	D	1950	2008	U	57	1,455,123	99	91	95	86	70	62	24
Washington													
1 DelBene	D	1962	2012	51	55	2,289,913	99	83	94	95	65	46	12
2 Larsen	D	1965	2000	56	61	1,112,278	97	91	95	90	55	50	5
3 Herrera Beutler	R	1978	2010	49	62	944,901	98	17	90	25	0	60	59
4 Newhouse	R	1955	2014	26	51	981,595	—	—	—	—	—	—	—
5 McMorris Rodgers	R	1969	2004	52	61	2,910,112	99	14	98	14	5	83	72
6 Kilmer	D	1974	2012	59	63	1,239,106	97	85	94	90	60	69	20
7 McDermott	D	1936	1988	77	81	581,723	97	91	99	100	100	23	8
8 Reichert	R	1950	2004	62	63	991,617	99	15	87	43	5	100	48
9 Smith	D	1965	1996	64	71	795,120	84	94	97	89	85	46	12
10 Heck	D	1952	2012	52	55	1,744,518	96	91	97	90	60	62	12
West Virginia													
1 McKinley	R	1947	2010	100	64	2,021,174	100	12	91	48	0	85	64
2 Mooney	R	1971	2014	36	47	2,010,181	—	—	—	—	—	—	—
3 Jenkins	R	1960	2014	100	55	1,647,575	—	—	—	—	—	—	—
Wisconsin													
1 Ryan	R	1970	1998	94	63	8,051,590	99	14	98	14	0	85	84
2 Pocan	D	1964	2012	100	68	896,400	99	92	99	100	100	23	12
3 Kind	D	1963	1996	100	56	1,162,176	98	94	94	86	60	62	20
4 Moore	D	1951	2004	71	70	1,045,919	98	94	99	90	85	38	8
5 Sensenbrenner	R	1943	1978	100	69	326,996	99	8	95	0	5	62	96
6 Grothman	R	1955	2014	36	57	1,191,796	—	—	—	—	—	—	—
7 Duffy	R	1971	2010	88	59	1,970,453	91	12	97	15	5	77	72
8 Ribble	R	1956	2010	100	65	1,066,298	99	6	96	14	10	92	80
Wyoming													
AL Lummis	R	1954	2008	76	66	300,949	99	8	97	5	5	69	88

(Table continues)

Table 5-11 *(Continued)*

Note: "—" indicates a newly elected representative (no basis for voting ratings) or data unavailable; "AL" indicates "at large"; "D" indicates Democrat; "P" indicates the candidate was nominated by party convention or caucus; "R" indicates Republican; "U" indicates the candidate received more than 99 percent of the vote or was unopposed and did not appear on the ballot. Information as of April 3, 2015. Table entries reflect those initially elected to serve in the 114th Congress.

[a] Two types of voting ratings are provided: Congressional Quarterly and interest group ratings. Congressional Quarterly calculates "VP," "PS," and "PU" scores for 2014 for members of the 113th Congress. "VP" indicates voting participation score (percentage of recorded votes on which a representative voted "yea" or "nay"). "PS" indicates presidential support score (percentage of votes on which the president took a position that the representative supported). "PU" indicates party unity score (percentage of votes on which a representative supported his or her party when a majority of voting Democrats opposed a majority of voting Republicans). Interest group ratings indicate the percentage of time a representative supported the group-preferred position on votes the group selects. The ratings are the 2013 scores provided by each group for anyone who qualified under each group's own rules. "AFL-CIO" (American Federation of Labor–Congress of Industrial Organizations) is a labor group; "ADA" (Americans for Democratic Action) is a liberal group; "CCUS" (Chamber of Commerce of the United States) is a business group; and "ACU" (American Conservative Union) is a conservative group. Voting participation and "ADA" scores are lowered by a member's failure to vote. Failure to vote does not lower the other scores.

[b] David Jolly (R) was initially elected in a special election on March 11, 2014.

[c] Curt Clawson (R) was initially elected in a special election on June 24, 2014.

[d] This representative had previously served in Congress (see "Year first elected" column) but did not serve in the 113th Congress and therefore has no voting ratings.

[e] Aaron Schock (R) resigned on March 31, 2015, amidst controversy over campaign funds. A special election to fill his seat is expected in September 2015.

[f] Louisiana election law calls for a primary open to candidates of all parties and held on the same day as the general election in the rest of the nation. If a candidate wins 50 percent or more of the vote in that primary, that candidate is declared elected and no runoff or "general election," normally held about a month later, occurs.

[g] Alan Nunnelee (R) died on February 6, 2015. Trent Kelly (R) won a special election for the seat on June 2, 2015.

[h] Alma Adams (D), Donald Norcross (D), and Dave Brat (R) all won two simultaneous elections in November 2014: a special election to serve in the 113th Congress and a general election for a full term beginning in the 114th Congress.

[i] Michael G. Grimm (R) resigned on January 5, 2015, after pleading guilty to tax evasion charges. Daniel M. Donovan Jr. (R) won a special election for the seat on May 5, 2015.

[j] Sean Maloney (D) ran uncontested for the nominations of both the Democratic and Working Families parties; he also ran for the Independence Party nomination but lost to Nan Hayworth.

Sources: "Biographical Directory of the United States Congress" (*http://bioguide.congress.gov*); CQ Press, U.S. Political Stats database, interest group ratings data compiled by J. Michael Sharp; *CQ Weekly*, March 16, 2015, 34–35, 44–45, 48–49 (*www.cq.com*); Federal Election Commission, "Congressional Candidate Table 7: Financial Activity of 2014 House Campaigns, January 1, 2013–December 31, 2014" (*www.fec.gov*); Office of the Clerk, U.S. House of Representatives, *Statistics of the Congressional Election from Official Sources for the Election of November 4, 2014* (*http://clerk.house.gov*); state election websites.

Table 5-12 The 114th Congress: Senate

State/senator	Party	Year born	Year first elected	Last election	% vote in last election Primary	% vote in last election General	Last campaign expenditures[a]	Voting ratings[b] VP	PS	PU	AFL-CIO	ADA	CCUS	ACU
Alabama														
Shelby	R	1934	1986	2010	84	65	$1,508,102	99	49	95	22	10	50	76
Sessions	R	1946	1996	2014	U	97	2,143,300	97	53	97	18	10	50	88
Alaska														
Murkowski	R	1957	2004	2010	49	39[c]	4,113,372	92	73	45	69	30	71	38
Sullivan	R	1964	2014	2014	40	48	7,797,250	—	—	—	—	—	—	—
Arizona														
McCain	R	1936	1986	2006	56	53	20,490,726	97	58	91	33	20	88	52
Flake	R	1962	2012	2012	69	49	9,556,220	99	63	82	28	15	88	71
Arkansas														
Boozman	R	1950	2010	2010	53	58	3,666,977	81	53	97	28	10	75	80
Cotton[d]	R	1977	2014	2014	U	56	13,948,938	99	9	99	19	0	92	92
California														
Feinstein	D	1933	1992	2012	49	63	17,152,230	92	99	99	100	100	50	4
Boxer	D	1940	1992	2010	81	52	17,113,918	91	98	99	100	100	38	4
Colorado														
Bennet	D	1964	2009	2010	54	48	10,875,815	98	99	99	100	85	38	8
Gardner[d]	R	1974	2014	2014	100	48	12,490,384	97	11	93	21	5	85	84
Connecticut														
Blumenthal	D	1946	2010	2010	U	55	8,718,286	99	98	99	100	100	50	4
Murphy	D	1973	2012	2012	67	55	10,436,219	99	99	99	100	100	50	4
Delaware														
Carper	D	1947	2000	2012	88	66	5,324,026	99	99	98	94	80	50	4
Coons	D	1963	2010	2014	U	56	5,456,856	97	99	99	100	85	50	4
Florida														
Nelson	D	1942	2000	2012	79	55	17,127,713	96	99	98	100	85	38	4
Rubio	R	1971	2010	2010	85	49	21,638,316	90	53	91	6	5	71	96

(Table continues)

231

Table 5-12 *(Continued)*

State/senator	Party	Year born	Year first elected	Last election	% vote in last election Primary	% vote in last election General	Last campaign expenditures[a]	VP	PS	PU	AFL-CIO	ADA	CCUS	ACU
Georgia														
Isakson	R	1944	2004	2010	100	58	7,644,579	97	64	83	33	10	63	54
Perdue	R	1949	2014	2014	31	53	14,196,681	—	—	—	—	—	—	—
Hawaii														
Schatz	D	1972	2012	2014[e]	49	67	5,156,058	87	98	100	100	100	38	4
Hirono	D	1947	2012	2012	57	63	5,644,499	100	99	99	100	100	38	0
Idaho														
Crapo	R	1951	1998	2010	79	71	2,515,883	100	48	98	6	0	63	88
Risch	R	1943	2008	2014	80	65	1,826,223	98	46	99	6	0	63	92
Illinois														
Durbin	D	1944	1996	2014	36	54	12,615,728	99	100	99	100	95	50	4
Kirk	R	1959	2010[f]	2010	57	48	14,146,756	96	66	85	38	40	88	44
Indiana														
Coats	R	1943	2010[g]	2010	39	55	3,612,863	98	65	87	22	10	88	83
Donnelly	D	1955	2012	2012	U	50	5,588,317	99	97	98	94	50	38	16
Iowa														
Grassley	R	1933	1980	2010	98	64	6,749,896	100	57	97	11	0	75	88
Ernst	R	1970	2014	2014	54	52	11,913,212	—	—	—	—	—	—	—
Kansas														
Roberts	R	1936	1996	2014	48	53	8,128,381	89	46	98	11	0	75	84
Moran	R	1954	2010	2010	50	70	5,965,285	85	52	96	19	0	75	80
Kentucky														
McConnell	R	1942	1984	2014	60	56	30,690,557	99	55	95	17	0	88	92
Paul	R	1963	2010	2010	59	56	7,756,095	98	53	94	0	0	75	96
Louisiana														
Vitter	R	1961	2004	2010	88	57	10,572,617	90	51	90	18	5	50	79
Cassidy[d]	R	1957	2014	2014	41	47	14,658,019	90	15	94	10	5	77	80
Maine														
Collins	R	1952	1996	2014	86	67	5,703,101	100	74	43	56	50	75	28
King	I	1944	2012	2012	—	53	2,888,522	99	96	95	100	85	38	13

	Party						Population							
Maryland														
Mikulski	D	1936	1986	2010	82	62	3,990,768	94	100	98	100	95	38	4
Cardin	D	1943	2006	2012	74	56	6,224,816	99	100	99	100	100	38	4
Massachusetts														
Warren	D	1949	2012	2012	100	54	42,211,677	99	99	97	100	90	57	4
Markey	D	1946	2013	2014[h]	98	59	17,857,729	97	99	97	100	—	67	—
Michigan														
Stabenow	D	1950	2000	2012	100	59	13,531,442	97	100	99	100	95	38	0
Peters[d]	D	1958	2014	2014	100	55	10,289,555	94	89	67	90	60	46	16
Minnesota														
Klobuchar	D	1960	2006	2012	91	65	8,944,477	99	99	99	100	85	38	4
Franken	D	1951	2008	2014	95	53	24,359,435	99	99	99	100	90	38	4
Mississippi														
Cochran	R	1937	1978	2014	99	60	8,018,305	71	91	62	28	10	63	60
Wicker	R	1951	2007	2012	89	57	2,203,166	98	91	61	28	10	63	60
Missouri														
McCaskill	D	1953	2006	2012	100	55	21,424,030	93	98	98	100	65	50	4
Blunt	R	1950	2010	2010	71	54	12,141,841	94	93	57	17	10	88	71
Montana														
Tester	D	1956	2006	2012	100	49	13,328,572	98	97	96	94	90	38	12
Daines[d]	R	1962	2014	2014	83	58	6,668,759	99	94	11	14	5	85	80
Nebraska														
Fischer	R	1951	2012	2012	41	58	5,176,461	100	99	57	17	5	75	76
Sasse	R	1972	2014	2014	49	64	5,864,653	—	—	—	—	—	—	—
Nevada														
Reid	D	1939	1986	2010	75	50	22,548,568	99	95	95	94	90	50	16
Heller	R	1960	2011	2012	86	46	9,192,588	98	84	61	22	5	88	83
New Hampshire														
Shaheen	D	1947	2008	2014	100	51	16,340,936	99	98	99	91	90	50	8
Ayotte	R	1968	2010	2010	38	60	3,540,079	98	73	64	17	20	100	68
New Jersey														
Menendez	D	1954	2006	2012	100	59	16,226,545	99	99	98	100	95	50	4
Booker	D	1969	2013	2014[i]	58	56	17,521,163	97	99	97	100	—	—	—

(Table continues)

Table 5-12 (Continued)

State/senator	Party	Year born	Year first elected	Last election	% vote in last election		Last campaign expenditures[a]	Voting ratings[b]						
					Primary	General		VP	PS	PU	AFL-CIO	ADA	CCUS	ACU
New Mexico														
Udall	D	1948	2008	2014	100	56	8,736,822	99	99	100	100	95	38	8
Heinrich	D	1971	2012	2012	59	51	6,720,126	99	97	99	100	95	38	12
New York														
Schumer	D	1950	2009	1998	U	66	18,143,840	99	99	100	100	95	38	4
Gillibrand	D	1966	2009	2012	U	72	14,257,872	98	96	99	100	90	38	0
North Carolina														
Burr	R	1955	2004	2010	80	55	4,770,832	97	58	94	22	10	63	84
Tillis	R	1960	2014	2014	46	49	10,513,963	—	—	—	—	—	—	—
North Dakota														
Hoeven	R	1957	2010	2010	100	76	2,909,158	99	60	94	33	10	88	60
Heitkamp	D	1955	2012	2012	100	50	5,498,044	99	95	94	100	70	38	12
Ohio														
Brown	D	1952	2006	2012	100	51	24,567,107	98	99	99	100	95	50	4
Portman	R	1955	2010	2010	100	57	15,054,910	96	63	89	39	15	75	64
Oklahoma														
Inhofe	R	1934	1994	2014	88	68	5,168,776	90	52	97	6	0	86	92
Lankford[d]	R	1968	2014	2014[j]	57	68	4,384,320	81	9	98	19	0	85	80
Oregon														
Wyden	D	1949	1996	2010	90	57	6,424,975	100	98	99	94	90	38	4
Merkley	D	1956	2008	2014	92	56	11,401,522	98	99	100	94	90	38	4
Pennsylvania														
Casey	D	1960	2006	2012	81	54	14,080,904	96	98	98	100	65	50	8
Toomey	R	1961	2010	2010	81	51	16,998,136	95	56	91	11	5	75	80
Rhode Island														
Reed	D	1949	1996	2014	100	71	4,649,761	99	99	98	100	100	50	4
Whitehouse	D	1955	2006	2012	100	65	5,183,335	99	99	99	100	100	50	4

South Carolina														
Graham	R	1955	2002	2014	56	54	11,348,821	93	60	85	33	20	63	68
Scott	R	1965	2014	2014^k	90	61	4,398,025	96	54	98	0	0	75	96
South Dakota														
Thune	R	1961	2004	2010	U	100	3,303,842	99	56	98	22	5	75	88
Rounds	R	1954	2014	2014	56	50	5,176,534	—	—	—	—	—	—	—
Tennessee														
Alexander	R	1940	2002	2014	50	62	9,378,379	92	68	83	39	5	100	60
Corker	R	1952	2006	2012	85	65	6,442,196	96	67	85	33	10	88	64
Texas														
Cornyn	R	1952	2002	2014	59	62	14,783,764	95	57	92	6	0	75	96
Cruz	R	1970	2012	2012	34	56	14,618,864	92	51	98	0	0	63	100
Utah														
Hatch	R	1934	1976	2012	66	65	13,135,929	97	65	84	29	10	75	75
Lee	R	1971	2010	2010	51	62	1,775,993	95	51	99	0	0	75	100
Vermont														
Leahy	D	1940	1974	2010	89	64	3,191,051	98	99	99	94	100	38	4
Sanders	I	1941	2006	2012	99	71	3,247,907	89	94	96	100	100	38	0
Virginia														
Warner	D	1954	2008	2014	P	49	18,112,444	98	99	98	89	65	63	4
Kaine	D	1958	2012	2012	U	53	17,918,247	98	100	99	94	85	50	0
Washington														
Murray	D	1950	1992	2010	46	52	14,873,696	99	99	100	100	95	43	5
Cantwell	D	1958	2000	2012	56	60	11,370,413	99	98	100	100	100	38	4
West Virginia														
Manchin	D	1947	2010	2012	80	61	3,660,906	98	89	87	89	50	50	28
Capito^d	R	1953	2014	2014	87	62	8,803,232	89	15	92	38	5	92	56
Wisconsin														
Johnson	R	1955	2010	2010	85	52	15,316,651	97	54	97	0	0	75	96
Baldwin	D	1962	2012	2012	U	51	15,650,797	99	99	99	100	90	50	4
Wyoming														
Enzi	R	1944	1996	2014	82	71	3,491,953	99	53	97	17	5	63	88
Barrasso	R	1952	2007	2012	90	76	2,523,386	99	52	97	18	0	75	88

(Table continues)

Table 5-12 *(Continued)*

Note: "—" indicates a newly elected senator (no basis for voting ratings) or data unavailable; "D" indicates Democrat; "I" indicates independent; "P" indicates the candidate was nominated by party convention; "R" indicates Republican; "U" indicates the candidate received more than 99 percent of the vote or was unopposed and did not appear on the ballot. Information as of April 3, 2015. Table entries reflect those elected to or continuing service in the 114th Congress.

a Figures for campaign expenditures can cover as many as six years, from January 1 of the year following the preceding election (or whenever the campaign registered with the Federal Election Commission during the six-year election cycle) through December 31 of the election year.

b For a description of the voting ratings, see note a, Table 5-11, this volume.

c Lisa Murkowski (R) lost the 2010 Republican primary but won the general election as a write-in candidate.

d The voting ratings for Shelley Moore Capito (R), Bill Cassidy (R), Tom Cotton (R), Steve Daines (R), Cory Gardner (R), James Lankford (R), and Gary Peters (D) pertain to their prior House service.

e Brian Schatz (D) was appointed to the 112th Congress to fill the vacancy caused by the death of Daniel Inouye. In 2014, he won a special election to serve the remainder of Inouye's term (ending January 3, 2017).

f Mark Steven Kirk (R) won two simultaneous elections in November 2010: a special election to serve in the 111th Congress and a general election for a full term beginning in the 112th Congress.

g Dan Coats (R) began his current Senate service with his election in November 2010. However, he previously served in the U.S. Senate, from 1989 to 1999.

h Edward Markey (D-MA) won the special election on June 25, 2013, to fill the vacancy caused by the resignation of John F. Kerry to become U.S. secretary of state. In 2014, Markey won the general election for a full term beginning in the 114th Congress.

i Cory Booker (D) won the special election on October 16, 2013, to fill the vacancy caused by the death of Frank Lautenberg. In 2014, he won the general election for a full term beginning in the 114th Congress.

j James Lankford (R) won the special election on November 4, 2014, to complete the remaining two years of the term of Sen. Tom Coburn (R), who resigned at the end of the 113th Congress on January 3, 2015.

k Tim Scott (R) was appointed by South Carolina governor Nikki Haley to fill the seat vacated by James W. DeMint upon DeMint's resignation on January 1, 2013, to take a position as president of the Heritage Foundation. In 2014, he won a special election to serve the remainder of DeMint's term (ending January 3, 2017).

Sources: "Biographical Directory of the United States Congress" (*http://bioguide.congress.gov*); CQ Press, U.S. Political Stats database, interest group ratings data compiled by J. Michael Sharp; *CQ Weekly*, March 16, 2015, 36, 43, 50 (*www.cq.com*); Federal Election Commission, "Congressional Candidate Table 5: Six-Year Financial Summary for Senate Campaigns," various years (*www.fec.gov*); Office of the Clerk, U.S. House of Representatives, *Statistics of the Congressional Election from Official Sources for the Election of November 4, 2014* (*http://clerk.house.gov*); state election websites.

6

The Presidency and Executive Branch

- **Presidents**
- **Ratings**
- **Backgrounds**
- **Cabinet and Staff**
- **Congressional Relations**
- **Civil Service Employment**
- **Regulations**

The presidency poses a special problem for those interested in collecting statistical data. The scope and variety of data available on the presidency are limited by the singularity of the office and how individual presidents change the office's organization and operation. The modern presidency has evolved since Franklin D. Roosevelt took office in the 1930s. Since then, the end of the Cold War and the rise of terrorism, the rapid developments in modes of communication, the growth of government power, and the shift in emphasis from conventions to primaries as a way of nominating presidential candidates have further changed the nature of the presidency and the characteristics of incumbent presidents. Indeed, analysts wishing to collect data on many points have found that there have simply been too few modern-day occupants of the Oval Office to sustain statistical analysis.

In spite of this seemingly insurmountable problem, the visibility of the president provides a considerable amount of relevant data. Of all elected officials, for example, only for presidents are public judgments about how well they are doing displayed prominently and repeatedly: the twists and turns in the public approval ratings of a president's job performance are themselves news items. Consequently, elsewhere in this book a graph is devoted to this subject alone—Figure 3-6 shows the overall presidential approval scores for Presidents Bill Clinton and George W. Bush as well as for President Barack Obama. But presidents are not judged only by the public or only while they are in office. At various times and in various ways, historians and political scientists have rated all the U.S. presidents (Table 6-2).

Apart from approval ratings (and, of course, presidential elections), the presidency has not been subjected to extensive statistical scrutiny. However, perhaps because the number of presidents has now reached forty-three (Table 6-1), some additional areas are beginning to receive systematic study.[1] The president's relationship with Congress is one such area. Information about presidential "victories" on votes in Congress (Table 6-7), the extent to which the president is supported by his own party and by the other party (Table 6-8), the number of vetoes presidents from Washington to Barack Obama have exercised (Table 6-9), and presidents' success in securing approval of their nominations (Tables 6-10 and 6-11) are all regularly tabulated and increasingly analyzed.

As discussed in Chapter 4, analysts are beginning to study media coverage of the president more systematically. In part, this study results from the extreme visibility of the president and of the federal government in general (Figure 4-1 and Table 4-17); it also stems from the changing relationships between the president and the press, as indicated, for example, by the considerable decline in press conferences since the 1930s (Table 4-3).

Compilations of various presidential characteristics and activities also have become more numerous or more meaningful as the number of presidents has grown. How individuals get to be president, for example, has been a subject of considerable interest (Tables 6-3 and 6-4). As shown in Chapter 7, presidential appointments have been assessed for their partisan characteristics (Table 7-6) and increasingly for their racial and sex distributions (Table 7-5).

The executive branch, apart from the president, has received little statistical analysis. Yet here too there is ample opportunity for meaningful tabulations, if not for t-tests and correlations. The tremendous size of the federal government (Tables 6-5 and 6-12) necessitates such an interest. The expanded involvement of the government in regulation (Table 6-13 and Figure 6-1) also compels attention. But these data also contain other more subtle and more significant messages. For example, the changing priorities of the nation and of particular presidents are reflected in such mundane listings as the size and of the White House staff over time (Table 6-6).

Thus, although the presidency is a source of data for conventional statistical analyses in only a few areas, the increasing numerical data available provide considerable insight into what traditionally has been viewed as an office of impressive singularity.

Note

1. Only forty-three persons have served as president, but President Barack Obama is known as the forty-fourth president because President Grover Cleveland is counted twice—his nonconsecutive terms make him the twenty-second and twenty-fourth president (*www.whitehouse.gov/about/presidents*).

Table 6-1 Presidents and Vice Presidents of the United States

President (political party)	Born	Died	Age at inauguration	Native of . . .	Elected from . . .	Term of service	Vice president
George Washington (F)	1732	1799	57	Va.	Va.	April 30, 1789–March 4, 1793	John Adams
George Washington (F)			61			March 4, 1793–March 4, 1797	John Adams
John Adams (F)	1735	1826	61	Mass.	Mass.	March 4, 1797–March 4, 1801	Thomas Jefferson
Thomas Jefferson (D-R)	1743	1826	57	Va.	Va.	March 4, 1801–March 4, 1805	Aaron Burr
Thomas Jefferson (D-R)			61			March 4, 1805–March 4, 1809	George Clinton
James Madison (D-R)	1751	1836	57	Va.	Va.	March 4, 1809–March 4, 1813	George Clinton
James Madison (D-R)			61			March 4, 1813–March 4, 1817	Elbridge Gerry
James Monroe (D-R)	1758	1831	58	Va.	Va.	March 4, 1817–March 4, 1821	Daniel D. Tompkins
James Monroe (D-R)			62			March 4, 1821–March 4, 1825	Daniel D. Tompkins
John Q. Adams (NR)	1767	1848	57	Mass.	Mass.	March 4, 1825–March 4, 1829	John C. Calhoun
Andrew Jackson (D)	1767	1845	61	S.C.	Tenn.	March 4, 1829–March 4, 1833	John C. Calhoun
Andrew Jackson (D)			65			March 4, 1833–March 4, 1837	Martin Van Buren
Martin Van Buren (D)	1782	1862	54	N.Y.	N.Y.	March 4, 1837–March 4, 1841	Richard M. Johnson
W. H. Harrison (W)	1773	1841	68	Va.	Ohio	March 4, 1841–April 4, 1841	John Tyler
John Tyler (W)	1790	1862	51	Va.	Va.	April 6, 1841–March 4, 1845	
James K. Polk (D)	1795	1849	49	N.C.	Tenn.	March 4, 1845–March 4, 1849	George M. Dallas
Zachary Taylor (W)	1784	1850	64	Va.	La.	March 4, 1849–July 9, 1850	Millard Fillmore
Millard Fillmore (W)	1800	1874	50	N.Y.	N.Y.	July 10, 1850–March 4, 1853	
Franklin Pierce (D)	1804	1869	48	N.H.	N.H.	March 4, 1853–March 4, 1857	William R. King
James Buchanan (D)	1791	1868	65	Pa.	Pa.	March 4, 1857–March 4, 1861	John C. Breckinridge
Abraham Lincoln (R)	1809	1865	52	Ky.	Ill.	March 4, 1861–March 4, 1865	Hannibal Hamlin
Abraham Lincoln (R)			56			March 4, 1865–April 15, 1865	Andrew Johnson
Andrew Johnson (R)	1808	1875	56	N.C.	Tenn.	April 15, 1865–March 4, 1869	
Ulysses S. Grant (R)	1822	1885	46	Ohio	Ill.	March 4, 1869–March 4, 1873	Schuyler Colfax
Ulysses S. Grant (R)			50			March 4, 1873–March 4, 1877	Henry Wilson

Rutherford B. Hayes (R)	1822	1893	54	Ohio	Ohio	March 4, 1877–March 4, 1881	William A. Wheeler
James A. Garfield (R)	1831	1881	49	Ohio	Ohio	March 4, 1881–Sept. 19, 1881	Chester A. Arthur
Chester A. Arthur (R)	1830	1886	50	Vt.	N.Y.	Sept. 20, 1881–March 4, 1885	
Grover Cleveland (D)	1837	1908	47	N.J.	N.Y.	March 4, 1885–March 4, 1889	Thomas A. Hendricks
Benjamin Harrison (R)	1833	1901	55	Ohio	Ind.	March 4, 1889–March 4, 1893	Levi P. Morton
Grover Cleveland (D)	1837	1908	55		N.Y.	March 4, 1893–March 4, 1897	Adlai E. Stevenson
William McKinley (R)	1843	1901	54	Ohio	Ohio	March 4, 1897–March 4, 1901	Garret A. Hobart
William McKinley (R)			58			March 4, 1901–Sept. 14, 1901	Theodore Roosevelt
Theodore Roosevelt (R)	1858	1919	42	N.Y.	N.Y.	Sept. 14, 1901–March 4, 1905	
Theodore Roosevelt (R)			46			March 4, 1905–March 4, 1909	Charles W. Fairbanks
William H. Taft (R)	1857	1930	51	Ohio	Ohio	March 4, 1909–March 4, 1913	James S. Sherman
Woodrow Wilson (D)	1856	1924	56	Va.	N.J.	March 4, 1913–March 4, 1917	Thomas R. Marshall
Woodrow Wilson (D)			60			March 4, 1917–March 4, 1921	Thomas R. Marshall
Warren G. Harding (R)	1865	1923	55	Ohio	Ohio	March 4, 1921–Aug. 2, 1923	Calvin Coolidge
Calvin Coolidge (R)	1872	1933	51	Vt.	Mass.	Aug. 3, 1923–March 4, 1925	
Calvin Coolidge (R)			52			March 4, 1925–March 4, 1929	Charles G. Dawes
Herbert C. Hoover (R)	1874	1964	54	Iowa	Calif.	March 4, 1929–March 4, 1933	Charles Curtis
Franklin D. Roosevelt (D)	1882	1945	51	N.Y.	N.Y.	March 4, 1933–Jan. 20, 1937	John N. Garner
Franklin D. Roosevelt (D)			55			Jan. 20, 1937–Jan. 20, 1941	John N. Garner
Franklin D. Roosevelt (D)			59			Jan. 20, 1941–Jan. 20, 1945	Henry A. Wallace
Franklin D. Roosevelt (D)			63			Jan. 20, 1945–April 12, 1945	Harry S. Truman
Harry S. Truman (D)	1884	1972	60	Mo.	Mo.	April 12, 1945–Jan. 20, 1949	
Harry S. Truman (D)			64			Jan. 20, 1949–Jan. 20, 1953	Alben W. Barkley
Dwight D. Eisenhower (R)	1890	1969	62	Texas	Pa.	Jan. 20, 1953–Jan. 20, 1957	Richard Nixon
Dwight D. Eisenhower (R)			66			Jan. 20, 1957–Jan. 20, 1961	Richard Nixon
John F. Kennedy (D)	1917	1963	43	Mass.	Mass.	Jan. 20, 1961–Nov. 22, 1963	Lyndon B. Johnson
Lyndon B. Johnson (D)	1906	1973	55	Texas	Texas	Nov. 22, 1963–Jan. 20, 1965	
Lyndon B. Johnson (D)			56			Jan. 20, 1965–Jan. 20, 1969	Hubert H. Humphrey

(Table continues)

Table 6-1 (Continued)

President (political party)	Born	Died	Age at inauguration	Native of . . .	Elected from . . .	Term of service	Vice president
Richard Nixon (R)	1913	1994	56	Calif.	N.Y.	Jan. 20, 1969–Jan. 20, 1973	Spiro T. Agnew
Richard Nixon (R)			60			Jan. 20, 1973–Aug. 9, 1974	Spiro T. Agnew Gerald R. Ford
Gerald R. Ford (R)	1913	2006	61	Neb.	Mich.	Aug. 9, 1974–Jan. 20, 1977	Nelson A. Rockefeller
Jimmy Carter (D)	1924		52	Ga.	Ga.	Jan. 20, 1977–Jan. 20, 1981	Walter F. Mondale
Ronald Reagan (R)	1911	2004	69	Ill.	Calif.	Jan. 20, 1981–Jan. 20, 1985	George H. W. Bush
Ronald Reagan (R)			73			Jan. 20, 1985–Jan. 20, 1989	George H. W. Bush
George H. W. Bush (R)	1924		64	Mass.	Texas	Jan. 20, 1989–Jan. 20, 1993	Dan Quayle
Bill Clinton (D)	1946		46	Ark.	Ark.	Jan. 20, 1993–Jan. 20, 1997	Al Gore
Bill Clinton (D)			50			Jan. 20, 1997–Jan. 20, 2001	Al Gore
George W. Bush (R)	1946		54	Conn.	Texas	Jan. 20, 2001–Jan. 20, 2005	Dick Cheney
George W. Bush (R)			58			Jan. 20, 2005–Jan. 20, 2009	Dick Cheney
Barack Obama (D)	1961		47	Hawaii	Ill.	Jan. 20, 2009–Jan. 20, 2013	Joseph R. Biden Jr.
Barack Obama (D)			51			Jan. 20, 2013–	Joseph R. Biden Jr.

Note: "D" indicates Democrat; "D-R" indicates Democratic-Republican; "F" indicates Federalist; "NR" indicates National Republican; "R" indicates Republican; "W" indicates Whig.

Source: Congressional Quarterly, *Presidential Elections, 1789–2004* (Washington, D.C.: CQ Press, 2005), 3; updated by the editors.

Table 6-2 Ratings of U.S. Presidents

Schlesinger (1948)	Schlesinger (1962)	Maranell-Dodder (1970)	Murray-Blessing (1982)[a]	Ridings-McIver (1989, 1996)	Schlesinger (1997)	Federalist Society-Wall Street Journal (2005)[b]	C-SPAN (2009)[b]	Rottinghaus-Vaughn (2015)
Great 1. Lincoln	*Great* 1. Lincoln	*Accomplishments of administration* 1. Lincoln	*Great* 1. Lincoln	*Overall ranking* 1. Lincoln	*Great* 1. Lincoln	*Great* 1. Washington	*Overall ranking* 1. Lincoln	*Overall ranking* 1. Lincoln
2. Washington	2. Washington	2. F. Roosevelt	2. F. Roosevelt	2. F. Roosevelt	2. Washington	2. Lincoln	2. Washington	2. Washington
3. F. Roosevelt	3. F. Roosevelt	3. Washington	3. Washington	3. Washington	3. F. Roosevelt	3. F. Roosevelt	3. F. Roosevelt	3. F. Roosevelt
4. Wilson	4. Wilson	4. Jefferson	4. Jefferson	4. Jefferson	*Near great* 4. Jefferson	*Near great* 4. Jefferson	4. T. Roosevelt	4. T. Roosevelt
5. Jefferson	5. Jefferson	5. T. Roosevelt	*Near great* 5. T. Roosevelt	5. T. Roosevelt	5. Jackson	5. T. Roosevelt	5. Truman	5. Jefferson
6. Jackson	*Near great* 6. Jackson	6. Truman	6. Wilson	6. Wilson	6. T. Roosevelt	6. Reagan	6. Kennedy	6. Truman
Near great 7. T. Roosevelt	7. T. Roosevelt	7. Wilson	7. Jackson	7. Truman	7. Wilson	7. Truman	7. Jefferson	7. Eisenhower
8. Cleveland	8. Polk/ Truman (tie)	8. Jackson	8. Truman	8. Jackson	8. Truman	8. Eisenhower	8. Eisenhower	8. Clinton
9. J. Adams	9. J. Adams	9. L. Johnson	*Above average* 9. J. Adams	9. Eisenhower	9. Polk	9. Polk	9. Wilson	9. Jackson
10. Polk	10. Cleveland	10. Polk	10. L. Johnson	10. Madison	*High average* 10. Eisenhower	10. Jackson	10. Reagan	10. Wilson
Average 11. J. Q. Adams	*Average* 11. Madison	11. J. Adams	11. Eisenhower	11. Polk	11. J. Adams	*Above average* 11. Wilson	11. L. Johnson	11. Reagan
12. Monroe	12. J. Q. Adams	12. Kennedy	12. Polk	12. L. Johnson	12. Kennedy	12. Cleveland	12. Polk	12. L. Johnson
13. Hayes	13. Hayes	13. Monroe	13. Kennedy	13. Monroe	13. Cleveland	13. J. Adams	13. Jackson	13. Madison
14. Madison	14. McKinley	14. Cleveland	14. Madison	14. J. Adams	14. L. Johnson	14. McKinley	14. Monroe	14. Kennedy
15. Van Buren		15. Madison	15. Monroe	15. Kennedy	15. Monroe	15. Kennedy	15. Clinton	15. J. Adams
		16. Taft		16. Cleveland			16. McKinley	16. Monroe
		17. McKinley		17. McKinley			17. J. Adams	17. G. H. W. Bush
		18. J. Q. Adams		18. J. Q. Adams			18. G. H. W. Bush	18. Obama
		19. Hoover		19. Carter			19. J. Q. Adams	19. Polk

(Table continues)

Table 6-2 (Continued)

Schlesinger (1948)	Schlesinger (1962)	Maranell-Dodder (1970)	Murray-Blessing (1982)[a]	Ridings-McIver (1989, 1996)	Schlesinger (1997)	Federalist Society-Wall Street Journal (2005)[b]	C-SPAN (2009)[b]	Rottinghaus-Vaughn (2015)
16. Taft	15. Taft	20. Eisenhower	16. J. Q. Adams	20. Taft	16. McKinley	16. Monroe	20. Madison	20. Taft
17. Arthur	16. Van Buren	21. A. Johnson	17. Cleveland	21. Van Buren	Average	Average	21. Cleveland	21. McKinley
18. McKinley	17. Monroe	22. Van Buren	Average	22. G. H. W. Bush	17. Madison	17. Madison	22. Ford	22. J. Q. Adams
19. A. Johnson	18. Hoover	23. Arthur	18. McKinley	23. Clinton	18. J. Q. Adams	18. L. Johnson	23. Grant	23. Cleveland
20. Hoover	19. B. Harrison	24. Hayes	19. Taft	24. Hoover	19. B. Harrison	19. G. W. Bush	24. Taft	24. Ford
21. B. Harrison	20. Eisenhower/Arthur (tie)	25. Tyler	20. Van Buren	25. Hayes	20. Clinton	20. Taft	25. Carter	25. Van Buren
Below average	21. A. Johnson	26. B. Harrison	21. Hoover	26. Reagan	21. Taft	21. G. H. W. Bush	26. Coolidge	26. Carter
22. Tyler	Below average	27. Hoover	22. Hayes	27. Ford	22. Van Buren	22. Clinton	27. Nixon	27. Coolidge
23. Coolidge	22. Taylor	28. Buchanan	23. Arthur	28. Arthur	23. Hayes	23. Coolidge	28. Garfield	28. Grant
24. Fillmore	23. Tyler	29. Fillmore	24. Ford	29. Taylor	24. G. H. W. Bush	24. Hayes	29. Taylor	29. B. Harrison
25. Taylor	24. Fillmore	30. Coolidge	25. Carter	30. Garfield	25. Reagan	Below average	30. B. Harrison	30. Hayes
26. Buchanan	25. Coolidge	31. Pierce	26. B. Harrison	31. B. Harrison	26. Arthur	25. J. Q. Adams	31. Van Buren	31. Garfield
27. Pierce	26. Pierce	32. Grant	Below average	32. Nixon	27. Carter	26. Arthur	32. Arthur	32. Arthur
Failure	27. Buchanan	33. Harding	27. Taylor	33. Coolidge	28. Ford	27. Van Buren	33. Hayes	33. Taylor
28. Grant	Failure		28. Reagan	34. Tyler	Below average	28. Ford	34. Hoover	34. Nixon
29. Harding	28. Grant		29. Tyler	35. W. H. Harrison	29. Taylor	29. Grant	35. Tyler	35. G. W. Bush
	29. Harding		30. Fillmore	36. Fillmore	30. Coolidge	30. B. Harrison	36. G. W. Bush	36. Tyler
			31. Coolidge	37. Pierce	31. Fillmore	31. Hoover	37. Fillmore	37. Fillmore
			32. Pierce	38. Grant	32. Tyler	32. Nixon	38. Harding	38. Hoover
				39. A. Johnson		33. Taylor	39. W. H. Harrison	39. W. H. Harrison
				40. Buchanan			40. Pierce	40. Pierce
				41. Harding			41. A. Johnson	41. A. Johnson

Failure	Failure	34. Carter	42. Buchanan	42. Harding
33. A. Johnson	33. Pierce	35. Tyler		43. Buchanan
34. Buchanan	34. Grant	Failure		
35. Nixon	35. Hoover	36. Fillmore		
36. Grant	36. Nixon	37. A. Johnson		
37. Harding	37. A. Johnson	38. Pierce		
	38. Buchanan	39. Harding		
	39. Harding	40. Buchanan		

Note: These ratings are derived from surveys of scholars. The sample sizes range from 49 to 846. In addition to these ratings, the Siena College Research Institute developed an alternative rating system based on scores given across twenty different categories. Using this method, it rated presidents in 1982, 1990, 1994, 2002, and 2010. See Douglas A. Lonnstrom and Thomas O. Kelly II, "The Contemporary Presidency: Rating the Presidents: A Tracking Study," *Presidential Studies Quarterly* 33 (2003): 625–634; and "America's Greatest & Worst Presidents—Siena's 5th Presidential Expert Poll (1982–2010)," Siena Research Institute, July 1, 2010. Additional ratings of the greatest and worst presidents can be found in previous editions of *Vital Statistics on American Politics*. Ratings of "presidential success" from a conservative/libertarian perspective can be found in Ivan Eland, *Recarving Rushmore* (Oakland, CA: Independent Institute, 2008).

[a] The rating of President Ronald Reagan was obtained in a separate poll conducted in 1989.

[b] An earlier rating by the same organization, with slightly different results, was conducted in 1999 (C-SPAN) or 2000 (Federalist Society). See previous editions of *Vital Statistics on American Politics*.

Sources: Henry J. Abraham, *Justices and Presidents: Appointments to the Supreme Court*, 2nd ed. (New York: Oxford University Press, 1985), 380–383; Robert K. Murray and Tim H. Blessing, *Greatness in the White House*, 2nd updated ed. (University Park: Pennsylvania State University Press, 1994), 16–17, 81; Arthur M. Schlesinger Jr., "Rating the Presidents: Washington to Clinton, "*Political Science Quarterly* (Summer 1997); "C-SPAN 2009 Historians Presidential Leadership Survey," (*http://legacy.c-span.org/PresidentialSurvey/presidential-leadership-survey.aspx*); "Presidential Leadership: The Rankings," Federalist Society—*Wall Street Journal*, September 12, 2005 (*www.opinionjournal.com*); William J. Ridings Jr. and Stuart B. McIver, *Rating the Presidents* (Secaucus, N.J.: Carol Publishing, 1997), xi; Brandon Rottinghaus and Justin Vaughn, "Expert Survey of Presidential Greatness," 2015 (*www.polsci.uh.edu/faculty/rottinghaus/rottinghaus.htm*).

Table 6-3   Previous Public Positions Held by Presidents, 1788–2013

Position	*Number of presidents holding position prior to presidency*	
	Pre-1900 (24)	Post-1900 (19)
Vice president	7	7
Cabinet member	7	3
U.S. representative	13	5
U.S. senator	9	6
U.S. Supreme Court justice	0	0
Federal judge	0	1
Governor	11	8
State legislator	16	5
State judge	1	2
Mayor	2	1
Diplomat, ambassador	7	2
Military general	11	1

Position	*Last public position held prior to presidency*	
	Pre-1900 (24)	Post-1900 (19)
Vice president		
Succeeded to presidency	4	5
Won presidency in own right	3	2
Congress		
House	1	0
Senate	3	3
Appointive federal office		
Military general	3	1
Cabinet secretary	3	2
Ambassador	2	0
Other civilian	1	0
Governor	4	6

Note: Included in the list of generals are Andrew Johnson, who held the rank of general when serving as military governor of Tennessee, and Chester A. Arthur, who held the rank of general when serving as quartermaster general. President Cleveland is counted only at his first term.

Source: Compiled by the editors from Robert G. Ferris, *The Presidents,* rev. ed. (Washington, D.C.: National Park Service, 1977); updated by the editors through President Barack Obama.

Table 6-4   Latest Public Office Held by Candidates for Democratic and Republican Presidential Nominations, 1936–2012

Public office[a]	Percentage of all persons polling at least 1 percent in Gallup Poll	Percentage of all Democratic and Republican nominees
President[b]	1	32
Vice president	1	15
U.S. senator	38	18
Governor	22	28
Cabinet officer	13	0
U.S. representative	10	0
Mayor	2	0
U.S. Supreme Court justice	1	0
All others	2	0
No public office	10	8
Total	100	101
	(N = 193)	(N = 40)

[a] Last or current office at time person first polled at least 1 percent support for presidential nomination among fellow partisans or was first nominated.
[b] Presidents Harry S. Truman and Gerald R. Ford received poll support for the presidential nomination only after they actually served in the office.

Source: William R. Keech and Donald R. Matthews, *The Party's Choice: With an Epilogue on the 1976 Nominations* (Washington, D.C.: Brookings Institution, 1976), 18; updated by the editors.

Table 6-5 The President's Cabinet, 2015

Cabinet office	Year established[a]	Current secretary[b]	Date confirmed	Number of paid civilian employees 1980[c]	2014[c]	Number of non–civil service positions[c]	Percentage of all positions
State	1789	John Kerry	1/29/2013	23,644	41,768	31,077	74
Treasury	1789	Jack Lew	2/27/2013	123,754	112,461	6,122	5
War	1789[d]						
Navy	1798[d]						
Interior	1849	Sally Jewell	4/10/2013	79,505	69,807	9,585	14
Justice	1870	Loretta Lynch	4/23/2015	56,426	114,055	48,109	42
Post Office	1872[e]						
Agriculture	1872[e]	Tom Vilsack	1/20/2009	122,839	94,083	7,518	8
Commerce and Labor	1903[f]						
Commerce	1913	Penny Pritzker	6/25/2013	46,189	43,182	9,140	21
Labor	1913	Thomas Perez	7/18/2013	23,717	16,796	1,697	10
Defense	1947	Ashton Carter	2/12/2015	972,999	723,175	126,975	18
Health, Education and Welfare	1953[g]						
Health and Human Services	1979	Sylvia Burwell	6/5/2014	158,644	71,862	12,587	18
Housing and Urban Development	1965	Julian Castro	7/9/2014	16,890	7,795	750	10
Transportation	1966	Anthony Foxx	6/27/2013	72,066	54,790	46,515	85
Energy	1977	Ernest Moniz	5/16/2013	21,729	14,802	1,869	13

Education	1979	Arne Duncan	1/20/2009	7,370	4,123	996	24
Veterans Affairs	1989	Robert McDonald	7/29/2014	235,501[h]	339,903	206,962	61
Homeland Security	2003[i]	Jeh Johnson	12/16/2013		185,870	71,894	39

Note: The Cabinet also includes the vice president. In addition, the following positions have the status of Cabinet-rank: White House chief of staff, Environmental Protection Agency, Office of Management and Budget, U.S. trade representative, U.S. ambassador to the United Nations, Council of Economic Advisers, and Small Business Administration.

[a] The year is that in which a department achieved cabinet status. The Offices of Attorney General and Postmaster General were created in 1789, but the executive departments were not created until later. A Department of Agriculture was established in 1862, but the commissioner did not achieve cabinet status until 1889.

[b] As of April 23, 2015.

[c] December 1980; September 2014. Non–civil service positions include excepted and senior executive service and are as of September 2014.

[d] Incorporated into Defense Department in 1947.

[e] Independent agency as of 1971.

[f] Split into separate departments in 1913.

[g] Split into Health and Human Services and Education in 1979.

[h] Figures are for the Veterans Administration, the agency that was upgraded on March 15, 1989, to the Department of Veterans Affairs.

[i] In January 2003, the Department of Homeland Security was organized with more than 180,000 employees drawn from other agencies.

Sources: "President Obama's Cabinet" (*www.whitehouse.gov*); year established: Ronald C. Moe, "The Federal Executive Establishment: Evolution and Trends," prepared for the U.S. Senate Committee on Governmental Affairs by the Congressional Research Service (Washington, D.C.: Government Printing Office, 1980), 26–27; *Congressional Quarterly Weekly Report* (1988), 3059; U.S. Office of Personnel Management, *Federal Civilian Workforce Statistics, Employment and Trends*, January 1981, 8–9, 11; September 2014, table 11 (*www.opm.gov*).

Table 6-6   White House Staff and Executive Office of the President, 1943–2014

Year	White House	Bureau of Budget/OMB[a]	Council of Economic Advisers	National Security Council	Office of Economic Opportunity	Office of Science and Technology Policy	Office of Administration	Office of the U.S. Trade Representative	Domestic Policy Staff/Office of Policy Development[b]	Total, executive office[c]
1943[d]	51	543								703
1944[c]	58	542								683
1945[c]	64	705								820
1946[c]	216	692	26							1,034
1947[c]	228	549	26							1,077
1948[c]	209	521	38	20						1,205
1949	243	517	36	17						1,240
1950	313	509	38	17						1,408
1955	366	422	33	27						1,221
1960	423	441	31	64						2,779
1965	292	506	45	39	1,768	75		24		3,307
1970	491	636	57	82	2,633	77		26	26	4,808
1975	525	664	48	85				56	55	1,801
1976	534	694	39	79		19		55	43	1,796
1977	387	721	36	68		44		52	41	1,637
1978	381	617	35	76		46	197	58	55	1,679
1979	418	638	36	73		44	180	70	60	1,918
1980	426	631	38	74		50	182	131	68	2,013
1981	378	679	38	65		13	190	139	48	1,674
1982	374	617	35	59		20	196	138	46	1,608
1983	376	619	34	61		23	213	139	39	1,622
1984	371	605	28	63		21	196	147	40	1,593
1985	362	569	32	61		17	193	152	38	1,549
1986	365	537	36	69		11	200	144	40	1,526
1987	375	573	31	56		11	199	155	37	1,604
1988	357	573	35	63		10	232	162	32	1,594
1989	370	536	32	62		20	213	164	37	1,640

1990	391	568	35	60	22	215	172	37	1,729
1991	358	608	36	61	39	241	181	33	1,797
1992	392	553	34	62	47	247	185	42	1,869
1993	392	522	31	52	35	185	177	38	1,570
1994	381	544	29	49	36	182	166	38	1,577
1995	387	522	28	44	34	182	165	30	1,555
1996	387	527	30	43	33	185	161	28	1,582
1997	389	507	28	43	34	178	154	29	1,591
1998	391	509	27	42	34	170	169	30	1,604
1999	393	525	28	40	33	180	180	28	1,651
2000	398	510	29	45	30	194	174	31	1,665
2001	382	509	32	49	19	198	201	33	1,652
2002	408	506	30	64	28	205	193	30	1,712
2003	401	502	29	57	31	216	198	31	1,717
2004	409	509	29	61	31	216	217	30	1,784
2005	411	473	24	61	30	221	210	27	1,697
2006	414	472	24	64	30	225	233	25	1,739
2007	419	476	23	59	32	224	226	22	1,707
2008	399	487	23	57	31	238	229	22	1,707
2009	423	517	24	63	27	226	234	24	1,769
2010	457	547	28	77	34	224	235	23	1,866
2011	464	545	26	74	35	226	236	23	1,875
2012	451	527	32	72	27	233	248	23	1,852
2013	454	456	27	69	34	236	235	23	1,761
2014	475	480	37	69	38	244	229	23	1,823

Note: In almost all instances, when no figures are shown the office did not exist as a separate entity. Data as of December of the year indicated, except 1947 (January), 1960 (October), 2009 (September), and 2014 (September). Data for additional years can be found in previous editions of *Vital Statistics on American Politics.*

[a] The Bureau of the Budget became the Office of Management and Budget (OMB) in 1970.
[b] The Domestic Policy Staff became the Office of Policy Development in 1981.
[c] Includes offices not shown separately.
[d] Total, executive office, excludes personnel in war establishments or emergency war agencies.

Source: U.S. Office of Personnel Management, *Federal Manpower Statistics, Federal Civilian Workforce Statistics, Employment and Trends,* quarterly release (www.opm.gov).

Table 6-7   Presidential Victories on Votes in Congress, 1953–2014

President (political party)/ year	House and Senate victories (percent)	House		Senate	
		Victories (percent)	Number of votes	Victories (percent)	Number of votes
Eisenhower (R)					
1953	89.2	91.2	34	87.8	49
1954	82.8	78.9	38	77.9	77
1955	75.3	63.4	41	84.6	52
1956	69.2	73.5	34	67.7	65
1957	68.4	58.3	60	78.9	57
1958	75.7	74.0	50	76.5	98
1959	52.9	55.6	54	50.4	121
1960	65.1	65.1	43	65.1	86
Average	69.9	68.4		70.7	
Total			354		605
Kennedy (D)					
1961	81.5	83.1	65	80.6	124
1962	85.4	85.0	60	85.6	125
1963	87.1	83.1	71	89.6	115
Average	84.6	83.7		85.2	
Total			196		364
L. Johnson (D)					
1964	87.9	88.5	52	87.6	97
1965	93.1	93.8	112	92.6	162
1966	78.9	91.3	103	68.8	125
1967	78.8	75.6	127	81.2	165
1968	74.5	83.5	103	68.9	164
Average	82.2	85.9		79.7	
Total			497		713
Nixon (R)					
1969	74.8	72.3	47	76.4	72
1970	76.9	84.6	65	71.4	91
1971	74.8	82.5	57	69.5	82
1972	66.3	81.1	37	54.3	46
1973	50.6	48.0	125	52.4	185
1974	59.6	67.9	53	54.2	83
Average	64.3	68.2		61.5	
Total			384		559
Ford (R)					
1974	58.2	59.3	54	57.4	68
1975	61.0	50.6	89	71.0	93
1976	53.8	43.1	51	64.2	53
Average	58.3	51.0		65.0	
Total			194		214

Table 6-7 *(Continued)*

President (political party)/ year	House and Senate victories (percent)	House		Senate	
		Victories (percent)	Number of votes	Victories (percent)	Number of votes
Carter (D)					
1977	75.4	74.7	79	76.1	88
1978	78.3	69.6	112	84.8	151
1979	76.8	71.7	145	81.4	161
1980	75.1	76.9	117	73.3	116
Average	76.6	73.1		79.7	
Total			453		516
Reagan (R)					
1981	82.4	72.4	76	88.3	128
1982	72.4	55.8	77	83.2	119
1983	67.1	47.6	82	85.9	85
1984	65.8	52.2	113	85.7	77
1985	59.9	45.0	80	71.6	102
1986	56.5	33.3	90	80.7	83
1987	43.5	33.3	99	56.4	78
1988	47.4	32.7	104	64.8	88
Average	62.2	45.6		77.9	
Total			721		760
G. H. W. Bush (R)					
1989	62.6	50.0	86	73.3	101
1990	46.8	32.4	108	63.4	93
1991	54.2	43.2	111	67.5	83
1992	43.0	37.1	105	53.3	60
Average	51.8	40.2		65.6	
Total			410		337
Clinton (D)					
1993	86.4	87.3	102	85.4	89
1994	86.4	87.2	78	85.5	62
1995	36.2	26.3	133	49.0	102
1996	55.1	53.2	79	57.6	59
1997	53.6	38.7	75	71.4	63
1998	50.6	36.6	82	66.7	72
1999	37.8	35.4	82	42.2	45
2000	55.0	49.3	69	65.0	40
Average	57.4	50.9		66.0	
Total			700		532
G. W. Bush (R)					
2001	87.0	83.7	43	88.3	77
2002	88.0	82.5	40	91.4	58
2003	78.7	87.3	55	74.8	119
2004	72.6	70.6	34	74.0	50

(Table continues)

Table 6-7   *(Continued)*

President (political party)/ year	House and Senate victories (percent)	House Victories (percent)	House Number of votes	Senate Victories (percent)	Senate Number of votes
2005	78.0	78.3	46	77.8	45
2006	80.9	85.0	40	78.6	70
2007	38.3	15.4	117	66.0	97
2008	47.8	33.8	80	68.5	54
Average	64.1	56.3		76.9	
Total			455		570
Obama (D)					
2009	96.6	94.4	72	98.7	79
2010	85.9	88.1	42	84.4	64
2011	57.1	31.6	95	84.3	89
2012	53.6	19.7	61	79.7	79
2013	56.7	20.9	86	85.2	108
2014	68.7	15.2	66	93.1	145
Average	68.2	41.5		88.1	
Total			422		564

Note: "R" indicates Republican; "D" indicates Democrat. Percentages based on the number of congressional votes supporting the president divided by the total number of votes on which the president had taken a position. The percentages differ slightly from those found in *Congressional Quarterly Almanac, Congressional Quarterly Weekly Report (CQ Weekly),* and Norman J. Ornstein et al.'s *Vital Statistics on Congress* because of corrections and consistent rounding of percentages to one decimal place. Averages are weighted by number of roll calls in each year.

Sources: Congressional Quarterly Almanac (Washington, D.C.: Congressional Quarterly, various years); *Congressional Quarterly Weekly Report (CQ Weekly)* (1992), 3894; (1993), 3473; (1994), 3620; (1996), 3428; (1998), 14; (1999), 76, 2972; (2001), 54; (2002), 142, 3237; (2004), 54–55, 2947–2948; (2006), 87; (2007), 50; (2008), 138–139, 3328; (2010), 118; (2011), 26; (2012), 106–107; (2013), 128; (2014), 178–179; (2015), 32–33.

Table 6-8   Congressional Voting in Support of the President's Position, 1954–2014 (percent)

President (political party)/year	House		Senate	
	Democrats	Republicans	Democrats	Republicans
Eisenhower (R)				
1954	44	71	38	73
1955	53	60	56	72
1956	52	72	39	72
1957	49	54	51	69
1958	44	67	44	67
1959	40	68	38	72
1960	44	59	43	66
Average	46.3	63.8	43.0	70.0
Kennedy (D)				
1961	73	37	65	36
1962	72	42	63	39
1963	72	32	63	44
Average	72.3	36.7	63.7	39.6
L. Johnson (D)				
1964	74	38	61	45
1965	74	41	64	48
1966	63	37	57	43
1967	69	46	61	53
1968	64	51	48	47
Average	68.4	43.2	58.0	47.6
Nixon (R)				
1969	48	57	47	66
1970	53	66	45	60
1971	47	72	40	64
1972	47	64	44	66
1973	35	62	37	61
1974	46	65	39	57
Average	44.1	64.2	40.9	61.7
Ford (R)				
1974	41	51	39	55
1975	38	63	47	68
1976	32	63	39	62
Average	37.3	59.7	42.5	62.4
Carter (D)				
1977	63	42	70	52
1978	60	36	66	41
1979	64	34	68	47
1980	63	40	62	45
Average	62.6	37.4	66.4	45.6
Reagan (R)				
1981	42	68	49	80
1982	39	64	43	74
1983	28	70	42	73
1984	34	60	41	76

(Table continues)

Table 6-8   *(Continued)*

President (political party)/year	House		Senate	
	Democrats	Republicans	Democrats	Republicans
1985	30	67	35	75
1986	25	65	37	78
1987	24	62	36	64
1988	25	57	47	68
Average	30.5	63.7	41.7	74.0
G. H. W. Bush (R)				
1989	36	69	55	82
1990	25	63	38	70
1991	34	72	41	83
1992	25	71	32	73
Average	29.7	68.7	42.8	77.3
Clinton (D)				
1993	77	39	87	29
1994	75	47	86	42
1995	75	22	81	29
1996	74	38	83	37
1997	71	30	85	60
1998	74	26	82	41
1999	73	23	84	34
2000	73	27	89	46
Average	74.2	31.0	84.3	38.4
G. W. Bush (R)				
2001	31	86	66	94
2002	32	82	71	89
2003	26	89	48	94
2004	30	80	60	91
2005	24	81	38	86
2006	31	85	51	85
2007	7	72	37	78
2008	16	64	34	70
Average	20.9	77.5	50.2	86.5
Obama (D)				
2009	90	26	92	50
2010	84	29	94	41
2011	80	22	92	53
2012	77	17	93	47
2013	83	12	96	40
2014	81	12	95	55
Average	82.0	19.1	93.9	48.4

Note: "R" indicates Republican; "D" indicates Democrat. Entries indicate the percentage of roll calls on which members voted in agreement with the president's position (based on a set of roll calls on which the president took a clear position). Averages are weighted by the number of such roll calls in each year, as shown in Table 6-7, this volume. Congressional Quarterly no longer provides information on absences, so "nonsupport" may include not voting on the roll call.

Source: CQ Weekly (2015), 31.

Table 6-9   Presidential Vetoes, 1789–2015, and Signing Statements, 1929–2015

| | | | | | Signing statements[a] | |
| | | | | | Those raising | |
Years	President	Regular vetoes	Vetoes overridden	Pocket vetoes	Total vetoes	constitutional concerns	Total
1789–1797	Washington	2	0	0	2	—	—
1797–1801	J. Adams	0	0	0	0	—	—
1801–1809	Jefferson	0	0	0	0	—	—
1809–1817	Madison	5	0	2	7	—	—
1817–1825	Monroe	1	0	0	1	—	—
1825–1829	J. Q. Adams	0	0	0	0	—	—
1829–1837	Jackson	5	0	7	12	—	—
1837–1841	Van Buren	0	0	1	1	—	—
1841–1841	W. H. Harrison	0	0	0	0	—	—
1841–1845	Tyler	6	1	4	10	—	—
1845–1849	Polk	2	0	1	3	—	—
1849–1850	Taylor	0	0	0	0	—	—
1850–1853	Fillmore	0	0	0	0	—	—
1853–1857	Pierce	9	5	0	9	—	—
1857–1861	Buchanan	4	0	3	7	—	—
1861–1865	Lincoln	2	0	5	7	—	—
1865–1869	A. Johnson	21	15	8	29	—	—
1869–1877	Grant	45	4	48	93	—	—
1877–1881	Hayes	12	1	1	13	—	—
1881–1881	Garfield	0	0	0	0	—	—
1881–1885	Arthur	4	1	8	12	—	—
1885–1889	Cleveland	304	2	110	414	—	—
1889–1893	B. Harrison	19	1	25	44	—	—
1893–1897	Cleveland	42	5	128	170	—	—
1897–1901	McKinley	6	0	36	42	—	—
1901–1909	T. Roosevelt	42	1	40	82	—	—
1909–1913	Taft	30	1	9	39	—	—
1913–1921	Wilson	33	6	11	44	—	—
1921–1923	Harding	5	0	1	6	—	—
1923–1929	Coolidge	20	4	30	50	—	—
1929–1933	Hoover	21	3	16	37	—	16
1933–1945	F. Roosevelt	372	9	263	635	—	44
1945–1953	Truman	180	12	70	250	—	107
1953–1961	Eisenhower	73	2	108	181	—	145
1961–1963	Kennedy	12	0	9	21	—	36
1963–1969	L. Johnson	16	0	14	30	—	177
1969–1974	Nixon	26[b]	7	17	43	—	117
1974–1977	Ford	48	12	18	66	—	137
1977–1981	Carter	13	2	18	31	—	228

(Table continues)

Table 6-9   *(Continued)*

						Signing statements[a]	
Years	*President*	*Regular vetoes*	*Vetoes overridden*	*Pocket vetoes*	*Total vetoes*	Those raising constitutional concerns	Total
1981–1989	Reagan	39	9	39	78	86	250[c]
1989–1993	G. H. W. Bush	29	1	15[d]	44	107	228
1993–2001	Clinton	36	2	1	37	70	381[e]
2001–2009	G. W. Bush	12	4	0[f]	12	127	161[g]
2009–	Obama	3	0	0	3[h]	10[i]	33[h]
	Total	1,499	110	1,066	2,565	—	—

Note: "—" indicates not available.

[a] Presidents issue "signing statements" in writing when signing legislation. Often these statements merely comment on the bill signed. Some statements involve more controversial claims by the president that some part of the legislation is unconstitutional and that he intends to disregard it or to implement it in ways he thinks is constitutional.

[b] Two pocket vetoes, overruled in the courts, are counted here as regular vetoes.

[c] The American Presidency Project lists 249 signing statements for Reagan.

[d] President George H. W. Bush attempted to pocket veto two bills during intrasession recesses. These two disputed vetoes are not included here.

[e] The American Presidency Project lists 383 signing statements for Clinton.

[f] President George W. Bush characterized his veto of H.R. 1585 as a pocket veto; however, the 110th Congress treated it as a normal veto. It is counted as a normal veto here.

[g] The American Presidency Project lists 162 signing statements for George W. Bush.

[h] Through March 16, 2015.

[i] Through 2011. See the source by Garvey for details.

Sources: Vetoes: Maeve P. Carey, "Regular Vetoes and Pocket Vetoes: An Overview," RS22188, Congressional Research Service, Washington, D.C., June 18, 2014, updated by the editors; signing statements (total), Hoover to Carter and Obama: John Woolley and Gerhard Peters, "Presidential Signing Statements," American Presidency Project (*www.presidency.ucsb.edu*); signing statements (those raising constitutional concerns and total), Reagan to G. W. Bush: Todd Garvey, "Presidential Signing Statements: Constitutional and Institutional Implications," RL33667, Congressional Research Service, Washington, D.C., January 4, 2012; signing statements (those raising constitutional concerns), Obama: Garvey, "Presidential Signing Statements."

Table 6-10   Senate Action on Nominations, 1937–2015

Congress		Received[a]	Confirmed	Withdrawn	Rejected[b]	Unconfirmed[c]
75th	(1937–1939)	15,330	15,193	20	27	90
80th	(1947–1949)	66,641	54,796	153	0	11,692
82nd	(1951–1953)	46,920	46,504	45	2	369
83rd	(1953–1955)	69,458	68,563	43	0	852
84th	(1955–1957)	84,173	82,694	38	3	1,438
85th	(1957–1959)	104,193	103,311	54	0	828
86th	(1959–1961)	91,476	89,900	30	1	1,545
87th	(1961–1963)	102,849	100,741	1,279	0	829
88th	(1963–1965)	122,190	120,201	36	0	1,953
89th	(1965–1967)	123,019	120,865	173	0	1,981
90th	(1967–1969)	120,231	118,231	34	0	1,966
91st	(1969–1971)	134,464	133,797	487	2	178
92nd	(1971–1973)	117,053	114,909	11	0	2,133
93rd	(1973–1975)	134,384	131,254	15	0	3,115
94th	(1975–1977)	135,302	131,378	21	0	3,903
95th	(1977–1979)	137,509	124,730	66	0	12,713
96th	(1979–1981)	156,141	154,665	18	0	1,458
97th	(1981–1983)	186,264	184,856	55	0	1,353
98th	(1983–1985)	97,893	97,262	4	0	627
99th	(1985–1987)	99,614	95,811	16	0	3,787
100th	(1987–1989)	94,687	88,721	23	1	5,942
101st	(1989–1991)	96,130	88,078	48	1	8,003
102nd	(1991–1993)	76,628	75,802	24	0	802
103rd	(1993–1995)	79,956	76,122	1,080	0	2,754
104th	(1995–1997)	82,214	73,711	22	0	8,481
105th	(1997–1999)	46,290	45,878	40	0	372
106th	(1999–2001)	46,952	44,980	25	0	1,947
107th	(2001–2003)	50,406	48,724	79	0	1,603
108th	(2003–2005)	59,655	48,627	39	0	10,989
109th	(2005–2007)	57,514	55,545	40	0	1,929
110th	(2007–2009)	45,453	44,677	74	0	702
111th	(2009–2011)	48,665	46,377	36	0	2,252
112th	(2011–2013)	44,987	44,111	44	0	832
113th	(2013–2015)	38,872	35,682	27	0	3,163

Note: Data for additional years can be found in previous editions of *Vital Statistics on American Politics.*

[a] Count includes those in the second session carried over from the first session.

[b] Category includes only those nominations rejected outright by a vote of the Senate. Most nominations that fail to win approval of the Senate are unfavorably reported by committees and never reach the Senate floor, having been withdrawn. In some cases, the full Senate may vote to recommit a nomination to committee, in effect killing it.

[c] Includes "returned" nominations. Nominations must be returned to the president unless confirmed or rejected during the session in which they are made. If the Senate adjourns or recesses for more than thirty days within a session, all pending nominations must be returned (Senate Rule XXI).

Sources: 1937–1999: *Congressional Quarterly's Guide to Congress,* 5th ed. (Washington, D.C.: CQ Press, 2000), 1: 295; 1999–2001: *Congressional Record—Daily Digest,* D45; 2001–2003: D456–D457; 2003–2005: D96–D97; 2005–2007: D158, D1173; 2007–2009: D80, D1336–D1337; 2009–2011: D1249; 2011–2013: D11, D210; 2013–2015: D195, D1161.

Table 6-11   Senate Rejections of Cabinet Nominations

Nominee	Position	President	Date	Vote
Roger B. Taney	secretary of treasury	Jackson	6/23/1834	18–28
Caleb Cushing	secretary of treasury	Tyler	3/3/1843	19–27
Caleb Cushing	secretary of treasury	Tyler	3/3/1843	10–27
Caleb Cushing	secretary of treasury	Tyler	3/3/1843	2–29
David Henshaw	secretary of navy	Tyler	1/15/1844	6–34
James M. Porter	secretary of war	Tyler	1/30/1844	3–38
James S. Green	secretary of treasury	Tyler	6/15/1844	[a]
Henry Stanbery	attorney general	A. Johnson	6/2/1868	11–29
Charles B. Warren	attorney general	Coolidge	3/10/1925	39–41
Charles B. Warren	attorney general	Coolidge	3/16/1925	39–46
Lewis L. Strauss	secretary of commerce	Eisenhower	6/19/1959	46–49
John Tower	secretary of defense	G. H. W. Bush	3/9/1989	47–53

[a] Not recorded.

Source: CQ Press Guide to Congress, 7th ed. (Washington, D.C.: CQ Press, 2012), 1:335.

Table 6-12   Number of Civilian Federal Government Employees and
Percentage under Merit Civil Service, 1816–2014

Year	Total number of employees[a]	Percentage under merit	Year	Total number of employees[a]	Percentage under merit
1816	4,837	—	1943	3,299,414	—
1821	6,914	—	1944	3,332,356	—
1831	11,491	—	1945	3,816,310	—
1841	18,038	—	1946	2,696,529	—
1851	26,274	—	1947	2,111,001	80.2
1861	36,672	—	1948	2,071,009	82.4
1871	51,020	—	1949	2,102,109	84.3
1881	100,020	—	1950	1,960,708	84.5
1891	157,442	21.5	1951	2,482,666	86.4
1901	239,476	44.3	1952	2,600,612	86.4
1910	388,708	57.2	1953	2,558,416	83.6
1911	395,905	57.5	1954	2,407,676	82.7
1912	400,150	54.3	1955	2,397,309	83.6
1913	396,494	71.3	1956	2,398,736	85.1
1914	401,887	72.8	1957	2,417,565	85.5
1915	395,429	73.9	1958	2,382,491	85.3
1916	399,381	74.3	1959	2,382,807	85.7
1917	438,500	74.5	1960	2,398,704	85.5
1918	854,500	75.2	1961	2,435,804	86.1
1919[b]	794,271	86.6	1962	2,514,197	85.9
1920[c]	655,265	75.9	1963	2,527,960	85.6
1921[c]	561,142	79.9	1964	2,500,503	86.1
1922	543,507	77.4	1965	2,527,915	85.2
1923	536,900	76.6	1966	2,759,019	85.8
1924	543,484	76.5	1967	3,002,461	82.8
1925	553,045	76.6	1968	3,055,212	84.1
1926	548,713	77.0	1969	3,076,414	82.9
1927	547,127	77.3	1970	2,981,574	82.3
1928	560,772	77.0	1971	2,862,894	84.1
1929	579,559	88.2	1972[d]	2,779,261	61.6
1930	601,319	87.9	1973	2,732,377	62.0
1931	609,746	76.8	1974[e]	2,893,118	57.0
1932	605,496	77.2	1975[e]	2,896,944	57.4
1933	603,587	75.6	1976[e]	2,883,134	57.6
1934	698,649	64.5	1977[e]	2,893,334	57.1
1935	780,582	58.3	1978[e]	2,929,100	57.3
1936	867,432	57.5	1979[e]	2,949,630	56.6
1937	895,993	59.4	1980	3,121,769	56.1
1938	882,226	63.8	1981	2,947,428	58.7
1939	953,891	69.5	1982	2,917,095	59.2
1940	1,042,420	69.7	1983	2,920,514	59.2
1941	1,437,682	68.9	1984	2,959,317	58.7
1942	2,296,384	—	1985	3,059,987	57.2

(Table continues)

Table 6-12   *(Continued)*

Year	Total number of employees[a]	Percentage under merit	Year	Total number of employees[a]	Percentage under merit
1986	3,061,210	56.6	2001	2,719,529	50.4
1987	3,125,635	56.2	2002	2,700,876	50.4
1988	3,126,171	56.0	2003	2,758,463	50.4
1989[f]	3,151,334	56.2	2004	2,735,359	49.9
1990	3,503,550	50.5	2005	2,728,432	48.8
1991	3,138,180	56.4	2006	2,718,917	48.8
1992	3,134,915	56.7	2007	2,715,395	48.6
1993	3,050,711	56.7	2008	2,758,468	48.6
1994	2,992,840	55.4	2009	2,823,174	49.2
1995	2,958,447	54.8	2010	3,328,530	43.3
1996	2,888,623	53.7	2011	2,869,548	53.4
1997	2,825,370	51.1	2012	2,800,715	54.0
1998	2,798,992	50.4	2013	2,745,887	54.2
1999	2,783,281	49.8	2014	2,719,422	53.8
2000	3,206,791	42.7			

Note: "—" indicates not available. As of June, except where indicated.

[a] Excludes employees of the Central Intelligence Agency and National Security Agency.
[b] As of November.
[c] As of July.
[d] Under the Postal Reorganization Act of 1970, U.S. Postal Service employees were changed from competitive (merit) service to excepted service.
[e] Excludes those employees in temporary and indefinite competitive status. In June 1973, 3.6 percent of federal civilian employees were in such service. In June 1980, 2.9 percent were.
[f] As of May.

Sources: 1816–1970: U.S. Bureau of the Census, *Historical Statistics of the United States* (Washington, D.C.: Government Printing Office, 1975), 1102–1103; 1971–2014: U.S. Office of Personnel Management, *Federal Civilian Workforce Statistics, Employment and Trends* (*www.opm.gov*).

Table 6-13   Major Regulatory Agencies

Agency	Year established	Agency head		Number of employees[a]
		Number	Title	
Consumer Product Safety Commission	1972	3	commissioner	522
Environmental Protection Agency	1970	1	administrator	16,918
Equal Employment Opportunity Commission	1965	5	commissioner	2,219
Federal Communications Commission	1934	5	commissioner	1,735
Federal Deposit Insurance Corporation	1933	5	board of directors	7,437
Federal Election Commission	1975	6	commissioner	333
Federal Energy Regulatory Commission	1977	5	commissioner	1,450
Federal Reserve System	1913	7	governor	1,873
Federal Trade Commission	1914	5	commissioner	1,131
Food and Drug Administration	1906	1	commissioner	16,646
National Labor Relations Board	1935	5	board of directors	1,572
Occupational Safety and Health Administration	1970	1	assistant secretary	2,170
Securities and Exchange Commission	1934	5	commissioner	4,217

Note: The Interstate Commerce Commission, established in 1887, was terminated on December 30, 1995. It was succeeded by the Surface Transportation Board.

[a] Federal Energy Regulatory Commission: 2013; all others: average number, October 2013 through June 2014.

Sources: Year established, agency head: *Federal Regulatory Directory,* 16th ed. (Washington, D.C.: CQ Press, 2014); number of employees: Federal Energy Regulatory Commission *(www .ferc.gov)*; Occupational Safety and Health Administration (*www.osha.gov*).

Figure 6-1   Number of Pages in *Federal Register,* 1940–2014

Number of pages

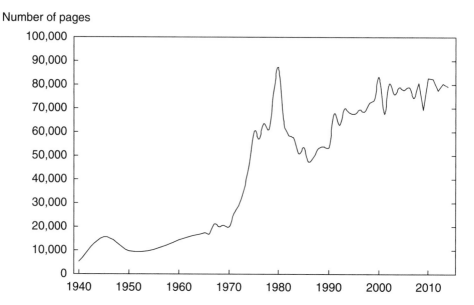

Source: Compiled from successive volumes of the *Federal Register* (Washington, D.C.: Government Printing Office).

7
The Judiciary

- **Federal and State Court Structures**
- **Supreme Court Justices**
- **Ratings**
- **Failed Nominations**
- **Federal Court Judges**
- **Supreme Court Caseloads**
- **Federal Court Caseloads**
- **Laws Overturned**

The judiciary, although one of the three "separate but equal" branches of government, is often considered beyond the political push and pull that characterizes the executive and legislative branches. Preoccupied with process, precedent, and the meaning of the law, the courts present a strikingly different appearance. Nevertheless, because they must grapple with the constitutionality of abortion or the death penalty and because they must pour practical meaning into ambiguous, generally worded statutes enacted by legislatures, the courts are squarely in the middle of the political process.

Even if the courts are considered political, are statistics essential to understanding the judiciary? They are for two reasons. First, the courts themselves have to deal with statistics. One line of cases, for example, has dealt with the question of racially disparate patterns in the imposition of the death penalty. It has been noted that proportionately more African Americans are on death row; in addition, defendants who kill whites are more likely to be sentenced to die than are those who kill blacks. Courts have had to decide whether the numbers they are given are accurate and meaningful as well as whether the defendant being tried is a victim of racial discrimination.

Other cases also often turn on conclusions drawn from numerical data—voting rights (Table 1-30), reapportionment and redistricting (Tables 1-20, 1-29, and 5-1), and school desegregation (Table 10-13) are three examples.

And although the courts do not explicitly take public opinion into account, they cannot help but be aware that cases often involve issues about which public opinion is strong and divided (for example, on abortion, Table 3-13, and same-sex marriage, Figure 3-16).

Statistics also provide useful insight into the operation of the judicial system. A single case does not lend itself to statistical analysis, but the large number, the hierarchy (Figure 7-1), and the geographical spread (Figure 7-2) of the federal courts, as well as the even greater variety of state courts and appointment methods (Table 7-1), suggest that numerical summarization aids comprehension.

Although the nature of the courts might suggest that appointments are merely a matter of judicial qualifications, the record indicates otherwise. Federal judicial appointments have always been subject to partisan considerations (Tables 7-2 and 7-6), and other characteristics of federal judges vary with the appointing president (Table 7-5). Partisan and ideological differences also explain part of the frustration presidents have encountered in making nominations to the Supreme Court (Table 7-4). As for more subjective judgments of court appointees, just as historians have judged presidents, legal scholars have evaluated Supreme Court justices (Table 7-3).

As they climbed dramatically, the growing caseloads of the courts became a major concern in recent decades (Tables 7-7 through 7-10 and Figure 7-3). The Supreme Court has managed to handle a crushing workload by deciding fewer cases by signed opinions (Table 7-7). In the lower federal courts, the workload per judge has risen sharply. The number of cases filed in district courts almost doubled between 1980 and 2005, but the number of judges increased by only one-third (Table 7-9). The number of appeals filed in the courts of appeals almost tripled over the same period before backing off slightly over the past few years, but the number of judgeships rose by less than one-third (Table 7-8).

Considerable information is also available on the nature of judicial work. For example, civil rather than criminal cases have accounted for much of the increased workload (Table 7-10), and they have dealt with a wide range of topics (Table 7-11). Dramatic changes also have occurred in the kinds of cases courts must deal with and in the ways they have responded. The Supreme Court, for one, struck down more federal, state, and local laws on constitutional grounds in the twentieth century than in the nineteenth (Table 7-12). Over the years, however, doctrinal trends changed. For example, beginning in the 1930s the Court rejected far fewer economic regulatory laws and increasingly struck down laws restricting civil liberties (Figure 7-4). All these examples demonstrate that statistics not only play an important role in how the executive and legislative branches undertake their responsibilities, but also are a necessary component of any understanding of the courts and their decisions.

Figure 7-1 The U.S. Court System

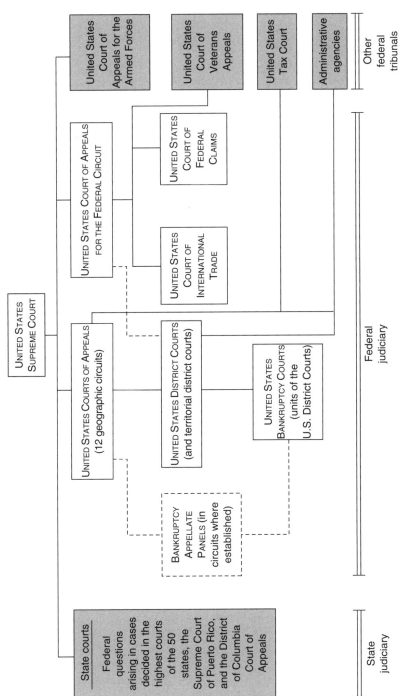

Source: Judicial Conference of the United States, *Long Range Plan for the Federal Courts (www.uscourts.gov/uscourts/FederalCourts/Publications/FederalCourtsLongRangePlan.pdf).*

Figure 7-2 The Thirteen Federal Judicial Circuits and Ninety-four District Courts

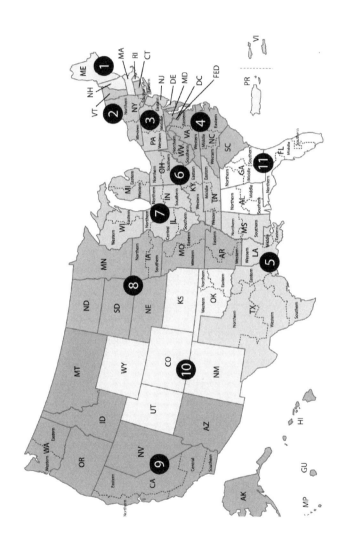

Note: Puerto Rico is part of the 1st Circuit; the Virgin Islands, the 3rd Circuit. The D.C. Circuit, not shown here, is also a geographic circuit. In addition, there is a Federal Circuit (see Figure 7-1, this volume).

Source: Administrative Office of the United States Courts (*www.uscourts.gov*).

Table 7-1   Principal Methods of Judicial Selection for State Appellate Courts

Partisan election	Nonpartisan election	Legislative appointment	Gubernatorial appointment	Merit plan
Alabama	Arkansas	South Carolina	California	Alaska
Illinois	Georgia	Virginia	Maine	Arizona
Louisiana	Idaho		New Hampshire	Colorado
New Mexico	Kentucky		New Jersey	Connecticut
Ohio	Michigan			Delaware
Pennsylvania	Minnesota			Florida
Texas	Mississippi			Hawaii
West Virginia	Montana			Indiana
	Nevada			Iowa
	North Carolina			Kansas
	North Dakota[a]			Maryland
	Oregon			Massachusetts
	Washington			Missouri
	Wisconsin			Nebraska
				New York
				Oklahoma
				Rhode Island
				South Dakota
				Tennessee
				Utah
				Vermont
				Wyoming

Note: "Merit plan" typically involves appointment by the governor from a list of candidates submitted by an independent or quasi-independent judiciary council or commission. For details on all selection methods, see notes in source.

[a] For North Dakota Supreme Court. North Dakota Temporary Court of Appeals judges are appointed by the Supreme Court.

Source: Council of State Governments, *The Book of the States, 2014* (Lexington, Ky.: Council of State Governments, 2014), 250–252.

Table 7-2 Supreme Court Justices of the United States

Seat number and justice	Party	Home state	Years on Court	Age at nomination	Years of previous judicial experience
Washington appointees					
1 John Jay	Federalist	New York	1789–1795	44	2
2 John Rutledge	Federalist	South Carolina	1789–1791	50	6
3 William Cushing	Federalist	Massachusetts	1789–1810[a]	57	29
4 James Wilson	Federalist	Pennsylvania	1789–1798[a]	47	0
5 John Blair Jr.	Federalist	Virginia	1789–1795	57	11
6 James Iredell	Federalist	North Carolina	1790–1799[a]	38	0.5
2 Thomas Johnson	Federalist	Maryland	1791–1793	59	1.5
2 William Paterson	Federalist	New Jersey	1793–1806[a]	47	0
1 John Rutledge	Federalist	South Carolina	1795	55	6[b]
5 Samuel Chase	Federalist	Maryland	1796–1811[a]	55	8
1 Oliver Ellsworth	Federalist	Connecticut	1796–1800	51	5
J. Adams appointees					
4 Bushrod Washington	Federalist	Virginia	1798–1829[a]	36	0
6 Alfred Moore	Federalist	North Carolina	1799–1804	44	1
1 John Marshall	Federalist	Virginia	1801–1835[a]	45	3
Jefferson appointees					
6 William Johnson	Jeffersonian	South Carolina	1804–1834[a]	32	6
2 H. Brockholst Livingston	Jeffersonian	New York	1806–1823[a]	49	0
7 Thomas Todd	Jeffersonian	Kentucky	1807–1826[a]	42	6
Madison appointees					
5 Gabriel Duvall	Jeffersonian	Maryland	1811–1835	58	6
3 Joseph Story	Jeffersonian	Massachusetts	1811–1845[a]	32	0
Monroe appointee					
2 Smith Thompson	Jeffersonian	New York	1823–1843[a]	55	16

J. Q. Adams appointee					
7 Robert Trimble	Jeffersonian	Kentucky	1826–1828[a]	49	11
Jackson appointees					
7 John McLean	Democrat	Ohio	1829–1861[a]	44	6
4 Henry Baldwin	Democrat	Pennsylvania	1830–1844[a]	50	0
6 James Wayne	Democrat	Georgia	1835–1867[a]	45	5
1 Roger B. Taney	Democrat	Maryland	1836–1864[a]	59	0
5 Philip P. Barbour	Democrat	Virginia	1836–1841[a]	52	8
Van Buren appointees					
8 John Catron	Democrat	Tennessee	1837–1865[a]	51	10
9 John McKinley	Democrat	Alabama	1837–1852[a]	57	0
5 Peter V. Daniel	Democrat	Virginia	1841–1860[a]	57	0
Tyler appointee					
2 Samuel Nelson	Democrat	New York	1845–1872	52	22
Polk appointees					
3 Levi Woodbury	Democrat	New Hampshire	1845–1851[a]	55	6
4 Robert C. Grier	Democrat	Pennsylvania	1846–1870	52	13
Fillmore appointee					
3 Benjamin R. Curtis	Whig	Massachusetts	1851–1857	41	0
Pierce appointee					
9 John A. Campbell	Democrat	Alabama	1853–1861	41	0
Buchanan appointee					
3 Nathan Clifford	Democrat	Maine	1858–1881[a]	54	0
Lincoln appointees					
7 Noah H. Swayne	Republican	Ohio	1862–1881	57	0
5 Samuel F. Miller	Republican	Iowa	1862–1890[a]	46	0

(Table continues)

Table 7-2 (*Continued*)

Seat number and justice	Party	Home state	Years on Court	Age at nomination	Years of previous judicial experience
9 David Davis	Republican	Illinois	1862–1877	47	14
10 Stephen J. Field	Democrat	California	1863–1897	46	6
1 Salmon P. Chase	Republican	Ohio	1864–1873[a]	56	0
Grant appointees					
4 William Strong	Republican	Pennsylvania	1870–1880	61	11
6 Joseph P. Bradley	Republican	New Jersey	1870–1892[a]	56	0
2 Ward Hunt	Republican	New York	1873–1882	62	8
1 Morrison R. Waite	Republican	Ohio	1874–1888[a]	57	0
Hayes appointees					
9 John M. Harlan	Republican	Kentucky	1877–1911[a]	44	1
4 William B. Woods	Republican	Georgia	1880–1887[a]	56	12
Garfield appointee					
7 Stanley Matthews	Republican	Ohio	1881–1889[a]	56	4
Arthur appointees					
3 Horace Gray	Republican	Massachusetts	1881–1902	53	18
2 Samuel Blatchford	Republican	New York	1882–1893[a]	62	15
Cleveland appointees (first term)					
4 Lucius Q. C. Lamar	Democrat	Mississippi	1888–1893[a]	62	0
1 Melville W. Fuller	Democrat	Illinois	1888–1910[a]	55	0
Harrison appointees					
7 David J. Brewer	Republican	Kansas	1889–1910[a]	52	19
5 Henry B. Brown	Republican	Michigan	1891–1906	54	16
6 George Shiras Jr.	Republican	Pennsylvania	1892–1903	60	0
4 Howell E. Jackson	Democrat	Tennessee	1893–1895[a]	60	7

	Party	State	Years		
Cleveland appointees (second term)					
2 Edward D. White	Democrat	Louisiana	1894–1910[a]	48	1.5
4 Rufus W. Peckham	Democrat	New York	1895–1909[a]	57	9
McKinley appointee					
8 Joseph McKenna	Republican	California	1898–1925	54	5
T. Roosevelt appointees					
3 Oliver W. Holmes	Republican	Massachusetts	1902–1932	61	20
6 William R. Day	Republican	Ohio	1903–1922	53	7
5 William H. Moody	Republican	Massachusetts	1906–1910	52	0
Taft appointees					
4 Horace H. Lurton	Democrat	Tennessee	1909–1914[a]	65	26
7 Charles E. Hughes	Republican	New York	1910–1916	48	0
1 Edward D. White	Democrat	Louisiana	1910–1921[a]	65	1.5[b]
2 Willis Van Devanter	Republican	Wyoming	1910–1937	51	8
5 Joseph R. Lamar	Democrat	Georgia	1910–1916[a]	53	2
9 Mahlon Pitney	Republican	New Jersey	1912–1922	54	11
Wilson appointees					
4 James C. McReynolds	Democrat	Tennessee	1914–1941	52	0
5 Louis D. Brandeis	Republican	Massachusetts	1916–1939	59	0
7 John H. Clarke	Democrat	Ohio	1916–1922	59	2
Harding appointees					
1 William H. Taft	Republican	Ohio	1921–1930	63	13
7 George Sutherland	Republican	Utah	1922–1938	60	0
6 Pierce Butler	Democrat	Minnesota	1923–1939[a]	56	0
9 Edward T. Sanford	Republican	Tennessee	1923–1930[a]	57	14
Coolidge appointee					
8 Harlan Fiske Stone	Republican	New York	1925–1941	52	0

(Table continues)

Table 7-2 *(Continued)*

Seat number and justice	Party	Home state	Years on Court	Age at nomination	Years of previous judicial experience
Hoover appointees					
1 Charles E. Hughes	Republican	New York	1930–1941	67	0
9 Owens J. Roberts	Republican	Pennsylvania	1930–1945	55	0
3 Benjamin N. Cardozo	Democrat	New York	1932–1938[a]	61	18
F. Roosevelt appointees					
2 Hugo L. Black	Democrat	Alabama	1937–1971[a]	51	1.5
7 Stanley F. Reed	Democrat	Kentucky	1938–1957	53	0
3 Felix Frankfurter	Independent	Massachusetts	1939–1962	56	0
5 William O. Douglas	Democrat	Connecticut	1939–1975	40	0
6 Frank Murphy	Democrat	Michigan	1940–1949[a]	49	7
4 James F. Byrnes	Democrat	South Carolina	1941–1942	62	0
1 Harlan Fiske Stone	Republican	New York	1941–1946[a]	68	0[b]
8 Robert H. Jackson	Democrat	New York	1941–1954[a]	49	0
4 Wiley B. Rutledge	Democrat	Iowa	1943–1949[a]	48	4
Truman appointees					
9 Harold H. Burton	Republican	Ohio	1945–1958	57	0
1 Fred M. Vinson	Democrat	Kentucky	1946–1953[a]	56	5
6 Tom C. Clark	Democrat	Texas	1949–1967	49	0
4 Sherman Minton	Democrat	Indiana	1949–1956	58	8
Eisenhower appointees					
1 Earl Warren	Republican	California	1953–1969	62	0
8 John M. Harlan	Republican	New York	1955–1971	55	1
4 William J. Brennan	Democrat	New Jersey	1956–1990	50	7
7 Charles E. Whittaker	Republican	Missouri	1957–1962	56	3
9 Potter Stewart	Republican	Ohio	1958–1981	43	4

Kennedy appointees					
7 Byron R. White	Democrat	Colorado	1962–1993	44	0
3 Arthur J. Goldberg	Democrat	Illinois	1962–1965	54	0
L. Johnson appointees					
3 Abe Fortas	Democrat	Tennessee	1965–1969	55	0
6 Thurgood Marshall	Democrat	New York	1967–1991	59	4
Nixon appointees					
1 Warren E. Burger	Republican	Minnesota	1969–1986	61	13
3 Harry A. Blackmun	Republican	Minnesota	1970–1994	61	11
2 Lewis F. Powell Jr.	Democrat	Virginia	1971–1987	64	0
8 William H. Rehnquist	Republican	Arizona	1971–1986	47	0
Ford appointee					
5 John Paul Stevens	Republican	Illinois	1976–2010	55	5
Reagan appointees					
9 Sandra Day O'Connor	Republican	Arizona	1981–2006	51	6.5
1 William H. Rehnquist	Republican	Arizona	1986–2005[a]	61	0[b]
8 Antonin Scalia	Republican	Illinois	1986–	50	4
2 Anthony M. Kennedy	Republican	California	1988–	51	12
G. H. W. Bush appointees					
4 David H. Souter	Republican	New Hampshire	1990–2009	50	13
6 Clarence Thomas	Republican	Georgia	1991–	43	1
Clinton appointees					
7 Ruth Bader Ginsburg	Democrat	New York	1993–	60	13
3 Stephen G. Breyer	Democrat	Massachusetts	1994–	55	15

(Table continues)

Table 7-2 (Continued)

Seat number and justice	Party	Home state	Years on Court	Age at nomination	Years of previous judicial experience
G. W. Bush appointees					
1 John G. Roberts Jr.	Republican	Maryland	2005–	50	2
9 Samuel A. Alito Jr.	Republican	New Jersey	2006–	55	15
Obama appointees					
4 Sonia Sotomayor	Democrat	New York	2009–	54	18
5 Elena Kagan	Democrat	New York	2010–	50	0

Note: Seat number 1 is always held by the chief justice of the United States.

[a] Died in office.
[b] Prior to appointment to associate justice.

Sources: Sheldon Goldman, *Constitutional Law: Cases and Essays* (New York: Harper and Row, 1987); previous judicial experience: Henry J. Abraham, *Justices and Presidents: Appointments to the Supreme Court*, 2nd ed. (New York: Oxford University Press, 1985), 56–58; *Congressional Quarterly's Guide to Congress*, 2nd ed. (Washington, D.C.: Congressional Quarterly, 1982), 786–788; updated by the editors.

Table 7-3 Ratings of Supreme Court Justices

Great dissenters	Lists of "great" justices				Blaustein and Mersky (1978) ratings of all justices				

Great dissenters

Zobell (1959)
W. Johnson
Curtis
Harlan I
Holmes

CQ (1990)
W. Johnson
Curtis
Harlan I
Holmes
Brandeis
Cardozo
Stone
Frankfurter
Brennan
T. Marshall

Lists of "great" justices

Hughes (1928)
J. Marshall
Story
Curtis
Miller
Field

Pound (1938)
J. Marshall
Story
Holmes
Cardozo

Frankfurter (1957)
J. Marshall
W. Johnson
Story
Taney
Curtis
Campbell
Miller
Field

Frank (1958)
J. Marshall
W. Johnson
Story
McLean
Taney
Curtis
Campbell
Miller
Davis
Field
Bradley
Waite
Harlan I
Brewer
Holmes
Moody
Hughes
Brandeis
Taft
Sutherland
Butler
Stone
Cardozo

Currie (1964)
J. Marshall
W. Johnson
Story
Taney
Miller
Bradley
Holmes
Brandeis
Hughes

Nagel (1970)
J. Marshall
W. Johnson
Story
Taney
Curtis
Campbell
Miller
Field
Bradley
Harlan I
Brewer
Holmes
Moody

Asch (1971)
Jay
J. Marshall
Taney
Miller
Harlan I
Holmes
Brandeis
Hughes
Stone
Cardozo
Frankfurter
R. H. Jackson
Black
Douglas
Warren

Schwartz (1979)
J. Marshall
Story
Holmes
Cardozo
Black
Warren

Blaustein and Mersky (1978) ratings of all justices

Great
J. Marshall
Story
Taney
Harlan I
Holmes
Hughes
Brandeis
Stone
Cardozo
Black
Frankfurter
Warren

Near great
W. Johnson
Curtis
Miller
Field
Bradley
Waite
E. D. White
Taft
Sutherland
Douglas

Average
Jay
J. Rutledge
Cushing
Wilson
Blair
Iredell
Paterson
S. Chase
Ellsworth
Washington
Livingston
Todd
Duval
Thompson
McLean
Baldwin
Wayne
Catron
McKinley
Daniel
Nelson
Woodbury
Grier
Campbell
Clifford
Swayne
Davis
S. P. Chase
Strong
Hunt
Matthews
Gray
Blatchford
L. Q. C. Lamar
Fuller
Brewer
Brown
Shiras
Peckham
McKenna
Day
Moody
Lurton
J. R. Lamar
Pitney
J. H. Clarke
Sanford
Roberts

Below average
T. Johnson
Moore
Trimble
Barbour
Woods
H. E. Jackson

Failure
Van Devanter
McReynolds
Butler
Byrnes
Burton
Vinson
Minton
Whittaker

(Table continues)

Table 7-3 *(Continued)*

Great dissenters	Lists of "great" justices			Blaustein and Mersky (1978) ratings of all justices		
	Frankfurter (1957)	**Nagel (1970)**	**Bradley (1993)**	*Near great*	*Average*	
	Bradley	Hughes	J. Marshall	R. H. Jackson	Reed	B. R. White
	Matthews	Brandeis	Holmes	W. B. Rutledge	Murphy	Goldberg
	E. White	Cardozo	Warren	Harlan II	T. C. Clark	T. Marshall
	Holmes	Black	Brandeis	Brennan	Stewart	
	Moody	Frankfurter	Brennan	Fortas		
	Hughes	Douglas	Black			
	Brandeis	R. H. Jackson	Harlan I			
	Cardozo	Warren	Douglas			
			Frankfurter			
			Cardozo			

Note: Blaustein and Mersky's ratings reflect evaluations by sixty-five law school deans and professors of law, history, and political science with expertise in the judicial process. Bradley's ratings reflect evaluations by ninety-six scholars (mostly political scientists) with expertise in the judicial process. Other ratings reflect the views of the individual compiler. State judges, not shown, were included in the lists by Pound (Kent, Gibson, Shaw, Ruffin, Cooley, and Doe) and Schwartz (Kent, Shaw, Vanderbilt, and Traynor). For more details, see the sources.

Sources: Albert P. Blaustein and Roy M. Mersky, *The First One Hundred Justices: Statistical Studies on the Supreme Court of the United States* (Hamden, Conn.: Shoe String Press, Archon Books, 1978), 37–40; Robert C. Bradley, "Who Are the Great Justices and What Criteria Did They Meet?" in *Great Justices of the U.S. Supreme Court,* William D. Pederson and Normal W. Provizer (New York: Peter Lang, 1993), 1–32.

Table 7-4   Supreme Court Nominations That Failed

Nominee	Date nomination received in Senate[a]	President	Action
William Paterson[b]	1793	Washington	withdrawn
John Rutledge[c]	1795	Washington	rejected, 10–14
Alexander Wolcott	1811	Madison	rejected, 9–24
John J. Crittenden	1828	J. Q. Adams	postponed
Roger B. Taney[b]	1835	Jackson	postponed
John C. Spencer	1844	Tyler	rejected, 21–26
Reuben H. Walworth	1844	Tyler	withdrawn
Edward King	1844	Tyler	tabled, 29–18
John C. Spencer	1844	Tyler	withdrawn
Reuben H. Walworth	1844	Tyler	motion to consider objected to
Reuben H. Walworth	1844	Tyler	withdrawn
Edward King	1844	Tyler	withdrawn
John M. Read	1845	Tyler	motion to consider unsuccessful
George W. Woodward	1845	Polk	rejected, 20–29
Edward A. Bradford	1852	Fillmore	tabled
George E. Badger	1853	Fillmore	postponed, 26–25
William C. Micou	1853	Fillmore	discharged
Jeremiah S. Black	1861	Buchanan	motions to consider unsuccessful
Henry Stanbery	1866	A. Johnson	no record of action
Ebenezer R. Hoar	1869	Grant	rejected, 24–33
George H. Williams[c]	1873	Grant	withdrawn
Caleb Cushing[c]	1874	Grant	withdrawn
Stanley Matthews[b]	1881	Hayes	postponed
William B. Hornblower	1893	Cleveland	no record of action
William B. Hornblower	1893	Cleveland	rejected, 24–30
Wheeler H. Peckham	1894	Cleveland	rejected, 32–41
Pierce Butler[b]	1922	Harding	no record of action
John J. Parker	1930	Hoover	rejected, 39–41
John Marshall Harlan II[b]	1954	Eisenhower	no record of action
Abe Fortas[c]	1968	L. Johnson	withdrawn
Homer Thornberry	1968	L. Johnson	not acted on
Clement F. Haynsworth Jr.	1969	Nixon	rejected, 45–55
G. Harrold Carswell	1970	Nixon	rejected, 45–51
Robert H. Bork	1987	Reagan	rejected, 42–58
Harriet Miers	2005	G. W. Bush	withdrawn

Note: Seven individuals were confirmed but declined to serve: Robert H. Harrison, 1789; William Cushing, 1796; John Jay, 1800; Levi Lincoln, 1811; John Quincy Adams, 1811; William Smith, 1837; Roscoe Conkling, 1882. One person, Edwin Stanton (1869), was confirmed but died before he could take his seat. In 1987 the nomination of Douglas Ginsburg was publicly announced by President Ronald Reagan but was withdrawn before the president formally submitted his nomination to the Senate.

[a] The date of the president's nomination and the date the nomination is received in the Senate are often, but not always, the same.
[b] Later nominated and confirmed (Taney as chief justice). See Table 7-2, this volume.
[c] For chief justice.

Sources: Henry B. Hogue, "Supreme Court Nominations Not Confirmed, 1789–2004," Congressional Research Service Report for Congress (*www.fas.org/sgp/crs/misc/RL31171.pdf*); Richard S. Beth and Betsy Palmer, "Supreme Court Nominations: Senate Floor Procedure and Practice, 1789–2011" (*http://assets.opencrs.com/rpts/RL33247_20110311.pdf*).

Table 7-5 Characteristics of Federal District and Appellate Court Appointees, Presidents Richard Nixon to Barack Obama (percent)

	Nixon appointees	Ford appointees	Carter appointees	Reagan appointees	G. H. W. Bush appointees	Clinton appointees	G. W. Bush appointees	Obama appointees
District courts								
Occupation								
Politics/government	10.6	21.2	5.0	13.4	10.8	11.5	13.4	19.2
Judiciary	28.5	34.6	44.6	36.9	41.9	48.2	48.3	42.8
Large law firm[a]	11.2	9.6	13.9	17.9	25.7	16.1	18.8	16.0
Moderate law firm[a]	27.9	25.0	19.3	19.0	14.9	13.4	10.0	12.0
Small/solo law firm[a]	19.0	9.6	13.9	10.0	4.7	8.2	6.1	7.2
Other	2.8	0.0	3.5	2.8	2.0	2.6	3.4	2.8
Experience								
Judicial	35.2	42.3	54.0	46.2	46.6	52.1	52.1	46.4
Prosecutorial	41.9	50.0	38.1	44.1	39.2	41.3	47.1	43.6
Neither	36.3	30.8	31.2	28.6	31.8	28.9	24.9	30.4
Political affiliation								
Democrat	7.3	21.2	91.1	4.8	6.1	87.5	8.0	80.4
Republican	92.7	78.8	4.5	91.7	88.5	6.2	83.1	6.8
Independent or other	0.0	0.0	4.5	3.4	5.4	6.2	8.8	12.8
Past party activism	48.6	50.0	61.4	60.3	64.2	50.2	52.5	49.6
Religion								
Protestant	73.2	73.1	60.4	60.3	64.2	—	—	—
Catholic	18.4	17.3	27.7	30.0	28.4	—	—	—
Jewish	8.4	9.6	11.9	9.3	7.4	—	—	—
Race/ethnicity								
White	95.5	88.5	78.2	92.4	89.2	75.1	81.2	64.0
Black	3.4	5.8	13.9	2.1	6.8	17.4	6.9	18.4
Asian American	0.0	3.9	0.5	0.7	0.0	1.3	1.5	6.4
Hispanic	1.1	1.9	6.9	4.8	4.0	5.9	10.3	10.8

Native American	0.4	0.0	0.3	0.0	0.0	0.5	—	—
Sex								
Women	41.2	20.7	28.5	19.6	8.3	14.4	1.9	0.6
Number of appointees[b]	250	261	305	148	290	202	52	179
Courts of appeals[b]								
Occupation								
Politics/government	8.5	18.6	6.6	10.8	6.4	5.4	8.3	4.4
Judiciary	59.6	49.1	52.5	59.5	55.1	46.4	75.0	53.3
Large law firm[a]	14.9	11.9	18.0	16.2	14.1	10.7	8.3	4.4
Moderate law firm[a]	4.3	6.8	13.1	10.8	9.0	16.1	8.3	22.2
Small/solo law firm[a]	0.0	3.4	1.6	0.0	1.3	5.4	0.0	6.7
Other	12.8	10.2	8.2	2.7	14.1	16.1	0.0	8.9
Experience								
Judicial	59.6	61.0	59.0	62.2	60.3	53.6	75.0	57.8
Prosecutorial	53.2	33.9	37.7	29.7	28.2	30.4	25.0	46.7
Neither	23.4	25.4	29.5	32.4	34.6	39.3	25.0	17.8
Political affiliation								
Democrat	87.2	6.8	85.2	2.7	0.0	82.1	8.3	6.7
Republican	0.0	91.5	6.6	89.2	96.2	7.1	91.7	93.3
Independent or other	12.8	1.7	8.2	8.1	3.8	10.7	0.0	0.0
Past party activism	46.8	67.8	54.1	70.3	66.7	73.2	58.3	60.0
Religion								
Protestant	—	—	—	59.4	55.1	60.7	58.3	75.6
Catholic	—	—	—	24.3	30.8	23.2	33.3	15.6
Jewish	—	—	—	16.3	14.1	16.1	8.3	8.9
Race/ethnicity								
White	68.1	84.7	73.8	89.2	97.4	78.6	100.0	97.8

(Table continues)

Table 7-5 *(Continued)*

	Nixon appointees	Ford appointees	Carter appointees	Reagan appointees	G. H. W. Bush appointees	Clinton appointees	G. W. Bush appointees	Obama appointees
Black	0.0	0.0	16.1	1.3	5.4	13.1	10.2	19.1
Asian American	2.2	0.0	1.8	0.0	0.0	1.6	0.0	6.4
Hispanic	0.0	0.0	3.6	1.3	5.4	11.5	5.1	6.4
Sex								
Women	0.0	0.0	19.6	5.1	18.9	32.8	25.4	46.8
Number of appointees	45	12	56	78	37	61	59	47

Note: "—" indicates not available. Statistics are for lifetime appointments to courts of general jurisdiction. Data for earlier years can be found in previous editions of *Vital Statistics on American Politics.*

[a] Large law firm: twenty-five or more partners and associates; moderate: five to twenty-four; small: two to four.
[b] Two recess appointments by Presidents G. W. Bush and Clinton are not included in these statistics.

Sources: Sheldon Goldman, "Bush's Judicial Legacy: The Final Imprint," *Judicature* 76 (April–May 1993): 287, 293; Elliot Slotnick, Sheldon Goldman, and Sara Schiavoni, "Writing the Book of Judges: Obama's Judicial Appointment Record After Six Years" (article manuscript).

Table 7-6 Federal Judicial Appointments of Same Party as President, Presidents Grover Cleveland to Barack Obama

President	Party	Percentage
Cleveland	Democratic	97.3
Harrison	Republican	87.9
McKinley	Republican	95.7
T. Roosevelt	Republican	95.8
Taft	Republican	82.2
Wilson	Democratic	98.6
Harding	Republican	97.7
Coolidge	Republican	94.1
Hoover	Republican	85.7
F. Roosevelt	Democratic	96.4
Truman	Democratic	93.1
Eisenhower	Republican	95.1
Kennedy	Democratic	90.9
L. Johnson	Democratic	94.5
Nixon	Republican	92.8
Ford	Republican	81.2
Carter	Democratic	89.1
Reagan	Republican	92.7
G. H. W. Bush	Republican	88.6
Clinton	Democratic	87.2
G. W. Bush	Republican	84.7
Obama	Democratic	81.5

Sources: Cleveland–Kennedy: Henry J. Abraham, *Justices, Presidents, and Senators: A History of U.S. Supreme Court Appointments from Washington to Bush II*, 5th ed. (Lanham, MD: Rowman and Littlefield, 2008), 54; L. Johnson–Obama: calculated from Table 7-5, this volume, and previous editions of *Vital Statistics on American Politics.*

Figure 7-3   Cases Filed in U.S. Supreme Court, 1880–2013 Terms

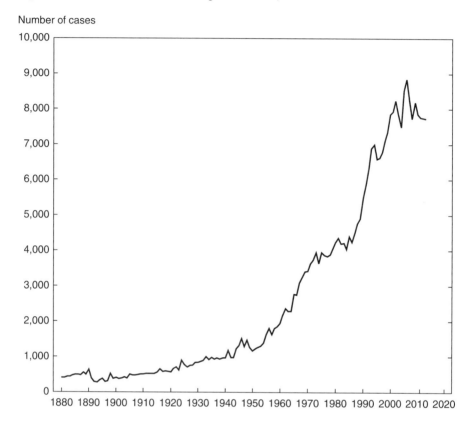

Number of cases

Note: Number of cases filed in term starting in year indicated.

Sources: 1880–2004: Lee Epstein, Jeffrey A. Segal, Harold J. Spaeth, and Thomas G. Walker, *The Supreme Court Compendium: Data, Decisions, and Developments,* 4th ed. (Washington, D.C.: CQ Press, 2007), 62–67; 2005–2013: "2006 Year-End Report on the Federal Judiciary," January 1, 2007; "2008," December 31, 2008; "2010," December 31, 2010; "2012," December 31, 2012; "2014," December 31, 2014 *(www.supremecourtus.gov).*

Table 7-7 Caseload of the U.S. Supreme Court, 1970–2013 Terms

Action	1970	1975	1980	1985	1990	1995	2000	2005	2008	2009	2010	2011	2012	2013
Appellate cases on docket	1,903	2,352	2,749	2,571	2,351	2,456	2,305	2,025	1,941	1,908	1,895	1,867	1,806	1,869
From prior term	325	431	527	400	365	361	351	354	345	328	337	315	303	303
Docketed during present term	1,578	1,921	2,222	2,171	1,986	2,095	1,954	1,671	1,596	1,580	1,558	1,552	1,503	1,566
Cases acted upon[a]	1,613	1,900	2,324	2,185	2,042	2,130	2,024	1,703	—	—	—	—	—	—
Granted review	214	244	167	166	114	92	85	63	78	69	76	59	83	68
Denied, dismissed, or withdrawn	1,285	1,538	1,999	1,863	1,802	1,945	1,842	1,554	—	—	—	—	—	—
Summarily decided	114	118	90	78	81	62	63	46	—	—	—	—	—	—
Cases not acted upon	290	452	425	386	309	326	281	322	—	—	—	—	—	—
Pauper cases on docket	2,289	2,395	2,371	2,577	3,951	5,098	6,651	7,575	7,021	7,388	7,167	7,082	6,997	6,706
Cases acted upon[a]	1,802	1,997	2,027	2,189	3,436	4,514	5,736	6,533	—	—	—	—	—	—
Granted review	41	28	17	20	27	13	14	15	9	8	14	7	10	8
Denied, dismissed, or withdrawn	1,683	1,903	1,968	2,136	3,369	4,439	5,658	6,459	—	—	—	—	—	—
Summarily decided	78	66	32	24	28	55	61	58	—	—	—	—	—	—
Cases not acted upon	487	398	344	388	515	584	915	1,042	—	—	—	—	—	—
Original cases on docket	20	14	24	10	14	11	9	8	4	6	4	3	3	5
Cases disposed of during term	7	7	7	2	3	5	1	4	1	2	2	1	0	0
Total cases available for argument	267	280	264	276	201	145	138	122	—	—	—	—	—	—
Cases disposed of	160	181	162	175	131	93	89	88	—	—	—	—	—	—
Cases argued	151	179	154	171	125	90	86	90	87	82	86	79	77	79
Cases dismissed or remanded without argument	9	2	8	4	6	3	3	1	1	4	2	1	2	3

(Table continues)

Table 7-7 (*Continued*)

Action	1970	1975	1980	1985	1990	1995	2000	2005	2008	2009	2010	2011	2012	2013
Cases remaining	107	99	102	101	70	52	49	31	48	40	43	31	45	40
Cases decided by signed opinion	126	160	144	161	121	87	83	82	83	77	83	73	76	77
Cases decided per curiam opinion	22	16	8	10	4	3	4	5	3	4	3	5	1	2
Number of signed opinions	109	138	123	146	112	75	77	69	74	73	75	64	73	67
Total cases on docket	4,212	4,761	5,144	5,158	6,316	7,565	8,965	9,608	8,966	9,302	9,066	8,952	8,806	8,580

Note: "—" indicates not available. The Supreme Court begins its regular annual session on the first Monday in October. This session, known as the October term, lasts about nine months. The year shown indicates when the term began. These data were previously provided by the Supreme Court in its unpublished statistical sheets. Beginning with the 2007 term, the Court no longer provides these statistical sheets to the public. Data for additional years can be found in previous editions of *Vital Statistics on American Politics.*

a For 1980–2005, includes cases granted review and carried over to next term, not shown separately.

Sources: 1970–1980: U.S. Bureau of the Census, *Statistical Abstract of the United States, 1977* (Washington, D.C.: Government Printing Office, 1976), 184; 1987, 168; 1985–2005: *The United States Law Week* (Washington, D.C.: Bureau of National Affairs), vol. 56, 3102; vol. 61, 3098; vol. 65, 3100; vol. 71, 3080; vol. 76, 3016; 2008–2013: U.S. Supreme Court, "Statistics as of June 30, 2009," *Journal of the Supreme Court of the United States, October Term 2008,* ii; "June 30, 2010," *October Term 2009,* ii; "June 29, 2011," *October Term 2010,* ii; "July 2, 2012," *October Term 2011,* ii; "June 27, 2013," *October Term 2012,* ii; "July 1, 2014," *October Term 2013,* ii (www.supremecourtus.gov/orders/journal.aspx).

Table 7-8 Caseload of U.S. Courts of Appeals, 1980–2014

	1980	1985	1990	1995	2000	2005	2010	2013	2014
Number of judgeships	132	156	156	167	167	167	167	167	167
Number of sitting senior judges	42	45	60	80	81	90	88	89	89
Number of vacant judgeship months	217.1	275.0	153.3	185.5	278.9	165.6	212.3	170.3	158.8
Appeals filed									
Prisoner	3,704	6,532	10,019	14,985	17,252	17,034	15,789	15,031	15,180
All other civil	12,141	18,660	18,631	21,630	23,501	21,666	19,593	21,233	21,878
Criminal	4,405	4,989	9,655	10,162	10,707	16,060	12,797	11,924	11,003
Administrative	2,950	3,179	2,553	3,295	3,237	13,713	7,813	8,287	6,927
Total	23,200	33,360	40,858	50,072	54,697	68,473	55,992	56,475	54,988
Appeals terminated									
Consolidations and cross appeals	2,704	2,669	3,839	3,177	2,740	2,317	2,379	2,647	2,878
Procedural	6,170	12,349	14,008	18,856	26,256	29,745	26,233	20,444	18,224
On the merits									
Prisoner	2,267	2,835	4,988	7,242	5,328	4,435	4,669	10,545	9,610
All other civil	5,861	9,208	9,563	11,293	13,497	12,443	11,025	12,140	12,905
Criminal	2,718	3,070	5,223	7,652	7,236	8,614	9,842	9,088	8,085
Administrative	1,167	1,256	1,169	1,585	1,455	4,421	5,378	3,529	3,514
Total on the merits	12,013	16,369	20,943	27,772	27,516	29,913	30,914	35,302	34,114
Total	20,887	31,387	38,790	49,805	56,512	61,975	59,526	58,393	55,216
Pending appeals	20,252	24,758	32,299	37,536	40,410	57,724	46,351	41,670	41,751
Per active judge[a]									
Termination on the merits	227	308	367	449	458	457	463	551	539
Procedural terminations	—	103	99	109	168	170	161	88	78

287

Note: "—" indicates not available. Data are for the twelve-month period ending on September 30. Data for additional years can be found in previous editions of *Vital Statistics on American Politics.*

[a] Includes only judges active during the entire twelve-month period.

Sources: 1980, 1985: Director of the Administrative Office of the United States Courts, *Federal Court Management Statistics 1985* (Washington, D.C.: Government Printing Office, 1985), 29–30; 1990: *1991*, 27–31; 1995: *1996*; 2000: *2001*, 31; 2005–2014: Administrative Office of the United States Courts (*www.uscourts.gov*).

Table 7-9 Caseload of U.S. District Courts, 1980–2014

	1980	1985	1990	1995	2000	2005	2010	2013	2014
Overall									
Filings	188,487	299,164	251,166	281,681	310,346	330,721	394,345	391,652	392,241
Terminations	180,245	293,545	245,014	259,336	306,211	347,196	419,178	362,228	359,835
Pending	199,019	272,636	273,301	268,197	290,167	323,914	377,952	391,788	423,082
Number (and percentage)	20,592	16,726	25,672	13,538	30,434	39,600	45,010	27,087	30,407
of civil cases over									
three years old	(11.7)	(6.6)	(10.6)	(5.6)	(12.2)	(14.9)	(15.8)	(9.0)	(9.0)
Number of judgeships	516	575	575	649	655	678	678	677	677
Vacant judgeship months	956.2	895.8	540.1	642.0	597.5	309.2	964.1	784.1	768.1
Per judgeship									
Civil filings	327	476	381	383	396	374	417	420	436
Criminal felony filings	38	44	56	51	78	87	130	120	107
Total filings	365	520	437	434	474	488	582	579	579
Pending cases	386	474	475	413	443	478	557	579	625
Terminations	349	511	426	400	467	512	618	535	532
Trials completed	38	36	35	27	22	19	20	19	18
Median time from filing to disposition (months)									
Criminal felony	3.7	3.7	5.4	6.6	6.5	7.3	6.9	7.3	7.5
Civil	8.0	7.0	9.0	8.0	8.2	9.5	7.6	8.5	8.3
Median time from filing to trial (months)									
Civil only[a]	15	14	14	18	20	23	24	26	26

Note: Data are for the twelve-month period ending on September 30. Data for additional years can be found in previous editions of *Vital Statistics on American Politics.*

[a] Time is computed from the date that the answer or response is filed to the date trial begins.

Sources: 1980, 1985: Director of the Administrative Office of the United States Courts, *Federal Court Management Statistics 1985* (Washington, D.C.: Government Printing Office, 1985); 1990: *1993*; 1995: *1996*; 2000: *2001*; 2005–2014: Administrative Office of the United States Courts (*www.uscourts.gov*).

Table 7-10   Civil and Criminal Cases Filed in U.S. District Courts,
1950–2014

	Civil cases		Criminal cases	
Year	Commenced	Terminated	Commenced	Terminated
1950	44,454	42,482	36,383	37,675
1955	48,308	47,959	35,310	38,990
1960	49,852	48,847	28,137	30,512
1965	67,678	63,137	31,569	33,718
1970	87,321	79,466	38,102	36,356
1975	117,320	103,787	41,108	49,212
1980	168,789	160,481	28,932	29,297
1985	273,670	269,848	39,500	37,139
1990	217,879	213,922	48,904	44,295
1991	207,742	211,713	47,035	41,569
1992	230,509	231,304	48,356	44,147
1993	230,597	227,316	46,098	45,280
1994	238,590	227,015	45,269	44,924
1995	248,335	229,820	45,788	41,527
1996	269,132	250,387	47,889	45,499
1997	272,027	249,641	50,363	46,887
1998	256,787	262,301	57,691	51,428
1999	260,271	272,526	59,923	56,511
2000	259,517	259,637	62,745	58,102
2001	250,907	248,174	62,708	58,718
2002	274,841	259,537	67,000	60,991
2003	252,962	253,015	70,642	65,628
2004	281,338	252,761	71,022	64,621
2005	253,273	271,753	69,575	66,561
2006	259,541	273,193	66,860	67,499
2007	257,507	239,678	68,413	67,851
2008	267,257	234,571	70,896	70,629
2009	276,397	263,703	76,655	75,077
2010	282,895	309,759	78,428	78,069
2011	289,252	303,158	78,440	79,839
2012	278,442	271,572	71,303	74,308
2013	283,087	257,057	69,642	69,601
2014	298,713	260,352	64,027	67,115

Note: Reports vary in the month used. Most are from the period ending on June 30 or September 30 of the year indicated.

Sources: 1950–1975: U.S. Bureau of the Census, *Statistical Abstract of the United States, 1971* (Washington, D.C.: Government Printing Office, 1971), 152; *1976*, 168; 1980–1999: Director of the Administrative Office of the United States Courts, *Annual Report of the Director of the Administrative Office of the United States Courts, Judicial Business of the United States Courts 1987* (Washington, D.C.: Government Printing Office, 1987), 7, 13; *1989*, 7, 12; *1991*, 7, 10; *1992*, 4, 6; *1994*; *1996*; *1998*, 16; *1999*, 16; 2000–2014, tables C, D (*www.uscourts.gov*).

Table 7-11   Types of Civil and Criminal Cases in U.S. District Courts, 2014

Civil cases	Percentage[a]	Criminal cases	Percentage
Contract actions	9.6	Drug offenses	31.5
Recovery of overpayments and enforcements of judgments	(0.8)	Immigration	26.5
		Fraud	11.6
Insurance	(3.9)	Traffic offenses	3.5
Other contract actions	(4.9)	Firearms and explosives	9.2
Tort actions	27.1	Larceny and theft	3.1
Personal injury, not product liability	(4.8)	Homicide, robbery, assault, and burglary	2.2
Product liability, personal injury	(21.2)	Embezzlement	0.6
		Forgery and counterfeiting	0.9
Personal property damage	(1.2)	Escape, aiding and abetting, and failure to appear	0.6
Statutory actions	60.5		
Prisoner petitions	(20.9)	All other	10.3
Civil rights	(11.7)		
Labor laws	(6.3)		
Social Security	(6.5)		
Intellectual property rights	(4.4)		
Bankruptcy	(0.9)		
Tax suits	(0.3)		
Other statutory	(9.5)		
Real property actions	2.8		
Total number of civil cases	298,713	Total number of criminal cases	83,779

Note: Data are for the twelve-month period ending on June 30, 2014. Data for earlier years can be found in previous editions of *Vital Statistics on American Politics.* Categories have changed slightly over the years.

[a] Percentages for subcategories may not sum to the category total due to rounding.

Source: Director of the Administrative Office of the United States Courts, *Annual Report of the Director of the Administrative Office of the United States Courts, Judicial Business of the United States Courts 2014* (Washington, D.C.: Government Printing Office, 2015), tables C-2, D-2 (*www.uscourts.gov*).

Table 7-12 Federal, State, and Local Laws Declared Unconstitutional by U.S. Supreme Court, by Decade, 1789–2014

Years	Federal	State and local
1789–1799	0	0
1800–1809	1	1
1810–1819	0	7
1820–1829	0	8
1830–1839	0	3
1840–1849	0	10
1850–1859	1	7
1860–1869	4	24
1870–1879	7	36
1880–1889	4	46
1890–1899	5	36
1900–1909	9	40
1910–1919	6	119
1920–1929	15	139
1930–1939	13	92
1940–1949	2	61
1950–1959	4	66
1960–1969	18	151
1970–1979	19	195
1980–1989	16	164
1990–1999	24	62
2000–2009	16	38
2010–2014	13	16
Total	177	1,321

Sources: Lawrence Baum, *The Supreme Court*, 11th ed. (Washington, D.C.: CQ Press, 2013); Lawrence Baum, Department of Political Science, Ohio State University, personal communication.

Figure 7-4   Economic and Civil Liberties Laws Overturned by U.S. Supreme
Court, by Decade, 1900–2014

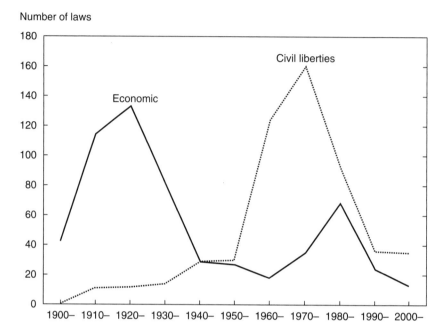

Number of laws

Note: Numbers for 2010–2014 are Economic, 6; Civil liberties, 17. Civil liberties category does
not include laws supportive of civil liberties. Laws include federal, state, and local. State and
local cases include those in which the Court held that a state law was preempted by federal law.

Source: Lawrence Baum, Department of Political Science, Ohio State University, personal
communication.

8

Federalism

- **Historical Data**
- **State Constitutional Provisions**
- **States and the Federal Constitution**
- **State and Local Governments and Employees**
- **Revenues and Spending**
- **Personal Income**
- **Intergovernmental Revenue Flows**

From a statistical point of view, a major problem in studying American government below the federal level is the fifty state governments and thousands of local government units that operate there (Table 8-7). Among other things, this large number of governments often makes it difficult for researchers to procure accurate, up-to-date information about all the relevant jurisdictions. Even for state-level data, a researcher often must turn to each of the fifty state capitals, or to fifty-one units if data about the District of Columbia are needed, or even more if Puerto Rico and areas such as the Northern Mariana Islands are included, which might be necessary to study delegates to the national party conventions. If a researcher's interest is in counties, cities, school districts, and the like, the data collection task can be enormous—well beyond the capacity of one person.

Fortunately, organizations and publications devoted to data collection have stepped up to the challenge. Some organizations, such as the Council of State Governments and the International City Management Association, are well established. The Council of State Governments has published *The Book of the States* since 1935, and the International City Management Association has issued *The Municipal Year Book* since 1934. Other sources are newer, such as the magazine *GOVERNING*, which began publication in 1987. Such groups and publications make data collection far easier and more systematic, and they ensure higher quality than in the past.

Even when data are available, a researcher can still be frustrated by the inevitable variety that occurs across units. Simple tables or one-sentence summaries are often inadequate. As revealed in Table 2-2 on financing state election campaigns, there is enormous variation among states. Similarly, state provisions for the initiative and referendum (Table 8-4) vary in important ways—in who proposes initiatives, whether they apply to statutes or the state constitution or both, and whether the state also provides for a legislative referendum.

In studying state and local governments, their interrelationships, and their relations with the federal government, a researcher must pay attention to details. Even more than usual, it is essential to read notes and check several sources. Differences in data collection procedures, the timing of data collection, and variations in the detail of reports all become important. The user also must keep in mind the purpose of examining the data. It takes a careful researcher to know when variations can be ignored and when they become so frequent or so large that they must be an explicit part of the analysis.

Despite improvements in data collection, states and localities must be approached directly for some information. Fortunately, this approach too has become easier, because the many searchable website directories now available provide the names of specific individuals and offices, typically with addresses, phone numbers, and e-mail addresses. Although the availability of such sources will still not make a project involving twenty-five or fifty states easy, at least one can gather missing information or exact details about specific states and localities.

Because of the surge in the availability of information over the last decade or so, it is now possible to take a serious look at cities, counties, states, and regions, and the relationships among all these governments. The tables in this chapter and others deal mainly with three kinds of information. The first is about specific states, often with an eye toward how states rank relative to one another. This information covers historical data and population, state constitutions, elected officials, provisions for direct democracy, economic provisions, and resources (Tables 8-1 through 8-6, 8-8, and 8-10 and Figures 8-1 and 10-4). The second is data on states and localities as a whole and how they differ from the federal government and from each other (Tables 8-7 and 8-9 and Figures 8-2 and 8-3). The third reflects the considerable emphasis placed on intergovernmental relationships because of the growing fiscal interdependence between federal and state governments, state and local units, and even directly between federal and local governments (Figure 8-4 and Tables 8-11 through 8-14).

As these tables amply demonstrate, students as well as professionals now have access to systematic information about all fifty states and increasingly about localities. Although users may have to make an extra effort to absorb all the details provided by these tables, they are rewarded by the new possibilities for research and understanding.

Table 8-1   The States: Historical Data

State	Date organized as territory	Date admitted to Union	Chronological order of admissions to Union
Alabama	March 3, 1817	December 14, 1819	22
Alaska	August 24, 1912	January 3, 1959	49
Arizona	February 24, 1863	February 14, 1912	48
Arkansas	March 2, 1819	June 15, 1836	25
California	[a]	September 9, 1850	31
Colorado	February 28, 1861	August 1, 1876	38
Connecticut	—	January 9, 1788[b]	5
Delaware	—	December 7, 1787[b]	1
Florida	March 30, 1822	March 3, 1845	27
Georgia	—	January 2, 1788[b]	4
Hawaii	June 14, 1900	August 21, 1959	50
Idaho	March 4, 1863	July 3, 1890	43
Illinois	February 3, 1809	December 3, 1818	21
Indiana	May 7, 1800	December 11, 1816	19
Iowa	June 12, 1838	December 28, 1846	29
Kansas	May 30, 1854	January 29, 1861	34
Kentucky	[a]	June 1, 1792	15
Louisiana	March 26, 1804	April 30, 1812	18
Maine	[a]	March 15, 1820	23
Maryland	—	April 28, 1788[b]	7
Massachusetts	—	February 6, 1788[b]	6
Michigan	January 11, 1805	January 26, 1837	26
Minnesota	March 3, 1849	May 11, 1858	32
Mississippi	April 7, 1798	December 10, 1817	20
Missouri	June 4, 1812	August 10, 1821	24
Montana	May 26, 1864	November 8, 1889	41
Nebraska	May 30, 1854	March 1, 1867	37
Nevada	March 2, 1861	October 31, 1864	36
New Hampshire	—	June 21, 1788[b]	9
New Jersey	—	December 18, 1787[b]	3
New Mexico	September 9, 1850	January 6, 1912	47
New York	—	July 26, 1788[b]	11
North Carolina	—	November 21, 1789[b]	12
North Dakota	March 2, 1861	November 2, 1889	39
Ohio	May 7, 1800	March 1, 1803	17
Oklahoma	May 2, 1890	November 17, 1907	46
Oregon	August 14, 1848	February 14, 1859	33
Pennsylvania	—	December 12, 1787[b]	2
Rhode Island	—	May 29, 1790[b]	13
South Carolina	—	May 23, 1788[b]	8
South Dakota	March 2, 1861	November 2, 1889	40
Tennessee	June 8, 1790[c]	June 1, 1796	16
Texas	[a]	December 29, 1845	28
Utah	September 9, 1850	January 4, 1896	45
Vermont	[a]	March 4, 1791	14

(Table continues)

Table 8-1   *(Continued)*

State	Date organized as territory	Date admitted to Union	Chronological order of admissions to Union
Virginia	—	June 25, 1788[b]	10
Washington	March 2, 1853	November 11, 1889	42
West Virginia	[a]	June 20, 1863	35
Wisconsin	April 20, 1836	May 29, 1848	30
Wyoming	July 25, 1868	July 10, 1890	44

Note: "—" indicates one of the original thirteen states.

[a] No territorial status before admission to Union.

[b] Date of ratification of U.S. Constitution.

[c] Date Southwest Territory (boundaries identical to Tennessee's) was created.

Source: Council of State Governments, *The Book of the States, 2014* (Lexington, Ky.: Council of State Governments, 2014), 505–506.

Table 8-2 State Constitutions

State	Number of constitutions[a]	Dates of adoption	Effective date	Present constitution Estimated length (number of words)	Number of amendments Submitted to voters	Number of amendments Adopted
Alabama	6	1819, 1861, 1865, 1868, 1875, 1901	November 28, 1901	376,006	1,209	880
Alaska	1	1956	January 3, 1959	13,479	42	29
Arizona	1	1911	February 14, 1912	47,306	274	151
Arkansas	5	1836, 1861, 1864, 1868, 1874	October 30, 1874	59,120	198	99
California	2	1849, 1879	July 4, 1879	67,048	894	527
Colorado	1	1876	August 1, 1876	66,140	340	158
Connecticut	2	1818, 1965	December 30, 1965	16,401	31[b]	30
Delaware	4	1776, 1792, 1831, 1897	June 10, 1897	25,445	145	145
Florida	6	1839, 1861, 1865, 1868, 1886, 1968	January 7, 1969	56,705	165	121
Georgia	10	1777, 1789, 1798, 1861, 1865, 1868, 1877, 1945, 1976, 1982	July 1, 1983	41,684	96	73
Hawaii	1	1950	August 21, 1959	21,498	133	110
Idaho	1	1889	July 3, 1890	24,626	212	125
Illinois	4	1818, 1848, 1870, 1970	July 1, 1971	16,401	19	12
Indiana	2	1816, 1851	November 1, 1851	11,476	79	47
Iowa	2	1846, 1857	September 3, 1857	11,089	59	54
Kansas	1	1859	January 29, 1861	14,097	126	96
Kentucky	4	1792, 1799, 1850, 1891	September 28, 1891	27,234	76	42
Louisiana	11	1812, 1845, 1852, 1861, 1864, 1868, 1879, 1898, 1913, 1921, 1974	January 1, 1975	69,876	248	176

(Table continues)

Table 8-2 *(Continued)*

State	Number of constitutions[a]	Dates of adoption	Effective date	Present constitution Estimated length (number of words)	Number of amendments Submitted to voters	Number of amendments Adopted
Maine	1	1819	March 15, 1820	16,313	205	172
Maryland	4	1776, 1851, 1864, 1867	October 5, 1867	43,198	264	228
Massachusetts	1	1780	October 25, 1780	45,283	148	120
Michigan	4	1835, 1850, 1908, 1963	January 1, 1964	31,164	73	30
Minnesota	1	1857	May 11, 1858	11,734	217	120
Mississippi	4	1817, 1832, 1869, 1890	November 1, 1890	26,229	161	125
Missouri	4	1820, 1865, 1875, 1945	March 30, 1945	69,394	177	115
Montana	2	1889, 1972	July 1, 1973	12,790	56	31
Nebraska	2	1866, 1875	October 12, 1875	34,934	354	230
Nevada	1	1864	October 31, 1864	37,418	233	137
New Hampshire	2	1776, 1784	June 2, 1784	13,060	289	145
New Jersey	3	1776, 1844, 1947	January 1, 1948	26,360	83	48
New Mexico	1	1911	January 6, 1912	33,198	298	160
New York	4	1777, 1822, 1846, 1894	January 1, 1895	44,397	301	225
North Carolina	3	1776, 1868, 1970	July 1, 1971	17,177	38	31
North Dakota	1	1889	November 2, 1889	18,746	271	154
Ohio	2	1802, 1851	September 1, 1851	53,239	287	172
Oklahoma	1	1907	November 16, 1907	81,666	360	193
Oregon	1	1857	February 14, 1859	49,016	495	253
Pennsylvania	5	1776, 1790, 1838, 1873, 1968	1968[c]	26,078	36	30
Rhode Island	2	1842, 1986	December 4, 1986	11,407	14	12
South Carolina	7	1776, 1778, 1790, 1861, 1865, 1868, 1895	January 1, 1896	27,421	687	498
South Dakota	1	1889	November 2, 1889	27,774	233	217

State	Number of constitutions	Dates of adoption[a]	Effective date of present constitution	Estimated length (number of words)	Number of amendments submitted to voters[b]	Number adopted
Tennessee	3	1796, 1835, 1870	February 23, 1870	13,960	62	39
Texas	5	1845, 1861, 1866, 1869, 1876	February 15, 1876	86,936	661	483
Utah	1	1895	January 4, 1896	17,849	169	117
Vermont	3	1777, 1786, 1793	July 9, 1793	8,565	212	54
Virginia	6	1776, 1830, 1851, 1869, 1902, 1970	July 1, 1971	21,899	56	48
Washington	1	1889	November 11, 1889	32,578	180	106
West Virginia	2	1863, 1872	April 9, 1872	33,324	122	71
Wisconsin	1	1848	May 29, 1848	15,102	194	145
Wyoming	1	1889	July 10, 1890	26,349	128	100

Note: Constitutions as of January 1, 2014. For more details on the constitutions, see source.

[a] The constitutions include those Civil War documents customarily listed by the individual states. In Connecticut and Rhode Island, colonial charters served as the first constitutions.

[b] Proposed amendments are not submitted to the voters in Delaware.

[c] Certain sections of the constitution were revised in 1967–1968. Amendments proposed and adopted are since 1968.

Source: Council of State Governments, *The Book of the States, 2014* (Lexington, Ky.: Council of State Governments, 2014), 10–11.

Table 8-3 Governors' Terms, Term Limits, and Item Veto

State	Length of term in 1900 (years)	Length of term in 2014 (years)	Year of change	Term limits	Item veto[a]
Alabama	2	4	1902	2–4	yes
Alaska	b	4		2–4	yes[c]
Arizona	b	4	1970	2–4	yes[c]
Arkansas	2	4	1986	2A	yes[c]
California	4	4		2A	yes[c]
Colorado	2	4	1958	2–4	yes[c]
Connecticut	2	4	1950	no limit	yes
Delaware	4	4		2A	yes
Florida	4	4		2–4	yes[c]
Georgia	2	4	1942	2–4	yes[c]
Hawaii	b	4		2–4	yes
Idaho	2	4	1946	no limit	yes[c]
Illinois	4	4		no limit	yes
Indiana	4	4		2–12	no
Iowa	2	4	1974	no limit	yes[c]
Kansas	2	4	1974	2–4	yes[c]
Kentucky	4	4		2–4	yes[c]
Louisiana	4	4		2–4	yes[c]
Maine	2	4	1958	2–4	yes[c]
Maryland	4	4		2–4	yes
Massachusetts	1	4	1920, 1966[d]	no limit	yes
Michigan	2	4	1966	2A	yes[c]
Minnesota	2	4	1962	no limit	yes[c]
Mississippi	4	4		2A	yes[c]
Missouri	4	4		2A	yes[c]
Montana	4	4		2–16	yes[c]
Nebraska	2	4	1966	2–4	yes[c]
Nevada	4	4		2A	no
New Hampshire	2	2		no limit	yes
New Jersey	3	4	1949	2–4	yes[c]
New Mexico	b	4	1916, 1970	2–4	yes[c]
New York	2	4	1938	no limit	yes
North Carolina	4	4		2–4	no
North Dakota	2	4	1964	no limit	yes[c]
Ohio	2	4	1958	2–4	yes[c]
Oklahoma	b	4		2A	yes[c]
Oregon	4	4		2–12	yes[c]
Pennsylvania	4	4		2–4	yes[c]
Rhode Island	1	4	1912, 1994[d]	2–4	no
South Carolina	2	4	1926	2–4	yes[c]
South Dakota	2	4	1974	2–4	yes[c]
Tennessee	1	4	1954	2–4	yes[c]
Texas	2	4	1974	no limit	yes[c]
Utah	4	4		no limit	yes[c]

Table 8-3 *(Continued)*

State	Length of term in 1900 (years)	Length of term in 2014 (years)	Year of change	Term limits	Item veto[a]
Vermont	2	2		no limit	no
Virginia	4	4		1–4	yes[c]
Washington	4	4		no limit	yes
West Virginia	4	4		2–4	yes[c]
Wisconsin	2	4	1970	no limit	yes[c]
Wyoming	4	4		2–16	yes

Note: 2A: Two terms, absolute; 2–4: Two terms, re-eligible after four years; 2–12: Two terms, eligible for eight out of 12 years; 2–16: Two terms, eligible for eight out of 16 years; 1–4: One term, re-eligible after four years.

[a] In all states the governor has the power to veto bills passed by the state legislature. Item veto refers to the power to veto items within a bill. Provisions to override vary, requiring as many as two-thirds of the legislators elected. For details, see *The Book of the States* in source.

[b] Oklahoma was admitted to the Union in 1907, Arizona and New Mexico in 1912, and Alaska and Hawaii in 1959. Oklahoma, Alaska, and Hawaii have always had four-year gubernatorial terms. Arizona started with two years. New Mexico started with four years, went to two years in 1916 and back to four years in 1970.

[c] Over appropriations only. In Wisconsin, the governor has a broader veto on appropriations bills.

[d] Massachusetts went from one year to two years in 1920 and from two years to four years in 1966. Rhode Island went from one year to two years in 1912 and from two years to four years in 1994.

Sources: Length of term in 1900 and year of change: Congressional Quarterly, *Gubernatorial Elections, 1787–1997* (Washington, D.C.: Congressional Quarterly, 1998), 2–3; all other: Council of State Governments, *The Book of the States, 2014* (Lexington, Ky.: Council of State Governments, 2014), 149–150, 154–155.

Table 8-4   State Provisions for Initiative and Referendum

| | Changes to constitution | | | Changes to statutes | | | |
| | Initiative | | Referendum | Initiative | | Referendum | |
State	Direct	Indirect	Legislative	Direct	Indirect	Legislative	Citizen petition
Alabama	no	no	yes	no	no	yes	no
Alaska	no	no	yes	no	yes	no	yes
Arizona	yes	no	yes	yes	no	yes	yes
Arkansas	yes	no	yes	yes	no	yes	yes
California	yes	no	yes	yes	no	yes	no
Colorado	yes	no	yes	yes	no	yes	yes
Connecticut	no	no	yes	no	no	no	no
Delaware	no	no	yes	no	no	yes	no
Florida	yes	no	yes	no	no	no	no
Georgia	no	no	yes	no	no	yes	no
Hawaii	no	no	yes	no	no	no	no
Idaho	no	no	yes	yes	no	yes	yes
Illinois	yes	no	yes	no	no	no	no
Indiana	no	no	yes	no	no	yes	no
Iowa	no	no	yes	no	no	no	no
Kansas	no	no	yes	no	no	no	no
Kentucky	no	no	yes	no	no	no	no
Louisiana	no	no	yes	no	no	no	no
Maine	no	no	yes	no	yes	yes	yes
Maryland	no	no	yes	no	no	no	yes
Massachusetts	no	yes	yes	no	yes	yes	yes
Michigan	yes	no	yes	no	yes	yes	yes
Minnesota	no	no	yes	no	no	no	no
Mississippi	no	yes	yes	no	yes	no	no
Missouri	yes	no	yes	yes	no	yes	yes
Montana	yes	no	yes	yes	no	yes	yes
Nebraska	yes	no	yes	yes	no	no	yes
Nevada	yes	no	yes	no	yes	no	yes
New Hampshire	no	no	yes	no	no	no	no
New Jersey	no	no	yes	no	no	no	no
New Mexico	no	no	yes	no	no	no	no
New York	no	no	yes	no	no	yes	no
North Carolina	no	no	yes[a]	no	no	no	no
North Dakota	yes	no	yes	yes	no	yes	yes
Ohio	yes	no	no	no	yes	no	yes
Oklahoma	yes	no	yes	yes	no	yes	yes
Oregon	yes	no	yes	yes	no	yes	yes
Pennsylvania	no	no	yes	no	no	no	no[b]
Rhode Island	no	no	yes	no	no	no	no
South Carolina	no	no	yes	no	no	no	no
South Dakota	yes	no	yes	yes	no	yes	yes
Tennessee	no	no	yes	no	no	yes	no
Texas	no	no	no	no	no	no	no
Utah	no	no	yes	yes	yes	no	yes

Table 8-4   *(Continued)*

State	Changes to constitution			Changes to statutes			
	Initiative		Referendum	Initiative		Referendum	
	Direct	*Indirect*	*Legislative*	*Direct*	*Indirect*	*Legislative*	*Citizen petition*
Vermont	no	no	yes	no	no	no	no
Virginia	no	no	yes	no	no	no	no
Washington	no	no	no	yes	yes	yes	yes
West Virginia	no	no	yes	no	no	no	no
Wisconsin	no	no	yes	no	no	no	no
Wyoming	no	no	yes	yes	no	no	yes

Note: An *initiative* may propose a constitutional amendment or develop state legislation and may be formed either directly or indirectly. The *direct initiative* allows a proposed measure to be placed on the ballot after a specific number of signatures has been secured on a citizen petition. The *indirect initiative* must be submitted to the legislature for a decision after the required number of signatures has been secured on a petition and prior to placing the proposed measure on the ballot. *Referendum* refers to the process whereby a state law or constitutional amendment passed by the legislature may be referred to the voters before it goes into effect. Three forms of referenda exist: (1) *citizen petition*, whereby the people may petition for a referendum on legislation that has been considered by the legislature; (2) *submission by the legislature* (designated in table as "Legislative"), whereby the legislature may voluntarily submit laws to the voters for their approval; and (3) *constitutional requirement*, whereby the state constitution may require that certain questions be submitted to the voters. For details, see source.

[a] Only the legislature can make statutory changes while in session. Proposed constitutional changes must be passed by the legislature and then are submitted to the citizens to be voted on.
[b] No provision for statewide referenda initiated by citizen petition. There are several county/local referenda that can be initiated by citizen petition.

Source: Council of State Governments, *The Book of the States, 2014* (Lexington, Ky.: Council of State Governments, 2014), 297–298.

Figure 8-1   Initiatives in the States, 1904–2014

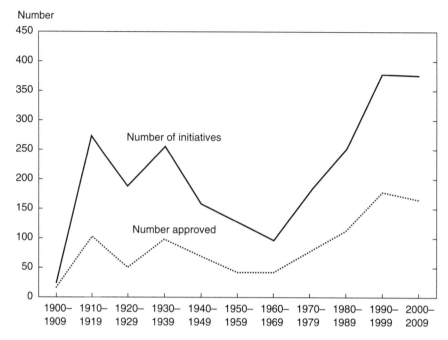

Note: Only initiatives—new laws placed on the ballot by petition—are included. The first use of the initiative was in 1904. The numbers do not include popular referendums or measures placed on the ballot by the legislature. From 2010 to 2014, there were 144 initiatives; 61 were approved.

Sources: 1900–2011: Initiative and Referendum Institute, "Overview of Initiative Use, 1900–2012," January 2013 *(www.iandrinstitute.org)*; 2012–2014: John Matsusaka, I and R Institute, personal communication.

Table 8-5 Incorporation of Bill of Rights to Apply to State Governments

Year	Issue (amendment)	Supreme Court case	Vote
[1868 Fourteenth Amendment to Constitution passed][a]			
1897	Eminent domain (V)	Chicago, Burlington & Quincy RR v. Chicago, 166 U.S. 266	9–0
1927	Freedom of speech (I)	Fiske v. Kansas, 274 U.S. 380	9–0
1931	Freedom of press (I)	Near v. Minnesota, 283 U.S. 697	5–4
1932	Counsel in capital criminal cases (VI)	Powell v. Alabama, 287 U.S. 45	7–2
1934	Free exercise of religion (I)	Hamilton v. Regents of the U. of California, 293 U.S. 245	9–0
1937	Freedom of assembly and petition (I)	De Jonge v. Oregon, 299 U.S. 353	8–0
1947	Separation of church and state (I)	Everson v. Board of Education of Ewing Township, 330 U.S. 1	5–4
1948	Public trial (VI)	In re Oliver, 333 U.S. 257	7–2
1961	Unreasonable searches and seizures (IV)	Mapp v. Ohio, 367 U.S. 643	6–3
1962	Cruel and unusual punishment (VIII)	Robinson v. California, 370 U.S. 660	6–2
1963	Counsel in all criminal cases (VI)	Gideon v. Wainwright, 372 U.S. 335	9–0
1964	Self-incrimination (V)	Malloy v. Hogan, 378 U.S. 1	5–4
		Murphy v. Waterfront Commission, 378 U.S. 52	9–0
1965	Confront adverse witnesses (VI)	Pointer v. Texas, 380 U.S. 400	7–2
1966	Impartial jury (VI)	Parker v. Gladden, 385 U.S. 363	8–1
1967	Obtaining and confronting favorable witnesses (VI)	Washington v. Texas, 388 U.S. 14	9–0
1967	Speedy trial (VI)	Klopfer v. North Carolina, 386 U.S. 213	9–0
1968	Jury trial in non-petty criminal cases (VI)	Duncan v. Louisiana, 391 U.S. 145	7–2
1969	Double jeopardy (V)	Benton v. Maryland, 395 U.S. 784	7–2
2010	Bear arms (II)	McDonald v. Chicago, 561 U.S. 742	5–4

Note: Enumerated rights not incorporated: grand jury indictment, trial by jury in civil cases, excessive fines and bail, and safeguards on quartering troops in private homes.

[a] The Fourteenth Amendment's due process clause is the basis for applying the Bill of Rights to the states.

Sources: Henry J. Abraham, *The Judiciary: The Supreme Court in the Governmental Process,* 9th ed. (Dubuque, Iowa: William C. Brown, 1994); updated by the editors; votes: *United States Reports* (Washington, D.C.: Government Printing Office, various years).

Table 8-6   Length of Time between Congressional Approval and Actual
Ratification of the Twenty-seven Amendments to the U.S.
Constitution

Amendment		*Time required for ratification*	*Year ratified*
I–X	Bill of Rights	2 years, 2.5 months	1791
XI	Lawsuits against states	11 months	1795
XII	Presidential elections	6.5 months	1804
XIII	Abolition of slavery	10 months	1865
XIV	Civil rights	2 years, 1 month	1868
XV	Suffrage for all races	11 months	1870
XVI	Income tax	3 years, 6.5 months	1913
XVII	Senatorial elections	11 months	1913
XVIII	Prohibition	1 year, 1 month	1919
XIX	Women's suffrage	1 year, 2 months	1920
XX	Terms of office	11 months	1933
XXI	Repeal of prohibition	9.5 months	1933
XXII	Limit on presidential terms	3 years, 11 months	1951
XXIII	Washington, D.C., vote	9 months	1961
XXIV	Abolition of poll taxes	1 year, 4 months	1964
XXV	Presidential succession	1 year, 10 months	1967
XXVI	Eighteen-year-old suffrage	3 months	1971
XXVII	Congressional salaries	203 years	1992

Sources: Congressional Research Service, *The Constitution of the United States: Analysis and Interpretation* (Washington, D.C.: Government Printing Office, 1973), 23–44 (92nd Cong., 2nd sess., S. Doc. 92-82); *Congressional Quarterly Weekly Report* (1992), 1423.

Figure 8-2   Government Employees: Federal, State, and Local, 1929–2013

Number of employees (millions)

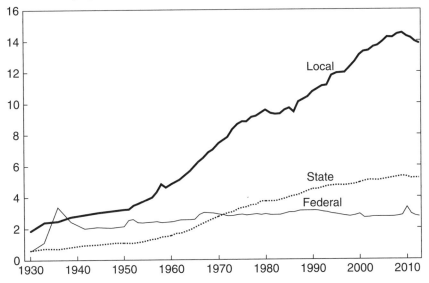

Note: No annual survey of government employment and payroll was conducted in 1996.

Source: 1929–1944, 1949, 1952, 1954, 1959, 1964, 1969–1992: U.S. Advisory Commission on Intergovernmental Relations, *Significant Features of Fiscal Federalism*, 1994, vol. 2 (Washington, D.C.: U.S. Advisory Commission on Intergovernmental Relations, 1994), 151; 1993–1994: (1995), 159; 1995–2013: U.S. Census Bureau *(www.census.gov/govs/apes.html)*; other years: U.S. Bureau of the Census, *Historical Statistics of the United States,* Series Y189-198 (Washington, D.C.: Government Printing Office, 1975), 1100.

Table 8-7 Federal, State, and Local Governments: Number of Units and Employees, 1942–2012

| Year | Federal government | State government | Local government | | | | | | Total |
			County	Municipal	School district	Township and town	Special district[a]	Local Gov't. Total	
1942									
Number	1	48	3,050	16,220	108,579	18,919	8,299	155,067	155,116
Employees (thousands)[b]	2,664	503[c]	333[c]	872[c]	—	223[c,d]	d	1,428[c]	5,915
1952[d]									
Number	1	50	3,052	16,807	67,355	17,202	12,340	116,756	116,807
Employees (thousands)	2,583	1,060	573	1,341	1,234	312[c]	c	3,461	7,105
1962									
Number	1	50	3,043	18,000	34,678	17,142	18,323	91,186	91,237
Employees (thousands)	2,539	1,680	862	1,696	2,161	449[c]	c	5,169	9,388
1972									
Number	1	50	3,044	18,517	15,781	16,991	23,885	78,218	78,269
Employees (thousands)	2,832	2,957	1,369	2,376	3,587	348	327	8,007	13,759
1982									
Number	1	50	3,041	19,076	14,851	16,734	28,078	81,780	81,831
Employees (thousands)	2,862	3,744	1,824	2,397	4,194	356	478	9,249	15,841
1992									
Number	1	50	3,043	19,279	14,422	16,656	31,555	84,955	85,006
Employees (thousands)	3,047	4,595	2,253	2,665	5,134	424	627	11,103	18,745
2002									
Number	1	50	3,034	19,429	13,506	16,504	35,052	87,525	87,576
Employees (thousands)	2,690	5,072	2,729	2,972	6,367	488	721	13,277	21,039

2007								
Number	1	50	3,033	19,492	13,051	16,519	37,381	89,476	89,527
Employees (thousands)	2,730	5,200	2,928	3,001	6,925	510	821	14,186	22,116
2012								
Number	1	50	3,031	19,519	12,880	16,360	38,266	90,056	90,107
Employees (thousands)	2,793	5,286	—	—	—	—	—	13,961	22,040

Note: "—" indicates not available. A census of governmental units is conducted every five years. Data for additional years can be found in previous editions of *Vital Statistics on American Politics*.

[a] Special districts include independent public housing authorities, local irrigation units, power authorities, and other such bodies.

[b] Month for employee counts varies across years. For details, see sources. Numbers include full- and part-time employees.

[c] Employees in other than education.

[d] Townships and special districts are combined.

Sources: 1942–1962: U.S. Bureau of the Census, *Historical Statistics of the United States* (Washington, D.C.: Government Printing Office, 1975), 1086, 1100; 1972–1992 governmental units: U.S. Bureau of the Census, *Census of Governments, 1987* (Washington, D.C.: Government Printing Office, 1988), vi; *1993, 3*; 1972–1992 employees: U.S. Office of Personnel Management, *Federal Manpower Statistics, Federal Civilian Workforce Statistics* (Washington, D.C.: Government Printing Office, various years); U.S. Bureau of the Census, *Public Employment in 1985* (Washington, D.C.: Government Printing Office, 1986), 2; *1989, vi*; *1992, vi*, ix; 2002 governmental units and employees: U.S. Census Bureau, 2002 Census of Governments, vol. 3, no. 2, "Compendium of Public Employment: 2002" (Washington, D.C.: Government Printing Office, 2002), ix, 2, 34; 2007 governmental units: U.S. Census Bureau, "Local Governments and Public School Systems by Type and State: 2007" (*www.census.gov*); 2007 employees: U.S. Census Bureau, "Summary of Public Employment and Payrolls by Type of Government: March 2007," 2007 Census of Governments (*www.census.gov/govs/cog*); 2012 governmental units: "Local Governments by Type and State: 2012" (*www.census.gov/govs/cog2012*); 2012 employees: Employment and Payroll Data, 2012 Census of Governments (*www.census.gov/govs/apes/historical_data_2012.html*).

Table 8-8   State Lottery Revenues (millions)

		Sales		Transfers[a]	
State	Year established	Fiscal year 2014	Change from previous year (percent)	Fiscal year 2014	Change from previous year (percent)
Arizona	1982	$724.0	4.5	$175.4	−0.6
Arkansas	2009	410.1	−6.7	81.5	−9.3
California	1985	5,034.7	13.2	1,357.0	5.6
Colorado	1983	545.0	−3.8	130.1	−4.1
Connecticut	1972	1,112.4	−0.9	319.5	2.4
Delaware	1975	597.2	−5.4	214.5	−9.5
District of Columbia	1982	216.2	−10.9	55.0	−19.6
Florida	1987	5,368.2	7.1	1,495.4	5.0
Georgia	1993	4,022.2	2.8	945.1	1.9
Idaho	1989	208.9	5.7	49.0	1.7
Illinois	1974	2,802.7	−1.4	815.4	2.8
Indiana	1989	1,018.7	9.2	250.7	11.6
Iowa	1985	314.0	−7.4	73.9	−13.0
Kansas	1987	258.1	5.1	74.3	−0.3
Kentucky	1989	858.9	1.4	225.5	0.8
Louisiana	1991	449.0	0.3	170.7	6.5
Maine	1974	230.1	1.1	51.9	−3.1
Maryland	1973	2,303.1	−0.6	941.7	2.2
Massachusetts	1972	4,838.5	−0.2	971.0	8.0
Michigan	1972	2,596.4	4.8	743.1	1.2
Minnesota	1989	531.5	−5.2	127.9	−5.4
Missouri	1986	1,158.1	1.5	267.3	−7.4
Montana	1987	53.3	−6.5	12.1	−7.6
Nebraska	1993	157.9	−1.8	38.0	−5.0
New Hampshire	1964	276.0	−1.0	72.5	−2.5
New Jersey	1970	2,901.6	2.8	965.0	0.0
New Mexico	1996	136.0	−4.1	40.9	−6.4
New York	1967	9,226.5	3.3	3,173.0	4.2
North Carolina	2006	1,839.3	8.8	503.1	5.1
North Dakota	2004	27.0	−3.2	7.8	−1.3
Ohio	1974	2,743.1	1.7	904.3	12.6
Oklahoma	2005	191.2	−4.5	66.9	−4.6
Oregon	1985	1,054.4	−1.4	516.7	−2.6
Pennsylvania	1972	3,799.6	2.7	1,081.5	1.3
Rhode Island	1974	837.9	8.0	376.3	−0.8
South Carolina	2002	1,264.4	5.4	323.4	7.6
South Dakota	1989	645.0	1.2	104.7	−2.7
Tennessee	2004	1,417.1	3.6	337.3	−0.7
Texas	1992	3,694.0	−15.6	995.5	−18.0
Vermont	1978	102.3	0.2	22.6	−1.3
Virginia	1988	1,810.8	7.2	538.6	10.7

Table 8-8   *(Continued)*

State	Year established	Sales Fiscal year 2014	Sales Change from previous year (percent)	Transfers[a] Fiscal year 2014	Transfers[a] Change from previous year (percent)
Washington	1982	595.1	4.5	148.3	6.5
West Virginia	1986	1,214.3	−8.6	—	—
Wisconsin	1988	568.8	0.5	168.3	8.0
Total United States		$70,153.5	1.8	$19,932.6	1.8

Note: "—" indicates not available. Amounts in current dollars. Data for additional years can be found in previous editions of *Vital Statistics on American Politics.*

[a] Transfers to beneficiaries are generally equivalent to "profits" (used in earlier reports) and refer to funds transferred to state-designated programs including state general funds. However, these transfers may not equal current-year profits due to individual reporting requirements and accounting policies in each jurisdiction.

Source: North American Association of State and Provincial Lotteries (*www.naspl.org*).

Table 8-9   State and Local Government Expenditures, by Function, 1902–2012 (percent)

Function	1902	1952	1962	1972	1982	1992	2002	2008	2009	2010	2011	2012
Education	23.3	27.0	31.5	34.6	29.4	28.5	29.1	29.1	28.5	27.6	27.3	27.6
Highways	16.0	15.1	14.7	10.0	6.6	5.8	5.6	5.4	5.2	5.0	4.9	5.0
Public welfare	3.4	9.0	7.2	11.1	11.1	13.5	13.7	14.3	14.5	14.7	15.5	15.4
Health	1.6	1.4	0.9	1.4	2.0	2.6	2.9	2.8	2.8	2.6	2.6	2.7
Hospitals	3.9	5.7	5.2	5.5	5.8	5.1	4.3	4.6	4.7	4.7	4.8	4.9
Police protection	4.6	3.0	3.0	3.2	3.2	3.0	3.2	3.2	3.2	3.1	3.1	3.1
Fire protection	3.7	1.9	1.6	1.4	1.3	1.3	1.3	1.4	1.4	1.3	1.3	1.3
Natural resources	0.8	2.5	1.9	1.6	1.3	1.1	1.1	1.1	1.0	0.9	0.9	0.9
Corrections	—	1.1	1.1	1.1	1.6	2.5	2.7	2.6	2.5	2.3	2.3	2.3
Sanitation and sewerage	4.7	3.2	2.8	2.5	2.9	2.8	2.5	2.5	2.5	2.4	2.4	2.4
Housing and community development	—	2.0	1.6	1.4	1.6	1.5	1.5	1.8	1.7	1.7	1.8	1.7
Parks and recreation	2.6	1.0	1.3	1.2	1.4	1.4	1.5	1.4	1.4	1.3	1.2	1.2
Financial administration	12.9	3.9	1.5	1.3	1.5	1.6	1.6	1.4	1.4	1.3	1.2	1.2
Other government administration	—	—	1.8	1.8	2.7	2.8	2.9	3.0	2.9	2.8	2.7	2.7
Social insurance administration[a]	—	0.6	0.6	0.6	0.4	0.3	0.2	0.1	0.2	0.2	0.2	0.2
Interest on general debt	6.2	1.8	2.9	3.2	3.8	4.8	3.7	3.6	3.5	3.4	3.4	3.5
Utilities	7.5	9.9	7.7	6.0	9.2	7.1	6.8	6.8	7.0	6.7	6.6	6.6

Liquor store expenditure	—	—	—	—	—	0.3	0.2	0.2	0.2	0.2	0.2	0.2
Insurance trust expenditure[b]	—	5.5	6.9	5.5	7.5	7.9	8.3	8.3	9.3	11.5	11.4	11.0
Other	8.8	5.4	5.8	6.6	6.7	6.2	7.0	6.5	6.3	6.2	6.0	6.0
Total direct expenditure (millions)	$1,095	$30,863	$70,547	$190,496	$524,817	$1,147,075	$2,044,331	$2,834,782	$2,988,979	$3,110,833	$3,155,285	$3,147,545

Note: "—" indicates not available. Amounts in current dollars. For 1902 to 1952, financial administration includes other government administration. For 1902 to 1982, the category utilities includes liquor store expenditures. Data for additional years can be found in previous editions of *Vital Statistics on American Politics*.

[a] Formerly, employment security administration.
[b] Unemployment compensation, employee retirement, workers' compensation, and other insurance trust.

Sources: 1902–1982: U.S. Bureau of the Census, *Census of Government, 1982* (Washington, D.C.: Government Printing Office, 1985), 32–33; 1987: U.S. Bureau of the Census, *Governmental Finances in 1987–88* (Washington, D.C.: Government Printing Office, 1990), 13; 1992–2012: U.S. Census Bureau, "United States State and Local Government Finances by Level of Government" (*www.census.gov*).

Table 8-10   Disposable Personal Income per Capita, by State, 1950–2013

State	1950	1960	1970	1980	1990	2000	2005	2010	2013
Alabama	$852	$1,403	$2,662	$6,955	$13,943	$21,355	$27,305	$31,279	$33,150
Alaska	—	2,703	4,559	13,057	19,937	27,081	34,113	41,984	45,600
Arizona	1,257	1,841	3,379	8,418	14,932	22,966	29,058	31,413	33,399
Arkansas	798	1,287	2,548	6,701	12,928	20,031	25,334	29,496	33,205
California	1,703	2,493	4,266	10,420	18,614	27,669	34,095	37,651	41,866
Colorado	1,383	2,055	3,550	9,288	17,003	28,865	34,037	37,538	41,137
Connecticut	1,695	2,438	4,398	10,551	22,815	33,837	41,376	47,594	50,743
Delaware	1,705	2,358	3,819	8,977	18,262	26,428	33,656	37,047	39,783
District of Columbia	2,009	2,379	4,273	10,378	22,400	33,441	48,308	61,900	65,507
Florida	1,204	1,822	3,559	8,752	17,398	25,392	32,470	35,537	37,332
Georgia	997	1,523	2,990	7,397	15,424	24,614	29,386	31,288	33,832
Hawaii	—	2,002	4,372	9,959	18,901	25,454	31,719	38,315	40,730
Idaho	1,239	1,683	3,183	7,708	13,868	21,577	26,968	29,691	32,746
Illinois	1,659	2,350	3,928	9,439	18,180	27,885	33,382	37,894	40,990
Indiana	1,403	1,964	3,319	8,168	15,331	23,983	28,076	31,327	34,573
Iowa	1,431	1,850	3,448	8,307	15,330	24,129	29,870	35,802	40,076
Kansas	1,354	1,921	3,377	8,616	15,921	24,833	29,978	35,274	39,660
Kentucky	914	1,459	2,811	7,173	13,544	21,725	26,104	30,097	32,579
Louisiana	1,037	1,534	2,787	7,669	13,687	21,059	26,792	34,405	37,307
Maine	1,114	1,724	3,069	7,450	15,222	23,230	28,846	34,073	36,790
Maryland	1,474	2,041	3,857	9,488	19,420	29,229	38,126	44,501	46,880
Massachusetts	1,503	2,177	3,861	9,021	19,549	30,795	38,475	45,103	48,808
Michigan	1,569	2,175	3,654	8,961	16,368	25,293	29,451	32,072	34,637
Minnesota	1,316	1,909	3,565	8,810	17,123	27,781	33,124	38,059	41,215
Mississippi	729	1,135	2,381	6,303	11,938	19,491	24,689	28,656	31,164
Missouri	1,308	1,948	3,381	8,124	15,492	24,330	29,358	33,480	36,452
Montana	1,535	1,861	3,228	7,936	13,693	20,770	26,513	31,694	35,045
Nebraska	1,464	1,950	3,364	8,010	15,996	25,063	31,332	36,493	42,244
Nevada	1,780	2,572	4,356	10,279	17,562	26,875	34,363	33,715	35,283
New Hampshire	1,242	1,958	3,406	8,664	18,016	29,286	35,401	41,296	46,071
New Jersey	1,646	2,358	4,218	10,053	21,163	32,334	38,950	45,227	48,012
New Mexico	1,110	1,715	2,849	7,467	13,313	20,196	26,439	30,784	32,816
New York	1,659	2,452	4,177	9,395	20,371	28,618	35,513	43,024	46,100
North Carolina	1,007	1,472	2,884	7,160	15,145	24,246	28,775	32,333	34,588
North Dakota	1,310	1,724	2,948	6,920	14,380	23,092	28,947	39,617	46,425
Ohio	1,467	2,115	3,591	8,746	16,341	24,758	28,927	32,815	36,442
Oklahoma	1,057	1,728	3,098	8,260	14,170	21,721	28,124	33,103	37,736
Oregon	1,495	1,986	3,427	8,705	15,709	24,544	28,546	32,337	35,015
Pennsylvania	1,417	2,037	3,563	8,725	17,091	26,002	31,857	37,606	40,917
Rhode Island	1,404	2,011	3,647	8,445	17,453	25,351	32,409	39,177	41,870
South Carolina	862	1,306	2,741	6,840	14,044	22,161	26,438	30,192	32,456
South Dakota	1,222	1,751	3,025	7,298	14,725	23,876	30,923	38,010	42,065
Tennessee	957	1,477	2,833	7,374	15,004	24,009	29,143	33,222	36,463
Texas	1,240	1,755	3,216	8,553	15,463	25,168	30,190	35,141	39,528
Utah	1,261	1,826	3,032	7,575	13,131	21,453	26,273	29,765	32,727
Vermont	1,073	1,719	3,162	7,593	15,527	24,535	30,942	36,833	40,894

Table 8-10   *(Continued)*

State	1950	1960	1970	1980	1990	2000	2005	2010	2013
Virginia	1,159	1,692	3,267	8,732	17,735	26,775	34,969	40,091	42,807
Washington	1,584	2,163	3,746	9,464	17,449	27,954	34,135	39,254	42,937
West Virginia	980	1,483	2,753	7,077	12,908	19,815	23,848	29,181	32,176
Wisconsin	1,376	1,982	3,463	8,764	15,716	25,079	30,524	35,114	38,331
Wyoming	1,591	2,062	3,472	10,167	16,056	25,312	35,271	41,047	46,028
United States	1,378	2,013	3,581	8,779	16,985	25,956	31,803	36,296	39,513

Note: "—" indicates not available. Amounts in current dollars. Data for additional years can be found in previous editions of *Vital Statistics on American Politics.*

Source: U.S. Department of Commerce, Bureau of Economic Analysis, Regional Economic Data, "State Annual Personal Income" (*www.bea.gov*).

Figure 8-3   Surpluses and Deficits in Federal, State, and Local Government Finances, 1948–2014

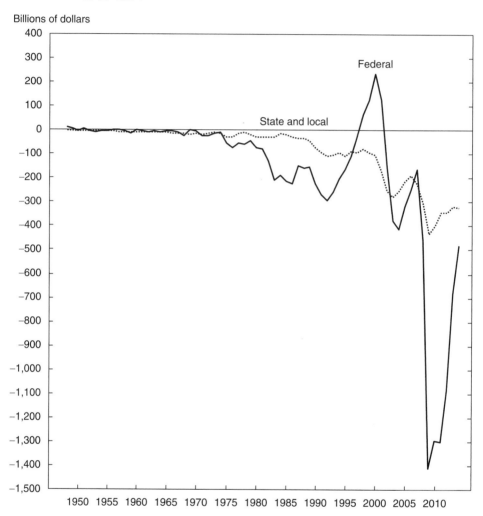

Note: Amounts in current dollars. State and local receipts and expenditures were subject to major revisions in 2003. The revisions made National Income and Product Accounts (NIPA) state and local government receipts and expenditures more comparable to the federal unified budget receipts and outlays. For details, see source and Brent R. Moulton and Eugene P. Seskin, "Preview of the 2003 Comprehensive Revision of the National Income and Product Accounts," *Survey of Current Business* (June 2003): 17–34.

Source: U.S. Office of Management and Budget, *Budget of the U.S. Government, Fiscal Year 2016, Historical Tables* (Washington, D.C.: Government Printing Office, 2015), Table 14.6.

Figure 8-4   State and Local Government Deficits Compared with Federal
Grants-in-Aid, 1948–2014

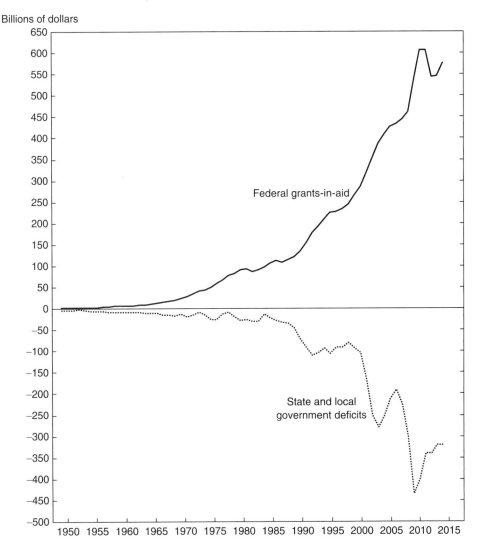

Note: Amounts in current dollars. See note to Figure 8-3, this volume.

Source: U.S. Office of Management and Budget, *Budget of the U.S. Government, Fiscal Year 2016,*
Historical Tables (Washington, D.C.: Government Printing Office, 2015), Tables 12.1 and 14.6.

Table 8-11   Federal Grants-in-Aid Outlays, 1940–2020

		Federal grants as a percentage of			
		Federal outlays[a]		State and	Gross
	Total grants-in-aid		Domestic	local	domestic
Year	(billions)	Total	programs[b]	expenditures[c]	product
1940	$0.9	9.2	—	—	0.9
1945	0.9	0.9	—	—	0.4
1950	2.3	5.3	—	—	0.8
1955	3.2	4.7	—	—	0.8
1960	7.0	7.6	18.0	14.3	1.3
1965	10.9	9.2	18.3	15.5	1.5
1970	24.1	12.3	23.2	19.6	2.3
1975	49.8	15.0	21.7	24.0	3.1
1980	91.4	15.5	22.2	27.3	3.3
1985	105.9	11.2	18.2	22.0	2.5
1990	135.3	10.8	17.1	18.7	2.3
1995	225.0	14.8	21.6	22.8	3.0
2000	285.9	16.0	22.0	21.8	2.8
2001	318.5	17.1	22.9	25.2	3.0
2002	352.9	17.5	23.2	26.3	3.2
2003	388.5	18.0	23.7	26.1	3.4
2004	407.5	17.8	23.9	25.0	3.4
2005	428.0	17.3	23.5	23.5	3.3
2006	434.1	16.3	22.4	23.3	3.2
2007	443.8	16.3	—	—	3.1
2008	461.3	15.5	21.2	22.0	3.1
2009	538.0	15.3	17.6	—	3.7
2010	608.4	17.6	23.4	26.4	4.1
2011	606.8	16.8	22.4	27.5	3.9
2012	544.6	15.4	16.2	24.5	3.4
2013	546.2	15.8	16.1	—	3.3
2014	577.0	16.5	21.2	23.6	3.3
2015 est.	628.2	16.7	20.8	—	3.5
2016 est.	651.7	16.3	20.6	—	3.5
2017 est.	678.1	16.1	—	—	3.4
2018 est.	709.3	16.0	—	—	3.4
2019 est.	736.3	15.8	—	—	3.4
2020 est.	749.8	15.3	—	—	3.3

Note: "—" indicates not available. Amounts in current dollars. Fiscal years. Data for additional years can be found in previous editions of *Vital Statistics on American Politics.*

[a] Includes off-budget outlays; all grants are on-budget.
[b] Excludes outlays for national defense, international affairs, and net interest and undistributed offsetting receipts.
[c] As defined in the National Income and Product Accounts.

Sources: Total grants, total federal outlays, and GDP: U.S. Office of Management and Budget, *Budget of the United States Government, Fiscal Year 2012, Historical Tables* (Washington, D.C.: Government Printing Office, 2011), 249–250; *2014,* 257–258; *2016,* Table 12.1; domestic programs and state and local expenditures: U.S. Office of Management and Budget, *Budget of the United States Government, Analytical Perspectives* (Washington, D.C.: Government Printing Office, various years), Trends in Federal Grants to State and Local Governments (table).

Table 8-12 Federal Grants-in-Aid to State and Local Governments, by Function, 1950–2016 (percent)

Function	1950	1955	1960	1965	1970	1975	1980	1985	1990	1995	2000	2005	2010	2014	2015 est.	2016 est.
Health	5	4	3	6	16	18	17	23	32	42	44	46	48	55	56	57
Income security	59	54	38	32	24	19	20	26	27	24	22	21	19	17	17	17
Education, training, employment, and social services	7	10	8	10	27	24	24	17	17	15	15	13	16	10	10	9
Transportation	21	19	43	38	19	12	14	16	14	11	11	10	10	11	10	10
Natural resources and environment	1	1	2	2	2	5	6	4	3	2	2	1	2	1	1	1
Community and regional development	—	2	2	6	7	6	7	5	4	3	3	5	3	2	3	2
General-purpose fiscal assistance	2	3	2	2	2	14	9	7	2	1	1	1	1	1	1	1
Agriculture	5	7	4	5	3	1	1	2	1	—	—	—	—	—	—	—
Other	—	—	—	—	—	1	2	1	1	1	2	1	1	1	1	1
Total	100	100	102	101	100	100	100	101	101	99	100	98	100	98	99	98

Note: "—" indicates 0.5 percent or less. Due to rounding, percentages may not sum to 100 percent. Data for additional years can be found in previous editions of *Vital Statistics on American Politics.*

Sources: 1950–1990: U.S. Office of Management and Budget, *Budget Baselines, Historical Data, and Alternatives for the Future* (Washington, D.C.: Government Printing Office, 1993), 429–432; 1995: U.S. Office of Management and Budget, *Budget of the U.S. Government, Fiscal Year 1997, Analytical Perspectives* (Washington, D.C.: Government Printing Office, 1996), 172–177; 2000: *2002,* 204–211; 2005: *2007,* 111–118; 2010: *2012,* 285–295; 2014–2016: *2016,* table 15-2.

Table 8-13   Fiscal Dependency of Lower Levels on Higher Levels of Government, 1927–2012

	Intergovernmental revenue as a percentage of total revenue		
Year	State from federal	Local from federal	Local from state[a]
1927	5.0	[b]	9.4
1934	27.3	1.3	20.7
1940	11.6	3.6	21.4
1946	9.4	0.1	21.9
1952	13.9	1.2	26.0
1957	14.2	1.2	25.2
1962	18.9	1.8	25.2
1965	20.2	2.2	32.5
1967	22.3	2.7	28.5
1970	21.6	2.9	30.2
1973	24.2	6.1	31.0
1977	22.4	8.4	30.7
1980	22.3	8.2	31.5
1983	19.3	6.2	29.1
1986	19.3	4.7	29.2
1989	18.4	3.3	29.6
1990	18.7	3.2	29.7
1991	20.4	3.1	29.8
1992	21.4	3.1	30.3
1993	22.0	3.1	30.3
1994	22.7	3.3	30.2
1995	22.3	3.5	30.7
1996	21.5	3.3	30.3
1997	20.7	3.4	30.5
1998	20.3	3.4	30.3
1999	20.7	3.3	31.1
2000	20.6	3.2	31.3
2001	24.4	3.3	31.9
2002	28.9	4.0	32.8
2003	26.5	4.0	32.5
2004	23.5	4.0	30.5
2005	23.5	4.0	30.6
2006	22.4	3.9	29.7
2007	20.4	3.7	29.0
2008	26.6	3.8	30.4
2009	42.0	4.3	32.4
2010	27.2	4.2	29.1
2011	25.4	4.3	28.8
2012	27.0	4.4	29.0

Note: Data for additional years can be found in previous editions of *Vital Statistics on American Politics*.

[a] Includes indirect federal aid passed through the states.
[b] Less than 0.1 percent.

Sources: 1927–1992: Calculated by the editors from U.S. Advisory Commission on Intergovernmental Relations, *Significant Features of Fiscal Federalism, 1994*, vol. 2 (Washington, D.C.: U.S. Advisory Commission on Intergovernmental Relations, 1994), 44; 1993–2012: U.S. Census Bureau (*www.census.gov*).

Table 8-14   Variations in Local Dependency on State Aid, 2012

Rank	State	Percentage	Rank	State	Percentage
1	Vermont	64.9	27	North Carolina	32.1
2	Arkansas	54.0	28	Virginia	32.1
3	Delaware	49.9	29	New York	31.4
4	New Mexico	48.2	30	Washington	31.3
5	Michigan	43.9	31	Kansas	30.9
6	North Dakota	41.6	32	Massachusetts	30.6
7	Minnesota	41.2	33	Tennessee	30.6
8	West Virginia	40.5	34	Utah	30.6
9	California	39.7	35	New Hampshire	29.1
10	Wisconsin	39.3	36	Maine	29.0
11	Mississippi	39.2	37	Illinois	28.8
12	Indiana	39.1	38	Maryland	28.4
13	Idaho	39.0	39	Missouri	28.3
14	Nevada	38.9	40	South Carolina	27.9
15	Wyoming	37.8	41	Connecticut	27.8
16	Alaska	36.1	42	Georgia	27.4
17	Kentucky	35.6	43	Texas	27.4
18	Montana	35.6	44	New Jersey	26.5
19	Pennsylvania	35.6	45	South Dakota	25.8
20	Ohio	35.1	46	Nebraska	24.7
21	Oregon	33.9	47	Rhode Island	24.1
22	Louisiana	33.8	48	Colorado	23.8
23	Oklahoma	33.5	49	Florida	22.1
24	Alabama	33.1	50	Hawaii	7.7
25	Iowa	32.3			
26	Arizona	32.1		Total	32.6

Note: Percentages reflect state transfers (including "pull-through" monies from the federal government) as a percentage of total local general revenues. Where ties occur, the rank order was determined by the second decimal. Data for earlier years can be found in previous editions of *Vital Statistics on American Politics*.

Source: U.S. Census Bureau, "State and Local Government Finances, by Level of Government and by State: 2012" (*www.census.gov*).

9

Foreign and Military Policy

- **Treaties and Agreements**
- **Military Engagements**
- **Military Personnel**
- **Expenditures**
- **Military Sales and Assistance**
- **Foreign Aid**
- **Investment and Trade**

Even researchers seeking to understand only U.S. domestic politics would find data on international relations essential. In the 1960 presidential campaign, for example, John F. Kennedy made the "missile gap" a major issue: the United States was falling behind the Soviet Union in its missile arsenal, which imperiled the defense of the free world. The actual existence of that missile gap has been disputed, but the charge fit in with Kennedy's pledge to get the country moving again and played well to the public in the aftermath of Sputnik and the U-2 incident. More recently, the events of September 11, 2001, the wars in Iraq and Afghanistan, and continuing acts of terrorism have made concerns that were once "foreign" very immediate.

Statistics related to foreign policy, especially its military aspects, may be difficult or impossible to find. After all, secrecy prevents publication of important information about U.S. defense capabilities. For example, the performance capabilities of spy satellites and the ability to fight computer hackers are understandably kept secret. Secret diplomatic and military initiatives also are undertaken by the Central Intelligence Agency and other organizations, and the public learns about these only later, if at all. One example is the sale of weapons to Iran in the 1980s (while the United States was publicly declaring that it would have nothing to do with that country) and the use of profits from these sales to support the Nicaraguan contras. Another example is the Central Intelligence Agency's pre–Iraq War assessments of weapons of mass destruction.

And yet despite these examples and the obvious need for secrecy in defense-related areas, a surprisingly wide array of data is available, in part because details about military hardware are not the only kinds of relevant information. As was especially evident during the 1960s, for example, public opinion on foreign policy is extraordinarily relevant and powerful information. But public opinion on U.S. involvement in world affairs has had its ups and downs (Table 3-16), and the public's judgment about whether foreign or domestic problems are "most important" has shifted sharply over time (Figures 3-11 and 3-12). Evaluations of U.S. involvement in Iraq (Figure 3-20) and the fight against terrorism (Table 3-18) have also fluctuated over time.

Diplomatic efforts, both current and historical, as well as international arms control and other agreements (Tables 9-1 and 9-2) are also relevant inasmuch as they are affected by and, in turn, affect domestic politics. The historical record of U.S. involvement abroad in both the distant and recent past (Tables 9-3 through 9-5) and its consequences for armed forces personnel (Table 9-6) serve as a reminder that the end of the "new world order" has not signaled a withdrawal from foreign engagements. Likewise, the number and placement of U.S. troops abroad remain important issues (Table 9-7). More obviously, data on military personnel are sometimes directly related to domestic concerns, as, for example, in the table on military personnel categorized by sex, race, and Hispanic origin (Table 9-8).

A variety of other information is closely related to both defense and domestic policy, and these kinds of data are emphasized here. Defense spending, for example, involves more than whether the United States has spent enough to defend itself. Elementary economics courses express the trade-off between defense and nondefense spending in terms of "guns or butter." Every dollar spent on weaponry means that a dollar less can be spent on social programs, tax reductions, and other politically worthy causes. Therefore, information on defense spending (Table 9-9 and Figure 9-1) is doubly relevant.

In information on defense spending, two elements arise. The first is the concept of "constant" versus "current" dollars. Current dollars are what people deal with every day. The price asked for goods is the price paid; whether the price has gone up more or less than other prices is not especially relevant. People may be aware that the prices of some goods have gone up (such as oil and gasoline in the 1970s and again in the 2000s) or down (such as many electronic products) more than others, but the price quoted is what is most significant. Constant dollars, by contrast, take into account what has happened to prices more generally (see Table 11-2 for the Consumer Price Index).

Thus, for example, most food clearly costs more in current dollars than it did years ago—in the 1960s one never heard of a loaf of bread that cost $4.00. Yet relative to other prices the cost of bread has fallen. Its price may have only doubled over a given period while other prices have tripled. In a meaningful sense, then, bread and other foods are cheaper than they used to be; the "real" cost of bread has been reduced.

Another, perhaps simpler way to express this concept is to say that constant dollar calculations take inflation into account. For defense spending, then, the question is whether, after inflation is taken into account, spending has increased. If spending has risen only as fast as inflation, the new budget will buy only as much as the previous budget, even though nominally—that is, in current dollars—it is larger. Because this issue of real versus current dollars is so significant, Table 9-9 and many of the tables in Chapter 11 express expenditures both ways.

The second element in presenting information on defense spending is the relevance of what other countries are doing (Table 9-10). Whether the United States is spending a lot or a little is a relative question. If foreign adversaries raise their spending, then perhaps the United States must do the same.

Economic and social dimensions are also relevant to U.S. foreign and military policy, and data about these are widely available. The slippage of the U.S. trade balance (Table 9-14) and the increasing foreign investment in the United States and U.S. investment abroad (Table 9-13) are two aspects of the economic context of recent foreign policy discussions. Foreign aid, whether in the form of military (Table 9-11) or nonmilitary (Table 9-12) assistance, is another part of economic foreign policy. Finally, immigration policy has social and economic implications, and changes in the flow of immigrants, along with future prospects, make it a most significant aspect of U.S. foreign relations (Tables 10-2 through 10-4 and Figure 10-2).

Despite the end to the Cold War, public opinion about wars, international agreements, previous conflicts, levels of defense spending, foreign aid, the balance of trade, and so on—and the data about them—remain as relevant as ever. The emergence of the United States as a world power in the twentieth century elevated the political significance of international relations, so that no overview of American politics would be complete without a look at foreign and military policy. Foreign policy has often proved critical in domestic politics, and that accounts for the numbers presented here.

Table 9-1   Treaties and Executive Agreements Concluded by the United States, 1789–2013

Years	Number of treaties	Number of executive agreements
1789–1839	60	27
1839–1889	215	238
1889–1929	382	763
1930–1932	49	41
1933–1944 (F. Roosevelt)	131	369
1945–1952 (Truman)	132	1,324
1953–1960 (Eisenhower)	89	1,834
1961–1963 (Kennedy)	36	813
1964–1968 (L. Johnson)	67	1,083
1969–1974 (Nixon)	93	1,317
1975–1976 (Ford)	26	666
1977–1980 (Carter)	79	1,476
1981–1988 (Reagan)	125	2,840
1989–1992 (G. H. W. Bush)	67	1,350
1993–2000 (Clinton)	209	2,048
2001–2008 (G. W. Bush)	136	1,998
2009–2013 (Obama)	19	1,045

Note: Number of treaties includes those concluded during the indicated span of years. Some of these treaties did not receive the consent of the U.S. Senate. Because of varying definitions of what comprises an executive agreement and their entry-into-force date, the numbers in the table are approximate.

Sources: 1789–1992: *Congressional Quarterly's Guide to Congress*, 5th ed. (Washington, D.C.: CQ Press, 2000), 219; 1993–2013: Office of the Assistant Legal Adviser for Treaty Affairs, U.S. Department of State.

Table 9-2   Major Arms Control and Disarmament Agreements

Issue	Participants
Nuclear weapons	
To prevent the spread of nuclear weapons	
Antarctic Treaty, 1959	51 nations
Outer Space Treaty, 1967	127 nations
Latin American Nuclear-Free Zone Treaty, 1967	33 nations[a]
Nuclear Non-proliferation Treaty, 1968	191 nations[a]
Seabed Treaty, 1971	117 nations
To reduce the risk of nuclear war	
Hot Line and Modernization Agreements, 1963	United States and Soviet Union
Accidents Measures Agreement, 1971	United States and Soviet Union
Prevention of Nuclear War Agreement, 1973	United States and Soviet Union
To limit nuclear testing	
Limited Test Ban Treaty, 1963	131 nations
Threshold Test Ban Treaty, 1974	United States and Soviet Union
Peaceful Nuclear Explosions Treaty, 1976[b]	United States and Soviet Union
Comprehensive Test Ban Treaty, 1996	183 nations[c]
To limit nuclear weapons	
ABM Treaty (SALT I) and Protocol, 1972	United States and Soviet Union
SALT I Interim Agreement, 1972[d]	United States and Soviet Union
SALT II, 1979[e]	United States and Soviet Union
Intermediate Range Nuclear Forces (INF) Treaty, 1987	United States and Soviet Union
Strategic Arms Reduction Treaty (START), 1991	United States, Russia, Belarus, Kazakhstan, Ukraine[f]
Strategic Arms Reduction Treaty, II (START II), 1993	United States and Russia[g]
Moscow Treaty on Strategic Offensive Reductions, 2002	United States and Russia
New Strategic Arms Reduction Treaty (New START), 2011	United States and Russia
Other weapons	
To prohibit use of gas	
Geneva Protocol, 1925	138 nations[a]
To prohibit biological weapons	
Biological Weapons Convention, 1972	182 nations[h]
To prohibit techniques changing the environment	
Environmental Modification Convention, 1977	85 nations
To control use of inhumane weapons	
Convention on Conventional Weapons, 1981	124 nations[i]

(Table continues)

Table 9-2   *(Continued)*

Issue	Participants
To limit conventional weapons	
Conventional Forces in Europe Treaty, 1990	30 nations[j]
To ban use, development, production,	
stockpiling of chemical weapons	
Chemical Weapons Convention, 1993	190 nations[k]

Note: "Participation" does not necessarily imply signing without reservations or ratification. In some instances, an agreement is no longer in force. For details, see sources.

[a] Number of parties and signatories as of April 2015.

[b] Ratified by the United States and entered into force December 1990.

[c] Number of parties and signatories as of April 2015. Not entered into force as of April 2015.

[d] Expired by its terms October 3, 1977.

[e] Never ratified. If the treaty had entered into force, it would have expired by its terms December 31, 1985.

[f] Ratified by the United States October 1992; entered into force December 1994. President Barack Obama and President Dmitri A. Medvedev of Russia signed an agreement on July 6, 2009, to cut deployed nuclear warheads and to reduce delivery systems, setting the stage for negotiations to replace the 1991 Strategic Arms Reduction Treaty that expired in December 2009.

[g] Ratified by the United States as of January 1996. Ratified by Russia in April 2000, but with amendments not approved by the U.S. Senate.

[h] Entered into force March 1975; number of parties and signatories as of April 2015.

[i] Entered into force December 1983. Number of parties and signatories as of April 2015. Full title of treaty is Convention on Prohibitions or Restrictions on the Use of Certain Conventional Weapons Which May Be Deemed to Be Excessively Injurious or to Have Indiscriminate Effects (and Protocols).

[j] Ratified by the United States December 1991; entered into force November 1992.

[k] Ratified by the United States April 25, 1997; took effect April 29, 1997. Number of parties and signatories as of April 2015.

Sources: U.S. Department of State (*www.state.gov*); notes "a," "c," "j," and "k": United Nations Office for Disarmament Affairs (*http://disarmament.un.org*); notes "h" and "i": United Nations Office at Geneva, "Disarmament" (*www.unog.ch*).

Table 9-3   Use of U.S. Armed Forces Abroad, 1798–2014

Decade	Number of instances	Example of use of armed forces
1798–1800	1	Undeclared naval war with France
1801–1810	4	Tripoli—First Barbary War
1811–1820	13	Caribbean—engagements with pirates, onshore and offshore
1821–1830	8	Cuba—fight, capture pirates
1831–1840	7	Fiji Islands—punish natives who attacked American explorers
1841–1850	8	China—after a clash at a trading post in Canton
1851–1860	22	Nicaragua—oppose William Walker's attempt to control country
1861–1870	13	Japan—several times, to protect American interests
1871–1880	5	Colombia—protect American interests in fighting over Panama
1881–1890	7	Hawaii—protect American interests
1891–1900	18	Philippine Islands—protect American interests; conquer islands
1901–1910	16	Colombia, Panama, Dominican Republic, Honduras, Nicaragua—protect American interests during civil turmoil
1911–1920	29	Honduras, China, Turkey, Mexico—protect American interests
1921–1930	15	Panama, Costa Rica—to prevent war over boundary dispute
1931–1940	7	Haiti—part of long-term stay to prevent chronic insurrection
1941–1950	13	Trieste—reinforce air forces after Yugoslav downing of plane
1951–1960	6	Korean War; Lebanon—protect against threatened insurrection
1961–1970	8	Vietnam War; Congo—airlift Congolese troops during rebellion
1971–1980	11	Lebanon—evacuate citizens fighting; Iran—rescue attempt
1981–1990	23	Libya—shoot down jets; Grenada—restore law and order
1991–2000	29	Persian Gulf War; Somalia—food aid; Haiti—oust military; Bosnia—keep peace; Yugoslavia—aid Kosovo
2001–2010	9	Afghanistan, Haiti, Iraq, Kosovo, Macedonia, Pakistan, Philippines, Somalia (pirates), Yemen
2011–2014	6	Afghanistan, Iraq, Libya, Pakistan, Somalia, Yemen

Note: The count of instances is necessarily approximate; for example, numerous engagements with pirates in the Caribbean between 1814 and 1825 are counted as only one instance. Five of the instances were declared wars: War of 1812 (1812–1815); Mexican War (1846–1848); Spanish-American War (1898); World War I (1917–1918); World War II (1941–1945). Others might be considered undeclared wars: undeclared naval war with France (1798–1800); First Barbary War (1801–1805); Second Barbary War (1815); Korean War (1950–1953); Vietnam War (1964–1973); Persian Gulf War (1991); Iraq War (2003). (Actions that covered more than one decade are counted as occurring in each decade.) The counts above do not include situations of nonmilitary conflict, such as use of the U.S. military to construct Ebola treatment facilities in Liberia. A detailed list of over five hundred incidents abroad appears in Benjamin O. Fordham and Christopher C. Sarver, "Militarized Interstate Disputes and United States Uses of Force," *International Studies Quarterly* (September 2001).

Sources: Ellen C. Collier, *Instances of Use of United States Armed Forces Abroad, 1798–1993* (Washington, D.C.: Congressional Research Service, 1993); updated by the editors based on reports in the *New York Times*.

Table 9-4 U.S. Personnel in Major Military Conflicts

Item	Civil War[a]	Spanish-American War	World War I	World War II	Korean War	Vietnam War	Persian Gulf War	Iraq War	Afghanistan War
Personnel serving (thousands)	2,213	307	4,735	16,113	5,720	8,744	2,233	1,500	832[b]
Average duration of service (months)	20	8	12	33	19	23	—	—	—
Casualties (thousands)									
Battle deaths	140	c	53	292	34	47	c	4.4	2.4[d]
Wounds not mortal	282	2	204	671	103	153	c	31.9	20.1[d]
Draftees: classified (thousands)	777	0	24,234	36,677	9,123	75,717	0	0	0
Examined	522	0	3,764	17,955	3,685	8,611	0	0	0
Rejected	160	0	803	6,420	1,189	3,880	0	0	0
Inducted	46	0	2,820	10,022	1,560	1,759	0	0	0
Cost (millions)[e]									
Current	$3,183	$283	$20,000	$296,000	$30,000	$111,000	$7,000[f]	$819,597[g]	$801,284[g]
Constant (2011)	59,631	9,034	334,000	4,104,000	341,000	738,000	11,700	—	—

Note: "—" indicates not available. For the Revolutionary War, the number of personnel serving is not known, but estimates range from 184,000 to 250,000; for the War of 1812, 286,730 served; for the Mexican-American War, 78,718 served. Periods covered are as follows: Spanish-American War: April 21, 1898, to August 13, 1898; World War II: December 1, 1941, to December 31, 1946; Korean War: June 5, 1950, to July 27, 1953; Vietnam War (personnel and draftees): August 4, 1964, to January 27, 1973; Vietnam War (deaths and wounded): January 1, 1961, to January 27, 1973; Persian Gulf War: August 1, 1990, to April 30, 1992; Iraq War: March 19, 2003, to December 31, 2011 (deaths and cost through April 22, 2015); Afghanistan War: October 7, 2001, to December 31, 2014 (deaths and cost through April 22, 2015).

[a] Union forces only. Estimates of the number serving in Confederate forces range from 600,000 to 1.5 million; cost for the Confederacy estimated at $1,000 million (current dollars) and $20,111 million (constant 2011 dollars).

[b] As of May 27, 2014.

[c] Fewer than five hundred.

[d] As of April 22, 2015.

[e] Original direct costs only. Excludes service-connected veterans' benefits and interest payments on war loans.

[f] Total costs estimated at $61.0 billion (in current dollars). Shown is the portion of that amount estimated to have been paid by the United States.

[g] Estimate of cost through April 22, 2015. Costs are approximations because costs are still being incurred. Does not include "complementary" costs such as spending for continuing care of returning veterans.

Sources: Noncost items, Civil War–Vietnam: U.S. Census Bureau, *Statistical Abstract of the United States, 2001* (Washington, D.C.: Government Printing Office, 2001), 332; personnel serving (Iraq): "Iraq by the Numbers" (*http://dpc.senate.gov/docs/fs-112-1-36.pdf*); (Afghanistan): "U.S. Military in Afghanistan by the Numbers" (*http://abcnews.go.com/blogs/politics/2014/05/u-s-military-in-afghanistan-by-the-numbers-2184-dead-19600-wounded/*); casualties (Iraq and Afghanistan): U.S. Department of Defense (*www.defenselink.mil/news/casualty.pdf*); cost (through Vietnam): "Costs of Major U.S. Wars," Congressional Research Service (*www.crs.gov*); cost (Persian Gulf): "Conduct of the Persian Gulf War, Final Report to Congress, April 1992," 725 (*www.ndu.edu/library/epubs/cpgw.pdf*); cost (Iraq and Afghanistan): National Priorities Project (*http://costofwar.com*).

Table 9-5 U.S. Military Forces and Casualties in Vietnam, 1957–1993

Year	Military forces (thousands)	Battle deaths				Wounded, nonfatal[a]	
		Total[a]	Killed	Died of wounds	Died while missing[b]	Hospital care (thousands)	No hospital care (thousands)
1957–1964	23.3[c]	279	197	10	72	0.8	0.8
1965	184.3	1,432	1,124	111	197	3.3	2.8
1966	385.3	5,047	4,142	579	326	16.5	13.6
1967	485.6	9,463	7,525	1,598	401	32.4	29.7
1968	536.1	14,623	12,624	979	959	46.8	46.0
1969	475.2	9,426	8,117	1,168	141	32.9	37.3
1970	234.6	4,230	3,486	555	189	15.2	15.4
1971	156.8	1,376	1,082	160	134	4.8	4.2
1972	24.2	361	205	28	128	0.6	0.6
1973–1993	0.0	1,118	0	22	1,068	[d]	[d]
Total	[e]	47,355	38,502	5,210	3,615	153.3	150.4

Note: Military forces as of December 31. All U.S. forces withdrawn by January 27, 1973. Discrepancies in total battle deaths and sum of categories for 1967, 1968, and 1973–1993 are found in the source.

[a] Casualties from enemy action. Deaths exclude 10,803 servicemen who died in accidents or from disease.
[b] Includes 114 servicemen who died while captured.
[c] For 1964 only.
[d] Fewer than fifty.
[e] Not applicable.

Sources: Military forces, battle deaths: U.S. Bureau of the Census, *Statistical Abstract of the United States, 1995* (Washington, D.C.: Government Printing Office, 1995), 365; wounded, nonfatal: *Statistical Abstract of the United States, 1987*, 328.

Table 9-6 Sexual Assaults, Amputations, Suicides, Traumatic Brain Injuries, and Friendly Fire Sustained by U.S. Military Personnel, 2001–2014

Year	Sexual assaults[a]	Sexual assaults at MSAs[b]	Amputations[c]	Suicides[d]	Traumatic brain injuries[e]
2001	—	—	45	147	11,619
2002	—	—	44	141	12,407
2003	—	—	134	160	12,815
2004	1,700	—	239	171	14,519
2005	2,374	42	246	152	15,531
2006	2,947	40	240	190	17,037
2007	2,846	34	274	197	23,217
2008	3,109	25	180	268	28,462
2009	3,472	41	168	309	28,877
2010	3,327	65	316	295	29,188
2011	3,393	80	362	301	32,625
2012	3,604	70	f	319	30,406
2013	5,518	61	f	259	20,250
2014	6,131		f	—	g

Note: "—" indicates not available. After a high rate of incidence in Operation Desert Storm (1991–1992), incidents of death by friendly fire have been reported to be rare: Operation Desert Storm: 25 (17% of all battle deaths); Iraq and Afghanistan Wars: 17 (about 1% of battle deaths), though up-to-date numbers are difficult to locate.

[a] Numbers are total reports of sexual assault made to the Department of Defense in the fiscal year ending in the year shown. Total reports include unrestricted reports (reports that are provided to command and/or law enforcement for investigation) as well as reports remaining restricted (reports that allow victims to confidentially access medical care and advocacy services without triggering an investigation). Numbers for 2007–2013 are higher than shown in earlier reports.

[b] Numbers are the total reports of sexual assaults at the military service academies during the academic program year ending in the year shown. The numbers are based on a survey of the cadets and midshipmen.

[c] Number of major upper (hand/wrist, forearm) and lower body (foot/ankle, leg) amputations. Some service members had both upper and lower body amputations; some had bilateral amputations. A total of 2,037 service members had major amputations over the twelve-year period 2000–2012. Source presented graphs only; numbers as read from graphs may contain slight inaccuracies.

[d] Numbers are death by suicide among active component service members. Source prior to 2008 presented graphs only; numbers as read from graphs may contain slight inaccuracies.

[e] Numbers represent actual medical diagnoses of TBI anywhere U.S. forces are located, including the U.S.

[f] Battle-injury major limb amputations—on average, about two-thirds of all amputations—through 2014 can be found in Congressional Research Service, *A Guide to U.S. Military Casualty Statistics: Operation Inherent Resolve, Operation New Dawn, Operation Iraqi Freedom, and Operation Enduring Freedom*, RS22452, November 20, 2014, 6.

[g] Through Quarter 2 of 2014: 12,082.

Sources: Sexual assaults: Department of Defense *Annual Report on Sexual Assault in the Military, Fiscal Year 2014*, 7 (*www.sapr.mil*); sexual assaults at MSAs: Department of Defense, *Annual Report on Sexual Harassment and Violence at the Military Service Academies*, Academic Program Year 2013–2014, 8 (*www.sapr.mil*); Amputations: *Medical Surveillance Monthly Report*, June 2012 (Silver Spring, MD: Armed Forces Health Surveillance Center, 2012), 4: Suicides, 2001–2007: *MSMR*, June 2012, 8; Suicides, 2008–2013: Department of Defense, *Suicide Event Reports, 2008–2013*; Traumatic brain injuries: Congressional Research Service, *A Guide to U.S. Military Casualty Statistics: Operation Inherent Resolve, Operation New Dawn, Operation Iraqi Freedom, and Operation Enduring Freedom*, RS22452, November 20, 2014, 4. Friendly fire: "Friendly Fire Deaths Rare" (*www.military.com*), March 11, 2006.

Table 9-7 U.S. Military Personnel Abroad or Afloat, by Country, 1972–2014 (thousands)

Country	1972	1975	1980	1985	1990	1995	2000	2005	2008	2009	2010	2011	2012	2013	2014
Outside United States[a]	628	517	502	515	609	238	258	291[b]	289[b]	263[b]	297[b]	205[b]	193[b]	—	80
Europe[a,c]	298	314	332	358	310	118	117	102	82	76	79	81	75	80	80
Germany	210	220	244	247	228	73	69	66	55	53	54	54	48	47	46
Greece	3	4	4	4	2	2	1	1	d	d	d	d	d	d	d
Iceland	3	3	3	4	3	2	2	1	1	d	d	d	d	d	d
Italy	10	12	12	15	14	12	11	12	10	10	10	11	11	12	12
Spain	9	9	9	9	7	3	2	2	1	1	1	2	2	2	2
Turkey	7	7	5	5	4	3	2	2	2	2	2	2	2	2	2
United Kingdom	22	21	24	30	25	12	11	11	9	9	9	9	9	13	14
Afloat	28	30	22	36	18	8	4	2	1	1	d	d	d	d	d
East Asia and Pacific[a]	275	156	115	125	119	89	101	79	69	48	44	56	52	58	57
Japan (includes Okinawa)	65	48	46	50	45	43	40	36	33	36	34	39	51	55	54
Korea, Rep. of	41	42	39	42	41	36	37	31	25	d	d	d	d	d	d
Philippines	17	15	13	15	14	d	d	d	d	d	d	d	d	d	d
Thailand	47	20	d	d	d	d	1	d	d	d	d	d	d	1	1
Vietnam	47	0	0	0	0	d	d	d	d	d	d	d	d	d	d
Afloat	51	28	16	20	16	13	23	12	10	11	9	16	6	—	—
U.S. outlying areas[e]	29	25	2	14	11	9	6	3	3	3	3	4	6	6	6

Note: "—" indicates not available. Data are for September except 2013 are for December. Data for additional years can be found in previous editions of *Vital Statistics on American Politics*.

[a] Includes troops in countries not shown.
[b] In addition, as of September 30 each year the following numbers of troops were in and around Iraq: 183,002 in 2003; 170,647 in 2004; 192,600 in 2005; 185,500 in 2006; 218,500 in 2007; 190,400 in 2008; 164,100 in 2009; 96,200 in 2010; and 92,200 in 2011. Also in and around Afghanistan: 19,500 in 2005; 21,500 in 2006; 25,240 in 2007; 32,300 in 2008; 66,400 in 2009; 105,900 in 2010; 109,200 in 2011; and 154,100 in March 2012.
[c] Western Europe and related areas.
[d] Fewer than five hundred.
[e] Primarily Guam and Puerto Rico.

Sources: 1972–1985: U.S. Bureau of the Census, *Statistical Abstract of the United States, 1977* (Washington, D.C.: Government Printing Office, 1977), 370; *1986*, 343; 1990–1995: U.S. Department of Defense, *Selected Manpower Statistics, Fiscal Year 1990* (Washington, D.C.: Government Printing Office, 1991), 44–47, 51, 176; *1995*, 1–6; 2000–2014: U.S. Department of Defense, *Worldwide Manpower Distribution by Geographical Area* (Washington, D.C.: Government Printing Office, 2000), (2005), 8–11, 38; (2006)–(2014).

Table 9-8 U.S. Active Duty Forces, by Sex, Race, and Hispanic Origin, 1965–2013

Year	Female			Black			Hispanic[a]			Total[b]	
	Officers	Enlisted	Total	Officers	Enlisted	Total	Officers	Enlisted	Total	Officers (thousands)	Enlisted (thousands)
1965	3.1%	0.9%	1.2%	1.9%	10.5%	9.5%	—	—	—	339	2,317
1970	3.3	1.1	1.4	2.2	11.0	9.8	—	—	—	402	2,664
1975	4.6	4.5	4.6	3.2	16.2	14.4	1.4	4.6	4.2	292	1,836
1976	5.0	5.3	5.2	3.6	17.1	15.2	1.3	4.6	4.2	281	1,801
1977	5.4	5.8	5.7	3.9	17.4	15.6	1.5	4.5	4.1	276	1,798
1978	6.2	6.5	6.5	4.3	19.3	17.3	1.6	4.5	4.1	274	1,788
1979	6.9	7.5	7.4	4.7	21.2	19.0	1.6	4.4	3.8	274	1,753
1980	7.7	8.5	8.4	5.0	21.9	19.6	1.2	4.0	3.6	278	1,759
1981	8.1	9.0	8.9	5.3	22.1	19.8	1.2	4.1	3.7	285	1,783
1982	8.6	9.0	9.0	5.3	22.0	19.7	1.2	4.1	3.7	292	1,804
1983	9.0	9.3	9.3	5.8	21.6	19.4	1.4	4.1	3.7	301	1,811
1984	9.4	9.5	9.5	6.2	21.1	19.0	1.4	3.9	3.6	304	1,820
1985	9.8	9.8	9.8	6.4	21.1	18.9	1.5	3.9	3.6	309	1,828
1986	10.1	10.0	10.1	6.5	21.2	19.1	1.7	4.1	3.7	311	1,845
1987	10.4	10.2	10.2	6.5	21.5	19.4	1.7	4.3	3.9	308	1,856
1988	10.7	10.4	10.4	6.7	22.0	19.8	1.8	4.5	4.1	305	1,819
1989	11.1	11.0	11.0	6.9	22.8	20.3	2.0	4.8	4.4	303	1,814
1990	11.4	10.9	10.9	6.9	22.9	20.5	2.1	5.0	4.6	304	1,762
1991	11.7	10.8	10.9	7.1	22.6	20.3	2.2	5.2	4.8	298	1,711
1992	12.0	11.3	11.4	7.2	22.0	19.8	2.3	5.5	5.0	281	1,551
1993	12.4	11.5	11.7	7.1	21.6	19.4	2.4	5.8	5.3	264	1,466
1994	12.8	12.0	12.1	7.3	21.4	19.2	2.6	6.0	5.4	253	1,380
1995	13.0	12.5	12.6	7.5	21.5	19.3	2.8	6.4	5.8	245	1,295
1996	13.4	13.2	13.2	7.8	21.8	19.6	3.0	6.9	6.3	233	1,225
1997	13.6	13.7	13.7	8.0	22.1	19.8	3.2	7.5	6.8	228	1,198

(Table continues)

Table 9-8 (Continued)

Year	Female			Black			Hispanic[a]			Total[b]	
	Officers	Enlisted	Total	Officers	Enlisted	Total	Officers	Enlisted	Total	Officers (thousands)	Enlisted (thousands)
1998	13.9	14.1	14.0	8.2	22.2	20.0	3.4	8.0	7.2	224	1,171
1999	14.0	14.2	14.2	8.3	22.0	19.8	3.7	8.5	7.7	227	1,179
2000	14.3	14.5	14.5	8.5	22.1	19.9	4.0	5.0	8.2	224	1,182
2001	14.6	14.8	14.8	8.8	22.1	20.0	3.9	9.4	8.6	223	1,181
2002	14.7	14.8	14.8	8.8	21.7	19.7	4.0	9.6	8.7	224	1,184
2003	15.2	14.9	14.9	8.9	20.6	18.8	4.5	9.8	9.0	235	1,227
2004	15.3	14.7	14.8	8.9	19.7	18.0	4.8	9.8	9.0	236	1,215
2005	15.3	14.3	14.5	8.9	19.1	17.4	4.9	9.8	9.0	234	1,179
2006	15.2	14.3	14.5	9.1	18.9	17.3	5.1	11.2	10.2	232	1,181
2007	15.1	14.1	14.3	9.1	18.5	17.0	5.2	11.4	10.4	230	1,177
2008	15.3	14.0	14.2	9.2	18.3	16.8	5.3	10.8	9.9	232	1,198
2009	15.5	14.0	14.3	9.3	18.1	16.7	5.4	11.7	10.7	237	1,210
2010	15.7	14.1	14.4	9.5	18.5	17.0	5.8	12.2	11.2	235	1,183
2011	15.9	14.2	14.5	9.5	18.4	16.9	5.8	12.3	11.2	237	1,171
2012	16.1	14.3	14.6	9.5	18.3	16.8	5.8	12.5	11.3	239	1,149
2013	16.4	14.5	14.9	9.4	18.5	17.0	6.0	12.8	11.6	239	1,131

Note: "—" indicates not available. Data for additional years can be found in previous editions of *Vital Statistics on American Politics*.

[a] Hispanics may be of any race. Data on percent Hispanic origin from 1971 to 1979 are based on male armed forces members only.
[b] Includes other races not shown separately.

Sources: 1965–1985: U.S. Bureau of the Census, *Statistical Abstract of the United States, 1976* (Washington, D.C.: Government Printing Office, 1976), 336; *1980, 375–376; 1984, 353; 1986, 341; 1987, 327; 1986–1988:* U.S. Department of Defense, unpublished data; 1989 (female, total officers, total enlisted): U.S. Department of Defense, *Selected Manpower Statistics, 1989* (Washington, D.C.: Government Printing Office, 1989), 78, 87, 101; 1989 (other): U.S. Department of Defense, *Defense 90 Almanac* (Washington, D.C.: Government Printing Office, 1990), 30; 1990–1998: Defense Equal Opportunity Management Institute, *Semi-Annual Race/Ethnic/Gender Profile of the Department of Defense Active Forces, Reserve Forces, and the United States Coast Guard* (Patrick Air Force Base, Fla.: Defense Equal Opportunity Management Institute—DEOMI, 1990), 24; (1991), 9; (1992)–(1998), 12; 1999–2002: Patrick Air Force Base (*www.patrick.af.mil*); 2003–2013: "Semiannual [now Annual] Demographic Profile of the Department of Defense and U.S. Coast Guard" (*www.deomi.org*).

Table 9-9   U.S. Defense Spending, 1940–2020

| | Annual percentage change[a] | | Defense outlays as a percentage of | |
| | Current dollars | Constant (2009) dollars | Federal outlays | Gross domestic product |
Year				
1940	—	—	17.5	1.7
1945	4.8	15.3	89.5	36.6
1950	4.4	3.4	32.2	4.9
1951	71.7	62.2	51.8	7.2
1952	95.6	88.0	68.1	12.9
1953	14.6	3.9	69.4	13.8
1954	−6.7	−8.2	69.5	12.7
1955	−13.3	−16.1	62.4	10.5
1956	−0.5	−6.1	60.2	9.7
1957	6.8	1.7	59.3	9.8
1958	3.0	−1.6	56.8	9.9
1959	4.7	−1.9	53.2	9.7
1960	−1.8	−0.9	52.2	9.0
1961	3.1	1.2	50.8	9.1
1962	5.5	5.3	49.0	8.9
1963	2.0	−2.2	48.0	8.6
1964	2.5	1.1	46.2	8.3
1965	−7.6	−7.4	42.8	7.1
1966	14.8	9.7	43.2	7.4
1967	22.9	19.0	45.4	8.5
1968	14.7	9.6	46.0	9.1
1969	0.7	−4.7	44.9	8.4
1970	−1.0	−5.8	41.8	7.8
1971	−3.5	−9.3	37.5	7.0
1972	0.4	−8.4	34.3	6.5
1973	−3.1	−9.6	31.2	5.7
1974	3.5	−3.1	29.5	5.3
1975	9.0	0.1	26.0	5.4
1976	3.6	−2.7	24.1	5.0
TQ[b]	c	c	23.2	4.7
1977	8.5	0.7	23.8	4.8
1978	7.5	0.7	22.8	4.6
1979	11.3	2.9	23.1	4.5
1980	15.2	4.2	22.7	4.8
1981	17.6	5.5	23.2	5.0
1982	17.6	8.3	24.8	5.6
1983	13.3	7.8	26.0	5.9
1984	8.3	3.5	26.7	5.8
1985	11.1	7.2	26.7	5.9
1986	8.2	5.8	27.6	6.0
1987	3.2	1.6	28.1	5.9
1988	3.0	0.5	27.3	5.6
1989	4.5	1.0	26.5	5.4

(Table continues)

Table 9-9   *(Continued)*

Year	Annual percentage change[a]		Defense outlays as a percentage of	
	Current dollars	Constant (2009) dollars	Federal outlays	Gross domestic product
1990	−1.4	−4.7	23.9	5.1
1991	−8.7	−13.4	20.6	4.5
1992	9.2	7.9	21.6	4.6
1993	−2.4	−3.5	20.7	4.3
1994	−3.2	−4.2	19.3	3.9
1995	−3.4	−5.4	17.9	3.6
1996	−2.3	−4.4	17.0	3.3
1997	1.8	0.3	16.9	3.2
1998	−0.9	−2.7	16.2	3.0
1999	2.5	0.3	16.1	2.9
2000	7.1	3.9	16.5	2.9
2001	3.5	−0.1	16.4	2.9
2002	14.3	10.4	17.3	3.2
2003	16.2	9.4	18.7	3.6
2004	12.6	8.5	19.9	3.8
2005	8.7	3.7	20.0	3.8
2006	5.4	1.0	19.7	3.8
2007	5.6	2.4	20.2	3.8
2008	11.8	7.6	20.7	4.2
2009	7.3	7.5	18.8	4.6
2010	4.9	4.6	20.1	4.7
2011	1.7	0.2	19.6	4.6
2012	−3.9	−4.9	19.2	4.2
2013	−6.6	−7.1	18.3	3.8
2014	−4.7	−6.2	17.2	3.5
2015 est.	−1.0	−2.3	15.9	3.3
2016 est.	3.0	1.4	15.4	3.3
2017 est.	−1.9	−3.6	14.3	3.1
2018 est.	−2.0	−3.8	13.4	2.9
2019 est.	−0.3	−2.2	12.7	2.7
2020 est.	1.3	−0.7	12.2	2.7

Note: "—" indicates not available.

[a] Change from prior year.
[b] Transition quarter, July–September.
[c] Not applicable.

Sources: Annual percentage change calculated from actual dollar amounts of defense spending in Table 11-3, this volume; percentage of federal outlays and GDP: U.S. Office of Management and Budget, *Budget of the U.S. Government, Fiscal Year 2016, Historical Tables* (Washington, D.C.: Government Printing Office, 2015), Table 6.1.

Figure 9-1   U.S. Defense Spending as a Percentage of Federal Outlays and of Gross
Domestic Product, 1940–2020

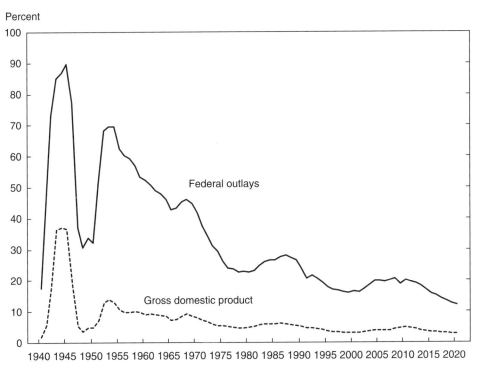

Note: Figures for 2015 through 2020 are estimates.

Source: Table 9-9, this volume.

Table 9-10 Military Expenditures: World, Regional, and Selected National Estimates, 1988–2014

Region[a]	Estimated expenditure (billions)										Percentage change, 1988–2014
	1988	1990	1995	2000	2005	2010	2011	2012	2013	2014	
Africa	$17.8	$17.7	$15.0	$19.5	$24.3	$34.6	$38.9	$40.4	$43.9	$46.5	161
North	3.7	3.8	4.6	5.2	7.9	12.1	15.2	16.3	17.9	19.2	419
Sub-Saharan	14.2	14.0	10.4	14.2	16.4	22.5	23.7	24.1	26.0	27.2	92
Americas	620.0	617.0	473.0	458.0	651.0	815.0	805.0	768.0	718.0	677.0	9
North	578.0	548.0	429.0	410.0	598.0	741.0	732.0	691.0	636.0	596.0	3
Central	3.9	4.0	4.6	5.3	5.1	7.5	7.8	8.5	9.0	9.8	151
South	37.9	64.9[b]	39.0	42.9	48.6	66.3	65.1	68.8	72.6	72.0	90
Asia and Oceania	142.0	153.0	179.0	204.0	261.0	356.0	371.0	388.0	403.0	423.0	198
Central and South Asia	23.5	24.5	27.8	36.0	46.2	61.7	62.9	63.2	63.7	65.0	177
East Asia	101.0	111.0	132.0	147.0	191.0	265.0	280.0	297.0	312.0	329.0	226
Oceania	17.9	17.8	18.5	20.1	23.4	29.3	28.8	27.8	27.6	29.5	65
Europe[c]	708.0	621.0	333.0	337.0	367.0	394.0	387.0	392.0	389.0	391.0	–45
Central and Eastern	411.0	321.0	59.0	55.0	75.0	96.0	101.0	112.0	116.0	125.0	–70
Western[c]	297.0	300.0	275.0	282.0	292.0	298.0	287.0	280.0	273.0	266.0	–10
Middle East[c]	75.3	93.4	76.5	97.4	112.6	139.0	141.0	151.0	165.0	173.0	130

Top-spending nations in 2014

Country	Estimated expenditure (billions)										Percentage of total world spending, 2014
	1988	1990	1995	2000	2005	2010	2011	2012	2013	2014	
United States	$557.5	$527.1	$411.6	$394.1	$579.8	$720.2	$711.3	$670.9	$617.7	$577.5	34.3
China	—	19.7	23.0	37.0	71.4	136.2	147.3	161.4	174.0	191.0	12.2
Russian Federation	371.1	291.1	33.8	31.1	46.4	65.8	70.2	81.0	84.8	91.7	4.8
Saudi Arabia	20.9	24.8	17.9	27.6	34.8	47.9	48.5	54.9	62.9	73.7	4.5
France	69.9	70.5	64.9	61.7	65.1	66.2	64.6	63.7	63.5	63.0	3.5

United Kingdom	58.2	58.8	48.4	48.0	58.1	62.9	60.3	57.7	55.3	54.9
India	18.1	18.8	19.6	27.7	36.1	49.2	49.6	49.5	49.1	50.0
Germany	47.2[d]	49.6[d]	53.2	50.6	47.0	49.6	48.1	49.3	48.2	46.6
Japan	45.7	47.8	56.8	60.3	61.3	59.0	60.5	60.0	59.4	59.0
Korea, Rep. of	13.7	15.1	19.3	20.0	24.7	29.9	30.9	31.5	32.4	33.1
Brazil	22.3	52.2[b]	22.9	25.2	26.5	38.1	36.9	37.6	37.9	37.3
Italy	38.0	36.9	32.5	43.1	42.3	38.9	38.1	35.4	34.0	31.0
Australia	15.4	15.3	16.3	18.0	21.4	27.0	26.6	25.7	25.4	27.1
United Arab Emirates	—	—	—	10.1	9.3	17.7	19.2	18.9	23.2	21.9
Turkey	9.4	13.1	15.8	20.6	15.7	17.0	17.1	17.5	17.9	18.0
World	1,563.0	1,502.0	1,076.0	1,115.0	1,416.0	1,738.0	1,744.0	1,740.0	1,719.0	1,711.0
Percentage change from previous year	—	-3.9	-28.4	3.6	27.0	22.7	0.3	-0.2	-1.2	-0.5

Note: "—" indicates not available. Amounts in constant 2011 U.S. dollars, market exchange rates. Regional figures do not always add up to totals because of rounding. Figures are estimates for China, the Russian Federation, and the United Arab Emirates in 1988 through 2014, for Australia in 1988 through 1995, for Brazil in 1988 through 1990, for Germany in 2013 and 2014, for the Republic of Korea in 1988 through 2000 and 2014, for Saudi Arabia in 1988 and 1990, and for the United Kingdom in 2010 through 2014. Some countries are excluded because of lack of data or of consistent time-series data. Totals exclude Cuba, Haiti, Iraq, Myanmar (Burma), North Korea, Somalia, Yemen (South), and Yugoslavia (former). For details on the derivations of the estimates as well as differences among countries and over time in what counts as military expenditures, see sources.

[a] For the country composition of the regions, see source "Military Expenditure by Region" (*www.sipri.org*).
[b] Due to the very high rate of inflation for Brazil in 1990, this figure is highly uncertain.
[c] Turkey was reclassified to the Middle East (from Western Europe) in the 1988–2014 SIPRI Military Expenditure database (see sources). The figures for Europe and Western Europe are therefore lower, and figures for the Middle East are higher, than in previous editions of the database and in this table from earlier editions of *Vital Statistics on American Politics*.
[d] Figures for Germany for 1988 and 1990 refer to the former Federal Republic of Germany (West Germany).

Sources: Adapted by the editors from Stockholm International Peace Research Institute, *SIPRI Yearbook 2015: Armaments, Disarmament and International Security* (Oxford, UK: Oxford University Press, 2014), and from the SIPRI Military Expenditure Database (*www.sipri.org/databases/milex*), "Military Expenditure by Region in Constant US Dollars, 1988–2014," "Military Expenditure by Country, in Constant (2011) US Dollars," and "Trends in World Military Expenditure, 2014." Reprinted by permission of SIPRI.

Table 9-11 U.S. Military Sales and Military Assistance to Foreign Governments, Principal Recipients, 1950–2013 (millions)

Country	Military sales								Military assistance[a]
	1950–2006	2007	2008	2009	2010	2011	2012	2013	1950–2013
Afghanistan	$469.9	$17.6	$7.0	$1.8	$10.5	$12.2	$4.2	$6.0	$191.7
Australia	10,846.6	750.8	889.7	373.6	914.2	731.8	638.7	637.1	0.0
Canada	4,782.5	239.5	467.6	517.6	382.4	399.6	288.5	310.9	0.0
France	2,465.8	45.0	57.3	58.3	112.2	132.1	125.1	185.9	4,097.8
Germany	14,210.2	204.9	172.6	161.1	293.1	159.5	141.8	150.3	884.8
Greece	9,672.6	200.6	196.6	1,251.2	277.6	149.0	163.4	61.9	1,673.2
Iran	10,704.9	0.0	0.0	0.0	0.0	0.0	0.0	0.0	766.7
Iraq	15.3	174.8	683.4	692.4	374.4	515.1	568.2	450.4	88.6
Israel	24,298.8	1,314.0	1,393.1	726.1	890.1	740.6	843.4	861.8	447.9
Italy	3,176.0	153.1	75.6	92.4	178.7	100.9	87.4	69.7	2,243.7
Korea, Rep. of	13,389.3	727.7	791.0	477.2	594.4	718.5	723.7	611.0	3,687.3
Netherlands	9,069.2	237.7	252.1	248.7	202.3	183.8	176.9	763.9	1,178.2
Saudi Arabia	63,251.5	1,007.8	894.6	1,713.7	1,587.1	1,405.2	1,551.1	3,497.0	23.9
Taiwan	23,486.1	771.1	611.6	638.7	695.4	767.0	877.9	810.3	2,554.6
Thailand	4,663.8	45.6	39.5	47.3	41.6	91.2	61.8	82.0	686.2
Turkey	12,540.9	181.7	306.0	306.1	251.0	876.4	1,243.1	760.8	3,170.3
United Kingdom	14,035.7	423.0	296.0	753.7	269.1	346.2	311.2	1,294.8	1,022.1
Vietnam	1.2	0.0	0.0	0.0	0.0	0.0	0.0	0.8	1,375.5
Total[b]	324,441.2	12,409.7	11,724.7	16,269.9	13,075.3	13,398.4	13,989.7	16,524.3	39,494.8

Note: Figures exclude training. Amounts in current dollars. Data for additional years can be found in previous editions of *Vital Statistics on American Politics.*

[a] Military assistance, especially to Europe, has been very low for a decade or more.
[b] Includes countries not shown.

Source: U.S. Defense Security Cooperation Agency, "Historical Facts Book as of September 30, 2013" (*www.dsca.mil*).

Table 9-12   U.S. Foreign Aid, Principal Recipients, 1962–2013 (millions)

Region/country	1962–2009	2010	2011	2012	2013
Asia[a]	$42,701	$4,299	$3,208	$3,514	$2,832
India	5,170	23	27	38	19
Indonesia	3,708	215	154	150	94
Korea, Rep. of	1,081	0	0	0	0
Pakistan	7,243	1,198	885	876	625
Philippines	3,989	57	74	83	90
Vietnam	4,610	20	17	59	38
Western Europe[a]	6,551	19	26	3	7
Eastern Europe[a]	7,200	254	219	124	157
Latin America and Caribbean[a]	29,837	1,321	1,093	808	757
Brazil	1,706	16	24	7	13
Costa Rica	1,408	3	3	3	3
Dominican Republic	1,255	34	31	23	18
El Salvador	3,909	30	60	28	52
Honduras	1,975	23	52	38	58
Jamaica	1,181	14	17	11	15
Middle East and North Africa[a]	81,698	1,656	1,375	1,516	2,849
Egypt/Arab Rep. of Egypt	26,210	288	224	132	291
Israel	32,126	5	5	3	0
Jordan	5,450	371	406	501	684
Morocco	859	22	26	15	20
Sub-Saharan Africa[a]	31,339	1,801	2,048	2,110	1,963
Kenya	1,372	110	143	177	102
Niger	424	42	19	67	21
Senegal	966	63	72	72	40
Somalia	656	40	134	182	104
South Sudan[b]	—	—	27	254	286
Sudan	2,917	412	422	148	133
Zaire/Dem. Rep. of Congo	1,316	87	88	112	112
Zambia	933	26	48	58	49
Zimbabwe	888	99	60	62	54
Eurasia[a]	11,253	630	439	522	298
Russia/Russian Federation	2,810	54	53	33	1
Ukraine	1,779	142	64	78	60
Oceania and other	270	21	32	11	16
Total[c]	262,824	11,771	10,111	11,324	11,775

Note: Amounts in current dollars. Shown are loans and grants made by the U.S. Agency for International Development and its predecessor agencies. Excluded are Food for Peace and "other" economic assistance. Data for individual years before 2010 can be found in previous editions of *Vital Statistics on American Politics.*

[a] Includes countries not shown separately.
[b] South Sudan became an independent country in 2011.
[c] Includes interregional aid.

Source: U.S. Agency for International Development, *U.S. Overseas Loans and Grants and Assistance from International Organizations, July 1, 1945–September 30, 2013* (Washington, D.C.: Government Printing Office, 2014) (*www.usaid.gov*).

Table 9-13   Foreign Investment in the United States and U.S. Investment Abroad, 1950–2013 (millions)

Year	All areas	Canada	Europe	Japan
Foreign direct investment in the United States				
1950	$3,391	$1,029	$2,228	—
1960	6,910	1,934	4,707	$88
1970	13,270	3,117	9,554	229
1980	83,046	12,162	54,688	4,723
1985	184,615	17,131	121,413	19,313
1990	396,702	30,037	250,973	81,775
1995	535,553	45,618	332,374	104,997
2000	1,256,867	114,309	887,014	159,690
2005	1,634,121	165,667	1,154,048	189,851
2006	1,840,463	165,281	1,326,738	204,020
2007[a]	1,993,156	201,924	1,421,325	222,695
2009	2,069,438	188,943	1,504,727	238,140
2010	2,280,044	192,463	1,659,774	255,012
2011	2,433,848	205,225	1,732,316	274,283
2012	2,605,755	217,800	1,857,270	299,121
2013	2,763,956	237,921	1,933,589	342,327
U.S. investment abroad				
1950	11,788	3,579	1,733	19
1960	32,778	11,198	6,681	254
1970	78,178	22,790	24,516	1,483
1980	215,578	44,978	96,539	6,243
1985	230,250	46,909	105,171	9,235
1990	430,521	69,508	214,739	22,599
1995	699,015	83,498	344,596	37,309
2000	1,316,247	132,472	687,320	57,091
2005	2,241,656	231,836	1,210,679	81,175
2006	2,477,268	205,134	1,397,704	84,428
2007[a]	2,993,980	250,642	1,682,023	85,224
2009	3,565,020	274,807	1,991,191	91,196
2010	3,741,910	295,206	2,034,559	113,523
2011	4,050,026	330,041	2,246,394	120,482
2012	4,384,671	346,080	2,443,287	125,286
2013	4,660,906	368,297	2,607,204	123,174

Note: "—" indicates not available. Amounts are in current dollars. Data for additional years can be found in previous editions of *Vital Statistics on American Politics.*

[a] There is a discontinuity between 2006 and 2007. See source for details.

Sources: 1950–1960: U.S. Department of Commerce, *Foreign Business Investments in the United States: A Supplement to Survey of Current Business* (Washington, D.C.: Government Printing Office, 1962), 34; 1970–2011: *Survey of Current Business,* August 1973, 50; September 1973, 24; August 1982, 21; August 1985, 63; August 1988, 65, 80; August 1992, 89; August 1994, 134; September 1998, 83; October 1998, 129; September 2003, 67, 119; September 2005, 134; September 2008, D-65, D-67; September 2010, D-69, D-71; September 2011, D-71, D-73; September 2014, Table 14 (Foreign Direct Investment in the US; US Direct Investment Abroad).

Table 9-14   U.S. Balance of Trade, 1946–2013 (millions)

Year	Balance on goods[a]	Balance on current account[b]	Year	Balance on goods[a]	Balance on current account[b]
1946	$6,697	$4,885	1980	−$25,500	$2,317
1947	10,124	8,992	1981	−28,023	5,030
1948	5,708	2,417	1982	−36,485	−5,536
1949	5,339	873	1983	−67,102	−38,691
1950	1,122	−1,840	1984	−112,492	−94,344
1951	3,067	884	1985	−122,173	−118,155
1952	2,611	614	1986	−145,081	−147,177
1953	1,437	−1,286	1987	−159,557	−160,655
1954	2,576	219	1988	−126,959	−121,153
1955	2,897	430	1989	−117,749	−99,486
1956	4,753	2,730	1990	−111,037	−78,968
1957	6,271	4,762	1991	−76,937	2,898
1958	3,462	784	1992	−96,897	−51,613
1959	1,148	−1,282	1993	−132,451	−84,806
1960	4,892	2,824	1994	−165,831	−121,612
1961	5,571	3,822	1995	−174,170	−113,567
1962	4,521	3,387	1996	−191,000	−124,764
1963	5,224	4,414	1997	−198,428	−140,726
1964	6,801	6,823	1998	−248,221	−215,062
1965	4,951	5,431	1999	−337,374	−295,531
1966	3,817	3,031	2000	−446,942	−410,756
1967	3,800	2,583	2001	−422,512	−395,328
1968	635	611	2002	−475,842	−458,087
1969	607	399	2003	−542,273	−521,342
1970	2,603	2,331	2004	−666,364	−633,768
1971	−2,260	−1,433	2005	−784,133	−745,434
1972	−6,416	−5,795	2006	−838,788	−806,726
1973	911	7,140	2007	−822.743	−718,643
1974	−5,505	1,962	2008	−833,957	−686,641
1975	8,903	18,116	2009	−510,491	−380,792
1976	−9,483	4,295	2010	−649,088	−443,930
1977	−31,091	−14,335	2011	−741,157	−459,344
1978	−33,927	−15,143	2012	−742,661	−460,749
1979	−27,568	−285	2013	−702,284	−400,254

Note: Amounts in current dollars and seasonally adjusted.

[a] "Balance on goods" measures the difference between the value of goods the United States imports and the value of goods the United States exports.
[b] "Balance on current account" is the broadest trade gauge, measuring the difference in imports and exports of merchandise trade and trade in services; also includes certain one-way flows of money into the United States such as pension payments.

Sources: 1946–1951: *Economic Report of the President* (Washington, DC: Government Printing Office, 2009), table B-103; 1952: (2011); 1953–1998: (2013), table B-103; 1999–2013: U.S. Department of Commerce, Bureau of Economic Analysis, "U.S. International Transactions Accounts Data," table 1 (*www.bea.gov*).

10

Social Policy

- **Population**
- **Immigration**
- **Medicare and Social Security**
- **Income Levels**
- **Public Aid**
- **Health Insurance**
- **Integration in Schooling and Employment**
- **Abortion**
- **Crime and Punishment**

The study of social policy might fairly be described as controversies informed by, but not settled by, statistics. No matter what the area, those on all sides of an issue try to support their arguments with the relevant data.

The data thought to pertain to questions and controversies about social policy are of many kinds and can be characterized in a variety of ways. First, there is factual information on, for example, how many whites, blacks, and Hispanics are below the poverty line (Table 10-9); what types of health care coverage are available and how many people are covered by health insurance (Tables 10-10 and 10-11); the historical pattern of immigration into the United States (Table 10-3 and Figure 10-2); how many unauthorized migrants are in the United States (Table 10-4); and how many crimes are committed in a given year (Table 10-16). Second, data are available on public opinion (see Chapter 3) and social policy. For example, social policy concerns not only the actual crime rate, but also what people think about crime—such as whether the courts are too easy on criminals (Table 3-15) and whether the death penalty is acceptable and desirable (Table 3-12). In another area, it matters not only what abortion rates are (Table 10-15), but also what people think and say about abortion (Table 3-13). One might also distinguish between data about the past or present and projections about the future. Much of the concern about Social Security payments and about health care costs revolves not just around present payments, but also around what to expect in the future (Tables 10-5 and 10-6, Figure 10-3).

Social policies are inherently controversial, and so too are the data relevant to such policies. The debate over how the 2000 U.S. Census was to be conducted illustrates the contentiousness surrounding how to determine even the basic facts of population counts (such as those in Tables 10-1, 10-2, and 10-4 or Figure 10-1). These population counts are important because the distribution of some federal funds as well as legislative apportionment turn on them. Even if analysts agree on a set of facts, they may disagree on the relevance of the material and its interpretation. Information about numbers of people without insurance coverage (Table 10-11), about the proportion of women and minorities elected to political office (Table 1-22 and Table 5-4), about the extent of crime and the number of people incarcerated (Tables 10-16, 10-18, and 10-19), and so on does not automatically answer causal questions (why the situation is as it is) any more than it answers normative questions (whether the existing situation is good and what should be done). As for projections, they often lead to special problems of inference. Any projection must be based on assumptions about what the future will be like. A note to Table 10-5, for example, might underscore the fact that no one can be certain now what health or Social Security costs will be in 2075.

Numerical and other data relevant to every social concern are available, but they are highly varied in type and always difficult to interpret. Information is provided here for a wide range of policies, including Medicare (Table 10-5), Social Security (Table 10-6 and Figure 10-3), income and poverty in general (Tables 10-7 through 10-9) and social welfare in particular (Figures 10-4 and 10-5), affirmative action in both the schools and in employment (Tables 10-12 through 10-14), abortion (Table 10-15), and crime and punishment (Tables 10-16 through 10-19). Often, a given set of data is relevant to more than one question. Information about poverty rates, for example, is relevant to questions about both social welfare and affirmative action. Because most debates about social policy involve expenditures, spending on other kinds of programs such as defense (Table 9-9), as well as overall taxation policies (Table 11-7), is also relevant.

In the face of enormous problems of inference, controversy about almost every fact, and the need to deal with future unknowns, one might well ask whether all these numbers are useful or necessary when discussing social policies. There are at least two answers to this question. The first is highly pragmatic. Some analysts will surely have factual information at their disposal; those who do not or cannot understand data and are unable or unwilling to provide any of their own will be hostage to others' information and interpretations.

Second, from a more theoretical perspective, although data are always subject to some error and interpretation, people often do agree on the facts and on roughly how they should be interpreted. There is no disagreement, for example, that—barring major unforeseen catastrophes or extremely large and unlikely changes in immigration—there will be a considerably smaller ratio of young people to old people over the next few decades. Knowing this does not solve the problems implicit in this fact, but it tells analysts that there will be problems and that the country needs to be thinking of solutions. It also suggests possible solutions—raising the retirement age, lowering Social Security payments, raising Social Security taxes, encouraging private pension plans so that the elderly need less government support, and so on.

In the area of social policy, as in other areas, data do not speak for themselves. They must be analyzed and interpreted. The facts alone will settle few arguments about causality or about normative questions. Still, data and an ability to interpret them are essential weapons in the arsenal of any well-educated social analyst, commentator, or student.

Figure 10-1   U.S. Population: Total, Urban, and Rural, 1790–2060

Population (millions)

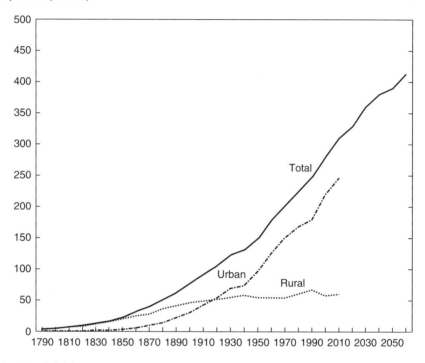

Note: For definitions, see sources.

Sources: Population, total, 1790–2000: U.S. Bureau of the Census, "Resident Population of the United States," April 2, 2001; total, 2010: U.S. Census Bureau, "Resident Population of the 50 States, the District of Columbia, and Puerto Rico: 2010 Census," December 21, 2010; total, 2020–2060: U.S. Census Bureau, "Projections of the Population and Components of Change for the United States: 2015 to 2060," December 2014; urban and rural, 1790–1990: U.S. Census Bureau, "Population: 1790 to 1990," March 31, 2001; urban and rural, 2000–2010: U.S. Census Bureau, "Urban, Urbanized Area, Urban Cluster, and Rural Population, 2010 and 2000: United States," 2010 Census *(www.census.gov)*.

Table 10-1   U.S. Population, 1790–2010, and State Populations, 2000–2030

Year	Resident population[a]	Year	Resident population[a]
1790	3,929,214	1910	92,228,496
1800	5,308,483	1920	106,021,537
1810	7,239,881	1930	123,202,624
1820	9,638,453	1940	132,164,569
1830	12,860,702	1950	151,325,798
1840	17,063,353	1960	179,323,175
1850	23,191,876	1970	203,302,031
1860	31,443,321	1980	226,542,199
1870	38,558,371	1990	248,709,873
1880	50,189,209	2000	281,421,906
1890	62,979,766	2010	308,745,538
1900	76,212,168		

State	Resident population[a]			Change (percent)	
	2000	2010	2030	2000–2010	2000–2030
Alabama	4,447,100	4,779,736	4,874,243	7.48	9.60
Alaska	626,932	710,231	867,674	13.29	38.40
Arizona	5,130,632	6,392,017	10,712,397	24.59	108.79
Arkansas	2,673,400	2,915,918	3,240,208	9.07	21.20
California	33,871,648	37,253,956	46,444,861	9.99	37.12
Colorado	4,301,261	5,029,196	5,792,357	16.92	34.67
Connecticut	3,405,565	3,574,097	3,688,630	4.95	8.31
Delaware	783,600	897,934	1,012,658	14.59	29.23
District of Columbia	572,059	601,723	433,414	5.19	−24.24
Florida	15,982,378	18,801,310	28,685,769	17.64	79.48
Georgia	8,186,453	9,687,653	12,017,838	18.34	46.80
Hawaii	1,211,537	1,360,301	1,466,046	12.28	21.01
Idaho	1,293,953	1,567,582	1,969,624	21.15	52.22
Illinois	12,419,293	12,830,632	13,432,892	3.31	8.16
Indiana	6,080,485	6,483,802	6,810,108	6.63	12.00
Iowa	2,926,324	3,046,355	2,955,172	4.10	0.99
Kansas	2,688,418	2,853,118	2,940,084	6.13	9.36
Kentucky	4,041,769	4,339,367	4,554,998	7.36	12.70
Louisiana	4,468,976	4,533,372	4,802,633	1.44	7.47
Maine	1,274,923	1,328,361	1,411,097	4.19	10.68
Maryland	5,296,486	5,773,552	7,022,251	9.01	32.58
Massachusetts	6,349,097	6,547,629	7,012,009	3.13	10.44
Michigan	9,938,444	9,883,640	10,694,172	−0.55	7.60
Minnesota	4,919,479	5,303,925	6,306,130	7.81	28.19
Mississippi	2,844,658	2,967,297	3,092,410	4.31	8.71
Missouri	5,595,211	5,988,927	6,430,173	7.04	14.92
Montana	902,195	989,415	1,044,898	9.67	15.82
Nebraska	1,711,263	1,826,341	1,820,247	6.72	6.37
Nevada	1,998,257	2,700,551	4,282,102	35.15	114.29

(Table continues)

Table 10-1 *(Continued)*

State	Resident population[a] 2000	Resident population[a] 2010	Resident population[a] 2030	Change (percent) 2000–2010	Change (percent) 2000–2030
New Hampshire	1,235,786	1,316,470	1,646,471	6.53	33.23
New Jersey	8,414,350	8,791,894	9,802,440	4.49	16.50
New Mexico	1,819,046	2,059,179	2,099,708	13.20	15.43
New York	18,976,457	19,378,102	19,477,429	2.12	2.64
North Carolina	8,049,313	9,535,483	12,227,739	18.46	51.91
North Dakota	642,200	672,591	606,566	4.73	−5.55
Ohio	11,353,140	11,536,504	11,550,528	1.62	1.74
Oklahoma	3,450,654	3,751,351	3,913,251	8.71	13.41
Oregon	3,421,399	3,831,074	4,833,918	11.97	41.28
Pennsylvania	12,281,054	12,702,379	12,768,184	3.43	3.97
Rhode Island	1,048,319	1,052,567	1,152,941	0.41	9.98
South Carolina	4,012,012	4,625,364	5,148,569	15.29	28.33
South Dakota	754,844	814,180	800,462	7.86	6.04
Tennessee	5,689,283	6,346,105	7,380,634	11.54	29.73
Texas	20,851,820	25,145,561	33,317,744	20.59	59.78
Utah	2,233,169	2,763,885	3,485,367	23.77	56.07
Vermont	608,827	625,741	711,867	2.78	16.92
Virginia	7,078,515	8,001,024	9,825,019	13.03	38.80
Washington	5,894,121	6,724,540	8,624,801	14.09	46.33
West Virginia	1,808,344	1,852,994	1,719,959	2.47	−4.89
Wisconsin	5,363,675	5,686,986	6,150,764	6.03	14.67
Wyoming	493,782	563,626	522,979	14.14	5.91
United States	281,421,906	308,745,538	363,584,435	9.71	29.20

Note: A counter with the U.S. Census Bureau's estimate of the current U.S. population can be found at *www.census.gov*. As of March 12, 2015 (8:30 a.m. CST), the count stood at 320,497,081. State and nation projections for 2030 shown are as of April 21, 2005. More recent population projections for the nation indicate that in 2030 the U.S. population will total 359,402,000 (U.S. Census Bureau, "Projections of the Population and Components of Change for the United States: 2015 to 2060 [Based on Census 2010]," December 2014).

[a] Resident population differs from apportionment population: "An area's resident population consists of those persons 'usually resident' in that particular area (where they live and sleep most of the time). A state's apportionment population, on the other hand, is the sum of its resident population and a count of overseas U.S. military and federal civilian employees (and their dependents living with them) allocated to the state, as reported by the employing federal agencies." United States Census 2000, "Resident Population" (*www.census.gov*).

Sources: U.S. Census Bureau, "Resident Population of the United States," December 28, 2000; "Resident Population of the 50 States, the District of Columbia, and Puerto Rico: 2010 Census," December 21, 2010; and "Interim Projections of the Total Population for the United States and States: April 1, 2000 to July 1, 2030," table A1, April 21, 2005 (*www.census.gov*).

Table 10-2 Foreign- and Native-Born U.S. Population, Characteristics, 2012

Nativity	Population	Percent
Total	313,914,040	100.0
Total native born	273,175,816	87.0
Total foreign born	40,738,224	13.0
Mexico	11,489,387	28.2
South and East Asia	10,443,902	25.6
Caribbean	3,882,592	9.5
Central America	3,172,307	7.8
South America	2,731,619	6.7
Middle East[a]	1,578,801	3.9
All other	7,439,616	18.3

English ability by age and country or region of birth (percent)

	Under 18 years			18 years and over		
	English only	English very well	English less than very well	English only	English very well	English less than very well
Total native born	80.4	16.0	3.6	91.4	7.2	1.4
Total foreign born	19.1	54.1	26.8	15.2	33.4	51.5
Mexico	2.1	69.0	28.9	3.5	24.5	72.0
South and East Asia	27.2	43.6	29.2	9.8	42.4	47.8
Caribbean	23.7	43.1	33.2	32.1	24.9	43.0
Central America	17.4	53.0	29.6	6.2	25.8	68.0
South America	13.0	68.1	18.9	15.5	38.2	46.3
Middle East[a]	10.9	64.1	25.1	11.4	47.8	40.8
All other	40.1	41.4	18.4	36.2	37.3	26.5

(Table continues)

353

Table 10-2 *(Continued)*

Educational attainment by country or region of birth (percent)

	Less than 9th grade	9th to 12th grade	High school graduate[b]	Some college	College graduate[c]	Advanced degree
Total native born	3.0	7.2	29.2	31.3	18.6	10.8
Total foreign born	19.5	11.2	22.1	19.2	16.5	11.6
Mexico	39.2	19.6	23.5	12.2	4.1	1.5
South and East Asia	9.5	6.5	15.6	18.5	28.7	21.2
Caribbean	13.7	11.9	30.1	24.8	12.8	6.7
Central America	33.2	14.3	25.2	17.2	7.4	2.6
South America	9.7	7.8	27.1	25.7	19.4	10.2
Middle East[a]	8.5	5.5	18.6	20.7	26.1	20.7
All other	7.1	6.0	22.4	25.6	20.7	18.2

Note: Table based on Pew Research Center's Hispanic Trends Project tabulations of the U.S. Census Bureau's 2012 American Community Survey, tables 2, 3, 21, and 23. The universe is the 2012 resident population for nativity and country or region of birth, the 2012 resident population ages five and older for language ability, and the 2012 resident population ages twenty-five and older for educational attainment.

[a] Middle East includes Afghanistan, Algeria, Egypt, Iran, Iraq, Israel/Palestine, Jordan, Kuwait, Lebanon, Morocco, Saudi Arabia, Sudan, Syria, Turkey, and Yemen.
[b] "High school graduate" refers to a person whose highest level of education achievement is a high school diploma or its equivalent, such as a General Educational Development (GED) certificate.
[c] "College graduate" refers to a person whose highest level of education achievement is a bachelor's degree.

Source: Pew Research Center's Hispanic Trends Project, "Statistical Portrait of the Foreign-Born Population in the United States, 2012," April 29, 2014 (*www.pewhispanic.org*).

Table 10-3 Immigrants to the United States, by Region of Origin, 1820–2013

Years	Europe				Asia[e]	Western Hemisphere			Africa and Oceania	Not specified	Total number (thousands)
	Northwestern[a]	Central[b]	Southern[c]	Eastern[d]		Canada	Mexico	Other[f]			
1820–1829	70.2%	4.5%	2.5%	0.1%	—	1.8%	3.0%	2.7%	—	15.2%	128.5
1830–1839	54.2	23.2	1.0	0.1	—	2.2	1.3	2.4	—	15.5	538.4
1840–1849	68.6	27.0	0.3	—	—	2.4	0.2	0.9	—	0.5	1,427.3
1850–1859	57.7	34.7	0.7	0.1	0.0%	2.3	0.1	0.6	—	2.6	2,814.6
1860–1869	54.2	35.0	0.9	1.3	2.6	5.7	0.1	0.5	—	0.9	2,081.3
1870–1879	48.4	30.0	2.4	3.6	4.9	11.8	0.2	0.6	0.4%	—	2,742.1
1880–1889	44.9	34.4	5.5	12.4	1.4	9.4	0.2	0.6	0.2	—	5,248.6
1890–1899	33.8	33.0	17.6	19.4	1.7	0.1	—	0.9	0.1	0.4	3,694.3
1900–1909	18.1	28.4	26.4	18.2	3.7	1.5	0.4	1.5	0.2	0.4	8,202.4
1910–1919	14.8	20.9	24.6	3.6	4.2	11.2	2.9	2.8	0.3	—	6,347.4
1920–1929	21.0	19.1	15.9	2.7	3.0	22.1	11.6	3.3	0.4	—	4,295.5
1930–1939	20.2	26.0	14.7	0.9	2.7	23.3	4.7	5.0	0.8	—	699.4
1940–1949	28.6	17.7	8.0	0.5	4.0	18.8	6.6	13.0	2.4	—	856.6
1950–1959	17.4	28.2	10.0	0.4	5.4	14.1	11.0	11.8	1.0	0.5	2,499.3
1960–1969	13.1	9.8	12.0	1.1	11.2	13.5	13.7	24.9	1.5	—	3,213.7
1970–1979	5.0	4.0	9.4	1.0	33.1	4.2	14.6	26.0	2.6	—	4,248.2
1980–1989	4.1	3.1	2.5	5.4	38.3	2.5	16.2	24.5	2.9	4.9	6,244.4
1990–1999	3.2	3.7	1.5	5.3	29.3	2.0	28.2	22.4	4.1	0.3	9,775.4
2000–2009	2.9	4.1	0.7	5.3	33.7	2.3	16.6	24.3	8.0	2.1	10,299.4
2010–2013	2.5	2.2	0.7	3.4	40.1	1.9	13.6	24.7	10.1	0.8	4,126.8

Note: "—" indicates less than 0.1 percent. Data for most years are for country of last permanent residence. See source for details.

a United Kingdom, Ireland, Finland, Norway, Sweden, Denmark, the Netherlands, Belgium, Switzerland, and France.

b Germany, Poland, Czechoslovakia (now the Czech Republic and Slovakia), Yugoslavia (currently includes Bosnia-Herzegovina, Croatia, Kosovo, Macedonia, Montenegro, Serbia, and Slovenia), Hungary, and Austria.

c Italy, Spain, Portugal, and Greece.

d Russia, Bulgaria, Romania, and "other Europe." Russia and surrounding areas were reported differently in various historical periods. See source for details.

e China, Hong Kong (China), India, Iran, Israel, Japan, Jordan, Republic of Korea, Philippines, Syria, Taiwan, Thailand, Turkey, and "other Asia."

f Caribbean and Central and South America.

Source: U.S. Department of Homeland Security, Office of Immigration Statistics, *Yearbook of Immigration Statistics, 2013* (Washington, D.C.: Government Printing Office, 2012), Table 2.

356

Figure 10-2 Immigrants to the United States, by Region of Origin, 1820–2013

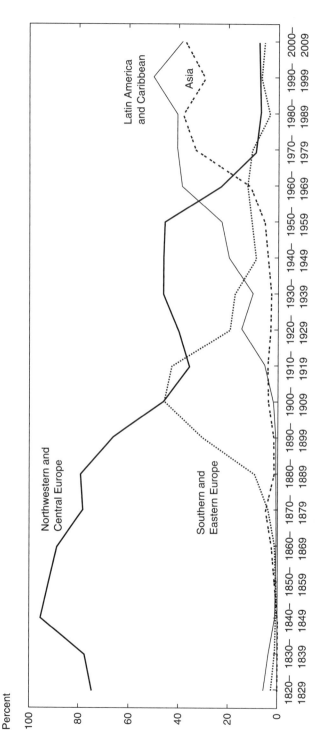

Note: Data for 2010–2013 can be found in Table 10-3, this volume.

Source: Table 10-3, this volume.

Table 10-4   Legal Status of Immigrants, 2010; Origins of Unauthorized Immigrants, 2012; and State Populations of Unauthorized Immigrants, 1990–2010

	Number (millions)	Percentage of foreign born living in United States
Legal status of immigrants		
Legal permanent resident (LPR) aliens	12.4	31
Naturalized citizens (former LPRs)	14.9	37
Temporary legal residents (such as students or temporary workers)	1.7	4
Unauthorized immigrants[a]	11.2	28
Total	40.2	100

	Number (millions)	Percentage of unauthorized immigrants
Unauthorized immigrants[a]: country/region of birth, 2012		
Mexico	5.9	52
Caribbean, Central America, South America	3.0	26
Asia	1.4	12
Europe or Canada	0.6	5
Middle East, Africa, or other	0.4	4
Total	11.2[b]	100[b]

	Estimated population (millions)			Percentage of unauthorized immigrants
	1990	2000	2010	2010
Unauthorized immigrants[a]: state of residence				
California	1.5	2.3	2.6	23
Texas	0.5	1.1	1.7	15
Florida	0.2	0.6	0.8	7
New York	0.4	0.7	0.6	5
New Jersey	0.1	0.3	0.6	5
Illinois	0.2	0.5	0.5	4
Georgia	0.0	0.3	0.4	4
Arizona	0.1	0.3	0.4	4
North Carolina	0.0	0.2	0.3	3
Maryland	0.0	0.1	0.3	3
Subtotal	3.0[b]	6.4[b]	8.2	73
Remaining 40 states and D.C.	0.5	2.0	3.0	27
Total, U.S.	3.5	8.4	11.2	100

(Table continues)

Table 10-4   *(Continued)*

Note: Demographic estimates based on U.S. Census Bureau, Current Population Surveys, March Supplements, with allowance for omissions. For details, see second source. Percentages calculated before rounding. The ten states listed are those with the largest estimated unauthorized immigrant populations in 2010. The estimated number of unauthorized immigrants in 2013 was 11.3 million, up from 8.6 million in 2000. Between 2000 and 2013, estimates of unauthorized immigrants peaked at 12.2 million in 2007.

[a] "Unauthorized" includes those entering the United States clandestinely without inspection, with fraudulent documents, or overstaying visas. *Undocumented immigrants, illegals, illegal aliens*, and *illegal immigrants* are kindred terms, but *unauthorized immigrants* more appropriately describes a group that includes those who enter the country with counterfeit documents and thus are not literally "undocumented."
[b] Due to rounding, the categories shown do not sum to the total or subtotal indicated.

Sources: Estimates of unauthorized immigrants in 2000, 2007, and 2013: Jeffrey S. Passel, Mark Hugo Lopez, D'Vera Cohn, and Molly Rohal, "As Growth Stalls, Unauthorized Immigrant Population Becomes More Settled," Pew Hispanic Center, September 3, 2014, 14; other data: Passel and Cohn, "Unauthorized Immigrant Population: National and State Trends, 2010," Pew Hispanic Center, February 1, 2011, 10, 11, 23; Passel, Cohn, and Rohal, "Unauthorized Immigrant Totals Rise in 7 States, Fall in 14," Pew Hispanic Center, November 18, 2014, 18 (*www.pewhispanic.org*).

Table 10-5   Hospital Insurance Trust Fund: Income, Expenditures, and Balance, 1991–2023 (billions)

Year	Income	Disbursements	Net increase in fund	Fund at end of year
1991	$88.8	$72.6	$16.3	$115.2
1993	98.2	94.4	3.8	127.8
1996	124.6	129.9	−5.3	124.9
1997	130.2	139.5	−9.3	115.6
1998	140.5	135.8	4.8	120.4
1999	151.6	130.6	21.0	141.4
2000	167.2	131.1	36.1	177.5
2001	174.6	143.4	31.3	208.7
2002	178.6	152.5	26.1	234.8
2003	175.8	154.6	21.2	256.0
2004	183.9	170.6	13.3	269.3
2005	199.4	182.9	16.4	285.8
2006	211.5	191.9	19.6	305.4
2007	223.7	203.1	20.7	326.0
2008	230.8	235.6	−4.7	321.3
2009	225.4	242.5	−17.1	304.2
2010	215.6	247.9	−32.3	271.9
2011	228.9	256.7	−27.7	244.2
2012	243.0	266.8	−23.8	220.4
2013	251.1	266.2	−15.0	205.4
2014	255.9	269.5	−13.6	191.7
2015	281.9	269.9	12.0	203.8
2016	300.3	283.2	17.1	220.8
2017	320.4	299.2	21.2	242.0
2018	342.0	322.0	20.0	262.0
2019	362.9	342.3	20.6	282.6
2020	383.9	366.3	17.5	300.1
2021	404.9	391.9	13.0	313.2
2022	425.9	419.1	6.8	319.9
2023	447.0	447.2	−0.2	319.8

Note: The Hospital Insurance Program (Medicare Part A) pays for in-patient hospital care and other related care for those ages sixty-five or older and for the long-term disabled. It represents roughly half of all Medicare expenses. Income for the fund is derived from a payroll tax on employees and employers. Figures for 1991 through 2013 represent actual experience. Figures for 2014 and beyond are "intermediate" projections; see sources for details. Amounts in current dollars.

Sources: 1991: U.S. Congress, House, "1992 Annual Report of the Board of Trustees of the Federal Hospital Insurance Trust Fund," 102nd Cong., 2nd sess., House Document 102–280, April 13, 1992, 14; 1993: 103rd Cong., 2nd sess., House Document 103–230, April 12, 1994, 14; 1996–2023: U.S. Department of Health and Human Services, "Annual Report of the Boards of Trustees of the Federal Hospital Insurance and Federal Supplementary Medical Insurance Trust Funds, Estimated Operations of the HI Trust Fund during Calendar Years, under Alternative Sets of Assumptions" (*www.cms.hhs.gov*).

Table 10-6   Social Security (OASDI)–Covered Workers and Beneficiaries, 1945–2090

Year	Covered workers[a] (thousands)	Beneficiaries[b] (thousands)			Covered workers per OASDI beneficiary	Beneficiaries per 100 covered workers
		OASI	DI	Total		
1945	46,390	1,106	—	1,106	41.9	2
1950	48,280	2,930	—	2,930	16.5	6
1955	65,066	7,564	—	7,564	8.6	12
1960	72,371	13,740	522	14,262	5.1	20
1965	80,539	18,509	1,648	20,157	4.0	25
1970	92,963	22,618	2,568	25,186	3.7	27
1975	100,193	26,998	4,125	31,123	3.2	31
1980	112,651	30,384	4,734	35,117	3.2	31
1985	120,312	32,763	3,874	36,636	3.3	30
1990	133,123	35,255	4,204	39,459	3.4	30
1995	140,976	37,364	5,731	43,096	3.3	31
2000	154,916	38,556	6,606	45,162	3.4	29
2005	159,212	39,961	8,172	48,133	3.3	30
2010	157,328	43,440	9,958	53,398	2.9	34
2011	158,988	44,388	10,428	54,816	2.9	34
2012	161,672	45,377	10,799	56,176	2.9	35
2013	163,221	46,517	10,954	57,471	2.8	35
2014	165,446	47,866	11,031	58,896	2.8	36
2015	167,493	49,377	11,108	60,485	2.8	36
2020	177,705	57,923	11,489	69,412	2.6	39
2025	182,644	65,509	12,058	77,567	2.4	42
2030	186,049	72,809	12,213	85,022	2.2	46
2035	189,841	77,752	12,545	90,297	2.1	48
2040	195,100	80,187	12,963	93,149	2.1	48
2045	200,717	81,430	13,694	95,124	2.1	47
2050	205,991	83,072	14,223	97,295	2.1	47
2055	210,763	85,475	14,723	100,198	2.1	48
2060	215,272	88,588	15,016	103,605	2.1	48
2065	220,022	91,742	15,470	107,212	2.1	49
2070	225,171	95,245	15,903	111,148	2.0	49
2075	230,524	98,430	16,252	114,681	2.0	50
2080	235,909	100,766	16,899	117,665	2.0	50
2085	241,094	103,890	17,509	121,399	2.0	50
2090	246,038	107,850	17,860	125,710	2.0	51

Note: "—" indicates not available; "OASI" indicates Old-Age and Survivors' Insurance; "DI" indicates Disability Insurance. Projections (2014–2090) are the "intermediate" projections; see source for details. Data for additional years can be found in previous editions of *Vital Statistics on American Politics.*

[a] Workers who pay OASDI taxes at some time during the year.
[b] Beneficiaries with monthly benefits in current-payment status as of June 30.

Source: U.S. Social Security Administration, "2014 OASDI Trustees Report," table IV.B2 (*www.ssa.gov*).

Figure 10-3   Social Security Receipts, Spending, and Reserve Estimates, 2014–2030

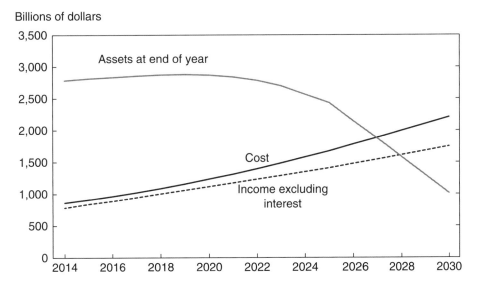

Billions of dollars

Note: Amounts in current dollars. Based on intermediate economic and demographic assumptions. Under these assumptions it is projected that the combined Old Age and Survivors Insurance (OASI) and Disability Insurance (DI) Trust Funds will become exhausted in 2033.

Source: U.S. Social Security Administration, "2014 OASDI Trustees Report," table VI.G8 (*www.ssa.gov*).

Table 10-7 Median Family Income, by Race and Hispanic Origin, 1950–2013

Year	Median income in current dollars				Median income in constant (2013) dollars				Annual percentage change in median income of all families	
	All families[a]	White alone[b]	Black alone[b]	Hispanic origin[c]	All families[a]	White alone[b]	Black alone[b]	Hispanic origin[c]	Current dollars	Constant dollars
1950	$3,319	—	—	—	$28,035	—	—	—	—	—
1955	4,418	—	—	—	33,587	—	—	—	6.8	5.5
1960	5,620	—	—	—	38,684	—	—	—	6.0	6.3
1965	6,957	—	—	—	44,990	—	—	—	5.9	4.3
1970	9,867	$10,236	$6,279	—	52,825	$54,800	$33,616	—	4.6	-0.2
1975	13,719	14,268	8,779	$9,551	54,008	56,169	34,560	$37,600	6.3	-1.8
1980	21,023	21,904	12,674	14,716	56,585	58,956	34,113	39,609	7.3	-3.4
1981	22,388	23,517	13,266	16,401	55,021	57,796	32,603	40,307	6.5	-2.8
1982	23,433	24,603	13,598	16,227	54,312	57,024	31,517	37,610	4.7	-1.3
1983	24,580	25,757	14,506	16,956	54,638	57,255	32,245	37,691	4.9	0.6
1984	26,433	27,686	15,431	18,832	56,447	59,122	32,952	40,215	7.5	3.3
1985	27,735	29,152	16,786	19,027	57,261	60,186	34,656	39,283	4.9	1.4
1986	29,458	30,809	17,604	19,995	59,737	62,476	35,698	40,547	6.2	4.3
1987	30,970	32,385	18,406	20,300	60,750	63,526	36,105	39,820	5.1	1.7
1988	32,191	33,915	19,329	21,769	60,910	64,172	36,573	41,190	3.9	0.3
1989	34,213	35,975	20,209	23,446	62,059	65,255	36,657	42,529	6.3	1.9
1990	35,353	36,915	21,423	23,431	61,082	63,781	37,014	40,484	3.3	-1.6
1991	35,939	37,783	21,548	23,895	59,945	63,021	35,941	39,856	1.7	-1.9
1992	36,573	38,670	21,103	23,555	59,494	62,905	34,329	38,317	1.8	-0.8
1993	36,959	39,300	21,542	23,654	58,671	62,388	34,197	37,550	1.1	-1.3
1994	38,782	40,884	24,698	24,318	60,279	63,546	38,388	37,797	4.9	2.7
1995	40,611	42,646	25,970	24,570	61,637	64,726	39,416	37,291	4.7	2.3

Year										
1996	42,300	44,756	26,522	26,179	62,536	66,167	39,210	38,703	4.2	1.5
1997	44,568	46,754	28,602	28,142	64,495	67,659	41,391	40,725	5.4	3.1
1998	46,737	49,023	29,404	29,608	66,703	69,966	41,965	42,257	4.9	3.4
1999	48,831	51,079	31,850	31,523	68,268	71,410	44,528	44,070	4.5	2.3
2000	50,732	53,029	33,676	34,442	68,626	71,733	45,554	46,590	3.9	0.5
2001	51,407	54,067	33,598	34,490	67,640	71,140	44,207	45,381	1.3	-1.4
2002	51,680	54,633	33,525	34,185	66,918	70,742	43,410	44,265	0.5	-1.1
2003	52,680	55,768	34,369	34,272	66,723	70,634	43,531	43,408	1.9	-0.3
2004	54,061	56,723	35,148	35,440	66,670	69,953	43,346	43,706	2.6	-0.1
2005	56,194	59,317	35,464	37,867	67,053	70,779	42,317	45,184	3.9	0.6
2006	58,407	61,280	38,269	40,000	67,481	70,800	44,214	46,214	3.9	0.6
2007	61,355	64,427	40,143	40,566	68,931	72,383	45,100	45,575	5.0	2.2
2008	61,521	65,000	39,879	40,466	66,560	70,324	43,145	43,781	0.3	-3.4
2009	60,088	62,545	38,409	39,730	65,257	67,926	41,713	43,148	-2.3	-2.0
2010	60,236	62,914	38,594	39,300	64,356	67,217	41,234	41,988	0.2	-1.4
2011	60,974	64,081	40,495	40,061	63,152	66,370	41,942	41,492	1.2	-1.9
2012	62,241	65,880	40,517	40,764	63,145	66,837	41,106	41,356	2.1	0.0
2013	63,815	67,255	41,588	42,269	63,815	67,255	41,588	42,269	2.5	1.1

Note: "—" indicates not available. Data for additional years can be found in previous editions of *Vital Statistics on American Politics.*

[a] Includes other races not shown separately.

[b] "White alone" and "black alone" refer to the fact that in the 2002 and later Current Population Surveys individuals could describe themselves as being of more than one race.

[c] Persons of Hispanic origin may be of any race.

Source: U.S. Census Bureau, "Current Population Reports, Historical Income Tables," table F-7 (*www.census.gov*).

Table 10-8   Persons below the Poverty Line, by Group, 2013

Group	Percentage of group that is poor	Group as a percentage of all poor people
Race/ethnicity		
White alone	12.3	66.1
White alone (not of Hispanic origin)	9.6	41.5
Black alone	27.2	24.4
Hispanic (of any race)	23.5	28.1
Family status		
Female householder, no husband present		
White alone	29.2	18.5
Black alone	42.5	13.0
Hispanic (of any race)	41.6	10.7
All other families		
White alone	6.9	25.5
Black alone	13.4	5.6
Hispanic (of any race)	16.0	12.5
Age		
Under 18 years	19.9	32.3
65 years and over	9.5	9.3
Residence		
Metropolitan residents	14.2	83.3
Nonmetropolitan residents	16.1	16.7
Region		
Northeast	12.7	15.5
Midwest	12.9	19.0
South	16.1	41.6
West	14.7	23.9
All persons	14.5	100.0

Note: The Current Population Survey asked respondents to choose one or more races. Shown are people who reported a single race of white or single race of black or African American. Hispanic origin may be of any race. For composition of regions, see Table A-1, this volume. Data for earlier years can be found in previous editions of *Vital Statistics on American Politics.*

Source: U.S. Census Bureau, *Income, Poverty, and Health Insurance Coverage in the United States: 2013* (Washington, D.C.: Government Printing Office, 2014), 13, 44–49.

Table 10-9   Persons below the Poverty Line, by Race and Hispanic Origin, 1959–2013 (percent)

Year	White	Black	Hispanic origin	Total
1959	18.1	55.1	—	22.4
1960	17.8	—	—	22.2
1965	13.3	—	—	17.3
1970	9.9	33.5	—	12.6
1975	9.7	31.3	26.9	12.3
1976	9.1	31.1	24.7	11.8
1977	8.9	31.3	22.4	11.6
1978	8.7	30.6	21.6	11.4
1979	9.0	31.0	21.8	11.7
1980	10.2	32.5	25.7	13.0
1981	11.1	34.2	26.5	14.0
1982	12.0	35.6	29.9	15.0
1983	12.1	35.7	28.0	15.2
1984	11.5	33.8	28.4	14.4
1985	11.4	31.3	29.0	14.0
1986	11.0	31.1	27.3	13.6
1987	10.4	32.4	28.0	13.4
1988	10.1	31.3	26.7	13.0
1989	10.0	30.7	26.2	12.8
1990	10.7	31.9	28.1	13.5
1991	11.3	32.7	28.7	14.2
1992	11.9	33.4	29.6	14.8
1993	12.2	33.1	30.6	15.1
1994	11.7	30.6	30.7	14.5
1995	11.2	29.3	30.3	13.8
1996	11.2	28.4	29.4	13.7
1997	11.0	26.5	27.1	13.3
1998	10.5	26.1	25.6	12.7
1999	9.8	23.6	22.7	11.9
2000	9.5	22.5	21.5	11.3
2001	9.9	22.7	21.4	11.7
2002	10.2	24.1	21.8	12.1
2003	10.5	24.4	22.5	12.5
2004	10.8	24.7	21.9	12.7
2005	10.6	24.9	21.8	12.6
2006	10.3	24.3	20.6	12.3
2007	10.5	24.5	21.5	12.5
2008	11.2	24.7	23.2	13.2
2009	12.3	25.8	25.3	14.3
2010	13.0	27.4	26.5	15.1
2011	12.8	27.6	25.3	15.0
2012	12.7	27.2	25.6	15.0
2013	12.3	27.2	23.5	14.5

Note: "—" indicates not available. Beginning in 2003, the Current Population Survey asked respondents to choose one or more races: for 2003 through 2013, white alone, black alone, Hispanic origin (of any race). The total includes other races not shown separately. Data for additional years can be found in previous editions of *Vital Statistics on American Politics.*

Source: U.S. Census Bureau, *Income, Poverty, and Health Insurance Coverage in the United States: 2013* (Washington, D.C.: Government Printing Office, 2014), 44–49.

Figure 10-4   Temporary Assistance for Needy Families (TANF) and Food
Stamp (SNAP) Benefit Levels as Percentage of Federal
Poverty Line, 2014

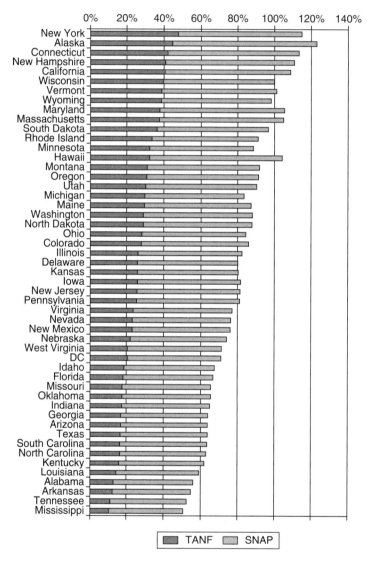

Note: The Temporary Assistance for Needy Families (TANF) program provides monthly cash benefits to eligible families with children. It is run directly by the states. Before 1996, it was known as the Aid to Families with Dependent Children (AFDC) program. The Food Stamp Program (now SNAP, or Supplemental Nutrition Assistance Program) provides monthly food stamp benefits to individuals living in families or alone, provided their income and assets are below the limits set by federal law. Benefit levels are for a single-parent family of three. For details, see source.

Source: Center on Budget and Policy Priorities, "TANF Cash Benefits Have Fallen by More Than 20 Percent in Most States and Continue to Erode," October 30, 2014 *(www.cbpp.org).*

Figure 10-5   U.S. Population Receiving AFDC/TANF and Food Stamps/
SNAP, 1970–2013

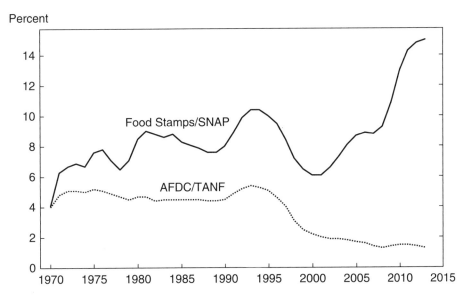

Note: See note to Figure 10-4, this volume.

Sources: U.S. Department of Health and Human Services (HHS), "Indicators of Welfare Depen-
dence: Annual Report to Congress 2008, Appendix A" *(http://aspe.hhs.gov/hsp/indicators08/index
.shtml).* Updated by personal communication from HHS.

Table 10-10   Health Insurance Coverage for the Noninstitutionalized U.S.
Population under Sixty-five, 1987–2013

	Uninsured		Insured (percent)			
Year[a]	Number (millions)	Percent	Employment-based[b]	Government[c]	Military[d]	Total population (millions)
1987	30.7	14.4	66.2	9.9	4.4	212.7
1988	32.4	15.1	66.0	10.0	4.2	214.7
1989	33.1	15.3	65.6	10.1	4.0	216.6
1990	34.4	15.7	64.1	11.5	4.0	218.8
1991	35.2	15.9	63.4	12.5	3.9	220.9
1992	38.3	16.9	61.3	13.4	3.7	226.4
1993	39.3	17.2	60.4	14.3	3.6	229.0
1994	39.4	17.1	64.4	14.1	4.2	230.8
1995	40.3	17.3	64.6	14.3	3.5	232.7
1996	41.4	17.6	64.8	14.0	3.3	234.9
1997	43.1	18.2	65.0	13.0	3.1	237.0
1998	43.9	18.4	65.8	12.4	3.2	239.3
1999	38.5	15.8	67.8	12.5	3.0	243.4
2000	38.2	15.5	68.3	12.9	3.1	246.0
2001	39.5	15.9	67.0	13.6	3.0	248.3
2002	41.8	16.6	65.7	14.2	3.1	251.7
2003	43.1	17.0	64.4	15.2	3.1	253.6
2004	43.0	16.8	63.9	16.0	3.2	256.0
2005	44.4	17.2	63.5	15.9	3.3	258.3
2006	46.5	17.8	62.9	15.9	3.0	260.8
2007	45.0	17.1	62.9	16.5	3.2	262.3
2008	45.7	17.3	61.9	17.8	3.3	263.7
2009	50.0	18.8	58.9	19.4	3.5	265.7
2010	49.2	18.4	58.6	19.8	3.6	266.8
2011	47.9	17.9	58.3	20.8	3.7	267.3
2012	47.3	17.7	58.4	21.0	3.7	267.8
2013[e]	44.7	16.7	57.1	21.4	1.2	267.8

Note: Persons may have more than one type of coverage; percentages may total to more than 100.

[a] Because of questionnaire changes in the Current Population Survey in 1994 and 1999, numbers are not strictly comparable over time.
[b] Group health insurance through current or former employer or union.
[c] Medicare or Medicaid. For 1999 and after, this category also includes other state programs for low-income individuals.
[d] Includes CHAMPUS (Comprehensive Health and Medical Plan for Uniformed Services)/Tricare, veterans, and military health care. In 2013, percent covered by VA care.
[e] In data year 2013, there were a series of changes to data collection operations that could have affected some estimates. See the source.

Sources: 1987–1998: U.S. Census Bureau, Health Insurance, "Historical Health Insurance Tables" (table HI-6); 1999–2009: "Health Insurance Coverage Status and Type of Coverage by State—Persons under 65: 1999 to 2009" (table HIA-6) (*www.census.gov*); 2010–2013: "Health Insurance Coverage Status and Type of Coverage by State for All People" (table HI05) (*www.census.gov*).

Table 10-11   Persons without Health Insurance, by Demographic Characteristics, 2013

	Uninsured	
Group	Number (millions)	Percentage of group population
Family status		
In families	31.4	12.3
Householder	10.5	12.9
Related children under 18 years	5.3	7.3
Related children under 6 years	1.8	7.6
In unrelated subfamilies	0.2	16.0
Unrelated individual	10.3	18.1
Race and Hispanic origin		
White	31.1	12.8
White, not Hispanic	19.1	9.8
Black	6.5	15.9
Asian	2.5	14.5
Hispanic origin (any race)	13.2	30.1
Age		
Under 18 years	5.4	7.3
Under 19 years[a]	5.9	7.6
19–25 years[a]	6.9	22.6
26–34 years	8.9	23.5
35–44 years	7.6	19.0
45–64 years	12.0	14.5
65 years and older	0.7	1.6
Nativity		
Native born	30.6	11.2
Foreign born	11.4	27.7
Naturalized citizen	3.0	15.9
Not a citizen	8.3	38.1

[a] These age groups are of special interest because of the Affordable Care Act of 2010. Children under the age of 19 are eligible for Medicaid/CHIP and individuals aged 19 to 25 may be a dependent on a parent's health plan.

Source: U.S. Census Bureau, *Health Insurance Coverage in the United States: 2013* (Washington, D.C: Government Printing Office, 2014), tables 2, 5 (*www.census.gov*).

Table 10-12 Persons Who Have Completed High School or College, by Race, Hispanic Origin, and Sex, 1940–2014 (percent)

	25 years and over						25–29 years					
	White[a]		Black[b]		Hispanic[c]		White[a]		Black[b]		Hispanic[c]	
Level/year	Male	Female	Male	Female	Male	Female	Male	Female	Male	Female	Male	Female
Completed four years of high school or more[d]												
1940	24.2	28.1	6.9	8.4	—	—	38.9	43.4	10.6	13.6	—	—
1947	33.2	36.7	12.7	14.5	—	—	52.9	56.8	19.6	24.7	—	—
1959	44.5	47.7	19.6	21.6	—	—	66.9	67.4	40.6	38.6	—	—
1970	57.2	57.6	32.4	34.8	—	—	79.2	76.4	54.5	57.9	—	—
1980	71.0	70.1	51.1	51.3	46.4	44.1	86.8	87.0	74.8	78.1	58.3	58.8
1990	79.1	79.0	65.8	66.5	50.3	51.3	84.6	88.1	81.5	81.8	56.6	59.9
2000	84.4	85.0	78.7	78.3	56.6	57.5	86.6	90.0	86.6	85.3	59.2	66.4
2005	85.2	86.2	81.0	81.2	57.9	59.1	84.3	87.1	86.4	86.5	63.2	63.4
2006	85.5	86.7	80.1	81.2	58.5	60.1	84.1	88.3	83.1	87.8	60.6	66.7
2007	85.3	87.1	81.9	82.5	58.2	60.6	84.2	89.0	86.9	87.7	60.6	70.6
2008	86.3	87.8	81.8	84.0	60.9	63.7	85.5	89.8	85.4	89.3	65.6	71.9
2009	86.5	87.7	84.0	84.1	60.5	63.3	87.0	89.9	88.6	89.2	66.2	72.5
2010	86.9	88.2	83.6	84.6	61.4	64.4	87.3	89.9	86.8	91.1	65.7	74.0
2011	87.4	88.6	83.8	85.0	63.6	65.1	87.1	90.8	87.6	87.8	69.2	74.3
2012	87.6	88.5	84.3	85.5	64.0	66.0	88.3	90.9	87.1	89.6	73.3	77.0
2013	88.0	89.2	84.0	86.0	64.5	67.9	88.0	91.1	87.1	92.1	73.2	78.9
2014	88.0	89.6	85.3	86.2	65.1	67.9	90.2	91.7	90.3	89.5	72.4	77.4
Completed four years of college or more[e]												
1940	5.9	4.0	1.4	1.2	—	—	7.5	5.3	1.5	1.7	—	—
1947	6.6	4.9	2.4	2.6	—	—	6.2	5.7	2.6	2.9	—	—
1959	11.0	6.2	3.8	2.9	—	—	15.9	8.1	5.6	3.7	—	—
1970	15.0	8.6	4.6	4.4	—	—	21.3	13.3	6.7	8.0	—	—

1980	14.0	7.7	8.1	9.7	6.2	25.5	22.0	10.5	12.5	8.4	6.9
1990	19.0	11.9	10.8	9.8	8.7	24.2	24.3	15.1	11.9	7.3	9.1
2000	23.9	16.3	16.7	10.7	10.6	27.8	31.3	18.1	17.0	8.3	11.0
2005	26.8	16.0	18.8	11.8	12.1	25.3	32.7	14.1	20.0	10.2	12.4
2006	27.1	17.2	19.4	11.9	12.9	25.0	31.7	14.9	21.6	6.9	12.8
2007	28.3	18.0	19.0	11.8	13.7	25.8	34.0	17.8	19.8	8.6	15.4
2008	29.1	18.7	20.4	12.6	14.1	26.7	35.9	18.7	22.3	9.9	15.5
2009	29.3	17.8	20.6	12.4	14.0	27.0	36.0	15.1	22.4	11.0	13.8
2010	29.9	17.7	21.4	12.9	15.0	28.8	36.9	14.8	22.9	10.8	16.8
2011	30.5	18.0	21.4	13.1	15.2	29.2	37.4	16.1	22.9	9.6	16.8
2012	30.8	19.2	22.9	13.3	15.8	29.9	37.5	18.5	26.2	12.5	17.5
2013	31.6	19.8	23.3	13.9	16.2	30.8	37.9	16.7	23.1	13.1	18.6
2014	32.3	20.4	23.7	14.2	16.1	31.6	38.2	19.5	23.4	12.4	18.3

Note: "—" indicates not available. Data for additional years can be found in previous editions of *Vital Statistics on American Politics.*

[a] For 1940 through 2000, data are for white persons only; for 2005 through 2014, data are for people who reported a single race of white.
[b] For 1940 through 1960, data are for black and other races; for 1970 through 2000, data are for black persons only; for 2005 through 2014, data are for people who reported a single race of black or African American.
[c] Persons of Hispanic origin may be of any race.
[d] Beginning in 2000, high school graduate or more.
[e] Beginning in 2000, bachelor's degree or more.

Source: U.S. Census Bureau, "Educational Attainment in the United States," table 1 *(www.census.gov).*

Table 10-13   School Desegregation, by Region, 1968–2011

Region/year	Percentage of black students in schools more than 50 percent minority	Percentage of Hispanic students in schools more than 50 percent minority	Percentage of black students in schools 90–100 percent minority	Percentage of Hispanic students in schools 90–100 percent minority
South				
1968	80.9	69.6	77.8	33.7
1972	55.3	69.9	24.7	31.4
1976	54.9	70.9	22.4	32.2
1980	57.1	76.0	23.0	37.3
1984	56.9	75.4	24.2	37.3
1988	56.5	80.2	24.0	37.9
1991	60.8	76.8	26.6	38.6
1994	63.4	75.6	—	38.0
1996	65.3	75.9	27.9	38.3
1998	67.2	76.1	29.7	39.1
2000	69.0	77.2	30.9	39.5
2001	69.8	77.7	31.0	39.9
2005	72.0	78.0	32.0	40.0
2009	74.0	79.4	33.4	41.3
2011	76.8	81.0	34.2	41.5
Border				
1968	71.6	—	60.2	—
1972	67.2	—	54.7	—
1976	60.1	—	42.5	—
1980	59.2	—	37.0	—
1984	62.5	—	37.4	—
1988	59.6	—	34.5	8.9
1991	59.3	37.4	33.2	10.8
1994	—	40.8	—	12.3
1996	63.2	43.5	37.3	12.6
1998	64.7	46.1	39.2	13.1
2000	67.0	49.2	39.6	13.4
2001	67.9	52.8	41.6	14.2
2005	70.0	57.0	42.0	17.0
2009	69.9	58.8	39.8	18.4
2011	73.2	59.9	41.0	20.0
Northeast				
1968	66.8	74.8	42.7	44.0
1972	69.9	74.4	46.9	44.1
1976	72.5	74.9	51.4	45.8
1980	79.9	76.3	48.7	45.8
1984	73.1	77.5	47.4	47.1
1988	77.3	79.7	48.0	44.2
1991	76.2	78.1	50.1	46.2
1994	—	77.6	—	45.1
1996	77.3	78.2	50.5	46.0
1998	77.5	78.5	50.9	45.7
2000	78.3	78.5	51.2	45.3

Region/year	Percentage of black students in schools more than 50 percent minority	Percentage of Hispanic students in schools more than 50 percent minority	Percentage of black students in schools 90–100 percent minority	Percentage of Hispanic students in schools 90–100 percent minority
2001	78.4	78.2	51.2	44.8
2005	78.0	77.0	51.0	45.0
2009	77.9	76.3	50.6	43.9
2011	79.4	76.6	51.4	44.2
Midwest				
1968	77.3	31.8	58.0	6.8
1972	75.3	34.4	57.4	9.5
1976	70.3	39.3	51.1	14.1
1980	69.5	46.6	43.6	19.6
1984	70.7	53.9	43.6	24.2
1988	70.1	52.3	41.8	24.9
1991	69.9	53.5	39.4	21.1
1994	—	53.1	—	21.8
1996	72.0	54.0	43.4	22.3
1998	72.8	55.6	45.5	24.1
2000	73.3	56.3	46.3	24.9
2001	72.9	56.6	46.8	24.6
2005	72.0	57.0	46.0	26.0
2009	71.6	58.8	44.3	27.0
2011	73.7	58.9	43.2	26.2
West				
1968	72.2	42.4	50.8	11.7
1972	68.1	44.7	42.7	11.5
1976	67.4	52.7	36.3	13.3
1980	66.8	63.5	33.7	18.5
1984	66.9	68.4	29.4	22.9
1988	67.1	71.3	28.6	27.5
1991	69.7	73.5	26.4	29.7
1994	—	75.9	—	32.1
1996	73.5	77.1	27.5	33.0
1998	74.0	78.3	28.8	35.2
2000	75.3	79.4	29.5	36.7
2001	75.8	80.1	30.0	37.4
2005	77.0	82.0	30.0	41.0
2009	78.1	83.7	29.5	43.2
2011	82.4	84.1	34.4	44.8
Total				
1968	76.6	54.8	64.3	23.1
1972	63.6	56.6	38.7	23.3
1976	62.4	60.8	35.9	24.8
1980	62.9	68.1	33.2	28.8
1984	63.5	70.6	33.2	31.0
1988	63.2	—	32.1	33.1
1991	66.0	73.4	33.9	34.0

(Table continues)

Table 10-13   *(Continued)*

Region/year	Percentage of black students in schools more than 50 percent minority	Percentage of Hispanic students in schools more than 50 percent minority	Percentage of black students in schools 90–100 percent minority	Percentage of Hispanic students in schools 90–100 percent minority
1994	67.1	74.0	33.6	34.8
1996	68.8	74.8	35.0	35.4
1998	70.1	75.6	36.5	36.7
2000	71.6	76.4	37.4	37.4
2002	73.0	77.0	38.0	38.0
2005	73.0	77.0	38.0	39.0
2006	73.1	78.7	38.4	43.1
2009	74.1	79.5	38.1	43.1

Note: "—" indicates not available. Data for 1968–1969 to 2011–2012 school years. "Total" data were not available for 2001 or 2011; regional data were not available for 2002 or 2006. For composition of regions, see Table A-4, this volume. Data for additional years can be found in previous editions of *Vital Statistics on American Politics.*

Sources: 1968–1980: Gary Orfield, testimony before the House Subcommittee on Civil and Constitutional Rights, *Civil Rights Implications of the Education Block Grant Program,* 97th Cong., 2nd sess., September 9, 1982, 67–72; 1984: Orfield, Franklin Monfort, and Melissa Aaron, "Status of School Desegregation 1968–1986," National School Boards Association, Alexandria, Va., 1989, 5, 7; 1988: Orfield and Monfort, "Status of School Desegregation: The Next Generation," National School Boards Association, Alexandria, Va., 1992, 3, 7–8; 1991: Orfield, "The Growth of Segregation in American Schools: Changing Patterns of Separation and Poverty Since 1968," National School Boards Association, Alexandria, Va., 1993, 9, © 1989, 1992, and 1993 National School Boards Association, all rights reserved; 1994: Orfield et al., "Deepening Segregation in American Public Schools," April 5, 1997, 11, 15; 1996: Orfield and John T. Yun, "Resegregation in American Schools," June 1999, tables 15, 19; 1998: Orfield, "Schools More Separate: Consequences of a Decade of Resegregation," July 2001, tables 9, 14, 18; 2000: Erica Frankenberg, Chungmei Lee, and Orfield, "A Multiracial Society with Segregated Schools: Are We Losing the Dream?" January 2003, tables 11, 29, 33, 37; 2001: Orfield and Lee, "Brown at 50: King's Dream or Plessy's Nightmare?" January 2004, tables 8, 9; 2002: Orfield and Lee, "Why Segregation Matters: Poverty and Educational Inequality," January 2005, table 4 (*www.civilrightsproject.harvard.edu*); 2005: Orfield and Lee, "Historic Reversals, Accelerating Resegregation, and the Need for New Integration Strategies," August 2007, tables 10, 14, 16, 17; 2006–2009: Orfield, John Kucsera, and Genevieve Siegel-Hawley, "*E Pluribus...*Separation: Deepening Double Segregation for More Students," September 2012, tables 2, 11; 2011: Orfield and Frankenberg, with Jongyeon Ee and Kuscera, "Brown at 60: Great Progress, a Long Retreat and an Uncertain Future," May 2014, tables 8, 11, B-1, B-3 (*http://civilrightsproject.ucla.edu*). Reprinted with permission of The Civil Rights Project/ *Proyecto Derechos Civiles* at UCLA.

Table 10-14   State and Local Government Employment and Salary, by Sex, Race, and Hispanic Origin, 1973–2013

| | Employment (thousands) | | | | | | | Median annual salary (thousands) | | | | | | |
| | Gender | | | | Minority | | | Gender | | | | Minority | | |
Year	Male	Female	Total	White[a]	Black[a]	Hispanic	Total[b]	Male	Female	Total	White[a]	Black[a]	Hispanic	Total[b]
1973	2,486	1,322	3,809	3,115	523	125	693	$9.6	$7.0	$8.6	$8.8	$7.4	$7.4	$7.5
1975	2,436	1,464	3,899	3,102	602	147	797	11.3	8.2	9.8	10.2	8.6	8.9	8.8
1980	2,350	1,637	3,987	3,146	619	163	842	15.2	11.4	13.3	13.8	11.5	12.3	11.8
1983	2,674	1,818	4,492	3,423	768	219	1,069	20.1	15.3	18.0	18.5	15.6	17.3	15.9
1985	2,789	1,952	4,742	3,563	835	248	1,179	22.3	17.3	19.9	20.6	17.5	19.2	18.4
1987	2,818	2,031	4,849	3,600	872	268	1,249	24.1	18.9	—	22.4	19.3	21.1	20.9
1989	3,030	2,227	5,257	3,863	961	308	1,394	26.1	20.6	—	24.1	20.7	22.7	22.1
1990	3,071	2,302	5,374	3,918	994	327	1,456	27.3	21.8	—	25.2	22.0	23.8	23.3
1991	3,110	2,349	5,459	3,965	1,011	340	1,494	28.4	22.7	25.5	26.4	22.7	24.5	—
1993[c]	2,820	2,204	5,024	3,588	948	341	1,436	30.6	24.3	27.7	28.5	24.2	26.8	—
1995	2,960	2,355	5,315	3,781	993	379	1,534	33.5	27.0	30.5	31.4	26.8	28.6	—
1997	2,898	2,307	5,204	3,676	973	392	1,529	34.6	27.9	31.2	32.2	27.4	29.5	—
1999	2,939	2,393	5,332	3,723	1,012	417	1,609	37.1	29.9	33.4	34.8	29.6	31.2	—
2001	3,080	2,554	5,634	3,888	1,077	471	1,746	39.8	32.1	36.2	37.5	31.5	33.8	—
2003	3,134	2,610	5,745	3,919	1,097	508	1,826	42.2	34.7	38.7	40.0	33.6	36.6	—
2005	3,185	2,644	5,829	3,973	1,100	532	1,856	44.1	36.4	40.3	41.5	35.3	38.9	—
2007	3,383	2,823	6,207	4,156	1,138	661	2,051	47.3	39.3	43.1	44.8	38.2	41.0	—
2009	3,239	2,742	5,980	3,976	1,145	601	2,004	50.3	41.5	46.1	47.6	40.3	44.8	—
2011	2,924	2,477	5,400	3,561	1,015	570	1,839	51.8	43.1	47.8	49.1	41.7	47.0	—
2013	3,055	2,568	5,623	3,671	1,057	634	1,952	52.5	43.8	48.5	49.9	42.0	46.8	—

Note: "—" indicates not available. Full-time employment as of June 30; excludes school systems and educational institutions. Amounts in current dollars. Data for additional years can be found in previous editions of *Vital Statistics on American Politics*.

[a] Non-Hispanic.

[b] Includes other minority groups, not shown separately.

[c] Reporting changes occurred in 1993 that affect comparability of 1993 and later numbers with earlier entries.

Sources: 1973–1991: U.S. Equal Employment Opportunity Commission, *State and Local Government Information Report* (Washington, D.C.: Government Printing Office, annual); 1993–2013: U.S. Equal Employment Opportunity Commission, *Job Patterns for Minorities and Women in State and Local Government*, annual, table 1 (full-time employment).

Table 10-15   Frequency of Legal Abortions, 1972–2011

	Total		White		Nonwhite	
Year	Number of abortions (thousands)	Percentage of pregnancies terminated by abortion	Number of abortions (thousands)	Percentage of pregnancies terminated by abortion	Number of abortions (thousands)	Percentage of pregnancies terminated by abortion
1972	587.0	15.5	455.0	14.9	132.0	18.2
1973	744.6	19.3	548.8	17.4	195.8	25.9
1974	898.6	22.0	629.3	19.6	269.3	31.6
1975	1,034.2	24.9	701.2	21.5	333.0	35.9
1976	1,179.3	26.5	784.9	23.0	394.4	38.9
1977	1,316.7	28.6	888.8	25.0	427.9	40.4
1978	1,409.6	29.2	969.4	26.1	440.2	39.6
1979	1,497.7	29.6	1,062.4	27.1	435.3	38.2
1980	1,553.9	30.0	1,093.6	27.4	460.3	39.2
1981	1,577.3	30.1	1,107.8	27.4	469.6	39.2
1982	1,573.9	30.0	1,095.3	27.1	478.7	39.2
1983	1,575.0	30.4	1,084.4	27.4	490.6	40.1
1984	1,577.2	29.7	1,086.6	26.8	490.6	39.2
1985	1,588.6	29.7	1,075.6	26.5	512.9	39.7
1986	1,574.0	29.4	1,044.7	25.9	529.3	39.8
1987	1,559.1	28.8	1,017.3	25.2	541.8	39.3
1988	1,590.8	28.6	1,025.7	25.0	565.1	38.9
1991	1,556.5	27.4	982.0	23.3	574.5	39.8
1992	1,528.9	27.5	943.5	22.9	585.4	40.5
1993	1,495.0	27.4	907.7	22.5	587.3	41.1
1994	1,423.0	26.6	855.8	21.6	567.2	41.0
1995	1,359.4	25.9	817.2	20.9	542.3	40.6
1996	1,360.2	25.9	796.9	20.5	563.3	41.1
1997	1,335.0	25.5	777.0	20.1	558.0	40.6
1998	1,319.0	25.1	761.9	19.6	557.1	40.4
1999	1,314.8	24.6	742.6	19.0	572.2	40.3
2000	1,313.0	24.5	732.7	18.7	580.3	40.3
2001	1,291.0	24.4	716.5	18.5	574.5	40.5
2002	1,269.0	23.8	705.8	18.1	563.2	39.8
2003	1,250.0	23.3	694.5	17.7	555.5	38.8
2004	1,222.1	22.9	673.8	17.3	548.3	37.8
2005	1,206.2	22.4	661.6	16.9	544.6	37.0
2006	1,242.2	22.9	681.4	17.0	560.8	36.6
2007	1,209.6	21.9	668.1	16.7	541.5	35.5
2008	1,212.4	22.5	—	—	—	—
2009	1,151.6	22.2	—	—	—	—
2010	1,102.7	21.7	—	—	—	—
2011	1,058.5	21.2	—	—	—	—

Note: "—" indicates not available. "Percentage of pregnancies terminated by abortion" indicates the percentage of pregnancies resulting in live birth or abortion that are terminated by abortion. The percentage is based on births occurring during the twelve-month period starting in July of that year (to match times of conception for pregnancies ending in births with those for pregnancies ending in abortion). Figures in 1983, 1986, 1993, 1994, 1997, 1998, 2001, 2002, 2003, 2006, and 2009 are estimated by interpolation of numbers of abortions.

Sources: 1973–1988: Stanley K. Henshaw and Jennifer Van Vort, eds., *Abortion Factbook, 1992 Edition: Readings, Trends, and State and Local Data to 1988* (New York: Alan Guttmacher Institute, 1992), 174–175; total, 1991–2011: Rachel K. Jones and Jenna Jerman, "Abortion Incidence and Service Availability in the United States, 2011," *Perspectives on Sexual and Reproductive Health* 46, no. 1 (2014): 3–14 (*www.guttmacher.org*); total, 1972, and white and nonwhite, 1972, 1989–2007: Guttmacher Institute, unpublished data. Reprinted with the permission of the Guttmacher Institute.

Table 10-16 Crime Rates, 1960–2013

Year	Violent crime					Property crime				Total
	Murder	Rape	Robbery	Aggravated assault	Total	Burglary	Larceny theft	Vehicle theft	Total	
1960	5.1	9.6	60	86	161	509	1,035	183	1,727	1,888
1965	5.1	12.1	72	111	200	663	1,329	257	2,249	2,449
1970	7.9	18.7	172	165	364	1,085	2,079	457	3,621	3,985
1975	9.6	26.3	218	227	481	1,526	2,805	469	4,800	5,281
1980	10.2	36.8	251	299	597	1,684	3,167	502	5,353	5,950
1985	7.9	36.7	209	303	557	1,287	2,901	462	4,650	5,207
1990	9.4	41.1	256	423	730	1,232	3,185	656	5,073	5,803
1995	8.2	37.1	221	418	685	987	3,043	560	4,591	5,276
2000	5.5	32.0	145	324	507	729	2,477	412	3,618	4,125
2004	5.5	32.4	137	289	463	730	2,362	422	3,514	3,977
2005	5.6	31.8	141	291	469	727	2,288	417	3,432	3,901
2006	5.8	31.6	150	292	479	733	2,213	400	3,347	3,826
2007	5.7	30.6	148	287	472	726	2,185	365	3,276	3,748
2008	5.4	29.8	146	278	459	733	2,166	315	3,215	3,674
2009	5.0	29.1	133	265	432	718	2,065	259	3,041	3,473
2010	4.8	27.7	119	253	405	701	2,006	239	2,946	3,351
2011	4.7	27.0	114	242	387	701	1,974	230	2,905	3,292
2012	4.7	27.1	113	243	388	672	1,965	230	2,868	3,256
2013	4.5	25.2	109	229	368	610	1,899	221	2,731	3,099

Note: Figures are rates per 100,000 inhabitants. For definitions of crimes, see the sources. Data for additional years can be found in previous editions of *Vital Statistics on American Politics.*

Sources: 1960–1985: U.S. Bureau of the Census, *Statistical Abstract of the United States, 1976* (Washington, D.C.: Government Printing Office, 1976), 153; *1987,*155; 1990: U.S. Department of Justice, Federal Bureau of Investigation, "Uniform Crime Reports: Crime in the United States, 2009," table 1 (*www.fbi.gov*); 1995–2013: "2013."

Table 10-17 Death Penalty in the States: Number of Executions, 1930–2015, and Number on Death Row, 2014

State	Method of execution[a]	Number executed									Number awaiting execution[c]
		1930s	1940s	1950s	1960s	1970s	1980s	1990s	2000s	2010s[b]	
Alabama	electrocution or lethal injection	60	50	20	5	0	7	12	25	12	198
Alaska	none	0	0	0	0	0	0	0	0	0	0
Arizona	lethal injection	17	9	8	4	0	0	19	4	14	123
Arkansas	lethal injection	53	8	18	9	0	0	21	6	0	33
California	lethal injection or lethal gas	108	80	74	30	0	0	7	6	0	745
Colorado	lethal injection	25	13	3	6	0	0	1	0	0	3
Connecticut	none	5	10	5	1	0	0	0	1	0	12[d]
Delaware	lethal injection	8	4	0	0	0	0	10	4	2	18
District of Columbia	none	20	16	4	0	0	0	0	0	0	0
Florida	electrocution or lethal injection	44	65	49	12	1	20	23	24	22	404
Georgia	lethal injection	137	130	85	14	0	14	9	23	11	90
Hawaii	none	0	0	0	0	0	0	0	0	0	0
Idaho	lethal injection	0	0	3	0	0	0	1	0	2	11
Illinois	none	61	18	9	2	0	0	12	0	0	0
Indiana	lethal injection	31	7	2	1	0	2	5	13	0	14
Iowa	none	8	7	1	2	0	0	0	0	0	0
Kansas	lethal injection	0	5	5	5	0	0	0	0	0	10
Kentucky	lethal injection	52	34	16	1	0	0	2	1	0	35
Louisiana	lethal injection	58	47	27	1	0	18	7	2	1	85
Maine	none	0	0	0	0	0	0	0	0	0	0
Maryland	none	16	45	6	1	0	0	3	2	0	4[e]

State	Method										
Massachusetts	none	18	9	0	0	0	0	0	0	0	0
Michigan	none	0	0	0	0	0	0	0	0	0	0
Minnesota	none	0	0	0	0	0	0	0	0	0	0
Mississippi	lethal injection	48	60	36	10	0	4	0	6	11	49
Missouri	lethal injection or lethal gas	36	15	7	4	0	1	40	26	16	39
Montana	lethal injection	5	1	0	0	0	0	2	1	0	2
Nebraska	lethal injection	0	2	2	0	1	0	3	0	0	11
Nevada	lethal injection	8	0	9	2	0	3	4	4	0	78
New Hampshire	lethal injection	1	0	0	3	0	0	0	0	0	1
New Jersey	none	40	14	17	1	0	0	0	0	0	0
New Mexico	none	2	2	3	10	0	0	0	1	0	2[f]
New York	none	153	114	52	1	0	3	12	0	0	0
North Carolina	lethal injection	131	12	19	0	0	0	0	28	0	160
North Dakota	none	0	0	0	0	0	0	0	0	0	0
Ohio	lethal injection	82	1	32	7	0	0	1	32	20	144
Oklahoma	lethal injection	34	13	7	6	0	0	19	72	21	49
Oregon	lethal injection	2	12	4	1	0	0	2	0	0	36
Pennsylvania	lethal injection	82	6	31	3	0	0	3	0	0	188
Rhode Island	none	0	0	0	0	0	0	0	0	0	0
South Carolina	electrocution or lethal injection	67	61	26	8	0	2	22	18	1	47
South Dakota	lethal injection	0	1	0	0	0	0	0	1	2	3
Tennessee	lethal injection	47	37	8	1	0	0	0	6	0	75
Texas	lethal injection	120	74	74	29	1	33	166	248	77	276
Utah	lethal injection	2	4	6	1	1	2	3	0	1	9
Vermont	none	1	1	2	0	0	0	0	0	0	0
Virginia	electrocution or lethal injection	28	35	23	6	0	8	65	32	5	8

(Table continues)

Table 10-17 *(Continued)*

State	Method of execution[a]	Number executed									Number awaiting execution[c]
		1930s	1940s	1950s	1960s	1970s	1980s	1990s	2000s	2010s[b]	
Washington	lethal injection or hanging	23	16	6	2	0	0	3	1	1	9
West Virginia	none	20	11	9	0	0	0	0	0	0	0
Wisconsin	none	0	0	0	0	0	0	0	0	0	0
Wyoming	lethal injection	4	2	0	1	0	0	1	0	0	1
U.S. government	g	10	13	9	h	h	h	0	3	0	63
U.S. military	lethal injection	h	h	h	h	h	h	0	0	0	6
Total[i]		1,667	1,284	717	191	3	117	478	590	219	3,035

a In some states, method depends on when sentenced. For details, see sources.
b Through April 21, 2015.
c As of October 1, 2014. On March 1, 2005, the U.S. Supreme Court ruled that it is unconstitutional to execute anyone who committed a crime while under the age of eighteen. Seventy-two death row inmates had been sentenced as juveniles (under eighteen at time of crime) as of December 31, 2004.
d On April 25, 2012, Connecticut repealed the death penalty. However, twelve inmates remain on death row.
e In spring 2013, the death penalty in Maryland was repealed. The sentences of the four inmates on death row were commuted in January 2015. This figure reflects the number of inmates on death row as of October 1, 2014.
f In March 2009, New Mexico repealed the death penalty. However, the act was not retroactive, leaving two people on the state's death row.
g The method of execution depends on the state in which the crime was committed.
h One hundred and sixty executions have been carried out under military authority since 1930.
i The national total counts inmates receiving multiple death sentences once. However, they are included in the state total for each state in which they were sentenced to death. Hence, the sum of the state totals will not necessarily equal the national total.

Sources: Number executed in 1930s–1970s: U.S. Department of Justice, Bureau of Justice Statistics, *Sourcebook of Criminal Justice Statistics—1989* (Washington, D.C.: Government Printing Office, 1990), 631; method; number executed in 1980s–2010s, number awaiting execution: Death Penalty Information Center (*www.deathpenaltyinfo.org*).

Table 10-18   Sentenced Federal and State Prisoners, 1925–2013

Year	Number of prisoners	Rate (per 100,000 population)[a]	Year	Number of prisoners	Rate (per 100,000 population)[a]
1925	91,669	79	1996	1,137,722	427
1930	129,453	104	1997	1,194,581	444
1935	144,180	113	1998	1,245,402	461
1940	173,706	131	1999	1,304,074	463
1945	133,649	98	2000	1,334,174	478
1950	166,123	109	2001	1,345,217	470
1955	185,780	112	2002	1,380,516	476
1960	212,953	117	2003	1,408,361	482
1965	210,895	108	2004	1,433,728	486
1970	196,429	96	2005	1,462,866	491
1975	240,593	111	2006	1,504,598	501
1980	315,974	139	2007	1,532,851	506
1985	480,568	202	2008	1,547,742	504
1990	739,980	297	2009	1,553,574	504
1991	789,610	313	2010	1,552,669	500
1992	846,277	332	2011	1,538,847	492
1993	932,074	359	2012	1,538,847	480
1994	1,016,691	389	2013	1,516,879	478
1995	1,085,022	411			

Note: Definition of prisoners has varied somewhat over the years. See source for details. Data for additional years can be found in earlier editions of *Vital Statistics on American Politics*.

[a] Prisoners with sentences of more than one year.

Source: 1925–2010: U.S. Department of Justice, Bureau of Justice Statistics, *Sourcebook of Criminal Justice Statistics*, Kathleen Maguire, ed., University at Albany, Hindelang Criminal Justice Research Center, Table 6.28.2011 (*www.albany.edu/sourcebook*); 2011–2013: U.S. Department of Justice, Bureau of Justice Statistics, "Prisoners in 2013," revised September 30, 2014, tables 1, 6 (*www.bjs.gov*).

Table 10-19   Estimated Number of Persons Supervised by Adult Correctional Systems, by Correctional Status, 2000, 2005, and 2010–2013 (thousands)

Year	Total correctional population[a]	Community Supervision			Incarcerated[b]		
		Total[a,c]	Probation	Parole	Total[a]	Local jail	Prison
2000	6,468	4,565	3,840	726	1,945	621	1,394
2005	7,056	4,947	4,163	784	2,200	748	1,526
2010	7,089	4,888	4,056	841	2,279	749	1,614
2011	6,990	4,814	3,971	854	2,253	736	1,599
2012	6,941	4,781	3,942	851	2,231	745	1,570
2013	6,899	4,751	3,911	853	2,220	731	1,575
Average annual percent change, 2000–2012	0.6	0.4	0.2	1.3	1.1	1.5	1.0
Percent change, 2012–2013	−0.6	−0.6	−0.8	0.2	−0.5	−1.8	0.3

Note: Estimates were rounded to the nearest 100 and may not be comparable to previously published BJS reports due to updated information or rounding. Counts include estimates for nonresponding jurisdictions. All probation, parole, and prision counts are for December 31; jail counts are for the last weekday in June. Detail may not sum to total due to rounding and adjustments made to account for offenders with multiple correctional statuses. Current data on the cost of incarcerating prisoners is not available. In fiscal 2010 it was estimated that the average annual cost per inmate varied from $14,603 (Kentucky) to $60,076 (New York), with an average cost per state of $31,979. In fiscal 2011 the average cost of incarceration for federal inmates was $28,893.

[a] Total was adjusted to account for offenders with multiple correctional statuses.
[b] Includes inmates held in local jails or under the jurisdiction of state or federal prisons.
[c] Includes some offenders held in a prison or jail but who remained under the jursdiction of a probation or parole agency.

Sources: Number of persons supervised: "Correctional Populations in the United States, 2013" (*www.bjs.gov*); Cost of incarceration: Christian Henrichson and Ruth Delaney, *The Price of Prisons: What Incarceration Costs Taxpayers* (New York: Vera Institute of Justice, 2012) (*www .vera.org*); "Annual Determination of Average Cost of Incarceration," *Federal Register*, March 18, 2013, 16711.

11
Economic Policy

- **Gross Domestic Product (GDP)**
- **Consumer Price Index (CPI)**
- **Federal Budget**
- **National Debt**
- **Tax Breaks**
- **Income Inequality**
- **Labor Unions**
- **Minimum Wages**
- **Unemployment**

Economic policy makers labor under the burden of an overabundance of numbers. Statistics recording various aspects of the economy's performance appear regularly—often monthly. These statistics are important, not simply because of the conditions they report, but also because of the way in which they filter into economic calculations: expectations about and reactions to indicators of past performance are critical determinants of how the economy performs in the future. Moreover, there is a direct link to politics, because the public's perceptions of economic performance help to shape choices in the voting booth. Properly or not, presidents often are blamed when the economy turns down and (less often) are praised when it recovers. President Ronald Reagan's public approval ratings plummeted as an economic downturn continued through 1982, as did President George H. W. Bush's ratings during the run-up to the 1992 election as his opponent Bill Clinton stressed economic problems (see Figure 3-5 in *Vital Statistics on American Politics 2007–2008* and Figure 3-14 in this volume). Subsequent economic recoveries played a substantial role in shaping the mood of the voters to secure Reagan's 1984 reelection in a landslide and President Clinton's reelection in 1996, though good times were not enough to propel Al Gore into office in 2000 nor to keep

President George W. Bush's ratings high in the face of growing criticism of the Iraq War (Figures 3-6, 3-14, and 3-20).

In even simple economic matters, fundamental issues and terms arise that distinguish the discourse from that in other areas of politics. One is the overall size of the economy, usually measured by the gross domestic product, or GDP (Table 11-1). Knowing what the GDP is and what it means is important even to a minimal understanding of economic statistics and policy. Without some sense of the size of the economy, one cannot make informed judgments about economic matters. For example, a trillion-dollar national debt is unquestionably large, but many argue that it needs to be assessed in terms of its relationship to the size of the total economy (Figure 11-2). Another case in point is the relative size of federal outlays, which almost always increase in total dollars (Table 11-3) but often not as a percentage of GDP (Figure 11-1).

A second key concept is that of constant dollars, which is explained in the introduction to Chapter 9 in connection with defense spending. Of importance here, the basis for many constant dollar calculations is the Consumer Price Index, or CPI (Table 11-2). This index reveals that a market basket of goods that cost $100 in 1982–1984 would have cost $29.60 in 1960. Unfortunately, although 1982–1984 is the base period in Table 11-2, other tabulations, such as those in Table 11-1, use a different base, making it more difficult to compare the data. However, the concept of a constant dollar is unchanged by which year is used as the base. (The identical CPI value is not always used as the basis for such adjustments, and here it is not possible to move precisely from the figures in Table 11-2 to those in Table 11-1. The matter of which CPI value to use has been in the news recently with discussion of whether the so-called chained CPI should be used in calculating increases on Social Security benefits.)

During the Reagan and George H. W. Bush presidencies, as well as during the first Clinton administration, the economic news was dominated by the annual deficit and the accumulating national debt. It was also part of the many economic discussions in the Obama administration. By 2001 the annual deficit had been eliminated, and the accumulated debt (as a percentage of GDP) had decreased (Figure 11-2), but that happy situation turned around quickly in 2002 and beyond. By 2005, taxes had been cut again at the federal level. The growth in the federal debt (Table 11-6) helps focus public attention on government spending and taxing as politicians and economists alike try to assess ways of reducing the gap between income and expenditures. Economic growth in the late 1990s and into the new century provided the basis for greater tax revenues to balance the budget and reduce the deficit as well as to justify a massive tax cut under President George W. Bush. But the economic downturn in 2008 and 2009, as well as long-term concerns such as the growth of Social Security and health care expenditures as the population ages, place constraints on future government spending and on the size of any tax cuts or increases. If taxes must be raised in the future, one means of doing so is through ending selective tax breaks (Table 11-7), some of which were curtailed in previous tax reforms.

Cutting government spending is another means of reducing the deficit. Alternatively, cutting spending may allow the government to cut taxes without increasing the nation's debt. Although federal budget outlays (Tables 11-3 and 11-4) may give the impression of vast sums and a variety of programs suitable for cuts, Table 11-5 reveals that mandatory programs now account for about 70 percent of federal budget outlays. An increasing proportion of the federal budget has become relatively uncontrollable from the president's standpoint. Reducing spending in the mandatory category would require that Congress rewrite laws affecting payments to which beneficiaries are entitled on the basis of past commitments. Programs that fall under this heading, such as Social Security, are known as entitlement programs.

Labor union membership, the minimum wage, unemployment, and inflation are four other noteworthy features of the economic landscape that merit inclusion when considering politics. Testament to critical economic trends with political ramifications are the long slide in the percentage of the workforce belonging to unions (Table 11-8), the effects of inflation on the minimum wage (Figure 11-4), the large-scale entry of women into the labor force since World War II (Table 11-9), the fluctuations in the annual unemployment rate since 1929 (Table 11-10), and the relatively high unemployment rates among black teenagers (Table 11-11).

Especially newsworthy in recent years has been the increasing gap between the wealthy and those less well-off. This is represented here with a figure showing changes in the mean income over the past half century of individuals at differing wealth levels (Figure 11-3).

Because economic issues are an important aspect of political policy making and because economic conditions affect voter choices, economic data rank among the most vital of vital statistics on American politics.

Table 11-1   Gross Domestic Product, 1929–2014 (billions)

Year	Current dollars	Annual percentage change	Chained (2009) dollars	Annual percentage change
1929	$104.6			
1930	92.2	−11.9	$966.7	−8.5
1935	74.3	11.1	939.0	8.9
1940	102.9	10.1	1,266.1	8.8
1941	129.4	25.7	1,490.3	17.7
1942	166.0	28.3	1,771.8	18.9
1943	203.1	22.4	2,073.7	17.0
1944	224.6	10.5	2,239.4	8.0
1945	228.2	1.6	2,217.8	−1.0
1946	227.8	−0.2	1,960.9	−11.6
1947	249.9	9.7	1,939.4	−1.1
1948	274.8	9.9	2,020.0	4.1
1949	272.8	−0.7	2,008.9	−0.5
1950	300.2	10.0	2,184.0	8.7
1951	347.3	15.7	2,360.0	8.1
1952	367.7	5.9	2,456.1	4.1
1953	389.7	6.0	2,571.4	4.7
1954	391.1	0.4	2,556.9	−0.6
1955	426.2	9.0	2,739.0	7.1
1956	450.1	5.6	2,797.4	2.1
1957	474.9	5.5	2,856.3	2.1
1958	482.0	1.5	2,835.3	−0.7
1959	522.5	8.4	3,031.0	6.9
1960	543.3	4.0	3,108.7	2.6
1961	563.3	3.7	3,188.1	2.6
1962	605.1	7.4	3,383.1	6.1
1963	638.6	5.5	3,530.4	4.4
1964	685.8	7.4	3,734.0	5.8
1965	743.7	8.4	3,976.7	6.5
1966	815.0	9.6	4,238.9	6.6
1967	861.7	5.7	4,355.2	2.7
1968	942.5	9.4	4,569.0	4.9
1969	1,019.9	8.2	4,712.5	3.1
1970	1,075.9	5.5	4,722.0	0.2
1971	1,167.8	8.5	4,877.6	3.3
1972	1,282.4	9.8	5,134.3	5.2
1973	1,428.5	11.4	5,424.1	5.6
1974	1,548.8	8.4	5,396.0	−0.5
1975	1,688.9	9.0	5,385.4	−0.2
1976	1,877.6	11.2	5,675.4	5.4
1977	2,086.0	11.1	5,937.0	4.6
1978	2,356.6	13.0	6,267.2	5.6
1979	2,632.1	11.7	6,466.2	3.2
1980	2,862.5	8.8	6,450.4	−0.2
1981	3,211.0	12.2	6,617.7	2.6

Table 11-1   *(Continued)*

Year	Current dollars	Annual percentage change	Chained (2009) dollars	Annual percentage change
1982	3,345.0	4.2	6,491.3	−1.9
1983	3,638.1	8.8	6,792.0	4.6
1984	4,040.7	11.1	7,285.0	7.3
1985	4,346.7	7.6	7,593.8	4.2
1986	4,590.2	5.6	7,860.5	3.5
1987	4,870.2	6.1	8,132.6	3.5
1988	5,252.6	7.9	8,474.5	4.2
1989	5,657.7	7.7	8,786.4	3.7
1990	5,979.6	5.7	8,955.0	1.9
1991	6,174.0	3.3	8,948.4	−0.1
1992	6,539.3	5.9	9,266.6	3.6
1993	6,878.7	5.2	9,521.0	2.7
1994	7,308.8	6.3	9,905.4	4.0
1995	7,664.1	4.9	10,174.8	2.7
1996	8,100.2	5.7	10,561.0	3.8
1997	8,608.5	6.3	11,034.9	4.5
1998	9,089.2	5.6	11,525.9	4.5
1999	9,660.6	6.3	12,065.9	4.7
2000	10,284.8	6.5	12,559.7	4.1
2001	10,621.8	3.3	12,682.2	1.0
2002	10,977.5	3.3	12,908.8	1.8
2003	11,510.7	4.9	13,271.1	2.8
2004	12,274.9	6.6	13,773.5	3.8
2005	13,093.7	6.7	14,234.2	3.3
2006	13,855.9	5.8	14,613.8	2.7
2007	14,477.6	4.5	14,873.7	1.8
2008	14,718.6	1.7	14,830.4	−0.3
2009	14,418.7	−2.0	14,418.7	−2.8
2010	14,964.4	3.8	14,783.8	2.5
2011	15,517.9	3.7	15,020.6	1.6
2012	16,163.2	4.2	15,369.2	2.3
2013	16,768.1	3.7	15,710.3	2.2
2014	17,418.3	3.9	16,085.3	2.4

Note: Data for additional years can be found in previous editions of *Vital Statistics on American Politics*.

Source: U.S. Department of Commerce, Bureau of Economic Analysis, "Gross Domestic Product," as of February 27, 2015 (*www.bea.gov*).

Table 11-2 Consumer Price Index, 1950–2014

Year	All items	Food	Shelter	Household energy services	Apparel and upkeep	Transportation Private[a]	Transportation Public	Medical care	All commodities	All services
1950	24.1	25.4	—	19.2	40.3	24.5	13.4	15.1	29.0	16.9
1955	26.8	27.8	22.7	20.7	42.9	26.7	18.5	18.2	31.3	20.4
1960	29.6	30.0	25.2	23.3	45.7	30.6	22.2	22.3	33.6	24.1
1965	31.5	32.2	27.0	23.5	47.8	32.5	25.2	25.2	35.2	26.6
1970	38.8	39.2	35.5	25.4	59.2	37.5	35.2	34.0	41.7	35.0
1975	53.8	59.8	48.8	40.1	72.5	50.6	43.5	47.5	58.2	48.0
1976	56.9	61.6	51.5	44.7	75.2	55.6	47.8	52.0	60.7	52.0
1977	60.6	65.5	54.9	50.5	78.6	59.7	50.0	57.0	64.2	56.0
1978	65.2	72.0	60.5	55.0	81.4	62.5	51.5	61.8	68.8	60.8
1979	72.6	79.9	68.9	61.0	84.9	71.7	54.9	67.5	76.6	67.5
1980	82.4	86.8	81.0	71.4	90.9	84.2	69.0	74.9	86.0	77.9
1981	90.9	93.6	90.5	81.9	95.3	93.8	85.6	82.9	93.2	88.1
1982	96.5	97.4	96.9	93.2	97.8	97.1	94.9	92.5	97.0	96.0
1983	99.6	99.4	99.1	101.5	100.2	99.3	99.5	100.6	99.8	99.4
1984	103.9	103.2	104.0	105.4	102.1	103.6	105.7	106.8	103.2	104.6
1985	107.6	105.6	109.8	107.1	105.0	106.2	110.5	113.5	105.4	109.9
1986	109.6	109.0	115.8	105.7	105.9	101.2	117.0	122.0	104.4	115.4
1987	113.6	113.5	121.3	103.8	110.6	104.2	121.1	130.1	107.7	120.2
1988	118.3	118.2	127.1	104.6	115.4	107.6	123.3	138.6	111.5	125.7
1989	124.0	125.1	132.8	107.5	118.6	112.9	129.5	149.3	116.7	131.9
1990	130.7	132.4	140.0	109.3	124.1	118.8	142.6	162.8	122.8	139.2
1991	136.2	136.3	146.3	112.6	128.7	121.9	148.9	177.0	126.6	146.3
1992	140.3	137.9	151.2	114.8	131.9	124.6	151.4	190.1	129.1	152.0
1993	144.5	140.9	155.7	118.5	133.7	127.5	167.0	201.4	131.5	157.9
1994	148.2	144.3	160.5	119.2	133.4	131.4	172.0	211.0	133.8	163.1

1995	152.4	148.4	165.7	119.2	132.0	136.3	175.9	220.5	136.4	168.7
1996	156.9	153.3	171.0	122.1	131.7	140.0	181.9	228.2	139.9	174.1
1997	160.5	157.3	176.3	125.1	132.9	141.0	186.7	234.6	141.8	179.4
1998	163.0	160.7	182.1	121.2	133.0	137.9	190.3	242.1	141.9	184.2
1999	166.6	164.1	187.3	120.9	131.3	140.5	197.7	250.6	144.4	188.8
2000	172.2	167.8	193.4	128.0	129.6	149.1	209.6	260.8	149.2	195.3
2001	177.1	173.1	200.6	142.4	127.3	150.0	210.6	272.8	150.7	203.4
2002	179.9	176.2	208.1	134.4	124.0	148.8	207.4	285.6	149.7	209.8
2003	184.0	180.0	213.1	145.0	120.9	153.6	209.3	297.1	151.2	216.5
2004	188.9	186.2	218.8	150.6	120.4	159.4	209.1	310.1	154.7	222.8
2005	195.3	190.7	224.4	166.5	119.5	170.2	217.3	323.2	160.2	230.1
2006	201.6	195.2	232.1	182.1	119.5	177.0	226.6	336.2	164.0	238.9
2007	207.3	202.9	240.6	186.3	119.0	180.8	230.0	351.1	167.5	246.8
2008	215.3	214.1	246.7	202.2	118.9	191.0	250.5	364.1	174.8	255.5
2009	214.5	218.0	249.4	193.6	120.1	174.8	236.3	375.6	169.7	259.2
2010	218.1	219.6	248.4	192.9	119.5	188.7	251.4	388.4	174.6	261.3
2011	224.9	227.8	251.6	194.4	122.1	207.6	269.4	400.3	183.9	265.8
2012	229.6	233.8	257.1	189.7	126.3	212.8	271.4	414.9	187.6	271.4
2013	233.0	237.0	263.1	194.8	127.4	212.4	278.9	425.1	187.7	277.9
2014	236.7	242.7	270.5	203.4	127.5	211.0	276.4	435.3	187.9	285.1

Note: "—" indicates not available. Data for 1982 through 1984 equal 100. Data beginning in 1978 are for all urban consumers; earlier data are for urban wage earners and clerical workers. Data beginning in 1983 incorporate a rental equivalence measure for homeowners' costs and therefore are not strictly comparable with earlier figures. Data for additional years can be found in previous editions of *Vital Statistics on American Politics.*

[a] Includes direct pricing of new trucks and motorcycles beginning with September 1982.

Sources: 1950–1955: *Economic Report of the President* (Washington, D.C.: Government Printing Office, 1995), tables B-59, B-60, B-61; 1960–1961: (2011), tables B-60, B-61, B-62; 1970–2012: (2013), tables B-60, B-61, B-62; 2013–2014: Table 1A. Consumer Price Index for All Urban Consumers (2015) (*www.bls.gov*).

Table 11-3   Federal Budget: Total, Defense, and Nondefense Expenditures, 1940–2020 (billions)

Year	Current dollars			Constant (2009) dollars		
	National defense	Non-defense	Total	National defense	Non-defense	Total
1940	$1.7	$7.8	$9.5	$25.5	$110.4	$135.8
1945	83.0	9.7	92.7	993.6	117.3	1,110.3
1950	13.7	28.8	42.6	167.8	255.9	423.5
1951	23.6	21.9	45.5	272.1	179.0	451.1
1952	46.1	21.6	67.7	511.5	161.3	672.8
1953	52.8	23.3	76.1	531.7	172.7	704.6
1954	49.3	21.6	70.9	488.3	148.8	636.6
1955	42.7	25.7	68.4	409.7	185.0	594.6
1956	42.5	28.1	70.6	384.8	202.7	587.7
1957	45.4	31.1	76.6	391.3	216.0	607.3
1958	46.8	35.6	82.4	385.0	232.0	616.8
1959	49.0	43.1	92.1	377.6	284.6	662.1
1960	48.1	44.1	92.2	374.3	278.9	653.4
1961	49.6	48.1	97.7	378.9	298.3	677.2
1962	52.3	54.5	106.8	399.0	339.8	738.7
1963	53.4	57.9	111.3	390.1	348.7	738.7
1964	54.8	63.8	118.5	394.5	379.6	774.2
1965	50.6	67.6	118.2	365.2	395.8	761.3
1966	58.1	76.4	134.5	400.5	442.3	842.9
1967	71.4	86.0	157.5	476.7	487.8	964.9
1968	81.9	96.2	178.1	522.5	530.4	1,052.8
1969	82.5	101.1	183.6	497.9	523.2	1,021.4
1970	81.7	114.0	195.6	469.0	561.1	1,030.3
1971	78.9	131.3	210.2	425.6	609.0	1,034.8
1972	79.2	151.5	230.7	389.8	675.5	1,065.0
1973	76.7	169.0	245.7	352.4	731.7	1,083.8
1974	79.3	190.0	269.4	341.3	755.8	1,097.2
1975	86.5	245.8	332.3	341.5	891.0	1,232.7
1976	89.6	282.2	371.8	332.4	954.3	1,286.5
TQ[a]	22.3	73.7	96.0	81.0	243.0	324.0
1977	97.2	312.0	409.2	334.6	985.7	1,320.5
1978	104.5	354.3	458.7	336.9	1,055.9	1,392.7
1979	116.3	387.7	504.0	346.8	1,061.9	1,408.7
1980	134.0	456.9	590.9	361.3	1,133.6	1,494.9
1981	157.5	520.7	678.2	381.1	1,162.9	1,543.9
1982	185.3	560.4	745.7	412.6	1,166.6	1,579.3
1983	209.9	598.5	808.4	444.6	1,185.8	1,630.4
1984	227.4	624.4	851.8	460.0	1,182.6	1,642.8
1985	252.7	693.6	946.3	492.9	1,268.5	1,761.3
1986	273.4	717.0	990.4	521.5	1,283.4	1,805.0
1987	282.0	722.0	1,004.0	529.6	1,249.4	1,778.9
1988	290.4	774.1	1,064.4	532.3	1,291.8	1,824.2
1989	303.6	840.2	1,143.7	537.5	1,350.1	1,887.7

Table 11-3   *(Continued)*

Year	Current dollars			Constant (2009) dollars		
	National defense	Non-defense	Total	National defense	Non-defense	Total
1990	299.3	953.7	1,253.0	512.2	1,496.7	2,008.6
1991	273.3	1,050.9	1,324.2	443.7	1,585.1	2,028.8
1992	298.3	1,083.2	1,381.5	478.8	1,561.2	2,040.1
1993	291.1	1,118.3	1,409.4	461.9	1,559.3	2,021.2
1994	281.6	1,180.1	1,461.8	442.4	1,616.4	2,058.8
1995	272.1	1,243.7	1,515.7	418.7	1,655.6	2,074.4
1996	265.7	1,294.7	1,560.5	400.2	1,691.6	2,091.8
1997	270.5	1,330.6	1,601.1	401.3	1,702.0	2,103.4
1998	268.2	1,384.3	1,652.5	390.6	1,760.9	2,151.4
1999	274.8	1,427.1	1,701.8	391.7	1,796.4	2,188.0
2000	294.4	1,494.6	1,789.0	406.9	1,837.5	2,244.3
2001	304.7	1,558.1	1,862.8	406.6	1,869.6	2,276.2
2002	348.5	1,662.4	2,010.9	449.0	1,967.8	2,416.9
2003	404.7	1,755.2	2,159.9	491.2	2,033.3	2,524.7
2004	455.8	1,837.0	2,292.8	533.0	2,078.6	2,611.7
2005	495.3	1,976.7	2,472.0	552.6	2,169.1	2,721.5
2006	521.8	2,133.2	2,655.1	558.1	2,267.5	2,825.7
2007	551.3	2,177.4	2,728.7	571.4	2,258.0	2,829.4
2008	616.1	2,366.5	2,982.5	614.9	2,373.4	2,988.2
2009	661.0	2,856.7	3,517.7	661.0	2,856.7	3,517.7
2010	693.5	2,763.6	3,457.1	691.3	2,725.2	3,416.4
2011	705.6	2,897.5	3,603.1	692.6	2,799.3	3,492.0
2012	677.9	2,859.1	3,537.0	659.0	2,705.7	3,364.7
2013	633.4	2,821.2	3,454.6	612.0	2,629.3	3,241.1
2014	603.5	2,902.6	3,506.1	574.2	2,664.7	3,238.9
2015 est.	597.5	3,161.1	3,758.6	560.9	2,865.4	3,426.2
2016 est.	615.5	3,384.0	3,999.5	568.8	3,010.6	3,579.3
2017 est.	603.9	3,613.9	4,217.8	548.2	3,150.5	3,698.5
2018 est.	592.0	3,831.3	4,423.3	527.2	3,268.8	3,795.8
2019 est.	590.4	4,062.2	4,652.6	515.5	3,387.4	3,902.9
2020 est.	598.0	4,288.4	4,886.4	511.8	3,497.0	4,008.8

Note: Data for additional years can be found in previous editions of *Vital Statistics on American Politics*.

[a] Transitional quarter when fiscal year start was shifted from July 1 to October 1.

Source: U.S. Office of Management and Budget, *Budget of the United States Government, Fiscal Year 2016, Historical Tables* (Washington, D.C.: Government Printing Office, 2015), Table 6.1.

Table 11-4 Federal Budget Outlays, by Function, 2000–2020 (billions)

Function	2000	2005	2010	2014	2015 est.	2016 est.	2018 est.	2020 est.
National defense	$294.4	$495.3	$693.5	$603.5	$597.5	$615.5	$592.0	$598.0
Human resources	1,115.5	1,586.0	2,386.6	2,525.5	2,734.6	2,884.8	3,088.2	3,450.7
Education, training, employment, and social services	53.8	97.6	128.6	90.6	136.8	106.3	125.6	139.4
Health	154.5	250.5	369.1	409.4	481.2	517.7	582.7	641.3
Medicare[a]	197.1	298.6	451.6	511.7	536.4	589.7	592.3	696.8
Income security	253.7	345.8	622.2	513.6	522.5	546.4	552.6	584.0
Social Security[a]	409.4	523.3	706.7	850.5	896.3	944.3	1,056.7	1,187.7
Veterans' benefits and services	47.0	70.1	108.4	149.6	161.4	180.3	178.3	201.5
Physical resources	84.9	130.1	88.8	59.2	143.1	148.5	155.5	163.5
Energy	−0.8	0.4	11.6	5.3	9.9	6.2	3.6	6.0
Natural resources and environment	25.0	28.0	43.7	36.2	41.7	44.3	46.4	45.4
Commerce and housing credit[a]	3.2	7.6	−82.3	−94.9	−28.6	−22.6	−22.3	−12.1
Transportation	46.9	67.9	92.0	91.9	92.9	98.7	107.2	109.8
Community and regional development	10.6	26.3	23.9	20.7	27.2	21.8	20.7	14.4
Net interest[a]	222.9	184.0	196.2	229.0	229.2	283.0	424.2	543.8
Other functions[b]	113.8	141.7	174.0	177.0	190.0	170.6	263.1	234.1
International affairs	17.2	34.6	45.2	46.7	55.0	56.0	52.4	51.8
General science, space, and technology	18.6	23.6	30.1	28.6	29.8	31.0	32.0	32.6
Agriculture	36.5	26.6	21.4	24.4	21.8	22.3	24.6	18.7
Administration of justice	28.5	40.0	54.4	50.5	58.7	58.5	61.2	64.3
General government	13.0	17.0	23.0	26.9	22.8	27.0	25.6	27.9
Undistributed offsetting receipts[a]	−42.6	−65.2	−82.1	−88.0	−135.8	−103.0	−99.8	−103.6
Total outlays[a]	1,789.0	2,472.0	3,457.1	3,506.1	3,758.6	3,999.5	4,423.3	4,886.4

Note: Amounts in current dollars. Fiscal year ending September 30. Due to rounding, numbers for individual categories may not sum to the subtotals and totals. Data for additional years can be found in previous editions of *Vital Statistics on American Politics*.

[a] Includes both on- and off-budget amounts.
[b] Includes other outlays not shown separately.

Source: U.S. Office of Management and Budget, *Budget of the United States Government, Fiscal Year 2016, Historical Tables* (Washington, D.C.: Government Printing Office, 2015), Table 3.1.

Figure 11-1   Federal Outlays as a Percentage of GNP/GDP, 1869–2020

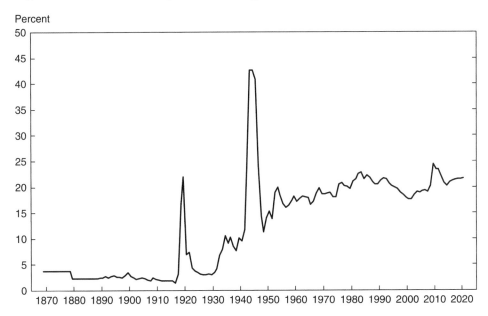

Note: Averaged by decade for 1869 through 1888. Percentage of gross national product (GNP) is shown through 1929, percentage of gross domestic product (GDP) thereafter. Figures for 2015 through 2020 are estimates.

Sources: 1869–1929: U.S. Bureau of the Census, *Historical Statistics of the United States* (Washington, D.C.: Government Printing Office, 1975), 224, 1,114; 1930–2020: U.S. Office of Management and Budget, *Budget of the United States Government, Fiscal Year 2016, Historical Tables* (Washington, D.C.: Government Printing Office, 2015), Table 1.2.

Table 11-5 Mandatory and Discretionary Federal Budget Outlays, 1975–2020 (billions)

Outlay	1975	1980	1985	1990	1995	2000	2005	2010	2015 est.	2019 est.	2020 est.
Mandatory and related program outlays, total[a]	$174.4	$314.6	$530.6	$752.4	$971.0	$1,174.3	$1,503.4	$2,109.9	$2,610.6	$3,471.3	$3,694.5
Health	7.1	14.7	23.9	42.8	93.4	124.6	200.1	303.7	421.4	559.9	580.1
Income security	46.7	75.8	109.8	125.2	184.6	212.3	291.6	552.6	455.2	501.9	511.1
Medicare	12.2	31.0	64.1	95.8	156.9	194.1	294.3	446.5	530.0	644.9	689.5
Social Security	63.6	117.1	186.4	246.5	333.3	406.0	518.7	700.8	890.8	1,114.8	1,182.1
Veterans' benefits and services	12.5	14.0	15.9	16.0	20.4	26.2	39.6	57.5	96.7	116.4	123.1
Undistributed offsetting receipts[b]	–13.6	–19.9	–32.7	–36.6	–36.8	–42.4	–65.1	–81.9	–90.3	–99.7	–102.4
Net interest[b]	23.2	52.5	129.5	184.3	232.1	222.9	184.0	196.2	229.2	483.5	543.8
Discretionary program outlays, total[a]	158.0	276.3	415.8	500.6	544.8	614.6	968.5	1,347.2	1,146.1	1,172.5	1,182.5
Domestic, total[a]	62.2	128.9	145.3	181.4	251.1	298.4	435.9	612.7	502.4	539.4	542.6
Education, training, employment, and social services	13.1	25.8	21.8	27.9	38.9	49.0	79.1	134.3	93.2	101.6	102.4
General science, space, and technology	4.0	5.8	8.6	14.4	16.7	18.6	23.6	30.0	29.7	32.3	32.5
Health	5.8	8.5	9.6	14.9	22.0	29.9	50.5	65.4	59.8	60.5	61.2
Income security	3.5	10.8	19.2	23.7	39.2	41.4	54.2	69.6	67.3	72.3	72.9
Natural resources and environment	8.1	15.5	15.1	17.8	21.9	24.9	30.4	42.5	38.1	39.4	39.7
Transportation	5.9	20.7	24.8	27.9	37.0	44.8	66.1	89.9	33.5	32.3	32.3
International affairs	8.2	12.8	17.4	19.1	20.1	21.2	39.0	45.6	55.2	52.2	51.4
National defense	87.6	134.6	253.1	300.1	273.6	295.0	493.6	688.9	588.6	580.9	588.5
Total outlays[c]	332.3	590.9	946.3	1,253.0	1,515.7	1,789.0	2,472.0	3,457.1	3,758.6	4,652.6	4,886.4
Mandatory program outlays as a percentage of total outlays	52.5	53.2	56.1	60.0	64.1	65.6	60.8	61.0	69.5	74.6	75.6

Note: Amounts are in current dollars. Due to rounding, numbers for individual categories may not sum to the subtotals and totals. Data for additional years can be found in previous editions of *Vital Statistics on American Politics.*

[a] Includes other outlays not shown separately.

[b] Includes both on- and off-budget amounts.

[c] Beginning in 2011, total outlays includes an allowance for future costs that is not displayed in the table by category.

Source: U.S. Office of Management and Budget, *Budget of the United States Government, Fiscal Year 2016, Historical Tables* (Washington, D.C.: Government Printing Office, 2015), Tables 8.1, 8.5, and 8.7.

Table 11-6   The National Debt, 1940–2020

Year	Debt held by the public (millions)	As a percentage of GDP	Year	Debt held by the public (millions)	As a percentage of GDP
1940	$42,772	43.6	1984	$1,306,975	33.1
1945	235,182	103.9	1985	1,507,260	35.3
1950	219,023	78.5	1986	1,740,623	38.4
1951	214,326	65.5	1987	1,889,753	39.5
1952	214,758	60.1	1988	2,051,616	39.8
1953	218,383	57.1	1989	2,190,716	39.3
1954	224,499	57.9	1990	2,411,558	40.8
1955	226,616	55.7	1991	2,688,999	44.0
1956	222,156	50.6	1992	2,999,737	46.6
1957	219,320	47.2	1993	3,248,396	47.8
1958	226,336	47.7	1994	3,433,065	47.7
1959	234,701	46.4	1995	3,604,378	47.5
1960	236,840	44.3	1996	3,734,073	46.8
1961	238,357	43.5	1997	3,772,344	44.5
1962	248,010	42.3	1998	3,721,099	41.6
1963	253,978	41.0	1999	3,632,363	38.2
1964	256,849	38.7	2000	3,409,804	33.6
1965	260,778	36.7	2001	3,319,615	31.4
1966	263,714	33.7	2002	3,540,427	32.5
1967	266,626	31.8	2003	3,913,443	34.5
1968	289,545	32.2	2004	4,295,544	35.5
1969	278,108	28.3	2005	4,592,212	35.6
1970	283,198	27.0	2006	4,828,972	35.3
1971	303,037	27.1	2007	5,035,129	35.2
1972	322,377	26.4	2008	5,803,050	39.3
1973	340,910	25.1	2009	7,544,707	52.3
1974	343,699	23.1	2010	9,018,882	60.9
1975	394,700	24.5	2011	10,128,187	65.9
1976	477,404	26.7	2012	11,281,131	70.4
TQ[a]	495,509	26.2	2013	11,982,713	72.3
1977	549,104	27.1	2014	12,779,877	74.1
1978	607,126	26.6	2015 est.	13,506,331	75.1
1979	640,306	24.9	2016 est.	14,108,492	75.0
1980	711,923	25.5	2017 est.	14,704,912	74.6
1981	789,410	25.2	2018 est.	15,314,954	74.3
1982	924,575	27.9	2019 est.	15,959,174	74.1
1983	1,137,268	32.1	2020 est.	16,634,696	74.0

Note: Amounts in current dollars. "GDP" indicates gross domestic product. Data for additional years can be found in previous editions of *Vital Statistics on American Politics*.

[a] Transitional quarter when fiscal year start was shifted from July 1 to October 1.

Source: U.S. Office of Management and Budget, *Budget of the United States Government, Fiscal Year 2016, Historical Tables* (Washington, D.C.: Government Printing Office, 2015), Table 7.1.

Figure 11-2   National Debt as a Percentage of GDP, 1940–2020

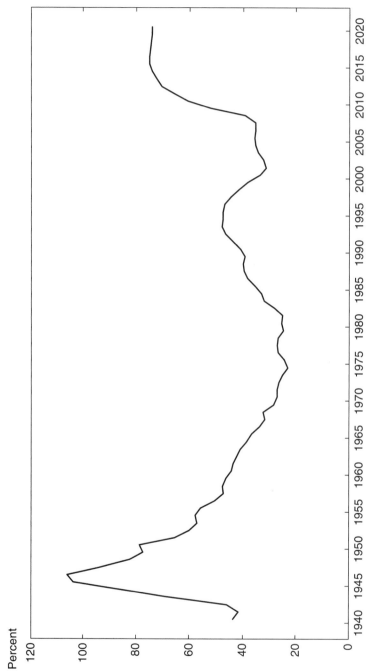

Note: Figures reflect debt held by the public and do not include debt held by federal government accounts. Percentages for 2015 through 2020 are estimates.

Source: U.S. Office of Management and Budget, *Budget of the United States Government, Fiscal Year 2016, Historical Tables* (Washington, D.C.: Government Printing Office, 2015), Table 7.1.

Table 11-7 Cost of Selected Tax Breaks: Revenue Loss Estimates for Selected Tax Expenditures, 2005–2024 (millions)

Type of tax expenditure	2005	2010	2015	2016	2018	2020	2022	2024
Commerce and housing								
Exclusion of interest on life insurance savings	$17,440	$18,410	$8,940	$12,490	$19,610	$25,710	$31,790	$35,690
Deductibility of interest on consumer credit	0	0	0	0	0	0	0	0
Deductibility of mortgage interest on owner-occupied homes	62,160	79,150	69,480	75,260	92,170	111,190	129,540	147,610
Deductibility of property tax on owner-occupied homes (now "real property")	19,110	15,120	33,120	35,520	40,980	46,730	52,400	58,450
Deferral/exclusion of capital gains on home sales[a]	35,990	22,160	36,930	39,560	45,390	52,090	59,770	68,580
Accelerated depreciation of machinery and equipment	4,370	22,650	−1,840	3,700	10,320	14,030	15,930	18,060
Investment credit, other than ESOPs, rehabilitation of structures, energy property, and reforestation expenditures	0	0	0	0	0	0	0	0
Education, training, employment, and social services								
Deductibility of charitable contributions (education)	2,880	3,310	4,310	4,620	5,390	6,140	6,850	7,530
Credit for child and dependent care expenses	3,060	3,470	4,510	4,590	4,780	4,950	5,180	5,400
Deductibility of charitable contributions, other than education and health	28,440	32,710	42,570	45,580	53,250	60,660	67,640	74,370
Health								
Exclusion of employer contributions for medical insurance premiums and medical care	118,420	160,110	206,430	216,080	236,640	267,950	305,610	350,670
Deductibility of medical expenses	6,110	9,090	7,080	7,660	8,090	10,530	14,250	19,700
Exclusion of interest on hospital construction bonds	1,470	2,390	2,650	2,850	3,490	4,330	5,130	5,860
Deductibility of charitable contributions (health)	3,190	3,670	4,780	5,110	5,970	6,800	7,590	8,340

(Table continues)

Table 11-7 *(Continued)*

Type of tax expenditure	2005	2010	2015	2016	2018	2020	2022	2024
Social Security and Medicare								
Exclusion of Social Security benefits								
Disability insurance benefits	3,600	7,040	8,310	8,580	8,620	8,780	9,160	9,690
OASI benefits for retired workers	19,110	21,440	27,080	28,300	31,110	33,640	35,330	36,580
Benefits for dependents and survivors	3,940	3,850	4,390	4,530	4,840	5,200	5,530	5,850
Income security								
Exclusion of workers' compensation benefits	5,770	6,770	9,990	10,090	10,290	10,490	10,710	10,920
Net exclusion of pension contributions and earnings								
Defined benefit employer plans	—	—	44,640	46,260	49,100	55,840	77,960	95,320
Defined contribution employer plans	—	—	68,040	73,910	79,380	92,750	108,470	122,340
Individual Retirement Accounts	3,100	12,630	17,240	18,270	20,240	21,930	25,100	27,010
Self-employed plans	9,400	13,820	25,480	28,020	33,740	40,450	47,850	56,600
Veterans' benefits and services								
Exclusion of veterans' death benefits and disability compensation	3,320	4,130	6,380	6,860	7,530	8,160	8,830	9,510
General-purpose fiscal assistance								
Deductibility of nonbusiness state and local taxes other than on owner-occupied homes	36,460	26,890	47,490	51,180	59,490	67,910	76,540	85,490

Note: Amounts in current dollars. Fiscal year basis. "ESOP" indicates Employee Stock Ownership Plan; "OASI" indicates Old Age and Survivors Insurance. Tax expenditures are defined as revenue losses attributable to provisions of the federal tax laws that allow a special exclusion, exemption, or deduction from gross income or that provide a special credit, a preferential rate of tax, or a deferral of liability. The Internal Revenue Service collected about $1.4 trillion in 2014 through individual income taxes. Losses shown are those for individuals. Data for additional years can be found in previous editions of *Vital Statistics on American Politics*.

[a] Prior to 1998, most capital gains on home sales were deferred, with an exclusion for those age fifty-five years and older. Beginning in 1998, most capital gains from home sales were excluded for those of all ages.

Sources: 2005: U.S. Office of Management and Budget, *Budget of the United States Government, 2007, Analytical Perspectives* (Washington, D.C.: Government Printing Office, 2006), 291–295; 2010: *2011*, 171, 246–251; 2015–2024: *2015*, 149, 234–239.

Figure 11-3   Mean Income Received by Each Fifth and Top 5 Percent of Families, 1966–2013

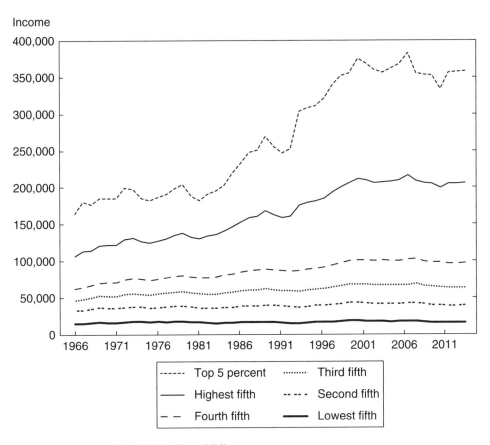

Note: Income is in 2013 CPI-U-RS adjusted dollars.

Source: U.S. Census Bureau, Current Population Survey, Annual Social and Economic Supplements (*www .census.gov*).

Table 11-8 Membership in Labor Unions, 1900–2014

Year	Membership (thousands)	Nonagricultural employment	Employed wage and salary workers	Labor force
		Percentage in unions		
1900	932.4	6.5		3.3
1905	1,947.1	10.8		6.0
1910	2,168.5	10.3		5.9
1915	2,597.6	11.5		6.6
1920	4,823.3	17.6		11.7
1925	3,685.1	12.8		8.2
1930	3,749.6	12.7		7.5
1935	3,649.6	13.5		6.9
1940	7,296.7	22.5		13.1
1945	12,254.2	30.4		22.8
1950	14,294.2	31.6		23.0
1955	16,126.9	31.8		24.8
1960	15,516.1	28.6		22.3
1965	18,268.9	30.1		24.5
1970	20,990.3	29.6		25.4
1975	22,207.0	28.9		23.7
1976	22,153.0	27.9		23.0
1977	21,632.1	26.2		21.8
1978	21,756.5	25.1		21.3
1979	22,025.4	24.5		21.0
1980	20,968.2	23.2		19.6
1981	20,646.8	22.6		19.0
1982	19,571.4	21.9		17.8
1983	18,633.6	20.7		16.6
1984	18,306.0	19.4		16.1
1985	16,996.0		18.0	14.7
1986	16,975.0		17.5	14.4
1987	16,913.0		17.0	14.1
1988	17,002.0		16.8	14.0
1989	16,960.0		16.4	13.7
1990	16,740.0		16.1	13.3
1991	16,568.0		16.1	13.1
1992	16,390.0		15.8	12.8
1993	16,389.0		15.8	12.7
1994	16,748.0		15.5	12.8
1995	16,360.0		14.9	12.4
1996	16,269.0		14.5	12.1
1997	16,110.0		14.1	11.8
1998	16,211.0		13.9	11.8
1999	16,477.0		13.9	11.8
2000	16,258.0		13.5	11.4
2001	16,387.0		13.4	11.4
2002	16,107.0		13.2	11.1
2003	15,776.0		12.9	10.8

Table 11-8   *(Continued)*

Year	Membership (thousands)	Percentage in unions Nonagricultural employment	Employed wage and salary workers	Labor force
2004	15,472.0		12.5	10.5
2005	15,685.0		12.5	10.5
2006	15,359.0		12.0	10.1
2007	15,670.0		12.1	10.2
2008	16,098.0		12.4	10.4
2009	15,327.0		12.3	9.9
2010	14,715.0		11.9	9.6
2011	14,764.0		11.8	9.6
2012	14,366.0		11.3	9.3
2013	14,528.0		11.3	9.3
2014	14,576.0		11.1	9.3

Note: Comparisons of 1983 and 1984 show that the counts by Troy and Sheflin are about one million members higher per year than the counts based on the Current Population Surveys reported by the U.S. Bureau of Labor Statistics in *Employment and Earnings*. In 1985–1996, self-employed workers whose businesses are incorporated are excluded from the union member count. After 1996, all self-employed workers are excluded. Wage and salary workers are workers who receive wages, salaries, commissions, tips, payment-in-kind, or piece rates in both the public and private sectors. Data for additional years can be found in previous editions of *Vital Statistics on American Politics.*

Sources: 1900–1984: Leo Troy and Neil Sheflin, *U.S. Union Sourcebook* (West Orange, N.J.: Industrial Relations Data and Information Services, 1985), 3–10, A-1, A-2; 1985–2000, membership and percentage of employed wage and salary workers: U.S. Department of Labor, Bureau of Labor Statistics, *Employment and Earnings*, January 1987 (Washington, D.C.: Government Printing Office, 1987), 219; (1988), 222; (1990), 232; (1992), 228; (1996), 214; (1997), 211; (1999), 219; (2001), 218; 2001–2014, membership and percentage of employed wage and salary workers: Bureau of Labor Statistics (*www.bls.gov*); 1985–2014, size of labor force: "Labor Force Statistics" (*www.bls.gov*).

Figure 11-4   Federal Minimum Wage Rates, 1950–2014

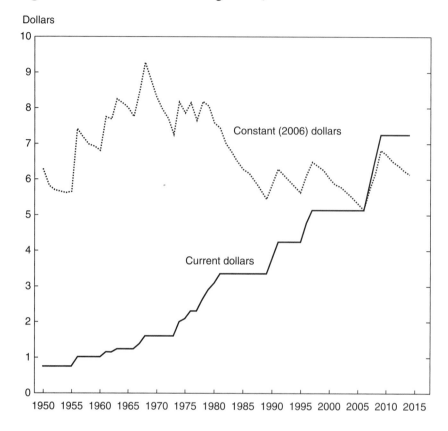

Note: Constant (2006) dollars are derived using the CPI-U index (Consumer Price Index for all urban consumers). Originally, the minimum wage was applicable generally to employees engaged in interstate commerce or in the production of goods for interstate commerce. Coverage was expanded in 1961 and again in 1966. In 1996 a subminimum wage was established for employees under twenty years of age during their first ninety consecutive calendar days of employment with an employer. In 2007 a bill was signed into law increasing the minimum wage to $7.25 over a two-year period, with the first increase in the summer of 2007.

Sources: Minimum wage: U.S. Department of Labor, "Federal Minimum Wage Rates under the Fair Labor Standards Act" *(www.dol.gov)*; consumer price index: Table 11-2, this volume.

Table 11-9   Civilian Labor Force Participation Rate, Overall and by Sex and Race, 1948–2014 (percent)

Year	Total	Male	Female	White	Black or African American[a]
1948	58.8	86.6	32.7	—	—
1950	59.2	86.4	33.9	—	—
1955	59.3	85.4	35.7	58.7	64.2
1960	59.4	83.3	37.7	58.8	64.5
1965	58.9	80.7	39.3	58.4	62.9
1970	60.4	79.7	43.3	60.2	61.8
1975	61.2	77.9	46.3	61.5	58.8
1980	63.8	77.4	51.5	64.1	61.0
1985	64.8	76.3	54.5	65.0	62.9
1990	66.5	76.4	57.5	66.9	64.0
1991	66.2	75.8	57.4	66.6	63.3
1992	66.4	75.8	57.8	66.8	63.9
1993	66.3	75.4	57.9	66.8	63.2
1994	66.6	75.1	58.8	67.1	63.4
1995	66.6	75.0	58.9	67.1	63.7
1996	66.8	74.9	59.3	67.2	64.1
1997	67.1	75.0	59.8	67.5	64.7
1998	67.1	74.9	59.8	67.3	65.6
1999	67.1	74.7	60.0	67.3	65.8
2000	67.1	74.8	59.9	67.3	65.8
2001	66.8	74.4	59.8	67.0	65.3
2002	66.6	74.1	59.6	66.8	64.8
2003	66.2	73.5	59.5	66.5	64.3
2004	66.0	73.3	59.2	66.3	63.8
2005	66.0	73.3	59.3	66.3	64.2
2006	66.2	73.5	59.4	66.5	64.1
2007	66.0	73.2	59.3	66.4	63.7
2008	66.0	73.0	59.5	66.3	63.7
2009	65.4	72.0	59.2	65.8	62.4
2010	64.7	71.2	58.6	65.1	62.2
2011	64.1	70.5	58.1	64.5	61.4
2012	63.7	70.2	57.7	64.0	61.5
2013	63.3	69.7	57.2	63.5	61.2
2014	62.9	69.2	57.0	63.1	61.2

Note: "—" indicates not available. Figures are for persons sixteen years of age and older. The participation rate is the percentage of adults who are either working or looking for work. For details on how employment and unemployment are measured, see "How the Government Measures Unemployment" (*www.bls.gov*). Data for additional years can be found in previous editions of *Vital Statistics on American Politics*.

[a] Black and other nonwhite prior to 1975.

Source: 1948: *Economic Report of the President* (Washington, D.C.: Government Printing Office, 1997), table B-37; 1950: (2001); 1955–1960: (2003); 1965: (2011); 1970–2012: (2013), table B-39; 2013–2014: *http://research.stlouisfed.org*.

Table 11-10   Unemployment Rate Overall, 1929–2014, and by Sex and
Race, 1948–2014 (percent)

Year	Civilian workers	Male	Female	White	Black or African American[a]
1929	3.2	—	—	—	—
1933	24.9	—	—	—	—
1939	17.2	—	—	—	—
1940	14.6	—	—	—	—
1941	9.9	—	—	—	—
1942	4.7	—	—	—	—
1943	1.9	—	—	—	—
1944	1.2	—	—	—	—
1945	1.9	—	—	—	—
1946	3.9	—	—	—	—
1947	3.9	—	—	—	—
1948	3.8	3.6	4.1	3.5	5.9
1949	5.9	5.9	6.0	5.6	8.9
1950	5.3	5.1	5.7	4.9	9.0
1951	3.3	2.8	4.4	3.1	5.3
1952	3.0	2.8	3.6	2.8	5.4
1953	2.9	2.8	3.3	2.7	4.5
1954	5.5	5.3	6.0	5.0	9.9
1955	4.4	4.2	4.9	3.9	8.7
1956	4.1	3.8	4.8	3.6	8.3
1957	4.3	4.1	4.7	3.8	7.9
1958	6.8	6.8	6.8	6.1	12.6
1959	5.5	5.2	5.9	4.8	10.7
1960	5.5	5.4	5.9	5.0	10.2
1961	6.7	6.4	7.2	6.0	12.4
1962	5.5	5.2	6.2	4.9	10.9
1963	5.7	5.2	6.5	5.0	10.8
1964	5.2	4.6	6.2	4.6	9.6
1965	4.5	4.0	5.5	4.1	8.1
1966	3.8	3.2	4.8	3.4	7.3
1967	3.8	3.1	5.2	3.4	7.4
1968	3.6	2.9	4.8	3.2	6.7
1969	3.5	2.8	4.7	3.1	6.4
1970	4.9	4.4	5.9	4.5	8.2
1971	5.9	5.3	6.9	5.4	9.9
1972	5.6	5.0	6.6	5.1	10.4
1973	4.9	4.2	6.0	4.3	9.4
1974	5.6	4.9	6.7	5.0	10.5
1975	8.5	7.9	9.3	7.8	14.8
1976	7.7	7.1	8.6	7.0	14.0
1977	7.1	6.3	8.2	6.2	14.0
1978	6.1	5.3	7.2	5.2	12.8
1979	5.8	5.1	6.8	5.1	12.3
1980	7.1	6.9	7.4	6.3	14.3

Table 11-10   *(Continued)*

Year	Civilian workers	Male	Female	White	Black or African American[a]
1981	7.6	7.4	7.9	6.7	15.6
1982	9.7	9.9	9.4	8.6	18.9
1983	9.6	9.9	9.2	8.4	19.5
1984	7.5	7.4	7.6	6.5	15.9
1985	7.2	7.0	7.4	6.2	15.1
1986	7.0	6.9	7.1	6.0	14.5
1987	6.2	6.2	6.2	5.3	13.0
1988	5.5	5.5	5.6	4.7	11.7
1989	5.3	5.2	5.4	4.5	11.4
1990	5.6	5.7	5.5	4.8	11.4
1991	6.8	7.2	6.4	6.1	12.5
1992	7.5	7.9	7.0	6.6	14.2
1993	6.9	7.2	6.6	6.1	13.0
1994	6.1	6.2	6.0	5.3	11.5
1995	5.6	5.6	5.6	4.9	10.4
1996	5.4	5.4	5.4	4.7	10.5
1997	4.9	4.9	5.0	4.2	10.0
1998	4.5	4.4	4.6	3.9	8.9
1999	4.2	4.1	4.3	3.7	8.0
2000	4.0	3.9	4.1	3.5	7.6
2001	4.7	4.8	4.7	4.2	8.6
2002	5.8	5.9	5.6	5.1	10.2
2003	6.0	6.3	5.7	5.2	10.8
2004	5.5	5.6	5.4	4.8	10.4
2005	5.1	5.1	5.1	4.4	10.0
2006	4.6	4.6	4.6	4.0	8.9
2007	4.6	4.7	4.5	4.1	8.3
2008	5.8	6.1	5.4	5.2	10.1
2009	9.3	10.3	8.1	8.5	14.8
2010	9.6	10.5	8.6	8.7	16.0
2011	8.9	9.4	8.5	7.9	15.8
2012	8.1	8.2	7.9	7.2	13.8
2013	7.4	7.6	7.1	6.5	13.1
2014	6.2	6.3	6.1	5.3	11.3

Note: "—" indicates not available. Figures for 1929 through 1947 are for persons fourteen years of age and older; 1948 and later figures are for persons sixteen years of age and older.

[a] Black and other nonwhite prior to 1972.

Source: 1929–1949: *Economic Report of the President* (Washington, D.C.: Government Printing Office, 1997), table B-33; 1950–1954: (2001); 1955–1958: (2003); 1959: (2007); 1960–1963: (2009); 1964–1965: (2011); 1966–1969: (2013), table B-42; 1970–2014: (2015), table B-12.

Table 11-11   Unemployment, by Race, Sex, and Age, 1955–2014 (percent)

	White				Black[a]			
	Male		Female		Male		Female	
Year	16–19	20 and older	16–19	20 and older	16–19	20 and older	16–19	20 and older
1955	11.3	3.3	9.1	3.9	13.4	8.4	19.2	7.7
1960	14.0	4.2	12.7	4.6	24.0	9.6	24.8	8.3
1965	12.9	2.9	14.0	4.0	23.3	6.0	31.7	7.5
1970	13.7	3.2	13.4	4.4	25.0	5.6	34.5	6.9
1975	18.3	6.2	17.4	7.5	38.1	12.5	41.0	12.2
1980	16.2	5.3	14.8	5.6	37.5	12.4	39.8	11.9
1985	16.5	5.4	14.8	5.7	41.0	13.2	39.2	13.1
1990	14.3	4.3	12.6	4.1	31.9	10.4	29.9	9.7
1991	17.6	5.8	15.2	5.0	36.3	11.5	36.0	10.6
1992	18.5	6.4	15.8	5.5	42.0	13.5	37.2	11.8
1993	17.7	5.7	14.7	5.2	40.1	12.1	37.4	10.7
1994	16.3	4.8	13.8	4.6	37.6	10.3	32.6	9.8
1995	15.6	4.3	13.4	4.3	37.1	8.8	34.3	8.6
1996	15.5	4.1	12.9	4.1	36.9	9.4	30.3	8.7
1997	14.3	3.6	12.8	3.7	36.5	8.5	28.7	8.8
1998	14.1	3.2	10.9	3.4	30.1	7.4	25.3	7.9
1999	12.6	3.0	11.3	3.3	30.9	6.7	25.1	6.8
2000	12.3	2.8	10.4	3.1	26.2	6.9	22.8	6.2
2001	13.9	3.7	11.4	3.6	30.4	8.0	27.5	7.0
2002	15.9	4.7	13.1	4.4	31.3	9.5	28.3	8.8
2003	17.1	5.0	13.3	4.4	36.0	10.3	30.3	9.2
2004	16.3	4.4	13.6	4.2	35.6	9.9	28.2	8.9
2005	16.1	3.8	12.3	3.9	36.3	9.2	30.3	8.5
2006	14.6	3.5	11.7	3.6	32.7	8.3	25.9	7.5
2007	15.7	3.7	12.1	3.6	33.8	7.9	25.3	6.7
2008	19.1	4.9	14.4	4.4	35.9	10.2	26.8	8.1
2009	25.2	8.8	18.4	6.8	46.0	16.3	33.4	11.5
2010	26.3	8.9	20.0	7.2	45.4	17.3	40.5	12.8
2011	24.5	7.7	18.9	7.0	43.1	16.7	39.4	13.2
2012	24.5	6.7	18.4	6.5	41.3	14.0	35.6	11.9
2013	—	6.2	—	5.7	38.5	12.9	—	11.3
2014	—	4.9	—	4.8	33.1	11.3	—	9.8

Note: "—" indicates not available. Data for additional years can be found in previous editions of *Vital Statistics on American Politics*.

[a] Black and other nonwhite prior to 1972.

Source: 1955–1960: *Economic Report of the President* (Washington, D.C.: Government Printing Office, 2003), table B-43; 1965: (2009); 1970: (2011); 1975–2012: (2013), table B-43; 2013–2014: *http://research.stlouisfed.org*.

Appendix
Definitions of Regions

Analyses of U.S. politics often involve breaking the nation down into groups of states in order to highlight tendencies and trends in different regions. For ease of reference, four regional definitions, used in various tables in this book, are shown here. These four, while prominent, by no means exhaust the various definitions of regions that have been employed in the study of U.S. politics.

Table A-1 Regions as Defined by the U.S. Census Bureau and by Pew Research

Northeast	Midwest	South	West
New England	East north central	South Atlantic	Mountain
Connecticut	Illinois	Delaware	Arizona
Maine	Indiana	District of	Colorado
Massachusetts	Michigan	Columbia	Idaho
New Hampshire	Ohio	Florida	Montana
Rhode Island	Wisconsin	Georgia	Nevada
Vermont	West north central	Maryland	New Mexico
Middle Atlantic	Iowa	North Carolina	Utah
New Jersey	Kansas	South Carolina	Wyoming
New York	Minnesota	Virginia	Pacific
Pennsylvania	Missouri	West Virginia	Alaska
	Nebraska	East south central	California
	North Dakota	Alabama	Hawaii
	South Dakota	Kentucky	Oregon
		Mississippi	Washington
		Tennessee	
		West south central	
		Arkansas	
		Louisiana	
		Oklahoma	
		Texas	

Sources: U.S. Census Bureau, "Census Regions and Divisions of the United States" (*www .census.gov*); and Pew Research, unpublished data.

Table A-2   Regions as Defined by Congressional Quarterly, *New York Times*/CBS News Poll, and Voter Research and Surveys

East	*Midwest*	*South*	*West*
Connecticut	Illinois	Alabama	Alaska
Delaware	Indiana	Arkansas	Arizona
District of Columbia	Iowa	Florida	California
Maine	Kansas	Georgia	Colorado
Maryland	Michigan	Kentucky	Hawaii
Massachusetts	Minnesota	Louisiana	Idaho
New Hampshire	Missouri	Mississippi	Montana
New Jersey	Nebraska	North Carolina	Nevada
New York	North Dakota	Oklahoma	New Mexico
Pennsylvania	Ohio	South Carolina	Oregon
Rhode Island	South Dakota	Tennessee	Utah
Vermont	Wisconsin	Texas	Washington
West Virginia		Virginia	Wyoming

Table A-3   Regions for Party Competition Table (Table 1-4) and Apportionment Map (Figure 5-1)

New England	*Middle Atlantic*	*Midwest*	*Plains*
Connecticut	Delaware	Illinois	Iowa
Maine	New Jersey	Indiana	Kansas
Massachusetts	New York	Michigan	Minnesota
New Hampshire	Pennsylvania	Ohio	Nebraska
Rhode Island		Wisconsin	North Dakota
Vermont			South Dakota

South	*Border*	*Rocky Mountain*	*Pacific Coast*
Alabama	District of	Arizona	Alaska
Arkansas	Columbia	Colorado	California
Florida	Kentucky	Idaho	Hawaii
Georgia	Maryland	Montana	Oregon
Louisiana	Missouri	Nevada	Washington
Mississippi	Oklahoma	New Mexico	
North Carolina	West Virginia	Utah	
South Carolina		Wyoming	
Tennessee			
Texas			
Virginia			

Table A-4   Regions for School Desegregation Table (Table 10-13)

South	Border	Northeast	Midwest	West	Excluded
Alabama	Delaware	Connecticut	Illinois	Arizona	Alaska
Arkansas	District of	Maine	Indiana	California	Hawaii
Florida	Columbia	Massachusetts	Iowa	Colorado	
Georgia	Kentucky	New Hampshire	Kansas	Idaho	
Louisiana	Maryland	New Jersey	Michigan	Montana	
Mississippi	Missouri	New York	Minnesota	Nevada	
North Carolina	Oklahoma	Pennsylvania	Nebraska	New Mexico	
South Carolina	West Virginia	Rhode Island	North Dakota	Oregon	
Tennessee		Vermont	Ohio	Utah	
Texas			South Dakota	Washington	
Virginia			Wisconsin	Wyoming	

Source: Gary Orfield and Franklin Monfort, "Status of School Desegregation: The Next Generation" (Alexandria, VA: National School Boards Association, 1992), 2.

Guide to References
for Political Statistics

General

Congressional Information Service. *American Statistics Index: A Comprehensive Guide and Index to the Statistical Publications of the U.S. Government.* Washington, D.C.: Congressional Information Service, 1973–. Annual, with monthly supplements. Available online at LexisNexis Statistical DataSets (*http://academic.lexisnexis.com*).

    Definitive guide, multiply indexed, to statistics "of probable research significance" in government publications; 1974 "Annual and Retrospective Edition" includes not only items in print but also significant items published over the preceding decade.

———. *Statistical Reference Index: A Selective Guide to American Statistical Publications from Sources Other Than the U.S. Government.* Washington, D.C.: Congressional Information Service, 1980–. Annual, with bimonthly supplements. Available online at LexisNexis Statistical DataSets (*http://academic.lexisnexis.com*).

    A complement to *American Statistics Index,* this resource indexes statistics from private and public sources other than the U.S. government.

Congressional Quarterly Weekly Report (*CQ Weekly* as of April 18, 1998). Washington, D.C.: Congressional Quarterly, 1945–.

    Newsweekly covering political developments in Congress, the presidency, the Supreme Court, and national politics; individual voting records on all roll call votes in the House and Senate; texts of presidential press conferences and major statements. *CQ Weekly* is available online with an individual or library subscription (*www.cq.com*).

Congressional Research Service. *The Constitution of the United States: Analysis and Interpretation.* Washington, D.C.: Government Printing Office, 2014. 112th Cong., 2nd sess., S. Doc. 112-9.

Not statistics-laden, but an essential document with commentary on and annotations of Supreme Court decisions and tables on proposed constitutional amendments pending and unratified, laws (congressional, state, and local) held unconstitutional by the Supreme Court, and Supreme Court decisions overruled by subsequent decisions. U.S. law requires a new edition every ten years with biennial supplements between editions to keep this work current.

Federal Statistics, *http://fedstats.sites.usa.gov*
Gateway to statistics from more than one hundred federal agencies.

FiveThirtyEight, *http://fivethirtyeight.com/*
Uses statistical analysis to tell compelling stories about politics and other fields.

Government Printing Office, *www.gpoaccess.gov/fdsys*
Provides free electronic access to publications of the federal government.

Harvard Institute for Quantitative Social Science, *www.iq.harvard.edu/*
Large collection of social science research data covering diverse topics.

Historical Statistics of the United States. Millennial ed. New York: Cambridge University Press, 2006.
Invaluable broad-ranging collection of more than twelve thousand time series covering the nation's history; often the series can be updated by the annual *Statistical Abstract of the United States* (see below).

Law Library of Congress, *www.loc.gov/law/index.php*
Established in 1832, has grown to become the world's largest law library with more than 2.65 million volumes. Some resources available online.

LexisNexis Statistical Insight, *http://academic.lexisnexis.com*
Online statistics from U.S. and state governmental publications, among others, and international governmental organizations.

Library of Congress, *www.loc.gov*
The largest library in the world, serves as the research arm of Congress.

Maier, Mark H., and Jennifer Imazeki. *The Data Game: Controversies in Social Science Statistics.* 4th ed. New York: Routledge, 2014.
Discussion of statistical source material, with an emphasis on inaccuracies, ambiguities, misinterpretations, and unavailability, as well as on the relationship between statistics and important social questions.

U.S. Census Bureau, *www.census.gov*
A primary source for population data, with links to federal government agencies and state data centers.

U.S. Census Bureau. *Statistical Abstract of the United States.* Washington, D.C.: Government Printing Office, 1879–. Annual. Since 2013, the *ProQuest Statistical Abstract of the United States.*

Strong, indispensable collection of nationally significant statistics from public and private sources on economics, politics, and society, and generally worth checking first. Also a useful guide to sources for additional statistics; indicates which time-series update those in *Historical Statistics of the United States* (see earlier entry).

U.S. Congress. *House. Constitution, Jefferson's Manual, and Rules of the House of Representatives of the United States*. Washington, D.C.: Government Printing Office. Biennial.
Solid reference on the Constitution with full notes on all ratifications; indexed.

Elections

Archer, J. Clark, Stephen J. Lavin, Kenneth C. Martis, and Fred M. Shelley. *Historical Atlas of U.S. Presidential Elections, 1788–2004*. Washington, D.C.: CQ Press, 2006.

Brunn, Stanley D., ed. *Atlas of the 2008 Elections*. Lanham, Md.: Rowman & Littlefield, 2011.

Archer, J. Clark, et al. *Atlas of the 2012 Elections*. Lanham, Md.: Rowman & Littlefield, 2014.
Maps showing regional voting patterns and context for U.S. presidential elections.

Burnham, Walter Dean. *Voting in American Elections: The Shaping of the American Political Universe since 1788*. Palo Alto, Calif.: Academica Press, 2010.
Discussion of problems in estimating turnout, references to other efforts, and extensive data on turnout and election results for president, the U.S. House, and more.

CQ Press. *Guide to U.S. Elections*. 7th ed. Washington, D.C.: CQ Press, 2016.
Superb collection of vote returns for presidential, gubernatorial, and U.S. House elections since 1824, electoral college votes since 1789, U.S. Senate elections since 1913, presidential primaries since 1912, and primaries for governor and senator since 1956 (in southern states since 1919); general and candidate indexes; biographies of presidential and vice presidential candidates; lists of governors and senators since 1789; discussions of and data on political parties and presidential nominating conventions throughout the nation's history.

CQ Press Voting and Elections Collection, *www.cqpress.com/product/CQ-Voting-and-Elections-Collection.html*
Online searchable database with information about individual races as well as summary information related to open-seat races, party switches, race competitiveness, and so on. Requires subscription.

DC's Political Report, *www.dcpoliticalreport.com*
Contain numerous links to candidates, political parties, election results, and governmental and political organizations.

Deskins, Donald R., Jr., Hanes Walton Jr., and Sherman C. Puckett. *The African American Electorate: A Statistical History.* Washington, D.C.: CQ Press, 2012.
Includes a variety of data on African American participation in and exclusion from voting and elections from colonial times through the election of Barack Obama.

————. *Presidential Elections, 1789–2008: County, State, and National Mapping of Election Data.* Ann Arbor: University of Michigan Press, 2010.
Unique feature: multicolor maps showing presidential election results at the county level.

Dubin, Michael J. *United States Congressional Elections, 1788–1997: The Official Results of the Elections of the 1st through the 105th Congresses.* Jefferson, N.C.: McFarland, 1998.
Complete, insofar as possible, returns for all U.S. House and Senate general elections; contains percentages for each Congress of representatives unopposed, seeking reelection, reelected, defeated, and first-termers.

————. *United States Gubernatorial Elections, 1776–1860: The Official Results by State and County.* Jefferson, N.C.: McFarland, 2003; *1861–1911,* 2010.
Detailed compilation of gubernatorial elections.

————. *United States Presidential Elections, 1788–1860: The Official Results by State and County.* Jefferson, N.C.: McFarland, 2002.
Detailed compilation of early presidential elections.

Federal Election Commission, *www.fec.gov*
Official source for data on campaign contributions and expenditures in federal elections.

Gans, Curtis. *Voter Turnout in the United States, 1788–2009.* Washington, D.C.: CQ Press, 2011.
Discussion of problems in estimating turnout and extensive data on turnout for president, the U.S. Senate and House, and state governors.

Glashan, Roy R. *American Governors and Gubernatorial Elections, 1775–1978.* Westport, Conn.: Meckler, 1979.
Details about state governors (such as birth dates, party affiliations, principal occupations, and terms of office) and election data. Continued in Mullaney (see below).

Kallenbach, Joseph E., and Jessamine S. Kallenbach. *American State Governors, 1776–1976.* Dobbs Ferry, N.Y.: Oceana Publications, 1977–1982.
Election results and biographical data on governors.

Klarner, Carl. Governors Dataset, *www.indstate.edu/polisci/klarnerpolitics.htm*
Dataset at the state-year level covering 1961 to 2012 (with limited coverage of earlier years for some variables) including demographic data about governors in office and data about terms and term limits.

McDonald, Michael. "United States Elections Project." *www.electproject.org*
Turnout data for U.S. elections since 1948, with an emphasis on the "voter eligible population," correcting for numbers of noncitizens, certain ex-felons, and others in the voting-age population who are ineligible to vote. Also offers data on and analyses of election administration and redistricting.

Mullaney, Marie. *American Governors and Gubernatorial Elections, 1979–1987*. Westport, Conn.: Meckler, 1988.
Continues the volume by Glashan (see earlier entry).

———. *Biographical Directory of the Governors of the United States, 1988–1994*. Westport, Conn.: Greenwood Press, 1994.
Details about state governors (such as birth dates, party affiliations, principal occupations, and terms of office). Continues earlier volume.

Nomination and Election of the President and Vice President of the United States. Washington, D.C.: Government Printing Office, 1960–. Quadrennial.
Compilation of federal and state laws and party rules governing nomination and election of the president.

Politico (elections), *www.politico.com*
Maps and tables of state- and county-level results for gubernatorial (and national) elections from 2002 to the present. Also has state polls about presidential primary and general elections, U.S. Senate, and some congressional district races.

Project Vote Smart, *www.votesmart.org*
Provides issue positions, biographical details, and campaign finance information on numerous candidates for president, Congress, and state legislatures, and information on statewide ballot measures.

Rusk, Jerrold. *A Statistical History of the American Electorate*. Washington, D.C.: CQ Press, 2001.
Includes lists and dates of election laws, initiative and referendum data, and measures of party competition, partisan swing, split-ticket voting, and partisan strength.

Scammon, Richard M., Alice McGillivray, and Rhodes Cook, eds. *America at the Polls: A Handbook of Presidential Election Statistics*. Washington, D.C.: CQ Press, various years.
Two volumes that span 1920 to 2004, providing popular votes (state and county) for president as well as state presidential primary results.

———. *America Votes: A Handbook of Contemporary American Election Statistics*. Washington, D.C.: CQ Press, Elections Research Center, 1956–.

Convenient compilation of vote totals and statistics by state for general elections and primaries for president, governor, and senator, principally since 1945 (comparable district-level data for members of Congress); county-level totals and statistics for most recent general election for president, governor, and senator; state maps with county and congressional district boundaries.

State legislative election returns, ICPSR Study No. 34297, *www.icpsr.umich.edu*
Comprehensive data on state legislative election returns from 1967 through 2010. Includes information on district and candidate attributes.

State partisan balance, *www.indstate.edu/polisci/klarnerpolitics.htm*
Dataset spanning 1937 to 2011 including information on partisan control of state legislatures, governors' offices, and state institutions.

U.S. Census Bureau, *www.census.gov*
Starting in 2005, demographic data on state legislative districts (above and beyond the racial/ethnic composition used for redistricting).

U.S. Census Bureau, Current Population Reports, Population Characteristics, Series P-20. *Voting and Registration in the Election of November [Year]*. Washington, D.C.: Government Printing Office, 1964–. Biennial.
Survey results on voter registration and turnout in presidential and midterm general elections for the nation and regions (and sometimes states and metropolitan areas) for various groups (*www.census.gov*).

Political Parties

Bain, Richard C., and Judith H. Parris. *Convention Decisions and Voting Records.* 2nd ed. Washington, D.C.: Brookings Institution, 1973.
Data on convention actions through 1972.

Congressional Quarterly. *National Party Conventions, 1831–2008.* 9th ed. Washington, D.C.: CQ Press, 2009.
Summarizes conventions, with results of ballots, nominees, and party profiles.

David, Paul T. *Party Strength in the United States, 1872–1970.* Charlottesville, Va.: University Press of America, 1972. Updated for 1972 in *Journal of Politics* 36 (1972): 785–796; for 1974 in *Journal of Politics* 38 (1974): 416–425; for 1976 in *Journal of Politics* 40 (1976): 770–780.
Measures of party competition in the states covering several offices and an admirably lengthy historical span.

Democratic National Committee, *www.democrats.org*
Republican National Committee, *www.rnc.org*
The Democratic and Republican Parties' official websites containing news releases, transcripts, video, and related material.

Campaign Finance and
Political Action Committees (PACs)

Campaign Finance Institute, *www.cfinst.org*
Center for Responsive Politics, *www.opensecrets.org*
CQ MoneyLine, *www.cqmoneyline.com*
National Institute on Money in State Politics, *www.followthemoney.org*
> Data on and analyses of campaign contributions and expenditures in federal and state elections.

Brasher, Holly. *Vital Statistics on Interest Groups and Lobbying*. Washington, D.C.: CQ Press, 2014.
> Data collected from disclosure forms filed by registered lobbyists. Information on the characteristics of lobbying organizations; how extensively organizations lobby on issues; lobbying Congress, the White House, and federal agencies; how much money is spent on lobbying.

The Campaign Disclosure Project, *www.campaigndisclosure.org*
> Database of campaign finance disclosure laws covering the fifty states, the District of Columbia, and the Federal Election Commission. Also includes a graded assessment of each state's disclosure programs.

Campaign Finance Information Center, *www.campaignfinance.org/linksstate .html*
> Lists sites offering state campaign finance data and indicates which states make it searchable.

Federal Election Commission. *Annual Report.* Washington, D.C.: Government Printing Office, 1976–.
> Cumulative figures since the mid-1970s on contributions and spending in federal election campaigns; also information on political action committee growth and activities (*www.fec.gov*).

Influence Explorer, *www.influenceexplorer.com*
> Tracks political contributions at the federal and state level. Also tracks earmarks, grants, and contracts by state.

Justice at Stake, *www.justiceatstake.org*
> Provides links to data on candidate fund-raising and advertising expenditures in state judicial campaigns.

Magleby, David B., ed. *Financing the 2012 Election: Assessing Reform.* Washington, D.C.: Brookings Institution, 2014.
> Coverage of fund-raising and spending in all phases of the presidential campaign; continues work by Alexander Heard and by Herbert Alexander on financing presidential campaigns since 1960.

Public Opinion

Note: Many universities and local news sources collect public opinion data within the state in which they are located. Cornell's Institute for Social and Economic Research (*www.ciser.cornell.edu/info/polls.shtml*) has a list of sources of polling data with a state or regional emphasis.

Gallup Poll, *www.gallup.com*
Inter-university Consortium for Political and Social Research, *www.icpsr .umich.edu*
Odum Institute, University of North Carolina, *www.irss.unc.edu/odum*
Pew Research Center for the People and the Press, *http://people-press.org*
Polling the Nations, *www.orspub.com*
Polling Report, *www.pollingreport.com*
> Online access to current and historical collections of public opinion poll data.

American National Election Studies. "Guide to Public Opinion and Electoral Behavior." *www.electionstudies.org*
> Tables and graphs showing public opinion, political participation, and electoral choice in American politics since 1952; responses to questions asked in the American National Election Studies.

Astin, A. W., et al. *The American Freshman: Forty Year Trends.* Los Angeles: Higher Education Research Institute, University of California, Los Angeles, 2007. *National Norms for Fall,* 1998–. Annual.
> Reports of national surveys of college freshmen, including attitudes toward jobs, subject interests, and liberalism/conservatism.

Opinion Research Service. *American Public Opinion Index.* Louisville, Ky.: Opinion Research Service, 1981–2000. Annual.
> Indexes scientifically drawn samples of national, state, and local universes.

POLL (The Public Opinion Location Library). Storrs, Conn.: Roper Center for Public Opinion Research. *http://ropercenter.uconn.edu*
> A computer-based information retrieval system for public opinion survey data. Extensive coverage for 1955 to the present; some coverage of earlier years. Subscription service with limited free access.

Public Opinion Quarterly. Chicago: University of Chicago Press, 1937–. Quarterly.
> Analysis of the mechanics and findings of survey research; regular thematic presentation of poll results.

Media

ABC News, *http://abcnews.com*
CBS News, *www.cbs.com*

CNN, *www.cnn.com*
C-SPAN, *www.c-span.org*
Fox News, *www.foxnews.com*
MSNBC, *www.nbcnews.com*
New York Times, *www.nytimes.com*
Time, *www.time.com*
USA Today, *www.usatoday.com*
Washington Post, *www.washingtonpost.com*

Broadcasting Publications. *Broadcasting Cablecasting Yearbook.* Washington, D.C.: Broadcasting Publications, 1982–. Annual. Continues *Broadcasting Cable Yearbook,* which combined *Broadcasting Yearbook* (1968–1979) and *Broadcasting Cable Sourcebook* (1973–1979).
 International directory of radio, television, and cable industries as well as related fields. Presents some statistical overviews.

Cable and TV Station Coverage Atlas, 1986. Indianapolis, Ind.: Warren Publishing, 1986–. Annual.
 Data on television stations and the growing reach of cable systems.

C-SPAN Archives. West Lafayette, Ind.: C-SPAN, 1987–. *www.c-spanvideo .org/videoLibrary*
 Records, indexes, and archives all C-SPAN programming; contains every program aired since 1987.

Dow Jones Factiva, *www.factiva.com*
 Online access to major U.S. newspapers, Dow Jones and Reuters's newswires, and business publications.

Editor & Publisher—The Fourth Estate. New York: Editor & Publisher, 1884–. Weekly.
 Weekly periodical covering the media.

LexisNexis, *www.lexisnexis.com*
 Wide-ranging material from journals, newspapers, reference books, and other sources. Includes databases, documents, maps, photographs, and more.

Media Tenor, *www.mediatenor.com*
 International organization monitoring and analyzing media content on topics that include U.S. electoral campaigns and government.

Newsbank, Inc., *www.newsbank.com*
 Online access to hundreds of U.S. and international newspapers and other sources.

Nielsen Audio, *www.nielsen.com/us/en/solutions/capabilities/audio.html*
 Reports of radio usage, including demographic and market analyses.

Nielsen Television Index. Northbrook, Ill.: A. C. Nielsen, 1955. Annual.

Overall and market section reports on television viewing and network program audiences.

Nielsen Wire, *http://blog.nielsen.com/nielsenwire/category/politics*
Data on audience ratings for political events and topics.

Proquest, *www.proquest.com*
Online access to major U.S. newspapers and magazines. Includes ProQuest Historical Newspapers—*New York Times* from 1851 and seven other major papers.

Television Digest. *Television and Cable Factbook.* Washington, D.C.: Television Digest, 1946–. Annual.
Data on cable, television, and related industries; published in two volumes: "Stations" and "Cable and Services."

Vanderbilt Television News Archive. Nashville, Tenn.: Vanderbilt University. *http://tvnews.vanderbilt.edu*
Archives of nightly network news since 1968.

Congress

Library of Congress, Thomas: Legislative Information, *http://thomas.loc.gov*
U.S. House of Representatives, *www.house.gov*
U.S. Senate, *www.senate.gov*

Balinski, Michel, and H. Peyton Young. *Fair Representation: Meeting the Ideal of One Man, One Vote.* New Haven, Conn.: Yale University Press, 1982.
Analysis of methods of apportionment of representatives among the states.

Barone, Michael, and Grant Ujifusa. *The Almanac of American Politics.* Washington, D.C.: National Journal, 1972–. Biennial.
Data-rich political analyses of each state, congressional district, representative, senator, and governor; current composition of committees; state maps with congressional district and county boundaries.

Biographical Directory of Congress, *http://bioguide.congress.gov/biosearch/biosearch.asp*
Biographical directory of the U.S. Congress, 1774–present.

Congressional Quarterly. *American Political Leaders, 1789–2009.* Washington, D.C.: CQ Press, 2009.
Material on more than eleven thousand members of Congress: age, religion, occupation, women, blacks, turnover, and shifts between chambers; data on congressional sessions, party composition, and leadership. Also includes

biographical summaries of presidents, vice presidents, Supreme Court justices, and governors.

————. *Congress A to Z.* 6th ed. Washington, D.C.: CQ Press, 2014.
Mostly essays but contains useful listings of hard-to-find material such as treaties killed by the Senate, impeachment trials, and women members of Congress.

————. *Congress and the Nation.* Washington, D.C.: Congressional Quarterly/CQ Press, 1965–. Quadrennial. Years 1945–1964 contained in one volume. Akin to *CQ Almanac* (see below), but each volume now covers a presidential term.

————. *Congressional Districts in the 2000s.* Washington, D.C.: CQ Press, 2003.
Profiles of each congressional district, with statistics on election returns, economic makeup, and demographics. Volume covering the 1990s published in 1993.

————. *Congressional Roll Call.* Washington, D.C.: Congressional Quarterly/CQ Press, 1974–. Annual.
Compilation of every roll call vote by every member of Congress and summary voting measures (ideology, party unity, presidential support, and voting participation).

————. *[Year] Congressional Staff Directory.* Washington, D.C.: Congressional Quarterly/CQ Press, 1959–2012. Biennial.
Names, addresses, phone numbers, and numerous biographies of senators' and representatives' personal staffs and the staffs of congressional committees and subcommittees. Discontinued.

————. *CQ Almanac.* Washington, D.C.: Congressional Quarterly/CQ Press, 1945–. Annual.
Each volume now covers legislation for a single session of Congress; appendixes contain particularly useful data on Congress and politics.

————. *Guide to Congress.* 7th ed. Washington, D.C.: CQ Press, 2012.
Massive, rich accounting of how Congress works and how it developed. Check here first for data covering all but the most recent years.

————. *Politics in America.* Washington, D.C.: CQ Press, 1981–. Biennial.
Data-rich political analyses of each state, congressional district, representative, and senator; current composition of committees; state maps with congressional district and county boundaries.

Congressional Research Service, *www.loc.gov/crsinfo/research*
Many Congressional Research Service documents can be found here.

CQ Press Congress Collection, *http://library.cqpress.com/congress*
Online, searchable database with biographical and roll call voting information on individual members of Congress as well as summaries of interest group ratings, key vote analysis, policy analysis, and so on. Requires subscription.

Freeman, Eric, and Stephan A. Jones. *African Americans in Congress.* Washington, D.C.: CQ Press, 2007.
   Stories of and original documents about the history of African Americans in the U.S. House and Senate.

Martis, Kenneth C. *Historical Atlas of Political Parties in the United States Congress, 1789–1989.* New York: Macmillan, 1989.
   ———. *The Historical Atlas of the United States Congressional Districts, 1789–1983.* New York: Free Press, 1983.
   Congressional-based perspective on the surge and decline of political parties.

Martis, Kenneth C., and Gregory A. Elmes. *The Historical Atlas of State Power in Congress, 1790–1990.* Washington, D.C.: Congressional Quarterly, 1993.
   Maps, tables, and text describing changes in apportionment among the states.

Martis, Kenneth C., and Gyula Pauer. *The Historical Atlas of the Congresses of the Confederate States of America.* New York: Macmillan, 1994.
   Maps, tables, and text describing Confederate districts, elections, and key votes.

Ornstein, Norman J., Thomas E. Mann, and Michael J. Malbin, eds. *Vital Statistics on Congress.* Publisher and frequency vary.
   Data on characteristics of members, elections, campaign finance, committees, staff, expenses, workload, budgeting, and voting alignments. Most data series stretch back to World War II, some longer.

Parsons, Stanley B., William W. Beach, and Michael J. Dubin. *United States Congressional Districts and Data.* 2 vols. Westport, Conn.: Greenwood Press, 1978, 1986.
   Demographic and geographic data about U.S. congressional districts between 1789 through 1883.

Parsons, Stanley B., Michael J. Dubin, and Karen Toombs Parsons. *United States Congressional Districts, 1883–1913.* New York: Greenwood Press, 1990.
   These two volumes cover 1883 and 1913; continues coverage of volumes listed earlier.

Sharp, Michael. *The Directory of Congressional Voting Scores and Interest Group Ratings.* 2 vols. 4th ed. Washington, D.C.: CQ Press, 2005.
   Contains voting scores (for example, presidential support) and interest group ratings (eleven groups, as available) for all members of Congress from 1947 to 2004.

Silbey, Joel, ed. *Encyclopedia of the American Legislative System: Studies of the Principal Structures, Processes, and Policies of Congress and State Legislatures since the Colonial Era.* 3 vols. New York: Scribner's, 1994–1996.
   A thorough treatment of the national and state legislatures.

Stewart, Charles, III, David T. Canon, and Garrison Nelson, eds. *Committees in the U.S. Congress, 1789–1946.* 4 vols. Washington, D.C.: CQ Press, 2002; Nelson and Stewart, eds., *1993–2010,* 2010.
  A comprehensive history of congressional committee membership.

Treese, Joel, ed. *Biographical Directory of the American Congress, 1774–1996.* Washington, D.C.: CQ Press, 1997.
  Biographies of U.S. senators and representatives to 1996.

U.S. Census Bureau. *Congressional District Atlas.* Washington, D.C.: Government Printing Office, 1960–. Frequency varies.
  Detailed maps of congressional districts.

———. *Congressional District Data Book.* Washington, D.C.: Government Printing Office, 1961–. Frequency varies.
  Census data by congressional districts, with maps. See also *www.census.gov.*

U.S. Congress. Joint Committee on Printing. *Official Congressional Directory.* Washington, D.C.: Government Printing Office, 1809–. Biennial (in recent years).
  Biographical data on current members and statistics on the sessions of Congress. Useful reference source on committees and subcommittees, foreign representatives and consular offices in the United States, press representatives, and state delegations.

Presidency and Executive Branch

The White House, *www.whitehouse.gov*

Compilation of Presidential Documents. Washington, D.C.: Government Printing Office, 1965–.
  Collection of presidential activities. Includes texts of proclamations, executive orders, speeches, and other presidential communications; supplements include acts gaining presidential approval, nominations submitted for Senate confirmation, and a list of White House press releases (*www.gpo.gov/fdsys*). Indexed.

Congressional Quarterly. *Federal Regulatory Directory.* Washington, D.C.: CQ Press, 1979–. Frequency varies.
  Extensive profiles of the major and minor regulatory agencies—more than one hundred in all.

———. *[Year] Federal Staff Directory.* Washington, D.C.: CQ Press, 1982–2012. Biennial.
  Names, addresses, phone numbers, and numerous biographies of key executives and assistants in the executive branch of the federal government. Discontinued.

————. *Guide to the Presidency and the Executive Branch.* 5th ed. Edited by Michael Nelson. Washington, D.C.: CQ Press, 2012.
Detailed coverage of numerous aspects of presidents and administrations. Focus on the institution complements CQ Press's volumes on Congress and elections.

————. *Washington Information Directory.* Washington, D.C.: CQ Press, 1975–. Annual.
Names, addresses, phone numbers, and heads of thousands of federal government and private, nonprofit agencies in and about Washington, D.C.

DeGregorio, William A., and Sandra Lee Stuart. *The Complete Book of U.S. Presidents.* 8th ed. Fort Lee, N.J.: Barricade Books, 2013.
Biographies of presidents and cabinet members.

Kane, Joseph Nathan, and Janet Podell. *Facts about the Presidents: A Compilation of Biographical and Historical Information.* 8th ed. New York: H. W. Wilson, 2009.
Chapter on each president and comparative statistics on all presidents.

Ragsdale, Lyn. *Vital Statistics on the Presidency: George Washington to George W. Bush.* 4th ed. Washington, D.C.: CQ Press, 2014.
Data largely on postwar presidents—their careers, elections, speeches and appearances, approval ratings, and congressional relationships—with some longer time series.

U.S. Government Organization Manual. Washington, D.C.: Government Printing Office, 1935–. Annual.
Official federal government handbook detailing the organization, activities, and current officials in legislative, judicial, and executive governmental units.

The Judiciary

Federal Judicial Center, *www.fjc.gov/history/home.nsf*
U.S. Courts, The Federal Judiciary, *www.uscourts.gov*
U.S. Supreme Court, *www.supremecourt.gov*
Federal court personnel, administration, procedures, and opinions.

The American Bench. Sacramento, Calif.: Reginald Bishop Forster and Associates, 1977–. Biennial.
Comprehensive listing of all judges in the United States, along with brief biographies of about eighteen thousand judges.

Biographical Directory of Federal Judges, 1789-present, *www.uscourts.gov/JudgesAndJudgeships/BiographicalDirectoryOfJudges.aspx*

Biographies of judges since 1789 on the U.S. District Courts, the U.S. Courts of Appeals, the Supreme Court, the former U.S. Circuit Courts, and the federal judiciary's courts of special jurisdiction.

Bureau of Justice Statistics. Courts Data Collections, *www.bjs.gov*
Collection of datasets on U.S. and state courts, including caseloads, court system organization and structure, numbers of and disposition of criminal and civil cases, governance of court systems; jury qualifications and verdict rules; processing and sentencing procedures for criminal cases.

Congressional Quarterly. *[Year] Judicial Staff Directory.* Washington, D.C.: CQ Press, 1986–2012. Annual.
Personnel listings for federal courts, maps of court jurisdictions, biographies of judges and staffs. Discontinued.

Cushman, Clare, ed. *The Supreme Court Justices: Illustrated Biographies, 1789–2012.* 3rd ed. Washington, D.C.: CQ Press, 2012.
Biographies of justices, including backgrounds, careers, and issues and cases on which they passed judgment.

Director of the Administrative Office of the United States Courts. *Annual Report.* Washington, D.C.: Government Printing Office, 1940–. Annual.
Numerous statistics on the kind, timing, and disposition of cases in the federal courts and on numbers and workloads of federal judges.

Epstein, Lee, Thomas G. Walker, Jeffrey A. Segal, and Harold J. Spaeth. *Supreme Court Compendium.* 6th ed. Washington, D.C.: CQ Press, 2015.
Data on characteristics of justices, caseloads, voting alignments, public opinion, and legal developments.

Friedman, Leon, and Fred L. Israel, eds. *The Justices of the United States Supreme Court.* 4th ed. New York: Facts on File, 2013.
Biography of each justice, including several typical opinions; tables showing acts of Congress held unconstitutional, decisions overruled by subsequent decisions, and summary biographical data.

Savage, David. *Guide to the U.S. Supreme Court.* 5th ed. Washington, D.C.: CQ Press, 2010.
Solid, broad coverage of the Supreme Court and development of the law; an excellent source that also refers readers to additional references.

State Court Caseload Statistics: Annual Report. Williamsburg, Va.: Conference of State Court Administrators and the National Center for State Courts, 1976–. Annual.
Data on judicial workloads in the state courts.

Federalism

Council of State Governments, *www.csg.org*
Library of Congress, State Government Information, *www.loc.gov/rr/news/
stategov/stategov.html*
National Governors Association, *www.nga.org*
The Pew Center on the States, *www.pewcenteronthestates.org*
> Information on the structure, personnel, and policies of individual states.

Alexander, Herbert E., and Mike Eberts. *Public Financing of State Elections: A Data Book and Election Guide to Public Funding of Political Parties and Candidates in Twenty States.* Los Angeles: Citizens' Research Foundation, 1986.
> Important compendium for understanding and comparing state regulation of campaign finances.

The Book of the States. Lexington, Ky.: Council of State Governments, 1935–. Biennial; annual since 2002.
> Definitive reference to the current data on state government activities across the board.

The County Year Book. Washington, D.C.: National Association of Counties and International City/County Management Association, 1975–. Annual.
> Surveys issues and trends in county government and administration; a reliable source of data on county government.

CSG State Directories. 3 vols. Lexington, Ky.: Council of State Governments, 1977–. Annual.
> Lists state elected officials; state legislative leadership, committees, and staff; state administrative officials by function. Originally issued as a supplement to *The Book of the States.* Previously biennial under various titles.

Dubin, Michael J. *Party Affiliations in the State Legislatures: A Year by Year Summary, 1796–2006.* Jefferson, N.C.: McFarland, 2007.
> Extensive data on states' electoral processes, term lengths, legislature size and membership by party, election dates, and more.

Federal Election Campaign Laws. Washington, D.C.: Federal Election Commission, 2008.
> Lengthy compilation of laws related to organization of campaigns, disclosure and reporting requirements, enforcement procedures, and so on.

Holli, Melvin G., and Peter Jones, eds. *Biographical Dictionary of American Mayors, 1820–1980.* Westport, Conn.: Greenwood Press, 1981.
> Covers 679 mayors in over a dozen cities; contains lists categorizing mayors by characteristics such as party, religion, and ethnicity.

Initiative and Referendum Institute, *www.iandrinstitute.org*
> State-by-state information about initiative and referendum processes; provisions and reports on current propositions. Database of the number and approval rate of initiatives in each state since 1904.

Lilley, William, III, Laurence J. DeFranco, Mark F. Bernstein, and Kari L. Ramsby. *The Almanac of State Legislative Elections.* 3rd ed. Washington, D.C.: CQ Press, 2007.
> Maps and statistical profiles of the geographic, economic, and political composition of state legislative districts.

————. *The State Atlas of Political and Cultural Diversity.* Washington, D.C.: Congressional Quarterly, 1997.
> Racial and ancestral makeup of top state legislative districts. Available diskette contains data on all state legislative districts.

Morgan, Kathleen O'Leary, and Scott Morgan, eds. *State Rankings 2014: A Statistical View of America.* Washington, D.C.: CQ Press, 2014. Annual.
> Compilation of state rankings in numerous categories. Feeds CQ Press State Stats database, *library.cqpress.com/statestats*. Database requires subscription.

The Municipal Year Book. New York: International City/County Management Association, 1934–. Annual.
> Reliable source for urban data and developments.

National Conference of State Legislatures, *www.ncsl.org*
> Compilations of laws and data on elections, redistricting, term limits, and other topics, as well as links to sites of individual state legislatures. Data about initiative and referendum availability and provisions across the U.S. Includes a state-by-state database of initiative and referendum legislation since 1993 and a state-by-state database of ballot measures since 1892.

State Legislative Sourcebook. Topeka, Kan.: Government Research Service, 1986–. Annual.
> A guide to finding detailed information on state legislative material, including offices, addresses, phone numbers, and price lists. State statistical abstracts. A list of state statistical abstracts (or near equivalents) can be found in recent editions of the *Statistical Abstract of the United States.* They are of widely varying quality.

State Yellow Book. New York: Leadership Directories, Inc., 1973–. Quarterly.
> Some statistics, but emphasizes contact information for executive and legislative branches, including departments, commissions, agencies, and legislative leadership and legislative committees. Continues State Information Book (*www.leadershipdirectories.com*).

Tax Foundation. *Facts and Figures on Government Finance.* Englewood Cliffs, N.J.: Prentice Hall, 1941–. Updated periodically.

Data on government revenues, spending, and debt at the federal, state, and local levels (*www.taxfoundation.org*).

U.S. Census Bureau. *Census of Governments.* Washington, D.C.: Government Printing Office, 1972–. Frequency varies.
Numbers and characteristics of governments, including special district governments dealing with subjects such as schools, parks and recreation, and sewage.

————. *City Government Finances; Government Finances; State Government Finances.* Washington, D.C.: Government Printing Office, 1909–; 1916–; 1965–. Annual.
These three series summarize government finances at the city and state levels; great detail for states and the larger cities.

————. *County and City Data Book.* Washington, D.C.: Government Printing Office, 1952–. Frequency varies.
Demographic, economic, health, agricultural, and other information about counties, cities, and towns. Presidential voting by county. Discontinued.

————. *State and Metropolitan Area Data Book.* Washington, D.C.: Government Printing Office, 1979–. Frequency varies. Discontinued.
Demographic, economic, health, education, and other data about states and metropolitan statistical areas.

Waters, M. Dane. *Initiative and Referendum Almanac.* Durham, N.C.: Carolina Academic Press, 2003.
History of, arguments about, and compendium of initiatives and referenda in American history.

Foreign and Military Policy

Cochran, Thomas B., et al. *Nuclear Weapons Databook.* Multiple vols. Cambridge, Mass.: Ballinger, 1984, 1987, 1989, 1994, 2005.
Comprehensive data on nuclear arsenals. Updated by the "Nuclear Notebook" section in each issue of the Bulletin of the Atomic Scientists.

Joint Chiefs of Staff. *Military Posture for Fiscal Year [Year].* Washington, D.C.: Government Printing Office. Annual.
Brief review of all aspects of military preparedness of the United States and of the world military environment.

The Military Balance. London: International Institute of Strategic Studies, 1959–. Annual.
Statistical analysis of military forces and defense spending; figures given for countries and regional organizations such as the North Atlantic Treaty Organization (NATO).

Patterns of Global Terrorism. Washington, D.C.: U.S. Department of State, 1983–2004, continued in *Country Reports on Terrorism.* Annual.
> Details on terrorist incidents around the world.

SIPRI (Stockholm International Peace Research Institute). *World Armaments and Disarmament: SIPRI Yearbook.* Stockholm: Almqvist and Wiksell; New York: Oxford University Press, 1970–. Annual.
> Overview of the arms race and efforts to promote disarmament; detailed data on world military spending (*www.sipri.org*).

United Nations, *http://untreaty.un.org*
> A large database of treaties and multilateral agreements. Requires subscription. Also contains references to hard copy publications.

U.S. Arms Control and Disarmament Agency. *World Military Expenditures and Arms Transfers.* Washington, D.C.: Government Printing Office, 1965–2000. Annual (title varies).
> A series of statistical accounts of military spending and the arms race.

Social Policy

Centers for Disease Control and Prevention, *www.cdc.gov*
Kaiser Family Foundation, *www.kff.org, www.statehealthfacts.org*
Medicaid, *www.medicaid.gov*
National Vital Statistics Reports. Previously titled *Monthly Vital Statistics Report.* Hyattsville, Md.: U.S. Department of Health and Human Services, 1952–. Varying numbers annually.
U.S. National Library of Medicine (National Institutes of Health), *www.nlm.nih.gov/hsrinfo/datasites.html*
> Sources of vast amounts of data, statistics, and survey results at the national, regional, and state level covering a range of health- and healthcare-related topics.

Anderton, Douglas L., Richard E. Barrett, and Donald J. Bogue. *The Population of the United States.* 3rd ed. New York: Free Press, 1997.
> Extensive description of the nation's population characteristics, focusing on the years since 1960; topics include poverty, income, housing, educational attainment, ethnicity, and migration.

Center for American Women and Politics, National Information Bank on Women in Public Office, Eagleton Institute of Politics, Rutgers University, *www.cawp.rutgers.edu*
> Various reports provide data on women in public office, electoral turnout of women, and so forth. Both historical and contemporary information.

Death Penalty Information Center, *www.deathpenaltyinfo.org*
State-level database of statistics related to capital punishment. Searchable database of executions since 1977. State-by-state historical and current information about death penalty laws and links to external reports and datasets on the topic of capital punishment.

Guttmacher Institute, *www.guttmacher.org/statecenter*
Information and data on state reproductive health laws and statistics. Includes data on pregnancy, abortion, availability of contraceptives, and funding and availability of family planning services and facilities. Interactive tools allow for comparisons of reproductive health policies across states.

Heaton, Tim B., Bruce A. Chadwick, and Cardell K. Jacobson. *Statistical Handbook on Racial Groups in the United States*. Phoenix, AZ: Oryx, 2000.
Contains a broad range of more than four hundred charts and tables on non-Hispanic whites, Native Americans, and African, Hispanic, and Asian Americans.

LGBT Human Rights Campaign, *www.hrc.org/resources*
Database of state laws and court decisions searchable by fourteen issue categories and state. Has maps that classify states on their degree of LGBT-friendliness. A "Municipal Equality Index" rates major U.S. cities on criteria relevant to LGBT legal protections.

National Directory of Latino Elected Officials, [Year]. Washington, D.C.: National Association of Latino Elected and Appointed Officials Education Fund. Annual.
Lists Hispanic elected officials by office and state (*www.naleo.org*).

Pew Hispanic Center, *http://pewhispanic.org*
Nonpartisan research organization conducting a broad range of demographic studies and opinion data on the Hispanic population in the United States.

The Sentencing Project, *http://sentencingproject.org*
Pro-reform advocacy website with state-by-state criminal justice data. Includes information on incarceration, racial disparity, drug policies, juvenile sentencing, felony disenfranchisement, and other topics.

The State of Black America. New York: National Urban League, 1976–. Annual.
Yearly review assessing the conditions of blacks in the nation.

University at Albany, Hindelang Criminal Justice Research Center. (Formerly Bureau of Justice Statistics.) *Sourcebook of Criminal Justice Statistics*. Washington, D.C.: Government Printing Office, 1974–. Annual in print through 2003.
Brings together nationwide statistical data on the criminal justice system, public opinion, illegal activities, persons arrested, judicial proceedings, and persons under correctional supervision (*www.albany.edu/sourcebook*).

U.S. Department of Education, National Center for Education Statistics. *Digest of Education Statistics.* Washington, D.C.: Government Printing Office, 1962–. Annual.

> Current data on school enrollments, teachers, retention rates, educational attainment, finances, achievement, schools and school districts, federal education programs, and so forth (*http://nces.ed.gov*).

U.S. Department of Education, Office of Educational Research and Improvement. *The Condition of Education: A Statistical Report.* Washington, D.C.: Government Printing Office, 1975–. Annual.

> Data survey of trends in elementary, secondary, and higher education. Data portray student characteristics and performance as well as fiscal, material, and human resources deployed in education (*http://nces.ed.gov*).

U.S. Department of Energy, Energy Information Administration. *Annual Energy Review.* Washington, D.C.: Government Printing Office, 1977–.

> Data on energy supply and disposition, exploration, and reserves (*http://eia.doe.gov/emeu/aer/contents.html*).

U.S. Department of Justice, Federal Bureau of Investigation. *Uniform Crime Reports for the United States.* Washington, D.C.: Government Printing Office, 1930–. Annual.

> Variety of charts and tables on types and frequencies of crimes, persons arrested, and law enforcement personnel; several forty-year trends (*www.fbi.gov/ucr/ucr.htm*).

Economic Policy

American Gaming Association's State of the States Survey, *www.americangaming.org*

> Data on the national and state-level economic impact of the casino and gaming equipment manufacturing industries. Also includes public opinion data and data on trends in casino patronage. See also, for state gambling laws, *www.gambling-law-us.com*.

The Economic Report of the President. Washington, D.C.: Government Printing Office, 1947–. Annual.

> Reviews the national economic situation; presents a substantial appendix with long time series of critical economic data (*www.gpo.gov/erp*).

The Economist. *Guide to Economic Indicators: Making Sense of Economics.* 7th ed. New York: Wiley, 2010.

> Explains some one hundred indicators, including information on their sources, reliability, and significance; provides guidelines for interpretation.

[Year] Historical Chart Book. Washington, D.C.: Board of Governors of the Federal Reserve System, 1965–. Annual.
> Long-range financial and business data, mostly from series maintained by the Federal Reserve Board.

Klarner, Carl. State Economic Dataset, *www.indstate.edu/polisci/klarnerpolitics .htm*
> Dataset at the state-year level covering 1929 to 2012 for selected variables including personal income, gross state product, expenditures, revenues, and housing prices.

Office of Management and Budget. *Budget of the United States Government.* Washington, D.C.: Government Printing Office. Annual.
> Multivolume annual presentation of data on federal revenues and expenditures. Although the details of the federal budget documents may be numbing to the uninitiated, even the novice might find the Historical Tables useful (*www.gpo .gov/fdsys/browse/collectionGPO.action?collectionCode=BUDGET*).

O'Hara, Frederick M. *Handbook of United States Economic and Financial Indicators.* 2nd ed. Westport, Conn.: Greenwood Press, 2000.
> Defines several hundred economic indicators culled from more than fifty sources; provides information on publication schedules and historical trends.

Tax Foundation, *http://taxfoundation.org*
> Data on taxes at the state and local level including income, sales, corporate, excise and property taxes, as well as data on business tax climates, tax burden, etc. Many of the data are up to date and available for a decade or more.

U.S. Bureau of Labor Statistics. *Employment and Earnings.* Washington, D.C.: Government Printing Office, 1961–. Annual.
> Various statistics on the nation's nonfarm workforce, including lengthy time series with data beginning in 1909 (*www.bls.gov*).

———. *Handbook of Labor Statistics.* Washington, D.C.: Government Printing Office, 1927–. Frequency varies.
> Collection of data on employment, unemployment, earnings, school enrollment and educational attainment, productivity, prices, strikes, and so forth (*www.bls.gov*).

———. *Monthly Labor Review.* Washington, D.C.: Government Printing Office, 1915–.
> Covers most Bureau of Labor Statistics series, presenting data on employment, hours, pay, strikes, prices and inflation, and so forth (*www.bls.gov*).

U.S. Council of Economic Advisers. *Economic Indicators.* Washington, D.C.: Government Printing Office, 1948–. Monthly.
> Data on total output, income, and spending; employment, unemployment, and wages; production and business activity; prices, currency, credit, and security

markets; and federal finance (*www.gpo.gov/fdsys/browse/collection .action?collectionCode=ECONI*).

U.S. Department of Agriculture. *Agricultural Statistics.* Washington, D.C.: Government Printing Office, 1937–. Annual.

Vast array of agricultural data, including politically relevant displays such as farm economic trends, price support programs, and agricultural imports and exports.

U.S. Department of Commerce. *Survey of Current Business.* Washington, D.C.: Government Printing Office, 1921–. Monthly.

Data on U.S. income and trade developments (*www.bea.gov/scb/index.htm*).

World Bank. *World Development Report.* New York: Oxford University Press, 1978–. Annual.

Analysis of and data on worldwide capital and economic indicators, with an emphasis on development (*http://econ.worldbank.org/wdr*).

Index

About the Authors

Harold W. Stanley is the Geurin-Pettus Distinguished Chair in American Politics and Political Economy at Southern Methodist University (SMU). In 1979, he joined the University of Rochester Department of Political Science and served as its chair from 1996 to 1999. Known as an expert in American national politics and electoral change in the South, Stanley currently serves as provost *ad interim* at SMU.

Richard G. Niemi is the Don Alonzo Watson Professor of Political Science at the University of Rochester. He is the coauthor of many books, including *Civic Education: What Makes Students Learn* and *Voting Technology: The Not-So-Simple Act of Casting a Ballot*. Niemi has written numerous articles on political socialization, voting, and legislative districting. He is currently doing research on civic education and voting.

CQ Press, an imprint of SAGE, is the leading publisher of books, periodicals, and electronic products on American government and international affairs. CQ Press consistently ranks among the top commercial publishers in terms of quality, as evidenced by the numerous awards its products have won over the years. CQ Press owes its existence to Nelson Poynter, former publisher of the *St. Petersburg Times,* and his wife Henrietta, with whom he founded *Congressional Quarterly* in 1945. Poynter established CQ with the mission of promoting democracy through education and in 1975 founded the Modern Media Institute, renamed The Poynter Institute for Media Studies after his death. The Poynter Institute (*www.poynter.org*) is a nonprofit organization dedicated to training journalists and media leaders.

In 2008, CQ Press was acquired by SAGE, a leading international publisher of journals, books, and electronic media for academic, educational, and professional markets. Since 1965, SAGE has helped inform and educate a global community of scholars, practitioners, researchers, and students spanning a wide range of subject areas, including business, humanities, social sciences, and science, technology, and medicine. A privately owned corporation, SAGE has offices in Los Angeles, London, New Delhi, and Singapore, in addition to the Washington DC office of CQ Press.